Beyond Black Hawk Down

Beyond Black Hawk Down

Intervention, Nation-Building,
and Insurgency in Somalia, 1992–1995

Jonathan Carroll

University Press of Kansas

© 2025 by the University Press of Kansas

All rights reserved

Published by the University Press of Kansas (Lawrence, Kansas 66045), which was organized by the Kansas Board of Regents and is operated and funded by Emporia State University, Fort Hays State University, Kansas State University, Pittsburg State University, the University of Kansas, and Wichita State University.

Library of Congress Cataloging-in-Publication Data

Names: Carroll, Jonathan (Military historian) author
Title: Beyond Black Hawk down: intervention, nation-building, and
    insurgency in Somalia, 1992–1995 / Jonathan Carroll.
Description: Lawrence, Kansas: University Press of Kansas, 2025 |
    Series: Modern war studies | Includes bibliographical references and
    index.
Identifiers: LCCN 2024060710 (print) | LCCN 2024060711 (ebook)
    ISBN 9780700638888 (cloth)
    ISBN 9780700638895 (ebook)
Subjects: LCSH: Operation Restore Hope, 1992–1993 | United Nations
    Operation in Somalia | Military assistance, American—Somalia | United
    Nations—Peacekeeping forces—Somalia | United States—History,
    Military—20th century | Somalia—History—1991– | BISAC: HISTORY /
    Military / General | POLITICAL SCIENCE / Colonialism & Post-Colonialism
Classification: LCC DT407.42 .C37 2025 (print) | LCC DT407.42 (ebook) |
    DDC 967.7305/3—dc23/eng/20250513
LC record available at https://lccn.loc.gov/2024060710.
LC ebook record available at https://lccn.loc.gov/2024060711.

British Library Cataloguing-in-Publication Data is available.

For my father, Alan, who loves a good story,
and my grandfather, Donal, the writer.

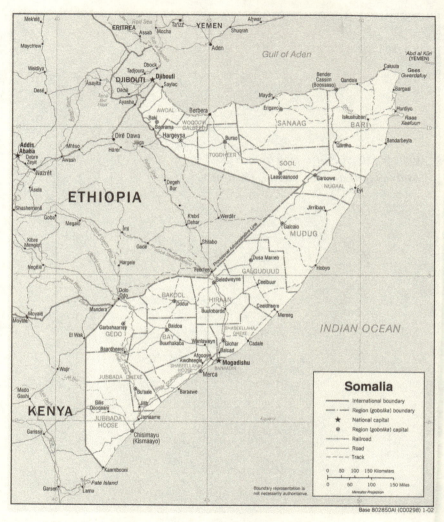

Map of Somalia, 1992

Contents

A photo gallery follows page 150.

Maps

Lastly to you, the reader. Many authors, indeed, many scholars, write books to showcase how smart *they* are. Those who know me personally will tell you that I am infuriatingly modest and all too willing to ignore my strengths and emphasize my weaknesses. So to you, the reader, if you not only enjoy this book but also learn something new, I thank you for your patience and time. This book is a true story of hope, tragedy, idealism, failure, ignorance, arrogance, and hubris. It is a story that needed to be told, and because historians are the arbiters of *our* story at large, I felt compelled to tell it. This is not *my* story of Somalia—I was four years old when the intervention started and seven when it ended. It is the story contained in countless archival documents, of which I am merely the interpreter. Before writing this book, I didn't know anyone who had been in Somalia; I had no axes to grind, no blame to throw, no scores to settle. That has not changed. But I had questions and couldn't find any book that had the answers. And so here we are. I got so frustrated that I went to Texas to write the book I was looking for. With that in mind, any errors in the pages that follow are mine alone.

Abbreviations

AAV	amphibious assault vehicle
APC	armored personnel carrier
ARFOR	Army Forces Somalia
ARG	Amphibious Ready Group
ASF	Auxiliary Security Force
AWSS	authorized weapons storage site
CAP	Combined Action Program
CDU	Christian Democratic Union
CENTCOM	United States Central Command
CFST	Coalition Forces Support Team
CIA	Central Intelligence Agency
CMOC	Civil-Military Operations Center
CSAR	combat search and rescue
HRS	humanitarian relief sector
ICRC	International Committee of the Red Cross
JTF	Joint Task Force
JTFSC	Joint Task Force Support Command
JULLS	Joint Uniform Lessons Learned System
MARFOR	Marine Forces Somalia
MDS	mass distribution site
MEF	Marine Expeditionary Force
MEU	Marine Expeditionary Unit
MPS	maritime prepositioning ships
NATO	North Atlantic Treaty Organization
NGO	nongovernmental organization
OFDA	Office of Foreign Disaster Assistance
QRF	Quick Reaction Force
RCT	Regimental Combat Team
REDHORSE	Rapid Engineer Deployable Heavy Operational Repair Squadron Engineers
ROWPU	reverse-osmosis water purification unit
RPG	rocket-propelled grenade

SDA	Somali Democratic Association
SDM	Somali Democratic Movement
SNA	Somali National Alliance
SNF	Somali National Front
SNM	Somali National Movement
SNPF	Somali National Police Force
SOAR	Special Operations Aviation Regiment
SPD	Social Democratic Party of Germany
SPM	Somali Patriotic Movement
SSDF	Somali Salvation Democratic Front
SSNM	Southern Somali National Movement
SYL	Somali Youth League
TNC	Transitional National Council
TPFDDL	time-phased force deployment data list
UAE	United Arab Emirates
UNDP	United Nations Development Program
UNICEF	United Nations International Children's Emergency Fund
UNITAF	Unified Task Force
UNLSC	United Nations Logistics Support Command
UNOSOM	United Nations Operation in Somalia
USAID	United States Agency for International Development
USC	United Somali Congress
USF	United Somali Front
WFP	World Food Program
WSLF	West Somali Liberation Front

A Note on Spelling

In the many works dealing with Somalia, a variety of spellings are used for place names, the names of individuals, and key terminology. Sometimes the spellings are based on the official national Somali orthography, but more often such terms are spelled phonetically for the reader's benefit. For example, the city of Baydhabo is normally spelled Baidoa, and the capital, Muqdishu, is written as Mogadishu. When it comes to the names of individuals, a similar practice has developed. In deference to the reader, Maxamed Farax Caydiid became Mohamed Farah Aidid. For the same reason, this book adopts the most frequently used spellings for the names of places and individuals. There is one exception: Aidid's name is usually spelled Aideed, but in his own letters he used Aidid. In this book, Aidid's own spelling is used throughout, with the alternative spelling retained in direct quotes from primary sources.

Acknowledgments

An Irishman from Kildare went to Texas to write a book about Somalia. That just describes how this project started. How it ended took the support, assistance, and measured tolerance of so many people. Among those at Texas A&M University, it is only fitting to first thank my adviser and mentor Professor Brian McAllister Linn, whose sage wisdom and timely advice was always on point and grounded in decades of experience as one of the field's foremost military historians. I also thank Professors Terry Anderson and Lorien Foote, valued mentors and friends; Professors Adam Seipp, John Schuessler, and Andrew Kirkendall; and the History Department's director of graduate studies, Professor Roger Reese, for his spirited, humorous, and forcefully delivered softball tips.

I am also eternally grateful for the professional assistance of General Anthony Zinni, US Marine Corps (retired); Professor Gordon W. Rudd; Colonel Randall Cochrane, US Army (retired); Captain Jeffrey Riedel, US Army (retired); Chief Warrant Officer Ben Johnson, US Army (retired); Lieutenant Colonel Thomas J. Daze, US Army (retired); Bob Breen; Robert F. Baumann; and Sepp Scanlin. I must also recognize another wise mentor, Professor James H. Willbanks, for his advice and kindness over the years. To the Society of Military History as a whole, thank you for not only providing me with a forum to test my arguments about Somalia but also for awarding what became this book the 2024 Edward M. Coffman First Manuscript Prize. At the University Press of Kansas, I was lucky to find an editorial team who believed in this project and made it a reality. I can't thank Joyce Harrison and Bill Allison enough. The same sentiments apply to readers Brian Drohan and Thijs Zaalberg for their fantastic suggestions.

I'm indebted to the staff of the US Army Heritage and Education Center in Carlisle, Pennsylvania; the US Marine Corps History Division in Quantico, Virginia; the US Army Center for Military History in Washington, DC; the 10th Mountain Division Museum in Fort Drum, New York; the United Nations Archives in New York; and the Irish Defence Forces Military Archives in Dublin. Thanks also to the Bush Presidential

Library in College Station, Texas, and the Clinton Presidential Library in Little Rock, Arkansas. The staffs' expert knowledge of the libraries' holdings was invaluable in putting this work together.

I was honored to receive significant funding support from Texas A&M's History Department for archival research and to present several chapters at both national and international conferences. My sincere thanks to the Morris family, which funds the annual Professor Brian McAllister Linn Research Fellowship in Military History, and to the Chapman family, which funds the David R. Chapman '67 Graduate Research Fellowship, both of which I was delighted to be awarded. I am similarly thankful for the support of many organizations, without which the countless hours of work, research, travel, and investigation that went into this book would not have been possible. I extend my sincere gratitude to the Bush School of Public Government and Service's Albritton Center for Grand Strategy, the 10th Mountain Division Foundation, and the Smith-Richardson Foundation for their support.

Writing this book was a passion project, but it was also maddening. It really was. And credit must be given to those who kept me sane and motivated, especially my closest friends who graciously tolerated me foisting drafts on them, chapter by chapter, over the years. I am grateful for my family's unwavering support, especially my aunt Linda, who never stopped asking questions, and, of course, my father. I must thank my two fellow historians from Florida, Ian Seavey and Ashley Vance, for their unwavering support from the start. I had the pleasure of sharing an office with Ian for many years, complete with his penchant for enjoying sick death metal riffs day in, day out. Foisting early drafts of this book on him, I think, constituted revenge. I also owe an awful lot to two other fantastic historians. Casey Ellisen, my battle buddy in the trenches, provided limitless faith, enthusiasm, and coffee that helped lock in the final chevrons that forged this book into what it now is. As for Nada Al-Jamal, ah sure listen! When times were tough, my brother Neil Richardson was always there to keep me going, as was Bryan Gerhart for our regular drink 'n' think sessions to discuss the world's problems. Kyra Renaud knows more about Somalia than she ever wanted to learn but, as my test audience, ensured that this book made sense, and the cups of tea and modest cheese boards made all the difference in the world. And without Jennifer, I never would have reached the point where I could have started this book, let alone become a historian. Thank you, thank you all.

Introduction

In 1994 two CIA operatives, under orders from the US national security adviser, arrived in the Horn of Africa posing as geologists. They spent weeks conducting mineral surveys to maintain their cover before setting up a meeting with General Mohammed Abdul Corp, the local warlord. Notorious for attacking UN peacekeepers and thwarting international efforts in the region, Corp was responsible for the deaths of twenty American soldiers. Claiming to have found rich deposits in the general's territory, these operatives lured Corp out into the wilderness, over-powered his bodyguards, and captured him. American Special Forces then arrived by helicopter to take him into custody. It seemed that Corp would finally face justice. But it was all fiction. For Tom Clancy, one of America's most popular techno-thriller authors, it was an apt scene to open his best-selling Jack Ryan novel *Debt of Honor*.[1]

Debt of Honor was published as the American public was struggling to come to terms with the disastrous Battle of Mogadishu. On 3 October 1993 a raid by US Special Forces to capture senior officials of General Mohamed Farah Aidid's Somali National Alliance went horribly wrong. Two Black Hawk helicopters were shot down, and eighteen Americans and hundreds of Somalis were killed. Almost immediately, President Bill Clinton announced that the United States was withdrawing from Somalia, confirming that, to those in Washington, the battle was seen as a catastrophic defeat. Always prone to incorporate contemporary events into fictional challenges, Clancy told a tale of triumphant American soldiers bringing a warlord to justice—a far more acceptable outcome than the visceral carnage in Mogadishu. The debt of honor, so to speak, was settled with the capture of the fictitious Corp, softening the reality that Aidid got away with it. But what was the perceived debt, and why did it need settling?

In December 1992 President George H. W. Bush announced to the American public and the world that the United States could no longer stand by and watch the worsening humanitarian disaster unfolding in Somalia. After two decades under the brutal socialist dictatorship of Mohamed Siad Barre, the country descended into civil war in 1988. The loose coalition of factions that ousted the Barre regime then turned on one another for control of the country. Shattered by war, drought, and famine, Somalia became the inspiration for the coining of a now familiar term, what Gerald B. Helman and Steven R. Ratner called a "failed state."[2]

The military intervention that followed can be divided into three phases. The first saw a minimalist response from a United Nations already beset by instability elsewhere in the world. With peacekeepers spread from Cambodia to Croatia to Lebanon, and with preparations under way to stymie the violent disintegration of Yugoslavia, only a small peacekeeping force, the UN Operation in Somalia (UNOSOM), could be sent to Mogadishu in September 1992. A concurrent US-led humanitarian airlift from Kenya tried to deliver food to the starving, only to have it fall into the hands of those who used hunger as a weapon. From frustration and failure came the second phase. In December 1992 Bush authorized Operation Restore Hope, a US-led coalition of nearly forty thousand troops from more than twenty nations christened the Unified Task Force (UNITAF). Sent to create a secure environment for the delivery of humanitarian aid unhampered by the warring factions, UNITAF enjoyed much—though often misunderstood—success, spurring the international community to launch the third phase.

In May 1993 the UN Operation in Somalia II (UNOSOM II) took over from UNITAF. With an explicit and historically unprecedented mandate to rebuild Somalia, UNOSOM II was the most ambitious nation-building operation in history at that point. And it was during this third phase that violence erupted between UN and US forces and those of the Somali National Alliance led by Aidid in what became known as the Summer War. Months of fighting culminated with the Battle of Mogadishu, the most intense engagement of US forces since the end of the Vietnam War, causing the impulsive withdrawal of all American forces and other key participants in March 1994. Severely depleted, the remaining UN forces withdrew ignominiously in March 1995, their attempt at nation building left in tatters.

Somalia was and continues to be a contentious and controversial post–Cold War episode. The Battle of Mogadishu ignited public and political outrage in the United States at the perception of soldiers dying when no vital American interests were at stake, prompting lasting bitterness toward the UN for stumbling naïvely down the perilous path of nation building while dragging the world's lone superpower along with it. As John R. Bolton, assistant secretary of state in the Bush administration, wrote, "Somalia was the wrong place and the wrong time to . . . experiment. The American dead prove that point."[3] Only weeks after leaving Somalia, the enduring political and public vitriol and indignation about the intervention meant that the Clinton administration refused to intercede in the Rwandan Genocide. The resonance of Somalia in the international psyche was such that when Mark Bowden recounted the events of 3 October 1993 in *Black Hawk Down: A Story of Modern War* in 1999, it became an international best seller.[4] Crowds then packed theaters in 2001 to see Ridley Scott's Academy Award–winning blockbuster movie adaptation. In 2003 players who successfully completed the video game *Delta Force: Black Hawk Down* were rewarded with a bonus level allowing them to covertly assassinate Mohamed Farah Aidid.[5]

The specter of Somalia haunted more than just the United States. The entire Canadian Airborne Regiment was disbanded because of its conduct during the intervention, while Italian and Belgian paratroopers stood trial for the rape of women and the torture of civilians. At the UN, ambitions for the world's policeman to evolve into a dynamic post–Cold War nation stabilizer and rebuilder lay in ruins, along with any chance of a second term for Secretary-General Boutros Boutros-Ghali. All this was undermined by going to war for the cause of peace in the world's first identifiable failed state. Dead and wounded peacekeepers in the hundreds; dead and wounded Somalis in the thousands, many of them civilians; dashed hopes, tragedy, shame, and disdain for a people blamed for not accepting the world's help—these are the lasting legacies of Somalia, resonating in the national memories of those countries that went there. This, perhaps, is the substantial debt Tom Clancy wanted settled.

Historiography of the Intervention in Somalia

The central and critical questions this book addresses are: What caused an intervention that started off so well, that embodied so much international optimism about the potential of the post–Cold War UN and the ability of militaries to do more than wage war, to derail so dramatically into the deadliest UN operation in the world at the time? And after it all went so wrong, what ultimately led to the cataclysmic failure in Somalia?

These questions have been at the core of a thirty-year-long scholarly debate in which historians, sadly, have played almost no role. Political scientists and scholars of international relations have long cited Somalia, though only in chapter-length, policy-oriented comparative analyses that measure the intervention against other UN and NATO operations of the 1990s, such as those in Bosnia, Haiti, Rwanda, and Kosovo. Karin von Hippel's *Democracy by Force*, Taylor B. Seybolt's *Humanitarian Military Intervention*, Lise Morjé Howard's *UN Peacekeeping in Civil Wars*, and Thomas R. Mockaitis's *Peace Operations and Intrastate Conflict* are just some examples of works that focus on defining terms such as "peacekeeping," "peace enforcement," and "humanitarian interventions" to identify *conceptual* flaws in such doctrines to explain what went so wrong in Somalia.[6]

Within this corpus of scholarship, several arguments have contested for dominance. One is that the UN mandates in Somalia were vague and ever-changing, shifting from peacekeeping to peace enforcement. According to Jane Boulden, the political and military goals of UNITAF were clear, but those of UNOSOM II were "less clear."[7] Another commonly cited explanation is based on the concept of consent—that the Somali population and political leaders did not consent to the intervention. Among others, Lisa Morjé Howard notes that Aidid never consented to UNOSOM II's presence, an operation that Michael Wesley claims intervened "against the will of some of the parties."[8] This lack of consent, Robert Cassidy concludes, was the "harbinger to the escalation of violence."[9] Another line of argument concerns the differences between UNITAF and UNOSOM II. In a decidedly predeterminant assumption that violence was inevitable, many scholars suggest that because UNITAF was larger and better armed, the ever-ambitious Aidid simply waited until UNITAF left and then attacked the qualitatively weaker UNOSOM II, whose nation-building mission was thwarting his quest for power.[10] Thomas Mockaitis concisely states this view, observing, "All the players knew that UNITAF was an interim force and could afford to wait it out."[11]

The most enduring indictment of what went wrong in Somalia came from General Sir Michael Rose, the British commander of the UN Protection Force in Bosnia. In a now infamous quote cited ad nauseam, Rose claimed UNOSOM crossed the "Mogadishu Line," an unhelpful phrase describing what he believed was the conceptual Rubicon between peacekeeping and warfighting.[12] In so doing, the UN lost the critical perception of being impartial in the eyes of the Somali population.

For decades, scholars have quoted or paraphrased Rose to argue that this loss of impartiality meant UNOSOM II had no credibility with the Somali people and essentially became just another faction in the civil war.[13] However, this quote, as well as the concept Rose was trying to articulate, is misunderstood and misrepresented.

Beyond Black Hawk Down challenges all these arguments. One unintended consequence of the popularity of Bowden's *Black Hawk Down* and the movie adaptation was a tendency for the public and academics to focus on one fifteen-hour battle, ignoring the broader context of the nearly three-year intervention of which it was a part. Therefore, given the focus by most scholars to find a *conceptual* reason for failure, the analysis thus far has been colored by hindsight and predeterminism. The critical nuances of the wider course of events have largely been ignored, as have the actions of the key personalities. The result is the intervention's reduction to a series of dates: the arrival of US marines as the vanguard of UNITAF on 9 December 1992, the massacre of Pakistani peacekeepers on 5 June 1993, the Battle of Mogadishu on 3 October 1993, and the American withdrawal in March 1994. Events in between these watersheds are largely ignored, as is the vital context that connects them.

For instance, the 5 June 1993 attack is commonly attributed to botched UN policy, with the Pakistanis as the main actors and no mention of the central role of American decision makers. The UN itself is treated as a ponderous, unthinking monolith instead of what it was: a vast bureaucracy of individuals who were often focused on furthering national interests that sometimes aligned with the UN mission and sometimes did not. Moreover, almost all works focus on the capital of Mogadishu, despite UNITAF and UNOSOM II occupying most of southern Somalia. Nor has there been any proper examination of UNOSOM II after the American withdrawal in 1994, despite the operation's continuation for another year. Consequently, there has been no objective evaluation that contextualizes the larger operations in Somalia and provides a proper examination of what occurred or what was achieved. This book aims to correct these omissions by providing a scholarly, multiarchival military history of the international venture into Somalia, exploring its trajectory and the successes and failures of this grand experiment.

The Argument

Beyond Black Hawk Down is a series of myth-busting course corrections, as each chapter makes a specific argument challenging the established narrative of what happened in Somalia. There are, however, three over-all contentions arguing for a fundamental reinterpretation of events. First, for the bulk of the two-and-a-half-year operation, violence was the exception, not the norm, in Somalia. The traditional narrative that the intervention lacked the consent of the populace and the political leadership, thus leading to widespread violence, is not supported by the evidence. This book demonstrates the exact opposite. Most Somalis, including political leaders such as Aidid and others, welcomed UNITAF and UNOSOM II. Aidid played a critical role in mobilizing consensus among Somali political factions to sign the UN-sponsored Addis Ababa Agreement, setting out the structure of a new government that UNOSOM II was entrusted with rebuilding. Even during the Summer War, from June to October 1993, only Aidid's faction fought against UNOSOM II, and only in a confined suburb of Mogadishu. During this war, which dominated media coverage, the rest of southern Somalia occupied by UNOSOM was peaceful. The remaining thirteen factions and most of the population remained enthusiastically supportive of the UN.

Second, the existing literature suggests that Aidid's uncompromising lust for power prompted him to attack UN forces on 5 June 1993, starting a war that culminated with the Battle of Mogadishu. Thus far, Aidid's motives have only been guessed at, with little evidence, and are largely dependent on his characterization as a warlord, a term with negative connotations. This has prevented an adequate analysis of his motivations and possible explanations for his behavior. Using previously untapped archival collections, this book argues that Aidid may not have been responsible for the violence that broke out in June 1993. Instead, fatal decisions and poor policies by key American officials in UNOSOM resulted in an outbreak of uncoordinated and random acts of violence that were then impulsively blamed on Aidid personally, prompting the escalation into a months-long conflict. The Battle of Mogadishu was thus not inevitable.

Last, although the intervention in Somalia failed, existing narratives misunderstand where that failure originated. Traditionally, the Battle of Mogadishu is presented as the critical juncture where the nation-building mission became unachievable. However, *Beyond Black Hawk Down* shows that in the six months after the battle, UNOSOM made great progress toward achieving its mandate and still enjoyed the support of the populace and most of the political factions. Even though UNOSOM was severely diminished after the withdrawal of US forces and other predominantly Western nations, the mission continued for another year because the indications of future success were tangible. The true failure came, in part, because institutionally, the UN was financially crippled. This is what forced many nations to leave UNOSOM, not violence by the Somalis. And when budgetary cuts whittled the mission down even further, there was neither the political will nor the money for UNOSOM to counter Aidid's moves to position himself as Somalia's leader once the UN left. Thus, this book argues that although the Battle of Mogadishu was a setback, and although the abandonment of Somalia by Western nations was damaging, financial shortages and political exhaustion ultimately proved fatal for what was, at the time, the most ambitious nation-building operation in history.

The end result in Somalia was not preordained. Failure was not rooted in the structural or systemic challenges inherent to nation building that dominate scholarship on the wars in Iraq and Afghanistan, nor does it rest with flawed concepts, doctrine, or theories. Instead, disastrous human decision making and miscalculation based on imperfect assumptions and flawed policies and influenced by national interest and personal prejudices made success impossible. And in a direct rebuttal of Rose, this book suggests that, in Somalia, the Mogadishu Line was not crossed at all.

To make these arguments, *Beyond Black Hawk Down* benefits from research in a dozen archives, including three collections of primary source materials not previously used in scholarly works on Somalia. The UNOSOM II collection at the UN Archives provided a wealth of documents from Somali faction leaders and senior UNOSOM officials, giving an on-the-ground look into UN operations and fundamentally challenging the traditional narrative of what happened in Somalia. The Irish Military Archives in Dublin provided excellent sources for events after the US withdrawal in 1994, as the Irish Defence Forces remained as part of the much-diminished UNOSOM. In addition, the US Army Center for Military History's Somalia Oral History Interview collection was an invaluable repository of hundreds of interviews conducted during the intervention itself, giving an honest appraisal of events as they were happening. As such, this book brings together the diverse perspectives of the United Nations, the United States. and other coalition countries and places the events of 3 October 1993 into the wider context of the overall intervention.

Somalia was a grand experiment in the post–Cold War world. In many ways, it was a journey into the unknown for the United States in a new unipolar world. American military power—the centerpiece for advancing US interests in the Cold War—now had to be used in new ways to maintain that influence in peacetime. And there was optimism that some of the burden of tackling global affairs could be shouldered by the United Nations. Freed from the diplomatic equivalent of a medically induced coma during the Cold War, the UN was now faced with instability, civil wars, and crises across the globe. Somalia thus became the precedent-setting demonstration of the role the UN could play in the new world order. The test was whether the international community could rebuild a nation literally from the ground up. For the United States, it was vital that the UN succeed in Somalia.

In the end, Somalia was seen as an unmitigated disaster, an episode best forgotten. Or, if remembered, it was with the caveat that the mission never could have worked. In a world where conflict is often driven by resource scarcity and the effects of climate change and where civil wars are becoming more frequent, the reality is that military interventions akin to Somalia will only become more common in the future. As such, beyond just an awareness of the result of past operations or an oversimplified summary of lessons learned, we need a nuanced understanding of what happened *on the ground*—what successes were achieved so they can be replicated, but more importantly, a sober analysis of what went wrong and, critically, why. When, on 4 November 1994, New Zealand's ambassador to the UN, Colin Keating, joined all members of the Security Council in deciding to withdraw UN forces from Somalia, leaving its mission of nation building tragically unfinished, he said, "A great deal has been written and said about the international community's intervention to help the Somali people. Too much of it has been sensationalized. There will be a need, before long, for a detailed and dispassionate analysis."[14] *Beyond Black Hawk Down* provides that analysis.

1 | The Collapse of Somalia
The Long Dark Road through Anarchy to Intervention

The UN . . . was totally absent.
—Mohamed Sahnoun, UN special representative to the secretary-general in Somalia[1]

Aidid was a professional soldier, educated, former ambassador to India, this guy was not a thug, he was a diplomat, a general.
—General Anthony C. Zinni, director of operations, Unified Task Force[2]

With the fall of the cities of Burao and Hargeisa to the Somali National Movement in 1989, the civil war against the authoritarian regime of Mohamed Siad Barre erupted in earnest. In New Delhi, the Somali ambassador to India had finished editing *Preferred Future Development in Somalia*, a collection of essays written by notable Indian politicians, scholars, and entrepreneurs. It included initiatives to improve the Somali education and agriculture sectors, integrate the nomadic population, and foster a prosperous tourist industry. Penning some essays, and no stranger to persecution from Barre himself, the ambassador wrote:

> It is a time of great expectations. . . . We have to select the right sort of leaders for this challenging task that lies ahead. There is no harm in anyone aspiring to be a leader . . . the model of healthy and functional democracy that we are planning to adopt in Somalia is such . . . [that] no one will be able to exploit the people by becoming President, Prime Minister or a big boss. May Allah . . . help us to usher in such an ideal democracy . . . for which we have been waiting for many many years.[3]

Shortly thereafter, the ambassador abandoned his post and went to Ethiopia to command a newly formed rebel militia fighting against Barre.[4] His name was Mohamed Farah Aidid.

Understanding Somalia's descent into civil war and anarchy, a collapse so complete that it required a new term to describe it—"failed state"—requires an awareness of Somali history.[5] The trajectory of this descent is critical to contextualizing the interventions by the United States and the United Nations and to understanding how the vying factions, their leaders, and the Somali people reacted to the first military intervention in the world's first failed state and, more importantly, why. Existing literature on this topic has two failings. The first is a tendency to downplay the civil war by merely acknowledging that it was a central contributor to the collapse. The second is the characterization of the various Somali faction leaders as African "warlords" whose motives extended no further than a rabid lust for power. This term has both racial and cultural overtones. The Somalis were called warlords, but not Radovan Karadzic or Ratko Mladic, whose names were synonymous with brutality and ethnic cleansing during the concurrent Bosnian War.[6] It is true that certain Somali leaders, such as Barre and his son-in-law Hersi Morgan, were as corrupt and violent as Charles Taylor, Idi Amin, and Joseph Kony. But for other so-called warlords, the term is inappropriate. Aidid was a former colonial police officer, a respected soldier and diplomat. Ismail Jumale Ossoble had been a human rights lawyer. Abdirahman Ahmed Ali Tuur, the first president of Somaliland, had been Somali ambassador to both East Germany and the United Arab Emirates. Ali Mahdi was a hotelier and businessman. None of them described themselves as warlords. The outside world applied that label. Caricaturing them as warlords has denied them agency in historical analysis as individuals and actors, whether noble, vain, egotistical, psychotic, or just dangerously ambitious. It is therefore important to explain events before the international community arrived in Somalia to contextualize the behavior and motivations of the various factions and their leaders and to describe the environment in which the outside world intervened militarily.[7]

Somalia and Colonialism

Despite being nearly homogeneously Sunni since the introduction of Islam in the eighth century, Somali culture and society fundamentally centered on the clan and subclan system. Historian Lee Cassanelli notes that "most Somalis . . . think of themselves first and foremost in terms of

their clan of origin."[8] Similarly, historian Mohamed Haji Ingiriis, a Somali himself, states, "no study on Somalia can leave out and ignore the importance of clan in their examination and analysis."[9] Five major clans (each with a number of subclans) dominate the system: Hawiye, Issaq, Darod, Dir, and Rahanweyn. Each clan derived its ancestry from Muslim saints who came to Somalia, such as Sheikh Darood (Darod clan) in the eleventh century and Sheikh Isahaaq (Issaq clan) in the thirteenth.[10] Sunnism was thus adopted and subordinated to an already existing societal framework that clearly delineated members of the shared community from outsiders. The central concept of *Diya*, or blood payment, used clan affiliation and ancestry to track debts and obligations for restitution, while *Heer*, a code of conduct, regulated conflict and disputes.[11] Clan affiliation was paramount, to the point that in Somali terms, anyone who could not trace their clan genealogy back to the seventeenth century was considered an "ignorant stranger."[12]

Nineteenth-century colonialism was a major shock to this system. Egyptians conquered northern Somalia in the 1870s and installed a brutal regime that was expelled by the Sudanese Mahdist Revolt in 1884.[13] Britain then established the Northern Somali Protectorate in 1886 in what became northeastern Kenya. Concurrently, French Somaliland was carved out. Italy then claimed Southern Somaliland in 1893, garrisoned the future Somali capital of Mogadishu, and expanded into the interior. Not all the colonizers were European. Ethiopia, under Coptic Christian Emperor Menelik II, simultaneously resisted European colonial encroachments and took the Ogaden region of Somalia. Thus, from 1870 to 1960, Somalis were ruled by Egyptians, Ethiopians, French, British, and Italians. Given the tenets of Somali culture and Sunnism, nationalists aspired to unite these five colonized regions into "Greater Somalia."[14] Indeed, the five-pointed star of the modern Somali flag represents this desire. The most famous attempt was the dervish resistance movement led by Mahammad Abdille Hassan, dubbed the "Mad Mullah" by the British. In a war that killed one-third of the population in northern Somalia, Hassan fought the British and Ethiopians from 1899 until his death in 1920.[15]

The Italian invasion of Ethiopia and East Africa in 1936 and the subsequent British invasion in 1941 gave Somalis hope that under either Italian fascism or British imperialism, Greater Somalia would be reconstituted. In both cases, colonial rule dominated. However, to erode residual Italian influence in the region during the Second World War, the British encouraged Somalis to organize politically. In 1943 the Somali Youth Club formed in Mogadishu as a nationalist political party for civil servants, police, and the educated middle class, dominated by the Darod clan. They renamed themselves the Somali Youth League (SYL) in 1947.[16]

After the war, the victorious powers decided the fate of Somalia through the Allied Council of Foreign Ministers. When the council's representatives visited Mogadishu, the SYL held massive rallies to showcase the appetite for independence—all to no avail. Possession being nine-tenths of the law, the British government attempted to retain Italian Somaliland. Earning accusations of imperialism from the United States and the Soviet Union, Westminster settled for British Somaliland once again, and the French retained French Somaliland. Heartened by the growing communist sentiment in Italy at the time, the Soviets argued successfully that Italian Somaliland should be returned to Rome. As for the Ogaden, Ethiopian Emperor Haile Selassie leveraged the American desires for military bases in Ethiopia and was granted the region despite widespread SYL protests.[17] By 1947, Somalia had simply returned to the colonial status quo ante.

The SYL movement for independence, however, could not be put back in the box. In 1949 the newly formed United Nations ruled that the postwar return of Italian Somaliland to Rome's control was only a temporary trusteeship; independence had to be granted by 1960. With a clearly defined timeline for sovereignty, nationalist fervor swept Somalia. The SYL swelled in membership and enjoyed landslide victories in the 1956 national elections, which created the first Somali administration in a century in preparation for independence in 1960. Concurrently, protests over political representation in British Somaliland opened elections to local parties with strong links to the overtly nationalist and centralizing SYL. Unification came in July 1960 as British and Italian Somaliland were granted independence. Britain retained the Somali regions in Kenya, and a referendum in French Somaliland on joining the new Somali Republic resulted in a French-aligned but independent Djibouti. Though considerable progress had been made, the division of Somalia based on the whim of the great powers in 1947 and the separation of the Ogaden at the behest of the United States left Somali nationalists bitter and with the perception that the UN had failed them.[18]

A Short-Lived Democracy

The newly independent Somali Republic, a parliamentary democracy, did not last the decade. The colonial period had shown Somali elites the value of political maneuvering and corruption, and the SYL used the new state as a vehicle for personal aggrandizement. Corruption was rife in elections, and the concerns of the average citizen increasingly took a backseat. Somalia became a one-party state under the SYL, which controlled 120 of 123 seats in the National Assembly by 1969. Notorious for patronage and nepotism based on clan affiliation, the SYL particularly favored the Darod clan, the largest in terms of population, which was concentrated in the south. This Darod-centric favoritism exacerbated clan tensions and prompted a minor revolt in 1961 when northern army officers refused to accept Darod superiors from the south. Though the regions were unified on paper, the differences between north and south reflected their respective colonial origins. Systems of education, health, and law differed in practice and in language: English versus Italian.[19] But also, as Gerard Prunier demonstrates, British colonialism in the north encountered little interference from the clans, which were successfully courted to ease the extraction of resources. The Italians, however, sought to civilize the Somalis in the south, often through subjugation and violence. This difference in colonial experiences led to tension when the SYL in Mogadishu asserted control in the north.[20]

Although the Somali Republic was Western leaning due to its politicians' emergence from British or Italian colonies, it also looked to the East, particularly for military assistance. In the early years of the republic, the idea of a Greater Somalia was so prevalent that the SYL government openly flirted with both Cold War superpowers to gain support for building and arming a powerful National Army to make final unification, particularly of the Ogaden, feasible. These entreaties were rebuffed by President Kennedy, as neighboring Ethiopia was a client-state of the United States, but Moscow offered a substantial military aid package. From 1963 onward, the Somali National Army was furnished with Soviet equipment and military advisers, while two thousand army officers received advanced military education at prestigious Soviet military academies. This created an ideological dichotomy between a democratic, if corrupt, political class and a growing Marxist outlook in the military.[21]

In 1964 Abdirizak Haji Hussein became prime minister of Somalia, pushing the republic even further into the Soviet sphere. Hussein had close ties to an overtly pro-Soviet senior army officer, Major General Mohamed Siad Barre, and made him commandant of the army. This set the stage for a premeditated military coup orchestrated by Barre with support from the Soviet KGB. By the late 1960s, government corruption and nepotism reached a zenith. Using his authority as army commander, Barre ordered soldiers to coerce the populace to vote for the SYL, engendering hatred toward the government and stoking discontent for his own advantage. On 15 October 1969 Abdirashid Ali Shermarke, the SYL president of Somalia and a Darod, was assassinated. The assassin was initially identified as one of Shermarke's bodyguards, with the suggestion of a personal motive for the killing. It was all meticulously planned, though. Shermarke was killed in a town that had experienced significant electioneering violence at the hands of Barre's troops, and the assassin was not a bodyguard but a specially recruited police officer who was promised money and protection by Barre loyalists.[22] When the SYL-dominated National Assembly tried to appoint another Darod as president, elements of the National Army, led by Barre and his loyalists, seized control in a bloodless coup sponsored by the Soviets.[23]

Barre's Autocratic Democratic Republic

After the coup, a newly formed Supreme Revolutionary Council appointed Barre president, and the country became the Somali Democratic Republic. An ardent Marxist-Leninist, Barre criticized the weakness and corruption of the SYL and established the Somali Socialist Democratic Party to impose what he termed "scientific socialism." According to I. M Lewis, the foremost scholar of Somali history and culture, scientific socialism marginalized clan identity and criminalized clan parochialism. In the new system, "salvation lay in honest toil, spurred on by the terse slogan: 'less talk and more work.'" Hagiography and iconography portrayed Barre as the "father" of Somalia, and its "'mother' was the Revolution."[24] Under Barre, the court system was militarized, and the death penalty was extended to most crimes. He was also a committed Somali nationalist, and his regime instituted a literacy program that shunned colonial languages such as English and Italian and introduced the first official orthography for the Somali written language. In the beginning, Barre was popular among Somalis, as de-emphasizing clan affiliation technically made all clans equal. Despite his initial overtures toward communist equality, Barre was an authoritarian ruler who quickly centralized his power base by having the other coup leaders executed. The Supreme Revolutionary Council was converted into a vehicle for Barre's cult of personality.[25]

Many historians have highlighted the contradictions in Barre's actions. On the surface, he tried to subordinate clannism in Somali society in favor of scientific socialism, yet he ensured that his own Marehan clan (a subclan of the Darod) occupied positions of power on the Supreme Revolutionary Council. His wife, Mama Khadiija, ran her own intelligence network. Nepotism also extended to the other Darod subclans—the Ogadeni and Dolbohante. The only non-Darod admitted into Barre's inner circle were those whose loyalty to the regime was beyond question. Essentially, despite the Marxist rhetoric, Barre leveraged the clan system to stay in power, and he used clan politics in a delicate balancing act to ensure that no rival clans could gain enough influence to truly compete with him. Anthropologist Catherine Besteman demonstrates that Barre's favoritism created a system of haves and have-nots in Somali society, which fueled the intensity of the civil war when it came.[26]

The combination of Barre's ideological views, Somalia's geostrategic location on the Horn of Africa as gatekeeper to the Indian Ocean, and the proximity of pro-West Ethiopia solidified Somalia's Cold War status as a client under the Soviet sphere of influence. Deliberately alienating the West, Barre established diplomatic relations with East Germany and North Vietnam, allowing the latter to fly Somali flags on its merchant ships.[27] With the assistance of Yuri Andropov and the KGB, Barre created the National Security Service. The *Gulwadaysha*, an ideological militia based on the Soviet *Druzhinniki*, emerged to report on political dissidents. Those who opposed Barre risked imprisonment or death, and civil servants were compelled to undergo forced "reeducation." In 1974 a new socialist indoctrination program was launched; all secondary schools were closed for a year and the students were sent into the bush to indoctrinate the nomadic population in scientific socialism. Soviet influence on Somali society became omnipresent. Of the few Somalis who obtained a university degree, 90 percent did so in Soviet or Soviet-influenced institutions.[28] When Somali sheikhs complained that Barre's increasingly dictatorial tendencies were interfering in Islamic lifestyles and subverting Koranic law, he executed ten of them and decreed that Islam no longer held sway in Somalia.[29]

Barre also sought increased military patronage from the Soviets just as their expulsion from Egypt in 1973 made Moscow eager to acquire a new regional client. Thus, the 1974 Soviet-Somali Friendship Treaty granted Soviet forces full basing rights; they constructed a naval base at Berbera for submarines to surge into the Indian Ocean and air bases at Baledogle, Hargeisa, and Galkayo. In return, Barre obtained a ten-year armaments program that furnished the National Army with modern T-54 main battle tanks, transforming it into the most powerful armored force in sub-Saharan Africa. The Soviets also provided MiG fighters and Ilyushin bombers and built an air defense missile complex and radar sites near Mogadishu.[30] In terms of size and capability, Somali military power quickly surpassed that of its Ethiopian neighbor—a fact not lost on Barre.

In 1974 Mengistu Haile Mariam and the Derg staged a Marxist coup against Emperor Haile Selassie in Ethiopia. The resulting instability presented Barre with an excellent opportunity to make Greater Somalia a reality by reclaiming the ethnically Somali Ogaden region of eastern Ethiopia. Barre began covertly arming and supplying the West Somali Liberation Front (WSLF), an Ogadeni paramilitary force fighting to secede from Ethiopia. Wise to Barre's ambitions, the Soviets tried to deter him from attacking their newest client-state, even sending Fidel Castro to Mogadishu to mediate with him, but to no avail. In 1977, Barre struck. Aided by the WSLF, the National Army penetrated deep into the Ogaden.[31]

This success was short-lived. In a clear display of picking a side, Soviet equipment and twenty thousand Cuban troops were sent to help the Ethiopians. Despite Barre's dogmatic devotion to Marxism, he was outraged at the Soviet support for Ethiopia. He poured more troops into the Ogaden, only to have them mauled by the Cubans and Ethiopians. The dream of Greater Somalia turned into a nightmare, and Barre became increasingly erratic. Somali officers were summarily executed for battlefield losses. Defeat in the Ogaden War was a watershed moment for Barre's regime. Greater Somalia was unachievable, Somali military power was shattered, and this pushed Barre's authoritarianism to new heights. The seeds of the future civil war were planted, and Barre's conduct ensured they would flourish.[32]

Ethnic Cleansing and the Emergence of Resistance

Because of Barre's brutality toward his own commanders in the Ogaden War, the Majerteen clan, which dominated the officer corps, attempted a coup in 1978. Like Barre's Marehan, the Majerteen was a subclan of the Darod, and he treated the coup as an intimate betrayal, responding with a campaign of clan-based persecution. The Majerteen ringleaders were executed; civilians, guilty only by association, were terrorized. Clan antagonisms were stoked when Barre invited more than six hundred thousand Ogadeni refugees and the WSLF remnant in Ethiopia to cross into Somalia.[33] Barre was rewarding the Ogadeni (another Darod sub-clan) and the WSLF for their wartime service and purchasing their continued loyalty by granting them land to settle and unleashing these new arrivals on the Majerteen. A similar fate befell the Issaq population in the northwest, which had criticized the political domination of Barre's Marehan clan. Through regime-sponsored terrorism, the goal was displacement of the Issaq and the Majerteen. The result was clan-based ethnic cleansing, rape, looting, and indiscriminate killing.[34]

Betrayed by the Soviet Union during the Ogaden War, Barre sought a new superpower patron, and the Cold War delivered. The Iranian Revolution and the Soviet invasion of Afghanistan in 1979 intensified the US focus on the Middle East to the point that the administration of Jimmy Carter articulated a policy of using force to defend national interests in the Persian Gulf region, with an emphasis on the oil industry. Lying adjacent to the Persian Gulf, Somalia was once again geostrategically important, this time to the United States. The timing could not have been better. The internationalization of the livestock market had hit Somalia hard, resulting in heavy borrowing from the International Monetary Fund and the World Bank. At its worst, inflation in Somalia fluctuated between 500 and 800 percent annually.[35] The National Army was also in a terrible state after the Ogaden War, and Barre faced growing discontent.

Beginning in 1980, the Carter administration commenced and the Reagan White House continued a program of economic assistance to Somalia, with the United States Agency for International Development (USAID) working to bolster the country's agricultural base. The Soviet-built port of Berbera became a key American naval hub for defending the Persian Gulf, while US Special Forces personnel advised the Somali military. American aid was predicated on Barre's promise to liberalize the economy and diversify his government politically.[36] Giving lip service to these promises, Barre published a new constitution in 1979 and created an elected Public Assembly. However, only members of his Socialist Party were eligible for election to this new body, after which the Public Assembly unanimously reappointed Barre president of Somalia. He ran unopposed for election in 1986, unsurprisingly winning 99.3 percent of the vote.[37]

At the same time, Barre's ethnic-cleansing campaign had borne significant fruit. The first organized resistance against his regime emerged from the Majerteen and Issaq clans. After their failed coup attempt in 1978 and Barre's harsh reprisals, armed groups of Majerteen fled into Ethiopia and formed the Somali Salvation Democratic Front (SSDF). The Issaq, politically marginalized and suffering at the hands of the Ogaden and WSLF militias, followed suit. Issaq officers in the army defected and, led by Abdirahman Ahmed Ali Tuur, formed the Somali National Movement (SNM) in April 1981 in London, determined to establish an independent Somaliland.[38]

Both the SSDF and the SNM sought to end Barre's rule and began guerrilla campaigns operating from across the Ethiopian border—the SNM in the northern Somaliland Issaq region and the SSDF in the Majerteen region of central Somalia. When the SSDF launched an offensive with Ethiopian assistance in 1982 near Galkayo, Barre pleaded for international assistance. The United States expedited arms shipments to Somalia and increased military aid to $80 million.[39] The incursion was put down by Barre's Marehan Red Berets, under the command of Colonel Mohamed Said "Hersi" Morgan. Once the dictator's personal bodyguard, Morgan's status skyrocketed after he married Barre's daughter in 1977. He subsequently graduated from the US Army's Command and General Staff College at Fort Leavenworth, a benefit of the US military aid program, before taking command of the Red Berets. Though a Majerteen himself, Morgan put his status in the regime above clan loyalty and destroyed the SSDF as an effective military force.[40]

Meanwhile, with the onset of famine in neighboring Ethiopia, economic aid and relief poured into Somalia, along with various humanitarian relief organizations. Working for USAID near the Ethiopian border, Michael Maren claimed that media reporting exaggerated the crisis by suggesting there were more than 1.5 million refugees in need of care, despite reports from USAID and the UN High Commissioner for Refugees that estimated the figure at four hundred thousand. More relief than necessary was flowing into the country, and Barre appropriated the excess supplies for his own purposes, fueling a black-market economy and controlling the population through weaponized hunger. Barre even used this foreign aid to support his campaign of ethnic cleansing. Refugee camps were built to house the Ogadeni streaming across the border, increasing the displacement of the Issaq. Even more egregious, Barre used relief supplies and military aid to arm and supply the WSLF and Ogaden militias, which were terrorizing the Majerteen and Issaq on his behalf. Between Barre's campaign of terror and the relief organizations' inadequacies, Maren argued, foreign aid was killing more Somalis and refugees than it was saving. Even more troubling, a USAID report showed that foreign aid accounted for two-thirds of the Somali economy.[41]

Maren would later write to warn of the dangers of fostering dependence on foreign aid in developing or fragile states; Somalia was his case and point. It was also Mohamed Farah Aidid's. In his writings, Aidid criticized Somalia's dependence on foreign aid and its inherent politicization. He condemned the fact that Somalia had consistently been receiving aid for thirty-three years.[42] It was not the form of foreign aid that Aidid criticized; he took issue with why the aid was provided and who benefited from it. The Soviets built the port of Berbera, and the United States expanded it and built the port of Kismayo, with both superpowers enjoying military benefits for doing so. Likewise, the Italians, British, French, and even Chinese all contributed to infrastructure projects that built hospitals, ports, airports, roads, and agricultural initiatives, as well as a satellite and telecommunications complex in Mogadishu. Despite all this, Aidid argued, this foreign aid was not being used to improve Somalia. Instead, foreign actors ingratiated themselves to the Barre regime to serve their own interests, directly facilitating the continued existence of a dictatorship that used that aid to brutally quash any dissent.[43]

The Issaq Genocide and Somali Civil War

In the early 1980s Barre focused primarily on fighting the SSDF guerrillas and slowly displacing the Issaq, with ethnic cleansing and low-intensity conflict confined to regions in northwestern Somalia. However, two events in May and December 1986 made wider civil war a certainty. In May, Barre was injured in an automobile accident. During his three-month-long recovery in a Saudi hospital, his regime hovered on the brink of implosion as competition emerged over who should take control of the country. On one side were the military officers on the Supreme Revolutionary Council; on the other were Marehan elites, including Barre's well-positioned family members. Barre's recovery made the issue moot, but the perceived challenge to his authority resulted in a ruthless purge of the officer corps and the release of his Red Berets on the population of Mogadishu to seek out dissidents, real or imagined. In December, the SNM assassinated the regional chief of the National Security Service in northwestern Somalia. In response, Barre promoted his son-in-law, Hersi Morgan, to the rank of general and sent him north as the military governor to quash the Issaq threat.[44] What had been regime-sponsored ethnic cleansing became genocide.

In a confidential letter to his father-in-law, Morgan explained that he was going to "liquidate" the "Isaak problem."[45] He used methods hauntingly similar to Nazi policies toward the Jews in the 1930s. Under Morgan's direction, Issaqs' property was confiscated, and their bank accounts were seized and "redistributed." Issaqs in government or military positions were purged, and Issaq-owned businesses were handed over to other clans. Under Morgan's authority, military courts imposed the death penalty, often without evidence of any crime. When the chief prosecutor of the northwest region balked at conducting what he considered unlawful executions, Morgan replaced him with the notoriously cruel Colonel Yusuf Muse, under whom the mass execution of Issaqs became commonplace, with communities forced to watch as a warning. Rape was widespread and used as a weapon of intimidation. Issaq students were beaten, shot, or imprisoned indefinitely for protesting the slaughter. Estimates vary, but the Center for Justice and Accountability estimated that two hundred thousand Issaqs were killed in a forgotten genocide.[46]

The violence unleashed by Barre throughout 1986 and 1987 turned the population against him. The other major clans feared it was only a matter of time before they too suffered the same fate as the Majerteen, the Issaq, and the population of Mogadishu. By April 1988, the instability in Somalia had become so severe that Barre relinquished claims to the Ogaden region and signed a nonaggression treaty with Mengistu in neighboring Ethiopia. The agreement mandated that neither country would assist any rebel organizations or allow them into their respective territories.[47] This ended the ability of the SNM and SSDF to shelter and train in Ethiopia, leaving them vulnerable to Morgan's ferocity. With its haven gone, it was now or never for the SNM. Taking the National Army by surprise, the SNM launched an all-out offensive across Somaliland in May 1988 that captured Burao and Hargeisa, the country's second largest city. Repressed Issaqs welcomed the SNM with open arms, and many joined the uprising. But one of the SNM's principal goals was to force the Ogadeni refugees back across the Ethiopian border. For the SNM, the Ogadeni were synonymous with Barre. Because of this, from the outset of the offensive, they attacked Ogadeni refugee camps and used the same methods Barre had visited on the Issaq: ethnic cleansing.[48] The Somali Civil War began in earnest. Far from being purely anti-Barre, clan-based violence became a hallmark of all sides. It was no longer the sole preserve of the Barre regime.

The National Army under Morgan quickly recovered and launched a counteroffensive that did not discriminate between the SNM and civilians. A survivor interviewed by Africa Watch described the relentless attacks on Hargeisa by Morgan's forces: "From dawn to dusk, day in and day out, and intermittently during the night, every night, there was shelling, bombing, people being slaughtered by soldiers in the streets, in their homes, and in all the places they sought refuge."[49] Casualty estimates ranged from five thousand to twenty thousand, earning Morgan the moniker the "Butcher of Hargeisa."[50] Elsewhere in Somaliland, any Issaq that Morgan thought might join the SNM offensive was arbitrarily imprisoned and often tortured or executed.

The depravity of Morgan's campaign was too big to ignore, prompting debate among US policymakers on whether to continue to support Barre's regime. General H. Norman Schwarzkopf, commander of US Central Command (CENTCOM), pressed Herman J. Cohen, assistant secretary of state for African affairs, to ensure access to Berbera for defense of the Persian Gulf. Cohen pointed out that with the international community and media criticizing Barre's methods and denouncing those that continued to support him, Congress would want to cut the flow of aid. Secretary of State James Baker informed Barre that if human rights abuses continued, aid would not be forthcoming. Frank T. Criggler, the US ambassador to Somalia, countered that, given the country's dependence on aid, continuing to provide it was the only way to influence Barre and perhaps bring about a settlement with the SNM. Nonetheless, ties were cut, and the aid stopped flowing. Maren suggested that with this curtailment, human rights abuses and violence only got worse. Barre had nothing left to lose.[51]

The United Somali Congress

Fighting that had been confined to the northwest and central regions quickly spread across Somalia. As fear and instability grew throughout the nation, the population fell back on their clans to distinguish friend from foe. Even Barre began to doubt anyone who was not Marehan. When he arrested General Aden Abdullahi Nur, his minister of defense and the highest-ranking Ogadeni in the administration, Ogadeni officers in the south formed the Somali Patriotic Movement (SPM) to resist Barre's regime. Barre's persecution of Mogadishu residents hailing from the Hawiye clan caused a mutiny of Hawiye Army officers in Galkayo in 1989. Influential Hawiye elites and intellectuals formed the United Somali Congress (USC) in Rome in January 1989. John Drysdale, a historian of Somalia acquainted with the key participants, credited Ismail Jumale Ossoble, a prominent civil rights lawyer, with formulating the initial USC strategy. Ossoble was renowned for defending those facing prosecution under the Barre regime—a job that resulted in his imprisonment on several occasions. Hedging its bets, the USC pursued a dual-track approach that was both open to negotiating with Barre and willing to overthrow him. Ossoble was considered the most likely candidate to replace Barre and enjoyed popular support. The problem was that Barre still controlled the National Army, which, though bruised, was still more powerful than the embryonic militias of the other factions. Thus, in addition to the USC's financial and organizational base in Rome, two satellite organizations were created: USC Mogadishu and USC Ethiopia. The former focused on negotiation options, and the latter set out to create a military force from those Hawiye who had mutinied.[52]

To lead the USC Ethiopia militia, Ossoble chose Mohamed Farah Aidid, who was stationed in New Delhi as the Somali ambassador to India. A member of the Habr-Gidr subclan of the Hawiye, Aidid was the logical choice. Born in 1934 in Beledweyne, Aidid served as a colonial police officer in Italian Somalia in the 1950s. After independence in 1960, he was commissioned as an army officer and quickly rose through the ranks, becoming army chief of staff by the time of the 1969 coup. Recognized as a competent and ambitious officer, Aidid was imprisoned for six years, along with other officers that Barre feared could be figureheads in any future coup against his regime. Notably, Aidid shared a cell with Colonel Abdullahi Yusuf, a future ringleader of the Majerteen rebellion and leader of the SSDF militia.[53] But Aidid's professional ability was so impressive that Barre released him just prior to the Ogaden War, promoted him to brigadier general, and tapped him to serve as the dictator's aide-de-camp. He was one of the few officers to emerge from the defeat with a reputation as a capable and respected commander. A rarity among officers of military forces on the periphery of the Cold War, Aidid attended both the Accademia Militare di Modena in Italy and the M. V. Frunze Military Academy in Moscow, enjoying the best military education open to NATO and Warsaw Pact officers. USC members donated funds to assist Aidid in defecting from his diplomatic post in New Delhi to command the USC Ethiopia forces, which then crossed into central Somalia to join the fray. On 2 October 1990 the USC, SNM, and SPM agreed to join forces. No separate peace with Barre was permissible. His defeat was the shared goal. After the Barre regime's destruction, the factions would form a provisional government, and democratic elections would be held.[54] Aidid later used this agreement as the basis for uniting several factions into a military and political coalition, the Somali National Alliance (SNA).[55] Barre was thus fighting the SNM in the north, the SPM in the south, and the USC in the center, and he was losing.

Even though Aidid's military campaign was under way, there were attempts at negotiation. In May 1990 a manifesto was published, written largely by Ossoble, calling for a national reconciliation conference. It was signed by 114 notable moderates, intellectuals, businessmen, and officials from both the Barre regime and the previous republic's administration. The "Manifesto Group" called for an end to the civil war, an end to repressive laws, a multiparty system, and constitutional reform. They claimed Somalis had enjoyed more rights under colonial rule than under Barre's repressive regime and urged him to step down. Among the signatories were Aden Abdullah Osman and Sheikh Mukhtar Mohamed Hussein, the first president and parliamentary president of the 1960 government, along with prominent members of USC Mogadishu. The Manifesto Group was naïve, however. Despite being squeezed militarily into a shrinking perimeter, Barre's approach toward internal dissent had not softened. Those signatories he could reach were arrested, some were killed, and the rest fled Mogadishu.[56] In a telling display of Barre's increasingly violent methods, he had his Red Berets fire into a crowd of spectators at a rally in Mogadishu who were guilty only of booing his arrival. The fighting raged on, and the destruction of Somalia worsened.[57]

At this point, fractures in the USC leadership began to appear. Aidid's forces were rolling back the National Army in a push toward

Mogadishu. His battlefield success earned him election as USC chairman in June 1990, but not all USC leaders accepted this, including one influential member in particular: Ali Mahdi Mohamed. Ali Mahdi had been a politician during Somalia's brief experience of democracy, which earned him a short stay in prison after the coup. He became a successful businessman and hotelier and helped finance Aidid's return from India.[58] Prominent within USC Mogadishu and a manifesto signatory, Ali Mahdi fled to Rome to escape Barre's retribution and found that the USC Rome membership was not pleased with Aidid's growing popularity. After his election as USC chairman, Aidid offered Ali Mahdi a position as secretary of the interior, but he refused. The real issue was a matter of clan and class competition. The Hawiye clan had two large but quite different subclans: the rural Habr-Gidr, hailing from the pastoral lands of central Somalia, and the urban Abgal in Mogadishu. Squeezed between the Abgal and Habr-Gidr were two smaller Hawiye subclans—the Hawadle and Murusade—also based in the capital. Ali Mahdi and his fellow Abgal in the USC felt threatened by the encroachment of the rural Habr-Gidr, personified by Aidid, on power positions within the Hawiye that the Abgal traditionally coveted.[59] Thus, a bloodless power struggle developed between Aidid and Ali Mahdi. The politically focused USC Rome and USC Mogadishu backed Ali Mahdi, and the USC Ethiopia militia backed Aidid.

The situation became more complex when Ossoble, the one candidate everyone could support to replace Barre, suddenly died. This created a vacuum that Aidid, Ali Mahdi, and the various wings of the USC sought to fill, but they all disagreed on who should fill it: a Habr-Gidr or an Abgal. The issue was temporarily tabled due to the war. Barre declared a state of emergency in December 1990 as Aidid's forces closed in on the capital. In desperation, the dictator appointed a new prime minister, an Issaq freshly released from prison after eight years, and promised free elections in the hopes of stemming the tide of violence against his regime. It was too little, too late. A general uprising began on 29 December, and Mogadishu descended into chaos.[60]

Operation Eastern Exit

On 2 January 1991, amid planning for Operation Desert Storm to liberate Kuwait from Iraqi forces, Major General Steven Arnold, the Third

Army operations officer for CENTCOM, was ordered to divert forces in the Persian Gulf to evacuate the US embassy in Mogadishu.[61] Ambassador James K. Bishop had cabled that his staff could not get to the airport because of fighting in the streets, and armed looters were assaulting the compound where five hundred people were sheltering.[62] This created a complex problem for CENTCOM planners. From their perspective, the wider situation in Mogadishu beyond the embassy walls was unknown. No one wanted a repeat of the Iran hostage crisis, but CENTCOM was focused on the imminent offensive against Saddam Hussein's Iraq. The Soviet-built air defense system outside Mogadishu created concerns about the feasibility of extraction by air. In the absence of any other options, two US Navy amphibious assault ships were dispatched from the Persian Gulf for Operation Eastern Exit, the evacuation of the US embassy in Mogadishu by helicopter.[63]

The helicopters were launched at extreme range due to Bishop's reports of violence, and the extraction team of US Marines and Navy SEALs was expecting to evacuate about one hundred Americans. They soon discovered that this was a gross underestimation. Responding to personal appeals from both the Soviet and British ambassadors, Bishop had dispatched teams to other embassies to retrieve their dignitaries, while others arrived at the US embassy gates hoping to be evacuated with the Americans. Somali police arrived and threatened to fire on the evacuation helicopters, and Bishop had to bribe their commander with thousands of dollars and the keys to the embassy's cars. With the compound under fire, the helicopters began shuttle runs, transporting 281 people from 32 countries to the ships offshore. The Italians launched a similarly successful evacuation of their embassy, Operation Ippocampo. Despite hundreds of Somalis sheltering in the compound, none of them were evacuated; nor did any try to rush the aircraft.[64] As the city was consumed by violence, they resigned themselves to their fate.

The End of Barre

Aidid's forces entered Mogadishu on 19 January, and Barre's desperation became palpable. Regime officials met with Aidid on 23 January and requested an immediate cease-fire. Barre claimed he had formed a new government composed of seventy-five Manifesto Group members and twenty-five regime appointees. In keeping with the principles of the

USC's agreement with the SNM and SPM, Aidid refused to consider anything other than unconditional surrender. During the night of 26 January, Barre slipped out of the Villa Somalia presidential palace with what remained of his forces under Morgan and left Mogadishu to the USC.[65]

With Barre's departure, the USC won a major victory, but the contest over its leadership resumed two days later. Without consulting any other faction, USC Mogadishu appointed Ali Mahdi as interim president of Somalia for twenty-eight days. Aidid, USC Ethiopia, and the other factions were outraged, especially when it emerged that Ali Mahdi's appointment had been decided by just four of the USC's 105-member congress. Seeing himself as Ossoble's heir apparent, Ali Mahdi had unilaterally seized power. Worse still, because of his Abgal support base in USC Rome, the Italian government immediately endorsed his presidency.[66] Aidid was in a difficult position. Although Mogadishu was in USC hands, it was divided between those who supported him and those who supported Ali Mahdi. Meanwhile, Barre was reconsolidating his forces in the interior. Aidid could either deal with Ali Mahdi or pursue Barre. He chose the latter. The civil war then entered its most destructive phase.

The parting shot of Barre's final expulsion from Somalia was a man-made humanitarian disaster encompassing widespread ethnic cleansing, destruction, famine, and starvation. After fleeing Mogadishu, Barre gathered what remained of the National Army, comprising mainly his Marehan clan, near Bardera and began advancing toward the divided capital. By April 1991, Barre had reached Afgooye, thirty kilometers outside Mogadishu. It was there, on 8 April, that Aidid's forces, with support from the SNM, decisively defeated Barre and then doggedly pursued him south for another battle near the port of Kismayo, where the local SPM helped deliver a second crushing defeat two weeks later. Barre retreated to the Bay region and its capital Baidoa, using a scorched-earth policy to hinder Aidid's pursuit, and encamped his forces there for months. The end of Barre's campaign to cling to power came in April 1992. He advanced from Baidoa toward Mogadishu and reached Wanleweyne, just outside the capital. Aidid was waiting for him. In two days of heavy fighting, Barre's forces were routed for the last time. The survivors fled into Kenya. Barre went into exile and turned over command to Morgan, who rebranded the battered remnants of the National Army the Somali National Front (SNF).[67]

With Barre's final defeat and exile, the unifying effect of an existential threat had disappeared. The dozen or more factions that emerged

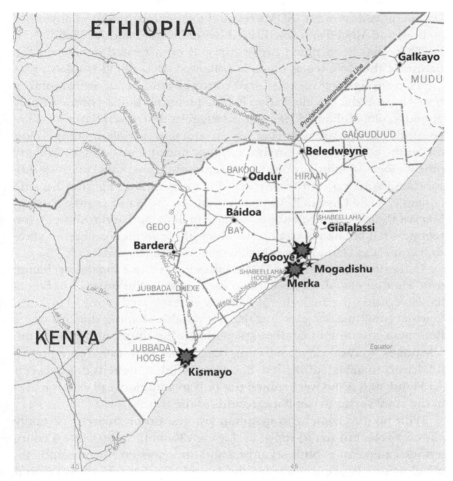

Major Battles between Barre and Aidid, 1991–1992

during the civil war turned on one another and began fighting along clan lines for regional and national control. In the south, the SNF fought both the SPM in Kismayo and the Dir clan's Southern Somali National Movement (SSNM) in Bardera. In the north, two Dir subclans, the Ise and Gadabursi, formed the United Somali Front (USF) and the Somali Democratic Association (SDA), which fought each other and the SNM. In central Somalia, the SNF fought a resurgent SSDF in a region also contested by Aidid's USC. In Baidoa, the Rahanweyn clan's Somali

Democratic Movement (SDM) resisted the encroachment of any other faction, and Mogadishu was divided between Aidid and Ali Mahdi.[68]

There has been much discussion and even heated debate on the nature of the violence as Somalia collapsed. Describing it solely as vying factions fighting for territorial control would be an oversimplification. Nor could it be called anarchy. Clan tensions boiling over certainly played a role. Mohamed Haji Ingiriis suggests that, given Barre's exploitation of clan divisions during his dictatorship, a violent competition for land, resources, and survival erupted once he was ousted. Military officers formed militias claiming to represent clans, subclans, and sub-subclans. With no clan strong enough to dominate, fighting became endemic.[69] Lee Cassanelli claims that due to the Barre regime's use of Marxist rhetoric to take ownership of Somalia's land and resources, the regime's fall created a vacuum in which these militias entered a zero-sum contest to claim these valuable resources for themselves.[70]

Catherine Besteman and I. M. Lewis engaged in a heated exchange over whether clan divisions explain the nature of the violence in Somalia. Given that the majority of factions were formed along clan lines, Lewis argued that the clan was the key variable shaping the civil war.[71] Besteman countered that this explanation is too simple and ignores the "cleavages" of race, class, and status that, in her view, were more powerful drivers than clan affiliation. She observed that the tensions between Ali Mahdi and Aidid were rooted not only in ambition and clan but also in the rural versus urban backgrounds of the two.[72]

With no government to maintain law and order, anarchy certainly played a role, but so did reprisals. Lidwien Kapteijns notes that a countrywide campaign of both organized and unorganized violence and ethnic cleansing broke out against the Darod clan because of its favored status under the Barre regime. Elements from all factions and clans participated, but the hallmark for Kapteijns was ordinary civilians attacking others based on clan affiliation.[73] Ingiriis observes that although several militias perpetrated such violence, these "reprisals were not clear-cut, but more complicated phenomena than assumed by many outsiders."[74] With Barre's defeat, the loss of a unifying goal meant that most faction leaders lost effective control over their forces—highlighting that most factions were loosely organized and poorly disciplined. Ingiriis largely exonerates the faction leaders from masterminding the ethnic-cleansing campaign against the Darod, writing, "how a group that could not control its rank-and-file could organise a clan cleansing campaign

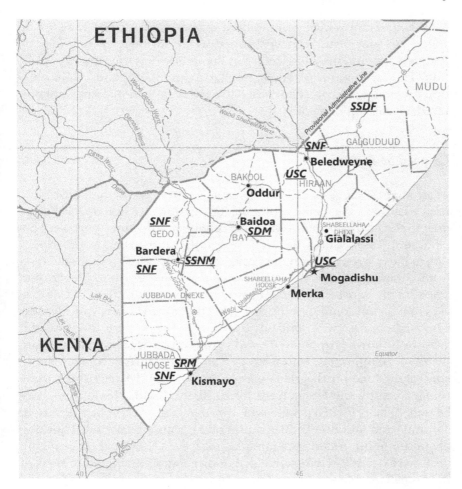

Approximation of Faction Concentrations, 1991–1992

was a puzzle to the rational mind."[75] This loss of control and pattern of unorganized, unrestrained reprisals meant that some groups that had opposed Barre, such as the SSDF and SPM, briefly fought the USC and SNM, fearing revenge for their clans' previous association with the regime.[76] It was, for Ingiriis, "a hostile, anarchic environment, over which no one could yield a real power."[77] After decades of oppression, the *Diya* tradition of blood payment reasserted itself with extreme prejudice among those thirsty for revenge.

Whether it was clan competition, dynamics of race or class, or revenge, no one factor can be blamed as the primary driver; they all featured prominently, and caught in the middle was the Somali population. The result was a total collapse. Barre was finally gone, but in every practical sense, Somalia had ceased to exist as a functional state and now faced a catastrophic famine.

Gripped by Famine

Later analysis suggests the famine came in three waves, demonstrating the cascading cataclysm of collapse. The first wave came in April 1991 during the civil war and peaked in September, affecting the lower Shabelle and Jubba valleys between Mogadishu and Kismayo, principally due to Barre's retreat from the capital toward Kenya. Ten thousand died in the fighting; hundreds of thousands more fled north to Mogadishu, where many perished as the infrastructure to support them did not exist. Others went south to Kenya, where refugee camps were quickly overwhelmed. Disease was rampant; banditry and rape were widespread.[78] Kenyan authorities opposed the influx of thousands of Somali refugees, many of them armed, who were perceived as a threat to maintaining control over the northeastern part of the country.[79] After visiting these refugee camps, the US ambassador to Kenya, Smith Hempstone, concluded, "The principal problem in this respect seemed to be the cussed, contrary, and obstinate individualism of the Somali character. They simply were not interested in digging latrines, even though their own children were dying."[80] Hempstone's prejudiced and inflammatory views of the Somali people would become infamous.

On 25 March 1991 Assistant Secretary of State Herman Cohen officially declared Somalia a disaster, triggering full mobilization of the Office of Foreign Disaster Assistance (OFDA) within USAID. OFDA's initial focus was managing displaced persons, casualties, and refugees from the civil war. Relief camps were bursting, and squalid camp conditions made militias an attractive option as factions and unaffiliated gangs solicited recruits with plundered relief supplies. Amidst the famine's first wave, OFDA director Andrew Natsios worked to bring UN relief agencies back to Somalia after their withdrawal during the exodus of all foreign dignitaries. Natsios offered to second a senior OFDA officer to the UN Office of Disaster Relief to coordinate efforts. This would have

relieved the UN, which was concerned about the violence, from having to send anyone itself. But the UN Security Office vetoed the offer over concerns about legal liability. Natsios then turned to the International Committee of the Red Cross (ICRC), which quickly commenced the largest relief effort since the Second World War, devoting 50 percent of its global resources to Somalia alone in 1991. Natsios also invited executives from the largest relief organizations to witness the growing disaster in Somalia firsthand, hoping to galvanize them to intervene. It worked.[81]

The famine's second wave began in late 1991, a direct result of Barre's scorched-earth policy as he retreated to the Bay region and its capital, Baidoa, home to the agrarian Rahanweyn clan. Encamped there for months, Barre's forces raped, killed, and plundered the Rahanweyn people, destroyed farm equipment, and caused a massive depopulation of the region. Already weakened by the first wave of famine, the second wave saw vulnerable Somalis—the old, the very young, and those injured in the fighting—succumbing to disease exacerbated by starvation; seventy thousand died.[82] Survivors fled into the surrounding regions of Bardera, Beledweyne, Oddur, and Mogadishu in search of relief.

The origins of this second wave were misunderstood at the time, and the level of destruction and displacement within the Bay region and the city of Baidoa was underappreciated. Relief efforts focused on the starving Somalis flooding into adjacent regions, without considering where they had come from. The ICRC initially refused to go to Baidoa, claiming there was no evidence of famine there. Relief did not reach the stricken city until April 1992, by which time the mortality levels had already peaked. Yet the aftereffects of the second wave were acutely felt everywhere as the internally displaced tried to survive. Within months, Somalia, a country of some seven million people, had one million displaced persons and four million facing starvation, disease, or some other form of humanitarian crisis. The final wave of the famine came in late 1992, with malaria, measles, and diarrhea sweeping across the land, killing thousands already compromised by hunger.[83]

With relief agencies present in only a small portion of the country, an accurate death count was, and is, impossible to calculate. Given its many large nomadic groups, estimating the population of Somalia itself proved elusive. One analysis suggests that 202,000 to 238,000 died during the famine in 1991–1992, with 80,000 more killed in the civil war and subsequent interfaction conflict.[84] Including the estimated 200,000 Issaqs killed in the Somaliland genocide, by the time the Unified Task

Force arrived in December 1992, about 518,000 had died—or one in every fourteen Somalis.

The USC Power Struggle Becomes War

As Somalia fell further into the grip of famine, the power struggle between Ali Mahdi and Aidid turned violent. To claim it was an arbitrary contest for dominance between "warlords" is both incorrect and an oversimplification. It evolved very quickly throughout 1991, with ebbs and flows. With Barre on the run and his regime on the ropes, all factions debated the future of Somalia. Although views on the path forward differed, there was broad consensus on one thing: no one wanted anything reminiscent of the Barre regime. Ali Mahdi's questionable appointment as president stoked fears that one dictator was replacing another. However, in the initial period, while Aidid was focused on finishing Barre off, the fact that all the factions were still talking instead of fighting meant there was hope that tensions would ease, making it possible to move forward with a new government. It was not to be.

The day before Ali Mahdi's twenty-eight-day interim term expired, the USC congress met in the Lafweyn Hotel in Mogadishu to consider the composition of the new government. Delegates had to scramble for cover when Ali Mahdi's militia suddenly fired into the hotel, although the motivation for the attack is unclear.[85] In any case, Ali Mahdi remained in power and announced his own reconciliation conference to discuss the future government, but it was canceled when many factions refused the invitation.[86] The central problem was that Ali Mahdi would not recognize Aidid as USC chairman, and Aidid would not recognize Ali Mahdi as president. In addition, most factions believed that Ali Mahdi had illegitimately seized power. This deadlock hindered the ability to tackle the growing crisis in Somalia—looting, fighting, and starvation. Nevertheless, attempts were made to break the impasse.

Italy and Egypt sponsored talks in Djibouti between the vying factions in May 1991, just after Barre was repulsed at Afgooye. There was no breakthrough, and Ali Mahdi continued to claim that his presidency was legitimate. Soon afterward, on 18 May, the SNM declared the independence of the Somaliland Republic. John Drysdale suggests that Ali Mahdi's unilateral assumption of the presidency without consultation stoked the SNM's fear of a return to Mogadishu-centric rule. Somaliland had been the lesser partner after unification in 1960 and then suffered horrifically under Barre. Unwilling to take the risk a third time, the SNM informed Ali Mahdi of its intention to secede and its hope that relations could remain cordial.[87]

In June, the Hawiye clan elders interceded, and Aidid and Ali Mahdi came to an agreement. The three USC branches would merge into one unified political entity, and a congress in July would elect a chairman. Whatever the result, the decision of the newly unified seven hundred–member congress would confer far more legitimacy than the questionable four-member quorum that had elected Ali Mahdi in the first place. Under the agreement, Ali Mahdi was also bound to abide by the policy decisions of the USC Central Committee. No one wanted another dictator. The new USC congress met in Mogadishu on 5 July 1991 and elected Aidid chairman with 72 percent of the vote.[88] Ali Mahdi finally accepted Aidid's position, and the USC Central Committee tasked Aidid with forming a new National Army. Soon after, Italy and Egypt sponsored a second round of talks in Djibouti (Djibouti II) that achieved broad agreement on several issues. Although neither Aidid nor Ali Mahdi attended personally, the conference decided on a 123-member parliament based on the pre-Barre democracy, a return to the 1960 constitution, and, importantly, the election of a president by the parliament, with the nominee chosen by the USC. When the USC nominated Ali Mahdi for a two-year term, Aidid had no objections, and he now recognized Ali Mahdi's position as president. Ali Mahdi was sworn in as interim president of Somalia on 18 August 1991.[89]

While all roads appeared to lead to reconciliation, irreconcilable differences arose almost immediately. The SSDF and SPM demanded cabinet posts in return for not challenging the presidential election, but instead, Ali Mahdi began arbitrarily filling government positions, in some cases selecting former Barre regime officials. He then attempted to amend the 1960 constitution to grant himself more executive powers. But Djibouti II had agreed on a constitutional president, not an executive one, and many factions and their leaders thought that Ali Mahdi was deliberately sidestepping Djibouti II and his agreement to follow USC Central Committee policies. In a supreme contradiction, while accepting the conference as the basis for his legitimacy as president, Ali Mahdi claimed that because he had not attended Djibouti II, he was not bound by it. Nor did he believe that the USC, especially under Aidid's chairmanship, should influence his actions more than any other party.

Ali Mahdi unilaterally appointed a prime minister in October 1991 and established a Council of Ministers that never convened, prompting Aidid to announce that he refused to recognize Ali Mahdi's self-appointed government.[90]

Ali Mahdi had money and Italian support, but Aidid had military power. Fighting broke out in Mogadishu on 13 November 1991. Ali Mahdi's militia struck first, attacking Aidid's headquarters.[91] It was Abgal versus Habr-Gidr, with the other Hawiye subclans caught in the middle. The Hawadle chose neutrality but leaned toward Aidid, while the Murusade were outwardly hostile to what they perceived as the rural Habr-Gidr's encroachment on their urban domain. By March 1992, thirty thousand had died in the fighting, and half a million were without power or water in the city—amid a worsening famine. The USC civil war went on unabated, punctuated only by Barre's second attempt to recapture Mogadishu, which resulted in his final defeat at Wanleweyne and exile in April.[92]

Competing theories exist to explain why fighting broke out between Aidid and Ali Mahdi. Blame is traditionally assigned to Aidid, with the established narrative citing his power-hungry inability to accept anyone else as the leader of Somalia. Did Aidid have ambitions? Certainly. But he was not alone in that regard. Drysdale, who knew him personally, argues that as far as Aidid was concerned, he had a legitimate case to be Barre's successor. As USC chairman, he had forced Barre out of Mogadishu and then twice repulsed his efforts to return. In addition, the first SYL prime minister elected in 1956 was, like Aidid, a member of the Habr-Gidr. He therefore claimed an ancestral lineage to the position, an argument not without merit in Somali society.[93] This rhetoric emerged, however, only after Ali Mahdi was perceived to be centralizing power in his own position as president, and only after he had reneged on agreements. This turning point is usually overlooked, hindering a proper analysis of what happened and why.

We cannot know what Aidid was thinking during these events, but his writings have probative value. He wrote of the importance of the return of democracy to Somalia. After independence, he claimed, the SYL had betrayed its promise of a government free from corruption, and this weakness facilitated Barre's efforts to turn the country into a "concentration camp." This historical experience, he observed, "warns us not to go in for that very model of democracy. . . . We cannot afford again to be cheated by such so-called representatives of the people" who, once elected, serve only their own interests. Aidid argued that Somalia should become a democracy enshrined in the constitution, rooted in Somali social, cultural, and Islamic norms. He envisioned a parliament elected by proportional and statistical representation through a competitive system of political parties that were national in character to avoid clan parochialism, and he championed constitutional amendments achieved through referenda. Somalis, he wrote, "did not shed their precious blood for any one tribe or political party."[94] With Ali Mahdi's pronounced preference for Abgal dominance and his arbitrary decisions to appoint government ministers and amend the constitution, it is not surprising that Aidid and the other factions that had suffered Barre's persecution resorted to violence in the face of presidential intransigence.

In December 1991—as Aidid and Ali Mahdi were fighting each other in Mogadishu, as the second wave of famine gripped Somalia, and as Barre slaughtered the Rahanweyn around Baidoa and prepared his final offensive to retake Mogadishu—UN Secretary-General Javier Perez de Cuellar received a letter from Omar Arteh Qhalib, Ali Mahdi's appointed prime minister, officially requesting UN assistance to deal with the deteriorating situation.[95] The international community was being summoned to intervene in Somalia. By the time this happened, though, most of the factions that had emerged as clan-based political movements had raised their own militias to confront the brutality of the Barre regime and the ensuing civil war. By necessity, politics and military power had become inseparable in Somalia.

2 | A Tale of Two Bureaucracies
The United Nations and United States Decide to Intervene in Somalia

I am more than ever convinced of the need for international military personnel to be deployed in Somalia.
— UN Secretary-General Boutros Boutros-Ghali[1]

Baidoa has become, as much of Somalia, a land of the living dead.
— Congressman Mervyn Dymally, chair of the House Subcommittee on Africa[2]

On 14 September 1992, surrounded by the ruins of the anarchic Somali capital, five hundred UN peacekeepers of the 7th Battalion of the Pakistani Frontier Force Regiment landed at Mogadishu airport. They were the first peacekeepers deployed under the United Nations Operation in Somalia (UNOSOM), intended to curb the violence hampering humanitarian relief efforts in the famine-stricken, war-torn state. Nine long months had passed since Omar Arteh Qhalib had pleaded with the UN Security Council to address the plight of Somalia.[3] Crippled by a civil war to excise the Barre regime and the subsequent fighting between Aidid and Ali Mahdi over Mogadishu, the Somali government had ceased to exist.

Getting UN peacekeepers into Somalia was a complex process fraught with frustration and delay not only because of UN doctrine and attitudes toward peacekeeping but also because of the wider political considerations of UN member states, principally the United States, and, more critically, the truly unique situation Somalia represented. This chapter tracks the decision-making processes that led to the deployment of UNOSOM and the rationale behind President George H. W. Bush's decision to send the largest number of American troops in history to the African continent. Understanding why it took so long for the international community to intervene in Somalia requires an acknowledgment that the crisis posed two unique challenges for the UN.

First, any UN peacekeeping deployment could, and did, founder on the issue of the host government's consent. Peacekeeping operations fell under Chapter VI of the UN Charter, "Pacific Settlement of Disputes." Article 36 therein enabled the Security Council to take action to encourage a peaceful settlement, such as introducing a peacekeeping force, but this action was dependent on one word: consent. Even though it is not mentioned in the UN Charter, obtaining the consent of the host government was a central principle of UN peacekeeping doctrine by the 1990s. It was not a legal requirement per se, but it aligned with the championing of state sovereignty espoused in Article 2 of the UN Charter. Consent was a practical necessity, conferring legitimacy, and it increased the likelihood that any peacekeeping mission would succeed with fewer casualties if the host government consented to its presence. But obtaining consent often proved difficult, as the UN experienced during the collapse of Yugoslavia.

In Somalia, there was no national government for the UN to deal with or to give consent. Ali Mahdi claimed the Djibouti II agreement legitimized him as president, but given his Barre-like attempt to centralize power, many factions disputed his authority, Aidid chief among them.[4] Who should the UN negotiate with? Worse still, many factions viewed the UN with contempt and suspicion for sponsoring the conference that had elected Ali Mahdi in the first place.[5] At the very least, the spirit of Chapter VI required consent from both Ali Mahdi and Aidid, but these two leaders were at war, and their control over their respective militias was sometimes uncertain. And consent from the always suspicious Aidid, when it came, was grudging, conditional, and subject to arbitrary revocation.

Second, UN efforts were unable to keep pace with the escalating violence. UNOSOM was originally created to monitor a cease-fire, which, though tentative, had been agreed to by Aidid and Ali Mahdi, and both had consented to the presence of UN military observers. The later expansion of UNOSOM to an armed security force due to the deepening crisis in Somalia required new consent from both leaders. Aidid's paranoia about UN favoritism toward Ali Mahdi frustrated this process, as he reacted to actions and perceived actions by the UN. However, even after deployment of the security force, the scale of the lawlessness and the crippling inadequacies of the UN forces meant that UNOSOM could not achieve its mission. This failure compelled the United States to intervene with Operation Restore Hope to reinforce the credibility of the UN as a force for maintaining international peace and security in the post–Cold War world.

The Cease-fire between Aidid and Ali Mahdi

When UN Secretary-General Javier Perez de Cuellar received Qhalib's appeal in December 1991, confronting the crisis in Somalia was a complex issue in practical terms.[6] Within the international community, Herbert Cohen, US assistant secretary of state for African affairs, argued that the perpetual violence in places such as Ethiopia, Sudan, Angola, Mozambique, and Liberia had created "conflict fatigue." UN peacekeepers were already heavily committed in Yugoslavia, Cambodia, and Namibia. The international community's resources were finite, and in a sea of competing crises, Somalia was, in Cohen's words, "out of luck."[7]

Perez de Cuellar's term as UN secretary-general was also ending. His successor, after a contentious election, was Boutros Boutros-Ghali. The sixty-nine-year-old former Egyptian foreign minister had run against Bernard Chidzero, Zimbabwe's finance minister, for the top UN position. The United States liked neither candidate, but Boutros-Ghali had the backing of France, Belgium, and most of the African states, giving him enough support to become the first UN secretary-general from the African continent.[8] A classified biography described him as "energetic, determined, and intellectual . . . [having] a vision of a world organization that can act as an agent for positive change."[9] After considering Qhalib's appeal, both Perez de Cuellar and Boutros-Ghali agreed that the UN should intervene in Somalia "for the restoration of peace."[10] As Marrack Goulding, UN undersecretary-general for peacekeeping, recalled, Boutros-Ghali was driven by a desire to correct what he perceived as the UN's neglect of African issues. To that end, James Jonah, undersecretary-general for political affairs, was sent to Mogadishu in January 1992.

The UN's first goal was to encourage Aidid and Ali Mahdi to declare a cease-fire. During Jonah's initial visit, the chief UN politico was so shocked by the ruined capital that he privately questioned whether any intervention would be worth the effort.[11] Nevertheless, when the UN Security Council met on 23 January 1992, it declared an arms embargo on Somalia and instructed Boutros-Ghali to engage the factions in negotiations. This he did by inviting both Ali Mahdi and Aidid to cease-fire negotiations in New York on 10 February. These talks, chaired personally by Boutros-Ghali, resulted in a cease-fire commitment from both factions, despite each delegation's refusal to meet the other in person. Jonah then drafted a plan for political reconciliation and a UN proposal to deploy military observers to monitor the cease-fire. On 3 March in Mogadishu, after much personal cajoling by Jonah, Aidid and Ali Mahdi signed the cease-fire plan, agreeing to disengage and restrain their forces, facilitate the flow of aid to alleviate the famine, and allow the deployment of UN observers.[12]

With a tentative cease-fire in place, the Security Council sent a technical team to Mogadishu led by David Bassiouni, the UN humanitarian coordinator for Somalia, to explore the practicalities of deploying the observers.[13] Bassiouni's recommendations were significant. He proposed a cease-fire monitoring group of fifty unarmed observers stationed on either side of the north-south "Green Line" dividing Mogadishu between Aidid and Ali Mahdi.[14] This force, Boutros-Ghali suggested, should be called the United Nations Operation in Somalia, shortened to UNOSOM. Bassiouni's team also developed a "90 Day Plan of Action" to provide 1.5 million Somalis with relief supplies and proposed "corridors" and "zones of peace" in Mogadishu to allow the delivery of those supplies in coordination with the ICRC, the World Food Program (WFP), and the UN International Children's Emergency Fund (UNI-CEF).[15]

UNOSOM was formally established on 24 April 1992 by Resolution 751, which also endorsed Bassiouni's recommendations for monitoring the cease-fire and the relief plan.[16] The fifty-strong unarmed observer force under the command of Pakistani Brigadier Imtiaz Shaheen was scheduled to arrive in Mogadishu on 10 July 1992.[17] Until then, with the cease-fire in place and holding, managing Somalia fell to the newly appointed UN special representative to the secretary-general and UNOSOM's civilian head, Ambassador Mohamed Sahnoun.[18] An Algerian diplomat, Sahnoun was chosen for his knowledge of African affairs and to increase the number of Africans in key UN positions. He arrived in Somalia on 4 May 1992 to find that the UN effort on the ground consisted of just himself. UNOSOM had no staff and no resources. His first report to UN headquarters in New York on 5 May was handwritten and sent by fax.[19] So equipped, Sahnoun often had to rely on what he termed "moral suasion to get things done."[20]

Aidid and Ali Mahdi: Two Views of the UN

Although both Aidid and Ali Mahdi welcomed UN involvement, they disagreed on what the UN's role should be. From the outset, Ali Mahdi repeatedly requested that a UN peacekeeping force be deployed, not just cease-fire observers. He sent a letter from the "Office of the President" on 25 March, "appeal[ing] to the United Nations . . . to urgently send to Somalia an international contingent in order to save this nation from total destruction."[21] He requested two light armored cavalry regiments, a tank battalion, an artillery battalion, and an air wing. Ali Mahdi also wanted a mechanized infantry brigade of forty-five hundred heavily armed troops for Mogadishu alone.

In contrast, Aidid opposed any peacekeepers on the ground, preferring to limit the UN's role to diplomatic mediation. For a variety of reasons, he was suspicious of the UN. For Aidid, the civil war was not over. At that point, Barre's forces were still encamped at Baidoa. The UN embargo was curtailing the supply of arms Aidid needed. He asked the UN to reconsider the embargo but did not openly oppose it.[22] Aidid also distrusted Boutros-Ghali personally. Egypt had supplied Barre with weapons during the civil war, and when he was Egyptian foreign minister, Boutros-Ghali had enjoyed cordial relations with the Barre regime and had endorsed Ali Mahdi's presidency. In a strictly confidential memorandum to a UNOSOM official, John Drysdale explained that Aidid's reticence toward the UN stemmed from Jonah's and Bassiouni's recognition of Ali Mahdi's office without any attempt "to analyse the underlying causes of the dispute within the USC."[23] When Jonah publicly announced that Ali Mahdi wanted UN peacekeepers in Somalia, Aidid feared they would be a vehicle for legitimizing his rival's claim to the presidency.[24]

Aidid's suspicions deepened when an Antonov transport aircraft made an unscheduled landing in Mogadishu carrying weapons and freshly printed Somali shillings for Ali Mahdi. The Antonov, which had previously been chartered by the WFP, carried UN markings and had not been repainted. Whether the Antonov was still under WFP contract at the time of delivery was hotly debated. The UN Office of Legal Affairs concluded that it was and suggested an investigation be undertaken in good faith. But for reasons that remain unclear, none ever took place, intensifying suspicions of UN favoritism among those factions that contested Ali Mahdi's presidency. For Aidid, this was irrefutable evidence of UN partiality toward his rival, and tensions in Mogadishu rose to palpable levels. The cease-fire seemed doomed. Brigadier Shaheen had only just arrived with his UNOSOM observers when Aidid demanded they leave Somalia immediately. Recognizing Aidid's influence, Sahnoun stepped in personally to engage in some shuttle diplomacy.[25] When Aidid calmed down, he agreed to let UNOSOM stay if Ali Mahdi forfeited the suspect currency. Sahnoun got Ali Mahdi to agree, and the fragile peace endured, but just barely. Aidid's distrust of the UN would only heighten in the coming months.

The Need for a UN Security Force

In June 1992 Mohamed Sahnoun reported to the UN:

> The support for relief services has been disappointing. . . . Over one million children are at risk, due to malnutrition, and will become the first casualties . . . if supplementary feeding programmes are not put in place or accelerated within the next few weeks. Some 4,500,000 people are in urgent need of food. Of the estimated seventy hospitals in Somalia in 1988, only fifteen remain partially operational today, and are totally dependent on external assistance.[26]

The UN estimated that the starving population needed 50,000 tons of food per month, so for the first six months of 1992, 300,000 tons was the minimum requirement. Yet by June 1992, cumulative deliveries by the WFP and the ICRC were just 18,857 tons and 53,900 tons, respectively.[27]

Associated Press journalists in Mogadishu reported on the growing chaos amidst the crisis. Mort Rosenblum wrote, "Somalia these days is a name on a map, and a nightmare, but it is no longer a country . . . foreign relief officials struggle against Somalis, to save Somalis from starving."[28] According to his colleague Greg Myre, "flights are sometimes diverted at the last minute due to gun battles on the tarmac at the main airport in Mogadishu. One German with the United Nations had his house burgled so frequently he had concrete furniture made."[29] In March a WFP relief ship was fired on as it approached the port in Mogadishu. ICRC and WFP aircraft were often looted at gunpoint on the tarmac immediately after landing. Banditry and the harassment of unprotected relief workers were endemic.[30]

With the breakdown in order threatening everyone's interests, Bassiouni negotiated a compromise between Aidid and Ali Mahdi in April 1992. They consented to the potential presence of "United Nations security personnel to . . . safeguard its activities in continuing . . . humanitarian relief."[31] It was more than monitoring and less than peacekeeping but something both sides could accept. Some key details were lacking, such as how many security personnel Bassiouni envisaged, when they would arrive, and how they would be armed. Critically, Aidid and Ali Mahdi consented only to a potential future eventuality, and only if they were consulted before any deployment was finalized.[32] Bassiouni cabled UN headquarters in New York and suggested a "security force" of five hundred peacekeepers based at Mogadishu's New Port. They would have no law-and-order responsibilities; their sole focus would be providing security for relief workers.[33]

This security force has become a contentious issue in the historiography of the intervention in Somalia. Of note, Bassiouni obtained this conditional consent and communicated his security force concept to the UN in April, just days before the Security Council passed Resolution 751 establishing UNOSOM. Commentators have since presented Resolution 751 as authorizing the security force deployment, which then, due to UN institutional dysfunction, took months to eventually arrive.[34] This narrative is incorrect. Although Resolution 751 created UNOSOM, a close reading shows that it authorized only the cease-fire monitoring mission of fifty unarmed observers. The language used in the resolution is important: a security force was agreed to "in principle."[35] The Security Council requested the submission of proposals for such a deployment, pending a future "decision." Because Bassiouni's agreement required Aidid and Ali Mahdi to approve any plans before they were finalized, Boutros-Ghali was instructed to gain their consent for the five hundred peacekeepers. At most, Resolution 751 endorsed the concept of a security force. Only consent could make it a reality.

Arguably, the incorrect narrative surrounding Resolution 751 stems from the conflation of its creation of UNOSOM as an administrative entity and the deployment of armed personnel months later in September 1992. In doing so, analysts failed to recognize that UNOSOM was created after the cease-fire agreement between Aidid and Ali Mahdi, which, at that point, necessitated only an unarmed military observer force to monitor the situation. In fact, once consent for a security force was obtained from Aidid, it was swiftly authorized not by Resolution 751

in April but by Resolution 775 in August, four months later. Just over two weeks after the passage of Resolution 775, the Pakistani battalion arrived in Mogadishu. The UN system could work quickly, but it depended on the critical factor of consent.

The fact that UNOSOM's mission was limited to cease-fire monitoring and that consideration of the proposed security force was tabled for future discussion reflected deep divisions within the various bureaus of the US State Department. Its Bureau of African Affairs argued that Somalia was a security issue, while the Bureau of International Organizations claimed the problem was food supply. These differences aside, there was consensus within the State Department that the UN was overextended globally and that, although the situation was tragic, Somalia held no vital interests for the United States. Consequently, as Assistant Secretary of State Cohen remembered, the American delegation on the Security Council blocked any UN deployment "for several months."[36] The justification for this obstructionism was that Congress and the American taxpayers were weary of paying for UN peacekeeping operations.[37] But Ali Mahdi's letter requesting forty-five hundred heavily armed troops hinted at the real cause. It far exceeded Bassiouni's recommendation of five hundred lightly armed troops. And the deployment of peacekeepers in any number could result in Somalia becoming the next Yugoslavia, sucking in UN forces with little progress to show for it. Thus, the Security Council, subject to American veto, could focus only on alleviating the humanitarian rather than security issues.

Expanding UNOSOM and Operation Provide Relief

The Security Council's reluctance and the Bush administration's unwillingness to authorize a larger peacekeeping deployment could last only so long, especially with growing public awareness of the crisis in Somalia. Throughout 1992, prominent policymakers took to the newspapers to advocate for action. In January, after visiting the devastated country, Republican Senator Nancy Kassebaum wrote, "it has reached the point where the world can no longer just watch as Somalia disintegrates into chaos and further death and suffering."[38] At the time, her appeal fell flat. But six months later, on 19 July, Somalia made the front page of the *New York Times*. Despite the presence of UNOSOM's cease-fire observer mission and various UN-sponsored relief plans, journalist

Jane Perlez conveyed the depths of the catastrophe at Baidoa. Replete with pictures of emaciated infants, Perlez's haunting exposé described twenty-five thousand Somalis with "rib cages protruding" lining up at soup kitchens for food, while "hundreds, too feeble to eat, died while they waited."[39]

The impact of Perlez's July exposé cannot be overstated. Regardless of questions of policy, doctrine, or consent, the credibility of the international community and the UN in the public eye equated to Somalis standing in line for food and dying of starvation. Just days after Perlez's story, Boutros-Ghali pushed to expand UNOSOM far beyond the potential security force of five hundred peacekeepers, aiming to "bring about an effective ceasefire throughout the [entire] country . . . with parallel efforts to promote national reconciliation. This will require . . . a presence in all regions and . . . an innovative and comprehensive approach dealing with all aspects of the Somali situation." UNOSOM, the secretary-general argued, should expand beyond cease-fire monitoring to establish four humanitarian zones in Berbera, Bossasso, Kismayo, and Mogadishu.[40] With Aidid still withholding final consent on the security force (for reasons discussed later), the concept of an *expanded* UNOSOM was acknowledged by the Security Council but not authorized. Instead, responding to the impact of Perlez's article and political lobbying, the Security Council instructed Boutros-Ghali to commence an "urgent airlift operation" to assist humanitarian efforts and to redouble his attempts to get consent for a security deployment.[41]

July and August 1992 saw a significant change in American policymakers' attitudes toward Somalia, notwithstanding debates in the State Department and conflict fatigue. Smith Hempstone, the US ambassador to Kenya, joined the op-ed circuit, writing in the *Washington Post*, "if the world averts its eyes and the rains do not come, the human suffering in the northeast will be on a scale unknown in Kenya's history."[42] His moral outrage aside, Hempstone privately cabled the State Department: "Tragic as the situation is in Somalia . . . [it] does not affect vital U.S. government interests. . . . The government should think, and then think again, before allowing itself to become bogged down in a quagmire."[43]

The UN's call for a humanitarian airlift, however, gave the Bush administration an opportunity to take meaningful action in a way that was visible to the public and the media. Assistant Secretary of State Cohen and OFDA director Andrew Natsios explored whether the United States could mount the airlift. Heavily influenced by Hempstone's private cable, the Joint Chiefs of Staff were extremely wary of getting involved.[44] Cohen recalled a rebuke from one representative of the Joint Chiefs, who said, "We plan for operations like Desert Storm. We do not plan for humanitarian airlifts that can be done more cheaply through civilian charter."[45] The State Department, the Department of Defense, and the National Security Council also remained adamant: resources were finite, and the United States and United Nations were suffering from conflict fatigue. Acting Secretary of State Lawrence Eagleburger broke the deadlock when he announced that Bush had personally ordered the State Department to be forward-leaning on Somalia. The policy tides were turning.

This shift in White House attitude had purely political motivations. Bush had been criticized for pushing for a UN deployment in Bosnia, expressly without committing US troops, only to vacillate on Somalia while his representatives on the Security Council stymied UN initiatives. Allegations circulated that racism was a factor. Critically, 1992 was a presidential election year, and Bush's rival, Arkansas Governor Bill Clinton, used the president's inaction to score points on the campaign trail, telling reporters, "Our support for the people of Somalia must not fade with the desperate images on our television screens."[46] Seeking a second term, and under pressure from the Republican Party and the Congressional Black Caucus to help the starving Somalis, Bush could not hesitate any longer.[47]

Bush's advisers presented him with two options. He could endorse the deployment of a UN security force, which the United States had previously blocked on the Security Council. Many in the Bush administration supported this option but doubted that Aidid would consent to it. The second option was provided by Fred Cuny, the owner of Intertect, a humanitarian consultancy firm in Texas. Cuny was a legend within the humanitarian relief community, epitomizing the impact nongovernmental actors could have on policymaking. After years of providing technical assistance to the UN, relief organizations, and the US government in disaster zones, Cuny had earned the sobriquet "Master of Disaster" and joined the OFDA in Somalia in 1992 to combat the famine.[48] Cuny proposed a "safe haven humanitarian intervention option," arguing that a US or UN force of three thousand could establish a safe haven in rural southern Somalia, the area worst affected, where no local militias could exist without being engaged. Bush chose neither option, instead striking a compromise between doing too much and doing nothing. The UN request for an emergency humanitarian airlift was the answer and, Bush hoped, would give him an election-year win. An airlift was highly visible both publicly and politically, and it was a low-risk undertaking that put few American lives in danger.[49] Despite objections from the State Department and the Department of Defense that Somalia could become a "bottomless pit," Bush authorized Operation Provide Relief just two days before accepting his party's nomination to run for reelection at the Republican National Convention.[50]

Under Operation Provide Relief, billed as a temporary initiative until a UNOSOM peacekeeping force was deployed, the United States supplied the aircraft—fourteen US Air Force C-130 Hercules planes capable of landing in austere environments—and the ICRC provided the relief supplies. The ICRC and WFP had already commenced an airlift into Baidoa, the epicenter of an area nicknamed the "Triangle of Death."[51] Established in Mombasa, Kenya, under the command of Marine Brigadier General Frank Libutti, Joint Task Force Provide Relief absorbed the existing airlift and expanded operations using military aircraft. Initially, Kenyan President Daniel Arap Moi refused to allow Mombasa to act as the bridge for Somali relief while Kenya was struggling under the weight of Somali refugees. Hempstone and Libutti negotiated with Moi and promised that for every four aircraft sent into Somalia, one would be sent to Kenya's refugee camps. Mogadishu was not a focus for the airlift. Because Aidid controlled the airport and Ali Mahdi controlled the seaport, flying into the divided capital would cause fighting over who controlled the valuable supplies. Consequently, Libutti had to use airfields or dirt airstrips in the interior. Additionally, the ICRC coordinator for Somalia insisted that the Red Cross be displayed on all the aircraft and that no armed personnel be onboard.[52]

In practical terms, relief organizations in Somalia requested supplies through the WFP office in Mogadishu, which the ICRC and WFP Regional Logistics Office in Nairobi then provided to Libutti for delivery. Given the policy of no armed personnel on relief flights, force protection was a concern for Libutti. Sorties into Somalia consisted of one or two C-130s landing or airdropping their cargo while a third circled above carrying teams from the US Army's 5th Special Forces Group—an airborne quick reaction force (QRF)—to deal with any aggression during unloading operations. On two occasions C-130s took hits from small-arms fire, but the QRF did not deploy. Operation Provide Relief commenced in late August and was quickly joined by the Royal Cana-

dian Air Force's Operation Relief on 12 September. Detachments from the British Royal Air Force also joined the airlift, as did the Luftwaffe in one of Germany's first military operations outside Europe since the end of the Second World War.[53]

Oblivious to the fragility of the international commitment, the WFP complained about the conduct of the airlift, particularly the perceived lack of flexibility: flight schedules could not be altered, only specific types of cargo could be carried, and flights were arbitrarily canceled over security concerns. The American aircraft were reaching the end of their service lives, leading to substantial maintenance requirements and questionable reliability. In one week, the WFP noted, twenty-six flights—one-quarter of those scheduled—were canceled.[54] Those complaints aside, the main issue with Operation Provide Relief was that it was simply not enough. The number of aircraft never exceeded twenty-five, and despite fourteen hundred flights by December 1992, only 2,700 tons of supplies a week were airlifted into Somalia, despite the minimum weekly requirement of 12,500.[55] Critics also noted that less food was being flown in, as the military aircraft carried less per plane compared to the previous ICRC and WFP airlift.[56]

The Provide Relief airlift ignored one fundamental fact: flying food into the country without any change in the security situation did more harm than good. Relief supplies fed the black market, encouraging more banditry. During the airlift, Philip Johnston, president of CARE USA, visited Mogadishu and noted that the city had seven hundred thousand residents and another six hundred thousand internally displaced persons; the water infrastructure had collapsed, there was no garbage collection, and human waste and bodies were piled up in the streets. At New Port, the unloading of relief supplies was glacial, as the Somalis were being paid per day and not by ship. Trucks loaded with supplies, regardless of faction or organization, were often looted right outside the port gates. Catherine Bertini, head of the WFP, estimated that 80 percent of relief supplies were being looted, and relief workers were increasingly being harassed, robbed, and even killed.[57] Relief was not reaching those in need. After returning to the United States, Johnston appeared on PBS's *MacNeil-Lehrer News Hour* to argue, "The UN, as the only capable entity in our world, has to put a unit in there and take over the administration of that country until they help the Somali population develop the capacity, again, to govern themselves."[58]

From Mogadishu, Mort Rosenblum reported:

It would be better to be elsewhere if the guy with the MiG rocket pod on his jeep ever hits the trigger . . . with no law and apparently less order, there are only "technicals," the aid workers' term for gun-studded jeeps that look more like a prop for Mad Magazine than Mad Max . . . the guns everyone packs are part of the scenery, like umbrellas in London, or baguettes in Paris.

Rosenblum described Aidid as "short and scrappy, with a demonic gaze," while Ali Mahdi "calls himself president of Somalia and fools no one."[59]

On 29 August a UNOSOM vehicle was ambushed. Two of Shaheen's observers, an Egyptian colonel and a Czech major, were wounded. Their three Somali guards were killed. That same day, armed militia attacked New Port using three tanks and stole twenty-five trucks full of supplies. The calls for a UN security force became thunderous.[60]

Aidid Finally Consents to a UN Security Force

With Brigadier Shaheen already in Mogadishu commanding the UNOSOM cease-fire observers, Pakistan volunteered the five hundred troops for Bassiouni's proposed security force. The Bush administration agreed to airlift them into Mogadishu once consent for their deployment was received.[61] And therein lay the problem. Aidid had agreed to the force in principle but had not yet been told the details. Already paranoid about Boutros-Ghali and the UN, the chief obstacle for Aidid was that he considered Bassiouni duplicitous. The number of personnel had not been discussed, and Aidid assumed the UN security force would consist of a few guards for UN facilities. He was shocked to learn of the battalion-sized force Bassiouni had proposed. One of Aidid's officials said such a force was tantamount to the "deployment of foreign troops in Somalia, which is not acceptable."[62] When Resolution 751 agreed to this, even only in principle, Aidid believed this violated the deal that he be consulted before any plans were finalized.[63]

Persuading Aidid fell to UN Special Representative Mohamed Sahnoun. He worked tirelessly to assuage Aidid's suspicions, even obtaining a promise from Ali Mahdi to resign his presidency once a meeting of Somali leaders could be convened. On 12 August Aidid finally agreed. The five hundred Pakistani peacekeepers would be allowed in, but perhaps remembering Ali Mahdi's previous request for a heavy combined-arms brigade, Aidid stipulated that the UN force have no artillery, air

support, or heavy weapons.[64] Sahnoun had achieved a breakthrough, but in New York, the UN secretary-general made two critical mistakes.

On 14 August Boutros-Ghali informed the Security Council of Aidid's consent for the security force. However, while Sahnoun was negotiating with Aidid for five hundred troops, a UN technical team had validated Boutros-Ghali's July proposal to enlarge UNOSOM across four zones in Somalia. Boutros-Ghali therefore pushed for this much larger deployment instead, expanding UNOSOM almost tenfold, to 4,626 personnel.[65] Assuming that consent for the former equated to consent for the latter, and with American obstructionism no longer an issue, the Security Council authorized the significantly larger deployment when it passed Resolution 775 on 28 August.[66] Boutros-Ghali's mistakes were failing to consult Sahnoun beforehand and assuming that Aidid's consent could be exploited to send nearly five thousand peacekeepers instead of five hundred.

The result should have been predictable. Sahnoun and Aidid both heard about Resolution 775 after the fact through the BBC World Service. Aidid was outraged. It looked like the UN was maneuvering behind his back again.[67] He refused to allow the increased UNOSOM deployment unless the five hundred–strong Pakistani battalion he had agreed to trained a Somali police force before any additional UN troops arrived. A police force, Aidid argued, would employ former militia members, preventing them from resorting to banditry, and would maintain order once UNOSOM left Somalia. Sahnoun and the UN refused Aidid's request, fearing that he would use the police force as a mechanism to rearm and train his forces.[68] Regardless of Aidid's objections, consent had been obtained for a UN deployment, and the five hundred troops of the Pakistani 7th Frontier Force Battalion were dispatched to Mogadishu.

The Bush administration had agreed to fly the Pakistanis into Mogadishu, but aircraft could not safely land and disembark troops in the middle of the chaotic city. Securing the airport before UNOSOM troops arrived fell to Libutti, Operation Provide Relief's commander. Mogadishu airport was controlled by a militia tenuously allied with Aidid, so Libutti met with Osman Atto, Aidid's top lieutenant and key financier, who assured him that US aircraft could land safely. However, Atto could not guarantee the cooperation of the various forces in Mogadishu that were not under Aidid's control. As a result, CENTCOM redirected the *Tarawa* Amphibious Ready Group (ARG) carrying the 11th Marine Expeditionary Unit (MEU) to Somalia to safeguard the UN deployment.

With the *Tarawa* lying off Mogadishu, the 11th MEU commander, Colonel Michael W. Hagee, sent his marines ashore to secure the airport. On 14 September 1992 the first of several US Air Force Lockheed C-141 Starlifter transports carrying the Pakistanis touched down.[69] Nine months had passed since the Somalis reached out for UN assistance, but barely two weeks after Resolution 775 authorized their deployment, the first armed UN troops arrived to provide security for aid workers and their relief efforts.

The Pakistani battalion came under UNOSOM's control and reported to Shaheen as force commander. Soon after, a small Australian contingent joined UNOSOM thanks to the efforts of Malcolm Fraser, the former Australian prime minster and inaugural president of CARE International. Fraser's daughter was a CARE relief worker in Baidoa. CARE Australia orchestrated a highly publicized flight of relief supplies from Melbourne to Mogadishu, and with domestic support and media attention growing, the Australian cabinet deployed a logistics unit to help UNOSOM regulate the delivery of aid.[70] Arriving in Mogadishu, the Australians immediately noticed the sorry state of the Pakistani battalion.

Lieutenant Colonel Kamal Aziz's 7th Frontier Force lived in the roofless buildings of a former Somali Air Force compound at the airport.[71] The Pakistanis' only means of communication with the outside world was an ancient Morse code radio. Shaheen complained to Marrack Goulding, UN undersecretary-general for peacekeeping operations, "Given the situation here . . . it is sufficiently volatile to merit . . . the need to furnish me with adequate, secure military communications facilities."[72] Being the sole UN force in-country, the Pakistanis had no logistics support, which forced them to buy food locally and boil water for drinking. In an instance of dark irony, the UNOSOM peacekeepers sent to help the starving were entirely dependent on the goodwill of those impoverished Somalis and the toleration of faction leaders for their continued existence. This was a stark contrast with the living conditions of the high-salaried staff of UN agencies and well-funded relief organizations, who enjoyed "far better working conditions and participated in a lively Western social circuit" that included fresh food and air-conditioning.[73]

What Aziz's battalion could do and where they could go remained unclear. All UNOSOM patrols and movements had to be cleared with Aidid and Ali Mahdi in advance; consent permeated all facets of UN peacekeeping operations.[74] The battalion was also in a precarious tactical position. Lightly armed in a major city, the Pakistanis were vastly outnumbered and outgunned by all the militias and factions in Mogadishu. The CIA estimated that Aidid's forces alone numbered at least two thousand.[75] Reflecting UNOSOM's inability to operate in Mogadishu as a security force, UN agencies and relief organizations hired Somali technicals to escort them around the city safely.[76] UNOSOM was too weak to coerce compliance from any Somali faction and too small to exert any influence outside its camp at the airport. In a damning indictment, six weeks after the Pakistanis arrived, Edith Lederer of the Associated Press wrote, "Hundreds, at least, still die every day and countless thousands survive on nothing more than grass, animal skins and meatless bones . . . some aid officials estimate bandits have looted half the 165,000 tons of food delivered this year."[77]

UNOSOM Comes under Fire in Mogadishu

To improve the coordination of relief efforts in Somalia, the UN Department of Humanitarian Affairs hosted a meeting in Geneva in October 1992. Chaired by Undersecretary-General for Humanitarian Affairs Jan Eliasson, the Geneva conference produced the 100-Day Action Programme for Accelerated Humanitarian Assistance. Developed by six UN agencies and thirty relief organizations, the 100-Day Action Programme mandated a massive infusion of food aid, "aggressive" expansion of supplementary feeding, the provision of basic health and immunization services, and the rehabilitation and recovery of civil society. The UN also agreed to assist relief organizations with protection, diplomatic negotiations, logistics support, funding, and a communications network.[78] To achieve these goals, Eliasson appointed Philip Johnston, president of CARE USA, to manage its implementation on behalf of UNOSOM.[79] But as Johnston arrived, the entire UNOSOM effort was severely undermined.

For months, Sahnoun had worked to ease tensions, seek consensus on peace initiatives, and lay the groundwork for political reconciliation. He was commended from all quarters for establishing a dialogue with every Somali leader. Even President Bush wrote to him personally, telling him, "Barbara joins me in wishing you success."[80] Yet Boutros-Ghali was concerned about Sahnoun's "warm relations" with Aidid and Ali Mahdi. Both Somali leaders facilitated relief shipments but demanded increasing portions of those shipments in return. Boutros-Ghali saw this as a protection racket paid for by the UN, and it was. Sahnoun openly criticized UN efforts, claiming on CBS's *60 Minutes* that intervening earlier would have saved more lives. Though seen as a "wild card," Sahnoun earned the respect of Somalis who were dubious of UN intentions.[81] For his part, Aidid was known to say, "I trust Sahnoun, but not Boutros-Ghali."[82] While hosting a conference of Somali intellectuals in the Seychelles, Sahnoun received a letter from Boutros-Ghali scolding him for being absent from his duty station in Somalia and ordering him to stop criticizing the UN. For Sahnoun, "it was more than one could tolerate from the UN bureaucracy that had inspired such criticism."[83] Despite colleagues' efforts to convince him otherwise, Sahnoun resigned.[84]

UNOSOM was now diplomatically leaderless, and Aidid was still obstructing the additional four thousand troops authorized by Resolution 775. The Security Council issued a stark warning, ostensibly to Aidid, that anyone obstructing UNOSOM deployments would be "responsible for aggravating an already unprecedented humanitarian disaster."[85] While Aidid's thoughts cannot be known, his subsequent actions and their timing cannot be viewed as anything other than a direct response to this indictment. With Sahnoun gone, Aidid ordered the immediate expulsion of the next highest ranking UNOSOM civilian official, David Bassiouni, claiming he was a coconspirator in the incident involving the UN-liveried plane filled with money and arms for Ali Mahdi. Aidid then proclaimed that Aziz's Pakistani battalion "would no longer be tolerated in the streets" and that any further UNOSOM deployment would be violently opposed. Concurrently, malicious rumors of a planned UN invasion of Somalia spread throughout Mogadishu.[86] The UN had weaponized the moral authority of the international community against him, and Aidid was responding in kind.

On 2 November 1992 Ismat Kittani replaced Sahnoun as UN special representative for Somalia. An Iraqi Kurd and former president of the UN General Assembly, Kittani complained to Boutros-Ghali that Sahnoun's warm approach toward Aidid, Ali Mahdi, and other faction leaders created an expectation that things would always go their way. Kittani reversed this paradigm, preferring to have the Somalis come to him instead of continuing to practice Sahnoun's shuttle diplomacy. When Kittani arrived in Mogadishu, he was invited to urgent talks by Aidid's chief diplomat, Mohamed Hassan Awale. Kittani rebuked the summons, considering it too blunt. After a more acceptable offer, the taciturn and prickly special representative met Aidid. According to John Drysdale, his political adviser, Kittani warned the Somali leader that the international community was tired of him obstructing the relief effort; he then upbraided Aidid for the poor etiquette of Awale's first invitation.[87] Kittani was blunt to the point of being confrontational, taking a firm approach in pursuing UNOSOM objectives. To his credit, he passed his first major test when relations with Aidid turned violent.

The militia that controlled Mogadishu airport consisted of the Hawadle, a Hawiye subclan that favored Aidid in the Mahdi-Aidid USC divide. The Hawadle extorted such exorbitant landing fees from relief agencies that the UN began canceling flights. Sensing an opportunity, Shaheen made the Hawadle an offer: UNOSOM's Pakistani battalion would take over security of the airport, enabling relief flights to recommence, if the Hawadle tempered their extortion. They agreed, and UNOSOM peacefully took control of the airport on 10 November. Hearing about the agreement with the Hawadle, again via the BBC, Aidid was furious. He raged that Shaheen's gambit was a deliberate attempt to undermine his support base and claimed that Boutros-Ghali had instructed "Governor Kittani" to take Somalia through a process of divide and rule. UNOSOM, he demanded, must immediately cede control of the airport or he would obstruct air traffic by installing antiaircraft emplacements. Kittani and Shaheen refused. The next day, Pakistani positions were heavily bombarded by Aidid's forces.[88] There were no UN casualties, and Kittani and Shaheen remained resolute: there would be no withdrawal. The airport represented decisive terrain in Mogadishu, and the delicate balance of power between Aidid and Ali Mahdi had fundamentally shifted, with consequences.

Scholars and commentators of the Somalia intervention overwhelmingly focus on Aidid as the sole antagonist, but Ali Mahdi was equally ruthless when his interests were threatened. His forces frequently hijacked relief convoys and UNOSOM vehicles at gunpoint. Just as Aidid responded violently to losing control of the airport, Ali Mahdi took a similar approach regarding New Port in Mogadishu. Johnston and Ali Mahdi had agreed that the latter's militia would prevent looting at New Port in return for 47 percent of incoming relief supplies, based on Ali Mahdi's control over 47 percent of the city. However, the divisive Somali president demanded not just 47 percent of supplies allocated to Mogadishu but 47 percent of everything coming in, regardless of its ultimate destination. He threatened to close New Port if he did not receive his

perceived fair share. Not long after he made that threat, a WFP relief
ship was struck by artillery fire while approaching the port. Ali Mahdi
claimed "rebels" were responsible but reported that his men had captured the culprits and the guns they had used. Inspecting the guns,
Brigadier Shaheen concluded they had not been fired recently, and he
believed Ali Mahdi was behind the attack.[89]

With this coercive message sent, Ali Mahdi then declared that too
much food was going to Aidid and warned that until UNOSOM took
over New Port, any relief ship attempting to dock would be shelled. With
just five hundred troops, Shaheen could not guard both the airport and
New Port. For two weeks, Mogadishu was off-limits to relief ships, and
residents suffered accordingly. Only after intense negotiations with Kittani did Ali Mahdi finally rescind this order on 23 November. But the
very next day, another WFP relief ship was shelled by his forces. Without
a secure environment, the WFP refused to operate and suspended all
shipments into Somalia.[90]

Peace Enforcement by "All Necessary Means": Bush Intervenes

The traditional UN responses designed for humanitarian or peacekeeping scenarios failed to curb Somalia's unique descent into crisis and
violence. That Aidid and Ali Mahdi bombarded the airport and shelled
relief ships with impunity demonstrated the fallacy of a UNOSOM security force, which, in the words of one Australian officer, was "tasked
to achieve the impossible."[91] By November 1992, this downward spiral
displayed to the world the weaknesses of traditional UN peacekeeping
doctrine in a far from traditional collapsed-state environment. Writing
to the Security Council on 27 November, Boutros-Ghali finally conceded that "the situation is not improving . . . it may become necessary
to review the basic premises and principles of the United Nations effort
in Somalia."[92]

Chapter VI of the UN Charter facilitated what is termed "traditional"
peacekeeping, designed to maintain peace and security. However, Chapter VII provided for the UN's use of force to maintain international
peace and security in a peace enforcement mission. Article 42 of that
chapter allowed the UN, as an organization, to use force in an enforcement role, but that provision had never been used in UN history—not

until Somalia, though that would come later. Historically, enforcement actions, though rare, were authorized instead under Article 41, which allowed a UN member state to use force under a Security Council resolution. In the past, Chapter VII resolutions had been passed in response to overt acts of aggression, such as the North Korean invasion of South Korea in 1950, the Argentine invasion of the Falklands in 1982, and the Iraqi invasion of Kuwait in the Gulf War.[93] Article 41 had never been invoked for a civil conflict or humanitarian crisis, and Article 42 had never been used. This changed during Boutros-Ghali's tenure as UN secretary-general with *An Agenda for Peace*.[94]

Shortly after taking office, Boutros-Ghali set out to improve the "capacity of the United Nations for preventive diplomacy, for peacemaking, and for peacekeeping."[95] *An Agenda for Peace* was the result. Article 2 of the UN Charter championed the primacy of member state sovereignty and thus the critical requirement of host-nation consent for any UN deployment. But Boutros-Ghali wrote in *An Agenda for Peace* that "the time of *absolute and exclusive sovereignty* . . . has passed; its theory was never matched by reality."[96] Boutros-Ghali argued that, with the Cold War at an end, the UN should be willing to invoke Article 42 when inaction would bring the UN into disrepute.[97] *An Agenda for Peace* articulated a major doctrinal shift away from traditional peacekeeping at a time when Somalia seemed immune to stability or progress. For the first time in UN history, Boutros-Ghali proposed dealing with a humanitarian crisis cum civil conflict by sidestepping consent and national sovereignty altogether and opting for peace enforcement under Chapter VII.

In November 1992, with UNOSOM efforts thoroughly frustrated, Boutros-Ghali presented the Security Council with five options on Somalia. The UN could withdraw completely and suffer international condemnation. The UN could push for the expanded UNOSOM deployment under Chapter VI, though Boutros-Ghali conceded that "the situation in Somalia has deteriorated beyond the point at which it is susceptible to the peacekeeping treatment."[98] The UN could execute a show of force in Mogadishu, as experts claimed this might coerce the Somali factions into cooperation. However, a US memorandum estimated that Aidid's forces outnumbered the Pakistanis four to one in Mogadishu; they also had Soviet-built tanks and artillery, of which Shaheen had none.[99] Three of the five options were thus unworkable for the UN.

The two remaining options reflected Boutros-Ghali's conviction that "international military personnel [had] to be deployed in Somalia."[100]

The Security Council could authorize an Article 41 enforcement mission led by a member state or, in an unprecedented move, the UN itself could organize and lead such an operation under Article 42. While advocating the latter, Boutros-Ghali conceded that the UN lacked the organizational capability and experience to lead such an unprecedented effort, and the member states were reluctant to subordinate their forces in a UN institutional experiment. Instead, he informed the Security Council that US Secretary of State Lawrence Eagleburger had conveyed a timely offer from President Bush to send a US-led coalition into Somalia.[101]

By November 1992, momentum for intervening in Somalia had gained traction in Washington, DC. Opinions were still divided, however, on what the US role should be. The commander of the airlift, General Frank Libutti, told the Joint Chiefs of Staff that Somalia would probably require a nation-building commitment lasting ten to fifteen years.[102] When Ambassador Smith Hempstone in Kenya was asked for his views, he infamously opposed intervention, provocatively invoking the American experience in Lebanon in the 1980s by writing, "If you liked Beirut, you'll love Mogadishu. To what end? To keep tens of thousands of Somali kids from starving to death in 1993 who, in all probability, will starve to death in 1994? It will take five years to get Somalia not on its feet but just on its knees."[103]

There were also strong advocates for going in, though. Principal among them was Fred Cuny, the "Master of Disaster." Though his earlier plan for Somalia had been rejected due to political considerations, Morton Abramowitz, president of the Carnegie Endowment for Peace, invited him to draft what became known as the Cuny Plan.[104] The Cuny Plan, which Abramowitz circulated among DC policymakers and the media, is significant because, with one notable exception, the subsequent American plan largely reflected it. Cuny suggested a multinational coalition led by twenty thousand US troops to establish "safe havens" in Somalia where relief agencies could operate free from attack by bandits or armed militias. The coalition's spearhead would be an MEU securing the Mogadishu port and airport before the main security force "of brigade to possibly division strength . . . drawn from US Army light infantry or airborne forces" arrived. Once a secure environment was established, Somalia could be handed over to a follow-on UN operation.[105]

The one major divergence between the Cuny Plan and what became known as Operation Restore Hope was Cuny's recommendation that coalition forces stay out of Mogadishu. He did not state the reason, but arguably it was the recognition that occupation of the capital, which was divided between Aidid and Ali Mahdi, could become politicized or bogged down in violence. In a stark appraisal, Cuny suggested that if Mogadishu was to be occupied, an armored division be deployed in the city. Failing that, Cuny recommended that the British, given their decades-long conflict with the Irish Republican Army, should "commit an experienced force ex Northern Ireland to manage the irregular urban warfare threat."[106]

The shape of any intervention, though, rested with the Deputies Committee of the US National Security Council, chaired by deputy national security adviser and retired US Navy Admiral Jonathan T. Howe. Meeting regularly throughout November 1992, the various departments and policymakers could agree on only two things. First, Operation Provide Relief could not continue. It was inefficient and costly and was not solving the crisis.[107] Second, there was no confidence that the UN could confront the catastrophic situation in Somalia. UNOSOM was surrounded and outgunned in Mogadishu. Memoranda called the enlarged UNOSOM deployment plan "seriously flawed" and "woefully inadequate."[108] The director of central intelligence claimed it would take three thousand troops to open a relief corridor from Mogadishu to just one major city in the interior. Worse still, the Deputies Committee doubted the UN could manage such a robust operation in a nonpermissive environment. In the committee's opinion, Somalia was simply beyond the UN. It concluded that if Aidid chose to escalate the violence, the United States was one of the few nations with the forces and the means to deploy into a hostile environment.[109]

Although the Deputies Committee agreed on these key points, intense debate centered on how the United States should intercede. From the State Department, Assistant Secretaries Herbert Cohen and Robert Gallucci and Undersecretary Frank Wisner argued in favor of intervening regardless of risk because of the "moral considerations" and to demonstrate "that the UN can act decisively in the post–Cold War world to end suffering."[110] The post–Cold War international order was on the line in Somalia. However, the deputies from State did not want to commit US combat troops. Instead, they recommended offering Boutros-Ghali assistance in forming a coalition for an enforcement mission with a quid pro quo of American logistical support and an ARG offshore to deter any attackers, ostensibly Aidid.[111] Interestingly, while proposing a US-supported intervention without American participation, the State

Department recommended that Boutros-Ghali and the UN develop a strategy for "reconstituting civil administration . . . and a plan for transferring its direction to representative Somali leadership."[112] Thus, as early as November 1992, the State Department was pushing for the UN to nation-build in Somalia.

The Department of Defense calculus was quite different. General Colin Powell, chairman of the Joint Chiefs of Staff, noted, "I was not eager to get us involved . . . but we were apparently the only nation that could end the suffering."[113] More importantly, there was growing anxiety among the Joint Chiefs and Defense policymakers that UNOSOM would collapse, requiring US intervention under far worse circumstances to extricate the UN force. For Defense officials, a proactive approach to Somalia was preferable. Powell and Undersecretary of Defense Paul Wolfowitz met with Cuny, who convinced them that a US-led intervention could work if it avoided politically sensitive Somali issues. Thus, Powell and Wolfowitz endorsed intervention with the limited objective of ensuring the delivery of aid.[114]

With the State and Defense Departments on different wavelengths regarding Somalia, Howe convened a Deputies Committee meeting on 23 November 1992 to discuss three courses of action. The minimalist approach envisioned a UN Chapter VII enforcement mandate with a drastically larger UNOSOM. The middle-of-the-road approach was the State Department's suggestion of an American-formed international coalition, with US participation limited to logistical support and over-the-horizon reinforcements provided by US forces stationed elsewhere in the region only if and when necessary. The third proposal was the sledgehammer approach of the Cuny Plan, a coalition involving American combat units for six months, after which Somalia would be handed over to the UN and a recruited and trained indigenous police force.[115]

The minimalist approach was dismissed out of hand. Representing the Joint Chiefs, US Army Lieutenant General Barry McCaffrey reiterated concerns about a UNOSOM collapse and claimed there was little faith in the UN mission. Moreover, he reported that the military services did not favor the State Department's proposal of over-the-horizon support to UNOSOM. Howe similarly challenged the State Department deputies, asking whether the United States would commit ground troops if UNOSOM got into trouble. A consensus emerged that the sledgehammer approach of a UN-authorized, US-led coalition had the best chance for success. Exerting total control over the affected areas of Somalia

with enough force to counter any faction that chose to fight it would raise the UN enforcement capability. General McCaffrey claimed this final option for Somalia was "resolvable by US forces" and was "a doable mission," and it could be implemented in weeks instead of the months it would take the UN to deploy.[116]

On 25 November 1992, the day before Thanksgiving, Bush was briefed on Operation Restore Hope, developed by CENTCOM based on the sledgehammer approach. It was an ersatz Cuny Plan. Powell personally endorsed the operation, telling Bush it was a mission US forces could achieve. Bush liked it but, having lost the 1992 presidential election, was concerned that it might interfere with the incoming Clinton administration and asked whether it could be completed before Inauguration Day on 19 January 1993. Powell and Secretary of Defense Dick Cheney said no. American forces would not get into Somalia before mid-December, and while the aim was a quick mission, it would not be finished before the inauguration. Aware that it would bleed over into Clinton's tenure, Bush authorized Operation Restore Hope. Powell ordered General Joseph Hoar, commanding general at CENTCOM, within whose territorial purview Somalia lay, to start preparations. And so it was that Bush dispatched Eagleburger to inform Boutros-Ghali that the United States was volunteering to lead a coalition into Somalia.[117]

The UN Security Council met on 3 December 1992 to consider the five options Boutros-Ghali had laid out for Somalia, Bush's offer to lead a coalition, and a draft resolution authorizing a US-led enforcement action under Chapter VII to use "all necessary means" to establish a secure environment in Somalia. The draft was written in the Pentagon to ensure that Operation Restore Hope would be a short mission with limited aims.[118] Ambassador Mumbengegwi of Zimbabwe noted, "The humanitarian imperatives of the Somali crisis cannot be met through conventional methods. . . . Somalia is a unique situation that warrants a unique approach." Ambassador Barbosa of Cape Verde suggested that Somalia posed the most serious challenge to "the full establishment of a new international order on Earth within which the United Nations has a capital role to play."[119] With that, a vote was called on Security Council Resolution 794, which was adopted unanimously.[120]

For the first time in history, the UN authorized the use of force for a military intervention in a member state without consent from that state. Resolution 794 was Boutros-Ghali's *Agenda for Peace* in action. Ambassador Perkins of the United States closed the meeting by saying, "The resolution before us expresses our commitment to resolving the human tragedy in Somalia . . . our military forces will remain . . . no longer than is necessary. We look forward to the early transition to an effective United Nations peace-keeping force."[121]

Various explanations for Bush's decision to intervene in Somalia have been presented over the years. One school of thought suggests it was one final altruistic gesture by the outgoing president. For example, Robert Patman wrote, "The moral tension between expectations of bountiful family reunions during a traditional national celebration in the United States and haunting TV images of starving Somalis apparently weighed heavily on President Bush."[122] Another school claims that Bush crumbled under the so-called CNN effect—media saturation of the plight in Somalia generating public and political pressure to do *something*.[123] Largely, these claims are not supported by the evidence. Matthew Baum dismissed the CNN effect argument by demonstrating that despite significant media coverage of the famine in 1991, Bush did not intervene. Similarly, reporting on Somalia peaked only after Bush announced the American intervention in 1992, not before.[124]

Significant debate also surrounded whether intervention in Somalia was preferable to getting involved in the emerging chaos in Bosnia—that committing troops to Africa was a convenient way of avoiding doing so in the Balkans.[125] In November 1992 the American delegation at the UN sent a cable stating that now was the time to promote a robust United Nations capable of enforcement missions in the post–Cold War world. Neither Somalia nor Bosnia were mentioned, but the cable argued that a precedent of UN enforcement needed to be set, and it was in the United States' interest to ensure that it succeeded.[126] To establish this precedent, Somalia appeared to be the easier option. On paper, the disparate Somali factions could be easily outgunned and outmaneuvered in a flat, arid country, reminiscent of the stunning US victory against Iraq in the Gulf War. Bosnia looked like a much tougher fight, with mountainous terrain and Croatian, Bosnian, and Serb forces fighting a brutal civil war using significant stocks of Soviet-era weaponry, not to mention the well-equipped Soviet-style Yugoslav Army, one of the largest in Europe at the time. Any enforcement mission in Bosnia, as the UN was learning, would be inherently difficult and would incur significant costs in lives and materiel. Powell denied that any Somalia versus Bosnia calculus existed, as the two situations were so fundamentally different that an either-or decision would not have been appropri-

ate. Somalia's situation was highly susceptible to resolution with a short, robust, and well-resourced operation, whereas Bosnia seemed invulnerable to outside intervention, requiring a significantly larger and longer commitment.[127] Somalia was low-hanging fruit for the US military at a time when going to Bosnia was not even being considered.

Today, Operation Restore Hope still stands as the largest deployment of American troops to the continent of Africa in history. However, the complex and nuanced decision-making process preceding its authorization relied far more on those around President Bush than on Bush himself. There was bipartisan support from Republicans and Democrats for intervening in Somalia, including from President-elect Bill Clinton.[128] The State and Defense Departments also argued for intervention, albeit with different approaches. Bush's personal altruism may explain why he authorized Operation Restore Hope, but it does not explain the conviction that intervention would actually work. Thus, the real driving force behind the belief that intervention was feasible came from the American military. The Joint Chiefs genuinely feared a UNOSOM collapse and chose to be proactive. As chairman of the Joint Chiefs, Powell's role was as pivotal as that of Bush himself. The post-Vietnam "Powell Doctrine," dictating overwhelming force to achieve clear goals, was as central to Restore Hope as it was to the Gulf War. Bush made the call, but Powell and others made the case for success, simplifying Bush's decision. It was a case of the military arguing to be proactive and intervene before UNOSOM collapsed, rather than an altruistic president coaxing a reluctant military to go where no vital US interests existed.

On 4 December 1992, the day after Resolution 794 was authorized, Bush addressed the American public and the world. "The United States alone cannot right the world's wrongs," he said. Bush lamented that "over a quarter-million people, as many people as live in Buffalo, New York, have died in the Somali famine," and he warned that 1.5 million more were at risk. There was no government in Somalia, law and order had broken down, and "anarchy prevails." An American-led coalition was going into Somalia "to open the supply routes, to get the food moving, and to prepare the way for a U.N. peacekeeping force. . . . We will not stay one day longer than is absolutely necessary. We do not plan to dictate political outcomes. So, to every sailor, soldier, airman, and marine who is involved in this mission . . . you're doing God's work."[129] Days later, US marines stormed the beaches of Mogadishu. The vanguard of thirty-nine thousand troops destined for Somalia had arrived.

3 | Deploying to the Moon
The Formation and Arrival of the Unified Task Force

Deploying to Somalia was like going to the moon: everything needed had to be brought in or built there.
> —General Joseph Hoar, commanding general,
> US Central Command[1]

The variety of international troops making up the coalition staff very quickly turned our headquarters into the bar scene from Star Wars.
> —Brigadier General Anthony Zinni, director of operations,
> Unified Task Force[2]

We didn't know much about Somalia. We didn't know much about Mogadishu. We didn't know much about the clans, and we didn't know a hell of a lot about the personalities.
> —Major General Steven Arnold, commanding general,
> US Army Forces Somalia[3]

In the small hours of 9 December 1992, US marines stormed the beaches of Mogadishu, the vanguard of nearly forty thousand troops participating in Operation Restore Hope. Buoyed from a post–Gulf War high, the United States and the Bush administration found it relatively easy to assemble the multinational coalition. On the largest deployment to Africa in history, Daniel P. Bolger wrote that US forces arrived "in style and power, as befits the legions of a superpower."[4] The reality, however, was far from a Roman procession worthy of Caesar. The formation of the Unified Task Force (UNITAF), as the Restore Hope coalition came to be known, and its initial occupation of southern Somalia were a rude awakening for the post–Cold War, post–Gulf War US military, which marketed itself as the "can-do" force, rapidly deployable across the globe.[5]

The problem was not armed opposition. Largely, there was none. But Somalia was an operating environment unlike anything the US military had ever experienced. It was not Saudi Arabia, South Vietnam, or Cold War West Germany. The infrastructure was in ruins, completely unable to handle the influx of tens of thousands of coalition personnel, dozens of ships, and hundreds of aircraft. It was assumed that Operation Restore Hope would proceed as smoothly as Desert Shield in Saudi Arabia or the frequent Cold War Reforger exercises of the 1980s. But in the words of one general officer, US and coalition forces went "from some of the most modern, highly developed, sophisticated port and airfield facilities in the world . . . to some of the very worst."[6] Somali airports and airfields were small, and many were badly damaged. Runways crumbled under the heavy transport aircraft as they landed. Seaports were too shallow for the massive logistics ships of the US Marine Corps' Maritime Prepositioning Force, an integral asset to American expeditionary operations tried and tested during the Gulf War.[7] The austere environment combined with the state of the country caused unprecedented challenges. Before UNITAF could help the Somali people, these challenges had to be overcome.

Joint Task Force Restore Hope

Before President Bush authorized Operation Restore Hope on 25 November 1992, CENTCOM was already planning a potential mission to Somalia due to the growing calls to intervene there. For the US military, Restore Hope was not only a multinational coalition but also a joint operation comprising elements from all the uniformed services. Doctrine mandated that one service take the lead and establish a headquarters staff to commence planning and organization, which would then assume command of all units—coalition and American—assigned to Joint Task Force (JTF) Restore Hope. Two corps-sized formations were candidates to lead JTF Restore Hope: the US Marine Corps' I Marine Expeditionary Force (I MEF) at Camp Pendleton, California, and the US Army's XVIII Airborne Corps at Fort Bragg, North Carolina. I MEF was chosen for several reasons.

Because Restore Hope was an expeditionary mission relying on offshore logistics due to the crippled Somali infrastructure, the Marine Corps was considered particularly well suited to lead it. Moreover, I

MEF's commanding officer, Lieutenant General Robert B. Johnston, had extensive experience managing coalition operations. He had served as General H. Norman Schwarzkopf's chief of staff during the Gulf War, overseeing a multinational force from thirty-five countries. Born in Scotland, Johnston was a veteran of Vietnam and Lebanon. He was quiet, welcomed input, and had a reputation for pragmatism. One of his senior officers remembered that Johnston "always looked like he stepped out of *Gentleman's Quarterly*."[8]

I MEF was also CENTCOM's designated humanitarian disaster response force after completing a May 1992 exercise based on a hypothetical earthquake in Ethiopia, Somalia's neighbor. Given the likelihood of being deployed, subunit commanders within I MEF had begun planning for a potential operation in Somalia.[9] Thus, I MEF's marines were hardly surprised when official word came on 27 November that they would lead JTF Restore Hope. Johnston was grand marshal at a parade in El Cajon, California, when CENTCOM commander General Joseph Hoar called to inform him that he would be the JTF commander.[10]

Within Johnston's leadership team was marine Brigadier General Anthony C. Zinni. Specializing in low-intensity conflict and humanitarian operations, Zinni was the deputy director of operations at US European Command and had coordinated the humanitarian airlift into the newly independent former republics of the Soviet Union after its dissolution. Zinni had also been deputy commanding general of Operation Provide Comfort in 1991, assisting the Kurds in northern Iraq. The commandant of the Marine Corps, General Carl E. Mundy, had assured Johnston that whatever he needed for Somalia, he would get. Johnston asked for Zinni and appointed him JTF Restore Hope's director of operations.[11]

For political and diplomatic guidance, Bush chose retired Ambassador Robert Oakley as presidential envoy to Somalia. A Texan and a graduate of Princeton, Oakley was a career foreign officer, serving in Saigon during the Vietnam War as his first assignment. Oakley's credentials included a tour as US ambassador to Somalia from 1982 to 1984, special assistant for national security affairs, and senior director of Middle East and North African affairs for the National Security Council under President Ronald Reagan. Before retiring, his final appointment was ambassador to Pakistan under Bush.[12] About Bush's choice, Boutros-Ghali said, "I admired Oakley; tall, lean, and articulately taciturn, he reminded me of the honest sheriff in a classic American cowboy movie."[13]

Defining the Mission

With Johnston's appointment as commanding general, planners focused on how JTF Restore Hope would enforce UN Resolution 794. Writing to Bush, Boutros-Ghali suggested a division of labor: UNOSOM would focus on relief efforts and political reconciliation while Johnston's command secured the environment. Boutros-Ghali also suggested that Johnston focus on Somali disarmament to pave the way for the "eventual transfer of responsibilities . . . to . . . an enlarged UNOSOM, perhaps with a modified mandate."[14] Disarmament was a contentious issue. All parties agreed that the population was vulnerable to militias, gangs, and criminals and that no societal or governmental restoration could occur in such an environment. Along with UN agencies and relief organizations, Boutros-Ghali pushed strongly for coercive disarmament of the country, believing that faction leaders such as Aidid, Ali Mahdi, and Hersi Morgan and their militias could then be marginalized to ease the process of rebuilding.[15] The Institute for National Security Studies concluded in December 1992 that "a significant reduction in weaponry . . . is the essential precondition for the success of Restore Hope. Peace, not food, is the real key to restoring the welfare of the Somali people."[16]

In contrast, Bush administration officials and senior US military leaders resisted the inclusion of disarmament in Restore Hope's mandate. From their perspective, this would increase the likelihood of American casualties, which, given the lack of vital interests at stake in the Horn of Africa, no American policymaker or legislator could support.[17] General Zinni noted that concerns about casualties stemmed from the reality that many Somali faction leaders and their militias were disciplined and experienced combat veterans. Hersi Morgan, the "Butcher of Hargeisa," had been trained by the US military, Aidid by the Soviet Union and NATO. Five factions, including Aidid's and Morgan's, had "credible" militias with "serious weaponry," Zinni recalled: "these guys could fight, and would fight."[18] There were also practical problems with widespread disarmament. According to Colonel F. M. Lorenz, Johnston's staff judge advocate, "virtually every male over the age of 12 in Somalia was armed."[19] At CENTCOM, Hoar believed disarmament "was neither realistically achievable nor a prerequisite for the core mission of providing a secure environment for relief operations."[20] Somalia was so flush with weaponry, Zinni quipped, that any buy-back program would bankrupt the US Treasury.[21]

Ultimately, the Pentagon drafted Resolution 794 to ensure that

Restore Hope was limited in duration and scope. Disarmament was a bridge too far. Hoar would later concede that "selective disarming as necessary would be an *implied* task," but at the time, any such phrasing was removed from Johnston's mission statement.[22] That mission statement read: "When directed by the [national command authority], [commander in chief Central Command] will conduct joint and combined military operations in Somalia, to secure the major air and seaports, key installations, and food distribution points, to provide open and free passage of relief supplies, to provide security for convoys and relief organization operations and assist UN/NGO's [nongovernmental organizations] in providing humanitarian relief operations under UN auspices."[23] Restore Hope was strictly a security mission, limited to establishing and maintaining a secure environment and ensuring that relief efforts were unimpeded. Militias or bandits would be engaged only if they showed hostile intent. There was no mention of disarmament, not even limited disarmament, and UNOSOM remained responsible for political reconciliation and coordination of the relief effort.

Developing the Plan

At CENTCOM and at Johnston's headquarters, planners had scant information about conditions in Somalia or its infrastructure, as the last American forces had left in January 1991 during Operation Eastern Exit. The capabilities of the various militias and their willingness to fight were unclear, as were the political issues and clan affiliations among factions.[24] Johnston told an interviewer, "We didn't have that level of intelligence when . . . trying to figure out how to peel this orange."[25] Zinni was more blunt: "I didn't know Somalis from salamis."[26] The country was littered with unmarked weapons caches and extensive minefields, yet the most detailed maps available were Soviet 1:100,000 scale, which did not align with US Air Force 1:250,000 maps.[27] When it came to reliable intelligence, planners conceded that "most of what [we] have is . . . from the press. With a couple of exceptions [we] are blind."[28] An intelligence picture of the Somali interior was constructed from the media and from those who had served in the Provide Relief airlift.[29] Thus, the only thing they knew for sure was that Mogadishu was in ruins, with a barely functioning airport and seaport, and most of the interior airfields consisted of dirt runways at best.

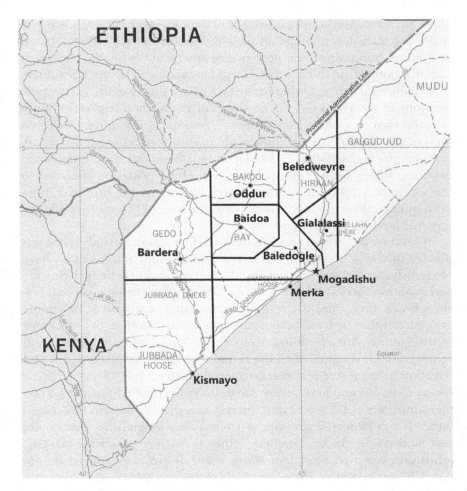

UNITAF Humanitarian Relief Sectors

Lacking detailed infrastructural information, Operation Restore Hope bore a striking resemblance to the Cuny Plan, which suggested that a Marine Expeditionary Unit secure Mogadishu's port and airport to allow the US Army to arrive in brigade or division strength to occupy the interior.[30] Key population centers would be secured and occupied, serving as hubs from which humanitarian relief and security operations flowed outward. Southern Somalia was divided into nine humanitarian relief sectors (HRSs)—Baidoa, Baledogle, Bardera, Beledweyne, Gialalassi, Kismayo, Merka, Mogadishu, and Oddur—each of which had one major population center and an airfield. The size of each HRS was based on natural boundaries, the presence of any faction's militia, and relief organization activity.[31] Each HRS would be managed by the US military or a coalition partner. Owing to the lack of intelligence, the geographic divisions of the HRSs did not account for established regional boundaries or clan or political affiliations.[32] Because the planners believed famine and instability were most acute in southern Somalia, the northeast regions and self-declared independent Somaliland were excluded from the intervention.[33] As such, Restore Hope would be confined to the southern 40 percent of the country, an area of one hundred thousand square miles, roughly equivalent to the state of Colorado or slightly larger than the United Kingdom.

With the operational concept defined, Operation Restore Hope was divided into four phases. In phase 1, marines would amphibiously seize Mogadishu's port and airport to enable the deployment of US Army and coalition forces and the flow of relief supplies into the capital. Marines would then seize the former Somali Air Force base at Baledogle to open another airhead before racing to secure Baidoa, the epicenter of the famine. After building up forces in Mogadishu, phase 2 would achieve the occupation of all the remaining HRSs. In phase 3, US and coalition forces would commence operations in each HRS to establish a secure environment and ensure the delivery of relief. Phase 4 would be the drawdown of US forces and the handover to a follow-on UN operation.[34] It was expected that phase 1—securing Mogadishu, Baledogle, and Baidoa—would be complete within thirty days of arrival (D+30). Johnston presented this plan, along with rules of engagement stating that US and coalition forces could "fire on any person or force that displayed hostile intent . . . [they] did not have to wait to be shot at."[35] The Joint Chiefs of Staff approved the plan, and Johnston and his staff assembled the various American elements of JTF Restore Hope.

Assembling US and Coalition Forces

In the interest of ensuring representation of all the military services, Johnston's I MEF headquarters staff grew to eight hundred personnel after army, navy, and air force staff were integrated. Johnston's deputy was an army major general; the intelligence and logistics staffs were headed by army officers with marine deputies; and personnel, operations, and plans were staffed by marines with army deputies.[36] Although the navy and air force contributed significant assets, Restore Hope was predominantly a US Army and Marine Corps operation. The marines contributed the bulk of Johnston's I MEF: elements of 1st Marine Division, 3rd Marine Aircraft Wing, and 1st Force Service Support Group. The army's XVIII Airborne Corps had considered using either the 101st or 82nd Airborne Division, but the 10th Mountain Division, the army's sole remaining "light" infantry division designed specifically for rapid deployment, was ultimately judged better suited for the mission's expeditionary nature.[37]

Johnston had overall command and reported directly to Hoar at CENTCOM. Reporting to Johnston were his senior component commanders. Major General Charles E. Wilhelm commanded 1st Marine Division and all US Marine Forces (MARFOR), and Major General Steven L. Arnold commanded 10th Mountain Division and all US Army Forces (ARFOR). Like Johnston, Oakley, and Zinni, Wilhelm and Arnold were Vietnam veterans. Wilhelm had previously served as deputy assistant secretary of defense for policy and missions, specializing in low-intensity conflict. Arnold had been Third Army's operations officer at CENTCOM during the Gulf War. As such, the American leaders of Restore Hope, both political and military, had experience working with coalition partners and were familiar with the nuances of conducting what are termed military operations other than war.

With the combat power of the 1st Marine Division and 10th Mountain Division, Restore Hope looked less like a humanitarian intervention and more like an invasion. This was intentional. The aim was to establish a secure environment essentially by intimidating the various factions and militias into behaving. This approach was emblematic of Joint Chiefs of Staff Chairman Colin Powell's "Powell Doctrine"—assembling overwhelming force to ensure that, in the event of hostilities, the United States would easily prevail with minimal casualties. The Powell Doctrine had shaped Operation Just Cause in Panama, Desert Storm in the Gulf War, and now Operation Restore Hope. At a press briefing, Secretary of Defense Dick Cheney pointedly remarked, "There should be no doubt in anybody's mind that we are prepared for hostilities should they occur. There should be no doubt about who would prevail." Powell then took the podium and explained that the coalition could force a settlement without the cooperation of the vying factions, if need be.

In Powell's words, "We wanted [the factions] to understand that. We wanted them to see that."[38]

Nearly twenty-eight thousand American personnel were going to Somalia, the majority coming from the 1st Marine and 10th Mountain Divisions. Yet many of them were not from combat units. Somalia required support units to reestablish utilities; repair roads, airports, and other infrastructure; and provide medical, communications, and logistics services. Nearly four thousand engineers from the army's 36th Engineer Group and the navy's 30th Naval Construction Regiment were needed simply to build the infrastructure required for the operation, along with the air force's 823rd Rapid Engineer Deployable Heavy Operational Repair Squadron Engineers (REDHORSE) to rebuild and repair airports. Thousands more soldiers from the army's 593rd Area Support Group and 7th Transportation Group were assigned to keep the coalition supplied across hundreds of miles of the austere interior, particularly with potable water. With disease rampant in the famine-stricken country, the army's 62nd Medical Group had to provide everything from shock trauma and triage facilities to epidemiology and veterinary services. Somalia was in ruins, and Johnston's force needed to be prepared for every possible contingency, which required military police, water purification teams, mortuary affairs personnel, explosive ordnance disposal units, and air traffic controllers.[39] And this was just the American forces.

Given that I MEF and the 10th Mountain Division were committed to participate in existing operational plans in the event of a conflict arising elsewhere in the world, forming a coalition in Somalia lessened the burden on the US military. Because Somalia was both an African and a Muslim country, Hoar and CENTCOM planners wanted a coalition that was culturally, regionally, and religiously acceptable to the Somalis. In addition to US forces, Hoar envisaged a "3-3-1" coalition of three African nations, three Arab nations, and one NATO partner.[40] When the call went out, the State Department was overwhelmed with volunteers. Each aspiring coalition partner completed a questionnaire regarding the forces it was offering, their capabilities and logistical needs, and the types of operations they were willing to participate in. Instead of the seven coalition partners the State Department was looking for, twenty-six countries offered forces, and twenty-one were accepted on the condition that they agree to serve under Johnston's command. For those nations unable to airlift their troops to Somalia, CENTCOM would arrange transport aircraft.[41]

Among the first to join were nations already committed to Boutros-Ghali's failed proposal to enlarge UNOSOM, including Canada, Australia, Belgium, and Egypt. With UN multilateralism a pillar of its foreign policy, Canada was a regular contributor to UN operations and had promised the Canadian Airborne Regiment to UNOSOM. When this was no longer an option, Canada agreed to join Johnston's coalition and increased its commitment by adding an armored squadron from the Royal Canadian Dragoons to form the 1,350-strong Canadian Airborne Regiment Battlegroup.[42]

The Australians were already serving with UNOSOM alongside the Pakistanis in Mogadishu. Public opinion was focused on the presence of CARE Australia in Baidoa, but when bandits embarked on a violent rampage in that city, Australian politicians uniformly supported joining the coalition. A task force was organized around the 1st Battalion, Royal Australian Regiment, for a seventeen-week deployment. This was acceptable to both the public and the government, and it was expected to strengthen Australia's relations with the United States.[43] Australian Prime Minister P. J. Keating announced:

> UNOSOM was slow to get underway . . . not structured adequately to deal with the problems it faced. Somalis continued to die. That is why we welcomed President Bush's action in offering to provide . . . a new coalition of forces that would try to enforce the peace in Somalia, not simply keep it . . . the contribution of about 900 personnel will be the largest commitment of Australian ground forces . . . in the last 20 years.[44]

Following Keating's announcement, Lieutenant General John C. Grey, chief of the Australian General Staff, wrote to US Army Chief of Staff General Gordon R. Sullivan that he was "proud to be again serving alongside your great Army, Merry Christmas."[45] The last time Australians had served under American command was in 1965, during the Vietnam War.

With Canada's participation, Hoar's goal of having one NATO member in Johnston's coalition was fulfilled. But five others joined too. Belgium and Turkey committed forces, as did Greece, in its first overseas mission since the Korean War. Despite ongoing French deployments with the UN in Cambodia and Yugoslavia, President Francois Mitterand was convinced by Health and Humanitarian Affairs Minister Bernard Kouchner to commit a substantial force of twenty-two hundred soldiers and marines, including elements of the elite French Foreign Legion.[46] Italy, though, was the largest contributor of all.

Many older Somalis remembered Italian colonial governance, and it was common to find that those aged thirty-five and older could still speak some Italian. For the first time since 1943, Italy had fought during the Gulf War, contributing a limited naval and air commitment. In Somalia, the Italian government wanted to increase its commitment to international affairs by deploying the Italian Army abroad for the first time. Intervening in Somalia was complex, though. Many political parties in Italy supported the mission, but others did not, especially as the country was experiencing an economic recession. There was also debate about the nature of the mission. Minister for Foreign Affairs Beniamino Andreatta claimed it was purely humanitarian, while Minister of Defense Salva Ando argued that the goal was disarmament. Economically, Italy had a vested interest in Somalia beyond its being a former colony, as a sizable portion of agricultural imports came from the ruined nation. The political complexities surrounding the largest Italian military operation since the Second World War were such that the thirty-two hundred troops from the Folgore Parachute Brigade and other ancillary units were in Somalia before the parliament voted its approval.[47]

Some of Johnston's senior staff feared that Italy's colonial past might cause tension with the Somali population, but an even bigger issue was local hostility toward Egypt, given Boutros-Ghali's former role as Egyptian foreign minister. Among Somalis, conspiracy theories abounded, including the rumor that Barre and Boutros-Ghali had hatched a plot for Egypt to take over Somalia's agricultural pastureland in the Jubba valley. Many Somalis were overtly anti-Egypt, and Egyptian troops were not well received when they arrived. Egypt, however, fulfilled the 3-3-1 strategy of having Arab and Islamic countries in the coalition. In fact, there were eight: Egypt, Morocco, Saudi Arabia, Tunisia, Pakistan, Kuwait, Turkey, and the United Arab Emirates.[48] Rounding out the 3-3-1 strategy were the African nations of Botswana, Nigeria, and Zimbabwe, which all sent small but very capable contingents.

For the coalition nations, the mission to Somalia had many names: Operation Oryx for the French, Deliverance for the Canadians, Solace for the Australians, Ibis for the Italians, and Equator Kiss for the Belgians. Some countries sent brigades; others sent battalions or companies. Some, such as France and Italy, sent forces with the full spectrum of military capabilities and armaments; others limited their contributions. Sweden sent a military hospital. New Zealand sent transport aircraft. India, participating in its first UN-authorized operation, sent a naval task force.[49] All told, coalition partners added more than eleven thousand troops to JTF Restore Hope, which now consisted of nearly thirty-nine thousand troops from twenty-two countries, all poised to descend on Somalia in the largest military intervention in Africa outside of the world wars.

Phase 1: D-Day Landings and the Occupation of Baledogle and Baidoa

Many residents of Mogadishu cheered when the first American F-14 Tomcats flew over the city in December 1992, cautiously dropping flares as decoys in case surface-to-air missiles were fired at them. There was still sporadic fighting in the city. Firefights between UNOSOM and Somalis, and between Somalis and Somalis, were nightly occurrences. But most Somalis eagerly awaited the coalition's arrival as the multinational fleet led by the USS *Ranger* Carrier Group appeared on the horizon.[50] Among the fleet was the US Navy's Amphibious Squadron Three, carrying Colonel Greg Newbold's 15th Marine Expeditionary Unit (MEU) spearheading the amphibious landings. Their mission was to seize New Port and the airport, the key real estate facilitating the coalition's deployment, as well as the former US embassy. The lack of reliable intelligence caused problems. Charts did not show the hazardous coral reefs off Mogadishu. There was no information on safe routes for landing craft or marine amphibious assault vehicles, and there were no estimates of Somali defensive positions.[51] In the early-morning darkness of 6 December, Navy SEALs carried out a reconnaissance of Green Beach, which abutted the airport, and Blue Beach, north of New Port in the former luxury riviera district from which Ali Mahdi's forces had shelled relief ships. Green Beach had favorable tides, space to unload landing craft, and safe paths through the coral. There also appeared to be no defensive preparations.[52] With a safe avenue to Green Beach, Newbold's 15th MEU awaited the assault order.

On 7 December President Bush authorized the launch of Operation Restore Hope.[53] The first boots on the ground belonged to Ambassador Robert Oakley, Bush's presidential envoy and the coalition's political head. Oakley met separately with Aidid and Ali Mahdi, instructing them to keep their forces away from Green Beach and 15th MEU's objectives. Both leaders took to the airwaves to warn Mogadishans away from

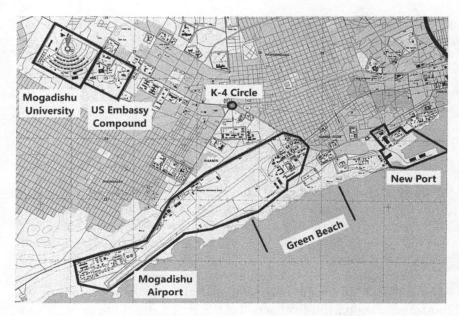

15th MEU Objectives on 9 December 1992 and Green Beach

the landing sites. Aidid added a message welcoming the Americans and persuaded the Murusade, an often hostile Hawiye subclan, to vacate their territory near the airport.[54] Aidid's chief lieutenant, Osman Atto, publicly promised "there will be no resistance," while his foreign affairs spokesman Mohamed Hassan Awale told reporters, "We are telling Somalis just to stay calm, not to feel threatened."[55]

Journalists from across the globe had flocked to Mogadishu to cover the long-anticipated arrival of the outside world. In a 4 December memo to all commanders, US Army Chief of Staff Gordon Sullivan emphasized, "We must get the story of the new, power-projection army into every American household . . . participation in Operation Restore Hope will have far-reaching consequences. . . . To sustain public support . . . we must get . . . the resulting coverage . . . to the American people, while their attention is rivetted."[56] Sullivan got far more than he bargained for when Pentagon officials leaked the landing timetable for Green Beach to the media, unbeknownst to Johnston, Newbold, or Oakley.[57]

In the early-morning darkness of D-day, 9 December, 1,305 marines from Newbold's 15th MEU launched a three-pronged amphibious assault on Mogadishu: 725 marines landed on Green Beach, 440 landed at the airport in helicopters, and 140 captured New Port using combat raider rubber craft.[58] Simultaneously, Navy SEALs landed on Blue Beach to ensure that no heavy weapons fired on the ships.[59] From the bridge of his flagship, USS *Tripoli*, Captain John Peterson, commanding Amphibious Squadron Three, watched the landings unfold. As he looked on, flashes erupted across Green Beach. Assuming the marines were under fire, he ordered the *Tripoli* to prepare to receive casualties, but there were none. What Peterson and Newbold did not know was that due to the Pentagon leak, nearly one hundred reporters had gathered on Green Beach with "cameras, strobe lights and notebooks in hand . . . like game park tourists seeing their first pride of lions."[60] Dazzled by the camera flashes and angered by the media presence, the marines responded to some desultory fire from New Port by surrounding a group of twenty-five reporters and Somalis. They "fired warning shots over their heads and ordered them face-down on the asphalt, M-16's aimed at their heads, barking at them not to move."[61] Peterson was "amazed that [Newbold's marines] didn't blow away a number of the international press."[62]

The French government condemned the intense up-front media coverage, calling it "a charity show . . . a circus."[63] This was not far off the mark. Newbold's marines found that their vehicles were stuck on Green Beach by a large sand berm, until an enterprising gunnery sergeant stole a nearby bulldozer to break through it.[64] Confusion ensued at the airport, where, inexplicably, the marines were unaware of the presence of Aziz's Pakistani UNOSOM battalion. Many of the Pakistanis could not speak English, and in the darkness, confusion reigned as both groups tried to identify their uniformed, armed counterparts.[65] Luckily, these were no more than hiccups, given that Oakley, Aidid, and Ali Mahdi had ensured a virtually unopposed landing. By noon on 9 December, the 15th MEU controlled New Port, had integrated with the Pakistanis to secure the airport, and had reclaimed the former US embassy compound.[66] Soon afterward, the first coalition forces, a company of the French Foreign Legion, landed at Mogadishu airport to reinforce the marines.

While guarding the key K-4 traffic circle outside the airport, the legionnaires and marines opened fire on an approaching bus that failed to stop, killing two civilians and wounding seven more who were evacuated to the *Tripoli* for treatment. Thus, the only casualties on 9 December were Somalis.[67] Newbold's landings were a complete success. The main arteries enabling the full deployment of JTF Restore Hope had been seized, manhandled journalists notwithstanding.

The next task for Oakley and Johnston was to ensure the continued cooperation of not only Aidid and Ali Mahdi but also UNOSOM. Oakley called a meeting on 11 December among Johnston and Zinni, representing JTF Restore Hope's military leadership; Aidid and Ali Mahdi as the principal faction leaders in Mogadishu; UNOSOM's force commander Brigadier Shaheen; and Ismat Kittani, the taciturn UN special representative. The two rivals for the leadership of Somalia had not met in over a year. No media were permitted, but many gathered outside the compound. Ali Mahdi protested the meeting taking place in Aidid-controlled territory and reportedly arrived looking like he expected to be murdered.[68] To assuage his fears and demonstrate the impartiality of coalition forces, Newbold's marines provided security for the meeting. Very quickly the tension between the two men eased. Kittani later reported, "The atmosphere was cordial bordering on euphoria. The two Somali leaders and their aides were ecstatic."[69]

Chairing the meeting, Oakley reiterated US support for UNOSOM and clarified that JTF Restore Hope's presence was paving the way for a sweeping UN operation to follow. To deter violence by the militias, he told Aidid and Ali Mahdi that the coalition had not come to fight but reminded them of America's swift victory in the Gulf War should any faction actively resist. With the stick subtly brandished, Oakley unveiled the carrot, promising to work as an honest broker for all sides of the Somali conflict. The coalition was there to help the country get back on its feet, and any faction that contributed to that goal would have a seat at the negotiating table. No offensive actions by one faction against another would be tolerated. Oakley was acutely aware that Aidid and Ali Mahdi were desperate for the United States to legitimize their respective claims to the leadership of Somalia, and he exploited this vulnerability over the course of the afternoon to reach a seven-point agreement.[70]

Oakley cajoled both men, reminding them of the value of being perceived as part of the solution rather than perpetuating the problem. The international media was right outside the door, waiting to report on whether an agreement had been reached; team players would enjoy the spotlight, and retrenchers would suffer the criticism. An immediate cease-fire was called, with an end of the division of Mogadishu along factional lines. Both men agreed to move their heavy weapons and fighting

vehicles outside the city in preparation for cantonment under coalition supervision. Johnston decreed that after forty-eight hours, any fighting vehicles that remained in Mogadishu would be destroyed, regardless of which faction they belonged to. Aidid and Ali Mahdi invited Oakley to watch as they signed the seven-point agreement. Then they both went outside to make magnanimous statements to the waiting journalists.[71]

Oakley's tactics worked. The next day, when technicals belonging to a Somali gang fired on American helicopters and were immediately destroyed in a clear show of US firepower, Aidid and Ali Mahdi publicly condemned the attack on coalition forces, at Oakley's request.[72] Not all parties were happy, though. Johnston, Oakley, and Zinni met separately with Shaheen and Kittani. Kittani resented the perception that UNOSOM had failed and America was now cleaning up the mess. Kittani bluntly claimed that regardless of statements to the contrary, the UN would not be taking over anytime soon and UNOSOM would not be involved with Restore Hope other than to deconflict the operations of both forces. Somewhat hypocritically, Kittani then asked that JTF Restore Hope be renamed to project an image of multinational co-operation. Oakley and Johnston agreed to Kittani's request to avoid the perception that America was grandstanding and to prevent any delay in the follow-on UN operation. On 11 December Zinni issued orders to all units that JTF Restore Hope would henceforth be known as the Unified Task Force, or UNITAF.[73]

With an unopposed arrival in Somalia and a declared cease-fire, Johnston turned to the remaining phase 1 objectives: securing Baledogle airbase and Baidoa, the principal city of the Bay region and the epicenter of the famine. To do this, Johnston built up forces for a series of leapfrogging maneuvers into the interior. With New Port and the airport secured, the 1st Marine Division's Regimental Combat Team 7 (RCT-7) under Colonel E. R. "Buck" Bedard arrived in Mogadishu. This freed up Newbold's 15th MEU to seize Baledogle in an air assault on 13 December. The Soviet-built airbase was in ruins. The buildings had no windows or plug sockets, wrecked MiG fighters littered the ramp, and the marines uncovered massive amounts of unexpended bombs and missiles. Just hours after the airbase's capture, the 10th Mountain Division's 2nd Battalion, 87th Infantry Regiment, landed at Baledogle.[74] As on D-day, the soldiers coming down the ramps of the transport aircraft were greeted by a "mob of about fifty cameramen and reporters."[75] The 2nd Battalion then took over Baledogle and the

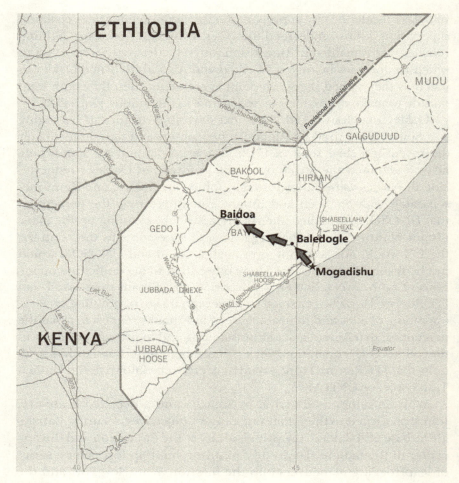

UNITAF Deployment Phase 1

nearby town of Wanlaweyne, allowing the 15th MEU to leapfrog again, this time to Baidoa.[76]

Newbold's marines joined French legionnaires for the occupation and relief of Baidoa with an air-ground convoy. On 16 December Baidoa airfield was seized in yet another unopposed air assault. Upon the approach of dozens of troop-laden helicopters, the local gangs that had been extorting "landing fees" dropped their weapons and fled. Simultaneously, a seventy-two-vehicle convoy entered the beleaguered town,

greeted by welcoming crowds. Prior to UNITAF's arrival, 50 percent of relief supplies sent to Baidoa were stolen. Within twenty-four hours, 90 percent of supplies were arriving unhindered. Not every relief convoy could be escorted from Mogadishu, but the mere presence of UNITAF forces deterred banditry and theft. Newbold announced that any weapons openly brandished in Baidoa would be confiscated. To emphasize this point, when the marines took fire from a compound on 18 December, it was surrounded by armored vehicles and helicopter gunships, and all its occupants were disarmed, marking "the first step of what [became] an aggressive policy of creating a secure environment by actively confiscating weapons."[77] The Powell Doctrine of overwhelming force was put into action on the streets of Baidoa.[78]

To the American soldiers and marines in the first units to arrive, Somalia was a shock. It was not just the hundred-degree heat and the oppressive humidity. General Zinni recalled that "driving through [Mogadishu] was like entering Stalingrad in 1942–43. Dead bodies, dead animals, and abandoned, burnt-out vehicles were scattered about the streets. Piles of garbage were everywhere . . . what could be called an economy . . . was conducted in the form of looting, pillage, or salvage."[79] While visiting one unit, Zinni was asked to provide rope so that dead animals could be dragged to the river to attract crocodiles so they could be killed. The crocodiles had been eating local children as they attempted to get drinking water.[80] Marines wrote in their diaries about the Somalis they encountered. One marine "saw anger and sorrow in their eyes, and when we passed by, they stared us down or averted their gazes altogether. None of them smiled. Theirs were the faces of a people who'd once had something good, only to have had it wrenched away and destroyed before them."[81] Another wrote:

> Noticed a boy . . . flies on his face, singing. Says a lot about that little boy. Character, in the face of adversity. He'll have flies on his face for the rest of his life, and he'll probably have to sell cigarettes to get food for years to come. . . . Give me food. We heard this a lot. But [military rations] would kill them so I started getting rid of the kids by asking *them* for chow. Puzzled some of them.[82]

In Mogadishu, Baidoa, and Baledogle, Americans digging defensive positions were horrified to find bodies buried all around them, victims of the civil war and famine.[83]

With the occupation of Baidoa on 16 December, phase 1 of Operation Restore Hope was complete, twenty-three days ahead of schedule. There were two main reasons for this. First, just as Oakley had arrived before D-day to ensure that Newbold's landing encountered no armed resistance, teams from his staff had preceded the arrival of the 15th MEU into Baledogle and Baidoa. These teams met with local elders, informed them that UNITAF was coming to provide security, and warned that hostile actions were not recommended. On Aidid's advice, these teams brought food and medical supplies to the local leaders as a sign of good faith, and as a result, there was little resistance to Newbold's arrival in these areas.[84] Second, the phase 1 deployment timetable was conservative and assumed that there would be armed resistance. Colonel Wallace Grayson, Zinni's deputy, remembered hearing at intelligence briefings that Aidid "was going to oppose this; there was going to be blood running in the streets, and all the hyperbolic rhetoric . . . and the news media started piling into Mogadishu airport. Suddenly [Aidid] holds a press conference and says I welcome the Americans."[85]

Before Newbold reached Baidoa, Johnston's staff realized that the various factions did not pose a substantial threat. The phase 2 expansion into the remaining HRSs could therefore be accelerated, especially as the international media and relief organizations were criticizing UNITAF for waiting in Mogadishu to build up forces to confront a threat that did not exist.[86] Johnston was reluctant to rush, however; he was concerned that rogue elements that had fled the capital ahead of UNITAF's arrival could use guerrilla warfare tactics to hamper the expansion into the interior. Nevertheless, he was under pressure to move quickly.[87] Thus, on 16 December Johnston ordered the commencement of phase 2. UNITAF's rapid leapfrogging continued, especially as coalition forces descended on Somalia. Yet, despite the completion of phase 1 ahead of schedule with almost no opposition and the beginning of phase 2, the harsh environment wreaked havoc on the broader deployment, especially the support forces needed to maintain and sustain UNITAF.

Unprecedented Logistical Challenges

In a deployment video shot in Somalia for the US Center for Army Lessons Learned, the narrator observes that, given the American strategy of deploying units from the continental United States, the quality of airports and seaports at the destination was vital for the strategic movement of troops and materiel. Referencing Somalia, the narrator notes that "while the deployment . . . has been small in relation to Operation Desert Storm, the airports and seaports are significantly more austere."[88] This was a profound understatement. With the possible exception of island-hopping in the Pacific theater during the Second World War, the US military had never deployed anywhere remotely like Somalia. In 1918 the American Expeditionary Force enjoyed the use of French infrastructure, and in 1942–43 British infrastructure was used to build up forces for the invasion of continental Europe. In South Vietnam, there were functioning ports and airports, a maintained road network, and utilities and infrastructure. During the Gulf War, Schwarzkopf's months-long buildup of forces used some of the most modern transportation facilities not only in the Middle East but in the world. Somalia had none of this.

According to one officer, "after the relatively benign environment of Operation Desert Shield/Desert Storm, Somalia came as a shock" up and down the American chain of command.[89] One CENTCOM planner noted, "In Saudi Arabia, we had a very robust infrastructure. We had ports that exceeded our shipping capacity. We had airfields close to that rich infrastructure . . . in Somalia the exact opposite was the case . . . infrastructure you need, such as electrical power, water, a trained labor force . . . there was nothing, absolutely nothing."[90] Marine Colonel Ray Cole, Wilhelm's operations officer, said it "was [like] going into the wild west in the 1850s and there was nothing there. . . . It has to be without parallel in that regard."[91] Another senior marine officer noted the "rude awakening" experienced by US forces who were expecting good facilities in Somalia, when the reality "was like camping out in a garbage dump with 5,000 of your closest friends."[92] Even General Hoar at CENTCOM would later write that it was "like going to the moon: *everything* needed had to be brought in or built there."[93] Somalia was not Desert Storm. And the unique challenges presented by a truly failed state with nonexistent infrastructure were compounded by American expectations shaped by the historical experience of deploying to functioning countries. This combination almost broke the most advanced military logistics system in existence. Before UNITAF could help any Somalis, it had to overcome not only the environment but also the poor quality of the country's infrastructure, especially the ports and airports.

New Port in Mogadishu was small; it had just two piers, four warehouses, and no ability to operate at night. Two sunken wrecks obstructed the harbor. Most cargo had to be unloaded by hand owing to the lack of machinery, and garbage and human refuse was everywhere. What little real estate the port had was split between UNITAF and the various relief agencies. Worse still, the Restore Hope planners decided to use the Military Sealift Command's Strategic Sealift Program of maritime prepositioning ships (MPSs) to supply UNITAF. MPSs were floating warehouses forward-deployed around the globe and loaded with vehicles, ammunition, and supplies. American troops simply flew into the area of operations, and MPSs arrived to supply them. They were a pillar of US military power projection and played a key supply role during the Gulf War. However, lacking adequate intelligence, planners were unaware that these ships were too deeply drafted to enter New Port. When the MV *Lummus* tried, it grazed the bottom.[94]

Three more MPSs arrived but could not dock. They all had small barges aboard to enable unloading from offshore, but the seas were too rough. These ships carried massive amounts of ammunition, medical supplies—including an entire combat support hospital—and construction materials for base camps and airport repair. All three sailed to Mombasa to unload in Kenya instead. However, two were forced to head back to base at Diego Garcia fully loaded; one was too large for Mombasa, and the other was refused entry because it was loaded with ammunition. The third ship off-loaded using its barges, which shuttled supplies from Mombasa to Mogadishu.[95] An astute logistics officer noted the irony of the US Army advertising itself as ready for operations in the Third World while being unable to dock at Mogadishu, a port similar in quality to most on the African continent. Concluding a memo with sage wisdom, the logistician wrote, "During this operation bigger is not better. . . . I've heard through the grapevine that the Army is attempting to purchase bigger ships for prepositioned cargo. Don't do [it]!"[96]

Unable to properly utilize these MPSs, significant amounts of supplies, especially construction materials and the hospital, had to be flown in instead. The hospital alone required twelve transport aircraft, and Mogadishu airport frustrated American logisticians as much as New Port had.[97] The airport sat right on the coast overlooking Green Beach, where Newbold's marines had landed on D-day. Its sole runway jutted out into the Indian Ocean. Of the two small ramps, the main ramp could fit only two US Air Force C-5 Galaxy or four C-141 Starlifter strategic lift aircraft at any one time. The smaller ramp was reserved for relief organizations. With no refueling facilities, aircraft had to land in Mogadishu with enough fuel for their return flights.[98]

The Australian air traffic controllers managing the airport described it in one word: chaos.[99] The control tower was made of shipping containers stacked on top of one another; it was so close to the runway that engine thrust shook the tower "to the point of collapse." Space was such an issue that it bordered on a catastrophe waiting to happen. In one incident, while a C-5 was taking off at night, its wing lights illuminated a blacked-out truck driving along the road running parallel to the runway, which fell within the massive aircraft's wing diameter. The pilots expected a collision, but the truck was low-slung enough that it fit under the wings and miraculously went between the engines without hitting them. Due to the shortage of space, troops frequently off-loaded aircraft by stacking supplies and parking vehicles on the runway itself, with one American unit establishing a major ammunition dump at the end of it.[100]

The small size of Mogadishu airport necessitated the seizure of Baledogle airbase during phase 1. The former was used for the UNITAF strategic airlift into Somalia, and the latter was used for tactical air operations within the country. Like everything in the failed state, both airports were in ruins from the civil war. When the first C-141 Starlifter landed at Baledogle airbase, one thousand feet of runway disintegrated under its weight, limiting the base to lighter aircraft and helicopter operations. The dusty environment also wreaked havoc on helicopters. Engine intakes repeatedly clogged, and visibility was nonexistent during takeoff and landing.[101] One American officer complained that the "dust at Baledogle has tremendous impact on aviation safety and maintenance. If we would have known what we know now, would we have established such an aviation hub there? McDonald's would have done a better study of any area to build a fast-food restaurant than we did at Baledogle."[102]

Somalia was completely unsuited to handle UNITAF's arrival, which constantly jostled for space with the ongoing relief effort. According to the Restore Hope deployment plan, Wilhelm's MARFOR and Arnold's ARFOR should have been fully deployed by 16 and 21 December, respectively. By 28 December, only 78 percent of Wilhelm's marines and 21 percent of Arnold's soldiers had arrived. By mid-January, half of ARFOR had not yet arrived.[103] Somalia made a mockery of America's power-projection, rapid-deployment post–Cold War strategy. By January 1993, the influx of coalition forces meant that Mogadishu had the busiest air and sea terminals in Africa. The airport handled anywhere from 87 to

444 aircraft operations per day, and in the space of thirty-five days, New Port unloaded 114,000 tons of cargo, 6,700 vehicles, 100 helicopters, 830,000 gallons of water, and 5 million gallons of fuel from 48 ships.[104]

Although the conditions in Somalia posed challenges for the US military, its own logistics system caused major problems too. Due to the limited seaport, massive amounts of equipment had to be flown into Mogadishu and Baledogle, disrupting the already tenuous situation at the airports. Arnold's ARFOR was initially promised twenty-eight transport aircraft a day, but this was reduced to twelve to free up aircraft to move other equipment due to the issues at New Port.[105] Consequently, the 10th Mountain Division, whose mission was to be "rapidly deployable" for crisis response, took more than a month to arrive.[106]

Compounding these problems, the logistics footprint was deliberately minimized to allow the quick redeployment of Johnston's troops once the mission was completed. Getting out quickly was preferable to logistical efficiency. Practically speaking, this meant that all equipment and supply stocks, even gasoline and potable water, were maintained only at thirty-day levels. Soldiers were limited to Meals Ready to Eat ration packs for the first thirty-four days in-country. Sustaining this minimum footprint was predicated on the use of MPSs. But when those ships could not off-load in Mogadishu, some supplies did not arrive for forty-five days, including construction materials for UNITAF base camps and airport and port repair. The harsh environment exacerbated the vulnerabilities of this minimal logistics footprint. In just one marine convoy to Oddur, eighty-four vehicle tires were destroyed due to the poor condition of the roads. Between Wilhelm's MARFOR and Arnold's ARFOR, there were insufficient spares to replace them, and such convoys were critical in Somalia.[107]

Given the heat and the arid climate, especially in the bone-dry interior, the supply of potable water was a constant and critical logistics issue. In the early weeks of Restore Hope, most vehicles were busy transporting food, water, and gasoline from Mogadishu across Somalia just to ensure the UNITAF forces' survival, not to help the Somalis. The 4,000 troops at Baledogle required 12,700 gallons of water per day; Arnold's ARFOR needed 40,000.[108] Drinking water was produced through Reverse Osmosis Water Purification Units (ROWPUs), as US Army medical units lacked the equipment to test whether the local water was safe for consumption.[109] ROWPU barges stood offshore and converted seawater to drinking water. But high seas frustrated the ROWPUs just as much as they did the MPSs. Moreover, the chemicals and equipment used to operate the ROWPUs were Desert Storm leftovers in short supply, and they were inadequate to produce water over a prolonged period. Coalition troops hated the taste of ROWPU water, so much so that bottled water had to be purchased and shipped in, further clogging up the already strained sea and air supply lines. Given the state of New Port, ships carrying bottled water had to be off-loaded by hand. It was discovered that MPSs carried tanks for building a water storage facility, but the specialized vehicles needed to off-load and transport them were lacking. Because remote UNITAF bases could not store water, it had to trucked in regularly from Mogadishu, traveling hundreds of kilometers on barely usable roads.[110]

Problems plagued every aspect of UNITAF's logistical effort. Of the nine fast sealift ships carrying the US Army's materiel to Mogadishu, two broke down en route carrying the very equipment needed to unload cargo at ports and airports. One MPS was detained by the Admiralty High Court in London due to an unpaid bill, which delayed its use and the supplies it carried. The MPS concept itself was stretched to the breaking point by Somalia. Nominally, each squadron of four ships was designed to supply 16,500 personnel for thirty days. Initially, CENTCOM planners determined that MPSs would supply only Johnston's headquarters and Wilhelm's 1st Marine Division, which almost met the 16,500-person limit. Even then, Johnston was told to avoid using too much of the MPS supplies. Then, on the cusp of deployment, he was informed the ships would also have to supply the ten thousand army personnel. After they arrived in Somalia, coalition forces were added, meaning that thirty-nine thousand troops were relying on an MPS squadron designed to supply less than half that number.[111]

With some UNITAF contingents 350 miles inland, the MPS system was setting records for supplying forces over great distances in difficult conditions. But with so many drawing from such a small pool, cascading shortfalls began to plague units as critical equipment was appropriated by those at the front of the line.[112] Confusion reigned as to whether the marines or the army owned the MPS cargo, who dictated the order of unloading, and who took precedence in terms of supply.[113] The only point of agreement was that American units took priority over coalition forces, nearly all of which depended on the United States for something, be it water, gasoline, or construction materials. Botswana, Tunisia, Zimbabwe, and Australia needed food; one nation even expected the Americans to pay its soldiers' salaries. Some requests were reasonable. The Tunisian contingent needed just four hundred gallons of water and one hundred gallons of gasoline daily. Others required significantly more; one UNITAF partner needed thirty-two thousand gallons of water and twenty-five thousand gallons of gasoline per day.[114]

Interservice rivalry also caused problems. In addition to disagreeing over MPS cargo, the marines and the army contested the allocation of space in the cramped New Port and airport. Every solution was ad hoc. A navy admiral became the "mayor" of New Port, even though no one had appointed him. The army assumed that it was in charge at Baledogle, while the marines were in charge at Baidoa. According to one observer, "A lot of time was spent by all involved just resolving who was to be in charge of different sites."[115] Marine Colonel John Holly complained that the army was too specialized; it always had excuses why its personnel could not do certain things. The army, Holly said, had one unit that filled water trucks and another that issued the water, with each refusing to do the other's job. In Holly's obviously biased opinion, the marines were the superior service and "ended up having to be the United Nations of the water site to keep [various army units] from fighting each other. . . . It's the most infuriating thing I've ever had to deal with."[116]

Command arrangements also caused frustration. With the MPS system strained, it was agreed that for the first fifty days of Operation Restore Hope, UNITAF logistics would be handled by the Marine Corps' 1st Force Service Support Group. After that, the US Army would take over logistics management with a bespoke entity called the Joint Task Force Support Command (JTFSC). Confusion ensued because even though the JTFSC was composed of only army units, it did not report to General Arnold, the commander of all army forces in Somalia. Also, due to its all-army composition, the JTFSC believed it was responsible for logistical support only to ARFOR, not to the marines or coalition forces. The ARFOR and JTFSC staffs clashed over the control of Baledogle airbase and then over the command of specific army units. The JTFSC appropriated all the medical units, leaving Arnold's 10th Mountain Division with a lone divisional surgeon dependent on his own personal equipment; he had to beg for three additional personnel to act as his assistants.[117]

The Time-Phased Force Deployment Data List

Perhaps the biggest issue for US forces in Somalia was the Time-Phased Force Deployment Data List (TPFDDL), pronounced *tip-fiddle*. The TPFDDL is a deployment plan—a complex roster of troops and materiel, the ships and aircraft needed to transport them, and a timetable of flights and sailings. Depending on the operation, the TPFDDL can be constructed specifically for one operation or adapted from a previous operation and amended where necessary. For Somalia, the TPFDDL caused mayhem for a multitude of reasons. First and foremost, the principal US commanders in Somalia had little or no access to the TPFDDL, while the various higher headquarters in the United States continually altered it and failed to communicate with one another or with the units preparing to deploy.

In one particularly egregious case, neither General Arnold nor his staff had access to the TPFDDL as they were preparing to deploy units of the 10th Mountain Division, and they were unaware of actions taken higher up the chain of command. The division was part of XVIII Airborne Corps, whose headquarters staff *did* have access to the TPFDDL and developed their own deployment plan, independent of Arnold's staff. Planners at CENTCOM, which had overall authority for Restore Hope, developed their own roster and argued with XVIII Airborne Corps about who was responsible for constructing the TPFDDL and deciding which units would deploy. When Secretary of Defense Dick Cheney arbitrarily set a limit of 10,200 army personnel for Restore Hope, XVIII Airborne Corps and CENTCOM disagreed over the limit for weeks, revising the personnel cap from 10,200 to 13,026 and then back to 10,200 and repeatedly adjusting the TPFDDL.[118]

In addition, CENTCOM and Arnold's 10th Mountain Division staff were planning for entirely different missions. For CENTCOM, the army's mission was to secure Baledogle only, although Baidoa was added later. Yet Arnold's staff was told to "assume ground defense of [Mogadishu] airfield, seaport [and] provide ground defense for an unspecified number of airfields, and to provide detention and life support for displaced personnel and enemy prisoners of war," a much broader mission requiring completely different units. Arnold's staff was concerned that such a mission "may totally consume the division."[119] Thus, CENTCOM and 10th Mountain were working on mutually exclusive deployment plans, with barely any coordination between the two. Arnold's staff was unaware of the 10,200-personnel cap; nor was it aware of the existence of the JTFSC or its mandate to take over the logistical effort from the marines. Only after Arnold's ARFOR units began to deploy was his staff informed that JTFSC units were counted in the army's 10,200-person limit, meaning that several of Arnold's units had to be cut or rerouted midstream. The result was chaos. Army units were told with little or no notice to deploy, to stand down, or that their mission had changed. One of Arnold's infantry battalions, already en route to Baledogle, changed course midflight to occupy Kismayo instead, while another on the verge of deployment was ordered to stand down to make room for JTFSC units.[120]

Another critical problem was that the TPFDDL for Restore Hope was not an original plan. CENTCOM planners had dusted off the version used in the Gulf War and simply deleted and added units where necessary. The TPFDDL was thus geared toward a war, not a humanitarian operation. As such, army combat units were sent to Somalia ahead of the support units required to supply them with fuel, food, water, and medical care. This would have made sense for a combat mission, but the marines had already secured Mogadishu airport, New Port, Baledogle, and Baidoa, and the Somalis were not a threat. One of Wilhelm's operations officers summed it up succinctly: "Classic dilemma, eaters and shitters consuming at an inordinate rate, with the guys that are supposed to satiate that consumption not even here."[121] It was late January when the 10th Tenth Mountain Division's operations officer conceded that "[our] initial response was to deploy . . . as we would for a wartime mission. We ended up front loading a lot of units' equipment . . . that later had to be removed."[122] This was an understatement. Fully one-fifth of all US equipment sent to Somalia was not needed due to the constantly changing TPFDDL. With units arbitrarily added to or removed from the deployment plan, more than nine hundred vehicles arrived in Somalia only to be reloaded and sent back.[123]

Because of the Gulf War TPFDDL, specialists trained to unload MPSs and to operate airports or seaports arrived last instead of first. Ships waited off Mogadishu, while the personnel trained to off-load them were still in the United States. Some units arrived without any ammunition, and vital water-producing equipment did not arrive until late January. Engineers tasked with repairing ports and airfields were also among the last to arrive, and they lacked the specialized equipment they needed because combat units' equipment took priority. Some essential engineering equipment took fifty days to arrive, meaning that route-proofing against mines was done with just a standard unprotected truck packed with sandbags instead of with armored dozers. On the road to Bardera, this truck ran over four mines that failed to detonate only because the Somali who planted them had removed the fuses when he heard the Americans were coming.[124]

Up and down the line, the TPFDDL caused chaos in Somalia and in the United States. By late December, members of the army's 62nd Medical Group knew their unit was deploying, but they did not know how many of them were going, their destination, or what their mission was. As it was about to depart, the unit, which was 48 percent female, was informed that Johnston's headquarters did not want any more female personnel in Somalia. Then the 62nd was told to leave 30 percent of its equipment behind. Finally, they were bumped from their flight because a public affairs team had priority. The 62nd Medical Group eventually deployed aboard US Air Force tankers because of the shortage of transport aircraft created by the knock-on effects of MPSs' inability to dock at Mogadishu.[125]

The TPFDDL frustrated the army, it frustrated the marines, it frustrated every level of the chain of command. No aspect of the deployment was unaffected. Eventually, the frustration reached Johnston, who ordered that no one could alter the TPFDDL without his express authorization.[126] But the damage had already been done. March Air Force Base had a "gigantic back-up of men and materiel the likes of which can only be imagined in the worst assembly line nightmare," with some units waiting two weeks to board a plane to Somalia.[127] Amidst the chaos, one marine squadron commander sarcastically considered writing a book entitled "How to Plan Deployment and Watch It Go Wrong."[128]

Phase 2: Expanding throughout Southern Somalia

With phase 1 complete, and despite the widespread logistical issues, US and coalition forces focused on phase 2—occupation of the remaining six HRSs in southern Somalia. America's UNITAF coalition partners were a mixed bag. Some contingents, such as the Australians and NATO members, were sizable and highly capable. Others were just as capable but small and logistically dependent on the Americans, particularly the African and Arab forces.[129] In fairness, though, some of these ill-equipped contingents were better trained for a mission in Somalia than the Americans were. The Botswanans, Nigerians, and Zimbabweans were much more adept due to their militaries' focus on bush fighting.[130]

Managing the coalition partners fell to the Coalition Forces Support Team (CFST). Established by Wilhelm, the MARFOR commander, the CFST oriented incoming coalition contingents, provided intelligence, assessed capabilities, and managed logistical needs. Wilhelm created the CFST because his headquarters at Mogadishu airport was "inundated with the senior officers of these arriving forces," who often appeared unexpectedly and lacked the ability to sustain their personnel.[131] Some nations sent liaisons ahead of their main force to smooth their eventual arrival in-country; they worked with the CFST to establish what HRS they would occupy and who they would report to.[132] General Zinni, UNITAF's director of operations, earned the nickname "Century 21 Man," as he was often required to greet the incoming coalition forces and quickly "sell" them the real estate in Somalia where they would be deployed.[133]

What emerged was a different command relationship for each coalition partner, depending on the forces they brought. Large contingents such as Italy, Canada, France, Australia, and Morocco, which were capable and logistically self-sustaining, were assigned their own HRSs and reported directly to Johnston as UNITAF commander. Smaller partners were assigned to a specific US service, depending on their operational capabilities and size. The smaller African and Arab contingents were assigned to Wilhelm and the marines who managed Mogadishu. This facilitated the ability to supply these logistically dependent forces, which, culturally and religiously, were best suited to work in the capital. India, with only a naval contribution, reported to Johnston's senior navy commander, while New Zealand and Germany, with only transport aircraft, reported to Johnston's senior air force commander. Belgium, with a midrange contingent, was assigned to ARFOR commander General Arnold.[134]

Relations between US and coalition forces were complex. US logistics personnel were suspicious that various contingents would take advantage of their generous supply system, even though the coalition partners were billed for everything they were given.[135] One American logistician wrote, "Limitations of support is something the Army must think through. . . . What is to stop the French from requesting copiers or TV sets from the U.S. forces. . . . Crafty coalition forces could take advantage of this uncertainty. . . . Without rules somebody will do something dumb."[136]

Coalition forces were also skeptical of the Americans. On the one hand, several US and coalition commanders had attended various American military schools and education programs together, which fostered cooperation. And to ensure coordination and cooperation across UNITAF, Johnston assigned CFST liaison officers to each of the various contingents. On the other hand, many contingents were leery of these liaison officers, believing they had been sent to spy on them. After fulfilling their supply requests, some requested that the CFST liaison be reassigned elsewhere.[137] This suspicion may have been driven by the presence of a team of American officers sent to Somalia to conduct extensive oral history interviews among the UNITAF coalition. Interviewees were asked about their country's military training regimes, weapons, capabilities, and officer education. The mutual mistrust was not helped by the fact that most US intelligence information could not be shared with foreign forces. This made multinational planning sessions difficult for American officers, who would "try to tell [coalition personnel] what an area looks like" without being able to show them reconnaissance photographs of it.[138]

The coalition's growing pains notwithstanding, the phase 2 occupation of the remaining six HRSs took less than fifteen days, achieving completion before the original phase 1 deadline. Using the same formula as before, Oakley or an aide visited the HRS first, met local elders, reassured them of UNITAF's aims, and advised them not to oppose its arrival. As more forces arrived, UNITAF again leapfrogged further inland and down the coast. For the most part, coalition forces were assisted in occupying their respective HRSs by either Wilhelm's 1st Marine Division or Arnold's 10th Mountain Division. On 20 December Belgian Lieutenant Colonel Marq Jacqmin led a joint Belgian–15th MEU amphibious landing at the port city of Kismayo, southern Somalia's only other major usable port. Meeting no resistance, Jacqmin's force secured the port, the airport, and the city within four hours, allowing transport aircraft to land with reinforcements. Once Kismayo was secured, the marines withdrew and were replaced by the 10th Mountain Division's 3rd Battalion, 14th Infantry Regiment, flown directly to Kismayo from Fort Drum, New York.[139]

Simultaneously, Wilhelm moved his headquarters from Mogadishu to Baidoa to support the occupation of HRS Bardera by marines from

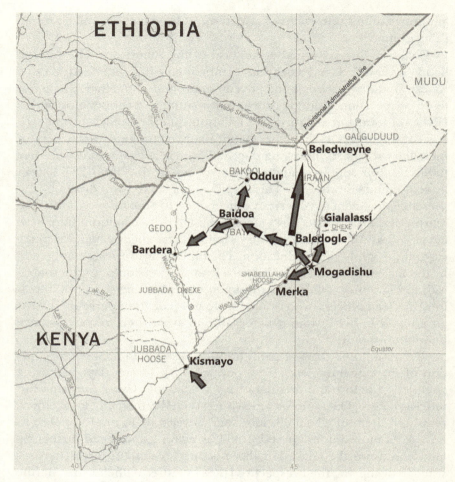

UNITAF Deployment Phase 2

Bedard's RCT-7 and HRS Oddur by Major General Rene Delhome's French brigade on 23 and 25 December, respectively.[140] Bedard's RCT-7 traveled the 450 kilometers from Mogadishu to Bardera on barely passable roads. The journey was made even harder by vehicles from nearly one hundred media organizations weaving in and out of the massive convoy, and some of the journalists had hired armed Somali technicals as escorts. Bardera was just as devastated as Baidoa had been. Relief organizations employed sixty full-time grave diggers to bury up to 350

bodies a day. Banditry was endemic, and the city was littered with ruined buildings and shot-up vehicles. Like Newbold in Baidoa, Bedard
met with five hundred community and clan leaders on Christmas Eve
1992. He banned weapons on the streets and disbanded the "quasi police force" that had been extorting locals. Bedard's marines then took
over security for relief convoys and patrolled the streets.[141]

On 27 December, again assisted by Wilhelm's marines, Major General Gianpietro Rossi's Italian Folgore Brigade occupied HRS Gialalassi.
Because the Italian government had shown a preference for Ali Mahdi,
who had established his branch of the USC in Rome during the civil
war, Johnston also assigned Italian troops to Mahdi's portion of Mogadishu.[142] By the time Bardera, Oddur, and Gialalassi were occupied, the
Canadian Airborne Battlegroup had arrived in Baledogle, intending to
take control of HRS Beledweyne, deep in the interior on the Ethiopian
border. Beledweyne was inaccessible due to poor roads and unmarked
minefields, so on 28 December, after flying 250 kilometers from Baledogle, the heliborne 10th Mountain Division's 2nd Battalion, 87th Infantry, took Beledweyne airfield. This allowed the Canadians to fly in from
Baledogle aboard C-130 transport aircraft.[143] As in other HRSs, there was
no local opposition in Beledweyne. Despite a leaflet drop warning locals
to stay away during the lodgment, thousands flocked to the airfield to
welcome UNITAF. Later that night, many of the locals fired their guns
wildly into the air in drunken celebration, forcing the Canadians to dig
foxholes as errant rounds landed within their camp.[144]

With the occupation of Merka by the US Army on 31 December
1992, the final HRS was under coalition control.[145] Phase 2 was complete weeks ahead of schedule, and across southern Somalia, UNITAF
was almost universally welcomed by hopeful Somalis. The last contingents to arrive were the Moroccans and the Australians. To relieve pressure on US forces, the Moroccans took over HRS Baledogle from the US
Army, which retained control of the airbase. And when the Australians
arrived, Zinni, once again selling real estate, offered them HRS Baidoa
to relieve Newbold's 15th MEU. Both the Australians and the Moroccans took over their respective HRSs on 16 January 1993.[146] Consequently, of the nine HRSs UNITAF controlled, the Canadians, Italians,
French, and Australians occupied one each (Beledweyne, Gialalassi,
Oddur, and Baidoa, respectively). Wilhelm's marines managed Bardera
by the Kenyan border and, along with the smaller Arab and African contingents, garrisoned Mogadishu. Meanwhile, Arnold's 10th Mountain

Division held Kismayo with the Belgians, Baledogle with the Moroccans, and Merka alone. By mid-January, there were 24,282 UNITAF troops in Mogadishu and 14,000 more spread across the other eight HRSs.[147]

On New Year's Day 1993, nearly one thousand Somalis gathered at the US embassy in Mogadishu to welcome President Bush just weeks before the inauguration of Bill Clinton.[148] Optimism and hope were in the air, and Aidid was no exception. He wished everyone at UNITAF headquarters a happy New Year and delivered a special cake made for the occasion. The icing on top of the cake depicted Bush and the aspiring Somali leader standing side by side under their respective flags. No one ate the cake, Zinni remembered, as "one of the troops noticed that it was the only thing around the place that never had flies on it."[149] In just twenty-two days, despite logistical mayhem, phases 1 and 2 of Operation Restore Hope had been completed with comparative ease and almost no opposition. UNITAF was now responsible for nearly one hundred thousand square miles of southern Somalia. Phase 3 could now begin.

4 | Pacification, Presence, and Overwhelming Force
Securing Somalia

I think they're safer here in Mogadishu than they are in some cities back in the States.
　　　　—Colonel Jack W. Klimp, commander, Task Force Mogadishu[1]

I compare our mission to taking someone with hysterics and slapping him out of it!
　　　　—Ambassador Robert B. Oakley, US presidential envoy to Somalia[2]

Across southern Somalia, UNITAF had swiftly completed phases 1 and 2 of Operation Restore Hope. Now it was time to fulfill the mandate of Resolution 794 and the Restore Hope mission: establish a secure environment. Of the nine HRSs, only Mogadishu and Kismayo presented security challenges. Elsewhere, violence was the exception, not the rule, for the six months UNITAF was present, from December 1992 to May 1993. These two cities demonstrate how the coalition approached its security mission and are representative of operations in the other seven sectors.

Mogadishu, Somalia's capital, was the single biggest security problem. Phase 1 of Restore Hope had involved securing New Port, the airport, and the US embassy compound. The rest of the city had been neglected to accelerate phase 2—expansion into the interior.[3] Managing the city was the responsibility of Major General Charles E. Wilhelm's Marine Forces Somalia (MARFOR). Keith Richburg of the *Washington Post* described Wilhem as a tough, no-nonsense marine, "the kind you'd expect Clint Eastwood to play in the movies."[4] Once the interior had been occupied, Wilhelm declared on 21 December 1992 that MARFOR's main effort was securing the capital.[5]

This was a daunting task. Mogadishu had one million residents, with an additional three hundred thousand internally displaced persons. It was also the center of inter-Hawiye tensions, divided between Aidid's Habr-Gidr and Ali Mahdi's Abgal but also contested by the Murusade, who were hostile toward the rural Habr-Gidr for encroaching on their urban territory.[6] Wilhelm's intelligence officer described Mogadishu as "a mosaic of clans and sub-clans and factional alliances that was just incredible."[7] Nevertheless, Wilhelm wanted to "turn Mogadishu back into a functioning city," and on 23 December he ordered marine Colonel Jack W. Klimp to develop a plan to "pacify" the capital.[8]

Wilhelm's choice of the word "pacify" was apt. Mogadishu was, as MARFOR's command chronology recorded, "in a state of anarchy . . . the only authority . . . was that of brute force."[9] Aidid and Ali Mahdi were abiding by the cease-fire and had cantoned their heavy weapons. But Mogadishans were still at the mercy of nonaligned gangs that roamed with impunity. Violence and crime were endemic. Klimp was ordered to make Mogadishu "favorable to the introduction of peacekeeping forces."[10] To that end, he developed a four-phase pacification plan: (1) intelligence collection, to create a target list of rogue gangs and arms caches; (2) presence, coalition patrolling, checkpoints, and convoy security to gain the support and confidence of the city's population; (3) direct action, which meant that all hostile factions or gangs would be "neutralized"; and (4) pacification, which, once achieved, would be maintained. Endorsing Klimp's plan, Wilhelm reiterated his desire for "intense peacemaking operations . . . to identify and neutralize the people, municipal regions, and activities which foster instability."[11]

Task Force Mogadishu

To execute the pacification plan, Task Force Mogadishu was established on 4 January 1993 under Klimp's command. It was a substantial force. From MARFOR came the 3rd Assault Amphibian Battalion, 3rd Light Armored Infantry Battalion, 3rd Battalion/11th Marines, and a detachment from the 1st Tank Battalion—all told, eighteen hundred marines with fifty armored amphibious assault vehicles and LAV-25 armored personnel carriers (APCs), four M1A1 Abrams main battle tanks, and 181 other vehicles. Task Force Mogadishu also included the smaller African and Arab contingents from Saudi Arabia, Egypt, Turkey, Botswana, Kuwait, the United Arab Emirates (UAE), Zimbabwe, and Pakistan, which were considered culturally and religiously acceptable to the

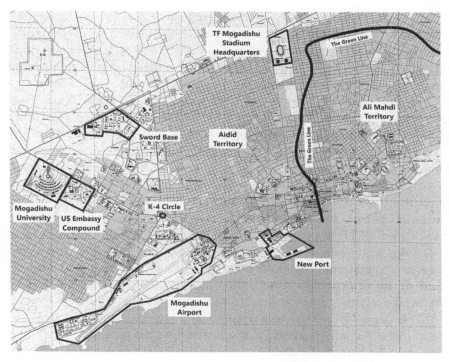

Mogadishu under UNITAF, 1992–1993

local population. Including coalition forces, Klimp commanded more than forty-five hundred heavily armed troops.[12]

Operationally, Task Force Mogadishu was subdivided into three "teams." The coalition contingents, along with 3rd Battalion/11th Marines, formed Team Secure, which garrisoned New Port and the airport, the US embassy compound, and the adjacent ruins of Mogadishu University, where UNITAF's headquarters and main base camps were located. Equipped with APCs, the 3rd Light Armored Infantry formed Team Convoy to escort relief convoys, and the 3rd Assault Amphibian Battalion formed Team Patrol to patrol the worst neighborhoods of Mogadishu.[13] The 1,198 marines of Team Patrol and Team Convoy were based at Mogadishu Stadium in the north of the city, a defensible installation that could accommodate armored vehicles and from which patrols could sortie outward.[14] The choice of the stadium was also a clear statement of intent. It sat squarely on the Green Line that divided Mogadishu between Aidid and Ali Mahdi territory.

Task Force Mogadishu began a herculean effort to secure the city with a campaign of urban patrolling, averaging between twenty and forty patrols per day from January 1993 onward.[15] To keep gangs and criminals off balance, patrols traveled in armored vehicles on different routes and at different times, dismounting seemingly at random to sweep a sector on foot before remounting to be dropped off somewhere else.[16] This presence campaign required innovation on the part of Klimp's marines. Under Marine Corps doctrine, units such as the 3rd Assault Amphibian and 3rd Light Armored Infantry Battalions were used to fast-paced mechanized and amphibious warfare operations, not policing an urban environment. However, with the expected threat limited to small-arms fire, the unconventional use of amphibious assault vehicles for urban armored patrols was deemed an "unmitigated success."[17] These patrols advertised UNITAF's presence and enhanced its visibility to build relationships with Somalis. Through interpreters, they also gathered intelligence directly from the locals on hostile groups and their arms caches and on the city's prolific arms trade operating from the Bakara Market in Aidid's territory and the Argentine Market in Ali Mahdi's.[18]

The need for interpreters resulted in a strange coincidence. With only three Somali speakers in the active-duty ranks, the US military searched for Somali-speaking civilians in the United States to serve as interpreters. Among the dozens of volunteers was the sole Somali speaker in the whole Marine Corps.[19] A veteran of the Gulf War, this reservist struck up a conversation with a journalist during the flight to Mogadishu, and the reporter naturally inquired how the marine happened to speak Somali. After the aircraft landed, the journalist hurriedly sought General Zinni to inform him that, unbeknownst to anyone, the reservist in question, Corporal Hussein Mohamed Farrah, was Aidid's son. Aidid had sent his family to the United States years previously, and after becoming a naturalized citizen, Farrah joined the Marine Corps. Given his father's identity, Corporal Farrah did not accompany patrols as an interpreter, for fear that he might be targeted by one of Aidid's rivals. And although Aidid knew of his son's presence, neither man reached out to the other. Farrah was assigned office duties in UNITAF headquarters and completed his tour without incident.[20]

For marine Lieutenant Colonel Edward Lesnowicz, commander of Team Secure, protecting UNITAF installations from potential attacks was challenging. Eight hundred troops alone were needed to guard the airport due to the poor state of the perimeter fences. Lesnowicz

assigned this task to his coalition contingents, as the logistical difficulties plaguing UNITAF's deployment meant that Egyptian, Kuwaiti, and Pakistani troops arrived long before their vehicles and equipment, relegating them to static security duties.[21] Although Team Secure's mission was to garrison UNITAF bases in Mogadishu, Lesnowicz also conducted a vigorous patrolling effort. He assigned the Saudi contingent the Medina district, where Islamic Relief, a Muslim relief organization, was based. The Turkish contingent, with its armored vehicles, was given a rarity in the city—a district with wide streets. The Botswanans' and Zimbabweans' light infantry were assigned to the more closely packed urban labyrinths, while the UAE garrisoned New Port.[22] Lesnowicz drove Team Secure hard. He told his troops that success was measured "in terms of hours in patrol zones; optimally 16 hours daily, minimally 12 hours daily . . . [and] I want to achieve peace through overwhelming firepower application should our presence fail to deter attacks on us or innocents."[23]

There was some desultory resistance to UNITAF from those who had previously extorted landing fees at the airport or operated illegal checkpoints, as they were now out of a job. Inaccurate sniper fire was a daily norm for marines based at the stadium, particularly at night and on Sundays, which Somalis believed was a Western holy day. This sniping was a nuisance that raised concerns about personnel being shot while sleeping at night. Every time incoming fire was taken, the marines were woken up and checked for wounds.[24] General Zinni recalled going outside at night to use a makeshift latrine, only to have rounds from sniper fire land around him. Humbled, Zinni's "appreciation for indoor plumbing . . . increased after that."[25]

Patrols also took sniper fire. Gangs or bandits would fire from a distance and then disappear. In most cases, there were no UNITAF casualties. However, on the night of 12 January, one of Lesnowicz's marine patrols was ambushed near the airport. After breaking contact, the patrol realized they were a man short. When they returned to the ambush site, they found Private Domingo Arroyo dead from a gunshot to the head, UNITAF's first fatality from enemy fire. The next day another marine was wounded by sniper fire near the stadium. To counter this threat, sniper teams from Reconnaissance Company, 5th Marines, established observation posts around the stadium, at the airport, and on the roof of the US embassy. In addition, with so many vehicles available and so many patrols, whenever personnel took fire, Klimp's forces rapidly converged on the bandits from several directions, a tactic that alleviated the threat over several weeks.[26]

The sniper threat was merely an annoyance. The real danger was friendly fire, as Mogadishu was a patchwork of UNITAF encampments and compounds. On the night of 11 January a Somali gunman fired three shots into the university compound. Lieutenant Colonel Leonard Sly, the 62nd Medical Group's executive officer, watched the response as Tunisians and American military police guarding the perimeter wall "immediately lit flares and put their machine guns on rock and roll . . . until [their] fingers got tired. . . . No one was hurt or wounded . . . the Tunisians and MPs fired 20,000 rounds. Some ratio!"[27] These twenty thousand rounds were fired over a friendly camp. On another occasion, Sly witnessed a Botswanan guard firing at an African American soldier he had mistaken for a Somali. Luckily, the shot missed. Thanks to one paranoid American noncommissioned officer from a medical unit, when a few shots rang out in the dark, his men were so convinced that Somalis were overrunning the university compound that they loaded their weapons and ran around in a panic, until their officers reminded them that their camp was surrounded by other UNITAF contingents.[28]

To prevent fratricide, Johnston's headquarters staff formed a Vital Area Security Committee to coordinate and regulate all defensive firing across coalition facilities to avoid friendly-fire incidents.[29] Another concern was coordination among the coalition forces, as the various contingents often encountered one another, unaware that friendly forces were operating in the same area, especially at night.[30] Lesnowicz, the Team Secure commander, blamed this lack of coordination on Wilhelm's MARFOR staff, who, in his opinion, failed to appreciate the experience and capabilities of the coalition forces. Lesnowicz recalled watching an American officer "teach" coalition partners how to eat a ration pack. In his words, this was "just absolute bullshit . . . [coalition officers] must have thought we were just the dumbest things in the world. In fact, looking at their faces, I'm thinking to myself, Jesus Christ this is embarrassing . . . that's the biggest problem that we got, is our own ethnocentrism."[31]

Violence: The Exception, Not the Rule

Although Task Force Mogadishu faced sporadic fire on occasion, with the exception of HRS Kismayo, violence really was the exception during

the UNITAF deployment. The international media received daily briefings from marine Colonel Fred Peck, director of UNITAF's Joint Information Bureau. Demonstrating the journalists' level of concern about safety, the first question Peck was asked at one briefing was whether a lifeguard could be posted at Mogadishu beach due to the presence of sharks.[32] During another, Peck joked about "opening up one of these briefings with a description of all the violent events of the last 24 hours and . . . at the end say 'oh, excuse me, I've got Pittsburgh here, let me find Mogadishu.'"[33] Peck's lighthearted deputy used one briefing to advertise T-shirts on sale in Mombasa with the slogan "You gotta *Provide Relief* before you can *Restore Hope.*"[34] With little violence to report, Keith Richburg of the *Washington Post* took note of a number of surreal events in the devastated capital. There was a formal party for the reopening of the US embassy and a black-tie banquet hosted by UNOSOM to raise funds for a refugee center. Journalists held nightly rooftop parties at the Al-Sahafi Hotel, where the international media resided. An outdoor movie theater opened with a screening of *Patton.* What the Somalis thought of a towering George C. Scott's opening monologue in front of the Stars and Stripes can only be imagined. For Richburg, Mogadishu was an "oddball fantasyland," a juxtaposition between the widespread poverty and tragedy inflicted on the Somalis and the party lifestyle of the Westerners working for the media, the UN, or relief agencies.[35]

Task Force Mogadishu's pacification campaign brought coalition personnel into constant contact with Somalis, and relations between them depended on several factors. Klimp recognized the value of being in good standing with the locals, especially clan elders. On 12 January Klimp met with Abgal elders, who offered their condolences for the loss of Private Arroyo and expressed anger over his death. To help stabilize the city, the elders offered to locate rogue groups and give the information to Task Force Mogadishu.[36] Two days later, Klimp met with elders from Aidid's Habr-Gidr, telling them, "America came here with an open mind, not a closed fist; to help all Somalis." Klimp asked them to help stop the sniping at marines. Somali casualties were not desirable, he explained, but UNITAF personnel would protect themselves if fired on. The Habr-Gidr elders told Klimp, "We are ready to give you any assistance we can."[37]

While clan elders responded well to UNITAF's presence, the attitudes of average Somalis varied. Many openly welcomed the coalition and the resultant stability. One report mentioned that the "local populace . . .

are glad to see Marines patrolling their city, but they fear the criminals will terrorize them when U.S. forces depart."[38] In most interactions, the locals were friendly, often warning coalition personnel of mines and bombs, surrendering weapons they owned or found, and revealing the locations of weapons caches or hostile groups. When coalition troops bathed in the ocean, crowds of bemused and curious Somalis gathered because they had never seen naked Caucasians before. In contrast, Somali youths threw rocks at UNITAF patrols or stole food and equipment from vehicles. The residents of Merka, remembering their colonial past, gathered on the shore and threw rocks at Italians who tried to land supplies there. The Italians wisely headed to Mogadishu's port instead.[39]

There were also religious tensions. In Baidoa, Australian soldiers rescued two teenage girls being stoned by a crowd that suspected them of intimate fraternization. Likewise, in Mogadishu, a Somali woman was "stripped, stoned, and knifed by a Muslim Fundamentalist" for her interactions with French troops.[40] When Australians uncovered a mass grave of nearly twelve thousand famine victims in January 1993, a riot almost broke out to protest Christians defiling the bodies of Muslims. The Australians, along with Oakley and senior UNITAF commanders, worked hard to emphasize coalition respect for Islam and for Somali cultural values.[41]

Many Somalis were unsure of the coalition's true intentions and feared what the UN had in store for Somalia's future.[42] With their country in ruins (and the internet and social media a decade away), Somalis eagerly consumed information on the radio and in newspapers. Both Aidid and Ali Mahdi had radio stations in Mogadishu, but neither could be relied on for objectivity. The most trusted radio station was the BBC Somali-language service, but even the BBC had spread erroneous reports about UNOSOM's takeover of Mogadishu airport. Fourteen newspapers competed in the capital for readership: four leaned toward Aidid; seven, including one English-language and one Italian publication, favored Ali Mahdi. Unsurprisingly, these publications blamed the other side for Somalia's problems while advocating for their respective leaders as the solution. Two newspapers were fundamentalist Islamic publications that supported neither leader but were "vehemently" anti-American, with one going so far as to declare Oakley the "real president of Somalia."[43] Information came in whatever flavor readers and listeners preferred.

To allay fears about the future, and to ensure that UNITAF's mission was clearly understood, the US Army and Oakley's staff established their own radio station and newspaper, both named *Rajo*—Somali for "hope." *Rajo* printed and broadcast information on UNITAF operations and relief efforts and readings from the Qur'an. Somalis who had come home to help their country were interviewed and profiled, and local poetry contests were held. *Rajo* was immensely popular, with a print distribution of eighteen thousand copies per day in Mogadishu and an additional eight thousand copies across the other HRSs.[44] Amidst the competing spin from Aidid's and Ali Mahdi's media, *Rajo* was the voice of objectivity. The newspaper was in such high demand that "Somalis literally fight for their own copy."[45]

One of the most popular aspects of *Rajo* was a comic strip devised by US Navy Petty Officer Abdul Elmi, who had left Somalia as a boy and returned as an interpreter. Elmi devised a Somali version of *Calvin and Hobbes* called *Celmi and Mandeeq*. Instead of a suburban boy and his stuffed tiger, Celmi, a young nomad, traveled Somalia with Mandeeq, his camel, and together they discussed the reconstruction efforts by UNITAF, the UN, and relief organizations. Elmi's choice of a hardy nomadic camel herder, a key facet of Somali culture and individualism, resonated positively with Somalis and helped convey UNITAF's efforts, goals, and impartiality.[46] *Rajo* worked hard to endear UNITAF to the population. It had to, because a growing problem was coalition troops' frustration with the locals.

With no real enemy to fight and violence rare, many senior American officers complained about "periods of activity punctuated by long periods of boredom."[47] One officer wrote in his diary, "With everything as quiet and uneventful as it is, I have to wonder . . . why are we here and what are we really doing."[48] One US Army press release authored by Staff Sergeant Cindy Killion provided an answer:

> I've been hearing more and more troops asking, "what are we doing here?" They haven't seen what I have seen. If they had they wouldn't wonder . . . there are two very different Somalias. The one that's visible . . . hordes of children gathering around military vehicles asking over and over again for food or water. . . . These kids aren't starving. Yes, they're poor. Yes, they're dirty and no, they're not in the best of health. But their bodies haven't turned on them . . . there are no bloated stomachs . . . and their faces just don't match the pictures we've seen. The match is found in the hidden Somalia . . . behind the walls of the therapeutic feeding centers. . . . That's the Somalia few soldiers see. Yet, that's the Somalia we came to rescue.[49]

If the Somali response to UNITAF was mixed, the reverse was also true. Killion was right. Most coalition personnel did not see the hidden Somalia. The troops' attitudes toward Somalis were defined not by the suffering they did not see but by their everyday experiences.

How American soldiers and marines viewed their mission in Somalia depended on their race, gender, and military specialty. In a revealing study by sociologists Laura Miller and Charles Moskos, white male combat personnel, termed "warriors," often perceived Somalis negatively and used excessive force against them or derogatory comments to describe them.[50] In contrast, support personnel—notably, women and African Americans—were more likely to be "humanitarians," viewing the Somalis positively and highly critical of violence and racism by their warrior comrades.

On the side of the humanitarians, one African American marine told reporters that he was eager to go to Somalia, "since our roots are there . . . it's good to be going over there to help people and not destroy them."[51] Likewise, female soldiers and marines saw Restore Hope as proof that gender was not a bar to serving in austere conditions, and a homosexual marine claimed it showcased why the ban on homosexuals in the US military should be lifted.[52] Many warriors, however, voiced their frustrations. A marine colonel argued that Restore Hope was a distraction and said, "Our mission shouldn't be humanitarian, our mission should be warfighting."[53] Another marine felt "anger toward the citizens of Mogadishu who protest our presence here. Don't they realize that, were it not for us, they would not be enjoying the relative peace and plenty which here this time exist? Being in this foreign and somewhat inhospitable land is a chore. Having to suffer the rebukes and refuse hurled our way by ungrateful Mogadishans is a burden that chafes."[54] One complained that "little importance was attached to establishing good relations with the locals. In one incident, (unfortunately not isolated) a marine officer pointed a loaded [grenade launcher] at an unarmed crowd while screaming at them at the top of his voice."[55]

Part of the problem was that the high operational tempo of Task Force Mogadishu was taking a psychological toll. Though the troops were welcomed on most street corners, sniper fire or stones being thrown at them was an ever-present possibility. By mid-January 1993, Klimp's marines were growing "increasingly impatient with the naturally curious Somalis, particularly when Somalis crowded them."[56] This impatience manifested in different ways. One officer complained that the emaciated and malnourished Somalis "are the slowest workers in the world—must be getting paid by the hour."[57] With nerves frayed and tempers short, one marine fatally shot a child approaching his Humvee carrying a box that he mistakenly thought was a bomb.[58] Across the coalition, troops started denigrating Somalis by referring to them collectively as "skinnies."[59]

What really infuriated UNITAF troops was thievery and looting by those desperate for food or anything that could be traded for food. Looters plagued every HRS and were often captured at the airport scavenging the food waste dumped near the perimeter fence by coalition personnel.[60] Over time, the exasperated soldiers got more aggressive in dealing with them. In Merka, the US Army held captured looters overnight in a storeroom dubbed "Motel 6" before releasing them—naked—the next morning.[61] In Baidoa, suspect locals were "restrained and given a talking to" by Australian troops in a practice called "adjusting Somali attitudes," perpetrated by those who believed physical retaliation was required to maintain respect.[62] Sometimes the intolerance boiled over into overt violence. In Mogadishu, an American soldier shot and killed a teenager for reaching into his Humvee and stealing his sunglasses. Looters were gunned down one night after scaling the walls of the US embassy compound.[63]

Realizing that morale and discipline were slipping, some commanders hired elderly Somalis to keep rampant children in line.[64] In an effort to find a compromise between shooting looters and doing nothing, many chose innovation. Antenna mounts or other implements dubbed "Somali be good sticks" were officially prohibited but widely used. Arriving coalition troops were advised to use tent pegs or ax handles "to literally beat [Somalis] off the trucks" to prevent theft.[65] General Zinni discovered marines testing rudimentary cattle prods to shock children who approached patrols or vehicles. He immediately put a stop to these experiments, fearing the backlash that would certainly result if CNN broadcast footage of white troops shocking African children.[66] "Somalis appreciated bayonets," one marine officer said. "They stop screwing with you when you put the bayonet on."[67] Intimidation through bayonet became so widespread that as early as 5 January, Johnston issued orders banning their use.[68]

Colonel Serge Labbe, the senior Canadian officer in UNITAF, lodged a complaint about Pakistani troops beating a Somali for no apparent reason, claiming it "reflects poorly on UNITAF and UN troops."[69]

But the Canadians were no strangers to excessive force. In Beledweyne, some Canadian officers led unauthorized patrols, leaving food and water out as bait to ambush would-be thieves. During one such patrol on 4 March 1993, two Somalis were ambushed and killed; one of them showed signs of being deliberately executed. In another incident on 16 March, sixteen-year-old Shidane Arone was captured by the Canadians, based on their suspicion that he was planning to steal. Arone was waterboarded, sodomized, and burned with cigarettes. He died in custody after being savagely beaten for hours.[70] Some of these acts came to light only years later. In 1997 photographs were uncovered showing Italian soldiers raping Somali women; others were accused of torturing detainees.[71] That same year, two Belgian paratroopers were convicted after photographs circulated of them dangling a boy over an open fire. Their lawyer defended their conduct as a "playful game meant to discourage the child from stealing."[72]

Recognizing a growing problem, Wilhelm distributed a "30-Day Attitude Adjustment Message." In it, he reminded marines that, "no matter how frustrating the situation became, the members of MARFOR had to avoid alienating the citizens of Mogadishu." He emphasized that 90 percent of Somalis were glad to see UNITAF.[73] Likewise, other UNITAF commanders stressed the importance of maintaining good relations with the Somalis. When American soldiers came across bandits robbing a truck during a nighttime patrol, a brief engagement ensued. Six Somalis were killed, only one of whom was a bandit. Unbeknownst to the soldiers, the bandits were hijacking a truck occupied by the owner and his family. The truck's owner, Abdi Noor Jeele, was wounded in the firefight, as was his mother; three of his sons were killed. In an effort to preserve UNITAF's standing with the populace, General Arnold, the ARFOR commander, arrived personally to investigate the incident and offer his condolences to Jeele.[74]

Mogadishu II: A Vietnam Solution to a Somalia Problem

After a monthlong campaign of patrolling and presence operations, Task Force Mogadishu had achieved a tenuous level of stability in the once anarchic city. Klimp reported to Wilhelm that while Operation Restore Hope was touted as a humanitarian mission, Task Force Mogadishu had found itself in a "low-intensity conflict."[75] This caused an interesting development at MARFOR headquarters, as Wilhelm devised a new plan—called Mogadishu II—to return the now pacified city to "functionality." Wilhelm took an innovative approach by dusting off a relic of the Vietnam War, the Combined Action Program (CAP).

Like many American field-grade and general officers in Somalia, Wilhelm was a veteran of the Vietnam War. His experience with pacification in that war undoubtedly influenced his plan to "pacify" Mogadishu. The main goal of Military Assistance Command Vietnam's pacification program had been to create security by gaining the acceptance of the Vietnamese people and by destroying the Vietcong and removing their ability to resist. Wilhelm's order to pacify Mogadishu sought the same result by saturating the city with patrols and targeting rogue elements.[76] A specifically Marine Corps initiative, CAP was just one of many pacification programs in Vietnam; small marine units dispersed, integrated with, and lived among the Vietnamese people "for the purposes of providing village level security, upgrading the local militia, consolidating intelligence operations, and conducting civic action and psychological operations."[77] CAP was based on "clear and hold" operations to prevent the Vietcong's return to rural areas and "to provide a continual security shield behind which the [Vietnamese government] could rebuild an atmosphere of security within which constructive development may take place, and to increase the inhabitants' ability and willingness to maintain that atmosphere."[78]

CAP focused on supporting nation-building efforts in three ways: giving away food, clothing, and school supplies; engaging in civil affairs projects such as road, school, marketplace, and infrastructure construction; and providing medical and dental outreach to locals.[79] After the Vietnam War, reports highlighted the successful aspects of CAP and recommended that it be utilized in the future. One report provided the fictional scenario of using CAP in an Islamic Middle Eastern country with a clan-based society, concluding, "There will be a need for, and opportunities to use, the Combined Action concept in the future . . . in the relatively small, lesser developed nations."[80] That described Somalia in a nutshell.

Wilhelm launched Mogadishu II on 17 January 1993. Marines were told "to build close ties with the members of the neighborhood in a conscious imitation of the Vietnam era Combined Action Program."[81] City streets were cleared of obstacles and debris to encourage the flow of people and trade. Task Force Mogadishu supervised the militias of

Aidid and Ali Mahdi as they dismantled all checkpoints and roadblocks across the city. Wilhelm divided Mogadishu into sectors that were categorized as either "stabilization" or "normalization." In both categories, UNITAF established permanent outposts with troops living among the Somalis. In stabilization districts, this presence was "authoritative," with a focus on ongoing patrols and direct-action pacification operations. In normalization districts, the presence was "benevolent," coupled with humanitarian assistance through civil affairs projects and medical outreach.[82]

One example was the Yashid district, inhabited by both Aidid and Ali Mahdi supporters and occupied by a company of marines under Captain Robert Abbott. Abbott interacted with the locals, showed them night-vision equipment to assure them that the marines could secure the district, and presented his garrison as integral to repairing the community. His efforts yielded results. Local elders helped locate bandits and criminals in Yashid, who were then neutralized.[83] Garrisoning a political and clan fault line, Abbott strove to ensure that his presence was seen as impartial. Marines started rebuilding Yashid's schools in a policy known as "sweat equity." To show impartiality, Abbott enlisted elders from both sides of the Hawiye divide and offered to remove ordnance from school yards if the elders provided Somalis to mark the mines' locations. If locals provided desks for classrooms, the marines would provide chairs. Abbott would not commit to any projects unless both sides contributed time and resources.[84] The "sweat equity" policy was remarkably effective. Collaborating with the locals, Abbott's marines cleared the streets of wrecked vehicles and rehabilitated food markets and schools. Weekly clinics were held, with marine surgeons treating thousands from dawn to dusk, alternating between Aidid and Ali Mahdi neighborhoods. Swiss nurses and German medics joined the clinics as word of these operations spread.[85]

Commanding Team Secure, Lesnowicz, also a Vietnam veteran, saw Mogadishu II as a "CAP without Vietnam. It's a CAP in an urban environment."[86] Even before Mogadishu II began, Lesnowicz ran civil affairs programs in the districts surrounding the airport. He justified this as "active defense," believing that security was a natural output of building good relations with Somalis. Lesnowicz asked local elders what they needed and provided health clinics by combining his medical staff with relief organizations that had supplies but no doctors.[87] The day Mogadishu II was launched, Lesnowicz's marines established eight small garrisons. Some were on the Green Line; one was in the gutted former Central Bank. Around these garrisons, life slowly returned to normal, with locals gathering under floodlights at night to socialize in safety.[88]

Mogadishu II enjoyed such quick success that, with UNITAF forces dispersed across the city, Wilhelm decided that Task Force Mogadishu had served its purpose and could be disbanded. On 22 January Klimp's command stood down; its units were reassigned to other HRSs or remained to garrison various sectors of the city. About the impact of his multinational task force, Klimp said, "Mogadishu was a changed city. . . . I think [Somalis are] safer here . . . than they are in some cities back in the States."[89] In light of the benign environment, UNITAF held an international soccer tournament at Mogadishu Stadium attended by thirty thousand Somalis who watched the Botswanans beat the Italians, the Americans, and the Pakistanis.[90] Wilhelm wrote:

> Mogadishu has improved dramatically. About half of the city has now reached the stabilization sub phase. Large scale fighting has left the city. There are no technicals . . . and weapons are no longer carried openly by Somalis. Somali merchants have reopened their shops throughout the city and there are several market centers which are now crowded from morning to late afternoon. Local elder groups have reorganized and are working to bring normal life back to their neighborhoods.[91]

Mogadishu was a changed city, even in the small Italian sector. The Italian government requested that the districts encompassing the Italian embassy and Old Port, falling within Ali Mahdi's territory, be assigned to its contingent. The Italians ran a campaign imitating Task Force Mogadishu's, patrolling, consulting with local leaders, conducting disarmament operations, providing food and medical services, and hosting soccer games. The security situation was stable, commerce and vibrancy were returning to the city, and reconstruction was proceeding. With Task Force Mogadishu's deactivation, Colonel Buck Bedard's RCT-7 took the lead in the capital and continued Mogadishu II operations.[92]

After partnering with Irish Concern to rebuild a large school in Ali Mahdi's territory in northern Mogadishu, Bedard hosted Generals Johnston and Zinni, Ambassador Oakley, and Aidid, who gave a speech thanking Bedard's marines and voicing his dedication to education.[93] In February Bedard established a permanent garrison in the Bakara Market, famed for its illegal arms sales and crime. A Zimbabwean contingent led by Major Vitalis Chigume, along with two platoons of US marines and a company each from Pakistan and Botswana, swept through the Bakara Market, confiscating all weapons. Chigume's task force occupied the East Africa Hotel at the heart of the market for weeks, conducting patrols, checkpoints, and weapons sweeps. Over time, just as in Yashid, locals helped Chigume locate weapons caches and recalcitrant bandits. Between 12 February and 30 March, more than a thousand weapons were confiscated, along with enough ammunition and explosives to equip a heavy battalion. Violence became the exception in the Bakara Market. Despite some sporadic sniping, only one UNITAF soldier was wounded during the entire operation, during which Nii Ali, a bandit notorious for terrorizing the locals, was shot dead.[94]

The activities of Task Force Mogadishu exemplified how all UNITAF forces not only asserted control over their respective HRSs but also achieved the chief goal of Operation Restore Hope and UN Resolution 794—establishing a secure environment in southern Somalia. Contingents in the other eight HRSs mirrored Task Force Mogadishu's clear demonstrations of military power. In Merka, Kismayo, Baidoa, and Bardera, the Australians, Americans, and Belgians were based at airfields, the gateway to resupply, and sortied into nearby towns and cities with day and night patrols to establish and maintain stability.[95]

In Beledweyne, Oddur, and Gialalassi, coalition forces were dispersed over the vast expanse of the Somali interior along the Ethiopian border. In HRS Oddur, the French were spread across twenty towns, in addition to their base at Oddur and the border regions.[96] In Beledweyne, the Canadians split their HRS into four zones: the town of Beledweyne itself, two zones straddling both sides of the Shabelle River, and one along the Ethiopian border.[97] Canadian mechanized and armored units patrolled the Shabelle River and the border region, while the infantry controlled Beledweyne. In HRS Gialalassi, the Italians occupied the three main population centers of Gialalassi, Balad, and Jawhar.[98] Thus, UNITAF occupied dozens of populations centers and regularly patrolled hundreds more. Did UNITAF control southern Somalia absolutely? Given the vast area of occupation, the answer is no. But UNITAF did control Mogadishu, Baidoa, Kismayo, and the principal cities. And outside these towns and cities, coalition forces may not have had a persistent presence, but they were free to go wherever they wanted whenever they wanted, and they enjoyed the uncontested ability to do whatever they wanted.

HRS Kismayo: Morgan versus Jess

Mogadishu was challenging for UNITAF because it was the capital and the largest population center. Kismayo was also challenging, but for entirely different reasons. In Kismayo, UNITAF was dealing less with the aftermath of famine or the task of policing a city and more with an ongoing civil war.[99] After Kismayo was initially secured on 20 December, Arnold's ARFOR headquarters established Task Force Kismayo, commanded by US Army Colonel Evan Gaddis. Under Gaddis was Lieutenant Colonel Marq Jacqmin's Belgian 1st Parachute Battalion and an armored reconnaissance company, as well as 10th Mountain's 3rd Battalion/14th Infantry Regiment under Lieutenant Colonel Victor Bero. Like its Mogadishu equivalent, Task Force Kismayo began intensive day and night patrols in the city.[100] Because HRS Kismayo was managed by the US Army, Arnold appointed 10th Mountain's assistant division commander, Brigadier General Lawson Magruder, as HRS commander.[101]

Leaving Kismayo garrisoned by the Belgians, Bero's battalion deployed across the HRS. In Jilib, ten thousand Somalis gave the American soldiers a "tumultuous welcome," with messages in broken English painted on the sides of buildings.[102] A drop zone was established, and German transport aircraft, flying just fifty feet off the ground, airdropped food and medical supplies to a town that had received no relief for the past three months. In Jamaame, soldiers, working with town elders and the WFP, went door to door delivering food. Bero's troops also discovered an anomaly in the town of Labadad, which was untouched by famine or war; even the bandits avoided it. It was a leper colony. Although residents had a 90 percent recovery rate, fear of infection kept bandits and militias away. Due to heavy flooding and the civil war, the bridges over the Jubba River had been destroyed or damaged, cutting large parts of HRS Kismayo off from the rest of Somalia. US Army engineers built two Bailey bridges over the Jubba—one at Buur Koy and one at Kamsuumo—on 22 and 27 January, opening the roads between Mogadishu and Kismayo.[103]

The biggest issue for Magruder and Task Force Kismayo was not feeding the starving but dealing with the violence between two hostile belligerents: the Somali National Front (SNF), led by General Hersi Morgan, and the Somali Patriotic Movement (SPM), a member of Aidid's Somali National Alliance (SNA), led by Colonel Omar Jess. During the civil war, Jess and Morgan had fought for dominance of Kismayo and the agricultural breadbasket of the Jubba valley.[104] Regardless of cease-fire agreements in Mogadishu, the fighting in Kismayo had continued, even after UNITAF's arrival. The conflict between Jess and Morgan was complex and emblematic of the clan-based fighting in the civil war.

Members of the SNF and SPM were predominantly Darod clan but belonged to different subclans. The SNF was Marehan, the same subclan as Siad Barre (Morgan's father-in-law). The SPM was divided among the Ogadeni, Absaame, and Harti, who had rebelled against Barre's brutal genocide and clan favoritism. These subclans were historically based in southeastern Somalia near the Kenyan border, and as a result, Kismayo's population was a mix of all of them. However, after Barre's exile, a split occurred in the SPM. Ali Mahdi's perceived power grab, which had so aggrieved Aidid, also alienated the Harti in the SPM, who joined Morgan's SNF. Thus, there were SPM on both sides—the Harti with Morgan against the Ogadeni and Absaame with Jess. As such, although it is easy to present the conflict as SNF versus SPM, the allegiances were complex.

When UNITAF arrived, Jess's forces held Kismayo, while Morgan's were out near the Kenyan border. Morgan commanded thousands of well-organized and disciplined troops, most of them former soldiers in the Somali National Army. Both Morgan and Jess were utterly ruthless. Morgan had presided over the Issaq genocide, while Jess's militia had kidnapped and executed hundreds of Morgan supporters in Kismayo. At the UN, reports of these executions detailed the killing of "whole families"—men, women, and children.[105] Task Force Kismayo discovered the mass graves outside the city, and though it was no secret that Jess was the perpetrator, no one was willing to testify against him.[106] In Kismayo, UNITAF was in the middle of an ongoing interclan war.

Magruder met Jess for what was described as "a one-way conversation." Magruder told the SPM leader that the same rules Aidid and Ali Mahdi had agreed to in Mogadishu applied in Kismayo—all heavy weapons cantoned, no weapons on the streets, and no interclan hostility—otherwise, UNITAF would respond decisively.[107] Jess agreed, claiming the SPM did not want any trouble, and had his militia stack their arms. To meet Morgan, Magruder boarded a helicopter and flew in the general direction of the Kenyan border, eventually spotting an SNF camp. Magruder landed, casually walked into the camp, and asked to speak to Morgan. The bewildered militiamen provided a radio frequency to reach the SNF leader, and a meeting was scheduled for the next day,

20 January. Magruder described Morgan as "a classic picture of the war-lord: designer sunglasses, gold rings, floral shirt, pearl handled revolver on his hip."[108] At the meeting, Morgan discussed his time at the US Army's Command and General Staff College at Fort Leavenworth, Kansas, noting that he had graduated ahead of Magruder. The general was blunt: the SNF was not to advance toward Kismayo or engage the SPM; if it did, UNITAF would retaliate. Morgan agreed and briefed Magruder on the locations of SNF forces, including a group closest to Kismayo at Beer Xaani.

Neither the SNF nor the SPM abided by Magruder's terms. On 24 January an SPM militia under Colonel Moallin was soundly defeated when it attacked the SNF at Beer Xaani. The next day Magruder ordered Morgan to withdraw his forces thirty kilometers west of Beer Xaani to put more space between the SNF and the SPM. Instead of moving west, Morgan's forces advanced east, toward Kismayo. Magruder radioed Morgan and twice ordered him to halt the advance, or else. Twice Morgan acknowledged the order, claiming the advance had been a mistake and saying his forces would withdraw. They never did. On Magruder's orders, US Army AH-1 Cobra attack helicopters descended on Morgan's forces. Warning shots were fired, which stopped the advancing convoy in its tracks as the SNF militiamen dismounted and fled on foot. Then the circling Cobras destroyed the entire convoy: six technicals, an armored vehicle, and several artillery pieces.[109]

Magruder's message to Morgan was that any infractions would earn a rapid response from UNITAF. Morgan, however, seemed willing to test the coalition's resolve. A week after his convoy's destruction, Morgan attacked Moallin's SPM forces while they slept, killing seventy and wounding fifty-seven.[110] Once again, Magruder ordered Morgan to withdraw, and this time Morgan complied and promised no more advances. To hold Morgan to his word, Magruder deployed the Belgian armored reconnaissance squadron at Beer Xaani between the SPM and the SNF. Additionally, Morgan was pressed to allow a US Army Special Forces detachment to reside at his main camp to report any movement of SNF forces.[111]

For the Belgians at Beer Xaani, sitting between the SPM and the SNF, the situation was tense. The Belgians were outnumbered, and just eight kilometers west was an SNF brigade of two thousand men whose commander vowed that "he is going to [Kismayo] no matter what."[112] SPM and SNF militia occasionally advanced toward each other, only to be engaged by the Belgians and driven away. Outwardly, Morgan's commanders seemed determined to capture Kismayo, but the situation within his camp was different. SNF officers spoke openly to the resident US Special Forces detachment, telling them that Morgan was unable to pay his troops, and their discipline was deteriorating. Sickness was also spreading through the camp; malaria was rife. One garrulous SNF colonel suggested that the best way to achieve peace was to "kill all the fighters, including Morgan, Jess, Aidid, and himself."[113] Despite the opinions of these SNF officers, the commander of the Special Forces detachment reported that Morgan was a "decent host" and his troops were "in excellent condition." At the same time, SNF officers claimed the residents of Kismayo hated the Belgians, who were allegedly mistreating them. They also complained that UNITAF allowed the SPM to maintain control of the city while the SNF soldiers were forced to live in the bush.[114]

Realizing that a direct confrontation with UNITAF would be suicidal, Morgan extended an olive branch. He requested that SNF and SPM elders meet to negotiate a peace and discuss the status of Kismayo. Organizing these talks fell to US Army Colonel Mark Hamilton. Having played a key role in mediating the end of the Salvadoran Civil War, Hamilton had been handpicked to go to Somalia by US Army Chief of Staff General Gordon Sullivan. Hamilton's personal efforts to get both sides talking repeatedly failed. The problem was Omar Jess. Several times, Morgan and the SNF elders agreed to a meeting but Jess objected and even used bribery and threats to convince SPM elders not to attend.[115] Jess viewed negotiations as a threat to his own power and status.

The consensus in UNITAF was that political pressure was needed "to remove Jess in order to have the first elders' meeting."[116] Luckily, Jess's obstinance did more than exasperate just Hamilton and Morgan. One member of the SPM executive committee was a CIA informer, and he revealed that Jess had tried and failed to muster support for another offensive against Morgan and the SNF. These repeated defeats had undermined confidence in Jess's leadership.[117] On 21 February SPM chairman Abdi Mahad broke ranks and, on behalf of the elders, agreed to meet with the SNF.[118] Unluckily, however, this breakthrough came too late. Just hours later, Jess's persistent unwillingness to talk resulted in the most violent incident that occurred during UNITAF's tenure in Somalia.

The Kismayo Incursion

At 01:20 on 22 February, Task Force Kismayo received reports that 150 Somalis had gathered at an intersection in the city and that "no units are aware of information pertaining to who this group of people might be." At 03:28, when fighting broke out, the situation was still unclear. Coalition helicopters were not in the air due to a lack of night-vision equipment and mechanical problems. Finally aloft at 06:18 with the sunrise, they reported a "massive exodus heading out of Kismayo."[119] Thousands were fleeing the city, and hundreds were headed for Jess's weapons cantonment, where his militia mobilized technicals and armored vehicles against a threat that Task Force Kismayo had not yet identified. Magruder ordered relief organizations to halt all operations in the city. In the past he had not hesitated to unleash UNITAF's firepower, but he now ordered the attack helicopters not to engage any armed Somali vehicles without his personal authorization. US aircraft flew over Morgan's camp near Beer Xaani and found that his forces were still there; they had not moved. Still unsure what was happening, Magruder took action to stop Jess's militia, adding to the chaos, and ordered the Belgians to surround his weapons cantonment, creating a tense standoff. Adding to the confusion, everyone from captured SPM militiamen to the estimated four thousand civilians fleeing Kismayo said that Morgan now controlled the city!

What had happened? A later investigation revealed that in the days before the attack, squad-sized groups of SNF dressed as nomads and led by Colonel Garem had infiltrated Kismayo to link up with urban Morgan supporters. A few had been intercepted by the Belgians, who established a screening perimeter outside the city, but it was not tight enough. In the early-morning darkness of 22 February, Garem's men attacked the homes of prominent SPM officials and Jess supporters. By 08:00, Garem had swept Kismayo from west to east, driving all SPM and Jess supporters before him, hence the mass exodus. Meanwhile, Jess's militia outside the city mobilized for a counterattack. Garem's men then dispersed to safe houses or fled Kismayo, leaving the city in anarchy.[120]

The UNITAF response to the attack was muted at first. Belgian troops did not want to hunt down an enemy that had blended in with the population in a dark city. At a press briefing, UNITAF spokesman Colonel Fred Peck justified this hesitancy by arguing that one of Task Force Kismayo's priorities was force protection. In his words, "that means looking out for our people. We are not going to throw them into a situation where they are subject to taking casualties without good reason."[121] It was a weak defense, given the coalition's mission of establishing a secure environment. Peck also rebutted claims that Garem's 200-man force now controlled a city of 150,000 that was also home to 1,600 coalition troops.

Kismayo was in an uproar. There was rioting and violence between Morgan and Jess supporters. Morgan denied ordering the attack yet cordially offered to move his forces into the city to help UNITAF restore order, which was probably his goal all along. Magruder declined, established a curfew, and worked to bring the rioting under control.[122] There was chaos and gunfire; women and children were killed. The bloodiest incident occurred when two grenades were thrown into a crowd at an ICRC hospital, killing fourteen and wounding more than twenty others, including a Belgian soldier. Moreover, throughout the night of 22–23 February, Task Force Kismayo intercepted militia from both sides trying to sneak into the city, leading to sporadic firefights that left three Belgians wounded, three SNF colonels taken prisoner, and heavy Somali casualties.[123]

Despite claims that Garem had attacked "against orders," there is compelling evidence that Morgan was personally responsible for the raid.[124] He had tested UNITAF's resolve to his detriment and then offered to negotiate for what he could not gain through military action. By late February, Kismayo had stabilized to the point that Bero's battalion was going home, leaving the Belgians solely responsible for the HRS. The SNF was unhappy about the American departure due to allegations of Belgian mistreatment of Somalis (which were true), but because the SNF also believed the Belgians favored Jess, it preferred to deal with the impartial Americans. There was, of course, the additional issue of Jess's refusal to negotiate. Fighting broke out as Bero's soldiers gathered at Kismayo airport to depart, which was hardly a coincidence. With Belgian control of Kismayo imminent, Morgan likely initiated the attack so he could offer to move his forces into the city to quell the unrest he had deliberately started. If this was his goal, it was successful only insofar as it delayed the US withdrawal. Bero's battalion stayed to stabilize and secure the city. The brutal nature of the interclan violence was exposed when Americans and Belgians found Somalis who had been mutilated and tortured. Some had had their intestines pulled out while they were still alive.[125]

On 23 February Oakley and Johnston wrote an open letter to Morgan condemning the attack and ordering him to remove his forces from Kismayo and the lower Jubba valley by midnight on 25 February. After that deadline, they promised, UNITAF would destroy all remaining SNF forces.[126] Jess was told not to retaliate or take any action against Morgan. Privately, Johnston vowed that if Jess and Morgan fought again, "all bets are off. We're going to go after them and destroy them."[127] To ensure clarity, leaflet drops and loudspeaker broadcasts warned Morgan's forces to leave "or risk destruction."[128] Morgan realized he had overplayed his hand. The SNF was now squarely in UNITAF's sights. Colonel Hamilton, the US Army negotiator, met with Morgan and SNF elders and persuaded them to withdraw without incident. The SNF militiamen in Kismayo surrendered their arms and left the city, while their heavy weapons and technicals were placed in cantonment under UNITAF surveillance. Hamilton then convinced Jess to do the same.[129] Stripped of its heavy weapons and under UNITAF escort, the SNF withdrew nearly two hundred kilometers to Dhoobley on the Kenyan border.[130]

Immediately after Morgan withdrew, SNF and SPM-Harti clan elders criticized Oakley and Johnston's ultimatum, accusing them of taking sides in the conflict and protecting Jess, the perpetrator of massacres in the city. These elders went so far as to call Operation Restore Hope Operation "Restore Genocide."[131] Although UNITAF had not taken sides in Kismayo, these elders' attitudes were understandable. The SNF suffered the greatest losses due to coalition action, but Morgan himself had provoked this retaliation. Despite these tensions, Hamilton built on the SPM's willingness to talk just prior to the raid. He was instrumental in finally hosting a meeting between SNF and SPM elders one week after the violence ended—"only the second time in recent history that they have met."[132] Both sides agreed to cooperate on security matters in the city, including the establishment of a local police force with members from both factions. Cooperation had replaced conflict. This was evident the next day when an American soldier shot a Somali armed with a grenade. Elders from both sides took to the streets to quell any protests and ensure that peace was maintained.[133]

Apart from the SNF-SPM cease-fire, the biggest consequence of Morgan's attack on Kismayo occurred in Mogadishu. In the days preceding Garem's infiltration, Aidid had informed Oakley that Morgan was planning to take action against Kismayo, hoping that a forewarned UNITAF would repulse the SNF. Obviously, with Jess and the SPM being allies, thwarting Morgan was advantageous to Aidid.[134] Oakley allegedly agreed to take preemptive action against Morgan but then later claimed that UNITAF could not follow through. John Drysdale, one of UNOSOM's political advisers, believed this about-face was due to Johnston's unwillingness to risk any casualties as US forces were withdrawing from Kismayo. A more likely rationale was that Oakley and Johnston wanted to maintain UNITAF impartiality by not taking sides in the clan conflict.

When Morgan attacked, Aidid was furious. Despite his warning to Oakley, UNITAF had done nothing. Aidid claimed to have a transcript of radio communications between Morgan and an unidentified US marine who allegedly agreed that some SNF militia could remain inside Kismayo, regardless of Oakley and Johnston's ultimatum that they leave. Aidid's paranoia peaked when the BBC inaccurately reported that Morgan controlled Kismayo, a feat Aidid believed was unachievable without UNITAF's help. To save face after fleeing Kismayo, Jess fanned the flames of this conspiracy theory. In Aidid's mind, it must have been UNITAF, and his propaganda machine went into overdrive. The next day, the first day of the Islamic month of Ramadan, Mogadishu was saturated with radio and loudspeaker broadcasts stating that UNITAF had allowed the SNF to attack Jess.[135] Provocative leaflets appeared, claiming that UNITAF had "hand-tied" the SNA and planned to restore Barre to power. They called for protests on 23 February, concluding that the "coming 24 hours is a preparation for war."[136]

These protests in Mogadishu were characterized as the most violent events since the intervention began, indicating just how peaceful the city had become under UNITAF's occupation. But their level of violence was a matter of debate. Describing the events of 24 February, Diana Schemo of the *New York Times* wrote, "The Somali capital exploded in violence . . . thousands of partisans of a major warlord [Aidid] stormed the streets . . . paralyzed the city, stopping traffic at the seaport and the airports . . . in a spree of looting and destruction."[137] This was grossly exaggerated media hype. Far from exploding in violence, the city's protests were confined to just a small portion of it. Protesters marched to the US embassy holding signs that read, "UNITAF—You have deceived us. . . . Are you here to help us, or loot us?"[138] A few of Bedard's marines were injured when rocks were thrown at them, primarily by women and children. On one occasion, marines fired warning shots. Johnston authorized the use of CS gas as a nonlethal alternative, but this was not necessary because the crowds had dispersed by noon.[139] Contrary to the panicked reporting of the press, the evidence supports the conclusion of a Pentagon spokesperson, who summed up the protest as "obviously well-choreographed . . . a bit of political theater."[140]

The next day, what began as largely peaceful protests by Aidid supporters escalated into a six-hour skirmish. An unknown gunman opened fire on Nigerian troops guarding the K-4 Circle, the key intersection linking the US embassy and UNITAF base at Mogadishu University with New Port and the airport. The K-4 Circle was also adjacent to UNOSOM headquarters and the Al-Sahafi Hotel, where the international media lodged, which might explain the sensationalized reporting. Bedard's marines and the Botswanans reinforced the Nigerians, sweeping the area before sunset. Three marines and two Nigerians were wounded. The firefight inflamed the protests. Oakley and Zinni warned that they would hold Aidid personally responsible for any further acts of violence. Zinni emphasized the point by tossing spent shell casings across the table and asking whether Aidid wanted to fight or talk.[141] Oakley instructed Aidid to get on the radio and tell his supporters to go home. Aidid's own deputy told him that UNITAF had not supported Morgan at all—in fact, quite the opposite. Pressed by Oakley and advised by his lieutenant, Aidid promptly called off the protests.[142]

After the K-4 firefight, Oakley, the *New York Times*, and others blamed Aidid for the attack on the Nigerians.[143] However, the evidence suggests that although Aidid orchestrated the protests, he had nothing to do with the attack. Drysdale was in a meeting with Aidid when the firefight began and witnessed the SNA leader frantically asking his aides what was happening.[144] In addition, Wilhelm's headquarters claimed the attackers were criminals trying to take advantage of the unrest.[145] Zinni's deputy, Colonel Wallace Grayson, believed a militia that was not loyal to Aidid had clashed with the Nigerians.[146]

A later investigation revealed that the perpetrators were the Murusade, the Hawiye subclan hostile to Aidid for encroaching on their territory in Mogadishu. That day, Murusade militia tried to force Habr-Gidr civilians out of a neighborhood they claimed was theirs. A firefight erupted that spilled over into the nearby K-4 Circle. After the attack, Colonel Michael Hagee met with both sides, who confirmed the sequence of events. The firefight had nothing to do with Aidid or the Kismayo incursion. It was, in Hagee's words, "completely outside what we were trying to do or what was going on."[147] An intelligence report in January had suggested that the Murusade would attack UNITAF and try to blame Aidid, hoping to provoke a violent response or at least discredit him.[148] The violent response never came, but in the court of public opinion and according to Oakley and the international media, Aidid was to blame. The Murusade strategy had worked.

On 23 February 1993 Turkish Lieutenant General Cevik Bir was briefed in Mogadishu by Johnston and Oakley on UNITAF's progress in Somalia. Bir had just been appointed force commander of a new UN operation in Somalia, UNOSOM II, set to take over from UNITAF in the coming months. Bir was told that in all the HRSs with the exception of Kismayo (which the SNF had raided the previous day), UNITAF had established a secure environment in accordance with Resolution 794.[149] Aidid's Kismayo-inspired and largely peaceful protest could be heard outside; the K-4 firefight that inflamed the protests had not happened yet. Except for the SNF infiltration of Kismayo, the February 1993 riots in Mogadishu and the K-4 firefight were the most violent events during UNITAF's tenure, but they were not excessively violent by any measure; they were judged to be violent only because of the relative absence of violence everywhere else in the months before and after. Responding to the *New York Times* report about Mogadishu "exploding," Wilhelm said, "We never lost control, no. It was represented in another light but that was pure sensationalism by the press. Blatant sensationalism."[150] Another senior marine officer argued that the riots were overhyped because events in Somalia had quieted down. Because violence was the exception, not the rule, "the vultures of the third estate were all over . . . it wasn't a big deal . . . nothing more than a hiccup."[151]

Hiccup was certainly an understatement, but between the events in Kismayo and Mogadishu on 22–24 February 1993 and UNITAF's withdrawal from Somalia on 4 May 1993, there were no notable acts of violence against coalition forces or anywhere they held sway. These two events were exceptional precisely because UNITAF had succeeded in its mission. On 6 March, just ten days after the infiltration of Kismayo—with the cease-fire between the SNF and SPM holding and Morgan banished to the Kenyan border—Bero's battalion handed over HRS Kismayo to the Belgian contingent and redeployed to the United States without incident.

During its six months in Somalia, UNITAF suffered eighteen fatalities—the same number US forces would suffer in the infamous Battle of Mogadishu in October 1993.[152] However, of the eighteen UNITAF fatalities, just three died from hostile actions—two US marines and a Saudi doctor. One marine committed suicide, and the remaining fourteen were simply unlucky. An Australian died from an accidental weapon discharge. Two soldiers drowned—an American in a swimming pool while on leave in Mombasa and an Emirati who fell into the water at Mogadishu port wearing full combat dress. Three Belgians and two Americans died when their vehicles hit mines, and two French, two Americans, and one Moroccan died in vehicle accidents. The last fatality was an unfortunate Belgian who, while climbing on an old Somali MiG at Kismayo airfield, accidentally triggered its ejector seat.[153] UNITAF had achieved its limited security mission, but as the next chapter shows, it also went far beyond it, embarking on an embryonic nation-building effort.

5 | Jump-Starting a Nation
UNITAF and Embryonic
Nation Building

UNITAF proceeded further and further into nation-building. We had gotten on this bus and now we didn't have a clue as to where it was going. We just knew we couldn't get off.

—Major Martin N. Stanton, US Army[1]

Senator, if there is a cache of weapons that we know exists that would pose a threat or if we find it, I am going to tell you that we'll take it.

—Lieutenant General Martin Brandtner,
director of operations, Joint Staff[2]

We are not here to rebuild the nation; but certainly, we're here to jump start it.

—Lieutenant Colonel Michael W. Sullivan, US Marine Corps[3]

In April 1993, as UNITAF was in the final stages of leaving Somalia, Jim Hoagland of the *Washington Post* lavished praise on the Pentagon for resisting "the dangers of *mission creep*, of getting pulled into local quarrels and taking on expanding, unfulfillable responsibilities. It is a success that deserves recognition, and encouragement."[4] Mission creep was a term with negative connotations harking back to the American descent into the Vietnam War, where objectives were vague, goalposts kept changing, and US forces became inescapably bogged down. In the case of Somalia, Hoagland was celebrating a job well done—the completion of a security mission meticulously limited in scope and duration. The only problem was, Hoagland got it wrong.

Once the security mission had been achieved and stability reigned in southern Somalia, something entirely predictable happened. Somalis who had weathered the storm were eager to rebuild, eager to help their country reemerge from the ashes. With no enemy to fight and witnessing firsthand the unprecedented suffering the population had endured, many coalition members decided to help. In some cases, UNITAF made conscious decisions to go beyond the provision of security; in others, these decisions were unavoidable, given the direction the wind was blowing. There were two principal reasons for this situation.

During President Bush's New Year's Day 1993 visit to Mogadishu, he and his national security adviser Brent Scowcroft met with the coalition leadership team: Lieutenant General Robert Johnston, UNITAF's commanding general; Ambassador Robert Oakley, Bush's presidential envoy; and Brigadier General Anthony Zinni, UNITAF's director of operations. Johnston asked the president what the plan was for Somalia and when a new UN mission would be taking over. Both Bush and Scowcroft shook their heads, as no such plan or timeline had been finalized.[5]

This indecision is often missed in the historiography of the intervention. That UNOSOM II eventually replaces UNITAF is taken as a foregone conclusion. In January 1993, though, such a handover was far from assured. This left UNITAF in uncharted waters. With the future uncertain, Oakley asked Johnston if UNITAF would support his efforts to initiate a peace process among the various factions in the interim, until the UN decided whether to commit. Johnston agreed.[6] UNITAF's mission in Somalia had just drastically changed.

The second reason for UNITAF's extension of its mandate was that Johnston gave coalition and HRS commanders wide discretion in running their sectors. Each sector was unique in terms of security issues and clan diversity, so commanders were given the latitude to solve their own regional problems and define what progress looked like.[7] In the words of Lieutenant Colonel David Hurley, commanding the Australians in HRS Baidoa, he had "virtually unlimited scope to conduct operations as [I] saw necessary." In Hurley's view, HRS commanders became military governors with "largely undefined powers and little political guidance."[8] Because of this, the nine HRSs became petri dishes of experimentation, based on how the various coalition partners, including the US Army and Marine Corps, interpreted their mission.

In the months-long interim between its deployment to Somalia and the arrival of a follow-on UN operation, UNITAF went far beyond a limited security mission and consciously veered into embryonic nation-building efforts. In Baidoa, the Australians rebuilt a judicial system; in Beledweyne, the Canadians rejuvenated the education system; in Gialalassi, the Italians created a postal system. In all the HRSs, coalition forces encouraged and empowered local residents to govern their own affairs and supported the reemergence of a nascent Somali police force. And, despite statements to the contrary, UNITAF—specifically, US forces—embarked on a widespread campaign of disarmament. Mission creep, far from being avoided, became the hallmark of UNITAF.

Empowering Somali Governance

In his television address announcing Operation Restore Hope to the world, Bush assured all, "We do not plan to dictate political outcomes."[9] Yet, with future UN participation uncertain, Oakley worked toward political reconciliation with the various factions and specifically with Aidid and Ali Mahdi. General Zinni recalled that Oakley "formed enough coordination committees to stagger Washington bureaucrats," believing that if the factions were talking, they would not be shooting.[10] Through these committees, Oakley got to know the faction leaders' personalities and motivations.[11] In Mogadishu, he established a Political Committee with every faction represented; Oakley himself represented UNITAF. A similarly diverse Security Committee was formed to deal with military issues and disarmament, with Zinni representing the coalition. These committees met daily on neutral ground, with UNITAF providing security.

This arrangement violated the agreement between Boutros-Ghali and Bush in terms of the UNOSOM-UNITAF division of labor: political efforts were UNOSOM's purview, and UNITAF handled security. Though admitting that Ismat Kittani should have led the negotiations as UN special representative, Oakley claimed the faction leaders believed the United States had more power to make things happen and chose to deal with him instead.[12] Zinni's deputy, Colonel Wallace Grayson, observed these meetings and noted that Oakley, Johnston, and Zinni did not act like the "ugly American," coming in and making decisions unilaterally or claiming they knew better than the Somalis.[13] It was during these meetings that Oakley recognized the differences between Ali Mahdi and Aidid. Ali Mahdi offered "few specifics" and frequently "consulted with his seven or eight advisors before responding," whereas Aidid "attended alone except for a note taker, did all the talking, and presented a number of points . . . very much the approach of a general who wished to show himself in full command."[14] Although faction leaders often asked UNITAF to lead the way on security policies or political initiatives, Oakley insisted that the coalition would not dictate the desired outcomes. Somalis had to take ownership of Somalia.

Faction leaders were encouraged to work together toward reconstruction and national reconciliation, but from the outset it was clear that Oakley did not want these men to be the sole arbiters of Somalia's future. At a December 1992 briefing, Oakley informed intelligence agencies that "efforts are underway, with some success, to isolate the warlords so that political leaders will emerge. [Oakley] cited Morgan [and] Jess . . . as prime targets for application of this attempt."[15] Aidid and Ali Mahdi were praised for their cooperation in establishing the cease-fire, as Oakley believed they "see the writing on the wall" and wanted to be part of the future government. But UNITAF's chief politico wanted a deliberate bottom-up marginalization of these men and their influence because he considered them "warlords." That label certainly fit Morgan and Jess but not Aidid and Ali Mahdi. Their rivalry and ambition aside, they were both popular and competent political leaders within their respective clans, and Aidid enjoyed a reputation for militarily ousting Somalia's previous dictator. Nevertheless, in Baidoa and Merka, the Australians and Americans excluded the SNA from local councils. In Kismayo, the Americans and Belgians bypassed Morgan and Jess and dealt directly with clan elders. In Baidoa, Hurley's Australian contingent empowered the Rahanweyn clan and their representative organization, the Somali Democratic Movement (SDM), which had been brutally persecuted by Barre's forces during the civil war. Hurley consulted the Rahanweyn elders on all matters and supported the SDM in regional governance, believing them to be the best hope for Baidoa to avoid the Aidid-Mahdi competition in Mogadishu.[16]

The motivations of Bush's presidential envoy were clear when he briefed State Department officials on 5 January 1993. Barely a month had passed since the coalition's arrival, but Oakley told all present that UNITAF was deliberately empowering the Somalis politically because, in the past, all power had derived from the "barrel of a gun."[17] It was a direct challenge to the power of the faction leaders. In all the HRSs, UNITAF commanders encouraged and supported local clan elders—who had traditionally steered Somali society before the Barre regime—to reassert their authority by forming local and regional councils. The Australians in Baidoa, the Canadians in Beledweyne, the French in Oddur, the Italians in Gialalassi, the US Marine Corps in Bardera, and the

US Army in Merka and Kismayo (along with the Belgians in the latter) all spurred the Somalis to govern their own affairs.[18] These councils mirrored the local and regional clan mix and espoused clan cooperation rather than clan competition. One situation report noted that "town elders in Merka, Kismayo and Afgooye [are] providing leadership to people," and the area was "showing signs of law and order returning."[19] After the Merka city council was established, one American officer observed that "shops opened up again, and [the city] returned to. if not quite normalcy, a sense of equilibrium."[20] In Beledweyne, Canadian Lieutenant Colonel Carol Mathieu let the interclan councils run the HRS under his supervision.[21]

Despite Bush's promise not to dictate political outcomes, that is precisely what Oakley was doing. Johnston recalled that he did not envisage the "extent of the political involvement that we would be drawn into, setting up village elder meetings." Though pointing out that the military commander was largely responsible for such efforts, Johnston did not interfere, as it was "what we hoped to bring to Mogadishu; some kind of a structure, a semblance of authority that came from the Somalis, not from us."[22] Wherever UNITAF went in southern Somalia, local governing councils followed.

Coalition Relations with Relief Organizations

Across southern Somalia, UNITAF's security mission involved interacting with relief organizations. In Mogadishu alone there were fifty-seven such organizations, often working independently of one another, UNITAF, and UNOSOM.[23] Managing these disparate groups fell to UNOSOM's humanitarian coordinator, former CARE president Philip Johnston, and just six staff members. With few resources and an obvious need to impose order, Johnston devised a cooperative initiative. In each HRS, he established a Humanitarian Operations Center, a regional forum where relief agencies and UNITAF could share information and coordinate efforts. Although this was a UNOSOM initiative, these forums became a joint UN-UNITAF effort. Within each Humanitarian Operations Center, UNITAF staffed a Civil-Military Operations Center (CMOC), where relief agencies could request direct coalition support.

Each Humanitarian Operations Center was headed by a UNOSOM official with two deputies: a civilian deputy from USAID, and a military deputy from UNITAF who ran the regional CMOC. The Mogadishu Humanitarian Operations Center was the central nexus, headed by Philip Johnston personally. Generals Johnston and Zinni chose marine Colonel Kevin Kennedy to run the capital's CMOC. Kennedy was the perfect choice, having previously worked as a liaison with relief organizations during Operation Provide Relief. To allay any concerns that the military was planning to take over the relief effort, Kennedy assured everyone that the CMOCs were there to assist, not to control.[24]

Through these CMOCs, the coalition assisted relief agencies in several ways, but they mainly provided armed escorts for relief convoys to prevent looting and banditry. On average, UNITAF escorted seventy long-haul relief convoys a month from Mogadishu alone. The Australians in Baidoa escorted four hundred convoys to 137 villages across their HRS. UNITAF engineers also repaired roadways to enable these convoys to travel deeper into the interior. In addition to escort duty, coalition forces frequently helped in other ways. The Beledweyne CMOC, run by the Canadian Airborne Regiment's executive officer, provided vehicle repair services to relief agencies and medical personnel to help the International Medical Corps run Beledweyne's hospital. In Baidoa, Australian troops worked alongside relief workers to distribute food in towns and villages, while medical personnel bolstered vaccination programs. Coalition contingents often secured relief organizations' funds in their headquarters, as Somalia had no electronic financial infrastructure.[25]

Doing too much came with risks, however. In Baledogle, American troops responding to an urgent request from the ICRC to prevent its warehouse in Wanlaweyne from being ransacked arrived to find three hundred looters who had to be driven away with fixed bayonets, rifle butts, and warning shots. Rather than dispersing, the large crowd surrounded Major Martin Stanton's troops, waiting to resume looting once they had departed. Stanton opted to distribute the food instead. He immediately regretted it, later writing, "The decision to hand out the food was an error . . . relief supplies were money . . . it was like handing out free money."[26] Stanton's men risked being overrun by the burgeoning mass. Conscious that warning shots "lose their value quickly," Stanton decided to "personally shoot one civilian adult male in the hopes the crowd would disperse. . . . I made this decision in cold sobriety." Luckily for the "man in a green knit cap" that Stanton had selected to shoot, friendly reinforcements arrived, and the situation was stabilized without any loss of life.[27]

Friction grew over the level of military support the relief organiza-tions wanted versus what UNITAF could provide. UNITAF was asked to guard relief facilities to prevent looting, and the response varied by locality. It boiled down to a numbers game. In Baidoa, Hurley deployed Australian troops to occupy relief organizations' compounds and use them as patrol bases. This was feasible in Baidoa, as all the compounds were conveniently located on one street. There was the added benefit of better living conditions for the Australian troops, who had access to beer, satellite phones, and "pretty young nurses from Ireland."[28] But what was possible in Baidoa was not practicable in Mogadishu. There were 585 properties—warehouses, offices, and residences—throughout the capital belonging to relief agencies, a security task far beyond UNI-TAF's resources.[29]

There was also a steep learning curve for military personnel staffing the CMOCs, who were not trained to deal with relief agencies or civil affairs operations. Hypersensitive about mission creep, CENTCOM had rejected proposals to send army civil affairs units to Somalia.[30] Thus, among the nearly thirty thousand Americans, just twenty-four came from the US Army's 96th Civil Affairs Battalion. Though not specifically trained for relief operations, they were better than nothing, so Zinni as-signed them to staff the CMOCs.[31] Likewise, across the coalition, it was personnel who could be spared—not those trained for the role—who ended up consulting with relief organizations. The Baidoa CMOC was run by Hurley's artillerists, who, without artillery pieces in-country, ful-filled a role they "had not trained for, nor had they expected to be in-volved in."[32] The I MEF command chronology summed it up succinctly: "everyone involved with the CMOC learned their job by doing it."[33]

Initially, many relief workers were reluctant to work with, or to even be perceived as working with, the military. They wanted to preserve an image of political and ideological impartiality and to avoid criticisms of military alignment from their donor communities. Over time, in the more remote locations in the interior, these groups welcomed the security, stability, and assistance coalition units offered, especially pro-tection from banditry and looting. In disparate locales, a relationship based on mutual respect formed over time. In Mogadishu, it was the exact opposite. The close proximity of the headquarters of UNOSOM, UNITAF, and most relief organizations, not to mention the political maneuvers of the Somali factions, brought the organizational cultures of all sides into collision. One camp was rigid and hierarchical, the other was not, and negative stereotypes swayed both sides.[34] According to one observer, many military officers believed relief organizations were disorganized, too independent, and anti-military and contained too many "young over-educated, self-righteous, incompetent, expatriate cowboys who merely came quickly into the area to 'do good' without considering how best to do it or what the consequences would be."[35] For their part, the expatriate cowboys were less than impressed with the military. They saw UNITAF as inflexible, too focused on its narrow mission, and filled with pedantic narcissists fixated on using the correct forms and adhering to regulations. Yet some also saw UNITAF as the solution to all their problems. The result was that, in Mogadishu, the expectations of relief workers were either too low or too high. They refused to relocate to UNITAF bases to facilitate the security of their compounds, then criticized the coalition's inability to secure six hundred locations.[36]

Running Mogadishu's CMOC, Kennedy stood on the fault line of this cultural pressure cooker. In his view, relief organizations were confrontational toward coalition personnel out of a "belief that humanitarian workers permanently occupied the moral high ground in all discussions." Kennedy, himself a marine, conceded that his colleagues were contemptuous of the young champions of morality for their ignorance of the logistics and security considerations inherent to any military operation. This was a "minority view," he claimed, but "held by sufficient numbers of commanders and staff officers to magnify its impact."[37] However, Kennedy also believed that tensions were less cultural and had more to do with relief workers enjoying far better living conditions than coalition personnel. The former had social lives, money, and freedom of movement; the latter did not. The result was that UNITAF personnel believed their redeployment home was being slowed by ignorant do-gooders enjoying an all too comfortable lifestyle.

The Somali Auxiliary Security Force

One of the most widespread initiatives undertaken by UNITAF was the rebuilding of an embryonic Somali police force. In a country defined by clan affiliation, the Somali National Police Force (SNPF) was an anomaly. Its members were clan-neutral and apolitical. In the waning years of the Barre regime, the SNPF had maintained law and order, not clan persecution. When the civil war escalated and spread, most police officers went home to ride out the storm with their families. The SNPF was a rare institution not stained by Barre's brutality and remained widely respected for being impartial across the spectrum of clan affiliations. After UNITAF arrived, and certainly when the coalition was firmly in control, former SNPF officers believed the storm had finally passed. Across all sectors, but particularly in Mogadishu, individual SNPF officers started showing up at random intersections to direct traffic or patrol their old beats. Where these officers appeared, local commerce was reinvigorated.[38] For the locals, UNITAF garrisons suggested security, but the SNPF represented a return to normalcy.

This development sparked debate over whether UNITAF should support the return of a Somali police force. The State Department, Department of Defense, CENTCOM, and even UNITAF's General Robert Johnston all believed that sponsoring a police force was mission creep. It went beyond the limited security mandate and, many claimed, was illegal. Section 660 of the US Foreign Assistance Act of 1961 barred the US military from supporting, funding, or training foreign police forces. Even Aidid and Ali Mahdi opposed a national force that was not controlled by their factions.

Conversely, former SNPF Commandant Ahmed Jama and various clan elders and religious leaders argued that a local police force would enhance stability. Others in favor were Philip Johnston, UNOSOM's humanitarian coordinator, and Lynn Thomas, the director of CARE. But the pivotal advocate was Oakley. Building such a force absolutely constituted mission creep, but a persuasive Oakley couched it in terms of force protection: local police would reduce the possibility of UNITAF casualties. These officers, he wrote, "spoke Somali, we didn't. They understood the body language, we didn't."[39] Local police, he argued, would free up UNITAF personnel for other tasks. This argument brought General Johnston around, as coalition forces were increasingly being sucked into police duties. For Johnston, a local police force represented an exit strategy, as UNITAF and any follow-on UN operations could leave only if there were some means of keeping order afterward. Twice the Bush administration rejected Oakley's proposals, despite his warnings that without a police force, UNITAF troops risked being killed while patrolling the alleyways of Mogadishu. This is exactly what happened to marine Private Domingo Arroyo. After Arroyo's death on 12 January, the White House reversed course and approved Oakley's initiative but refused to provide any resources for it.[40]

The police force that eventually emerged did so only through the goodwill of others and the efforts and innovation of key personalities who believed in it. Starved of resources, Oakley turned to Aidid and Ali Mahdi for support. They agreed to create a ten-member police sub-committee to vet, select, and shape this embryonic force. Six members were former SNPF officers, including Ahmed Jama, while the two rivals appointed two members each for political balance.[41] One of Ali Mahdi's appointees was his closest adviser, Brigadier General Ahmed Jilao. A Barre loyalist, Jilao had been a career officer in the dreaded secret police and kept files on prominent Somalis.[42] The political appointees tried to sway the committee, but in keeping with the reputation of the SNPF, the six former officers led by Jama remained politically neutral and focused on mobilizing the new police force.[43]

A regular attendee at police subcommittee meetings was UNITAF's provost marshal, US Army Lieutenant Colonel Stephen Spataro. He was assigned to coordinate coalition support and resources for the project. Initially, these meetings were tense affairs polarized by clan affiliations and conducted entirely in Somali, as members claimed they could not speak English. As time went on, the sessions assumed a more cooperative tone, with members intermingling regardless of clan. The subcommittee even became more accepting of Spataro, and its members suddenly gained the ability to speak to him in English. The key issue was whether the police force should be national, regional, or confined to Mogadishu. Jama argued that a national force could disarm the militias and bring order to the country. Aidid's and Ali Mahdi's loyalists supported this view, hoping to control the force and boost their respective leader's political legitimacy. A lack of resources, however, meant that only a constabulary force of three thousand officers for Mogadishu was possible, and all members had to have at least two years of verified prior service in the SNPF.[44]

There were concerns about how this force might influence any future UN-led nation-building efforts. As such, it was agreed that the force would not be a new SNPF per se but an interim Auxiliary Security Force (ASF). Command of the ASF was offered to Ahmed Jama, who refused and proposed that an American should be chief of police to ensure clan impartiality. UNOSOM's Ismat Kittani also insisted that a non-Somali oversee the ASF due to the impact on future UN operations. Consequently, General Anthony Zinni was appointed the ASF's chief of police. The subcommittee vetted and appointed division- and district-level

ASF officers, who then spread the word among former SNPF officers to report to their old stations. They came first in the hundreds and then in thousands. However, they had no equipment, vehicles, or weapons. Most of the stations were dilapidated, lacked electricity and running water, and, in many cases, had no roofs. Spataro toured every ASF station in Mogadishu, often finding old SNPF flags flying overhead and poorly attired but proud ASF officers already on duty. He arranged for coalition engineers to rehabilitate the dilapidated buildings, including the former SNPF Academy.[45]

The ASF had its first operational test after two weeks of basic training. On the Green Line that divided Ali Madhi's and Aidid's territories in Mogadishu, both sides' supporters were stoning marines who were attempting to repatriate residents who had been displaced during the civil war. With the SNPF's long-standing reputation of respect among the locals, Oakley suggested using the ASF instead. Spataro had grave concerns, writing, "Here were U.S. Marines in full combat gear, unable to control a very volatile situation, and [I'm] sending a bunch of ragtags to slaughter . . . in rags—old police shirts, pants, and their old blue berets."[46] One hundred ASF officers, including five women, were trucked to the Green Line armed only with broken tree branches as batons. As they marched past the heavily armed marines and into the ongoing riot, the rocks suddenly stopped flying. Residents on both sides cheered as they welcomed the SNPF's return to the streets. Then, as if the riot had never happened, the repatriation continued without further incident. Spataro was "stunned." Commenting on the ASF officers patrolling the streets of what had been, until very recently, one of the most dangerous cities on earth, one marine officer said, "They are motivated. They have to be out there every day. It's like me telling you I'm not going to pay you . . . give you any uniforms . . . give you any vehicles . . . give you any weapons, now go clean Mogadishu up."[47] The ASF's potential was clear, but until the officers were properly supported and equipped, ragged old uniforms and branches as weapons would limit that potential.

Resourcing and equipping the ASF fell to Spataro and CARE's Lynn Thomas.[48] Labeling the ASF a "security force" rather than a police force allowed US forces to skirt the strictures of the Foreign Assistance Act, enabling Spataro to provide tacit support. This, of course, was semantics, as the ASF was undoubtedly a police force, fostering a more secure Mogadishu through law enforcement. The reality was that UNITAF could maintain its support of the ASF only if it did not draw too much attention. For example, staff officers at CENTCOM were so concerned about the legalities that they directed Spataro to personally sign for all equipment provided to the ASF. Unwilling to be directly liable for millions of dollars of equipment that probably was not coming back, but hoping to capitalize on the ASF, Spataro and Thomas looked elsewhere for help.

Faction leaders, UNITAF coalition partners, and UNOSOM were all approached to help the ASF. In an encouraging sign of cooperation, Ali Mahdi offered thirty-five vehicles in poor condition, which Aidid paid to have repaired. The Italian and Japanese governments offered additional vehicles and uniforms. UNOSOM found boots, berets, and radios. The police subcommittee asked Spataro about weapons for the ASF, as building the force and its supporting infrastructure would be useless if it could not be defended. This was an easy problem to solve, given the veritable arsenal of weaponry confiscated by UNITAF, and Spataro recommended that General Johnston approve the limited issuing of weapons to the ASF for station defense.[49]

Recognizing the ASF's potential to be a force for good, Spataro was determined to make it a success. In a 27 January memo he wrote, "They wouldn't look like the NYPD, but they wouldn't look like Barney Fife either . . . [they] probably won't pass the ACLU tests, we will have corruption, brutality, extortion, and anything that can go wrong will go wrong. We will never have a 100% solution, but we have at least a 60% solution. Bottom line, lead, follow, or get the h___ out of the way."[50] As uniforms, weapons, vehicles, and buildings were being obtained, one persistent problem was pay. No one was willing to pay the ASF, yet the officers kept reporting for duty every day. And around ASF stations and in areas where officers patrolled, commerce and stability returned, laughter could be heard, and a semblance of normalcy reigned for many Mogadishans.[51]

On 6 February the ASF began its largest operation in Mogadishu: the mass distribution site (MDS) feeding program. The MDS was organized by CARE and the WFP, funded by the OFDA, and supported by nine other relief organizations. The goal was to end starvation in the capital and lower black-market prices by saturating the city with free food. Thirty-five sites across the city would each distribute ten metric tons of wheat a day, giving each Somali a ration of two kilograms per day. Relief organizations ran the MDSs, MARFOR transported the wheat, and the ASF provided the "key element"— crowd control.[52]

For the duration of the MDS program, one thousand ASF officers, often dressed in rags and armed only with rudimentary batons, kept order while 175,000 people received food each day. Most Somalis respected the ASF and remained calm while waiting in line. Some did not. Three ASF officers were shot, two of whom died. After the second day of the program, CARE insisted that the ASF officers be paid salaries. Philip Johnston of UNOSOM was similarly impressed by the ASF and eventually obtained a UN commitment to seek funding for salaries from the international donor community. It was not until April 1993, though, that the ASF officers in Mogadishu received their first pay.[53]

By May 1993, Mogadishu had an ASF thirty-five hundred strong, including sixty female officers. Although Oakley, General Johnston, and Spataro had initially envisaged supporting an ASF in the capital, former SNPF officers also returned to work in towns and cities across the country. These regional and local ASFs were not influenced or controlled by factions in Mogadishu. Instead, many were deliberately shepherded by whatever UNITAF coalition partner held sway in the area. The Baidoa ASF was started by Newbold's 15th MEU to create "kiddies patrols" of marines and former SNPF officers to keep children out of dangerous areas, such as the airport runway.[54] After the Australians took over, a small and entirely Somali-operated Criminal Investigation Division was established. Its sole vehicle was confiscated from imprisoned bandit Ali "James Bond" Salaad, so named because he had inscribed "007" on the license plate.[55]

Five days after arriving in Kismayo, General Lawson Magruder met the former city police chief, his deputy, and the local prison warden. They asked Magruder to follow them around the corner, where 170 SNPF officers waited in uniform and in formation, "ready to go back to work." Magruder was aware of the Foreign Assistance Act but recalled "I sure as heck saw an opportunity to use a viable force."[56] In Beledweyne, the Canadians enlisted former police officers for joint patrols to secure key local infrastructure, resulting in a 350-person ASF. The chief of the Canadian Defense Staff personally traveled to Beledweyne to present the local ASF chief with a brand-new Toyota Land Cruiser. In HRS Bardera, marine Lieutenant Colonel Michael Sullivan enthusiastically supported the local ASF, arguing that although US law prohibited the training of foreign police forces, if only former officers were used, no training would be required. That nuance, coupled with calling the force the ASF, left Sullivan feeling legally in the clear to support it. Across southern Somalia, proto-ASFs emerged, always with coalition encouragement. The French trained and equipped an ASF in Oddur, the Italians in Gialalassi, and the US Army in Merka.[57]

The quality and capabilities of these regional ASFs varied, but their worth as a culturally astute interlocutor between UNITAF and the population was recognized by all. Oakley wrote, "In five of every six of them [cities or towns], including Mogadishu, the police performed effectively . . . they knew how to control crowds, and the people obeyed them."[58] By May 1993, the Australians had so much confidence in the Baidoa ASF that most city policing duties were handed over to it. Both the US Department of Justice's International Criminal Investigation and Training Assistance Program and the UN sent teams to evaluate the ASF in Mogadishu. Both organizations endorsed it and recommended funding for a force of five thousand in the capital as part of a national force of twenty thousand. To ensure uniformity and quality, Spataro traveled to each HRS to standardize the recruitment, training, and equipping of these forces, optimistically observing, "It just may be successful and actually work."[59] There were some problems, of course. In a few isolated cases, it was discovered that ASF officers were not former SNPF at all or were collaborating with bandits or factional militias, despite an intelligence background check. Where this occurred, the UNITAF HRS commander and local elders cooperated to root out and replace such individuals.[60] By April 1993, there were forty-four hundred ASF officers in seventeen major towns and cities, excluding those in the capital.[61]

UNITAF: Limited Intervention or Military Occupation?

The ASF solved the problem of UNITAF having to function as both military occupier and police. But a host of new problems arose when the ASF started to arrest suspects. What should be done with violators of the law, and what law held sway in the absence of a functioning Somali government? This was a major quandary, as UNITAF's intervention was unprecedented in terms of legal jurisprudence. Did UNITAF have the power to prosecute criminals? If so, under what law and by what court? More critically, did UNITAF's presence constitute a military occupation under international law? If so, UNITAF had legal responsibilities in terms of providing a certain level of governance.

This caused a debate between General Johnston's headquarters and the Australian contingent over what UNITAF's legal obligations were or should be. The Australians believed their control of HRS Baidoa was a legally recognized occupation and that the HRS commander, Lieutenant Colonel D. J. Hurley, was the equivalent of a "military governor" under Protocol I of the Fourth Convention of the Hague Regulations governing the laws of war. Hurley's Australians had enthusiastically assisted Baidoans in creating a regional ASF and rebuilding the judicial system, believing they were legally obligated to do so. Major Michael Kelly, Hurley's legal officer, argued that UNITAF's assumption of control over Somali ports and airspace, usually a preserve of national sovereignty, met the test of a legal occupation under the Hague Convention. General Hoar at CENTCOM and General Johnston disagreed. They viewed Somalia as a quick intervention with a limited scope—an in-and-out mission—whereas a legally recognized occupation could keep UNITAF in Somalia indefinitely. When Kelly communicated his legal opinion, Johnston's headquarters responded that an occupation had not taken place, and CENTCOM decreed that Operation Restore Hope was a purely humanitarian mission, not an occupation.[62]

Despite CENTCOM's ambitions for a limited mission, UNITAF was in Somalia, and if this was not an occupation, who was responsible for preventing Somali-on-Somali criminal violence? What was the policy on detainees arrested by the ASF or coalition forces? The more CENTCOM and Johnston's headquarters resisted the suggestion that UNITAF was an occupation force, the more questions emerged, and there were no easy answers. For instance, the initial policy on detainees was limited to cases in which the coalition's mission was being impeded. This caused embarrassment when the international media reported on a Somali woman who was viciously attacked in Mogadishu while US marines and French troops looked on, unsure what to do because the incident was not impeding their mission.[63]

Issuing additional guidance on 24 December 1992, Johnston clarified that coalition personnel were obliged to protect the population from attack, crime, and civil disobedience. Detention was reserved for exceptional circumstances and serious crimes such as rape, torture, murder, and inhumane treatment or when the failure to detain would be an embarrassment to US or UN forces. Somalis could be detained for more than twenty-four hours only with the approval of Johnston's headquarters and could be interrogated only on a "voluntary" basis.[64] What voluntary interrogation meant was anyone's guess, and after twenty-four hours, where were detainees supposed to go?

For some commanders, particularly in Mogadishu, where the early weeks of the intervention saw rampant crime, Johnston's policies were seen as cumbersome. Commanding RCT-7, Colonel Buck Bedard complained about the "inordinate amount of time and resources to get a guy detained."[65] Lieutenant Colonel Edward Lesnowicz of Team Secure had "two rapists that it took a three-star general to personally sign their incarceration. . . . It's like we wanted to bring Perry Mason to Mogadishu, crazy."[66] Detaining violent criminals only to see them released due to the lack of a proper policy for dealing with them was demoralizing for UNITAF troops. ASF officers became reluctant to make arrests, fearing reprisals when the suspects were quickly released. Far worse, UNITAF was losing credibility with the populace, being perceived as unable to provide protection from criminals.[67]

The conditional nature of Johnston's detainee policy necessitated another update in February 1993, which made it even more complex, arguably to avoid UNITAF being responsible for any detainees. A detainee could be held for forty-eight hours by the HRS commander. After that, if there was inadequate evidence to establish a prima facie criminal case, the detainee had to be released. If a valid case existed, the suspect was sent to the university compound in Mogadishu for another evaluation period of seventy-two hours while Johnston's staff judge advocate team examined whether "probable cause" existed for detention. If so, the suspect was sent to Mogadishu Prison, a facility that Spataro found to be operated "very professionally," even though prisoners were fed only every two days.[68] But again, this created problems, because now individuals were being arrested and incarcerated without a trial. How long were they to be confined for? And if they were they awaiting trial, by what entity?

One solution, proposed by Johnston's staff judge advocate, was to hold military tribunals under Article 5 of the Third Geneva Convention. These tribunals would decide whether detainees should be treated as prisoners of war. There was even a short-lived suggestion that UNITAF should create a war crimes tribunal after the massacre in Kismayo by Omar Jess came to light. Most detainees were not enemy combatants, though; they were criminals. The judge advocate of the US Department of the Army countered that the Geneva Convention applied only to international hostilities. Because Somalia was a humanitarian operation, detainees were not entitled to the same status as enemy combatants or prisoners of war, nor were the coalition's legal obligations as rigorous as those under international law. Everything pointed to the need for a judicial process, but any such endeavor required UNITAF to acknowledge its legal status as an occupying force. With the ASF arresting violators and criminals, UNITAF's desire for a limited mission was overtaken by events. Both the Security Committee and the police subcommittee argued, rightly, that the ASF could not make the law, enforce it, and convict criminals; a judicial system was needed.[69]

The Baidoa Judiciary

Just as former SNPF officers took the initiative and began to patrol their old beats, former judicial officers contacted Colonel Lorenz, Johnston's staff judge advocate, and proposed to reconstruct the judiciary. Chief among them was Abdullahi Ossoble Barre, a former supreme court judge and no relation to the former dictator. On 3 March 1993 Lorenz and Kelly hosted a meeting at UNOSOM's headquarters with Barre and other lawyers and judicial officers. Despite the location, Kittani refused to participate or even endorse the meeting for fear that UNOSOM would be responsible for any initiatives emerging from it. And, as Kelly and Lorenz were the only coalition personnel present, UNITAF's support was also largely nonexistent. The American position was that UNITAF was not an occupying force. Kelly and the Australians believed the opposite and felt obligated to help the Somalis rebuild their judiciary, if only in HRS Baidoa.[70] And that is precisely what happened.

Working with Kelly and the Australians, Judge Barre tracked down surviving judiciary members in the Bay region. Collectively, this proto-judiciary shunned the brutal laws of the Barre regime and readopted the postindependence 1962 Somali Penal Code. Much like Somalia itself, the 1962 Code was a melting pot reflecting the country's diverse colonial history. It was based on the 1931 Italian Penal Code, with Somali and Islamic additions. In a matter of weeks, the Australians and Somali judges in the Bay region had rebuilt a small but functional judicial system. Every main town had a district court; Baidoa, the regional capital, hosted the regional court and a court of appeals. The Australians collocated the courts with ASF stations, provided troops for security, refurbished prisons, and trained ASF officers and prison guards. Kelly criticized the American leadership in UNITAF and UNOSOM for not supporting the Bay region's court system. Johnston's headquarters claimed it was mission creep, and UNOSOM refused to pay the judiciary. Nevertheless, the Australians put all members of the judiciary on the rolls of the Baidoa ASF at the highest officer grade. UNOSOM never checked the names, so Somali judges and lawyers were paid through creative accounting.[71]

With a rebuilt court system, Somalis in the Bay region petitioned to regain property stolen by factions or militias during the war, and Australian troops joined the Baidoa ASF in enforcing court orders and repatriating stolen property. But the biggest case, capturing the attention of UNITAF, UNOSOM, and nearly all relief organizations, involved the bandit known as Gutaale. Gutaale had used an armored vehicle to crush fifteen women and children and had killed sixteen more civilians in another incident. The Bay regional court issued a warrant for his arrest, and Australian troops hunted him down. Gutaale was connected to a regional militia aligned with Aidid's SNA, prompting fear that witnesses, judges, and jurors would be intimidated or killed. However, no such abuses occurred. Gutaale was found guilty, sentenced to death, and promptly executed. The execution caused tension in the US State Department, as General Zinni was still the nominal chief of police, and it looked like the US military was endorsing the execution of Somali criminals.[72]

By March 1993, the Australians had re-created a judiciary that was operating independently and effectively. This highlighted the reality that the various members of the UNITAF coalition had vastly different interpretations of the mission in Somalia. For the Americans, a judiciary was mission creep; for the Australians, it was a legal obligation. The Australians were not alone in this interpretation. In Beledweyne, the Canadian contingent's legal team also worked to rebuild the region's judicial system, though with less success than the Australians. The Canadians departed before these efforts yielded fruit.[73] The Canadians' main effort, however, was a school system. Schools in Somalia had been closed for two years, so Lieutenant Colonel Carol Mathieu's Canadians worked to reopen them. Canadian engineers rebuilt or rehabilitated school buildings, while Mathieu's three-person civil affairs team, in conjunction with UNICEF, located, retrained, and certified three hundred teachers and sorted fifteen thousand children into classes. In April 1993 the first school was reopened in Beledweyne by retired US Admiral Jonathan Howe, who had chaired the Deputies Committee meetings in Washington, DC, in November 1992. Howe had just been appointed the new UN special representative to Somalia for the UN follow-up deployment that, by this point, was set to replace UNITAF: UNOSOM II.[74]

The Canadians and Australians were not alone in undertaking ambitious projects. In HRS Gialalassi, the Italians not only reestablished a postal service and refuse collection but also attempted to give Somalis in their HRS and the Italian sector of Mogadishu a semblance of health care through *Circuiti Operativi Umanitari* (Operational Humanitarian Channels). Detachments of sixty Italians, including doctors and nurses, lived in villages and towns for weeks on end, providing medical care and ensuring access to clean water before moving on to do the same elsewhere. More than four thousand Somalis received critical medical treatment. Despite initial concerns about Italy's colonial past, these efforts resulted in Italian troops being welcomed and treated warmly wherever they went. The Italians were joined in medical initiatives by the Moroccans, who established a hospital in Mogadishu that treated eight thousand patients a month.[75]

As UNITAF commanding general, it was up to General Johnston to try to reign in just how deep the coalition got involved in Somalia. He had reluctantly agreed to support the ASF but then withheld support for the judiciary in Baidoa. Another line in the sand became medical care for Somalis. Stricken by famine and war, Somalia had hundreds of thousands in need of care, and like the Italians and Moroccans, medical units throughout the coalition provided treatment. Johnston viewed UNITAF's mission as limited to security, but he supported deviations when there was a benefit, even a tangential one, to the security environment. He was not heartless; nor was he blind to the scale of the suffering. But with extraordinarily little medical infrastructure in the country, the treatment of Somalis raised the question of how much care should be provided when there was no chance of maintaining that standard of care after UNITAF left. Should the medical treatment provided be based on Western standards or local norms? For instance, the well-intentioned personnel of the US Army's 86th Evacuation Hospital opened its doors to the sick and injured, leaving the 104-bed hospital full, with "no local hospital of equivalent capability to accept them in transfer" and no room for UNITAF casualties if they occurred.[76]

As early as 19 December 1992, Johnston issued guidance to all commands: "The Somalian population is facing very serious medical and dental problems. Severe malnutrition and the many tropical infectious diseases are the main concerns. The lack of basic public health measures, adequate food supply, poor oral hygiene and an effective medical/dental care infrastructure are the underlying causes of this crisis." However, Johnston clarified, the mission of American medical units was to care for UNITAF personnel only. "No additional personnel or supplies have been allocated for humanitarian services to the local population."[77] The only Somalis UNITAF was obligated to care for were those injured as a direct result of coalition actions. Johnston's guidance was based on pure practicalities. UNITAF had significant medical assets—more than were needed, in hindsight—but caring for everyone who needed treatment would exhaust and overwhelm the coalition's medical capabilities and create the expectation of a level of care that could not be maintained. There was also the sticking point of relief organizations, which saw the medical treatment of the famine-stricken populace as their preserve and, in some cases, viewed UNITAF's benevolent medical activities as competition, complicating the already tense civil-military relationship.[78]

Therefore, when US troops in Mogadishu found a Somali with a gunshot wound to the head, they were told to provide first aid only, not evacuate him to a hospital because UNITAF had not caused the injury. That said, soldiers often could not in good conscience ignore suffering when they encountered it. Three Somalis injured in a bus accident were brought to the 86th Evacuation Hospital and placed on ventilators, even though UNITAF did not cause their injuries. But the commander of the 86th was given a harsh ultimatum: the hospital could continue to care for the injured Somalis, but they were to be taken off the ventilators if the machines were required to treat American casualties. Luckily, no such dilemma presented itself.[79]

Other commanders found loopholes that allowed them to continue helping the sick and wounded. When the chief surgeon at Johnston's headquarters directed US forces to cease medical support to civilians, claiming it was the relief organizations' responsibility, Lesnowicz equated this with being told "to sit here [and] watch people starving and dying from disease."[80] He approached Team Secure's coalition partners, who were more than willing to provide medical care to locals and could safely ignore orders from the American chief surgeon. Lesnowicz gleefully told an interviewer, "The coalition can tell [the chief surgeon] to go eat shit and die and that's what they're doing."[81] For the most part, Johnston's guidance was heeded only by American forces. Coalition partners continued to provide medical care where and when they could.

By September 1993, the Moroccan hospital in Mogadishu celebrated treating its one hundred thousandth patient.[82]

Disarming Southern Somalia

Coalition support of the ASF had taken advantage of an unforeseen but fortuitous opportunity. In contrast, UNITAF's disarmament campaign was something American policymakers had expressly stated the coalition would not do. When the Restore Hope mission statement was defined, Boutros-Ghali, the UN, and relief organizations had argued that Somalia should be effectively disarmed. CENTCOM and the Pentagon rejected this goal as being too risky and, given the amount of weaponry, unachievable. Moreover, Generals Johnston and Hoar claimed disarmament was not part of the mission. If the US military could not disarm New York City or Los Angeles, Hoar argued, it could not disarm Mogadishu.[83]

Yet the messaging on disarmament varied. At a press briefing on 4 December 1992, on the eve of UNITAF's deployment, Secretary of Defense Dick Cheney replied, "We might," when asked if the coalition would disarm the Somalis.[84] Hoar also backtracked during another press briefing, saying, "I don't think that I had said we're not going to disarm the Somalis . . . in the process of executing the mission . . . there is going to be a reduction in arms and I think that's key . . . what we're trying to achieve is arms control."[85] When Hoar was told that Johnston had stated unequivocally that "disarmament is not the mission," Hoar said, "Of course we're going to disarm" to facilitate the political process. Even Oakley contributed to the mixed message, telling State Department officials, "Our mission is not to disarm, our mission is to protect humanitarian operations. It's been spelled out I don't know how many times," only to say, "What we're trying to do is take away the most dangerous weapons, thereby changing the balance from war to peace and from empowerment by weapons to empowerment by other means and shifting the whole thing."[86] Despite CENTCOM and the Pentagon's resistance to including disarmament in the mission statement, senior American civilian and military leaders displayed a serious case of policy schizophrenia.

Interestingly, when he wrote to President Bush on the passage of Resolution 794 in December 1992, Boutros-Ghali did not ask for Somalia to be totally stripped of its weapons. Specifically, the UN secretary-general asked that "at least the heavy weapons of the organized factions are neutralized and brought under international control and that the irregular forces and gangs are disarmed."[87] Later, in his memoir, Boutros-Ghali criticized the Pentagon and the Bush administration for not doing this.[88] Yet UNITAF not only delivered what Boutros-Ghali requested but also went further, launching a widespread disarmament campaign across all nine HRSs.

After UNITAF's arrival, the initial approach to the factions' heavy weapons was containment. In accordance with their seven-point agreement, both Aidid and Ali Mahdi voluntarily cantoned their heavy weapons and vehicles in a dozen authorized weapon storage sites (AWSSs) across Mogadishu. Their respective militias were allowed to guard these sites, but the removal of weapons was expressly forbidden. AWSSs became common in the other HRSs too, where coalition commanders successfully negotiated with local militias to canton their heavy weapons, tanks, artillery, and APCs.[89] Any other heavy weapons or caches discovered after the cantonment grace period were subject to confiscation.

The cantonment strategy fulfilled Boutros-Ghali's request that the factions' heavy weapons be confiscated. UNITAF's attitude toward small arms, however, was different: out of sight, out of mind. Only weapons openly brandished on the streets risked seizure. This caused problems, as locals often armed themselves against the threat of banditry, especially when traveling across the country.[90] In Afgooye, US marines under Captain Robert Abbott were disarming Somalis at a road bridge. Major General Charles Wilhelm, MARFOR commander, was personally supervising the operation and, when he saw the fury of those being disarmed, ordered Abbott to return their weapons. Later, Abbott was told to resume confiscating weapons but "only take guns away from the bad guys . . . then the big question is, who are the bad guys?"[91] Frustrated by the conflicting orders, Abbott had his marines apply "the [National Rifle Association] rule": if his men believed the weapons were for home defense, they could be retained; if not, they were confiscated. Similar disarmament operations occurred on a much larger scale. Task Force Mogadishu launched Operations Clean Sweep I and II, specifically targeting small arms carried openly on the streets, which netted a thousand weapons.[92]

Clean Sweep II took place on 5 January 1993 and provoked an unintended response. On 6 January, a Task Force Mogadishu patrol took fire from SNA militia guarding two of Aidid's AWSSs. Available evidence does not suggest why the militia opened fire, but they may have assumed that after Clean Sweep II, the next target for disarmament was their AWSSs. Aidid was out of the country at the time, so UNITAF informed his deputy, Brigadier General Ali Mohamed Kedeye Elmi, that the militia had violated the seven-point agreement, meaning that the two AWSSs were "invalidated." They would be surrounded, and all the weapons and fighting vehicles inside would be taken.[93] The first AWSS was deserted and was quickly seized. The second was guarded by the militia that had fired on the patrol. Klimp had Task Force Mogadishu's APCs and Abrams tanks surround the AWSS, while Cobra helicopter gunships circled overhead. Loudspeakers were used to appeal to the militiamen to surrender. But inside the AWSS, they had access to Aidid's best weaponry, including tanks and plentiful ammunition. They chose to fight.

When the militia mounted a tank and several antiaircraft guns, Task Force Mogadishu and the Cobras "hammered the Somalis" in a twenty-minute fusillade, according to one witness. Klimp's marines refrained from using tank rounds or missiles for fear of civilian casualties, and they alternated between firing and calling for the militia to surrender. Clearly outmatched, the militiamen gave up. Twelve men were captured, and four M47 Patton tanks, French and Soviet APCs, and dozens of heavy artillery pieces, mortars, and technicals were impounded. The marines were surprised, given the overall state of Mogadishu, to find all this equipment well maintained and serviceable.[94] Task Force Mogadishu noted that the AWSS incident "demonstrated to the criminals and bandits of Mogadishu what happens when they try to shoot U.S. Marines. [We] swiftly and forcefully smashed the Somali resistance."[95]

After the AWSS incident, General Johnston issued a new policy on weapons in HRSs: "UNITAF will stabilize and expand security . . . by reducing weapons, and the visibility of weapons."[96] Except for weapons stored in AWSSs and those used by faction leaders' bodyguards, all heavy weapons and small arms in Mogadishu were to be confiscated. HRS commanders were given complete discretion on the disarming of their regions.[97] Johnston had transitioned from the containment of heavy weapons and the confiscation of visible small arms to a campaign of widespread disarmament. The other HRS commanders followed suit.

Task Force Mogadishu began an extensive disarmament campaign. Between 9 and 20 January, weapons caches across the city were raided. An artillery park holding dozens of howitzers was demilitarized, along with fifteen bunkers filled with ordnance. Weapons and ammunition were seized by the truckload. On one occasion, Task Force Mogadishu received panicked reports of Somali-manned tanks in the city. Marines in M1 Abrams tanks raced to the scene and found four Soviet-made T-55s in a field. When one of the T-55s moved its turret toward them, the marines prepared to open fire, only to discover at the last moment that children were playing inside the abandoned tanks.[98]

That Johnston was serious about disarmament was demonstrated on 11 January when Task Force Mogadishu was ordered "to confiscate all weapons within [the] Bakara Market."[99] The Bakara Market was the heart of the local arms trade, and even Aidid endorsed the raid to remove a major source of crime and instability.[100] The Bakara Market was surrounded and 850 marines combed the area, going door to door using mine detectors and searching under floors for hidden arms. The task force reported that "the local population received the operation well, many expressing very positive support." Seven truckloads of ordnance were captured, including thousands of artillery and mortar rounds, hundreds of landmines, small-arms ammunition, and, worryingly, heat sensors for Soviet antiaircraft missiles.[101] As one marine battalion commander noted, "We aggressively took every weapon in sight . . . we really went through the Bakara . . . like a hot knife through butter."[102] The sweep was such a blow to the black market that one Somali approached a UNITAF patrol to report that an assassination plot against Oakley was planned for the following day, 12 January—a plot that ultimately came to naught.[103] That said, it is perhaps more than a coincidence that Private Domingo Arroyo, UNITAF's first fatality, was killed that same day, right after the Bakara Market raid.

Across southern Somalia, the coalition conducted dozens of cordon and search operations. Towns or city blocks were sealed off, and detailed searches were conducted.[104] One search in Baidoa netted "over 20 tons of ordnance."[105] In Afgooye, a missile complex was discovered, with thirty bunkers filled with thousands of mines, artillery rounds, fifty SA-7 surface-to-air missiles, and two hundred truckloads of ammunition. In Buurhakaba, local children were paid in food and coffee to reveal the locations of hidden weapons caches or mines; several sites a day were identified and dealt with by UNITAF engineers. In Baidoa, Oddur, and Gialalassi, the Australians, French, and Italians, respectively, confiscated thousands of weapons.[106]

Often, the Somalis themselves took the lead in disarmament. One of Ali Mahdi's colonels contacted the Italians and asked them to confiscate twenty-six hundred cases of machine gun ammunition, six hundred cases of mortar rounds, fifty cases of rocket-propelled grenade (RPG) rounds, and forty cases of grenades, with "no other explanation."[107] Clan elders in Habare invited the Australians to disarm the town to create a safe environment for their children, welcoming Australian engineers with food and drink before escorting them to the already gathered weaponry. Residents also enthusiastically helped UNITAF locate unmarked minefields, of which there were many.[108] Just as the AWSS incident prompted Task Force Mogadishu to sweep the capital clean of weaponry, the aftermath of Morgan's raid saw Task Force Kismayo work decisively to make Kismayo a "weapons free zone . . . [with] no weapons of any kind in the city," a campaign that netted, among other things, twenty-eight tons of torpedoes.[109] UNITAF had the power to disarm southern Somalia and used it. Not every weapon was confiscated, but the effort was deliberate and widespread.

The Consequences of Disarmament

Although disarmament contributed to stability and security, it worsened the already tense relations with relief organizations. In the chaotic environment before UNITAF arrived, these groups had commonly hired armed Somali guards for security, a practice that continued after the coalition's arrival because UNITAF could not be in all places at all times. Somali guards were paid exorbitant wages, and many of them were also members of factional militias. Within UNITAF, these competing loyalties reminded many of Vietnam. As one senior marine officer put it, "You might have a guy working inside the U.S. compound by day and he was a [Vietcong] by night."[110] One UNITAF memo equated legitimizing the use of armed Somali guards by relief agencies to legitimizing armed Somali factions.[111]

In the view of most UNITAF personnel, these armed guards were suspicious and duplicitous. Relief organizations were in a difficult position, however, as firing these well-paid guards risked violent retaliation. UNICEF's Sean Deveraux and Kurt Lustinburger of the ICRC were both murdered by Somalis formerly employed as guards. When the disarmament campaign began, these guards were just as likely to have their weapons confiscated as anyone else. Tensions soared between the coalition and the relief organizations, as many hired guards refused to work unarmed and vulnerable to bandits. Debates raged at the CMOC, with relief workers arguing that if UNITAF could not secure their facilities—an impossibility in Mogadishu—armed local guards were a critical necessity.[112]

An initial compromise was reached. Hired guards could register for authorization to carry a personal weapon and would receive a pink identification card. These pink cards did not carry a photograph of the registered owner, so coalition units, either unaware of the system or out of an abundance of caution, often disarmed the cardholders anyway.[113] Relief workers complained to Colonel Kennedy at the CMOC, demanding the return of their guards' weapons. In ironic scenes, relief agency staff reluctant to be associated with the military left Kennedy's office "burdened with recovered AK-47s and M-16s."[114] The worthless pink cards were eventually replaced by blue cards that at least carried a photograph of the registered owner and details about the weapon. However, the bearer of a blue card was allowed to vouch for accompanying armed Somalis who had no such cards.[115]

Among commanders, particularly Bedard in Mogadishu, this was unacceptable. Bedard's position was, "any weapons that I see . . . in the city I'm taking those weapons and I'm taking the blue cards."[116] For Bedard, armed Somali guards were justifiable when traveling across the country, but not in the capital. The zeal with which the marines of RCT-7 disarmed these guards led Kennedy, himself a marine, to believe that there was a "fundamental antagonism toward humanitarian organizations from some elements of UNITAF." Kennedy suggested this enmity came from officers who wanted to strictly adhere to the limited security mission and saw facilitating relief organizations as extra responsibilities at best or as creating another uncontrollable element in an already chaotic environment at worst.[117] Thus, a cycle was established where UNITAF disarmed Somali guards, relief workers recovered the weapons and rearmed their guards, and the guards were often disarmed again. As a result, civil-military relations remained sour.

Justifying Mission Creep

Given the uncertainty of whether a follow-on UN operation would replace UNITAF, the coalition went far beyond establishing a secure environment in southern Somalia. Local and regional governing councils

were deliberately empowered, and national security and political committees were created. The ASF was encouraged and stewarded in every
HRS, along with a regional judiciary in Baidoa, an education system in
Beledweyne, and a postal system in Gialalassi. Despite Hoagland's ill-
informed celebration of UNITAF's avoidance of mission creep in the
Washington Post, UNITAF had exceeded its mission mandate, and everyone knew it. Across the coalition, personnel worked hard to justify
this situation by claiming that it facilitated the security mission. The
US Army's 10th Mountain Division, responsible for HRSs Baledogle,
Merka, and Kismayo, included a paragraph titled "Mission Creep" in its
after-action report:

> Most of the examples of mission creep have to do with the mission itself. . . .
> To get military forces out of the security business, local security forces must
> function once again . . . to establish these forces some type of local council
> or "government" must exist. . . . As town councils began to stand up and the
> local elders were empowered once again, civic action projects were begun
> by [UNITAF] units to help the community recover.[118]

Despite CENTCOM and State Department claims that the ASF was mission creep, 10th Mountain argued the opposite, as the erstwhile police
force contributed to stability and security in towns and cities.

The intervention in Somalia brings into question the utility of the
concept of mission creep. Operation Restore Hope's mission statement
mandated a limited mission to create a secure environment, but at the
same time, a UNITAF political plan included initiatives to develop local
administration, regional police forces, basic health systems, employment
opportunities, and a basic education infrastructure.[119] Simultaneously,
UNITAF headquarters voiced concerns when individual unit commanders, seeing the suffering in Somalia, did their best to alleviate it. All
commanders were ordered to "remind soldiers of all ranks . . . of their
obligation to mission accomplishment, as well as the suffering population, and where the dividing line falls . . . well-meaning commanders
must focus on . . . assisting the [relief organizations] in their efforts, not
usurping [their] mission."[120]

But with the latitude and independence Johnston extended to all
HRS commanders, many believed that what they were doing fostered a
secure environment or that their activities were an implied task derived
from the mission statement. Commanding RCT-7, Bedard acknowledged, "We are way over and above what we came here and what we

should be doing. But . . . as you progress along and get this thing going, that vacuum is there, and these people want to move forward in certain areas. We're doing more than stabilization and normalization in my opinion."[121] Zinni's deputy, Colonel James Egan, claimed the activities conducted by UNITAF were implied in the mission "to accomplish this broad goal of establishing adequate levels of security. . . . Implied tasks are repair the roads, repair the bridges, restore power, restore water. There is no civilian infrastructure so there has to be something from a law enforcement perspective, so those things are all implied."[122] Colonel Wallace Grayson agreed with Egan's reasoning, saying, "We knew specifically what the mission was, but there were a lot of implied tasks that you could pull out of that: disarmament becomes an implied task."[123]

In Baidoa the Australian commander, Lieutenant Colonel D. J. Hurley, wrote, "Mission creep, in some cases 'mission stretch,' had occurred. In some instances, this was by default, in others deliberate decisions were made to widen the scope of operations. The decision . . . reflected the pace at which developments were happening on the ground and UNITAF's and the UN's inability to provide timely advice and policy guidance."[124] Major Martin Stanton, operations officer for the US Army's garrison in Merka, also lamented the lack of guidance from higher headquarters. Stanton wished UNITAF had developed a long-term strategy beyond the provision of security because, "as it was, [we] proceeded further and further into nation building. We had gotten on this bus and now we didn't have a clue as to where it was going. We just knew we couldn't get off."[125]

It could be argued that mission creep emanated from the latitude Johnston gave to HRS commanders or from taking advantage of opportunities that presented themselves. Robert Oakley deserves some responsibility for going beyond the security mandate. Oakley had chaired meetings in October and November 1992 with prominent Somalis at the US Institute for Peace, and they had advised him what UNITAF should achieve during the intervention: Disarmament was a must, and regional police forces should be established. Somalia needed a tailored regional approach, not a national one. Close contact must be maintained with factional leaders, and the UN had to be more active in promoting dialogue and political reconciliation. Last, Somali structures of authority must be rebuilt at local, village, subregional, and regional levels.[126]

Oakley took what he heard at those meetings and operationalized it through the coalition. In briefings, he discussed deliberately marginal-

izing the faction leaders to allow political leaders to emerge, saying that
"disarmament will end the psychological terror which permits the warlords and thugs to dominate the people . . . deprivation of weapons leads
to deprivation of political power."[127] When Vice President Al Gore asked
Oakley in March 1993, "What about our endgame—are we headed in
the right direction?" Oakley replied, "We're playing it right. It's a three
phased operation. First, we accomplished our original goal . . . provide a
secure environment for delivery of relief operations. Second, we need to
empower civil society and create a climate conducive to reconstruction.
And finally, we need to pluck the war lords' feathers."[128] Oakley made
what might have been his only serious gaffe when he repeated this last
part to a reporter, saying, "You take one feather at a time and the bird
doesn't think there's anything terrible going on. Then one day he finds
out he can't fly."[129] Such opinions about the goal of the disarmament
campaign were not well received by Aidid, Ali Mahdi, or the other faction leaders.

Was UNITAF guilty of mission creep? Absolutely. Most commanders
knew full well they were going beyond the mission's parameters. Limiting mission creep was impossible when nearly forty thousand troops,
dozens of governments, and numerous government departments were
involved. The belief that mission creep could be limited implied absolute control over the operating environment, which was a fallacy in
Somalia. But the critical factor overlooked is why this happened. For
Johnston, Oakley, Zinni, and the UNITAF coalition, future UN participation in Somalia was uncertain. In such a vacuum, Zinni argued, the
benefits of an open dialogue with the warring factions and the independent reemergence of a local police force represented opportunities that
were too good to ignore. In Zinni's words, "You could term it as mission
creep, but in reality, it was mission necessity."[130] UNITAF had come to
Somalia to create a secure environment; it had done that and more,
even embarking on an embryonic nation-building effort. Now UNITAF
was getting off the bus, so to speak, as the UN was taking over with a new
operation. Whereas UNITAF had become a benevolent nation builder
by accident, UNOSOM II would oversee the largest deliberate attempt
at nation building in history.

Aircraft carrier USS *Ranger* en route to Somalia, December 1992. Showcasing the optimism felt by the international community at the outset of the intervention, the crew assembled on the flight deck to spell out "Restore Hope." (National Archives and Records Administration)

The 15th Marine Expeditionary Unit's amphibious assault vehicles coming ashore on Green Beach in Mogadishu in December 1992, shortly after Operation Restore Hope began. Coalition vessels can be seen offshore in the distance. (US Marine Corps photograph)

Mogadishu from the air. What was once considered the glamorous riviera of Mogadishu's Old Port is now filled with ruined and damaged buildings after the civil war. New Port and its two warehouses can be seen in the distance in the top left. (Tenth Mountain Division Collection)

Mogadishu airport was the busiest airport in Africa during the intervention. But with just one runway, no refueling facilities, and limited ramp space, the influx of UNITAF was challenging, especially as the airport had to be shared with humanitarian relief agencies. Here, a US Air Force C-5 Galaxy is unloading beside the main terminal buildings. (Department of Defense photograph)

Mogadishu Stadium became a key base for both UNITAF and UNOSOM. It sat astride the Green Line dividing Mogadishu between Ali Mahdi and Aidid. (10th Mountain Division Collection)

The K-4 Circle, a key thoroughfare in Mogadishu connecting the airport and New Port to the US embassy and university compounds, was the site of several engagements during the intervention. (Department of Defense photograph)

Ambassador Robert Oakley, US presidential envoy and the political head of UNITAF, at a ceremony marking the construction of a bridge in HRS Kismayo by US Army engineers. Behind him to the left is US Army Brigadier General Lawson Magruder, HRS commander. (US Army photograph)

US President George H. W. Bush visits Mogadishu on New Year's Day 1993. He is escorted from his helicopter by UNITAF's commanding general, marine Lieutenant General Robert B. Johnston. (Department of Defense photograph)

One of UNITAF's achievements was the reconstitution of the Somali police as the Auxiliary Security Force (ASF). Respected for being an impartial arbiter, the ASF was very effective at maintaining law and order. Here, an ASF officer in his trademark blue beret oversees a gathering in a town in HRS Kismayo. (10th Mountain Division Collection)

Boutros Boutros-Ghali was the first UN secretary-general from Africa. Aidid distrusted Boutros-Ghali owing to his former post as Egyptian foreign minister, and the Clinton administration considered him unpredictable. Here, Boutros-Ghali is inspecting a Pakistani guard of honor during a visit to Mogadishu. (National Archives and Records Administration)

UNOSOM II's controversial special representative, retired US Navy Admiral Jonathan Howe, pictured here as a rear admiral in 1984. As deputy national security adviser, Howe presided over the National Security Council meetings in 1992 where the decision was made to intervene in Somalia. He later became the political head of UNOSOM II. (National Archives and Records Administration)

Assisting Howe was UNOSOM II's deputy force commander, US Army Major General Thomas Montgomery. A decorated Vietnam War veteran, Montgomery was handpicked by US Army Chief of Staff General Gordon Sullivan and presided over some of the heaviest fighting during UNOSOM II's mission. (Department of Defense photograph)

UNOSOM II's force commander, Turkish Lieutenant General Cĕvik Bir. As the violence intensified in Mogadishu, Bir's job became increasingly difficult when various contingents refused to participate in offensive operations against Aidid. (National Archives and Records Administration)

UNOSOM II was the first overseas deployment of large numbers of German soldiers since 1945. Here, a German soldier hands out candy to Somali children in Beledweyne. (Department of Defense photograph)

Given the violence between Morgan and Jess, weapons sweeps and checkpoints became routine for the Belgian contingent in Kismayo. Two of its members are pictured here searching a car and its owner. (National Archives and Records Administration)

Radio Mogadishu, Aidid's radio station, became a major point of contention in the weeks leading up to the Summer War. It is visible in the right foreground after being destroyed from the air on 12 June 1993. The holes in the roof from gunship rounds are clearly visible. (10th Mountain Division Collection)

Across Somalia, UNITAF was welcomed by the population. Here, US Army Brigadier General Lawson Magruder (sitting second from the right) is welcomed to a town in HRS Kismayo. Sitting to his right and smiling is Lieutenant Colonel Victor Bero, commander of the 3rd Battalion/14th Infantry Regiment, whose men occupied HRS Kismayo in conjunction with the Belgians. (10th Mountain Division Collection)

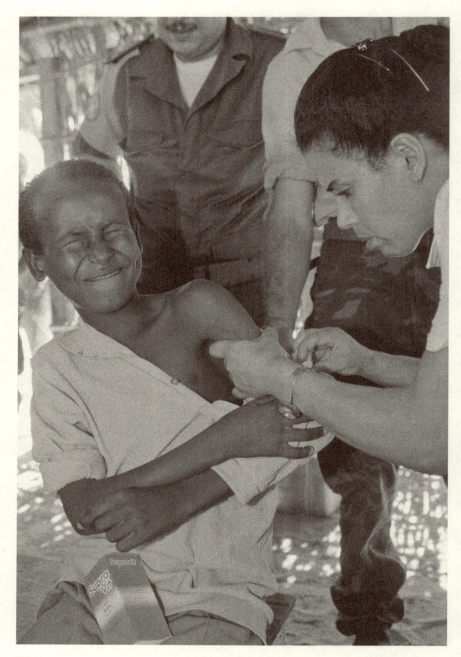

Nearly 750,000 Somali children received vaccinations during the intervention. Here, a child is being vaccinated by a nurse at the Moroccan hospital in Mogadishu. Moroccan medical personnel treated more than 100,000 Somalis in what came to be known as "Little Morocco." (National Archives and Records Administration)

Mogadishu airport became the focus for SNA mortar barrages during the Summer War. As a result, sandbag revetments were constructed around American Black Hawk helicopters to protect them from nearby impacts. (10th Mountain Division Collection)

The men of Bravo Company, 3rd Battalion/75th Ranger Regiment, on Mogadishu beach in September 1993. US Army Rangers formed the backbone of Task Force Ranger, sent to Mogadishu to hunt down Aidid or, failing that, undermine the SNA as an organization. (US Army photograph)

After the Battle of Mogadishu on 3 October 1993, the men of Task Force Ranger held a memorial service at the airport. In front of the Little Bird helicopters and beneath the American flag is a row of upturned rifles adorned with helmets, one for each of the dead. Major General William Garrison, Task Force Ranger's commander, can be seen leading the service (center left). (US Army photograph)

Critical to the relief of Task Force Ranger was the assistance of the Pakistani and Malaysian contingents, which did not hesitate to help on 3 October. Here, Montgomery is pictured awarding members of the Malaysian contingent the UNOSOM medal. (National Archives and Records Administration)

Brigadier General Anthony Zinni established a rapport with Aidid while serving as UNITAF's director of operations. He later returned to Mogadishu with Oakley to obtain the release of Chief Warrant Officer Michael Durant. In March 1995 he returned to Somalia again as a lieutenant general and commander of Operation United Shield, the final evacuation of UNOSOM. Zinni was in the last amphibious assault vehicle to leave Somalia. (National Archives and Records Administration)

6 | The Reluctant Crusader
UNOSOM II Takes over in Somalia

We must continue to do all in our power to encourage the United Nations to assume control of the situation . . . to get them into the nation building business.
— General Gordon S. Sullivan, US Army chief of staff[1]

There was no precedent for the Organization to follow as it embarked on this course, no example but the one it was about to set, and there were many unanswered questions about the undertaking.
— UN official history on Somalia[2]

UNITAF provided the shock and power to force rapid change. Forward momentum is established. Now the stage is set for rapid political, social, and cultural advancement if the proper agencies can be put in place.
— Lieutenant General Robert Johnston,
commanding general, UNITAF[3]

On 5 May 1993 President Bill Clinton decorated Lieutenant General Robert Johnston on the White House lawn and congratulated the Unified Task Force for the "largest humanitarian relief operation in history." "One can now envision a day," Clinton said, "when Somalia will be reconstructed as a functioning civil society." UNITAF had "set the stage and made it possible . . . to complete the work of rebuilding and creating a peaceful, self-sustaining, and democratic civil society."[4] But America's involvement with Somalia did not end that day on the White House lawn.

In 1996 Colin Powell, former chairman of the Joint Chiefs of Staff, published his memoir, *My American Journey*. Regarding the October 1993 Battle of Mogadishu, he wrote, "This was the quicksand that the UN 'nation-building' mission had sucked us into."[5] Referring to UNITAF's successor, UNOSOM II, Powell criticized the UN for dragging a reluctant United States into a much deeper involvement in Somalia, the clear implication being that Americans had died as a result. Memoirs, of course, are often idealized recollections of events. In truth, long before UNOSOM II took over from UNITAF in May 1993, the nation-building goal in Somalia was known to all, including Powell; it was a course deliberately set and enthusiastically encouraged by the United States. With the Cold War over and the United States no longer having the power or the budget to be the world's policeman, the Clinton administration viewed Somalia as the precedent-setting test case for a new, robust UN capable of shouldering some of the burdens in an increasingly unstable world. The United States put such value on UN success in Somalia that the level of American involvement in and influence on UNOSOM II's mission, structure, and leadership made it just as much of a US-led effort as the UNITAF coalition that preceded it.

Results of the Unified Task Force

On 19 January 1993 Edward Perkins, US ambassador to the United Nations, addressed the UN Security Council. Phases 1 and 2 of Operation Restore Hope were complete, Perkins said. Most Somalis had welcomed UNITAF, and the factions had cantoned their heavy weapons; a secure environment had been created. By this stage, UNITAF had secured all nine HRSs, Task Force Mogadishu was disbanding after its pacification campaign in the capital, and the ASF had emerged in several towns and cities. Sufficient progress had been made, Perkins argued, for Boutros-Ghali to start planning for the follow-on UN mission that would replace UNITAF in Somalia: UNOSOM II.[6]

To quantify the success Perkins lauded, Zinni's operations staff had developed a set of progress indicators that evaluated each HRS based on the status of its ASF and local councils, level of banditry, status of factional militias, and disarmament. Each HRS was then categorized as volatile, unstable, stable, or secure.[7] By January 1993, these assessments were encouraging, indicating that local governing councils and regional ASFs were emerging to take control of their localities, banditry was decreasing, disarmament was progressing, and the factional militias were largely maintaining the cease-fire.[8] Only two problem areas were identified: Kismayo, due to the potential for SNF-SPM violence (which later happened), and Mogadishu. Competition between Aidid and Ali Mahdi was not the concern in the capital; it was criminal gangs and bandits trying to fill the vacuum in the city now that the factions had stopped fighting. A January status report noted, "Mogadishu is not ready for a handoff. If all goes according to plan, sometime around 1 [February], a strong, well-trained, and tough peacekeeping force should be able to do the job."[9]

Central to the claims of UNITAF's success was Johnston's January 1993 commander's assessment. The Green Line that had divided Mogadishu for so long was now a thriving market. Weapons were no longer seen in the streets, with "captured ammunition quantities . . . so large they defy accurate accounting."[10] Johnston cited ongoing feeding and vaccination programs, the ninety-four million meals delivered to Somalis, and the repair and upgrading of eight airfields and more than a thousand kilometers of roads. "Leadership entities were identified and given stature and credibility based on what best worked in each area," Johnston reported. The death toll in Mogadishu had plummeted from 150 a day to between 5 and 15. The factions, Johnston said, were "largely neutralized," and "it is currently felt that all HRSs could immediately be transferred to a peacekeeping mission." So confident was Johnston that UNITAF had achieved its mission that he was quoted as sending a message to CENTCOM saying, "War is over, we won, it's time to come home."[11]

Boutros-Ghali had a slightly different perspective. Beginning as early as 19 December 1992, just ten days after UNITAF's arrival, the United States had pressed the secretary-general for solid plans and a timeline for UNOSOM II to take over. Like UNITAF, the United States wanted the new UN operation to have a Chapter VII peace enforcement mandate, as events had shown that the traditional approach of consent-based Chapter VI peacekeeping—demonstrated by the original UNOSOM— was unworkable in Somalia. Essentially, the United States now wanted the UN to pursue the fifth option Boutros-Ghali had presented to the Security Council in November 1992: a UN-commanded peace enforcement mission under Article 42 of the UN Charter—the first of its kind in UN history. When he first presented this option, Boutros-Ghali had warned that the UN lacked the organizational capability and experience to lead such a venture, fearing that member states would be reluctant to volunteer military personnel in what amounted to an institutional experiment.[12] Boutros-Ghali was clearly nervous. Somalia needed a "long haul" effort, he wrote, and UNOSOM II as envisaged by the Americans would be a journey into the unknown. Impulsive decision making, he feared, could "plunge Somalia back into anarchy." Despite the American pressure, a prudent Boutros-Ghali told the Security Council that he wanted to gauge the success of UNITAF before developing detailed plans for UNOSOM II. Privately, he also told US officials that he wanted to wait until after Clinton's inauguration, to ensure continued American support for the next phase of the intervention.[13]

This prudence manifested itself when Boutros-Ghali set two conditions for any transition to UNOSOM II. First, UNITAF had to neutralize the factions' "heavy weapons" and ensure that "irregular forces and gangs are disarmed."[14] Between cantonment and the widespread disarmament campaign prompted by the AWSS incident in Mogadishu, the first condition was on course to be met. The second was trickier. Boutros-Ghali wanted UNITAF to take control of all of Somalia, not just the southern 40 percent of the country. His view was that UNITAF's limited area of operations gave Somali militias a sanctuary where the coalition could not disarm them. However, American policymakers had refused an all-country deployment during the planning of Restore Hope, as famine and instability were limited to the southern regions.[15] Debates over this second condition caused a stalemate between the United States and the UN, as the Americans had no appetite for expanding the coalition's area of responsibility. The result was that no timeline for a transition had been established, explaining why Bush and Scowcroft told Johnston, Oakley, and Zinni on New Year's Day 1993 that plans for a UN takeover were still unclear.

After Perkins's mid-January appeal for the start of preparations for UNOSOM II, Boutros-Ghali was still wary. Planning had begun, the secretary-general told the Security Council, the new UN force would deploy across the entire country, and a force commander would soon be appointed. He acknowledged both Johnston's and Perkins's reports but argued that the security situation was still tenuous. There was still sporadic sniping in Mogadishu, and marine Private Arroyo and an ICRC relief worker had recently been killed.[16] Regardless of progress indicators, the secretary-general was not yet convinced that UNITAF had achieved its security mission. In fact, when he visited Mogadishu on 3 January, he encountered anti-UN and anti–Boutros-Ghali protests, mainly from Aidid supporters.[17] At UN headquarters in New York on 16 January, Colonel Bruce Osbourne, Australia's military attaché, attended a planning meeting for potential contributors to UNOSOM II. Afterward, he was left with the impression that "the U.S. is chafing at the bit to get out, while the UN is clearly dragging its feet."[18] Johnston was eager to redeploy UNITAF, but Boutros-Ghali was still worried about the UN taking over too early.

The same day as that planning meeting, US Undersecretary of State Frank Wisner chaired a conference in Washington, DC, for diplomats representing UNITAF's coalition partners. The transition from the Bush administration to the Clinton administration was under way, and Wisner assured all present that "the change in administrations will not alter our commitment to Somalia."[19] UNITAF, Wisner said, would seamlessly transition to a stronger, better-equipped UNOSOM II. Wisner's briefing was hopeful, emphasizing continued American cooperation with and support of the UN. Yet the change of administrations in January 1993 heralded a slew of new actors on the American side. Perkins was replaced by Clinton's new appointee as US ambassador to the UN, Madeleine Albright, and her first job was to negotiate the prompt handover from UNITAF to UNOSOM II. This push was heavily influenced by President Clinton's desire to leverage American influence and military power to bring an end to the ongoing Bosnian War. When it was suggested that the United States should leave Bosnia to the Europeans, Clinton's response was, "We can't do that without giving up our whole position in the world."[20] For Clinton, the Balkans represented a way to ensure the United States' continued relevance in European affairs now that the Cold War was over. To do that, the burden of Somalia needed to be shifted to the UN. As such, in one of their first encounters, Boutros-Ghali explained that the UN was not yet ready or equipped to take over, and Albright "told the Secretary General he had no choice, U.S. troops would leave whether the UN was prepared to take their place or not."[21]

Drawdown of the Unified Task Force

By any objective assessment, UNITAF had achieved its security mission and more with its deliberate forays into nation building. Getting out of Somalia quickly was now CENTCOM's priority. On 21 December 1992, two days after Boutros-Ghali communicated his two conditions for a transition to UNOSOM II, Johnston canceled the deployment of American units still scheduled to arrive in Somalia, as the threat from militias had been overestimated. A week later, before phase 2 was complete or phase 3 had even begun, Johnston's headquarters staff started planning for phase 4 of Operation Restore Hope—the eventual handover to the UN. Johnston optimistically scheduled the transfer for 20 January 1993, with the coalition withdrawing over the following ninety days.[22] This timeline did not pan out, especially as Zinni's progress indicators suggested that Mogadishu would not be ready for the UN until February at the earliest. Nevertheless, given the paucity of violence, Johnston started sending American troops home.

While Ambassador Perkins addressed the UN Security Council on 19 January, equipment and vehicles were loaded onto the MPS fleet in Mogadishu, and the 3rd Battalion, 9th Marines, left for home.[23] From February onward, the United States decreased its forces—from the bulk of two divisions, 1st Marine and 10th Mountain, to one heavy brigade from each. At the UNITAF press briefing on 19 February, Colonel Fred Peck announced that another three thousand American troops were departing Somalia. Journalists asked whether this was designed to increase pressure on the UN to take over. Peck rebuffed that suggestion, pointing out, rightly, that the force reduction was based on the stable security environment and the emergence of the ASF. Johnston similarly defended this drawdown as being a reflection of the operating environment.[24] Three days later, Morgan's infiltration of Kismayo would undermine claims of UNITAF-imposed stability. However, at the time of Peck's briefing, the first steps had been taken to establish UNITAF's successor.

On 10 February Boutros-Ghali announced that the force commander of UNOSOM II would be Turkish Lieutenant General Cevik Bir.[25] A competent officer and chief of operations on the Turkish General Staff, Bir was America's choice, not the UN's.[26] Within days of Clinton's inauguration, Undersecretary of State Wisner, who remained in his position despite serving in the Bush administration, recommended to Les Aspin, the new secretary of defense, that the force commander should "preferably [be] a Turk, who was acceptable" to the United States.[27] Given his nervousness about the UN's first peace enforcement mission, Boutros-Ghali was open to suggestions. In his first meeting with Clinton, he told the president, "The U.N. is a very weak institution. As an old Egyptian civil servant, I thought Egypt was the worst bureaucracy that existed. However, the U.N. is much worse. It needs a lot of work."[28] The Clinton administration wanted Somalia to be a successful demonstration of the new post–Cold War UN, and Boutros-Ghali was eager for the world's sole superpower to underwrite the effort. What came next was a privately orchestrated marriage of convenience. A classified memorandum to US Secretary of State Warren Christopher dated 1 February began by stating, "This is a sensitive subject . . . Boutros does *not* want to give the impression [America has] either a proxy or a veto in this area. Boutros [said] we could provide a name, provided this fact did not become public, or even known within the UN. We have suggested a Turkish three-star general, and we believe the UN will request the right man."[29]

About the choice of Bir, CENTCOM's General Hoar later said, "We wanted to get a new commander . . . and we wanted to get a Muslim; this would work better."[30] Bir's religion mattered little, as the original UN-OSOM force commander, Pakistani Brigadier Imtiaz Shaheen, was also a Muslim. What really mattered was American influence in UNOSOM II. Turkey was a NATO partner, and Bir was personally acquainted with Colin Powell, chairman of the Joint Chiefs of Staff. Furthermore, Bir's deputy was US Army Major General Thomas Montgomery, the personal choice of US Army Chief of Staff General Gordon Sullivan.[31] Despite its multinational character, beneath the UN façade, the senior military positions within UNOSOM II were either selected by the United States or filled by Americans themselves.

To get an idea of what they were in for, Bir and Montgomery traveled to Mogadishu for a briefing at UNITAF headquarters on 23 February. They were told that in all the HRSs, weapons were no longer visible on the streets, disarmament operations were progressing, and local governing councils and ASF detachments had been established. All HRSs were stable and ready for UNOSOM II. The sole remaining concern was the small risk of bandits attacking unescorted relief convoys. There were two exceptions to this otherwise glowing report. The new leadership duo was warned that although half of Mogadishu was "stable" and the other half "fair," the Murusade were a "wildcard" that "will not honor [the] ceasefire, [and] will attempt to regain territory."[32] In Kismayo, the difficulties with Morgan and Jess were laid bare, as the violent infiltration of that city had happened only twenty-four hours ago. Nevertheless, Bir and Montgomery were assured that Somalia was ready for UNOSOM II. The timing of their visit could not have been worse, coinciding with the Aidid-inspired protests in the wake of the Kismayo raid and the firefight caused by the Murusade at the K-4 Circle. As Johnston was persuading the pair to take ownership of Somalia, Montgomery recalled "smoke from burning tires wafted through the room and a machine gun on the roof fired a burst at a suspected sniper across the street."[33]

The raid on Kismayo, and its aftermath in Mogadishu, again brought Boutros-Ghali's wariness to the fore. He argued that UNITAF had *not* created a secure environment, writing, "It was the uniqueness of the situation in Somalia that led to the adoption of Resolution 794 by the Security Council . . . I must emphasize that the unique features of the situation continue to prevail. There is still no effective functioning government in the country. There is still no organized civilian police force. There is still no disciplined national armed force . . . the atmosphere of lawlessness and tension is far from being eliminated."[34]

Instead of using Kismayo and Mogadishu to delay the transition, which was now an inevitability, Boutros-Ghali crafted a disclaimer in case the new operation did not live up to its potential. "UNOSOM II," he wrote, "[will] be the first operation of its kind to be authorized by the international community. . . . The task ahead [will] not be easy. UNOSOM II might frequently come under criticism for acts of omission or commission."[35] The secretary-general hinted that despite their best attempts, Somalia could regress into chaotic violence. After all, UNITAF covered only 40 percent of the country, whereas UNOSOM II would have to encompass its entirety to enforce the cease-fire and continue the disarmament campaign until a newly organized national army could be created. Unlike UNITAF's security mission, UNOSOM II would have to manage governmental and political rehabilitation. Somalia as a nation needed to be rebuilt.

Because of this herculean task, Boutros-Ghali claimed in a report to the Security Council in March, UNOSOM II "will not be able to implement the above mandate unless it is endowed with enforcement powers under Chapter VII of the Charter."[36] The lack of consent could not hamper UNOSOM II, as it had its peacekeeping predecessor. Boutros-Ghali was now arguing that the UN should mount its first ever peace enforcement mission under Article 42 in Somalia, with a mandate for nation building—precisely what he had complained the United States was pressuring the UN to do in January. The only difference was that, by March, UNITAF was drawing down, and the UN had no choice but to take over. It was a monumental task that had potential but was also fraught with risk, and the secretary-general knew it.

The Addis Ababa Agreement: A Framework
for Somalia's Future

There was one major development in March 1993 that allayed fears of Somalia sliding back into anarchy, and that was significant progress in reconciling the disparate factions. Under the original UNOSOM-UNITAF division of labor, the former was responsible for political and national reconciliation efforts. With that purview, Boutros-Ghali had invited fourteen factions, including Aidid's and Ali Mahdi's wings of the USC, to a UN-sponsored meeting in Addis Ababa on 4–5 January 1993 (Addis I). The UN sought factional cooperation to develop a framework for Somali national reconciliation and to schedule a formal conference to crystalize it.[37] Ismat Kittani urged all faction leaders to attend. Aidid initially refused, citing the litany of UN transgressions the previous year and the oft-repeated conspiracy theories surrounding Boutros-Ghali's support of Siad Barre during the secretary-general's tenure as Egypt's foreign minister. In the end, the SNA leader agreed to attend not because of Kittani's entreaties but because of Oakley's. Eager for the UN to take over, Bush's presidential envoy convinced Aidid to tone down the rhetoric, emphasizing that the UN was there to stay. If Aidid wanted a seat at the table, he needed to cooperate. Torn between believing the UN favored Ali Mahdi and not wanting to be left out in the cold, Aidid agreed to attend because Addis I was only a noncommittal "preparatory" meeting.[38]

Addis I was far more productive than anyone anticipated. Scheduled to last just two days, it went on for eleven. Unexpectedly, the representatives of the fourteen factions became so thoroughly engrossed in cross-party meetings that they did not want to stop talking. Addis I resulted in three encouraging agreements signed by all factions: the seven-point agreement, the cease-fire and disarmament agreement, and the scheduling of a National Reconciliation Conference (Addis II).[39] Under the seven-point agreement, signed personally by Aidid, Omar Jess, Hersi Morgan, and Ali Mahdi's representative, all factions committed to an immediate countrywide cease-fire and agreed to cooperate with all international organizations inside and outside Somalia, allow the free movement of peoples throughout the country, and establish mechanisms for cross-faction dialogue at Addis II.[40] With the cease-fire and disarmament agreement, all factions acquiesced to the cantonment of heavy weapons under UNITAF or UNOSOM II supervision and agreed that all militias would withdraw from cities and towns until a process was established for their disarmament and eventual demobilization.[41] As for Addis II, Mogadishu was originally suggested as the venue, but damage to the city made Addis Ababa a more appropriate choice.[42]

On 15 March 1993 Addis II commenced, sponsored by the UN and chaired by Guinean Ambassador Lansana Kouyate. In scope and attendance, Addis II dwarfed January's preparatory meeting. In addition to UN and international delegates, nearly eight hundred Somalis convened to determine what their future government should look like. These delegates were not limited to the principal factions. Of the 250 official representatives, 119 came from the factions, 80 were religious and community leaders, and 51 were nonpolitical delegates representing various Somali business, intellectual, and women's advocacy groups.[43] Anyone who had a stake in the future had a seat at the table.

The delegates also understood that the specifics of UNOSOM II were being finalized, including its mission, size, and duration. Ahead of Addis II, Boutros-Ghali had communicated to all participants that the conference was a critical opportunity for them to take ownership of their country. If Addis II did not yield tangible results, the UN would have no choice but to impose a trusteeship on the nation. The message was crystal clear: either the Somalis stepped up and worked together, or the UN would govern Somalia.[44] With the consequences of failure clearly defined, the delegates galvanized to ensure that Addis II was a success, and it was.

The two-week conference saw all factions renew their commitment to the cease-fire and disarmament, but the keystone was the Addis Ababa Agreement.[45] During the deliberations and negotiations, an impasse developed surrounding how much power should be concentrated in Mogadishu under any new government. Aidid and the SNA argued for a strong central government with legislative and executive powers and with regional and district governance based on candidates elected from the factions. Most other factions, hypersensitive to anything reminiscent of Barre, wanted a weaker central government and elections based on clans, not factions. Kouyate on behalf of the UN and President Meles Zenawi of Ethiopia tried to broker a compromise, but by 27 March, no breakthrough was forthcoming. Kouyate and Zenawi both decreed that if no agreement was reached that night, the conference would end and all the factions would lose credibility with UNOSOM II. Delegates from the Somali women's groups suggested to Kouyate that the faction representatives be locked in a room until they reached an agreement. It worked.[46]

The resulting Addis Ababa Agreement, signed on 27 March 1993, mandated a pseudo-federal three-tier system of governance based on district and regional councils under an interim Transitional National Council (TNC).[47] The TNC would reestablish and manage new organs of civil administration and act as a caretaker until a national government could be established within two years. In practice, the TNC would consist of seventy-four council seats as the top tier of governance for the entire country, not just the southern portion. Even though Somaliland had declared independence, there was hope that the SNM would rejoin the new nation. Filling the seats was based on a simple process that focused on broad clan and factional representation. The 1990 administrative map of Somalia had eighteen administrative regions, each of them subdivided into districts. Under the Addis Ababa Agreement, each district would elect twenty-one members to create a district council. Each district council would then select three of its elected members to form a regional council. In turn, each regional council would appoint three of its members to the TNC. In a move encouraged by Kouyate, Oakley, and Boutros-Ghali, the agreement required that at least one of the three members sent to the TNC from each regional council be a woman. The eighteen regional councils would thus fill fifty-four of the TNC's seventy-four seats. For the remaining twenty, each faction was allotted one seat, giving them national representation without the ability to overpower regional interests. The final five seats were reserved for representatives of Mogadishu, as the nation's capital.[48]

Although the Addis Ababa Agreement was light on the finer details of implementation and left several matters still to be clarified, it afforded a two-year period to establish the regional and district councils and the TNC and put Somalia on the road to national and political reconstruction. The text of the agreement exemplified the hopes and aspirations for the future. Its conclusion stated, "Emerging from the darkness of catastrophe and war, we Somalis herald the beginning of a new era of peace. . . . It is a message we must pass on to our children, and our grandchildren, that the proud Somali family . . . can once again become whole."[49]

There was one disturbance during Addis II. On 16 March the SPM-Harti, allied with Morgan's SNF, took control of Kismayo, despite the presence of UNITAF's Belgian contingent. Most of the urban population was SPM-Harti, and they managed to push out the small remaining pockets of Jess supporters in a sudden coup de main not nearly as violent as the February incursion.[50] Aidid insisted that Addis II be paused so he could return to Kismayo to investigate what had happened. In Oakley's view, the SNA leader was concerned that UNITAF had somehow colluded with Morgan, and he thought Aidid was posturing to improve his political position at the conference.[51] However, Aidid returned on 22 March, in time to play a pivotal role in the proceedings.

Throughout the conference, Kouyate and Zenawi played the role of mediators. But the unlikely voice of compromise and conciliation when political issues seemed intractable was Aidid. Usually immoveable to the point of violence, Aidid displayed his skills as a former ambassador and worked hard to show his potential as a statesman. Even before the conference, he had convinced his SNA allies to allow community leaders, academics, and women's rights groups to participate.[52] Critically, as interim president of Somalia—an office still not recognized by many of the factions—Ali Mahdi could not be a signatory to the Addis Ababa Agreement. Instead, the chairman of his faction, Mohamed Qanyare Afrah, signed on behalf of the USC. Afrah was a Murusade, though, meaning that the agreement had no Abgal signatories. In a stunning move, recognizing that the largest Hawiye subclan needed to be represented and the consequences of exclusion avoided, a charismatic Aidid convinced all the signatories to guarantee his longtime rival a seat on the TNC. That gesture inspired Ali Mahdi to warmly embrace Aidid before all those present. Kouyate called Aidid "one of the strongest supporters to the Agreement" and central to the success of the conference. In fact, the SNA leader was awarded the privilege of delivering the closing address.[53] If Aidid's brand had been tarnished by the February violence in Mogadishu, Addis II brought him back into favor by March.

Opinions on the significance of the Addis Ababa Agreement differed among UN officials who attended the conference. Leonard Kapungu, UNOSOM II's director of political affairs, was cynical, writing, "There is no doubt that all of them . . . meant what they pledged. But when they . . . settle back in their clan-oriented environment, it is doubtful whether they would resist looking at Somalia through the personal and clan lenses they are so much accustomed of doing."[54] Kouyate was optimistic, dismissing the pessimism and cynicism of those like Kapungu, who thought the factions should not have dominated the negotiations. Kouyate wrote that, like it or not, the goal of Addis II was national reconciliation, and the factions "are the largest political unit of the Somali national base . . . reconciliation will have to start somewhere. The Addis Ababa Agreement is certainly an encouraging start."[55] Collectively, the signatories now entrusted UNOSOM II to oversee the agreement's implementation. The goal was ambitious: the creation of a national government by February 1995.

UNOSOM II's Mission: Nation Building

Going forward, the mission in Somalia was unequivocally nation building. Despite Powell's later criticism that the UN dragged the United States down that path, he was well aware of it at the time and made no objections. As far back as the November 1992 Deputies Committee meetings that decided the United States should intervene, the State Department wanted the UN to nation-build in Somalia.[56] Then, on 5 January 1993, just weeks after UNITAF arrived, Army Chief of Staff General Gordon Sullivan wrote to Powell: "We must continue to do all in our power to encourage the United Nations to assume control of the situation . . . to get them *into the nation building business.*"[57] At the time, Powell acquiesced. It was only years after he retired—a week before the disastrous Battle of Mogadishu—that he suddenly took a post hoc revisionist approach.

The newly empowered Clinton administration was also fully behind the nation-building effort in Somalia. Anthony Lake, Clinton's national security adviser, saw UNOSOM II's mission as an experiment in how to use military power to establish a semblance of a stable country.[58] In March 1993 Ambassador David Shinn testified before the House Committee on Armed Services and said, "We expect to use [American] influence to encourage the rebuilding of political institutions at the local, regional, and national levels simultaneously."[59] Even Clinton's remarks from the White House lawn on 5 May expressed these same sentiments. UNOSOM II, he said, "is a reflection of the new era we have entered, for it has Americans participating in new ways."[60] So enamored was Clinton with UNITAF's success that in a briefing with Johnston, Zinni, and Powell, he asked how many of these operations the US military could do simultaneously. Zinni recalled that "Powell . . . jumped back a little, . . . like 'oh god, [Clinton's] gonna turn us into humanitarian warriors or something.'"[61] For the United States, Somalia was going to demonstrate to the world what a new, robust post–Cold War UN could achieve.

That the United States fully endorsed the nation-building mission is evidenced by American efforts to ensure that its candidates were appointed to leadership positions in UNOSOM II. Both Force Commander Bir and his deputy, Montgomery, were US choices. Allegedly, the initial non-American choice for deputy force commander faked a heart attack to enable Montgomery's appointment.[62] The political leadership of UNOSOM II was just as Americanized. Ismat Kittani, the terse UN special representative to Somalia, had cancer, and speculation was rife about who would replace him. "Whoever takes his job," Keith Richburg wrote in the *Washington Post*, "will need the same mix of toughness and personal diplomacy that Oakley has shown to be effective here."[63] The top UN choice to replace Kittani was Guinean Ambassador Lansana Kouyate (who would go on to chair Addis II), but a classified memo to Clinton's national security adviser said it was "essential that an American fill this position."[64] Again, American influence was mobilized in support of their preferred candidate. Based on Lake's personal recommendation, Clinton offered the position of UN special representative to Somalia to retired US Navy Admiral Jonathan Howe. His formal appointment was announced on 5 March 1993, and Kouyate was named his deputy.[65]

Before retiring in 1992, Howe had enjoyed a successful thirty-five-year naval career, but it is unclear what made him the preferred candidate as the political and diplomatic head of UNOSOM II. He spent half his service on submarines, destroyers, and cruisers and the other half as a military adviser in the Washington, DC, bureaucracy, including a stint as assistant to the chairman of the Joint Chiefs of Staff in 1987–89. Howe's last assignment was a dual role as NATO commander in chief for Allied Forces Southern Europe and commander of US Naval Forces Europe. He then became Bush's deputy national security adviser, presiding over the Deputies Committee meetings that endorsed Operation Restore Hope. Howe was not a diplomat and had no expertise in either nation-building operations or working with the UN. Despite these shortcomings and his previous position in a Republican administration, Howe was headhunted for the special representative job by Clinton's national security adviser.[66]

Opinions on Howe were polarized. He would later be described variously as a "dedicated and selfless public servant" and a "kind of real-life Dr. Strangelove."[67] In his memoirs, Boutros-Ghali described him as "unfailingly calm and openly cooperative toward everyone. I never regretted my decision to make Howe my special representative for Somalia."[68]

This was painfully diplomatic praise for someone who had essentially been foisted on UNOSOM II. Journalist Scott Peterson was probably most accurate, describing Howe as a "too-polite career military man and born-again Christian whose appointment was described by one American official as 'the miscasting of the century.'"[69]

In fairness to Boutros-Ghali, he did not simply bend under US pressure to appoint Bir, Montgomery, and Howe. There was a quid pro quo. At a February meeting with the UN secretary-general, US Secretary of State Warren Christopher made an offer. "We are prepared to make a significant contribution," Christopher said, "contingent on achieving a satisfactory UN Security Council resolution . . . for a successful UNOSOM II force, and assurances that the UN will pursue the humanitarian and political tracks as I have outlined. If [we] obtain your assurances in these areas, the U.S. is prepared to contribute in three areas."[70]

First, the US Army would provide a quick reaction force (QRF) for UNOSOM II—a strategic reserve ready to react to any violence that occurred. This QRF comprised an army light infantry battalion, an aviation battalion of transport and attack helicopters, and support units. Initially, the QRF was supposed to be maintained offshore, but the French government refused to keep ground troops in Somalia unless the United States did the same.[71] This was the main reason Montgomery was appointed UNOSOM II's deputy force commander, as he was also the commander of all US forces in Somalia. Howe recalled that Montgomery's appointment was "a mechanism that served the purpose of making the U.S. comfortable with the arrangement for the [US] forces that were left behind."[72] If American troops engaged in combat, the Pentagon wanted an American in command.

But it was not as clear-cut as Montgomery simply commanding US combat units. While Bir commanded UNOSOM II, any action taken by the QRF had to be cleared with CENTCOM beforehand. Hoar thus retained "final approval 'authority' for all command decisions involving US forces."[73] Montgomery was "authorized to make the executive decision," but only in situations "that exceed the capability of UNOSOM II . . . and require emergency employment of immediate combat power for a limited period or for show of force operations."[74] This arrangement created two separate chains of command: one from Bir to the UN forces under his control, and one from CENTCOM, through Montgomery, to US forces. Though Montgomery nominally reported to Bir as UNOSOM II's force commander, when it came to the QRF, Hoar was the gatekeeper.

Second, Christopher offered "staff support for this peacekeeping operation."[75] CENTCOM seconded forty-seven staff officers to serve at Bir's force headquarters. Bir's assistant, press officer, head of operations, and deputy heads of the intelligence, logistics, and communications staffs were all American officers.[76] In addition, military planners were sent to bolster the staff in the Peacekeeping Department at UN headquarters in New York.

Third, given the US military's unsurpassed logistical capabilities and the UN's complete lack thereof, Christopher assigned a US Army Area Support Group calling itself the UN Logistics Support Command to manage UNOSOM II's logistics. All this support, Christopher said, would "provide a strong signal of U.S. commitment to UNOSOM's success."[77]

Large numbers of American troops had never served in a UN-led operation, but now nearly four thousand were participating in UNOSOM II under what was called Operation Continue Hope. Hoar at CENTCOM had wanted a complete US withdrawal, but maintaining forces in Somalia was part of the compromise to entice Boutros-Ghali into a speedy transition.[78] It was an offer he could not refuse.

UNOSOM II's Structure and Composition

When the call went out, there was no shortage of nations volunteering for UNOSOM II, largely due to UNITAF's success.[79] Nineteen of the coalition's twenty-one participants opted to remain in Somalia as part of UNOSOM II. Australia and Canada agreed to stay, but with much smaller commitments. Both countries had contributed well over a thousand personnel to UNITAF, but Australia provided only a movement control platoon for UNOSOM II, and Canada sent just five staff officers for its force headquarters. Due to their progressive approach in Baidoa, the Australians were considered a serious loss. US Vice President Al Gore and General Colin Powell personally approached Australia's Foreign Affairs Minister Gareth Evans and asked the Australians to remain in Somalia. The Baidoans themselves asked the Australians to stay. The Rahanweyn SDM in Baidoa proposed that if Hurley's troops missed their families, the locals would gladly welcome them to the city and house them. But Evans would not budge. The Australians were already involved in six UN operations, and the government had promised to reduce overseas deployments.[80]

Other coalition members that stayed with UNOSOM II increased their commitment. India, which had provided only a naval task force for UNITAF, offered an infantry brigade of five thousand, instantly becoming UNOSOM II's largest troop contributor.[81] Pakistan was a close second. Indo-Pakistani relations were tense, as both countries were locked in the long-simmering Siachen War in Kashmir. Tensions were so high that the Indian enthusiasm to commit to UNOSOM II was initially tempered by Pakistani propaganda that "Hindus will be shooting" Muslims in Somalia.[82] It was therefore decided that the Indian brigade would deploy much later, in September 1993. Though deadlocked in Kashmir, these two countries left their differences behind and cooperated frequently during their shared deployment to Somalia.

Joining the slew of old faces in Somalia were some new ones. Bangladesh, South Korea, Norway, Malaysia, Nepal, Romania, Ireland, and, most notably, Germany participated in UNOSOM II. In the newly reunified Germany, UNOSOM II prompted a fierce constitutional debate on the contentious issue of military deployments outside of Europe. The German Basic Law, or *Grundgesetz*, allowed military deployments only for mutual security alliances, such as NATO commitments, or for overt humanitarian operations. This had prevented German Chancellor Helmut Kohl and his Christian Democratic Union (CDU) government from sending a token naval force to the Gulf War. Kohl and the CDU wanted to open a new chapter of multilateralism with a foreign policy of "never again alone." Deploying the German armed forces, the *Bundeswehr*, on military operations outside continental Europe thus became an attractive foreign policy tool.[83]

Kohl started with small deployments to overtly humanitarian missions in Kurdistan under Operation Provide Comfort and with the UN in Cambodia. Then Kohl pledged 1,640 troops to Somalia, the first German deployment abroad with a mandate to use force since the end of the Second World War. The CDU logic underpinning Kohl's pledge was that if the Basic Law allowed military deployments under the auspices of mutual security alliances, enforcing a UN resolution should be just as legal as participating in NATO. Challenges by German opposition parties, principally the Social Democratic Party and the Free Democratic Party, failed in the Constitutional Court, which supported the CDU's legal interpretation and claimed that German credibility would be damaged if Kohl reneged on his pledge. It was perhaps not a coincidence that three days after pledging these troops, Kohl and the CDU applied for Germany to have a seat on the UN Security Council, causing further criticism from opposition parties. Nevertheless, the *Bundeswehr* was going to Somalia.[84]

Bir and Montgomery were leading a force of twenty-eight thousand troops in five brigades, plus a logistics support group. An additional twenty-eight hundred civilian staff worked in administrative divisions dealing with political affairs, humanitarian relief, judicial reform, and police support.[85] Despite being ten thousand personnel lighter than UNITAF, UNOSOM II had slightly more combat power. Johnston's coalition had twenty-nine battalion-sized combat units; UNOSOM II had thirty-four. UNITAF had included a substantial amount of service and support units, but the improved infrastructure in Somalia meant that UNOSOM II could forgo large medical and engineering units.

Three of the five brigades would replace coalition forces in Mogadishu, Kismayo, and Baidoa; the remaining two would expand outside UNITAF's area of operations, into Galkayo and Somaliland. The new force was numerically smaller than its predecessor but was expected to cover the entire country. This was justified, given that the size of UNITAF had been based on an estimated threat that never materialized on the ground. In addition, the ASF had now been established. As Johnston pointed out, it took a lot more troops to establish security than to maintain it.[86] In principle, UNOSOM II should be able to do more with less. In keeping with the Addis Ababa Agreement, control of Somalia would be transferred to civilian governmental institutions once they were rebuilt, and then UNOSOM II would depart, leaving behind a functioning state.[87]

UN Resolution 814: The "Mother of All Resolutions"

On 26 March 1993, the day before Aidid and Ali Mahdi embraced in Addis Ababa, the UN made history. The Security Council was rife with enthusiasm for a proposal later termed the "mother of all resolutions." Resolution 814, just like the resolution underpinning UNITAF, had been specifically crafted and drafted in the Pentagon by policymakers in the State and Defense Departments.[88] In discussing Resolution 814, all members were vocally supportive of UNOSOM II and of the UN's unprecedented action to implement the Addis Ababa Agreement. Ambassador Pedauye of Spain noted, "The exceptional nature of the situation in Somalia . . . has made necessary the adoption of equally exceptional measures . . . this operation is without precedent . . . its proposed objectives are as laudable as they are ambitious."[89]

It was Madeleine Albright, though, who really summed up the watershed moment. The United States, she said,

> has been pleased to join . . . a military mission of mercy unprecedented in size or purpose . . . we will embark on an unprecedented enterprise aimed at nothing less than the restoration of an entire country as a proud, functioning, and viable member of the community of nations. This is a historic undertaking. We are excited to join it and we will vigorously support it. . . . We are soberly conscious of the fact that this . . . engages the world community *to provide the most comprehensive assistance ever given to any country, but . . . with few lessons and no models to guide our path.*[90]

Resolution 814 passed unanimously and with much aplomb, authorizing UNOSOM II under Article 42 of the UN Charter to nation-build with a Chapter VII peace enforcement mandate.[91] The UN was now empowered to be the trailblazer of post–Cold War idealism regarding the utility of military power in situations other than war. And that trail would be blazed in Somalia.

From its inception, UNOSOM II was unprecedented in almost every way. It was the largest UN mission in terms of personnel, though it would soon be surpassed by the UN Protection Force's thirty-nine thousand-strong operation in Bosnia and Croatia during the Yugoslav wars. It was the first UN-led Chapter VII peace enforcement mission and the first time US, German, or Indian troops had served under UN command in large numbers.[92] By 1993, UNOSOM II amounted to the largest and most ambitious deliberate nation-building operation in history. All that was left was for Howe and Bir's force to take over from UNITAF.

The Operational Transition: UNITAF to UNOSOM II

In Mogadishu, Johnston and Zinni were anxious for the handover, especially as some elements of UNITAF were not remaining as part of UNOSOM II. Chief among them was the US Marine Corps, as Operation Continue Hope was a US Army commitment. Johnson was particularly annoyed at what he considered the UN's lethargy. "Christ," he raged, "they've known they were coming to Somalia for eight months."[93] UN-

OSOM II's chief of staff, Canadian Brigadier General James Cox, met with UNITAF's operations team in March. Afterward, marine Colonel Brian Egan told Johnston that UNOSOM "won't have all the stuff we need here as fast as we'd hoped. . . . As this is the first operation under Chapter VII of the charter, the UN . . . is having a hard time accepting the early primacy of military operations. They haven't done anything like this before."[94] As March became April, UNOSOM II's personnel trickled rather than poured into Somalia, with the ultimate handover date set as 4 May 1993.[95]

To ensure a smooth transition, the 24th Marine Expeditionary Unit (MEU) aboard the USS *Wasp* Amphibious Ready Group arrived off the coast just as Resolution 814 passed. Its mission was to demonstrate the ongoing American commitment to Somalia and send a clear message to UNITAF's problem area, Kismayo. To remind all factions that the US military still had freedom of movement and could reach any potential adversary, Colonel Matthew Broderick, the MEU commander, landed a marine company in Kismayo that then marched 180 kilometers to Morgan's camp at Dhoobley, just to show the SNF that it could. Broderick then undertook a similar march to Jess's camp at Jilib. Heliborne raids to conduct weapons sweeps were carried out in towns and villages across the HRS, and the Jubba River saw intensive marine operations. For three weeks, Broderick alternated his demonstrations of force between Morgan and Jess. The SPM and SNF were on notice: US forces were not picking sides, and transgressors could be struck with impunity. Broderick and the 24th MEU met no resistance and steamed for the Persian Gulf in late April, assuming that its message had been received and understood.[96]

With Somalia just two weeks away from belonging to Howe and UN-OSOM II, US Ambassador Sheldon Krys outlined what Howe should focus on as UN special representative. Successful nation building, Krys said, depended not only on UNOSOM II but also on the Somalis themselves. Specifically, he encouraged Howe to get the judicial system back online and to build on the progress made by the Australians in Baidoa. UNOSOM II should "identify geographical areas with highest likelihood of an early return to acceptance of, and reliance upon, a judicial system. Allocate resources to those areas first."[97] Krys suggested that Howe's staff establish a Public Affairs Office to get the Somalis on board and to emphasize the "seamless transition" from UNITAF and demonstrate that "the power of enforcement is undiminished."[98] But most important, he reminded Howe that Somalia represented a test of the post–Cold War UN.[99]

Visiting Somalia on 6 April, Colin Powell said "no" when journalists asked if he saw any problems with the transition. Elaborating, he said, "I don't think the people of Somalia will see much change." The only difference the chairman of the Joint Chiefs identified was that Bir "will be more into nation building than we were."[100] He was only half right. France, Italy, and Belgium were staying, so HRSs Oddur, Gialalassi, and Kismayo would see no changes. As the Canadians and Australians were leaving, the Italians and French moved into Beledweyne and Baidoa, respectively, serving as placeholders until the newly participating German and Indian contingents arrived. The only delays were in Bardera and Mogadishu, occupied by the US Marine Corps, which would be leaving. The transition would not be complete until troops arrived to relieve them.[101]

In practical terms, as Colonel Brian Egan explained, "The way we're going to do it is once the entire UNOSOM staff gets here, gets up and running, we will spend probably a week working side-by-side [in the headquarters] and then one morning we just won't come to work."[102] This desk-sharing plan was frustrating for some, as Johnston's headquarters was staffed almost completely by Americans who were used to working a certain way. They were now trying to hand over their duties to Bir's staff from more than a dozen countries with different staff processes and training standards. As an example, during the drafting of UNOSOM II's rules of engagement, determining the circumstances in which deadly force was authorized fell to a Belgian officer with no legal experience.[103]

By 23 April, only 28 percent of UNOSOM II's twenty-eight thousand troops had arrived.[104] The Indian brigade was not scheduled to arrive until September, and several other contingents, including the Irish, Germans, and Malaysians, would be deploying over the summer. Despite troops shortfalls, General Bir was confident that he had enough forces in place to maintain the secure environment. Out of concern, though, Howe asked Johnston and Zinni whether UNITAF could remain until June. The answer was an unequivocal no. The 4 May date had been set, UNITAF had achieved its mission, and staying longer would require a new mission authorized by the president. Clinton had already committed to support UNOSOM II, and UNITAF would not stay beyond the agreed date.[105]

Luckily for Howe, the stability UNITAF brought to Somalia, reinforced in Kismayo by the 24th MEU, provided a benign environment that forgave UNOSOM II's slow arrival. On 10 April the US Army's 10th Mountain Division formally established elements of its 1st Brigade as UNOSOM II's QRF. Based in Mogadishu, they were poised to be air-lifted anywhere in the country if necessary.[106] On 26 April, at a ceremony attended by Johnston, Howe, and Bir, Colonel Buck Bedard formally transferred responsibility for Mogadishu from the US Marine Corps to Brigadier Ikram ul Hasan's Pakistani brigade from UNOSOM II.[107] The Unified Task Force was leaving Somalia.

The Somalia UNITAF Gave to UNOSOM II

On the eve of UNOSOM II's takeover, the key question is, what did the Somalia it inherited look like? UNITAF's final situation report on 21 April 1993 stated: "The situation as the UN prepares to assume control has changed. The factions that paralyzed and virtually destroyed Somalia have been largely neutralized. This was done through negotiation from strength, backed by a willingness to use force in response to unaccept-able acts . . . the factional political and military leaders are negotiating and working out points of agreement . . . long suppressed community leaders are emerging."[108] Mogadishu was now the busiest airport on the African continent. Gunshot wounds in the capital had decreased from fifty a day to five. Sacks of wheat had dropped in price from $100 to $7, while an AK-47 that cost $50 in November 1992 had skyrocketed to $1,000.[109] In Beledweyne, the Canadians reported that they had "virtu-ally ended all of the violence and the countryside is now stable enough that crops are being planted and there are no food shortages to speak of."[110] UNITAF had transformed Somalia. In his final report, Johnston concluded that the coalition "provided the shock and power to force rapid change. Forward momentum is established. Now the stage is set for rapid political, social, and cultural advancement."[111]

As April turned to May, UNITAF dissolved as contingents departed or were integrated into UNOSOM II. Howe and Bir were now respon-sible for the most ambitious nation-building operation in history. The aim was a functioning Somali government by February 1995. As Howe recalled, "Optimistically we were hoping we could meet the goal that the Somalis themselves had established in the Addis Ababa accords."[112] The mission, specifically crafted in the Pentagon, was known to all, with few dissenters. The UN did not suck anyone into nation building; it was a course specifically and collectively charted, including by the United States. As UNOSOM took over, Powell's advice to Montgomery was to avoid making Somalia an "American show," but do not allow it to fail.[113]

The last members of UNITAF to depart were Generals Johnston and Zinni. To the sounds of Pakistani bagpipers and drummers, both men attended a short ceremony on 4 May at the US embassy compound in Mogadishu as Johnston's personal three-star flag was lowered and replaced by the UN flag, officially marking the end of UNITAF and the ascendancy of UNOSOM II. Johnston briefly addressed the crowd, commenting on the success of Operation Restore Hope. He then turned to Bir and said, "It's all yours."[114] Before parting ways, Bir asked Johnston for his thoughts on what threats UNOSOM II could expect to face. At most, Johnston responded, protests would be the worst of it.[115] With that, the UNITAF commanding general and his director of operations headed for Mogadishu airport. On the way, Zinni recalled that Johnston stopped their Humvee, got out, looked around, and said, "I give it thirty days and it will all come apart."[116]

Just thirty-two days later, on 5 June 1993, violence erupted between the SNA and UNOSOM II. It marked the start of a war that would culminate months later in the Battle of Mogadishu. The question is why.

7 | 5 June 1993

I am deeply disturbed and outraged by the unnecessary death of so many Somalis and UN troops last Saturday.
—Mohamed Farah Aidid, SNA leader[1]

It was very clear to us that it was Aidid.
—Admiral Jonathan Howe, UNOSOM II special representative[2]

If you hate someone you should not allow it to affect policy—the UN's credibility is at stake.
—Mohamed Hassan Awale, senior SNA official[3]

Without investigation, blame for the attacks of 5 June was laid on the USC/SNA.
—UN Commission of Inquiry, February 1994[4]

On 5 June 1993 Pakistani units from UNOSOM II inspected five weapons cantonments belonging to Aidid's SNA militia in Mogadishu. Returning to base along 21 October Road, a company of the 10th Battalion, Baloch Regiment, was caught in the open when the streets around their convoy erupted in gunfire. Heavy machine guns and rocket-propelled grenades (RPGs) tore into the soft-skinned vehicles and their occupants, many of whom wore no body armor. A mile away, another squad from the Baloch Regiment was attacked by a mob of men, women, and children. Twenty-five Pakistanis were killed, fifty-seven were wounded, and ten were missing. Some victims reportedly had their eyes gouged out or their limbs severed; one peacekeeper's testicles were cut off.[5] It was a shocking slaughter of those who had come to help Somalia rebuild, and this attack marked the beginning of a campaign of violence in Mogadishu between UNOSOM II and the United States on one side and Aidid's SNA on the other.

In the historiography of the intervention, the events of 5 June are

188 | CHAPTER 7

infamous. Nearly all works present Aidid as the personal architect, with authors proposing various hypotheses to explain his motivations.[6] In *The Effort to Save Somalia*, Walter Poole wrote that Aidid was "evidently worried" that UNOSOM was undercutting his ambition for power.[7] The US Forces Somalia after-action report argued that "Aideed had little respect for [UNOSOM]."[8] Even though he had left Somalia by then, Oakley suggested that UNOSOM's weakness compared to UNITAF "sent a message of irresolution to Aideed [which he] took as an opportunity."[9] A rushed and flawed investigation by Professor Tom Farer on behalf of the UN concluded that the passivity of the original UNOSOM operation in 1992 led Aidid to believe that the "risks [of attacking] . . . appeared acceptable."[10] Others have argued that Aidid believed UNOSOM intended to use the weapons inspections to destroy or shut down Radio Mogadishu, the SNA's propaganda station.[11] Although one author argued that the radio station's proximity to an AWSS was mere "chance," it was undoubtedly the UN's target on 5 June.[12]

Most of these works follow Mark Bowden's characterization of Aidid as "a clever and ruthless killer," nothing more than a warlord on a bloody quest for personal power.[13] In a few cases, the Pakistanis conducting the inspection are blamed specifically, and the UN more broadly. General Hoar at CENTCOM incorrectly claimed the Pakistanis inspected the AWSS without giving prior notice to the SNA.[14] For his part, Oakley blamed the UN, suggesting—again incorrectly—that the inspections had been ordered by "the UN military side without consulting the UN political side."[15] Likewise, an account by the US Army Center of Military History noted that "UNOSOM II" decided to conduct the inspections.[16]

The dominant narrative surrounding the events of 5 June is deeply flawed. There is little analysis of the weeks preceding the outbreak of violence. The Pakistani troops are presented as the sole actors, and the UN is treated as a monolithic entity in which the role of individual decision makers is ignored, particularly the Americans leading UNOSOM II. Jonathan Howe, its political head, was a retired US Navy admiral and former deputy national security adviser in the Bush administration. The force commander was the American-backed Turkish Lieutenant General Cevik Bir, and Bir's deputy was US Army Major General Thomas Montgomery. Although most narratives mention only the Pakistanis, American personnel were part of the inspection team sent to Radio Mogadishu on 5 June.

In the traditional story of Somalia, the events of 5 June are presented as an unprovoked attack on UN peacekeepers. However, from the moment UNOSOM II took over from UNITAF on 4 May 1993, tensions with the SNA escalated because of several incidents that put the two sides on a collision course. Avoidable miscalculations, misinterpretations, and poor decision making raised the temperature to boiling point in Mogadishu, and on 5 June the city boiled over. The violence was not inevitable. Contextualizing why 5 June happened requires not only an understanding of the events leading up to it but also a recognition that Aidid may not have orchestrated the attacks at all.

The First Clash: The Addis Ababa Addendum

The first sign of friction between the political factions and UNOSOM emerged in April, before the handover from UNITAF, and it concerned the Addis Ababa Agreement. That framework for the future Somali government, agreed to by all factions on 27 March, was the guiding light for UNOSOM's nation-building mission. However, in two key areas it lacked specificity on how certain provisions would be met. Under the agreement, district councils would be formed, and selected members would then form regional councils. Each of these regional councils would send three delegates to the Transitional National Council. The problem was that the Addis Ababa Agreement did not specify how these regional councils would choose their three candidates for the TNC. For this reason, even though the Addis II conference concluded on 27 March, all the signatories remained for several days and signed a second agreement on 30 March.[17] In this addendum, all the signatories agreed that the factions would select the three TNC candidates from the regional councils. Furthermore, the factions would establish a committee to draft a charter setting out the guiding principles of the TNC, to be approved once that body was formed.

There was nothing secret or nefarious about this second agreement. It was, for all intents and purposes, the signatories' attempt to clarify the process. It recognized that each district and regional council would undoubtedly reflect the locality's clan or faction composition. The addendum sought to ensure consistency in the selection of TNC members and to provide a mechanism if any regional council with a mixture of clan or faction representatives became stalemated when selecting candidates. In that case, the factions would "iron out their differences" in Addis Ababa. As for the TNC charter, the Addis Ababa Agreement stated that the charter would be written after the TNC was formed. Arguably, this was doing things backward, so the leaders decided to draft the guiding principles of future Somali governance before that government was created. In some quarters, it was thought that this addendum gave the factions more influence on the process of government formation, but it was accepted by the same leaders who had signed the Addis Ababa Agreement, and these signatories were the political representatives of their clans and subclans.

Like the Addis Ababa Agreement, this addendum should have been seen as an encouraging sign of factional cooperation, but it was not received that way. When the factions started to form the charter drafting committee in April and sought UNOSOM's assistance, they were rebuffed. The UN refused to recognize this addendum; only the provisions of the original Addis Ababa Agreement would be enforced.[18] Thus, as early as April, tensions had emerged between UNOSOM and all factions—not just Aidid's—over who held sway on political reconstruction. The situation would gradually worsen over the course of May.

The Second Clash: Kismayo

On the night of 6 May, two days after the formal transition from UNITAF, Omar Jess and 150 of his SPM militia advanced on Kismayo, hoping to wrest the city from Hersi Morgan's SNF. The SPM attack was stopped cold by the Belgians in a short but sharp fight that resulted in one Belgian wounded and forty SPM casualties. As force commander, General Bir took a hard line. He had just told both Jess and Morgan that they were prohibited from entering Kismayo. When Jess tried to explain the attack by claiming that his troops merely wanted to return home, Bir put the SPM leader under house arrest and ordered him to use his influence to ensure stability in the contested city.[19]

The next day, with Jess in tow, Aidid met with Ambassador Lansana Kouyate, UNOSOM's deputy special representative and Howe's political second, who had chaired Addis II. Aidid assured Kouyate that Jess and the SPM would not cause any more trouble and reiterated his support for the political reconstruction process.[20] The lopsided UN victory on 6 May, however, left Jess irate. Just as he had with UNITAF in February, Jess claimed that UNOSOM had colluded with Morgan. From Jess's perspective, Morgan had infiltrated the city in February and then again in March, twice bypassing the same Belgians who had just forcefully prevented the SPM from doing the same.[21]

Because of Jess's failed attack, the American QRF—the US Army's 1st Battalion, 22nd Infantry Regiment—was deployed to bolster the Belgians in Kismayo and maintain stability on the Kenyan border for the remainder of May and into June. This freed the Belgians to conduct weapons sweeps outside the city and functioned as a show of force to support clan elders from both sides of the Morgan-Jess conflict as they tried to reassert control. This left only one company of the QRF in Mogadishu, where tensions were rising between UNOSOM and the SNA.[22]

The Third Clash: The Galkayo Conference

On 4 April, one month before UNOSOM II took over in Somalia, Mohamed Hassan Awale, Aidid's minister for foreign relations, met with one of Howe's senior officials and offered a proposal. Aidid wanted to host a conference in May between his Habr-Gidr and the Majerteen Somali Salvation Democratic Front (SSDF) to discuss an end to hostilities in the central Mudug region and its capital of Galkayo, an area neither UNITAF nor UNOSOM controlled. Awale asked UNOSOM to support the Galkayo conference by transporting and accommodating delegates and to attend as observers.[23] He also invited Howe, as UNOSOM's political head, to deliver the opening address.

Given the focus on the handover from UNITAF, Aidid did not receive an answer until 8 May. Kouyate enthusiastically agreed to the proposal, writing to Aidid, "Admiral Howe has agreed to open the meeting and to deliver the concluding speech during the closing session. UNOSOM accepts to exercise the status of observers during the different sessions of the conference . . . [and] to consider any other role as deemed necessary for the success of the meeting."[24] Many in the Political Division, including John Drysdale, believed the Galkayo conference and the possibility of achieving stability in the central region would benefit the entire country.[25] With UN support in hand, Aidid wrote to Howe "to express my deep appreciation for your cooperation, understanding and support to the peace initiative. I wish to assure you that SNA will cooperate fully with UNOSOM II so that it can succeed in its mission to assist the Somali people overcome their current difficulties."[26]

Quite suddenly, though, everything changed. The Galkayo conference became a major point of contention between Aidid and UNOSOM throughout May 1993. A central actor in the events surrounding the 5 June attacks who has largely escaped notice is April Glaspie.[27] The former US ambassador to Iraq, Glaspie sparked controversy when she allegedly suggested to Saddam Hussein that military action against Kuwait, which led to the Gulf War, would not provoke a response from the United States. In the aftermath, she appeared before Congress for what one reporter described as the "Capitol Hill version of the OJ Simpson trial."[28] Losing her ambassadorship, Glaspie was ousted from the American delegation at the UN by Madeleine Albright after the Clinton administration moved into the White House. The State Department seconded Glaspie to UNOSOM II to serve as Howe's political adviser. As Paul Houston of the *Los Angeles Times* opined, "What better way to save a career that's been nose-diving . . . than to face down a group of Somali warlords?"[29] Glaspie may have been determined to avoid another accusation of being overly conciliatory. Of her tenure in Somalia, Rupert Cornwell of the *Independent* wrote, "If she had ever been soft on Saddam, she most certainly was not so on the warlord Mohammed Aideed."[30]

In mid-May Kouyate was temporarily recalled to New York. As Drysdale observed, Kouyate's departure led to a "marked deterioration in relations" with Aidid, and a previously cordial relationship was "brought to an end."[31] In Kouyate's absence, Glaspie was made acting deputy special representative, and she went from being Howe's political adviser to being his second. In this role, she became central to the tensions over the Galkayo conference. According to Drysdale, on Glaspie's advice, Howe responded harshly to Aidid's letter of thanks and turned the conference proposal on its head. Aidid was informed that, under the Addis Ababa Agreement, all factions had to take part in any reconciliation conferences, and the Galkayo conference excluded the other factions. Furthermore, Resolution 814 mandated that any such negotiations were to be managed by the UN. On that basis, Howe wrote, he would not be a guest at a conference that, by rights, he should be hosting.[32]

This disagreement between Howe and Aidid centered on differing interpretations of what UNOSOM's job actually was. According to Howe and Glaspie, Resolution 814 gave UNOSOM the authority to *manage* all political reconciliation and military affairs under its Chapter VII enforcement mandate. Aidid believed that such efforts fell to the Somalis themselves, with UNOSOM taking a supporting role to *assist* where necessary.[33] Who was right? Resolution 814 had two sections defining UNOSOM II's mandate and codifying where Howe had enforcement powers and where he did not. Military matters, force protection, and disarmament were all listed under Chapter VII, giving Howe enforcement authority. Political reconciliation, however, was covered in a preceding section of the resolution, which stated that UNOSOM's role was to "assist the people of Somalia."[34] Aidid's interpretation was correct. Howe was overreaching, but this was not acknowledged by a UN Commission of Inquiry until 1994.[35]

In May 1993 a white paper circulated within UNOSOM's Political Division entitled "Galcayo as Keystone." It argued that UNOSOM should quickly deploy to the Mudug region—a move that most factions, including Aidid's SNA, supported. However, "Galcayo as Keystone" also warned that if Aidid successfully concluded his peace conference with the SSDF, he would be free to bring his forces from Mudug to Mogadishu, but if UNOSOM arrived before any peace was concluded, these militias could be disarmed.[36] Furthermore, UN suspicion was aroused because the head of the SSDF delegation for the Galkayo conference was Colonel Ahmed Abdullahi Yusuf. Yusuf and Aidid were close, having served together in the National Army, and they shared a cell when imprisoned under the Barre regime. Yusuf was not, however, the chairman of the SSDF; Abshir Mussa was, and it was well known that Mussa and Yusuf were rivals. To Glaspie and, by extension, Howe, Yusuf's presence at the conference suggested that Aidid was trying to foment a pro-SNA coup within the SSDF.[37] Whether this was true is unclear, but Glaspie was determined to thwart what she saw as a conspiracy. She became known among the UN staff as the "Iron Lady" for her unyielding attitude.[38] Supporting rather than hosting Aidid's conference risked showing favoritism, which "was unacceptable to UNOSOM II."[39]

The profound hostility toward Aidid within the senior ranks of UNOSOM was not due solely to personalities. Bir's military adviser, US Army Lieutenant Colonel Thomas J. Daze, recalled that the US State Department had apparently determined that no "warlord" could be allowed to become the head of any new government.[40] The political ascension of any of these faction leaders, the State Department argued, would undermine any lasting peace. The logic here is inexplicable. This policy disqualified all of Somalia's existing political leaders, and it directly contravened Addis II, where the UN recognized these same individuals as being key to political reconstruction. Moreover, although Glaspie and others were working for UNOSOM, they were pursuing national policies completely at odds with the UN mission and mandate. How this could do anything other than cause tension is hard to fathom. It perhaps explains some of Glaspie's actions, though she seemed to take a particularly hard line. This policy manifested itself in a confidential memo sent to Howe on 16 May from an anonymous staffer identified only as "Walter." It urged UNOSOM to develop a strategy to marginalize the "warlords." Walter argued that Aidid was unsure of his relationship with UNOSOM and "is very worried that he is losing control of the process . . . and he's right. When he fully realizes this loss, we could see him return to his strongarm tactics, at which point we should arrest him . . . once a thug usually means always a thug. Conversions to responsible politics are rare." Walter suggested that if Aidid could not be arrested, he should be removed through bribery instead, a tactic Walter had found highly effective in Africa.[41] No Aidid- or SNA-sponsored violence had yet occurred in Mogadishu. As such, Walter's memo advised the creation of a scenario in which Aidid and others could be marginalized or arrested in the future.

During the UNITAF phase, Aidid had a cordial and cooperative relationship with Oakley on political matters. But Glaspie was dictating who could host and who could attend the Galkayo conference and what the agenda would be, even though this was beyond UNOSOM's remit. Abshir Mussa, chairman of the SSDF, told her that he knew about the planned conference between Yusuf and Aidid and was comfortable having Yusuf represent his faction. Nevertheless, Glaspie insisted that Mussa attend. She then dictated that the conference be chaired not by Aidid but by former Somali president Aden Abdullah Osman. This choice was inflammatory. Osman despised Aidid, and upon arriving in Mogadishu, his first act was to demand Aidid's arrest. Glaspie then went further and deemed that the conference had to be open to all national factions and the agenda would include resolving the recent violence in Kismayo. Glaspie thus turned Aidid's regional conference with a limited focus into a third Addis Ababa conference, giving every faction a say on matters that, according to Aidid, involved only the SNA and SSDF. With his plans thoroughly frustrated, Aidid took to the airwaves and voiced his displeasure on Radio Mogadishu, the SNA's propaganda station in the capital.[42]

Through Glaspie, UNOSOM was not being a kingmaker, but it was certainly making clear who was in disfavor at court. Political reconciliation would be under UN control, with UNOSOM as the gatekeeper. Glaspie's confrontational attitude toward Aidid was encouraged by none other than his longtime rival Ali Mahdi. An astute operator, Ali Mahdi used the SNA-UNOSOM tensions to his advantage. He denounced Aidid for obstructing political reconciliation and galvanized twelve factions under his leadership to create the "Group of 12," a pro-UNOSOM alliance opposed to the SNA.[43] Tom Farer's investigation into the 5 June attacks found that Glaspie "openly manifested sympathy for one of Aideed's most important political opponents [Ali Mahdi] . . . and was less than discreet about her hostility to Aideed."[44]

Meeting with Omar Halim from UNOSOM's Political Division on 2 June, Mohamed Hassan Awale complained that instead of carrying out Resolution 814 and assisting in political reconciliation, UNOSOM was "acting like a government."[45] Hinting at Glaspie's hostility, Awale sardonically advised Halim, "If you hate someone you should not allow it to affect policy—the UN's credibility is at stake."[46] Frustrated and isolated, Aidid went ahead with his conference, and despite all the furor it caused, on 2 June the SNA and SSDF agreed to disarm their militias and hand over their weapons to UNOSOM. On 3 June, in a joint letter, Aidid and Yusuf extended the olive branch and again invited Howe to deliver the closing address.[47] Apparently, Howe did not reply.

The Fourth Clash: Radio Mogadishu and AWSS Inspections

In a country with a literacy rate of only 30 percent and the cultural primacy of oral tradition, Somalis were avid radio listeners.[48] For the SNA and its supporters, Radio Mogadishu was the station of choice. This became another point of contention, given Aidid's on-air criticism of UNOSOM and its leaders for their interference in the Galkayo conference. These broadcasts have been characterized as Aidid spewing "vicious diatribe" in an anti-UN campaign that reached "fever pitch" prior to 5 June.[49] However, according to Drysdale, these broadcasts were not worthy of concern. Fluent in Somali, he recalled that Radio Mogadishu mentioned UNOSOM in twenty broadcasts from 1 May to 3 June 1993, and Aidid spoke eight times. In Drysdale's opinion, only four of these speeches were "mildly critical" of UNOSOM with regard to Jess's attack on Kismayo, the Galkayo conference, and its rebuffing of the SNA.[50] Another speech thanked Howe, Kouyate, and the UN for their assistance to Somalia. Similarly, a 1994 UN investigation singled out only one egregious broadcast on 11 May in which Aidid claimed the United States and UN were trying to "colonize" Somalia.[51] Reporting from Mogadishu, Michael Maren also reviewed broadcast transcripts and concluded that, though provocative, they were no worse than what might be heard on American talk radio.[52] Nevertheless, Howe requested that Aidid tone down the inflammatory rhetoric. Perhaps feeling unfairly singled out, Aidid proposed that a committee be set up to monitor the content of all radio stations. This never happened.

Radio Mogadishu became another lightning rod. Glaspie, Drysdale recalled, had an "obsession" with the radio station and threatened to resign if nothing was done about it.[53] Within UNOSOM circles, discussions were held on whether Radio Mogadishu should be seized or taken off the air. In mid-May, with the dispute over the Galkayo conference ongoing, Brigadier Ikram ul Hasan's Pakistani brigade was ordered to draw up plans to disable the radio station. They were joined in this effort by a team from the US Army's 5th Special Forces Group. Glaspie was not alone in wanting Aidid taken off the air. On 12 May the vice-chairman of Ali Mahdi's USC met with UNOSOM officials and said, "If UNOSOM is for freedom and democracy it should take over the radio station."[54] Then, while Aidid and Yusuf were attending their conference, Ali Mahdi personally approached Howe with a proposal dated 31 May. This new initiative suggested using an inspection of the SNA's AWSSs in Mogadishu to access Radio Mogadishu.[55]

The timing of decisions regarding these inspections is vitally important. General Bir, UNOSOM's force commander, left Somalia on 31 May for UN headquarters in New York to discuss operational and logistical matters with Kofi Annan, undersecretary-general for peacekeeping operations, and his chief military adviser, Canadian Major General Maurice Baril. Bir wanted to highlight UNOSOM's lack of aircraft and staff shortages, which were "having a major effect on the operational capability" of force headquarters.[56] That same day, Ali Mahdi proposed taking over Radio Mogadishu, and UNOSOM records noted that "plans [are] being formulated regarding short-notice inventories of the AWSSs located in and around Mogadishu."[57] At this pivotal juncture in the intervention, with Bir and Kouyate out of the country, both the political and military leadership of UNOSOM was temporarily all American. Howe was the special representative, Glaspie was filling in for Kouyate as his deputy, and in Bir's absence his deputy, US Army Major General Thomas Montgomery, commanded all coalition forces. This American trio made the decision to inspect the SNA's AWSSs.

The official justification for the inspections was to take an inventory of the SNA's heavy weapons, as there was a suggestion that some had been removed. Resolution 814 gave UNOSOM a mandate to disarm the militias, so inspections were a fulfillment of that mission. Although some authors believe that the inspections were solely for this purpose and Radio Mogadishu was not an objective, the evidence clearly shows otherwise. Radio Mogadishu was collocated with an SNA AWSS, and the inspections were a cover to get close to the source of Glaspie's ire. Even among UNOSOM staff, many knew the goal was to knock out Radio Mogadishu; a senior UNOSOM officer later told UN investigators that this was indeed the case. The US Forces Somalia after-action report noted that the inspections would allow UNOSOM to verify whether Radio Mogadishu was actually an AWSS or defined as such by the SNA to exclude other factions from using the facility. Significantly, this report also claimed the inspections would verify "the real use of the facilities [and] UNOSOM would be able to recommend the disestablishment of the site, if necessary."[58] The focus on seizing or disabling Radio Mogadishu was so blatant that even Aidid and the SNA were aware of rumors that it was the real target.[59]

Under UNITAF, AWSSs had been established by all factions across the country. In Mogadishu, both Aidid and Ali Mahdi had cantonment sites for their heavy weapons and fighting vehicles. Even though the inspections were a barely veiled cover for targeting Radio Mogadishu, Montgomery planned to inspect the AWSSs belonging to both militias so as to appear impartial, with no indication of favoritism. There was a problem though. On 2 June the Italian commander overseeing Ali Mahdi's portion of Mogadishu informed Montgomery that the AWSSs belonging to Mahdi's militia had been disestablished months earlier. No one had informed UNITAF or UNOSOM II. This fundamentally changed the situation, as the inspections, coupled with UNOSOM's well-known desire to neutralize Radio Mogadishu, would now be perceived as a provocative targeting of the SNA. Montgomery nevertheless decided to proceed.[60]

There was an established procedure for inspections. Factions were normally given twelve hours' notice beforehand to ensure there were no misunderstandings. The job of conducting the inspections was assigned to the Pakistani brigade, and its commander, Brigadier Hasan, was worried about the potential for a violent clash with the SNA, given the well-known tensions with UNOSOM leadership and the barely concealed objective of the inspections. He suggested to Montgomery that either no notice be given or no inspections take place until the SNA's response to the notification had been communicated to his brigade.[61] Montgomery opted to follow the regular notification procedure and drafted a letter to Aidid, informing him that the five AWSSs belonging to the SNA would be inspected on the morning of 5 June. Montgomery referred the draft to Howe, who showed it to Glaspie. Despite this obviously dangerous move, there were no objections. Drysdale remembered that "Howe did not inform other political officers in UNOSOM II of the contents of the letter, nor did he seek their advice."[62] As for Radio Mogadishu, when the Pakistani brigade had originally been ordered to make plans to neutralize the facility, Hasan claimed his men lacked the technical expertise for such a mission. Because of this, US Special Forces personnel were ordered to accompany the Pakistanis to "survey the radio installation."[63]

On the evening of Friday, 4 June, a Muslim holy day, US Army Lieutenant Colonel Kevin McGovern, UNOSOM II's deputy intelligence officer, accompanied by fellow army Lieutenant Colonel Timothy Byrne and three Australian soldiers, arrived at Aidid's residence.[64] McGovern was met by Colonel Abdi Qaybdiid, a senior SNA security official, who informed him that Aidid was not home, as he was concluding his conference with Yusuf and the SSDF. McGovern delivered Montgomery's letter to Qaybdiid, whose response upon reading it was either "this is unacceptable . . . this means war" or the less confrontational but still negative reaction that the SNA needed time to respond, but if UNOSOM insisted on carrying out the inspections, it could lead to war.[65] Qaybdiid was told it was not a proposal but a declaration. McGovern informed his superior, Italian Colonel Giuseppe Pirotti, the head of UNOSOM intelligence, of Qaybdiid's response, who then informed Montgomery in a memo.

What Montgomery did next is debated. The US Forces Somalia after-action report, the writing of which he personally supervised, is the only source that claims the SNA warning was passed on to Brigadier Hasan. However, this claim is suspect, as it shifts all responsibility away from the Americans who made the decisions. Multiple sources and a UN investigation concluded that Hasan and his command were not warned of the

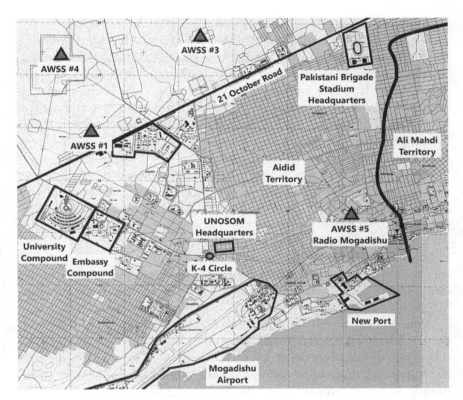

Somali National Alliance Authorized Weapon Storage Sites in Mogadishu, 1993

SNA's hostile response. That Hasan, already conscious of the prospect for violence, deployed his lightly armed units to carry out the inspections in soft-skinned vehicles, with some personnel not wearing body armor, confirms that they were not expecting trouble, as no warning had been received.[66]

The Sum of All Clashes: 5 June 1993

At 07:00 on 5 June 1993, Hasan's Pakistani brigade commenced the inspections of five SNA AWSSs, numbered 1, 3, 4, 5, and 9, in Mogadishu. On the northwestern outskirts of the city, the 6th Punjab was assigned AWSSs 1 and 4 and the 10th Baloch was assigned AWSS 3; outside the city, the 1st Sind Regiment would handle AWSS 9; and in the city center, almost on the Green Line that divided Aidid and Ali Mahdi territory, the 7th Frontier Force—the original UNOSOM battalion that arrived in September 1992—was assigned AWSS 5, collocated with Radio Mogadishu. Hasan's troops escorted the inspection teams, consisting of American and Australian officers from UNOSOM force headquarters and a team from the US Army's 5th Special Forces Group sent to survey Radio Mogadishu, categorize weapons sites, and, ominously, "update target folders for future use if necessary."[67]

Hasan timed the inspections to occur simultaneously. AWSS 3 was guarded by fifty SNA militiamen who were cowed into submission by an American AH-1 Cobra attack helicopter that practiced mock strafing runs, not so subtly implying the consequences if they chose to resist.[68] At AWSS 4, the inspection team met nothing more than some "verbal resistance."[69] After a few hours, all the inspections had been concluded successfully. In some of the sites there were fewer weapons than inventories suggested; in others, more. It was at AWSS 5, collocated with Radio Mogadishu, that the trouble started.

Veterans of the 7th Frontier Force claim they were accompanied by two American Special Forces personnel in plain clothes. While the inspection team inventoried AWSS 5, the SNA guards reportedly told the Americans there were no weapons at the adjacent Radio Mogadishu broadcast facility. Nevertheless, the Americans used hammers to break the locks and gain entry, which caused "visible agitation" among the growing crowd of Somali onlookers.[70] Word spread quickly that the UN was breaking into Radio Mogadishu, and by 08:30, two hundred Somalis had gathered outside AWSS 5 to protest.[71] This escalated when a man in the crowd was shot as he tried to take a weapon from a Pakistani soldier. The inspections at Radio Mogadishu and AWSS 5 ended at 09:30, and the inspection team and 7th Frontier Force withdrew without further incident. But the word was out, and the spark had been lit.

Less than a mile away, twelve Pakistani soldiers guarding Feeding Point 20, one of the MDS distribution sites, were attacked by a mob of men and women armed with everything from machetes and clubs to RPGs and grenades. Three Pakistanis were killed and six were captured, one of whom died in captivity. Pakistanis nearby at Strongpoint 50 heard the attack and proceeded to Feeding Point 20 in four APCs, only to be ambushed and forced to withdraw. Across southern Mogadishu, sporadic violence against UNOSOM broke out. Howe remembered, "There

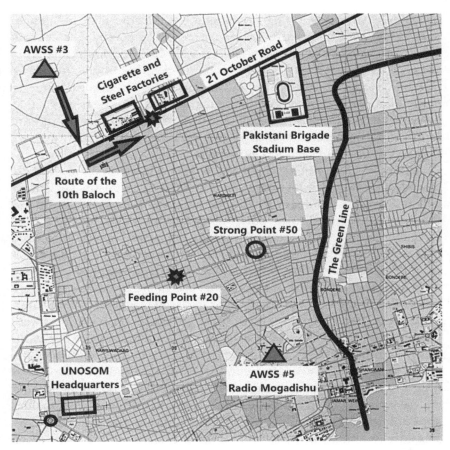

Locations of 5 June 1993 Attacks on Pakistani Forces

were demonstrations and shooting all over town . . . there was a major eruption."[72] UNOSOM's force headquarters and administration build-ings were fired on, as was the US embassy compound.[73]

The worst came at 10:00. Returning from AWSS 3, the Pakistani company from 10th Baloch turned left onto 21 October Road as they headed back to their base at Mogadishu Stadium. That road was an SNA stronghold lined with militia barracks at the cigarette factory and the steel factory. Half an hour after the attack at Feeding Point 20, SNA militia on 21 October Road poured fire into the Pakistani convoy with heavy machine guns and RPGs from these factories.[74] The volume of fire was later cited as suggesting premeditation; that the SNA militiamen were firing from their barracks was ignored. The company from 10th Baloch was caught in a merciless kill zone. As reinforcements came from the stadium, they too took fire. Pakistani dead and wounded littered 21 October Road, and UNOSOM and Hasan's brigade tried to come to their aid. At 11:00 Hasan requested tank support, but the nearest tanks belonged to the Italians at Balad, far outside Mogadishu. They did not arrive at the ambush site until 16:00. Until the Italian tanks arrived, UNOSOM deployed what forces it could.[75]

The bulk of the American QRF, UNOSOM II's reserve, was still deployed hundreds of miles to the south in Bardera and Kismayo, leaving only one infantry company to join the action in the capital as the rest of the QRF scrambled to get back to Mogadishu. A Company of the 1st Battalion, 22nd Infantry, sortied from the university compound, moved up 21 October Road, and reached what remained of the Pakistanis at 12:46.[76] Under continuous SNA fire, American troops dragged the Pakistani dead and wounded out of the streets. At 13:20 American Cobra and Italian Mangusta attack helicopters arrived to suppress the SNA in the factories, but due to the close quarters at the ambush site, they were unable to tell friend from foe and accidentally wounded three Pakistanis before withdrawing.[77] A Company's arrival, however, forced the SNA militia to pull out of the two factories overlooking the road. By 14:00, it was over. Twenty-five Pakistanis were dead, fifty-seven were wounded, and ten were missing. Three Americans were also wounded. SNA casualties were unknown but presumed to be high, and undoubtedly many civilians were caught in the cross fire.[78] It was the deadliest single-day attack on UN peacekeepers since the Congo in 1961.

Was Aidid Responsible for 5 June?

The 5 June violence in Mogadishu was a turning point. Almost immediately, the mission in Somalia transitioned from humanitarian nation building to an intentional manhunt that became an unintentional counterinsurgency campaign. But the critical question is, where does the responsibility for 5 June lie? In 1993 the easy answer was to blame Aidid, the SNA leader, personally, which is exactly what the UN, the United States, and the international community did. Aidid was undoubtedly ambitious, and the civil war showed he was willing to fight doggedly to attain his goals, ergo, he ordered a premediated ambush of UNOSOM personnel. That the attacks were perpetrated in part by SNA militia, especially on 21 October Road, is beyond question. An examination of the evidence, however, suggests that Aidid had no part in ordering the attacks. The uncomfortable reality is that the months of violence that followed 5 June were predicated on a flawed and impulsive assignment of blame.

Ever since the intervention, there was no shortage of accusers who blamed Aidid for 5 June. But the logic underpinning such arguments was weak. Howe, for example, claimed:

> It was Aidid. I was very careful not to say it was Aidid until we had more evidence, at least publicly, but . . . it was in his interests to attack the UN forces . . . to have all the international people pack up and leave. And I think he saw that striking a blow to the Pakistanis who had replaced the Americans in South Mogadishu, which was his territory, was a way to get the UN to leave.[79]

Howe neglected to elaborate on why it was in Aidid's interests to attack, and his analysis ignored that the Pakistani brigade had always been in southern Mogadishu. The same units had served there under UNITAF.

On 7 June Aidid wrote to Howe. Denying responsibility and claiming that the sudden onset of violence had caught him by surprise, the SNA leader was "deeply disturbed and outraged by the unnecessary death of so many." The population of Mogadishu had revolted independently, he argued. In his words, "When the Somali people gathered around the Radio studio to peacefully protest against the takeover, the Pakistani troops opened fire on the crowd killing instantly several people. With this killing the situation went out of control." Aidid queried why UN personnel had gone into the radio station unannounced. "Even if UNOSOM II officials wished to maintain [an] element of surprise, they could invite the proper SNA officials to accompany them in the very moment they were going to the studio." Despite the events, Aidid remained conciliatory, telling Howe, "I fully agree with you that issues can be, and I believe should be, resolved by discussions and dialogue. I wish to state once again that the SNA has been and will be willing and ready to cooperate fully with UNOSOM II for the good and well being of the Somali people and Somalia." That said, Aidid demanded "an investigation of the incident conducted by impartial and neutral experts to determine conclusively the responsible party."[80] He would wait a long time to get it.

On the afternoon of 5 June, Howe cabled Kofi Annan at UN headquarters in New York, informing him of the attacks. In the initial draft, Howe wrote that no seizure of Radio Mogadishu "had taken place, nor was it intended." This was patently false. Although the radio station was not seized on 5 June, its seizure had been UNOSOM's focus for weeks. Howe's draft continued: "While Aidid and the USC/SNA are denying it, today's activities appear to be a calculated, premeditated series of major ceasefire violations." With this sentence, Howe established means and opportunity, but use of the word "appear" implied some unanswered questions. Plus, there was no motive. The draft was typed, but in the margins was a handwritten revision to be added to the end of this sentence: " . . . meant to challenge and intimidate UNOSOM II."[81] In the final version sent to Annan, the sentence read: "Today's activities appear to be a calculated, premeditated series of major ceasefire violations *meant to challenge and intimidate UNOSOM II*."[82] The added revision constructed a motive with absolutely no evidence and presented a series of events that had yet to be investigated as a deliberate attack with an identifiable goal. And a deliberate attack to intimidate UNOSOM required a chief architect.

At Howe's invitation, Professor Tom Farer of American University came to Mogadishu to investigate the events of 5 June. Less of an investigator and more of a prosecutor, Farer reached some highly subjective conclusions. He did not consider any suspect other than Aidid; the SNA leader's culpability was presumed from the outset, and an argument was constructed to make the assignment of blame simple. It was a combination of circumstantial evidence and outright assumptions. In Farer's opinion, the 5 June attacks had to be premeditated because they were simultaneous and because the SNA forces on 21 October Road had heavy weapons positioned to attack Pakistani reinforcements coming from the stadium. This reasoning ignored that the attack on Feeding Point 20 occurred half an hour before the ambush on 21 October Road and that, because the SNA barracks were located at the cigarette and steel factories, heavy weapons were readily at hand. Farer's investigation included only UN witnesses; there was no Somali or SNA input. When John Drysdale was asked whether, due to his connections to Aidid and the SNA, he could persuade any Somalis to contribute to Farer's inquiry, he convinced five, including a top SNA official, to do so. However, these Somalis were reluctant to go to UNOSOM headquarters for fear of being arrested, and Howe would neither grant them safe passage nor allow Farer to leave the fortified compound to talk to them.[83]

Constrained as he was, Farer relied on what he considered two smoking guns. He cited the testimony of an unnamed "credible witness" who claimed to have seen Aidid congratulate members of the SNA after the ambush. Farer also cited a captured SNA memorandum that discussed "future military operations" against UNOSOM II as proof that the SNA perceived itself to be at war with the UN. He wrote, "That belief would be baseless unless SNA had launched the 5 June assault."[84] That incriminating document, however, was not obtained until later in June during UNOSOM's retaliatory offensive, the power of which could only lead the SNA to believe it was at war with the UN. At that point, it was. Farer concluded that because Aidid knew the inspections were taking place and had a readily available militia, "a large and complex body of evidence leads ineluctably to the conclusion not simply that General Aidid had the requisite means, motive and opportunity [to attack], but that he had that trinity uniquely. . . . The corresponding risks may well have appeared acceptable."[85] But were they?

When the evidence and the various accounts of 5 June are considered, the chronological sequence of events and the crucial element of geography present a different picture. The violence started at AWSS 5–Radio Mogadishu when the Pakistanis killed a Somali at around 09:00. At 09:30 the Pakistanis at Feeding Point 20 were attacked. Shortly afterward, the various UN facilities in Mogadishu began to take sporadic fire. Half an hour later, at 10:00, the Pakistanis were ambushed on 21 October Road. The violence on 5 June spread radially, outward from Radio Mogadishu and across the city. It was no secret that UNOSOM wanted to shut down Radio Mogadishu. For all the SNA militiamen on 21 October Road knew, 10th Baloch was heading not back to their base at the stadium but to reinforce the UN at Radio Mogadishu. With violence now spreading across the city because of the belief the radio station had been shut down, the SNA opened fire. It is a hard hypothesis to prove, but it is the most compelling argument when one considers the weakness of Aidid's incentive to attack. Significantly, all the violence began after the inspections were completed. As such, they were not the trigger. And earlier that day, on their way to conduct the inspections, the Pakistanis had passed the very same SNA-held factories on 21 October Road without incident.

Farer was correct in claiming that Aidid had the means and the opportunity to conduct the attack. But he failed to establish any motive. He claimed that UNOSOM had curtailed Aidid's influence, so "guns would no longer trump all other sources of influence."[86] Consequently, 5 June was Aidid's bid to oust UNOSOM efforts to reconstitute the police and judiciary and ensure that he was the principal gatekeeper for the rebuilding of Somalia. Disarmament, however, was something that all factions had agreed to under UNITAF, including Aidid and Ali Mahdi, whose influence was just as curtailed. All factions then formalized disarmament again under the Addis Ababa Agreement, which Aidid was instrumental in achieving. He also supported the rebuilding of the ASF. Even with the Galkayo conference, Aidid did not try to bypass UNOSOM; instead, he wanted the UN to play the very role Resolution 814 had set out for it. And if Aidid was concerned about his political power diminishing, it was not evident in any of his correspondence with UNOSOM officials.

Farer's conclusion was far too simple; he presented Aidid as impulsive and, frankly, idiotic. Bloody as they were, the attacks on 5 June amounted to an ambush of just one company of Pakistanis and another squad at a feeding site. Aidid had the forces to make Mogadishu highly unstable, as the subsequent months of violence would show. But the CIA estimated that he had no more than five hundred militiamen in Mogadishu.[87] Aidid could not destabilize all of Somalia or militarily defeat the UN. The 5 June incidents were far too small to do anything more than bring the SNA into direct conflict with the UN and the United States, which was underpinning the military effort. Aidid was an accomplished, intelligent, and calculating professional soldier trained by NATO and the Soviet Union. He had seen both UNITAF and UNOSOM respond decisively to violence, and it is impossible to identify any convincing reason for him to conclude that ambushing one company of Pakistanis would be in his interest or in any way advantageous. Farer's investigation certainly did not provide one, and neither did anyone else.

In the days and months after the attack, evidence emerged that supported Aidid's claim that the Mogadishans had acted independently. Reporting from Mogadishu, Michael Maren interviewed many who claimed that Aidid did not order the attack and that the violence had begun when Somalis heard that UNOSOM was attacking Radio Mogadishu.[88] General Anthony Zinni, UNITAF's director of operations who twice returned to Somalia, heard the same testimony. He said, "I talked to people afterwards that were not Aidid supporters, far from it, [and] they felt that [the violence] was spontaneous."[89] Zinni recalled that the chief of the Mogadishu ASF, who was not an SNA supporter, claimed that Aidid did not order the attacks but took credit in the aftermath, believing it would boost his legitimacy with the city's populace.[90] There is no record of Aidid taking credit for 5 June, but if he did, it was the only miscalculation he was guilty of making.

It was not until February 1994 that a formal UN Commission of Inquiry came to quite different and uncomfortable conclusions about 5 June. Zambian Chief Justice Matthew Ngulube chaired the commission, which included Ghanian Lieutenant General Emmanuel Erskine, a former UN force commander in Lebanon, and the chief of the Finnish Defense Staff, Lieutenant General Gustav Haaglund. The commission's report was initially kept under wraps at the UN.[91] Established to "find facts," not "ascribe blame," it chided Farer's conclusions for being based on "circumstantial evidence." The commission's investigation was everything Farer's was not. UNOSOM's failings were laid bare: the mishandling of the Galkayo conference that put the UN and SNA on a collision course, the misinterpretation of the Resolution 814 mandate, the plans to neutralize Radio Mogadishu, and the failure to warn the Pakistanis of Qaybdiid's response. The commission concluded that UNOSOM was supposed to assist the Somalis with political reconciliation, not force a solution on them.[92]

Although several SNA members participated in the inquiry, Aidid refused invitations to meet with the commission. He doubted its objectivity because it was not "free from the influence of the UN Secretary-General who himself is a part of the June 5 controversy." Given the tenor of Farer's investigation, this reluctance is perhaps understandable. Aidid instead suggested a non-UN-led investigation chaired by a former head of state "like Jimmy Carter."[93] Even without Aidid's cooperation, the commission's conclusions were seismic. In direct contrast to Farer, who found Aidid personally guilty, the commission found no evidence that Aidid authorized the 5 June attacks nor any evidence of premeditation or preplanning by the SNA. It was "quite possible," it wrote, that "the attacks on 5 June were orchestrated by the SNA on the spur-of-the-moment after the inspections had begun." The real culprit, however, was UNOSOM's Political Division, as "inappropriate political advice contributed to the misjudgment of the sensitivity and timing of the inspections."[94] This was undoubtedly a criticism of April Glaspie, whose actions were singled out as "one example of an evident political miscalculation."[95]

The commission's findings were initially withheld not only because they constituted an admission of several completely avoidable mishaps but also because of what had happened in the interim between 5 June 1993 and the publication of the commission's report in February 1994. By that time, more than one hundred UN and US personnel had been killed and hundreds more wounded in the violence that followed 5 June, a campaign that culminated with the disastrous Battle of Mogadishu. For the Somalis, the casualties numbered in the thousands, many of them civilians. The commission concluded that "without investigation, blame for the attacks of 5 June was laid on the USC/SNA . . . and the authorization of punitive action against the SNA leadership . . . was adopted by the Security Council the next day."[96] The cold reality was that the months of violence and the many lives lost were predicated on a mistake, that the uncompromising attitudes of Howe, Glaspie, and others put UNOSOM on an avoidable collision course with the SNA. But none of these reasoned conclusions mattered; they came far too late.

The UN-Authorized Manhunt: Resolution 837

On 6 June Mogadishu was described as "stable and quiet but tense."[97] The previous evening, Aidid had gone on the air. He congratulated Somalis on defending their "homes, religion, and your country" and then appealed for calm, saying, "God is my witness . . . I ask the Somali people to observe order."[98] At UN headquarters in New York, however, the outrage was palpable. Pakistani Ambassador Jamsheed Marker requested "an urgent meeting of the Security Council to discuss the recent developments in Somalia."[99] He submitted a draft of a pointedly decisive resolution for consideration. It instructed "the Force Commander of UNOSOM II to take all necessary measures against those responsible, including their arrest, detention and conviction, for the armed attacks [and] to urgently enquire into the incident, with particular emphasis on the role played by General Aidid and authorizes General Aidid's arrest and detention if his complicity in the attack is established."[100]

Marker's draft confirms the immediate focus on Aidid as the chief architect of 5 June, undoubtedly because of Howe's inflammatory cable. Once again showing the United States' disproportionate influence on the UN mission in Somalia, the draft resolution was sent to the Joint Staff at the Pentagon for review. Aidid's name was removed at the personal request of General Colin Powell, chairman of the Joint Chiefs. Revised and sanitized, the draft resolution was sent back to Madeleine

Albright's delegation for consideration at the emergency session requested by Marker.[101]

The meeting was heated. Marker assured the Security Council:

> The grave and tragic losses which we have sustained in Somalia, as a result of the deliberate actions of a bunch of murderous warlords and thugs, will in no way diminish our commitment to peacekeeping efforts of the United Nations. . . . We owe it to them . . . who embraced martyrdom in the cause of peace, that their sacrifice will not be in vain, and that it will lead to peace in the tortured land of Somalia.

Curiously, most took pains not to mention Aidid by name. Marker never mentioned him. Neither did Albright, who settled for condemning the "actions by certain factional leaders of the USC" and promising that "those who would challenge the authority of this body . . . will pay a heavy price for ignoring the Council."[102]

Only Ambassador Arria of Argentina said what every council member was thinking and revealed the true thrust of the resolution. Aidid, Arria said, "is nationally and internationally recognized as primarily responsible for the destruction of Somalia and for thousands and thousands of crimes against his people . . . the Secretary-General, apart from ordering his arrest and detention, will be able to proceed to trying him so that he may later be punished appropriately."[103] Aidid, of course, was far from solely responsible for the collapse of Somalia, but with passions inflamed and emotions high, Resolution 837 was unanimously approved with "little debate, and no dissent."[104] The Security Council, alarmed by the actions of the forces "apparently belonging" to the SNA in direct violation of the Addis Ababa Agreement and Resolution 814, and condemning radio broadcasts inciting violence against UNOSOM II, decreed that those responsible for 5 June would be brought to justice. Radio Mogadishu would be neutralized. Member states were encouraged to accelerate the deployment of their forces to Somalia and to provide tanks, APCs, and attack helicopters for use by UNOSOM II.[105]

From mid-April to early June 1993, Howe, Glaspie, and Montgomery, through poor decision making, a misinterpretation of the mandate, and the deliberate targeting of Aidid, created an incredibly combustible environment in Mogadishu. One spark was all that was needed, and it came on 5 June.

Mohamed Hassan Awale visited UNOSOM's director of political affairs, Leonard Kapungu, on 8 June. Awale was "just dropping in to have a cup of Zimbabwe tea with me," Kapungu noted.[106] Nonchalantly sipping his tea, Awale told Kapungu that the events surrounding the AWSS inspections "looked very strange." Delivering the notification letter on a Muslim holy day, Awale said, was like "delivering letters to the Secretary-General on Sunday at 4pm." He told Kapungu that those within the SNA thought it had been a deliberate setup. Setup or not, Resolution 837 announced the hunt for a fugitive and declared that UNOSOM was going to war.

8 | The Fatal Attraction of Mogadishu
The Summer War, June–October 1993

Whether they wait him out, root him out, starve him out, bomb him out or induce a henchman to sell him out, whether he is seized next month or next year, whether he is tried in Mogadishu, Geneva or the Hague, before or after stability returns to Somalia, all matters less than the United Nations' determination to persevere.
> —Theodore C. Sorensen and Christopher B. Jochnik,
> *Los Angeles Times,* June 1993[1]

We are confronting civil wars, divided societies, without a government, where militias and warlords rule. . . . Before people said, "Where is the UN?" and accused us of doing too little. Now . . . we are accused of doing too much.
> —Kofi Annan, UN undersecretary-general for peacekeeping[2]

We waded ashore in Somalia to feed the hungry. Now our gunships hover over Mogadishu shooting rockets into crowded villas. It is the humanitarian's ultimate nightmare. Famine relief turns into counterinsurgency.
> —Charles Krauthammer, *Time,* July 1993[3]

Sixteen helicopters, packed with US Army Rangers and Special Forces operators, skirted the rooftops of Mogadishu. Their target was a high-level SNA meeting attended by Aidid's principal advisers. Helicopters hovered over the building where the meeting was taking place and in the surrounding streets, disgorging their passengers. In a matter of minutes, they had captured two dozen attendees. On the verge of withdrawing, an orbiting UH-60 Black Hawk helicopter was shot down by SNA fire. Within the next twenty minutes, a second Black Hawk was shot down, while a third, crippled and heavily damaged, limped back to base. It was Sunday, 3 October 1993. The Battle of Mogadishu, one of the most intense engagements of US forces since the Vietnam War, had begun.

The events of the Battle of Mogadishu itself are well known, given the popularity of Mark Bowden's book *Black Hawk Down* and Ridley Scott's

2001 film adaptation, though without the context of the broader intervention in which it occurred. UN and US forces stumbled into an unplanned months-long counterinsurgency campaign that commenced after the 5 June attacks. Confined to the portion of Mogadishu that was loyal to Aidid, this campaign against an absolute minority of the population had strategic consequences for the intervention in Somalia. For the United States, its credibility and that of the UN was at stake. For Aidid, his position as leader of the SNA and, in his mind, the future leadership of Somalia were on the line. Once it started, both sides escalated, resulting in a four-month insurgency in Mogadishu that Somalis called the Summer War.[4] To understand the causes of the Battle of Mogadishu, it is critical to understand the war itself because, tragically, after months of bloodshed and stalemate, the battle occurred after the Clinton administration decided to seek a negotiated end to the conflict.

The UNOSOM Offensive: June–July 1993

After 5 June, Mogadishu was transformed. The *Los Angeles Times* condemned Aidid for the "most flagrant defiance of U.N. authority in 32 years."[5] Humanitarian workers and UNOSOM's civilian staff fled to the safety of Nairobi. Mogadishans took shelter or chose a side. For the first time in months, weapons were brandished openly in the streets. SNA militia established defensive positions on rooftops and hastily constructed roadblocks to impede UN movement.[6] Sporadic fire pocked UNOSOM bases, frustrating American pilots because force headquarters would only authorize strikes on clearly identifiable targets, which, one pilot complained, "was almost impossible" in the urban labyrinth.[7]

The SNA was preparing, but so was UNOSOM. On 8 June Jonathan Howe held a "marathon meeting" of his senior military leadership, where it was decided to go on the offensive against the SNA. Howe was reportedly reluctant, but April Glaspie was strongly in favor of a military response to 5 June.[8] She was not alone. A State Department cable to the US mission at the UN on 10 June urged action against Aidid to "send a strong message beyond Somalia. Dealing effectively with Aideed would establish a positive precedent for UN efforts to maintain international peace and security . . . it will be important to emphasize the leadership role of the UN."[9] With UN credibility on the line, the Pentagon and UN headquarters became inundated with urgent requests for reinforcements. From Hoar at CENTCOM, Boutros-Ghali in New York, and Howe in Somalia, requests came in for a level of firepower that had not been seen in a UN operation since the Korean War.[10] A retaliatory offensive was in the offing. Mogadishu was "saturated with a vast arsenal of hidden illegal weapons" that needed to be confiscated.[11] More than that, Resolution 837 mandated that the SNA and Radio Mogadishu be neutralized to "establish the effective authority of UNOSOM."[12] While UN military power was building, Howe warned Ali Mahdi's Group of 12 not to try to take advantage of the tensions. The pro-UNOSOM, anti-SNA alliance agreed and uniformly condemned the 5 June attacks.[13]

In the early-morning darkness of 12 June, a lone US Air Force AC-130 gunship droned over Mogadishu. A modified C-130 Hercules transport aircraft, this gunship was equipped with fuselage-mounted artillery pieces for bombarding ground targets. Without warning, Radio Mogadishu was leveled from the air at 04:00, the first act in a coordinated assault on SNA facilities across the city. Cobra attack helicopters laid waste to tightly packed SNA tanks and armored vehicles parked at two AWSSs, while another was air-assaulted by American troops from the QRF. The loitering AC-130 then shattered the cigarette factory, the key SNA bastion during the 5 June attacks. Two more SNA weapons caches, along with thirty vehicles in a makeshift technical factory, were destroyed the next day.[14] Howe took to the airwaves to explain the strikes, blaming the SNA for "using Radio Mogadishu to incite Somalis against the international community."[15] The bulk of the SNA's heavy weapons had been annihilated.

UNOSOM's success was quickly overshadowed by a public relations nightmare. The next day, 13 June, Somalis held an anti-UN protest at the K-4 Circle as Pakistani troops watched. No one knows to this day who fired the first shot. The Pakistani commander claimed the SNA fired on his troops and allegedly fired into the crowd to implicate the Pakistanis and discredit UNOSOM. Fourteen protesters were killed and twenty wounded in full view of the Sahafi Hotel, the favored residence of the international media. Some journalists said the SNA was not present and the Pakistanis simply opened fire indiscriminately in revenge for 5 June. Shocked UN officials were asked pointedly whether these troops would be prosecuted, while commentators suggested the killings allowed Aidid to present himself and the SNA as victims. Just in case he was asked about 13 June, President Clinton's press talking points emphasized regret over the loss of life and adopted a strategy of demoniz-

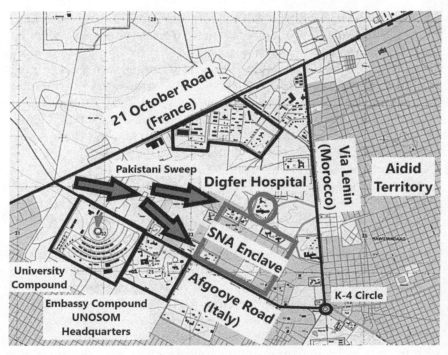

UNOSOM Cordon and Search Operation, 17 June 1993

ing Aidid: "He is a criminal. He is responsible for the civil war that raped his country and in which over 300,000 people died."[16] It was a gross exaggeration to blame Aidid for Barre's crimes, but such was the media furor. UNOSOM staff were encouraged to lie about the SNA being the perpetrators to cover up a major scandal.[17] It was not the last blunder.

UNOSOM's largest and last offensive came just days later, on 17 June. Howe and Bir moved to capture or kill the SNA leadership and neutralize any remaining weapons caches in Mogadishu by targeting the SNA "enclave."[18] This small neighborhood of homes belonging to Aidid, Omar Jess, Osman Atto, and other officials was conveniently located just down the street from UNOSOM's now fortified headquarters at the US embassy compound. Gunships would reduce the homes from the air, while UNOSOM ground forces sealed off the enclave. The French covered 21 October Road, the Italians the Afgooye Road, and the Moroccans Via Lenin. With this outer cordon established, two Pakistani battalions would sweep the enclave to capture weapons and SNA leaders.

Altogether, thirty-five hundred UNOSOM troops were involved, with the American QRF held in reserve. Given the high-profile nature of the operation, both Howe and Boutros-Ghali requested US Special Forces to assist, but this was refused.[19]

Destruction rained down from above in the early morning of 17 June as AC-130s pounded the SNA enclave. The Italians, French, and Moroccans established their cordon, and the Pakistanis commenced their sweep. One hundred SNA militia were captured, along with weapons and documents. As the sweep progressed, desultory and sporadic sniper fire increased, while crowds of protesters approached and probed the outer cordon. After the 13 June protest, the Moroccans on Via Lenin were determined to maintain discipline and not fire into the crowd. However, a group of women suddenly threw grenades among the Moroccans, causing heavy casualties. With their attention focused on the now hostile crowds, the Moroccans then took withering fire from behind.[20]

The SNA enclave was dominated by Digfer Hospital, overlooking Via Lenin. The Pakistanis had not searched it, and unbeknownst to anyone, the SNA had fortified it. Machine gun fire relentlessly poured into the Moroccans. With crowds of Somalis swarming the Moroccans and the hospital full of patients, UNOSOM helicopters were unable to attack the SNA militia without killing civilians or their comrades. Four Moroccans, including their regimental commander Colonel Ben Namous Abdullah, were killed and forty-one were wounded, including the executive officer. The French contingent fought its way down Via Lenin to relieve them. The events of 17 June cost UNOSOM seven dead and fifty-seven wounded; the estimated 150 SNA casualties undoubtedly included civilians. It was later reported that Aidid had escaped his villa just minutes before it was leveled by gunships and took refuge in Digfer Hospital.[21]

That same evening, Howe announced, "I have instructed Lieutenant General Bir . . . to arrest General Mohammed Farah Aidid," under the authority of Resolution 837, on the charge of crimes against humanity, "conspiracy to conduct premeditated attacks against UN forces," and "endangering civilians and UN personnel through organized incitement of violence."[22] The investigations into 5 June had not yet started, but Howe was arguably trying to distract from the disaster of that morning. Urged by officers in force headquarters, he offered a $25,000 reward for information leading to Aidid's capture. This paltry sum never stood a chance. The SNA leader responded with a $1 million bounty on

Howe and $500,000 more for Montgomery; "Animal Howe" became a commonly painted adornment on city buildings.[23]

Coalition Fragmentation

Despite being characterized by Boutros-Ghali as "successful in neutralizing weapons and command and control structures that were used to stir up violence in the southern sector of Mogadishu," the 17 June operation was a failure.[24] No SNA leaders were captured or killed. Worse still, it caused friction among the contributing nations within UNOSOM. The Moroccans were outraged that the Pakistanis had failed to sweep Digfer Hospital.[25] Australian staff officers blamed the operation on the "reluctance of the United States to commit ground forces and the lack of cooperation between disparate national forces."[26] Several nations criticized the irony of UNOSOM launching assaults during a peace operation, and concerns about the level of violence bled over into the public sphere. In the *Washington Post* on 20 June, Jennifer Parmalee wrote, "It's tempting to brand [Somalis] as incorrigible and ungrateful, impossible to understand and perhaps not worth the effort. It's even more seductive if we're thinking of abandoning ship. After all, we tried to feed them and look what it got us?" But getting rid of Aidid, Parmalee warned, was not the answer, as "other warlords wait in the wings. Ali Mahdi . . . may cut a respectable figure in his Italian-made suits, but his militias are every bit as blood-soaked as those of Aidid."[27]

After 17 June the French and Moroccan governments prohibited their forces from conducting offensive operations in Mogadishu. UNOSOM was bolstered by three infantry battalions from Zimbabwe, Egypt, and Malaysia and a Pakistani tank regiment. However, unsuited to urban warfare, the Zimbabwean light infantry was sent to Baidoa. The Egyptians reinforced the airport security perimeter, while the Malaysians, whose battalion was mechanized, became UNOSOM's armored reserve.[28] Just weeks into the conflict, no nation wanted to become the next Pakistan or Morocco and suffer heavy casualties, especially contingents that were uncomfortable with UN methods in Somalia. Italy was an example of both.

Italian troops had served credibly in UNITAF. But under UNOSOM, the Italian government and the UN were at odds from the beginning, fueled initially by the unfulfilled expectation that Italian officers would hold senior positions in Bir's headquarters. This was necessary, the government in Rome argued, to justify its contribution of such a large contingent. After 5 June Kofi Annan, UN undersecretary-general for peacekeeping, received complaints from Italian officials that their contingent in Mogadishu was not being informed of operational decisions in advance. Brigadier General Bruno Loi, the Italian commander in Somalia, then complained to the media about American forces entering his sector of Mogadishu unannounced and stirring up hostility. This caused a shouting match between Loi and Bir. Annan asked Italian officials to "authoritatively" rein in their commander, but the Italians responded that if they were kept in the loop, there would be no problem. On and on it went. The Italian parliament was split between those who wanted Italy involved in UNOSOM come what may and those who wanted a very visible senior Italian presence in the decision-making circle. The crux of the issue was revealed when Foreign Affairs Minister Beniamino Andreatta wrote to Boutros-Ghali and complained that UN-OSOM headquarters was dominated by Americans.[29]

Exacerbating tensions were rumors, rife during the intervention and still circulating, that the Italians were feeding information to the SNA, unilaterally negotiating with the group, or bribing it not to attack.[30] There is little to substantiate these charges. There were negotiations, but the context matters. Directed personally by General Loi, five hundred Italian troops supported by tanks and APCs launched a cordon and search operation near Mogadishu's pasta factory on the morning of 2 July. An SNA stronghold, the pasta factory dominated one end of 21 October Road, controlling the critical route into and out of the city. Loi's men were greeted by stone-throwing protesters but successfully completed their sweep. When his troops passed the pasta factory as they returned to base, it erupted with fire from SNA militia. What the Italians did not know was that to avoid capture, Aidid constantly moved around the city. On 2 July he was reportedly in a building near the pasta factory, and the SNA assumed the Italians were aware of his location. Italian tanks and APCs, assisted by QRF Cobras, fired into the pasta factory before Loi ordered a withdrawal. Three Italians were killed and twenty-nine wounded, leaving 170 Somali casualties behind.[31]

After the Battle of Checkpoint Pasta, Rome directed Loi to cease offensive actions against the SNA, just as the French and Moroccans had been ordered. Instead, he was told to negotiate with the SNA if possible.[32] This was not an effort to collude with the SNA or to seek

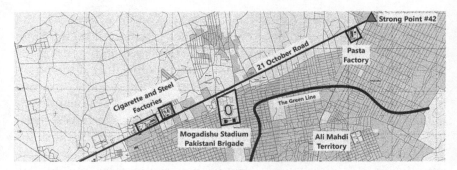

Battle of Checkpoint Pasta, 2 July 1993

a unilateral settlement. It was emblematic of the Italian government's discomfort—and the Italian public's uneasiness—with the violent direction UNOSOM was taking. From then on, though, Italian reluctance to engage the SNA prompted rumors among the coalition that something nefarious was afoot. Italian troops avoided calling in airstrikes because Loi believed civilian casualties were counterproductive, which led to more criticism from UNOSOM. Indeed, Loi was judged harshly for withdrawing from the pasta factory. Provocative—and false—tales spread that Italian troops had not even returned fire during the engagement.[33]

This new Italian attitude was on display when Bir ordered Loi to retake Strongpoint 42, which had been abandoned on 2 July. On 9 July Italian forces negotiated with the SNA for a peaceful reoccupation of Strongpoint 42. Loi achieved his mission, but not the way Bir wanted. His diplomatic approach was derided as reducing UNOSOM's effectiveness. Others accused the Italians of bribery and enabling the SNA to gain access to weaponry. The rumors persisted unabated, and Bir's military assistant recalled that Italian Colonel Giuseppe Pirotti, the head of UNOSOM intelligence, was excluded from briefings on upcoming operations because many believed he would leak the plans to the SNA. Loi had his orders from Rome, and he saw that talking first helped maintain peace in the Italian sector of the city.[34]

This softer approach caused a very public clash with the UN when Kofi Annan unilaterally announced that Loi was being relieved and sent home, indicted for obeying Rome's orders over UNOSOM's. Annan accused the Italians of undermining the "ethical integrity of the UN."[35] The hard-liners in the Italian parliament were outraged, publicly rebuking Annan with a reminder that they, not the UN, determined who commanded Italian forces in Somalia. Defense Minister Fabio Fabbri wrote directly to Les Aspin, Clinton's secretary of defense, rejecting any suggestion of collusion by pointing out that at one point Italian troops had an opportunity to capture Aidid, only to be told by force headquarters "to desist from intervening." "It is patently obvious," Fabbri chided, "that one does not spontaneously offer to capture a person with whom one has special relations."[36] The uproar caused the Italian contingent in Mogadishu to be moved to the interior because, according to Boutros-Ghali, the Italians had a "diversity of views . . . about some modalities of the implementation of the United Nations mandate."[37] Privately, Minister Andreatta had supplied this exact phrase to Boutros-Ghali, as he was concerned that the Italian hard-liners would demand a complete withdrawal from Somalia if a suitable reason for their redeployment was not provided. Appeasing these hard-liners further, Minister Fabbri told the media that the move was "a very singular way to avoid the real problem"—that UNOSOM's strategy was turning the Somalis against them.[38]

To say that the escalating violence caused a lack of unity within UNOSOM would be a fair assessment but also an oversimplification. Strain within the coalition was rooted in different approaches to fulfilling the UN mandate. The Italians were just one high-profile example. The reality was that everyone answered to someone in Somalia. Anytime Howe or Bir planned a move, it had to be cleared in New York by Kofi Annan or Maurice Baril, his military adviser. Because of this strain, Montgomery became frustrated by a growing "lack of aggressiveness" within UNOSOM. Coalition contingents checked with their national governments before participating in operations, especially if there was the potential for violence, which frequently drew the ire of American officers. This was hypocritical, as every time Montgomery wanted to use the QRF he had to clear it with Hoar at CENTCOM, who had to refer it to the State and Defense Departments in Washington, DC.[39] But, believing this passivity was putting American troops at risk, Montgomery received clearance from Hoar to begin using the QRF as a force protection measure.[40] Though couched as ensuring the safety of US personnel, in actuality, American combat units took over the fight against the SNA and the hunt for Aidid.

The SNA Counteroffensive and Operation Michigan

On 6 July the first mortar rounds fired by the SNA landed on Mogadishu airport. That same day, six Somalis working for UNOSOM were murdered in the city. Throughout July the SNA harassed UN forces with sporadic gunfire on UNOSOM installations, sniper fire against patrols, and attempts to breach secure compounds. Between 6 July and 31 August the airport, UNOSOM force headquarters at the US embassy compound, Sword and Hunter logistics bases, and the QRF base at the university were subjected to more than one hundred mortar bombardments.[41] Ambushes were so regular that UN-marked vehicles were parked at New Port, and UNOSOM leased unmarked cars flying Somali flags to avoid being targeted by the SNA.[42] All the while, casualties mounted.

In Washington, Deputy Secretary of Defense William Perry remembered that "what had started off as a humanitarian operation was turning out to be an insurgency."[43] UNOSOM's campaign had yielded no tangible successes, several contingents had been ordered by their governments not to engage, the SNA was not quelled, and Aidid had not been brought to justice. In Howe's words: "There were a whole bunch of ambushes going on of convoys trying to go out and work with justices and do other missions. . . . There were shootings going on all over and mortars coming in on the compounds. We'd gotten to the point where we needed to do something because of the attacks . . . to get back to reality in terms of the military side of the equation."[44] That something, born of frustration, was the most controversial act of the entire intervention: Operation Michigan.

The home of Colonel Abdi Qaybdiid was identified by UNOSOM intelligence as a regular meeting place for the highest echelons of the SNA, including Aidid. On 12 July six American Cobra attack helicopters surrounded the "Abdi house." Howe and Montgomery decided not to give the occupants any warning or an opportunity to surrender, which Howe described as "one of those awful, agonizing, tough choices."[45] The Cobras unleashed a four-minute barrage of two thousand cannon rounds and sixteen missiles into the house while a meeting was taking place.[46] Operation Michigan was, in Montgomery's words, "a very precise, and very decisive operation, and the intent was to kill bad guys, to decapitate part of the command staff that were making the decisions about the attacks on the United States and the United Nations."[47] The SNA command staff were not in the Abdi house on 12 July.

Many Habr-Gidr were unhappy with the Summer War. Some blamed

the war on Aidid's leadership. Abdikassim Salad Hassan, a Habr-Gidr and Barre's former deputy prime minister, proposed a cease-fire. He met with leaders from Habr-Gidr and other SNA clans on 11 July. A negotiated peace appealed to those who feared the war would mean their political ostracization from any future Somali government. It was therefore decided on 11 July that a six-member SNA delegation would approach UNOSOM to discuss a cease-fire. Beforehand, a meeting would take place at the Abdi house on 12 July to brief the wider Habr-Gidr and SNA clan leaders on the initiative. John Drysdale had informed Howe that Habr-Gidr clan leaders were interested in talking, but unfortunately, Howe's response was that the hunt for Aidid took priority.[48] It would not be the last peace overture to be rebuffed.

Whether the 12 July meeting was a war council or a peace conference, the Abdi house attack was hugely controversial. How many died was a major point of contention because the figure varied wildly. The US Army's 1st Battalion, 22nd Infantry Regiment from the QRF, which conducted the raid, claimed thirteen were killed and seven wounded. The QRF headquarters reported seventeen deaths. UNOSOM force headquarters recorded twenty-seven.[49] According to UNOSOM, among the dead were the SNA's propaganda chief, Aidid's "chief planner," the leader of the Habr-Gidr clan, and Abdi Qiir-Deed, who had allegedly planned the 5 June attacks. A press release claimed the successful destruction of a "terrorist planning center."[50]

Aidid presented a vastly different narrative. He put the death toll at seventy-three and not only supplied a videotape of the building after the strike but also trucked the bodies to the Sahafi Hotel for the international media to see. UNOSOM derided Aidid's estimate as "grossly exaggerated."[51] The International Red Cross estimate was actually higher: 54 dead and 174 wounded. Scott Peterson, a journalist covering Mogadishu, rushed to the Abdi house and saw "bodies all over the place, they were mincemeat."[52] He was lucky. Four other journalists who arrived at the scene later were killed by an enraged mob.[53] Drysdale, who knew several of the dead personally, agreed with Aidid's figures. African Rights published a scathing report on UNOSOM human rights abuses in July 1993, condemning the strike for killing women and children as well as Habr-Gidr religious leader Sheikh Hassan Abdi Naleye and Sheikh Mohamed Iman Elmi Gelle, the religious leader of Aidid's own Sa'ad subclan.[54] For Somalis, Drysdale said, the Abdi house strike was "a deed for which there could be no atonement."[55]

When Operation Michigan was proposed, coalition disquiet meant that no contingent apart from the American QRF was willing to carry it out.[56] If anything, the strike at Abdi house had deepened those tensions, with one report noting that the "violent, sudden, and unilateral nature of the attack disturbed some coalition partners."[57] Chief among them was Italy. Just hours after the strike, Defense Minister Fabbri told reporters that UN combat operations should end and diplomatic and political dialogue with the SNA must resume.[58] Italian Prime Minister Carlo Azeglio Ciampi reiterated complaints about an "American-dominated" force headquarters fixated on the manhunt for Aidid and even threatened to withdraw from Somalia because UNOSOM was becoming "a military intervention almost as an end in itself, against the wishes of those who are carrying it out."[59]

The day after the strike, Howe received an unsigned memo. The author was later identified as Ann Wright, a career State Department official, former US Army officer, and the senior member of UNOSOM's Justice Division, who would later describe the Abdi house attack as "slaughter."[60] Wright's memo asked whether Resolution 837 authorized "lethal force against all persons without possibility of surrender," or "did the Security Council allow that persons suspected to be responsible for attacks against UNOSOM . . . would have the opportunity to be . . . judged in a neutral court of law?" Wright's missive encapsulated the acute discord within UNOSOM after six weeks of insurgency. She pointedly asked Howe "whether the UN should hold itself to a higher standard of conduct toward [a] civilian population it has been asked to assist" and criticized the willingness of US forces to conduct a strike that others would not. Wright ended with an appeal—a subtle suggestion that force should not always be the first choice in Somalia. She urged Howe instead "to use the experience, contacts, and ideas your advisors in these fields bring to UNOSOM to provide as complete a picture of the probable consequence of military actions."[61] Echoing these sentiments, nine UNOSOM officials resigned in protest for what they saw as a targeted assassination carried out under the guise of the UN, an institution that, in their opinion, should uphold a higher moral standard. Keith Richburg of the *Washington Post* obtained the memo and reported the widespread disaffection over the strike. His exposé was so damning that UN Undersecretary-General for Political Affairs James Jonah contacted Howe and urgently asked for his comments "so that we can prepare a response."[62]

Due to the backlash, Operation Michigan was the last deliberate at-

THE FATAL ATTRACTION OF MOGADISHU | 223

tack against the SNA by UNOSOM or the QRF. Nevertheless, the US after-action report on Somalia claimed that the strike "strengthened UNOSOM II's military position in Somalia by severely damaging the command control structure of the SNA militia [and] created an opportunity for some of his [Aidid's] opponents to seize power . . . [by breaking] the cycle of harassment and guerilla tactics used against UNOSOM II."[63] This was pure fantasy. If anything, it had the opposite effect. The attack galvanized the Habr-Gidr's and SNA's support for Aidid. Many Somalis, even those unaffiliated with the SNA, refused to work for UNOSOM or help it in any way. But more than that, the Abdi house attack pushed the SNA to target US forces specifically in retaliation. An SNA spokesperson whose father had died in the attack summed up the thirst for revenge: "There was no more United Nations, only Americans, and if you could kill Americans, it would start problems in America directly."[64]

From 5 June to 31 July, between UNOSOM operations and incessant SNA ambushes, snipers, and mortar attacks, 39 peacekeepers died and 160 were wounded. The violence increased markedly after the Abdi house attack. In July the SNA launched twenty-five mortar barrages on UNOSOM facilities. In August the number rose sharply to eighty-nine, and there were more than one hundred in September. UNOSOM became the deadliest operation in the world, accounting for 50 percent of all UN fatalities in 1993. Incessant mortars, small-arms fire, and RPGs against UN bases became the nightly routine in Mogadishu, particularly for the American QRF based at the university. UN and US forces responded by lighting up the sky with illumination flares and firing tracer rounds from heavy machine guns into suspected SNA positions.[65] Bir's military assistant, Lieutenant Colonel Thomas Daze, recalled that the Tunisians had recoilless rifles on the perimeter wall of the embassy compound, and every evening they would engage SNA snipers in the city. According to Daze, the sound of the heavy rounds echoing in the dark was just "a normal night in Mogadishu."[66]

To counter the mortar threat, counterbattery radar was installed to locate where the mortars were fired from. Frequently, QRF Cobras and Black Hawks with snipers on board took off to locate and destroy the SNA position after the first rounds impacted. On rare occasions, mortar crews were engaged and destroyed from the air. Most often, though, they were long gone before the helicopters arrived overhead. SNA militia constantly moved their mortars around the city, quickly firing from one location before moving again. Sometimes the SNA took over relief organizations' compounds just long enough to fire and then disappeared before the QRF could respond.[67]

With mortars wreaking havoc, the QRF began "Eyes over Mogadishu" helicopter missions. Every night, two Black Hawks flew from 22:00 to 06:00, patrolling the skies to locate and engage mortar crews. Unsurprisingly, Mogadishu airport was bombarded eighty-two times to thwart US helicopter operations and to close the air bridge connecting UNOSOM to resupply and reinforcement. In this effort the SNA was partially successful, with one barrage destroying one helicopter and damaging five more on the tarmac. On 20 August the airport was officially closed to commercial traffic due to constant mortar fire, as well as the belief that the SNA had obtained SA-7 surface-to-air missiles, although this threat never materialized. Mogadishu was still open to military aircraft, and US Air Force C-5 Galaxy and C-141 Starlifter transports continued to bring in equipment and personnel. Because the SA-7 was a heat-seeking missile, QRF Black Hawks provided "wide-body" escorts, flying alongside these massive transports during their final approach to offer an alternative hot target rather than the aircrafts' engines.[68]

Mortars were not the only danger. After 12 July it was rumored on the streets that the SNA was offering a bounty for every American killed. On 8 August four American military policemen patrolling the airport perimeter died when their Humvee was destroyed by a command-detonated mine so powerful it left a seven-foot-deep crater. On 19 August another mine wounded four American troops, and six more were injured in a blast three days later.[69] In revenge for the Abdi house attack, SNA militia were using command-detonated mines exclusively to target American personnel.

This provoked a decisive reaction from the United States. The CIA claimed that "arresting Aideed offers UNOSOM's best opportunity to restore credibility to the UN peacemaking mission."[70] Responding to public and political outcry over US troops dying in Somalia, Madeleine Albright took to the *New York Times* to argue that instability would spread beyond Somalia if it were not checked. She also issued a rallying call against Aidid, who, she wrote, sought "to return Somalia to anarchy. . . . Normally the UN is criticized for doing too little. [Now] it is being criticized for doing too much. . . . For Somalia's sake, and ours, we must persevere."[71] The credibility of the UN, the United States, and the international rule of law was at stake in Mogadishu. And for the United States at least, perseverance meant escalation.

Task Force Ranger and Operation Gothic Serpent

Since June, Howe had repeatedly asked for US special operations forces to capture or kill Aidid. On his behalf, the UN made similar requests to France and Australia, to no avail. Initially, Hoar gave Montgomery permission to use the QRF to capture Aidid. But the assault helicopter and light infantry battalions were trained for conventional operations, not the type of small-unit surgical raids required for a manhunt. Nevertheless, the first QRF rotation—the US Army's 3rd Battalion/25th Aviation Regiment and 1st Battalion/22nd Infantry from the 10th Mountain Division—trained for a "snatch" mission to disable Aidid's vehicle from the air using snipers or to launch a heliborne raid to capture him in his hideout. Several snatch missions were attempted in July, but none were successful.[72] As Major John Evans, the 1st Battalion/22nd Infantry's intelligence officer, recalled, "Either intelligence was not accurate enough, or higher headquarters aborted the mission."[73] In late July Evans and the rest of the QRF completed their tour and departed Somalia. They were replaced by a second rotation—the composite helicopter task force, Task Force Raven, and the 2nd Battalion/14th Infantry. Arriving in the midst of an ongoing insurgency in Mogadishu, the new QRF was untrained for snatch missions and was so busy with operations in the city that it had no time to train for Aidid's capture.[74]

Montgomery supported Howe's repeated requests for special operations forces. In his words, "We had a mandate to capture Aidid. But . . . we did not have the capability to capture him. . . . My position was, if you want us to capture Aidid, then you have to give us the resources to do it, and I don't have them."[75] At CENTCOM, however, Hoar "refused to believe that the key to solving Somalia's problems lay in seizing one man."[76] In the Pentagon, Colin Powell and Secretary of Defense Les Aspin agreed with Hoar. Outside Somalia, the consensus was that Aidid should be "marginalized" politically, but he was not "the center of gravity." UNOSOM's main effort should be political reconciliation. From the Pentagon's perspective, sending Special Forces could turn a "UN versus Aidid" situation into a "US versus Aidid" situation.[77] But from the SNA's perspective, because of the Abdi house strike, it already was the United States versus Aidid.

Throughout July and August SNA attacks increased. Aidid remained at large, and Howe's weekly requests for Special Forces became daily appeals. In July he invited an American interagency assessment team led by Ambassador David Shinn to Mogadishu to see the situation for themselves. Though reportedly told by both Bir and Montgomery that there "was no military solution in Somalia," Shinn was lobbied heavily by Howe, and when he returned to Washington, he recommended that Powell and Aspin send Special Forces to Somalia.[78] By early August, the mood in Washington was shifting in Howe's favor, and the catalyst came with the deadly 8 August mine attack on American military policemen. Both Powell and Hoar attributed their agreement to send Special Forces to capture Aidid to this single incident.[79] After promising to take "appropriate action" against those responsible for detonating the mine, President Clinton recalled that Powell "came to me with a recommendation that I approve a parallel American effort to capture Aidid, though he thought we had only a 50 percent chance of getting him, with a 25 percent chance of getting him alive . . . [to which] I agreed."[80] This parallel effort was Task Force Ranger.

Shortly after the 5 June attacks, the US Army's elite Special Forces Operational Detachment—Delta, commonly known as Delta Force, was put on alert for a potential deployment to Somalia code-named Operation Caustic Brimstone. Fifty Delta Force operators would enter Mogadishu covertly and capture Aidid. However, after the Abdi house strike and the August mine attacks, Caustic Brimstone was increased in size and firepower and given a new code name: Gothic Serpent. The mission was the same, but the force was increased substantially. The 450-strong Task Force Ranger, comprising elite Special Forces personnel from all the US military services, assembled at Fort Bragg. Joining the original Caustic Brimstone Delta Force contingent were US Navy SEALs, US Air Force pararescuemen, a company of Army Rangers, and elite aviators from the 160th Special Operations Aviation Regiment (SOAR).[81] Commanding Task Force Ranger was Major General William Garrison, the head of Joint Special Operations Command. Garrison's mission was to "increase security in Mogadishu by dismantling the high infrastructure of the Somali National Alliance."[82] What this really meant was that the mission was to capture or kill Aidid or, failing that, to target the principal leaders of the SNA.

During the Vietnam War, Garrison had participated in the Phoenix Program, rooting out and eliminating members of the Vietcong. Then, from 1985 to 1989, Garrison personally commanded Delta Force before taking charge of Joint Special Operations Command in 1992. In this last posting he had assisted in the hunt for drug lord Pablo Escobar in Colombia. Among those sent to Bogota and Medellin at the time were Colonel William Boykin, commander of Delta Force, and Lieutenant Colonel Gary Harrell, commander of Delta's C Squadron. Given their experience in Colombia tracking the world's most notorious drug lord, Garrison brought Boykin and Harrell with him to Mogadishu, along with covert intelligence-gathering units.[83] Hunting those who did not want to be found was Garrison's profession.

Used to operating in secrecy, Garrison, Boykin, and Lieutenant Colonel Daniel McKnight, commander of the 3rd Ranger Battalion, traveled to Mogadishu in disguise. The rest of Task Force Ranger was not so inconspicuous. The international media could not help but notice six massive C-5 Galaxy transports landing on 27 August and disgorging 450 personnel and sixteen heavily armed assault helicopters. Task Force Ranger's identity and its mission were broadcast to the world. Despite Montgomery being the commander of all US forces in Somalia, Garrison reported directly to Hoar at CENTCOM, creating a second chain of command in Mogadishu. Montgomery and Garrison had a good relationship, though; they had both served two tours in Vietnam and understood that their respective missions were different—the former focusing on UNOSOM's broader effort in Somalia and the latter on the narrower hunt for Aidid.[84]

For that pursuit, Garrison devised a plan. After establishing a presence in Mogadishu, his men would target Aidid personally. Should he evade capture, Garrison would then focus on neutralizing key SNA officials to learn Aidid's whereabouts or force him to surface. Task Force Ranger set up an operations center on the north ramp of Mogadishu airport, and Garrison's men lived in a dilapidated hangar. Secrecy was paramount. No one, either from UNOSOM or from the other conventional US military units, was allowed access. Nevertheless, Task Force Ranger's presence was public, and so were its operations, but for the wrong reasons.[85]

On the night of 29 August Task Force Ranger was welcomed to Somalia with a mortar barrage that hit both the operations center and the hangar, wounding five. Garrison retaliated by raiding the "Lig Legato" compound, where UNOSOM intelligence claimed Aidid had recently been spotted. As Boykin, the Delta Force commander, recalled, "Aidid gave us the finger. We gave him the finger right back."[86] In a heliborne assault, the men of Task Force Ranger breached the compound, cleared the buildings, and arrested everyone inside. As it turned out, it was not an SNA safe house but a UN Development Program (UNDP) office.[87]

The UNDP's Larry De Boice lodged a formal complaint with Howe when he and his colleagues living at the Lig Legato compound were detained and interrogated by Task Force Ranger. Accused of being an Aidid sympathizer, De Boice was quizzed as to why his staff was living there and why there was so much cash onsite. For months, De Boice told his captors, UNOSOM had failed to relocate his staff into one of the fortified compounds, and cash was a necessity in a country with no functioning banking services.[88] Garrison's inaugural foray resulted in an embarrassing and public failure. Journalists around the world had a field day, reporting, "Crack American troops looked a laughingstock last night after a daring mission turned into a military farce of Hollywood proportions" and "Whoops: Delta Force does it again. . . . The people who brought the world Operation Desert Disaster in the wilds of Iran . . . have chalked up another humiliation."[89] In Washington, Colin Powell was so incensed that he had to "unscrew myself from the ceiling." Garrison was told that all future operations had to be cleared with Hoar at CENTCOM before they were launched.[90] So chastened, Task Force Ranger focused on targeting Aidid personally.

Like they had with Escobar, Garrison's men relied on a major intelligence-gathering effort to hunt Aidid. Agents from every intelligence agency came to Mogadishu to parse through imagery from daily reconnaissance flights, signals intercepts, and reports from dozens of informants. They relied heavily on informants, whose reports were often embellished to encourage American forces to attack rival clans or factions. Informants were also a perishable resource. The most reliable source working for the CIA accidentally shot himself in the head playing a game of Russian roulette. Mogadishu was rife with sightings of the SNA leader. Forty missions were planned but ultimately not launched because the intelligence on Aidid's whereabouts was questionable at best. In addition, Task Force Ranger personnel struggled to distinguish one Somali from another.[91]

On 6 September an old Soviet military compound was raided based on intelligence that Aidid was there. Seventeen prisoners were taken; none were Aidid.[92] A week later, while visiting the Italian embassy, Garrison's men claimed they spotted Aidid speeding away in a car. Despite the unlikelihood of Aidid visiting an embassy located in Ali Mahdi's territory, the car was followed and a raid ensued. General Ahmed Jilao, a key UNOSOM ally, was captured along with dozens of others simply because he looked like Aidid. Jilao unsuccessfully sued Task Force Ranger

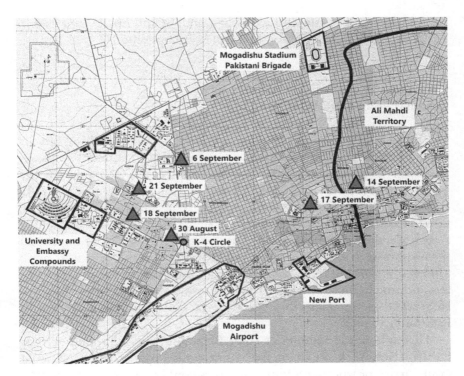

Task Force Ranger Operations, 30 August–21 September 1993

for damages.[93] As one of Garrison's men put it, "Aidid had become like Elvis, people saw him where he wasn't."[94] Reporting on the manhunt, Rick Atkinson wrote that "soldiers nearly became convinced that Aidid was working in the airfield mess hall."[95] By mid-September, Aidid was still at large, so Garrison began targeting senior SNA officials to flush him out and to undermine the SNA's organizational leadership. This yielded quick results.[96]

On 18 September Task Force Ranger attempted to capture Osman Atto, Aidid's right-hand man and chief financier. The media arrived during the raid, and Delta operators threw flash grenades to keep them from being injured during the firefight. Atto escaped, but only briefly. The CIA had placed a homing beacon inside an ivory cane that was intended to be given to Aidid as a gift via an informant. The cane was passed to Atto instead. On 21 September helicopters homed in on the beacon as Atto was traveling in his car. His vehicle was disabled from the air, and Atto was pursued to a nearby building and finally captured in Task Force Ranger's sixth and first successful operation.[97]

Consumed by Mogadishu: Failure and Exhaustion for UNOSOM II

The environment Task Force Ranger operated in was anything but benign. Between UNOSOM and the QRF there were fifteen thousand troops in Mogadishu; Garrison's men were hunting a fugitive in the middle of an insurgency, while UNOSOM contingents and the QRF engaged in heavy fighting across the city. The day Atto was captured, three Pakistanis were burned alive and seven were wounded half a mile away when their APC took an RPG hit to its fuel tank. Mortar attacks on the airport were so frequent that Garrison's men set up a mortar pool: whoever bet on the right time slot for an impact won the pot. No one was immune to these barrages. During a visit on 10 September, General Hoar was forced to take cover when mortars interrupted his lunch with Pakistani troops.[98]

Throughout the summer of 1993, Bir sought constant updates from Baril in New York on when the contingents promised to UNOSOM would arrive or whether additional forces could be found. UNOSOM's authorized strength was twenty-eight thousand, but by early September, only twenty thousand troops were in Somalia. There were still large contingents slated to arrive in late 1993. The Nepalese and Bangladeshis were sending a battalion each, but Bir's hopes rested on the five thousand–strong Indian brigade.[99] Alongside the Pakistanis, the well-equipped and powerful Indian brigade might be sufficient to "break the log jam" in Mogadishu and "clear the city."[100]

Bir's optimism was dashed for two reasons. First, many governments whose contingents had yet to arrive opposed their troops' participation in UNOSOM's war in Mogadishu. The Irish and Koreans had been barred from the city by their respective governments, as was the German logistics force. German political sensitivities meant that its contingent was prohibited from even transporting weapons or ammunition to UNOSOM combat units. The Indian government also decreed that the Indian brigade could not be deployed in Mogadishu, partly due to the war but also due to concerns about having Indian and Pakistani troops near each other.[101] This undermined any plans to secure the capital. Second, in August the Belgian and French governments announced that their troops would be withdrawing from Somalia by December 1993 and January 1994, respectively. This meant that new garrisons were needed for Kismayo in the south and for Baidoa and Oddur in the interior. Though his main effort was Mogadishu, Bir's most powerful combat force, the Indian brigade, would have to replace the French and Belgians.[102] UNOSOM could never amass enough forces to concentrate on stabilizing Mogadishu.

With capable contingents leaving and others unwilling to serve in Mogadishu, Bir was desperate for troops and begged both Howe and Baril to find more. He requested another brigade (at least) for Mogadishu and asked a coalition nation to provide a division-level headquarters to manage UNOSOM troops in the capital. This last request was telling, as Bir was conceding that the fight against Aidid had consumed UNOSOM force headquarters. His staff was "controlling tactical, operational and strategic level operations" instead of focusing on the broader nation-building mission.[103]

The war really had consumed UNOSOM. The situation was so acute that at one point Bir was willing to use the Indian brigade in Mogadishu regardless of any political repercussions. Pakistan volunteered more troops and a divisional headquarters, and Egypt offered to provide the extra brigade.[104] But when Bir learned that the Egyptians would not arrive until 1994, he had to resort to musical chairs–style redeployments to free up forces from the interior to stabilize Mogadishu. "We cannot do it with the forces currently here," he told Howe.[105] Newly arrived Indian units relieved Zimbabweans in Oddur and Moroccans at Baledogle, which in turn freed up Pakistanis in Merka to go to Mogadishu.[106]

These troops were sorely needed as the tensions between the UN and the Italians manifested on the streets of Mogadishu. On 5 September, with the Italians moving outside the city, Nigerian troops replaced them in northern Mogadishu. The locals did not want the Italians to leave and protested the arrival of the Nigerians. At Strongpoint 42, the Nigerian commander was confronted by a clan elder who said there could be no handover without the locals' agreement. The Nigerian officer tried to explain the situation, but the elder simply walked away. Moments later, gunfire peppered the streets around the Nigerians, who scrambled for cover. Another Nigerian platoon at a nearby strongpoint was badly mauled while trying to reach their comrades at Strongpoint 42. Seven Nigerians were killed, ten were wounded, and one was taken

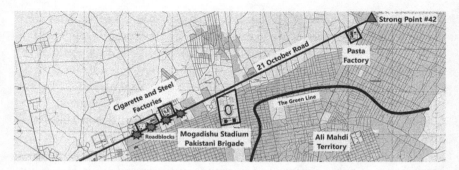

Operation Red Sweep, 9 September 1993

prisoner.[107] The Italians blamed the incident on one Nigerian who "lost his nerve" and fired into the crowd, while the Nigerians accused the Italians of setting up the ambush.[108] Why did this firefight happen? A subsequent meeting between Somalis from northern Mogadishu and UNOSOM representatives suggests an answer. Locals expressed their anger over the Italians' departure from the city, complaining that Americans were killing them from the air while Pakistanis killed them in the streets.[109] Whatever the agitation between Italy and UNOSOM, many Somalis felt they stood a better chance under the former.

On 9 September UNOSOM launched a concerted effort to reestablish control of 21 October Road—the main road running through Mogadishu and connecting the capital to the interior. At one end, it joined the main roads to Baledogle and Baidoa; at the other end, by the pasta factory, it joined the routes to Gialalassi and Beledweyne. However, 21 October Road was dominated by SNA positions at the cigarette and pasta factories and obstructed by seven roadblocks. Bir was determined to clear the road and regain a critical route for resupplying northern Mogadishu and the interior; otherwise, UNOSOM's logistics and freedom of movement would be severely hampered.

The road-clearing effort was called Operation Red Sweep. Four Pakistani M48 tanks and four M113 APCs would proceed up 21 October Road, escorting American combat engineers as they dismantled the roadblocks all the way to the pasta factory using two bulldozers.[110] Somali crowds gathered to watch as the first two roadblocks were cleared with nothing more than sporadic fire from the SNA. At the third, Pakistani tanks were forced to fire main gun rounds due to the increasing opposition. Red Sweep foundered on the fourth roadblock. The SNA knocked out one of the Pakistani tanks, an American bulldozer broke down, and a truck was disabled by an RPG. Task Force Raven's Cobra gunships arrived overhead to find a burning tank, Americans and Pakistanis pinned down, and five hundred to a thousand Somalis advancing on them.[111]

To avoid a repeat of 5 June, Colonel Michael Dallas, the QRF commander, designated the area a "free fire zone," ordering his gunships to disperse the crowds with cannon fire. It was not enough. After firing thirteen hundred rounds and exhausting their ammunition, Dallas authorized the use of rockets, leaving a "substantial but undetermined number of SNA militia killed and wounded," with civilians caught in the middle.[112] With one dead and six wounded, the Pakistanis and the American engineers ceased their advance and withdrew. Adding insult to injury, some locals stole the remaining bulldozer and attempted a getaway before Cobras destroyed it from the air.[113] The SNA had successfully denied the UN the use of the road. Coalition engineers were forced to build a bypass around the capital, which, according to one American officer, "physically represented the complete failure and hopelessness of the UN effort."[114]

The QRF fared no better conducting cordon and search operations near UNOSOM facilities to sweep for weapons and mortar crews. Somali guards working for relief organizations were disarmed if they did not possess blue or pink identification cards.[115] Captain Michael Whetstone, commanding C Company of the US Army's 2nd Battalion/14th Infantry (part of the QRF), described his approach to dealing with Somalis:

> If kids threw rocks, we'd throw rocks back. If our enemy fired a pistol, we'd fire our M16s. If our enemy fired a rifle, we'd fire machine guns. If they fired a machine gun, we'd fire AT-4 rockets. And if they are bold enough to fire an RPG in our direction, all bets were off. . . . God help those who put up a fight. . . . Infantry soldiers can be a lot like rogue cops when their lives are on the line. A Somali would be asked through an interpreter to remain calm and more or less accept his fate. Those who didn't were manhandled to the ground, had their wrists secured behind their backs with a plastic zip binding, and were whisked away.[116]

Whetstone's approach was indicative of the environment most troops in Mogadishu found themselves in. On 15 August his company was joined by intelligence operatives to successfully capture the perpetrators of the 8 August mine attack.[117]

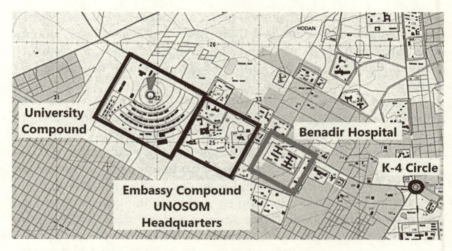

University
Compound

Benadir Hospital

K-4 Circle

Embassy Compound
UNOSOM
Headquarters

QRF Cordon and Search Operation, 13 September 1993

The QRF's biggest engagement came in mid-September, during Task Force Ranger's manhunt. SNA mortar positions were identified near Benadir Hospital, just five hundred meters from the US embassy and the QRF base at the university. At dawn on 13 September, two infantry companies, including Whetstone's, swept two compounds near the hospital code-named Loki and Thor. At Loki, the hospital's former blood bank, Whetstone's company captured a sleeping SNA mortar crew. While his men were loading their detainees, SNA militia began firing RPGs from the hospital. The fire was so intense that Whetstone's withdrawal route was blocked. His men had to use explosives to create an exit in the compound wall. To cover their retreat, they fired twenty antitank rockets at the hospital. The salvo was so intense, Whetstone recalled, that "fighters could be seen falling off the building."[118]

The other infantry company fared worse. They were pinned down against the outside wall of the US embassy by withering SNA fire, eight hundred meters away from a gate they could not get to. In a desperate attempt to reach safety, they tried to blow a hole in the reinforced embassy wall, but the wall held. One hundred militia then attacked the embassy compound from two sides. With the company trapped, Colonel Dallas ordered Task Force Raven to "get anything airborne to suppress the enemy."[119] Cobras began gun runs on SNA positions, while Black Hawk door gunners and snipers on the embassy wall joined the melee.

Inside the compound, soldiers and civilian staff from UNOSOM gathered on rooftops to watch the firefight, "drinking sodas, laughing and exchanging jokes."[120] This revelry dissipated when incoming mortars scattered the spectators, who were not wearing body armor or helmets. After a two-hour firefight that left three Americans wounded and heavy SNA casualties, the company was able to return to base.[121]

From August to October, Task Force Raven helicopters from the QRF expended 38,440 rounds of cannon ammunition and fired 500 rockets and 80 missiles in Mogadishu.[122] Colonel Lawrence Casper, who replaced Dallas as QRF commander, did not exaggerate when he wrote, "During the pivotal months of September and October 1993, Task Force [Raven] was the single most dominant military force in the Somali theatre of operations. The outcome of each major engagement was largely determined by the . . . sound employment of attack and assault helicopters. The damage inflicted on the forces of the SNA militia was unmatched by any other combat force in Somalia."[123] Montgomery later told reporters, "There are plenty of people in the United States who still don't know that this was a war, is a war."[124]

A Helicopter-Rich Environment

After the Battle of Mogadishu, the prevailing narrative promulgated by veterans and by those within the US military education system was that the SNA had recognized the operational centrality of American helicopters. Then, taking advantage of Task Force Ranger's use of the same tactics in each of its seven operations, the SNA focused on shooting down a helicopter. This narrative was reinforced by subsequent statements from Aidid that he aimed to down an aircraft so that his forces could engage the Americans in a pitched battle.[125] But this narrative does not reflect the evidence. Although there were isolated SNA attempts to target American helicopters, they were uncoordinated at best and fell far short of being a concerted effort.

Mogadishu airport was home to Task Force Raven's fifty-two helicopters. Thirty Russian Mil helicopter transports contracted by UNOSOM to airlift supplies into the interior were also based there.[126] The skies above Mogadishu were constantly filled with low-flying helicopters. Task Force Raven flew "Eyes over Mogadishu" and reconnaissance missions, wide-body escorts, and transport flights in addition to supporting American and UNOSOM troops engaged by the SNA. Reconnaissance flights typically flew low during daylight hours. One veteran remembered being "able to make out the facial features on the people in the streets below. . . . If we were over a bad part of town, some of the kids flipped us off and threw rocks at the bird."[127] Pilots often flew low over the Swedish hospital in the university compound to catch glimpses of topless nurses sunbathing on the roof. One officer remarked that this was "a welcome distraction in a country where the women . . . were clothed from head to foot."[128]

Added to the air traffic from the QRF and UNOSOM was that of Task Force Ranger. The embarrassing Lig Legato raid had undermined any secrecy surrounding the mission, so, with the element of surprise lost, Garrison opted for desensitization. Every day, often more than once a day, his entire sixteen-helicopter fleet loaded up and flew across Mogadishu in formation, skirting the rooftops and sometimes hovering over random buildings. Task Force Ranger's presence could not be concealed, but with these constant flights, they could obscure whether they were conducting a genuine raid or a feint.[129] Garrison also varied his methods and timing. Some raids were launched at night, others during the day. Sometimes troops were extracted by helicopter, sometimes by ground vehicles; in one instance, helicopters were not used at all.[130] Thus, any assertions that Task Force Ranger used a consistent tactical formula are incorrect.

Low-flying helicopters, particularly American helicopters, were a constant presence above Mogadishu. Black Hawks, Hueys, Cobras, and Kiowas filled the skies. Yet the vast majority were not shot down by the SNA or even fired on. Despite hostilities starting on 5 June, the first report of "possible RPG fire" against a helicopter was not until 20–21 August.[131] Definitive SNA use of RPGs against a helicopter was confirmed on 24 August. Then, on 2 September, a Task Force Raven Black Hawk was hit by a 57mm antiaircraft gun. One soldier on board was wounded, the first in-flight injury caused by the SNA.[132] Task Force Raven's after-action report highlighted that there was no prescribed doctrine for combat search and rescue by aviation units if a helicopter was shot down. In such a scenario, it stated, it was "every 'pilot for him/herself.'" The only existing response was the deployment of a team of mechanics to repair a downed helicopter in a secure area; there was no procedure for securing one in a hostile urban environment.[133]

Aviators were advised that the best defense against RPGs was to fly at high speed at an altitude of one hundred feet to make the aircraft more difficult to hit.[134] The RPG threat was dismissed by many. Task Force Ranger's Lieutenant Larry Perino recalled that "the prevailing attitude . . . was that RPG fire was ineffective in bringing down helicopters."[135] This confidence is understandable. American helicopters, especially Black Hawks, were ubiquitous in Somalia after four months of combat operations. During that time, the RPG threat had been sporadic to the point of being negligible. The chief threat to helicopters was mortar barrages on the airport ramp—until a Black Hawk was shot down.

Courage Five-Three: The First Black Hawk "Down"

At 01:00 on 25 September, *Courage Five-Three* was one of two Task Force Raven Black Hawks conducting an "Eyes over Mogadishu" mission. Piloted by Chief Warrant Officers Dale Shrader and Perry Alliman, *Courage Five-Three* was refueling when mortars hit the airport. Lifting off immediately to locate the mortar crew, they were flying at one hundred feet and at high speed when a single RPG impacted the underside of the aircraft. The blast ruptured the fuel cells and engulfed the cabin in flames. Piloting the other Black Hawk that night, Lieutenant Jeffrey Riedel heard Shrader on the radio: "I'm hit, I'm hit, we're on fire, we're going down." Shrader and Alliman struggled to stay aloft, hoping to land at UN-controlled New Port. The flames in the cabin spread, burning both pilots and rendering their night-vision optics useless. Then the engine failed. Riedel watched *Courage Five-Three* go into a "somewhat controlled descent," followed by a "significant impact" and explosion.[136] *Courage Five-Three*, the first Black Hawk "down" in Somalia, had crashed in an SNA stronghold near Radio Mogadishu.

The QRF scrambled. Accompanied overhead by Task Force Raven's Cobras and Black Hawks, Whetstone's company mobilized to reach the crash site before the SNA did. UN forces did the same. A Pakistani patrol was repulsed by the SNA en route to the crash site. Whetstone arrived to find *Courage Five-Three* "totally destroyed, most of it was either ash, or in a molten pool working its way down the street."[137] They found no survivors. All that remained of one of the crew was "femurs, ribcage, and skull . . . the rest was just ash." The fire burned too hot for Whetstone's men to search the wreckage. Making matters worse, two hundred SNA militia had arrived first. Whetstone's company was engaged immediately, and three American soldiers were seriously wounded. Gathering what remains could be found, Whetstone was forced to withdraw under fire.[138]

The initial RPG hit killed an observer from the 10th Mountain Division, and the final impact killed *Courage Five-Three*'s crew chief and door gunner. But Shrader and Alliman, though seriously wounded, had survived. Long before Whetstone and the QRF arrived, Shrader, sometimes carrying Alliman, evaded and exchanged fire with the SNA militia advancing on the crash site. After exhausting their pistol ammunition, they headed for New Port. A Somali found the two injured and defenseless pilots and guided them to a nearby Emirati patrol from UNOSOM that had sortied from New Port in search of them.

The downing of *Courage Five-Three* exposed the serious issues Task Force Ranger would face little more than a week later. The Black Hawk went down at 01:10. Whetstone and his men departed the university at 02:00 and reached the wreckage at 04:00.[139] The SNA had been able to mobilize faster. Yet later that same day, during a UNOSOM press briefing, Captain Tim McDavitt dismissed the seriousness of the *Courage Five-Three* incident, telling reporters, "I don't call it significant. I call it rather ... an unlucky shot for ... an RPG is not a precise weapon."[140] McDavitt was not alone in suggesting that it was a fluke. Members of Task Force Ranger, and even Montgomery in Senate testimony, put it down to bad luck; they all concluded that an RPG was not an antiaircraft weapon.[141] The UH-60 Black Hawk was, after all, a resilient post–Vietnam War platform designed specifically to withstand the Cold War European battlefield. But what was neither acknowledged nor realized at the time was that the Black Hawk's design process took no account of the dangers of RPGs.[142]

The Policy Change to Negotiation

By September 1993, Task Force Ranger had not neutralized Aidid or the SNA leadership, and the QRF and UNOSOM forces stumbled from one bloody engagement to another. The international community, the United States in particular, was tiring of Somalia. Immediately after the Abdi house strike, Lansana Kouyate, who had resumed his post as deputy special representative, met with the staff of UNOSOM's Political Division for "an exchange of views . . . to avoid further escalation and make progress." One staffer noted that communicating with the SNA, and especially with Aidid's Habr-Gidr, was difficult, given that many of the leaders had been killed on 12 July. The "brainstorming" session concluded that negotiation was preferable and that Aidid should be pressured to leave Somalia "without publicity."[143]

At the time, the policy of negotiation failed to gain traction, amounting to just one backroom pitch behind closed doors. Then Aidid made the first of several peace overtures in August. Aidid appealed directly to former US President Jimmy Carter (in a still classified letter) to act as a mediator with the Clinton administration and to press for an independent commission to investigate the events of 5 June. Several Habr-Gidr clan members living in the United States approached the State Department with the same request. Carter wrote to National Security Adviser Anthony Lake, Secretary of State Warren Christopher, and US Ambassador to the UN Madeleine Albright, arguing for an easing of hostilities with Aidid.[144] However, Carter's appeal fell on deaf ears, as any plans for mediation were being actively "discouraged" by senior White House officials.[145] At this stage, Task Force Ranger had just arrived in Somalia. There may have been confidence that Garrison would bring Aidid in, so why negotiate?

For Boutros-Ghali, too, negotiation was not an option. He took to the *New York Times* to address growing criticisms of UN actions in Somalia. "In these and other peace operations," he wrote, "critics have failed to recall, or misunderstood or even knowingly disregarded requirements of resolutions that their governments may have voted for or even helped draft . . . if this is to succeed, governments can expect to act multilaterally or unilaterally, but not . . . both ways at the same time."[146] The message was clear. UN actions were not the will of the secretary-general but the collective desire of its member states, as agreed on in the Security Council. Nations could not agree to a UN resolution authorizing a manhunt, for example, and then criticize it in action. Boutros-Ghali's views on negotiation were undoubtedly colored by the relative detachment and comfort of UN headquarters in New York. On the ground in Mogadishu, with flares and gunfire lighting up the sky every night, a potential settlement was not dismissed out of hand.

On 3 September Aidid reached out again through John Drysdale, Howe's political adviser and a senior member of UNOSOM's Political Division, offering a cease-fire and the opening of a "mutual dialogue." Howe rejected this after the firefight with the Nigerians two days later, believing that Aidid was not being genuine. Nevertheless, several UN-

OSOM civilian officials, Drysdale included, continued secret negotiations with the SNA throughout September to explore a cease-fire, but after Howe "passed up . . . several chances to make peace," Drysdale resigned in protest.[147]

The reality was that in Washington and among senior American officials in Mogadishu, there was no appetite for negotiation. Aidid was a "warlord," and it would undermine US credibility to deal with someone who had been demonized for months and portrayed—inaccurately—as the reason for Somalia's collapse. In Mogadishu, Robert Gosende, Oakley's replacement as presidential envoy, cabled the State Department on 6 September and stated, "Any plan for negotiating a truce with Aidid's henchmen should be shelved. We should refuse to deal with perpetrators of terrorist acts."[148] He advocated escalation against the SNA to sweep and secure Mogadishu. "If we're going to take a military approach, we should take it and not pussyfoot around," he argued.[149]

Gosende's suggestion prompted vehement opposition from none other than Hoar at CENTCOM. Hoar was not in favor of negotiation, though; he was just opposed to sending any more US troops into the cauldron. UNOSOM had lost control of Mogadishu, he claimed, and escalation could be achieved only by using US forces, owing to the coalition partners' reluctance to engage the SNA. Concerned that American troops would have to do the heavy lifting if Gosende's appeal was successful, Hoar cabled Frank Wisner, undersecretary of defense for policy, and Colin Powell on 8 September. "After four months of operations with extraordinary help from the U.S.," Hoar told them, "the U.N.'s successes have been modest. . . . Control of Mogadishu has been lost . . . if the only solution . . . is a large-scale infusion of troops and if the only country available to make this commitment is the United States, then it's time to reassess. . . . The U.N. is attempting too much too quickly in Somalia."[150]

Hoar believed that regardless of an increase in forces, the UN experiment in nation building had failed. Gosende, in contrast, believed that conceding failure would severely damage American credibility, but then he wavered. On 17 September, just two weeks after suggesting escalation and after two peace overtures from Aidid had been rebuffed, he pushed for a complete about-face, sending a cable to the State Department entitled "The Making of a Deal."[151] In it, Gosende suggested giving Aidid his independent investigation of 5 June and even allowing members of the Habr-Gidr clan to participate. In return for a cease-fire,

Aidid would be offered exile until the investigation was concluded. Gosende believed this would be a win-win. If Aidid accepted, the war would be over; if not, he would alienate himself from the rest of the SNA for prolonging the fighting, potentially easing his capture by Garrison and Task Force Ranger.[152]

Why the change? Task Force Ranger had carried out four unsuccessful operations. American confidence that Aidid could be caught was waning. The same was happening in Washington, where congressional frustration with the lack of progress in Somalia was becoming outright opposition. Samuel P. Huntington wrote in the September issue of *Joint Forces Quarterly*, "The United States has no interest in which clan dominates Somalia. . . . It is morally unjustifiable and politically indefensible that members of the Armed Forces should be killed to prevent Somalis from killing one another."[153] Even Tom Farer, who had led the initial highly prejudicial investigation into the events of 5 June, argued that "without a change in direction, the U.N. operation is headed for a rendezvous with disaster." Aidid, Farer said, was not a "mercenary thug" but a clan leader, chosen in an "essentially democratic process." Removing him would not end the war; it would escalate it further. Farer conceded that Glaspie and the American leadership in UNOSOM had marginalized Aidid, even though he had "played by the rules." Farer concluded that the chase for Aidid should end, as nation building can be accomplished only around "existing centers of power."[154]

And so it was that Secretary of State Christopher met Boutros-Ghali on 20 September. Christopher warned the secretary-general of the precarious state of American public and political support for the mission and outlined Gosende's proposal to offer Aidid exile. Boutros-Ghali responded that Resolution 837 mandated Aidid's capture—a mandate, he reminded Christopher, that the United States had shaped and supported—and only a new resolution could change that mandate.[155] In a letter to Christopher five days later, Boutros-Ghali reiterated that he was "obliged to make every effort to bring Aidid to justice. I know that you understand and support this position." "At the same time," he continued, "my mind is not closed to other ways of neutralizing Aidid. . . . However, confidentiality has to be maintained." Thus, negotiation could be pursued only if it was not public knowledge. Boutros-Ghali's letter to Christopher clarifies that making Somalia a precedent-setting success for the post–Cold War UN was the absolute priority. Credibility was paramount, and the United States had to stay the course in Somalia. If US resolve "should weaken," he warned, it "would have a devastating effect on your and my efforts to strengthen the capacity of the United Nations to contribute to a better world . . . it would also represent a humbling of the United Nations and of the . . . United States." While giving tacit support to negotiating with Aidid, the UN secretary-general still maintained that there were "no practicable alternatives" to the manhunt.[156]

Regardless of the desire to maintain confidentiality, the Clinton administration unilaterally pursued the negotiation track from late September onward. In the corridors of the Pentagon, with congressional pressure to leave Somalia mounting, Powell was presented with three options by the Joint Staff. First, the United States could withdraw by 15 November, which could cause an exodus of UNOSOM coalition members, undermining the future of the operation. Second, withdrawal by 1 January 1994 increased UNOSOM's viability and avoided any link being drawn to the failure to apprehend Aidid. Third, departing by 1 April 1994 gave UNOSOM the best chance to go forward. Powell conferred with Hoar, who, in agreement with Gosende's new position, recommended negotiation and the offer of exile. At a White House briefing on 25 September, Powell, armed with these recommendations, advised that the United States either send more troops to Somalia or change its policy.[157] Thus, with both the US military and the State Department pushing for a negotiated settlement, Clinton had a choice to make.

On 27 September Clinton addressed the UN General Assembly. In his lengthy speech, he mentioned Somalia only twice. Toward the end, however, he said, "The United Nations simply cannot become engaged in every one of the world's conflicts. If the American people are to say yes to U.N. peacekeeping, the United Nations must know *when to say no*."[158] On the surface, it was a warning that, with ongoing UN operations in Bosnia, Mozambique, and Cambodia and new missions starting in Haiti and Rwanda, the UN was stretched too far. But, given the timing of events in Somalia, it could only be seen as a veiled indictment of the UN being overly ambitious—and an indication that American support had its limits, despite the United States' push for the ambitious UNOSOM mandate Clinton was now criticizing. That America had reached its limit was made clear the next day when Elaine Sciolino reported in the *New York Times* that the Clinton administration would now focus on isolating Aidid politically, not capturing him. It was, she wrote, "a clear admission that the military campaign . . . has failed."[159]

Operational Consequences of the Policy Shift

The decision to pursue a negotiated settlement with Aidid and the SNA had major consequences in Somalia. Prior to the attack on the Nigerians, Operation Red Sweep, and the Benadir Hospital firefight, Montgomery had requested reinforcements. In his words:

> There was an increase in the number of ambushes on the roads. There was an increase in numbers of mortar attacks against us, against our facilities and the Headquarters, our casualties started to go up . . . it was becoming increasingly difficult . . . the United Nations forces were becoming increasingly timid, and I really began to be worried about my capability to protect my force, as the U.S. Commander.[160]

On 26 August he had submitted an informal request to Major General Waldo Freeman, Hoar's deputy at CENTCOM, for substantial reinforcements, including a mechanized battalion with Bradley armored fighting vehicles, an artillery battery, and an air cavalry troop. Freeman responded that Hoar would travel to Mogadishu to discuss Montgomery's request in person.[161] When Hoar arrived on 9 September, he told Montgomery his request "wouldn't fly because the United States wanted out of Somalia, wanted to lower our troop presence, rather than increasing it." Hoar had just cabled Powell and Wisner the previous day about reassessing the commitment of US forces to Somalia, so his lukewarm attitude toward Montgomery's request was not surprising. It is unclear whether Montgomery knew that Hoar was central to the ongoing debate on US policy in Somalia. Nevertheless, Hoar hinted that a much smaller request might be approved. As such, Montgomery submitted a "formal" and much diminished request directly to Hoar on 14 September, asking for just a company-sized force of Bradley vehicles, Abrams tanks, and artillery "at the earliest feasible date." "U.S. forces are at risk without it," he ended.[162]

This second request became highly controversial. It was later claimed that instead of following procedure and forwarding the request to the Joint Staff at the Pentagon, Hoar sent it directly to Powell. When the Senate Armed Services Committee held hearings and asked the Pentagon for documents related to the second request, it responded that "no written documentation has been found pertaining to these questions."[163] When Hoar himself testified before the Senate, almost every response he gave was redacted in the *Congressional Record*.[164]

Barton Gellman of the *Washington Post* later excoriated Hoar. In a piece exposing Hoar's opposition to any further deployment of American forces to Somalia, Gellman revealed that, "for reasons that remain unclear," Hoar waited until 22 September before forwarding Montgomery's request to Powell, who was retiring as chairman of the Joint Chiefs of Staff on 30 September. Gellman questioned why Hoar delayed forwarding the request to Powell while at the same time he sent three cables indicating that he was "absorbed much less by the need for reinforcements than by the wish to encourage withdrawal from a humanitarian enterprise that had long since bogged down in guerilla war."[165] When Hoar finally sent the request, he included his own views on the political ramifications of granting it. Powell brought the request and Hoar's opinions to Secretary of Defense Les Aspin. Unsurprisingly, given the political climate and the policy shift toward negotiation, Aspin refused to send Montgomery any reinforcements.[166] After all, the war was now supposedly over.

The motivations of CENTCOM's commanding general are hard to discern. Hoar invited Montgomery to make the second request and then sat on it. Simultaneously, he encouraged the policy shift toward a negotiated settlement with the SNA. Hoar had to know that the longer he waited to forward Montgomery's request, the less receptive the political climate in Washington would be. He may have been thinking of the bigger strategic picture, waiting to see what the final policy decision would be. Or he may have been stuck between a subordinate making politically unacceptable demands for reinforcements amidst an insurgency and an increasingly risk-averse Pentagon and White House. Likewise, Montgomery asked for reinforcements knowing that he would probably be turned down. Arguably, it was an attempt to avoid future blame and career fallout, given that US forces were now bogged down. However, with casualties mounting from command-detonated mines in a frustrating counterinsurgency campaign, his request for armored vehicles made sense. Between the two, Hoar is far more culpable because, critically, when the policy shift came on 28 September, he did not issue new orders reflecting the change toward negotiation. Garrison's orders to hunt Aidid remained in place, and Montgomery's use of the QRF in Mogadishu was allowed to continue.

Thus, on 3 October 1993 staff in the Pentagon were formalizing the proposals to negotiate with the SNA. The war would end; Aidid would be granted foreign exile, pending an independent investigation of his

culpability for 5 June; and a US withdrawal was scheduled for 31 March 1994. Their work was suddenly interrupted by breaking news from Mogadishu. Two Black Hawk helicopters had been shot down, and American forces were embroiled in a major engagement.[167]

9 | The Battle of Mogadishu

*The Intelligence for the operation was good. The execution of the assault
went flawlessly. It took less than 10 minutes.*
> —Sean J. Darragh, deputy assistant secretary of defense[1]

*There are plenty of people in the United States who still don't know that this
was a war.*
> —Major General Thomas Montgomery, commander, US Forces
> Somalia, deputy force commander, UNOSOM II[2]

We probably have made Aideed into a hero.
> —Brigadier Ikram ul-Hasan, commander, Pakistani brigade[3]

Sunday, 3 October, was a day off for Task Force Ranger. But for the
QRF, the morning began with a medevac. A Humvee carrying a marine
counterintelligence team and a Somali interpreter was destroyed by a
command-detonated mine near New Port, close to where *Courage Five-
Three* crashed the previous week. The interpreter was killed, one marine
was trapped in the wreckage, and two others were slightly wounded. In a
daring move, the pilots of a Task Force Raven Black Hawk circling overhead, *Courage Six-Eight*, landed in the streets to evacuate the ambulatory
survivors. However, the marines refused to leave their trapped comrade.
With a Somali crowd approaching the extremely vulnerable helicopter
and reports of gunfire, the pilots of *Courage Six-Eight* reluctantly took off.

Moments later, another Black Hawk, *Courage Seven-Three*, arrived.
Pilots Lieutenant Jeffrey Riedel and Chief Warrant Officer Ben Johnson watched *Courage Six-Eight* coming out and heard Task Force Raven
headquarters prohibit any further landings due to the gunfire. But with
the marines trapped in a hostile part of town, Riedel and Johnson disregarded orders and landed. Riedel left the idling Black Hawk and ransacked nearby houses. Eventually finding a shovel, Riedel, with the help
of his door gunner, crew chief, and the two wounded marines, freed the

trapped man. They retrieved the eviscerated body of the Somali interpreter, reboarded *Courage Seven-Three,* and took off.[4] It was a successful and gutsy medevac, and Riedel and Johnson were decorated for their actions. Bravery aside, if this had happened on any other day, it would have been unremarkable. It is not mentioned in most accounts of 3 October, but evidence suggests that Task Force Raven's landings that morning influenced events later that afternoon.[5]

Unbeknownst to UNOSOM or Task Force Ranger, the SNA had scheduled a high-level meeting later that day near the Olympic Hotel. Two of Aidid's top advisers, Omar Salad Elmi and Mohamed Hassan Awale, were due to attend. Garrison learned of the meeting only by chance. He had compiled a target list of known SNA leaders and their associates to be detained—individuals who might have knowledge of Aidid's whereabouts. One of the men on the list contacted the Mogadishu CIA chief, claimed his inclusion was a mistake, and offered information about the meeting in return for being removed from it.[6] With only Osman Atto in custody after six operations, this was an opportunity for Garrison to deal a decisive blow to the SNA.

The entirety of Task Force Ranger was mobilized for the raid: sixteen helicopters—eight Black Hawks and eight AH/MH-6 Little Birds. The plan was relatively simple. Four Black Hawks would carry a security force from B Company, 3rd Ranger Battalion, commanded by Captain Michael Steele. From each of the four helicopters, sixteen Rangers would fast-rope into the streets around the building, creating a four-corner perimeter and sealing it off from SNA reinforcements. Four Little Birds and two Black Hawks would carry an assault force of forty Delta operators under Captain Austin S. Miller, which would hit the meeting itself. The nimble Little Birds would land on top of the building, while the rest of Miller's men fast-roped from the larger Black Hawks. The goal was a simultaneous raid on the building from the roof and the ground floor to capture all attendees.[7] The remaining four Little Birds were gunships, available to provide air support if needed. Of the two remaining Black Hawks, one carried Garrison's only reserve, a Special Forces combat search and rescue (CSAR) team in case one of the helicopters went down. The other was the command-and-control aircraft carrying Lieutenant Colonel Gary Harrell, commanding Delta Force's C Squadron, whose operators made up the assault force, and Lieutenant Colonel Tom Matthews, commanding 1st Battalion, 160th SOAR, whose helicopters and aviators were part of Task Force Ranger. Garrison would supervise the raid from his operations center at the airport. Once the prisoners were secured, a convoy of nine Humvees and three trucks manned by Rangers under Lieutenant Colonel Daniel McKnight, commander of 3rd Ranger Battalion, would transport everyone back to the airport.[8] From start to finish, the raid was expected to take thirty minutes. Given the secretive nature of Task Force Ranger's operations, neither the QRF nor UNOSOM was informed beforehand.

Sitting on the airport ramp, rotors spinning, the sixteen fully laden helicopters waited to go. The Somali informant had been told to confirm the meeting location by parking his car outside the target building, which he did after initially parking in front of the wrong building out of fear of the SNA. With that, the launch code word was given: "Irene."[9] The heliborne assault began at 15:42. Almost immediately, the helicopters came under intense fire from RPGs, a level of resistance never before seen during the intervention. Dust clouds kicked up by rotor wash were the only protection as the Black Hawks hovered to allow the Rangers and Delta operators to rope down to the streets. At 15:53 McKnight's convoy moved toward the target building. Within five minutes, one of his trucks was knocked out by an RPG. Despite the resistance, Miller's assault force captured twenty-four SNA officials, including Elmi and Awale. By 16:04, the mission was complete. Miller loaded his prisoners into McKnight's vehicles, and the security force was preparing to collapse the perimeter and withdraw to the airport. It had taken twenty-two minutes from start to finish. But then it all went wrong.[10]

At 16:20 *Super Six-One*, an orbiting Black Hawk piloted by Chief Warrant Officer Clifton Wolcott, was struck in the tail rotor by an RPG. There were eight men on board. As he spun out of control, Wolcott radioed, "Six-One's going down. Six-One's going down," before crashing in the SNA section of Mogadishu, roughly half a kilometer from the target building.[11] A new plan was rapidly formulated on the ground. Miller's assault force and Steele's security force would fight their way through the streets to the crash site on foot to secure it and retrieve any survivors. McKnight's convoy, with the SNA prisoners aboard, would collect everyone there and head back to the airport. Meanwhile, at 16:24 *Star 41*, a much smaller Little Bird piloted by Chief Warrant Officers Karl Meier and Keith Jones, landed right beside the wreckage of *Super Six-One*, hoping to evacuate some of the survivors before the advancing SNA militia reached them. The first person they saw, a Delta operator, was firing at the SNA; he still wore "his black helmet, but his face was a mask of blood,

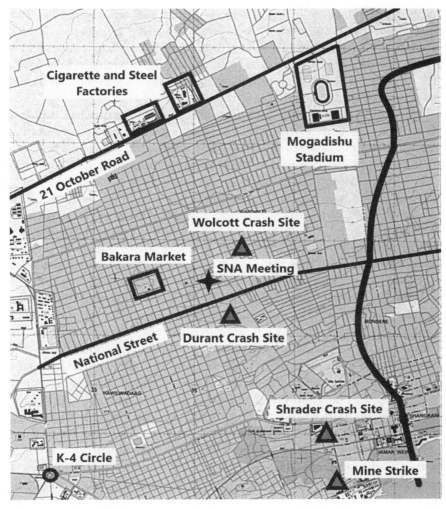

Task Force Ranger Raid, 3 October 1993

and part of it looked crushed in."[12] The two pilots began firing at the militia from the cockpit and watched as two wounded survivors were hit again and collapsed. Under fire, Jones left the cockpit to drag each of the men back to *Star 41*. Meier was repeatedly ordered to take off, but his response was, "[I'm] not leaving without my co-pilot."[13] Just as Jones got the two men aboard, Meier saw the first Rangers arrive on foot to secure the crash site. As *Star 41* took off for the hospital at the airport, the Black Hawk *Super Six-Eight* arrived with a CSAR team of medics and Special Forces operators to rope down to add to the growing perimeter and treat the remaining wounded. *Super Six-Eight* was struck by several RPGs, but the pilot managed to hold the severely damaged helicopter in a hover until the entire CSAR team had deployed, and then he barely made it back to the airport.[14]

With the CSAR team committed and Miller and Steele's men en route to or arriving at the crash site, Garrison had used every option available to him. Task Force Ranger had trained for a downed helicopter scenario in the previous days, ironically, using Wolcott's *Super Six-One*. The inclusion of a CSAR team accounted for the possibility of a downed helicopter, but it did not allow for two. At 16:41 another orbiting Black Hawk, *Super Six-Four* piloted by Chief Warrant Officer Michael Durant, was hit by an RPG in the tail rotor. Durant turned the stricken aircraft toward the airport, but the rotor tore apart and *Super Six-Four* went down. Garrison had nothing left to commit. All his forces had been sent to Wolcott's crash site, taking casualties in the process.[15]

The local SNA commander in the area was Colonel Sharif Hassan Giumale, a career army officer trained in both Soviet and NATO military academies. The SNA had divided the city into eighteen sectors connected by a radio network, with duty officers constantly on watch. Giumale took advantage of this network and mobilized militia units to converge on the two crash sites and ambush Miller and Steele's men in the streets. The goal was to isolate Task Force Ranger and prevent any reinforcements from reaching them.[16] He was partially successful. McKnight's convoy got lost in the urban labyrinth of Mogadishu while trying to locate the first crash site. Twice they passed within one block of it, without realizing how close they were. Giumale's forces created roadblocks and poured weapons fire into McKnight's thin-skinned vehicles. With the number of casualties mounting, McKnight was ordered to return to base to rearm and regroup. Miller and Steele were ordered to dig in and hold the perimeter around *Super Six-One* until a relief mission could reach them. Garrison later testified, "There's not a force in the world that can take on the personnel that we had . . . in a perimeter defense."[17]

All that could be spared for Durant's *Super Six-Four* were two Delta snipers. Circling overhead in *Super Six-Two*, Master Sergeant Gary Gordon and Sergeant First Class Randall Shughart repeatedly volunteered to secure the second crash site alone, despite not knowing when or if a relief force could reach them. Garrison reluctantly acceded. Gordon and Shughart reached Durant's crash site, defending it against militia and hostile crowds until they were overwhelmed and killed. Durant, badly injured, was captured. Shughart and Gordon were both posthumously awarded the Medal of Honor, the first recipients since the end of the Vietnam War. At 17:27, after delivering the two snipers, *Super Six-Two* was hit by an RPG. The blast severed the leg of a third Delta sniper on board and rendered the copilot unconscious. Veering away, *Super Six-Two* crash-landed at New Port. In a little over an hour, half of Task Force Ranger's eight Black Hawks had been shot down or forced to crash-land due to enemy fire. A fifth, *Super Six-Six*, was rendered unflyable by SNA fire later that evening after dropping supplies and ammunition to Steele and Miller at Wolcott's crash site.[18]

Fully engaged, Garrison turned to the QRF. At 16:29, after Wolcott was shot down and the CSAR team committed, he asked Montgomery to ready the QRF to assist if necessary. Once Durant was shot down, it became necessary. Lieutenant Colonel William David's 2nd Battalion/14th Infantry mobilized, and Whetstone's C Company was dispatched to the airport as the initial reaction force. With orders to secure Wolcott's crash site, Whetstone departed the airport in a convoy at 17:03. They reached the K-4 Circle and proceeded up Via Lenin, headlong into an SNA ambush at National Street. Giumale's tactics to prevent US reinforcements from getting through resulted in two destroyed Humvees and several casualties. Whetstone's company was not strong enough to punch through alone. "The vehicles were totally shot up, every windshield was spider-webbed, nearly every tire was blown out," a veteran remembered.[19] David ordered Whetstone back to the airport.[20]

A new rescue plan was needed. With ninety men between them, Miller and Steele were holding Wolcott's crash site, but Durant's had been overrun. McKnight's convoy was badly mauled, as was Whetstone's company. A much stronger force was needed to relieve Task Force Ranger, and the QRF lacked armored vehicles. Garrison now asked Montgomery for UNOSOM's assistance. As deputy force commander, Montgomery had put the Pakistanis, Malaysians, and Italians on standby, as they had the most armored vehicles. The Pakistani brigade was deployed throughout Mogadishu, and the Malaysians were UNOSOM's armored reserve. The Italians were too far away to help, being outside the city in Balad. Unaware that an operation had been launched until they were told it had gone wrong, the Pakistanis and Malaysians did not hesitate to make their forces available. At the same time, Colonel Lawrence Casper, the QRF commander, readied his entire command—Task Force Raven's helicopters and David's 2nd Battalion/14th Infantry—for the rescue operation.[21]

As the sun set on 3 October, thirty-two Pakistani and Malaysian APCs and four Pakistani tanks, along with their crews, assembled at New Port. This armored convoy would carry two of David's rifle companies, his antitank platoon, and more than forty Rangers and Special Forces personnel.[22] Because the SNA had repulsed Whetstone on Via Lenin, and given the difficulties McKnight's convoy had experienced trying to negotiate the warrens of the city, the rescue convoy would move from New Port east across the Green Line into Ali Mahdi's territory, turn north, and then turn west onto National Street, approaching Miller and Steele from the opposite direction. The two crash sites were north and south of National Street. David's armored convoy would advance up this main thoroughfare and stop to allow his two companies to disembark—one heading for each crash site—while the convoy stayed on National to keep the escape route open. David's companies would collect all the survivors from both crash sites, and the convoy would then head for the Pakistani base at Mogadishu Stadium nearby. National Street was also the dividing line for air operations; Task Force Ranger helicopters covered north of National and Wolcott's crash site, while Task Force Raven aviators handled everything south, including Durant's crash site.[23] This was critical, because until the convoy arrived, the beleaguered men at the crash sites would have to rely on the four Little Bird gunships to hold the SNA at bay. Their mini-guns, by one estimate, fired 170,000 rounds that night.[24]

The UNOSOM armored convoy under David's command left New Port, with the Pakistani tanks in the lead, at 23:10. Following the plan, the convoy turned onto National at 23:54 and advanced west toward the crash sites. The SNA poured fire into the vehicles. Overhead, one helicopter pilot observed "two layers of mass confusion—air and ground."[25] Despite dividing the airspace, Task Force Raven and Task Force Ranger helicopters were in such proximity that two of their Black Hawks, one from each task force, almost collided. On the ground, SNA resistance caused three APCs to take a wrong turn, forcing the convoy to halt in the kill zone. These three APCs were then ambushed and disabled. Task Force Raven Cobras were firing in "danger close" proximity to the convoy—so close, in fact, that David ordered them to withdraw. The shrap-

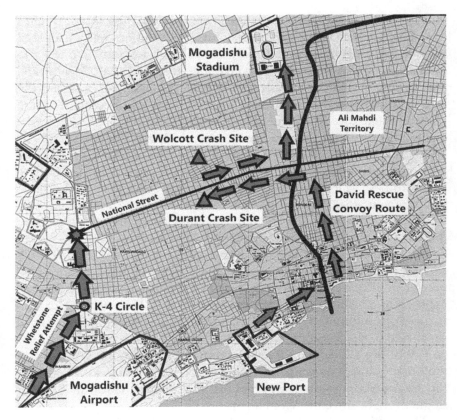

Task Force Ranger Relief, 3–4 October 1993

nel and debris from their cannon fire caused the men in the armored vehicles to close their hatches to avoid injury, reducing their ability to fire back at the SNA. As the fight went on, the tanks, 1950s-era M48 Pattons, ran out of fuel. Braving enemy fire, their Pakistani crews got out to refuel them manually.[26]

The armored convoy inched along National for ninety minutes under intense fire until David was informed at 01:37 that he was nearing Wolcott's crash site to the north. His two rifle companies disembarked; A Company under Captain Drew Meyerowich headed north toward Steele and Miller's perimeter, while Whetstone's C Company headed south. They found no bodies at *Super Six-Four* and, after fruitlessly calling Durant's, Gordon's, and Shughart's names into the night, used thermite grenades to destroy the wreckage before departing. Meyerowich's company reached Miller and Steele at 01:54, but there was a problem. Wolcott had been killed in the crash, and his body was pinned under the fuselage of *Super Six-One*. It would take time to cut him out. Meanwhile, after searching Durant's crash site, Whetstone's company rescued the American platoon that had made a wrong turn and been ambushed. Finding them alive but their APCs damaged and disabled, Whetstone loaded them into his vehicles and headed to Mogadishu Stadium.[27]

At 03:38 David reported that he needed another hour to extricate Wolcott's body and was still taking constant fire from SNA militia. The Pakistani base at the stadium was warned to prepare to receive a large influx of casualties. Then it was discovered that there was not enough room in the convoy for all of Steele and Miller's men; fifteen would have to follow the convoy on foot. By 05:50, as the sun was rising, Wolcott's body was finally free. After a six-hour-long engagement, the convoy began to withdraw. For Task Force Ranger, it had been fifteen hours. The specter of fifteen exhausted men running behind the armored convoy, exposed to SNA fire, was unacceptable to David. He ordered the convoy to stop so the men could be loaded on top of the vehicles. On the short ride to the stadium, Meyerowich warned all troops not to fire as crowds of pro-UN Somalis lined the route of the battered vehicles and their badly bloodied occupants. Some cheered them on—a surreal sight for the American soldiers who had just endured the US Army's largest single firefight since the Vietnam War.[28]

The Battle of Mogadishu ended when David's convoy entered the relative haven of the stadium. It was 06:35 on 4 October 1993. Which side won was debatable, but the cost was high. Among the rescuers, David's two companies suffered two killed and twenty-four wounded. The Pakistanis and Malaysians suffered one dead and twelve wounded. For Task Force Ranger, the toll was sixteen dead, fifty-seven wounded, and Durant missing in action. All told, between US and UN forces, nineteen were dead and ninety-three wounded. For the SNA, a very conservative estimate was 1,126 casualties, including civilians.[29]

The traditional narrative of what went wrong on 3 October 1993 for Task Force Ranger is that the repetitive use of the same tactics convinced the SNA that helicopters were critical to US military operations. This is incorrect. Task Force Ranger varied its operations; its seven missions were not executed in the same manner, and the skies over Mogadishu provided the SNA with a shooting gallery of low-flying helicopters, most of which flew unchallenged for four months. The disaster was attribut-able to something else. In December 1993 American troops would dis-cover an SNA monument to the Battle of Mogadishu. It was constructed not from the wreckage of Wolcott's and Durant's Black Hawks but from the wreckage of the marines' Humvee destroyed on the morning of 3 October—an attack that led to two Black Hawks landing in the streets for the very first time just hours before an important SNA meeting. For the Somalis, the Battle of Mogadishu did not begin in the afternoon of 3 October; it began that morning. The evidence suggests that seeing Black Hawks land in the streets of Mogadishu spurred the SNA to mobi-lize an unprecedented level of defense to protect that meeting, arguably to prevent a repeat of the 12 July Abdi house attack.[30]

The Battle of Mogadishu on 3–4 October 1993—or the Black Hawk Down incident, as it is commonly referred to—was the culmination of a counterinsurgency campaign that began after the 5 June attacks on Pakistani peacekeepers. Once this conflict started, due to a series of miscalculations and dangerous decision making, both sides escalated to win credibility, with the international community for one side and the population for the other. But when the fight for credibility eventually became too exhausting for the Clinton administration, the policy shift toward negotiation was not communicated to Garrison or Montgomery. The true tragedy of the Battle of Mogadishu was that it should not have happened.

There was no question that Task Force Ranger and the QRF had taken a mauling, but US and UNOSOM forces believed the SNA had been bloodied to the breaking point. Many assumed the next move would be to decisively finish off Aidid and the SNA, but it was not to be. After four long months that left scores of US and UN personnel dead, hundreds more wounded, and Somali casualties impossible to calculate, the war was over.

Impact and Aftermath of the Battle of Mogadishu

On 4 October Fatun M. Hassan, the chargé d'affaires of the Somali Mission at UN headquarters in New York, wrote to the Security Council "on behalf of all peace-advocating Somalis." Expressing sorrow at the previous days' "brutal incidents," Hassan appealed to Aidid and the SNA to "resort to civilized ways for resolving national problems and expressing their grievances." Patently aware that international outrage over the battle could lead to the abandonment of Somalia, Hassan walked a fine line. He reminded the Security Council that not all Somalis were fighting UNOSOM: "The world must not forget . . . there are a minimum of twelve other factions that are signatories to the Addis Ababa agreements . . . that are supportive of the United Nations efforts." But Hassan also chided the UN focus on Mogadishu, writing that Somalis wanted resources devoted to other areas of the country as well, "so that the world could appreciate the stark contrast" between those places and southern Mogadishu. Claiming "neither the legitimacy nor the moral authority to impose my wishes on the international community," he begged the Security Council "to maintain their support to [UNOSOM] to avoid a greater loss and a lasting tragedy."[31]

Hassan was right to be concerned. The battle was a major turning point. The future of the intervention was in danger the moment Task Force Ranger lifted off for a raid in pursuit of a policy that had already ended. Despite the heavy casualties, Task Force Ranger personnel did not view the battle as a defeat. Lieutenant Larry Perino wrote, "[We] were severely outnumbered, but still accomplished [our] mission."[32] And it was true: Task Force Ranger had captured the intended targets. Garrison's men were not the only participants who held this view. Whetstone of the QRF wrote, "American and UN forces had clearly and utterly defeated the enemy."[33] In Washington, even though no marines participated, the commandant of the Marine Corps, General Carl E. Mundy, sent a message to "all units and personnel involved . . . in respect and admiration for the fighting qualities shown by every American who took part."[34]

In contrast, US intelligence estimates suggested that, for the SNA, 3 October was a disaster.[35] Aidid had suffered irreplaceable losses, providing an opportunity to definitively remove the SNA as a threat to UNOSOM's mission once and for all. Garrison's men were eager for another engagement. Staff Sergeant Matthew Eversmann, a veteran of 3 October, wrote that "reinforcements from the States were inbound immediately; more Special Forces, more Rangers, AC-130 gunships to fly twenty-four hours a day. Yes, the next fight was going to be brutal. The gloves were off."[36] Major General Norman Williams, commanding the UN Logistics Support Command, noted that American soldiers in Mogadishu "really wanted to get out and fight."[37] Their fervor was shared by General Bir, who agreed on 4 October to a proposed offensive against the weakened SNA. Montgomery, as both UNOSOM's deputy force commander and commander of US forces in Somalia, concurred, as did Garrison with Task Force Ranger.[38] None of the senior US or UN leadership saw the battle as a watershed in terms of policy. The campaign against Aidid, as far as they were concerned, was not over.

For the American public and politicians in Washington, DC, 3 October was a disaster conveyed by unforgettable reportage. "Americans were outraged and astounded," Clinton wrote in his memoir.[39] In December 1992 Americans had watched President Bush tell the nation that US troops were doing "God's work" to end starvation in Somalia. Then in May 1993, on the White House lawn, Clinton had personally congratulated UNITAF on the "largest humanitarian relief operation in history."[40] At the time, Clinton had pointedly remarked that Somalia was "not combat" and emphasized that "we cannot be the world's policeman." From June to September, the media had reported the growing insurgency and frustrating manhunt for Aidid before finally announcing that the policy was changing to one of negotiation.

Then, on Monday, 4 October, Americans watched as CNN cut coverage of the October coup in Moscow to announce unconfirmed reports that an American soldier had been captured in Mogadishu.[41] Minutes later, ABC News anchors reported the "worst battlefield tragedy in several years . . . 48 hours of massive violence" that left "12 American soldiers killed, 78 wounded and 3 helicopters shot down."[42] The SNA released video of captured *Super Six-Four* pilot Michael Durant, which was broadcast across the world.[43] His battered and bruised face adorned the front cover of *Time* under the caption, "What in the world are we doing?"[44] CNN showed disturbing footage of Somalis desecrating the bodies of Durant's crew members, dragging them naked through the streets of Mogadishu. Congressional representatives and their staffs were besieged by thousands of phone calls and letters from citizens demanding to know what America was doing in Somalia.[45] Politicians wanted answers too, and they wanted someone to blame. Clinton would receive a letter three days after the battle signed by 142 Republican congressmen claiming that "Americans deserve an explanation for . . . a national tragedy."[46]

The Senate Armed Services Committee met in closed session on the evening of 4 October for a briefing from Lieutenant General John J. Sheehan and Rear Admiral Mike Cramer, the respective directors of operations and intelligence for the Joint Staff. Opening the session, Republican Senator Strom Thurmond was somber: "Twelve U.S. soldiers died last night, 75 were wounded, and now, to cap the bad news, American prisoners are in the hands of the Somalis. This is no small matter . . . it is clear things have gone terribly wrong in Somalia . . . Aideed and his thugs have killed Americans, it is in the national interest to teach them a lesson. . . . What is at stake is U.S. credibility and prestige."[47] Cramer and Sheehan then walked the committee through the battle, arguing that the raid was successful but the unprecedented level of SNA resistance was unexpected.

Both were then peppered with questions: What was the mission in Somalia? Who was in command of US forces? Was the whole country embroiled in violence? Would removing Aidid end the violence? Sheehan and Cramer gave balanced answers: The mission was to support UN-OSOM in achieving its mandate. US forces were under Montgomery's command, not the UN's. The violence was confined to Mogadishu. And no, although Aidid was the "most charismatic, most dominant" leader opposing the coalition, he was not the only one.[48] The committee chair, Democratic Senator Samuel Nunn, asked whether there was a military solution in Somalia, and Sheehan said no. That earned a rebuke from Senator Robert Smith, who demanded to know why America was conducting military operations if there was no military solution. "Why are we doing this?" Smith asked emphatically. "What is the military objective here, General?"[49]

Sheehan and Cramer returned for another closed session on 7 October, when they were quizzed on command arrangements. Committee members were now searching for someone to hold responsible. UN-OSOM, the two men testified, was led by a Turkish general, but US forces reported to Montgomery, who was also Bir's deputy. Both repeatedly clarified that at no point were US combat forces under UN command.[50] From Mogadishu, Montgomery had submitted written answers to the senators' questions and explained that he had not ordered the raid. Task Force Ranger was controlled by CENTCOM and was not part of his command.[51]

Sheehan deflected where possible. He testified that the Joint Chiefs of Staff had resisted deploying Task Force Ranger, but the UN had forced the issue. Senators Nunn and John Warner then cornered Sheehan and asked, if CENTCOM commanded Task Force Ranger and the Joint Chiefs were against its deployment, who made the decision to do so? In truth, the answer was Colin Powell, chairman of the Joint Chiefs, but Sheehan evaded. At first, he seemed not to understand the question; then he claimed to be unable to "tell you a person's name" before settling on vague generalities: "It was a decision the inter-agency process made," he said.[52] Montgomery later complained about political "finger pointing," saying in an interview, "You've got 25,000 staffers on the congressional staff, and you didn't know that there was a UN mandate that the United States authored in the Security Council . . . that clearly set out the expanded mission? Give me a break. . . . It was infuriating."[53]

The questioning then turned to Montgomery's September request for armored reinforcements that Secretary of Defense Les Aspin turned down. Montgomery clarified that his request had nothing to do with any raids he was planning and restated that Task Force Ranger was not under his command. Senators queried why Montgomery did not have armored forces on standby for the raid and why it took so long for Task Force Ranger to be relieved. Were UN forces to blame for the delay? Montgomery was honest and said that he had the QRF on standby but not UN armored forces, as "there was no specific intelligence . . . that indicated US or UN forces would meet the degree of resistance actually experienced in that area."[54] Once it was clear that Task Force Ranger was in trouble, he immediately mobilized UNOSOM's armored forces. To his credit, Montgomery repeatedly praised the Pakistanis and Malaysians for unhesitatingly volunteering to assist. Montgomery was trying to emphasize that UN forces were not to blame for the casualties while avoiding pointing out that Garrison had launched the raid without notifying UNOSOM or the QRF beforehand.

The committee requested documents from the Joint Staff and the Department of Defense concerning Montgomery's appeal for reinforcements. The response was, "No written documentation has been found pertaining to these questions."[55] Sheehan then testified that Hoar did not follow normal procedure and send Montgomery's request to the Joint Staff for consideration; instead, he sent it directly to Powell. Now the committee had someone to blame. Hoar was called to testify on 13 October regarding Montgomery's armor request. Curiously, every response by Hoar during that session was redacted from the *Congressional Record*. However, the committee's comments and questions were not, and Hoar was pointedly asked why he allowed the hunt for Aidid to continue unabated, even though he knew the policy had changed in September from offensive operations to pursuit of a negotiated settlement.[56]

The Battle of Mogadishu continued to cast a long shadow in the Senate. Both Garrison and Montgomery would appear in person in May 1994 to answer questions about who was in command, what the mission was, and who should be held responsible. Garrison was direct and unequivocal in his testimony, declaring from the outset that Task Force Ranger's mission was to "apprehend" Aidid and that he reported directly to Hoar at CENTCOM, not UNOSOM. Committee members tried to connect Montgomery's failed request for armor with the fatalities suffered on 3 October and to determine whether UNOSOM had slowed the relief of Task Force Ranger. Garrison and Montgomery were questioned about these issues in numerous ways, but both officers held firm. Montgomery said, "There was not a second's hesitation" from the Malaysians and Pakistanis.[57] Garrison surprised the committee members by telling them he had deliberately taken his time to organize the relief effort. At Wolcott's crash site, Garrison told them, Task Force Ranger was "not pinned down. [They] could have fought [their] way out any time [they] chose to do so."[58] Garrison was exaggerating on that point. Miller and Steele were surrounded, had no vehicles, and would have faced the impossible task of fighting their way out on foot and carrying their dead and wounded through the streets of Mogadishu.

Garrison's most powerful testimony came when he soberly pointed out that most of Task Force Ranger's fatalities had occurred as they were moving on foot to Wolcott's crash site, not after the defensive perimeter around the wreckage had been established. Confident in the strength of this perimeter, Garrison had taken the time to ensure that the rescue plan was adequate and that the relief force was properly organized and strong enough to break through. He did concede, however, that if American armor had been sent to Somalia, the relief convoy might have arrived sooner, but because most of the fatalities occurred in the initial stages of the battle, this armor might not have made a difference.[59]

The Senate Armed Services Committee asked for a formal Senate investigation into the Battle of Mogadishu. In September 1995, nearly two years after the battle, its findings were published. The Senate blamed "policymakers" in the Clinton administration for deploying Task Force Ranger "against professional military advice."[60] Powell and Hoar were portrayed as soldiers who reluctantly went along with the plan due to their belief in "civilian control" of the military.[61] "The policy of going after Aideed was a flawed policy," Hoar was quoted as saying. Likewise, Powell claimed he had resisted going after Aidid, but because Garrison wanted the job and Montgomery and Howe wanted Aidid dealt with, he had no choice. "I will go along," he testified, "since as a general principle I believe in supporting the commander in the field."[62] Secretary Aspin was on holiday when Powell called to say that both he and Hoar believed Task Force Ranger was the answer. Based on that professional military advice, which the Senate claimed was absent, Aspin authorized the deployment. The report was largely a whitewash. The only truly reputable assertion coming out of it was from Montgomery, who said, "I think the U.S. gave Aideed a victory he didn't win."[63] He was right.

The Senate was not alone in seeking answers in October 1993. To a staggering degree, Clinton seemed to be personally ignorant of what was going on in Somalia—or at least he claimed to be. When asked whether he knew about Montgomery's request for reinforcements at the time, he said, "No. And I was talking to General Powell on a very regular basis about this whole thing. This was not something that anybody brought to me directly."[64] When he read Keith Richburg's 11 November *Washington Post* article explaining Gosende's proposal for a deal with Aidid, Clinton sent a handwritten note to his national security adviser asking, "Tony, What *is* the deal here?"[65] His claims of ignorance continued. When he met the widow of one of those who died in the battle months later, she asked him why the raid was launched when the decision had been made to negotiate? "I was surprised when I heard about the raid," Clinton told her. "Do you mean you had no knowledge of the decision to launch the raid?" she asked. "No, I did not," he answered.[66]

This is hard to reconcile. According to Elizabeth Drew's book on the Clinton presidency, Clinton was told on 3 October that the raid had begun just as he was leaving for California. The next day, learning of the casualties during a conference call, he demanded to know what the UN had asked American troops to do that had led to the battle and why no one had informed the White House what UNOSOM was up against.[67] So, to the bereaved widow, he was either lying or demonstrating just how out of touch he really was. Years later, Clinton would confide in British Prime Minister Tony Blair during a phone call that the Battle of Mogadishu "was the lowest point of my presidency. It was a goddamned nightmare. I felt personally responsible for that kid's body being dragged through the streets."[68]

In his memoir, Clinton offered a convoluted explanation for his role in the battle that "haunted" him: "I was responsible for an operation I approved in general but not in particulars. . . . I did not envision anything like a daytime assault in a crowded, hostile neighborhood. . . . I thought I was approving a police action."[69] The reality was that Somalia had never been a priority for the Clinton administration. Before 3 October, his cabinet met to discuss ongoing events in Bosnia eighteen times but not once to discuss Somalia.[70] He was criticized for missing the warning signs of disaster, given that Howe, Glaspie, and Gosende were hard-liners who were willfully marginalizing a recognized political leader in Somalia.[71] Secretary of State Warren Christopher conceded to reporters, "We were not sufficiently attentive."[72]

With public outrage over the battle, most Clinton officials opted for deflection—implying that the UN was to blame. Christopher claimed that he had tried to dissuade Boutros-Ghali from continuing the manhunt. "I thought that he had [got] the message," Christopher said. Aspin did the same thing, criticizing UNOSOM for its inability to rapidly relieve Task Force Ranger.[73] Clinton joined in, explaining at a White House press briefing, "The United Nations asked the United States to attempt to arrest [Aidid]."[74] He later wrote that Americans demanded to know "why were [US] forces doing Boutros-Ghali's and Admiral Howe's bidding?"[75] Thus, despite Task Force Ranger being under CENTCOM's command and UNOSOM contingents immediately responding to Montgomery and Garrison, a narrative of a tragedy was born, and the UN was the scapegoat. It was a grossly inaccurate narrative, but it allowed the White House and its charismatic first-term president to escape the scandal relatively unscathed.

Clinton was also saved by Garrison, who took full responsibility for what happened. Writing in a letter that the mission was a success and that the loss of the second helicopter was the cause of the problems, he ended by saying that the "authority, responsibility, and accountability . . . rests here . . . with the TF Ranger commander, not in Washington. President Clinton and Sec. Aspin need to be taken off the blame line."[76] Aspin, however, did not escape. The UN could not be blamed for his refusal to send Montgomery reinforcements. "Had I known at that time what I knew after the events of Sunday," he said, "I would have made a very different decision. This is my decision, somebody has to make the decision. This is the decision that I get paid for, and I made the decision as best I could with the information and the knowledge that I had at the time."[77] Aspin resigned in February 1994, falling on his own sword.

In the days following 3 October, CIA Director James Woolsey was invited to the White House for a National Security Council meeting on

Somalia. This was the first such meeting he had been invited to and, by his recollection, the first attended by Clinton. Woolsey had been asked to deliver an intelligence assessment, but administration officials focused on public relations and who would provide background information for the *New York Times* and *Washington Post*. It was announced that Ambassador Robert Oakley was being sent back to Somalia to "set up a coalition government" and negotiate the release of Durant. According to Woolsey, he spoke up to inform the group that there was no chance of establishing any coalition government between Aidid and Ali Mahdi; clan warfare was the history of Somalia, and it would continue to be. An awkward silence descended, and then the conversation on public relations continued unabated.[78]

Damage control through public relations seemed to be the main priority for the White House. Some efforts were intended to provide good optics. For example, Clinton could meet the returning bodies of the fallen at Andrews Air Force Base because that was what President Reagan had done after the 1983 Beirut bombing. Reagan's remarks that day, the proposal said, "were among the most powerful of his presidency."[79] Some efforts went too far. When a *New York Times* article mentioned "bitter and grousing" soldiers in Whetstone's company after the battle, White House staffers suggested that such griping to the press demonstrated a "leadership problem," implying that disciplinary action might be taken against David as the battalion commander, the very man who had led the rescue of Task Force Ranger.[80]

On 6 October an SNA mortar hit the hangar housing Task Force Ranger at Mogadishu airport, killing one and wounding twelve others.[81] The public and political outrage, as George Church described in *Time*, "coalesced into a roar: Get out. All the way. And never mind what precedent a pullout set for future U.N. peacekeeping operations."[82] The next day Clinton addressed the nation and the world. Echoing the public's "anger and horror" over the desecration of dead Americans, he again implied a UN connection to the battle by claiming the dead had been "taking part in an international effort to end the starvation of the Somali people." Substantial reinforcements were heading for Mogadishu, which, he assured his audience, "will be under American command," another suggestion that American forces had been led astray by the UN. Clinton presented Somalia as a house on fire, and US forces had saved the occupants. The embers remained, he warned, but it was time for "other firefighters to take our place." Explaining that an immediate withdrawal would damage American credibility internationally and invite a return to anarchy, he announced the complete withdrawal of American forces from Somalia by 31 March 1994.[83]

Clinton's speech received a mixed response in Mogadishu. The withdrawal angered American troops, who relished a renewed offensive against the SNA. Whetstone wrote, "Much like Tet in Vietnam, American and UN forces had clearly and utterly defeated the enemy, only to have the government fold when they had the upper hand . . . politicians pulled defeat from the mouth of victory."[84] Two days later, Aidid announced a unilateral cease-fire.[85] Whether this was prompted by Clinton's speech is unclear. US forces had announced their withdrawal, and Aidid's capitulation was most likely due to the significant number of SNA casualties. His influence was waning due to war weariness, and he may have been afraid UNOSOM would continue the war regardless of Clinton's announcement. Bir had agreed to go on the offensive after the battle, and UN forces remained unbloodied, unlike the SNA. And when Clinton said substantial reinforcements were going to Somalia, he meant it. But the Battle of Mogadishu would cast a shadow on the United States for a long time to come.

10 | Caught in a Dangerous Interlude
Charting the Course for UNOSOM amidst the Settling Dust

We are presently caught in a dangerous interlude. Political stalemate com-
bined with no clear force end state and outline of military tasks prevents the
formulation of a coherent near-term military strategy.
    —Lieutenant General Cevik Bir, UNOSOM II force commander[1]

How can I plan if you just walk out of Somalia? You Americans insist that
I hire Admiral Howe. So, I hire him. . . . Then things go wrong. Then you
blame him. Then you blame me for relying on him. I can't function this way.
    —Boutros Boutros-Ghali, UN secretary-general[2]

I leave here with a very good conscience . . . with a guarded optimism about
what lies ahead . . . for the Somalis, well, we can't guarantee their safety for
the rest of their lives.
    —General John Shalikashvili, chairman of the Joint Chiefs of Staff[3]

In telling the story of Somalia, the literature has always focused on Mogadishu, but events in the capital were not representative of the rest of the
country. For UNITAF, Mogadishu was the exception, not the rule, and
the same was true for UNOSOM. The considerable progress achieved
elsewhere from June to October 1993, during the Summer War, is often
ignored.[4] UNOSOM had developed a plan for rebuilding Somalia by
focusing on a critical trinity: reestablishing the police, restoring a functioning judiciary, and creating the Transitional National Council (TNC),
the embryonic governing body set out in the Addis Ababa Agreement
as the precursor to a future Somali government. In the words of Martin
Ganzglass, an adviser to UNOSOM's Justice Division, the UN "had to
rebuild and leave behind a [system] capable of preventing Somalia from
descending again into the chaos of civil war."[5] UNOSOM capitalized
on the goodwill and support for UNITAF among the population in the
interior to make significant gains in spite of the Summer War, which

was confined to Mogadishu. In July Marc Grossman, executive secretary of the State Department, noted these unsung developments in a memo: "The current reporting . . . is extremely limited. The main story line continues to be Aideed. Success stories are occurring outside Mogadishu. The famine is over. Crops are beginning to be harvested. Political reconstruction from the grassroots level up is occurring . . . reporters are not picking up on these stories."[6] Even more critically, also overlooked was the rapid progress made after the Summer War ended.

Even as the Summer War was ongoing, the nation-building mission was progressing in the interior—slowly at first, but then at a rapid pace after the Battle of Mogadishu. Contrary to opinions that the battle signaled the end of any hope of progress in Somalia, October 1993 to March 1994 was actually the most successful period of UNOSOM's tenure. But any headway made was undermined—not fatally, but substantially—by Western forces' exodus from Somalia. This chapter tracks UNOSOM's efforts outside Mogadishu during the war and then explores the immediate aftermath and consequences of the Battle of Mogadishu and the subsequent Western withdrawal. Significantly, this battle ended only the war, not the possibility of UN success.

Nation Building Outside Mogadishu: Howe's "Ticket Out"

Broadly speaking, UNOSOM's nation-building plan sought to capitalize on UNITAF's achievements. In May 1993 Martin Ganzglass and Ann Wright from UNOSOM's Justice Division presented their ambitious reconstruction plan for the judiciary and police force to Kofi Annan, UN undersecretary-general for peacekeeping. They hoped to replicate the "Baidoa model" of courts and police, created by the Australians during the UNITAF phase, in the rest of the country. The Justice Division aimed to train ten thousand police by October 1993, with that number increasing to eighteen thousand by March 1995. The Baidoa model of a three-tier court system—district court, regional court, and court of appeals—would be expanded to all regions. Collaborating with Somali representatives, the Justice Division would select qualified members of the new judiciary and vet and hire one thousand Custodial Corps prison staff to manage the rehabilitated prison system. For a relatively modest $45 million, the new police-court-prison system would lower the costs of

UN peace enforcement by fostering social stability.[7] Howe, UNOSOM's special representative, allegedly described this plan as the UN's "ticket out," and former Somali police officers, judges, and magistrates eagerly supported it.[8]

In New York, Annan endorsed the plan but added a caveat. Funding would not commence until the Somali district and regional councils were created, as mandated by the Addis Ababa Agreement. Ganzglass later called this decision "strategically flawed," reasoning that Resolution 814, which enshrined the mandate for nation building, prioritized the speedy creation of a police force, thus fostering stability from the ground up. Annan's decision meant that reconstruction had to wait until midlevel governance had emerged. Ganzglass cited broad support for the ASF to argue that there was no reason to delay launching the reconstruction program.[9] Though worthy of criticism in hindsight, Annan was not necessarily wrong at the time. In mid-May 1993 the war with the SNA had not begun, and creating district and regional councils did not seem unrealistic (as proved by how rapidly they emerged after the war ended). No one, not even Annan, could have foreseen the Summer War. When it broke out in June, Howe and Bir redirected UNOSOM's military resources toward Aidid and the SNA, while civilian staff either hunkered down or evacuated to Nairobi.

The Summer War interrupted nation-building efforts temporarily but did not stop them. Considerable advances were achieved elsewhere. The Addis Ababa Agreement set out the criteria for establishing the district and regional councils that would, in turn, elect members to the TNC. Despite the fighting in Mogadishu, Ambassador Lansana Kouyate, UNOSOM's deputy special representative, traveled throughout Somalia—not just in the southern, UN-controlled portion of the country—helping Somalis establish district councils. The first was formed on 3 July 1993 in Buurhakaba in the Bay region. Baidoa, the regional capital, formed its council the next day. By the end of July, twenty-one district councils had been created in various cities and towns, including Gialalassi, Oddur, Merka, Afgooye, and Balad. Although no council was formed in Mogadishu due to the fighting, the local response was overwhelmingly positive.[10] And although some councils were set up hastily and their effectiveness and efficiency varied, they were an undeniable sign of progress.

The headway made in the interior was not limited to political reconciliation. In the city of Kismayo—UNITAF's toughest challenge—UN-

OSOM negotiated the Jubbaland peace agreement. UNOSOM's Political Division believed that national reconciliation could be achieved only if regional conflicts were resolved first. As a constant source of instability, Kismayo was the logical place to prioritize. Clan elders there were tired of the endless conflict between Morgan and Jess, so UN mediators bypassed the two bitter rivals and dealt directly with the elders. From May to August 1993, 152 elders from twenty clans, with UNOSOM assistance, formulated the Jubbaland agreement, enabling the free movement of peoples in Somalia's most contested city and bringing a temporary end to the violence.[11]

These were successes, but it would be an oversimplification to suggest that the war was not detrimental to nation-building efforts. In a 14 July letter to one of Howe's aides, UN political affairs officer Angelina Eichhorst voiced concerns that political and humanitarian efforts appeared to be on hold. Writing from Nairobi, where UNOSOM's civilian staff had been evacuated to, Eichhorst explained that representatives from the factions had requested UN assistance or meetings but had received no response. Some had had no interaction with UNOSOM since the Addis Ababa Agreement in March. Eichhorst wrote, "They were all [signatories to the agreement] and they all were completely ignored afterwards."[12] Mohamed Qanyare Afrah, chairman of Ali Mahdi's USC and spokesperson for the pro-UN Group of 12 coalition, complained bitterly of being treated like "lepers" by Howe.[13] Similarly snubbed, the chairs of the SNF and SPM "deplored UNOSOM's obsession with General Aidid" and demanded that the UN work with factions that clearly wanted to cooperate.[14] With the violence contained in Mogadishu, Eichhorst recognized that there was both the potential for progress elsewhere and an appetite in the pro-UN factions to make it a reality. She tried to convince Howe that "it is really not desirable to have hundreds of expatriates remain hunkered down in Mogadishu, or like we are, exiled in Nairobi, waiting for the better days, when there is so much work that can and should be done in other parts of the country."[15]

During the months of war, UNOSOM was dispersed across southern Somalia in four brigade sectors; the Indians amounted to a fifth, but they did not arrive in strength until after the war. Kismayo and most of the Kenyan border fell within the Belgian sector. The French brigade was headquartered in Baidoa, with the now huge French sector also encompassing Bardera and Baledogle, garrisoned by the Botswanans and Moroccans, respectively, while the Greeks and Zimbabweans were sta-

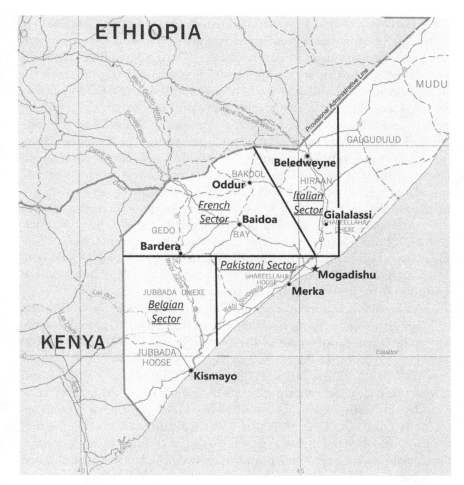

UNOSOM II Sectors of Responsibility, 1993

tioned in Waajid. Most UN forces were deployed in the Pakistani sector, along with the American QRF; this sector included the capital and the port town of Merka, both of which were the responsibility of the Pakistani brigade. The Italian brigade managed the fourth and final sector covering Gialalassi and Beledweyne (previously separate HRSs under UNITAF), with the German logistics task force based at Beledweyne.[16]

By August 1993, although casualties were mounting steadily in Mogadishu, stability reigned in Bardera, Baidoa, Oddur, Beledweyne, and even Galkayo, outside UNOSOM's area of responsibility. The French, Italians, and Moroccans conducted successful weapons sweeps, largely without resistance and with no casualties.[17] On 9 August Brigadier General Maurice Quadri, commanding the French brigade, informed Bir that he wanted to hand over more responsibilities to the Baidoa district and regional councils and requested increased support for the judiciary, police, and education system. Quadri reported, "To my mind the civilian action of UNOSOM shall now take precedence on military action. . . . I am aware that this program is ambitious . . . but [the] time has come to put it in concrete form."[18] Baidoa was almost ready to be self-sustaining, exemplifying the dichotomy between the level of violence in Mogadishu compared to the rest of the country. From the start of the Summer War on 5 June to the Battle of Mogadishu on 3 October, UNOSOM did not suffer a single fatality outside the capital due to hostile action. Bandits in the interior occasionally targeted UNOSOM convoys, but in four months the only casualties were two Belgians who were wounded in an ambush near Kismayo in July.[19]

The 1996 UN report on Somalia claimed that "while the bloodshed in Mogadishu was making headlines around the world, gains were being made throughout much of the rest of Somalia."[20] This assessment was echoed by the US Forces Somalia after-action report, which noted that UNOSOM efforts outside the capital "flourished."[21] In addition to the Jubbaland agreement, the SSDF in Galkayo announced that it would voluntarily disarm its militia. Even Hersi Morgan was in disarmament talks with UNOSOM. In Baidoa, businesses had recovered, resulting in what US forces described as a "booming" local economy. Furthermore, through coordination between UNOSOM and more than forty relief organizations, starvation had ended, and 750,000 children had been vaccinated against disease. Seventy thousand were attending primary schools, exceeding pre–civil war enrollment. Hospitals were reopening, as were child-care clinics. Livestock exports had recommenced.[22] Resistance to UNOSOM is often portrayed as being uniform across the population, but this is incorrect. Of the fifteen factions that signed the Addis Ababa Agreement, only one was fighting in a confined part of the capital. For most Somalis, there was no Summer War and no resistance against UNOSOM.

True, this progress was slow to start, but it was enough to encourage Kofi Annan to launch the reconstruction plan even though only a fraction of the district councils and no regional councils had been formed. He held a meeting of twelve key UN member states in New York on 3 August to elicit their financial support to train ten thousand police officers by December 1994 instead of October 1993, assuring them that UNOSOM's resources and efforts would be concentrated in areas of Somalia that were stable.[23] From Annan, the plan went to Boutros-Ghali, who, when conveying it to the Security Council for authorization, highlighted that "significant gains have been made" outside Mogadishu. Boutros-Ghali recommended the creation of two UN-supported police academies, with local police under the control of the district and regional councils until the TNC was established.[24]

On 22 September, the day after Task Force Ranger captured Osman Atto and three days before *Courage Five-Three* was shot down, the Security Council passed Resolution 865, officially authorizing the judicial reconstruction plan, or Howe's "ticket out" of Somalia.[25] This was no surprise, as Secretary of State Warren Christopher had just told Boutros-Ghali that the United States was opting to negotiate with Aidid, and any kind of progress would change the narrative of the UN mission in Somalia from one of endless violence to one of a country rising from the ashes. Although UNOSOM was embroiled in warfare in the capital, Resolution 865 gave it key benchmarks for measuring a successful mission. Two weeks later, though, the Battle of Mogadishu threw the future of UN involvement in Somalia into question, and in the wake of Clinton's announcement of a US withdrawal, American military power descended on the Horn of Africa.

Joint Task Force Somalia

On 10 October, after Aidid declared a cease-fire, Mogadishu enjoyed its first night without gunfire in months. Earlier that day, the USS *New Orleans* Amphibious Ready Group (ARG) carrying the 13th MEU appeared on the horizon. It was quickly joined by the aircraft carrier USS *Abraham Lincoln* and its support ships, as well as the USS *Guadalcanal* ARG carrying the 22nd MEU. More than four thousand additional soldiers poured into Mogadishu, including a powerful armored task force from the US Army's 24th Infantry Division with thirty Abrams main battle tanks, forty-two Bradley infantry fighting vehicles, and twenty Paladin self-propelled howitzers. Loitering offshore like a coiled spring were an additional sixteen thousand sailors and marines with forty more armored vehicles, sixty helicopters, and fifty-six carrier attack aircraft.[26] Somalis had rejoiced as jets roared over Mogadishu in December 1992, heralding UNITAF's arrival. Now, nearly a year later, apprehension was in the air at the sight of carrier aircraft, as many wondered whether the war would continue.

Howe later recalled, "The kind of force we got after October 3 . . . which wasn't allowed to do much was actually the kind of force that would have probably been a deterrent to an Aidid or anybody else that really didn't see the UN succeeding in its interests. It probably would have prevented that from happen[ing] and made that peaceful track work."[27] By the end of October 1993, UNOSOM had 29,284 personnel in Somalia. With the massive influx of Americans, international military forces reached their peak strength for the entire intervention, totaling 46,984 troops, or almost 10,000 more than UNITAF at its peak.[28]

Despite being powerful enough to crush the SNA, these reinforcements had a different mission. All American combat units in Mogadishu—those newly arrived and preexisting units of the QRF such as Task Force Raven and David's 2nd Battalion/14th Infantry—were organized under a new headquarters: Joint Task Force (JTF) Somalia. Created by Hoar after Clinton's withdrawal speech, JTF Somalia's mission was to protect all US forces in the country and to ensure that logistical lines of communication remained open until the final American withdrawal at the end of March 1994.[29] Hoar forbade offensive operations against Aidid and the SNA. As the JTF Somalia after-action report noted, "Political and military leaders were reluctant to put troops at risk to achieve in the near-term what could be futile in the long-term."[30]

There had been two separate American chains of command prior to the Battle of Mogadishu. Montgomery served as both UNOSOM's deputy force commander and commander of all US forces, except for Garrison's Task Force Ranger. Both Montgomery and Garrison reported to Hoar at CENTCOM. JTF Somalia further complicated this situation. Believing that Montgomery had too many responsibilities, and to reassure the public that American troops were not under UN command, Hoar gave JTF Somalia to newly promoted US Army Major General Carl F. Ernst. A Vietnam and Gulf War veteran, Ernst had been the deputy chief of staff for the US Army's Training and Doctrine Command.[31] For day-to-day matters, Ernst ostensibly reported to Montgomery. But in terms of achieving his mission, Ernst reported directly to Hoar. Ernst had far more resources and staff than Montgomery, and their relationship was fractious. The complex chain of command—where, depending on the circumstances, Ernst either answered to Montgomery or was his equal—did not help matters.

The command complexities did not end there. The naval forces and marines offshore were not under Ernst's command. They were split into three distinct cohorts. Rear Admiral Joseph Dantone, commanding the *Abraham Lincoln* Carrier Group, established a "gentleman's agreement" to cooperate with Ernst and JTF Somalia. This agreement continued when Rear Admiral Arthur Cebrowski and his *America* Carrier Group relieved the *Lincoln*. As for the two ARGs offshore, two more chains of command developed. The two MEUs were loosely combined under Brigadier General Richard Vercauteren as Marine Forces Somalia, while the naval vessels carrying them came under Rear Admiral James Perkins. Thus, depending on the time frame, CENTCOM had five or six separate commanders reporting from Somalia: Montgomery, Ernst, Perkins, Vercauteren, either Dantone or Cebrowski, and Garrison, until Task Force Ranger departed on 17 October.[32] It was confusing and inefficient, and personalities clashed. Joining this mix on 10 October to negotiate Durant's release was Robert Oakley.

Oakley and Zinni Meet Aidid

Oakley was selected as Clinton's new presidential envoy to Somalia because of the relationship he had developed with Aidid during UNITAF. His mission was to get things back on track to form a government, as set out by the Addis Ababa Agreement, and to obtain Durant's unconditional release. He brought along another veteran known to Aidid: Anthony Zinni, UNITAF's former director of operations. En route to Somalia, Oakley and Zinni, using Ethiopian President Meles Zenawi as an intermediary, obtained Aidid's agreement to meet in person. They arrived in Mogadishu just as JTF Somalia was pouring into the country, and Zinni recalled that the situation was tense and confused. Howe was not happy to see Oakley and seemed disinterested in Aidid's cease-fire, earning him a pointed reminder that regardless of his UN position, "the president of the United States is your boss."[33]

The date of the meeting with Aidid is unclear, but it most likely took place on 12 October. To facilitate the parley, Zinni had to ensure that all operations against the SNA had ended. He shuttled from headquarters to headquarters trying to navigate the new "hodgepodge of military commands."[34] Bir promised Zinni that UNOSOM would not make any moves but warned that he did not control US troops. Montgomery followed suit but pointed out that he did not command Task Force Ranger. Garrison was highly supportive of the meeting, not least because some members of Task Force Ranger were still missing and he wanted Zinni to ask Aidid if the SNA had any American remains or prisoners. Garrison then warned Zinni that JTF Somalia had arrived in-theater under Ernst, who subsequently advised Zinni that Vercauteren controlled the two MEUs offshore. Eventually, with assurances obtained from the various commanders that their forces would stand down, Oakley and Zinni went to meet the SNA leader.

Paranoid about being captured, Aidid had agreed to meet only under certain conditions. On a nondescript but predetermined street corner in Mogadishu, an armored SUV carrying Oakley and Zinni pulled up. Their marine escort in accompanying Humvees then left, per these conditions. As the lone SUV waited, a curious bystander knocked on the window and asked for asylum in the United States. Then an SNA convoy of heavily armed technicals arrived to escort them to Aidid's safe house, led by a person Zinni described as the Somali equivalent of "Arnold Schwarzenegger . . . the biggest Somali I have ever seen in my life." Before they set off, this SNA commander took Zinni aside and said, "No more, no more, no more killing, no more fighting." In Zinni's view, the recent battle had taken a severe and very visible toll on the SNA militia.[35] After driving a circuitous route at high speed through the warrens of the city to avoid being followed, Oakley and Zinni arrived at a compound on 21 October Road.

If Aidid had been shaken by recent events, he did not show it. In front of an SNA film crew, he warmly embraced both Zinni and Oakley. He then presented his cabinet, reminiscing that it had changed since the UNITAF days. Upon being introduced to the SNA "minister for tourism," Zinni chortled to Aidid, "Tourism . . . you gotta be kidding me!" "You have to plan ahead," Aidid quipped.[36] Sitting at a conference table holding pens and paper with the SNA letterhead, the participants discussed Durant. Oakley was blunt: nothing less than an unconditional release was acceptable; there would be no negotiating. Aidid countered that UNOSOM was holding high-level SNA prisoners captured by Task Force Ranger, including Osman Atto, Omar Salad, and Mohamed Hassan Awale. UNOSOM had arrested and detained 740 Somalis, and 50 were still being held in an island prison off the coast.[37] Aidid offered a prisoner exchange, but Oakley refused and reiterated there would be no negotiating. In any case, those prisoners were being held by the UN, not the United States. Oakley promised to check on their condition but pointed out that, without a gesture from the SNA, no goodwill would be forthcoming. A disappointed Aidid agreed to release Durant, especially after Oakley observed that JTF Somalia would flatten Mogadishu if it was forced to rescue him. The discussion then turned to another topic, and Aidid's calm veneer slipped. The SNA had declared a unilateral cease-fire, but UNOSOM had not reciprocated. In a telling move hinting at the state of SNA forces post 3 October, Aidid urged Oakley and Zinni to prevail on the UN to declare a cease-fire and formally end the Summer War.[38]

The meeting was then interrupted by the sound of helicopters overhead. Apprehension skyrocketed among the SNA cabinet and militia. Outside, Oakley and Zinni were greeted by thousands of leaflets in the air stating, "Wanted! $25,000 Reward, General Aidid, dead or alive." The SNA was "furious," Zinni remembered, and "Oakley looks at me like, I thought I told you to shut down all operations."[39] On returning to the US embassy compound, Zinni tracked down the wayward officer who had ordered the leaflet drop. Firmly chastened, he claimed no one had told him to cease operations—yet another example of the cumbersome American command arrangements.

The meeting with Aidid created one problematic narrative about the Battle of Mogadishu that has persisted to this day. Zinni asked Aidid to describe the battle from the SNA perspective. American forces and Task Force Ranger, Aidid said, always used helicopters in their offensive operations during the war. As such, he planned to shoot one down and then engage American forces in a large-scale battle.[40] Aidid's statement was taken at face value, and this became the accepted explanation for the cause of the battle, a narrative called into question in the preceding chapter.

It also dispels an urban legend that emerged in the post-9/11 revisionism of Somalia: the suggestion that al-Qaeda contributed to 3 October by training the SNA to shoot down helicopters.[41] Zinni had heard "unsubstantiated" reports of al-Qaeda offering support to the SNA or rumors that Aidid was thinking about enlisting such support, but he never saw anything in Somalia to corroborate these claims or any evidence of al-Qaeda's involvement in the events of 3 October. According to Scott Peterson, who interviewed many SNA personalities on this issue, they laughed "at this claim that bin Laden helped them . . . they never even heard of [him] until he began boasting about Somalia years later."[42]

Aidid was also known to be opposed to Islamic fundamentalism or the imposition of Sharia law in Somalia.[43] At the meeting, Oakley raised the issue of any future collaboration with al-Qaeda, warning Aidid that associating with an avowedly anti-American terror group could have dire consequences. In Zinni's words, "Aidid got it, just gave a little nod."[44] There is little evidence that al-Qaeda participated in the Battle of Mogadishu, and whatever proficiency the SNA had developed in shooting down helicopters did not come from that quarter. Perhaps undermining the al-Qaeda connection once and for all was the case of Giancarlo Marocchinio, an Italian citizen and illegal arms trafficker. UNOSOM arrested and deported Marocchinio a week before the battle for furnishing Aidid with "anti-aircraft technology and training."[45]

On 14 October Aidid held his first press conference in months. He was buoyant but conciliatory. To the world, he praised Clinton for choosing a different strategy and emphasized that the UN should assist Somalis. He said he never left Mogadishu during the manhunt for him and the United States "never came close" to catching him.[46] He went on to announce that Durant was being released, along with a Nigerian peacekeeper captured in September. Severely injured in the helicopter crash, Durant was delivered to the Red Cross that afternoon.

Aidid's desire for the UN to recognize his unilateral cease-fire was rewarded. After four months of costly violence, member states wanted the mission in Somalia to return to nation building and political reconciliation. But there was still a desire to find out what had really happened on 5 June to start it all. This curiosity was piqued when Clinton was asked at a press conference on the day Durant was released, "Do you think there's a possibility that Aideed was not directly responsible for the attack on the Pakistani UN forces?" Clinton tried to evade and then said, "You asked me a question about Aideed personally. I can't answer that."[47] Days later, Anthony Lake received a memo noting that it was now "essential that a serious and independent tribunal be convened to determine responsibility for the attacks on the Pakistani peacekeepers . . . we will be exposed to serious critique as well as public outcry if . . . Aideed is not subjected to a rigorous and credible investigation."[48] Aidid was finally getting his impartial investigation.

On 16 November, six weeks after the Battle of Mogadishu, the Security Council passed Resolution 885, suspending all attempts to arrest or bring to justice those "who might be implicated" in the 5 June attacks.[49] It was an armistice that gave Aidid a chance to come back into the fold and allowed the UN to refocus on its mission. But Resolution 885 also established the Commission of Inquiry, whose February 1994 report would ultimately conclude that Aidid was not personally responsible and that the violence was a result of poor decision making and UNOSOM's rash assignment of blame without an adequate investigation.

UNOSOM's Success after Black Hawk Down

Resolution 865, passed on 22 September 1993, set the priorities for UNOSOM's nation-building plan in Somalia: a rebuilt police force, a functioning judiciary and prison system, and the TNC. With Resolution 865 in hand, the UN secretary-general now had to account for the consequences of the Battle of Mogadishu and the announcement that the United States was pulling out. Tensions were high at UN headquarters. Boutros-Ghali recounted an exchange with Madeleine Albright and Warren Christopher on 8 November. They asked about his plan going forward, and he responded angrily, saying, "How can I plan if you just walk out of Somalia? You Americans insist that I hire Admiral Howe. So, I hire him. Then you want him to report directly to Tony Lake at the National Security Council, who then gives him his instructions from Washington. Then things go wrong. Then you blame him. Then you blame me for relying on him. I can't function this way."[50]

In his November 1993 report, Boutros-Ghali presented his case for continuing the nation-building mission. The crux of his argument was that Mogadishu was the exception to the UN's overall progress in Somalia. He stated, convincingly, that the major problems of the humanitarian crisis necessitating the intervention had been "successfully addressed." Somalia's agricultural sector was back on its feet, with 250,000 livestock exported since April. Civilian maritime shipping traffic into Mogadishu had increased tenfold since January. More children were attending school than before the civil war. More importantly, thirty-nine district councils had been formed, as well as six regional councils. Seven hundred members of, or candidates for, these councils had completed a UN administrative training program. With this progress in local governance,

Boutros-Ghali estimated that the TNC could be formed by January 1994. Noting that UN member states had risked the lives of their soldiers on what was perceived to "be a somewhat ill-defined objective," the UN secretary-general argued that significant gains had been achieved, but they could easily be lost. The UN, he wrote, "must not abandon Somalia in view of the incontrovertible desire of the Somali people for the continued presence of UNOSOM II in their country."[51]

With his rationale for continuing the mission set out, Boutros-Ghali next voiced his concern about UNOSOM's ability to continue without the United States. As always, he presented a menu of options to the Security Council. UNOSOM could continue with a Chapter VII peace enforcement mandate in the hopes that Aidid and the SNA would cooperate, while being ready to act once again if they did not. UNOSOM would require an extra brigade, $1 billion, and, most importantly, member states' acceptance of the risk of violence. Alternatively, UNOSOM could revert to traditional consent-based peacekeeping under Chapter VI in one of two ways: continued political dialogue and relief operations with a diminished force of sixteen thousand, or a drastic reduction to five thousand to control just the ports and airports while helping UN agencies provide relief and train local police forces. These two last options depended, largely or wholly, on the goodwill and cooperation of the factions. Warning that national reconciliation might fail "despite the best efforts on the part of all concerned," Boutros-Ghali appealed to the Security Council to carefully consider which option to pursue, as the cost of failure could be the resumption of civil war. "In that event," he wrote, "UNOSOM II, without the required resources, might become a hapless spectator to the tragedy."[52]

The progress outside Mogadishu was undeniable, as was Boutros-Ghali's belief that the UN must persevere. The Security Council renewed the nation-building mandate until 31 May 1994 but held off on deciding which version of UNOSOM to adopt until February. Exemplifying the international community's weariness, the Security Council urged the swift reconstruction of judicial institutions and civil governance, noting that "the people of Somalia bear the ultimate responsibility for national reconciliation and reconstruction of their own country."[53]

UNOSOM now had breathing room to capitalize on the progress made in the interior, but in Mogadishu, the strategy for achieving this was unclear to General Bir. Three options had been proposed for UNOSOM, but it would be months before the Security Council chose one.

In a memo, Bir asked Howe what the "end state" was after 31 March 1994. Coercive disarmament was not feasible if the Security Council chose to return to consent-based peacekeeping, and fighting the SNA was out of the question, given the political climate after the battle. Clearly frustrated, he wrote, "We are presently caught in a dangerous interlude. Political stalemate combined with no clear force end state and outline of military tasks prevents the formulation of a coherent near-term military strategy."[54] In limbo, and with the future unclear, UNOSOM's military and civilian personnel focused on the most pressing issues at hand. For the former, it was a scramble to find forces to replace those of the nations withdrawing from UNOSOM. For the latter, the priority was furthering the goals of Resolution 865—Howe's "ticket out." And in this, rapid gains were made.

The unrecognized reality is that while the Battle of Mogadishu was certainly a low point in the intervention, the subsequent period from October 1993 to March 1994 was the most progressive in terms of achieving the goals set out in Resolution 865. By January 1994, 6,737 trained police were operating from more than one hundred stations across southern Somalia, often in joint patrols with UNOSOM. The criminals they arrested were processed through a judicial system that included a three-tier court system in Mogadishu, with fifteen district courts, five regional courts, and five appeals courts operating elsewhere. The new judiciary had a staff of more than three hundred, in addition to the seven hundred Custodial Corps personnel who ran the refurbished prisons in Mogadishu and Hargeisa.[55] The system was fragile and still needed UN support, but the judicial reconstruction plan was working.

There were similarly encouraging signs related to local governance. With the fighting now over, UNOSOM's Political Division had the personnel and the time to deal with matters other than Mogadishu, and councils were rapidly established. This was hugely significant because, by early 1994, the SNM in Somaliland had decided to remain independent. This meant that the remainder of Somalia encompassed thirteen regions with eighty districts. By 21 March 1994, as Western forces were leaving, fifty-five of these eighty districts had councils, as did eight of the thirteen regions. Of the nine HRSs formerly occupied by UNITAF, three (Oddur, Baidoa, and Gialalassi) had district and regional councils in place and functioning, with another three (Bardera, Beledweyne, and Merka) lacking just one of their district councils. Councils were also up and running in regions outside UNOSOM's current area of responsibility, in anticipation of extending the operation to central and northeastern Somalia. The only region that had no district councils and therefore no regional council was Mogadishu, which was still divided between Aidid and Ali Mahdi. But, excluding the fourteen districts in the city, fifty-five of the sixty-six districts outside Mogadishu had representative local governance.[56]

This was an astonishing and underappreciated success, especially given the creation of some councils outside UNOSOM's area of responsibility. Arguably, this progress was possible because coalition forces peaked at nearly fifty thousand troops, while Aidid's SNA was bloodied, disorganized, and concerned about another crushing UN offensive. In this moment of pause—with one side politically unable to attack and the other fearing an attack anyway—real progress was made. But a critical contributing factor was JTF Somalia. Even though Hoar at CENTCOM had prohibited offensive operations against the SNA, Ernst's interpretation and execution of his mission kept Aidid and the SNA off balance and wondering whether the war might suddenly reignite.

The Soldier-Statesman and the Warfighter

The frustratingly complex American command arrangement made friction between Montgomery and Ernst unavoidable. According to Colonel Lawrence Casper, who had commanded the QRF under Montgomery but now reported to Ernst as part of JTF Somalia, the two men could not have been more different. The former was a "consummate soldier-statesman," Casper wrote, ideally suited to coalition operations, while the latter was "focused entirely on warfighting."[57] Ernst saw JTF Somalia as a coiled spring, ready to go on the offensive if the SNA or any faction, for that matter, wanted to fight. "If we were going to get into a fight," Ernst later explained, "we didn't want it to be rifle against rifle. We made that decision early on. We would use maximum, overwhelming force."[58] Montgomery, however, advised Ernst that Hoar wanted a more cautious approach. A personality clash was inevitable. Ernst resented Montgomery trying to dictate JTF Somalia's posture, while Montgomery thought Ernst was marginalizing UNOSOM. Caught in the middle, Casper often heard the same information through two very different filters; one man was seemingly determined to retake Mogadishu, and the other wanted to leave without kicking the hornets' nest.[59]

Ernst had his engineers build a massive base outside the city to allow his armored forces to retain freedom of movement, seal off the city if necessary, and avoid getting bogged down in the streets. Christened "Victory," the nickname of the 24th Infantry Division, whose units built it, this base symbolized the supreme irony that, for the United States, success meant leaving, preferably with no additional casualties. Protecting Victory Base were eighteen kilometers of triple concertina barbed wire, ten kilometers of fencing, and half a million sandbags. It was a fortress, a bastion of force protection. At Victory Base and the other UNOSOM installations, Ernst's snipers had clearance to fire on anyone operating a technical or crew-served weapon.[60]

Though offensive operations were forbidden, Hoar instructed Ernst to conduct displays of force as a deterrent against any SNA aggression. Ernst took this order literally throughout November and December 1993. Some operations were merely suggestive. "Eyes over Mogadishu" missions continued, but reinforced with marine gunships from the offshore MEUs. Navy SEALs conducted surveys to identify beaches for amphibious assaults. Around Victory Base, Ernst's units trained incessantly to rescue the crew of a downed helicopter.[61] Other operations were much more overt and intended to send a clear message, principally to Aidid. AC-130 gunships held weekly live-fire exercises above Mogadishu, as did Abrams tanks and Bradley fighting vehicles on the ground.[62] Due to the complex command relationships, Ernst could use the offshore naval or marine forces only with CENTCOM's approval. He circumvented this restriction through "gentleman's agreements" with his naval and marine counterparts to conduct operations that they labeled "exercises."[63]

Ernst's zeal bordered on goading the SNA into attacking. From 11 to 14 November 1993, JTF Somalia and the offshore marines conducted Operation Show Care, consisting of coordinated helicopter and amphibious landings in Merka. It was billed as providing "medical and dental assistance to the people," but its true objective was sending "a strong message to Somali clan leaders concerning the mobility and capability of US forces." Show Care included a "turn-away" landing whereby seaborne marines conducted an amphibious feint, turning away from the beaches at the last moment. The landing site was defended by militiamen who "reportedly abandoned their positions there in fear."[64] The choice of Merka was not random; the SNA had recently made moves toward the port town. And although Show Care could certainly be viewed as a deterrent operation, it was also provocative. Just one militiaman opening fire would provoke a major response. Similar actions were launched in Mogadishu. In Operation More Care in early December, the capital was buzzed by A-6 Intruders and F-18 Hornets from *America*'s air wing, while Ernst's artillery displayed its firepower. At the same time, armored columns sortied into the city from Victory Base to demonstrate the Americans' freedom of movement. Amphibious landings carried marines who "seized" Old Port and "captured" New Port and the airport before marching through Mogadishu to Victory Base. City leaders lodged protests ahead of More Care, but as JTF Somalia's after-action report noted, "The mission was completed anyway, sending a strong signal to the Somali clans that US forces were not afraid to maneuver and did not need their approval to conduct operations."[65]

Force protection through deterrence came to a head when Ernst proposed reopening 21 October Road. Controlling the main logistical artery in the city would add credibility to the threats of force that kept the SNA subdued. Dismissing the existence of the purpose-built bypass road, Ernst's plan was to have JTF Somalia's armor and artillery units take positions north of and parallel to 21 October Road to provide fire support. The 22nd MEU would then land east of Mogadishu to close off the road at the pasta factory. Once these forces were in place, the Pakistani brigade and Malaysian battalion from UNOSOM would advance up 21 October Road and clear it, under the cover of *America*'s carrier wing. The plan left nowhere for the SNA to go; its militia could either surrender or fight. If they fought, JTF Somalia was positioned to bombard them into submission in the same area where the war had started on 5 June.

Requiring a division's worth of troops to execute, this would have been the largest military operation of the intervention, had it proceeded. It could have been decisive during the war if there had been sufficient forces to carry it out at the time. Now, however, Montgomery was completely opposed to the operation and thought it was too risky. Ernst disagreed, arguing that Aidid would not react, and he began holding rehearsals, deploying his units, and coordinating with the Pakistanis and Malaysians. Here again, the vague command structure caused confusion. During a visit to Somalia, Lieutenant General James Ellis, commanding US Third Army, was briefed by Ernst on the imminent operation; then he walked the short distance to UNOSOM force headquarters and heard from Montgomery that it was not happening. Montgomery could not order Ernst to stand down, so he went to Bir, who as force commander prohibited coalition forces from participating. Without UN forces, Ernst was unwilling to put American troops' lives at risk, so he had to call it off.[66] So acute was the acrimony that Ernst was ultimately removed from command of JTF Somalia and replaced by his deputy, marine Brigadier General Peter Pace, who "saw the writing on the wall" in terms of US policy in Somalia.[67] Unfortunately for Ernst, he was a warfighter who arrived after the war was over.

From December 1993 onward, with Ernst gone and Pace in charge, JTF Somalia's demonstrations of force gave way to a bunker mentality as the focus became the American withdrawal in March. At Victory Base, soldiers complained to reporters about boredom. They had arrived expecting to fight, and what they perceived as their superiors' risk-averse mentality was not well received. One told the *Washington Post*, "I'm just playing spades and eating [rations]." Another argued, "I think this mission is worthless, they've got these big vehicles here, and we're doing nothing." One of JTF Somalia's operations officers conceded to reporters, "It doesn't make a whole lot of sense to the men. They're sent out to build [Victory Base] and it will be finished just about the time they're supposed to leave Somalia."[68] America, though, was not the only country leaving.

Who's in and Who's Out

In November 1993 there were 46,984 military personnel from more than twenty countries in Somalia or offshore.[69] But between December 1993 and March 1994, there was an exodus of predominantly Western forces. On 14 October Boutros-Ghali attended a meeting of the Organisation of African Unity in Cairo, chaired by Egyptian President Hosni Mubarak, to discuss the future of UNOSOM. Referencing this meeting in his memoir, Boutros-Ghali quoted Mubarak as saying, "As soon as the United States pulls out of Somalia, all the other countries will follow. The French, the Belgians, and all the Western countries will pull out as soon as the Americans leave. And one hour after the U.S. leaves, I will pull out also."[70] The US Forces Somalia after-action report suggested that Clinton's 7 October announcement that America was withdrawing encouraged other nations to do the same.[71] However, this narrative of an American-led exodus, or even that the Battle of Mogadishu was the main driver, is not entirely accurate.

In August, months before the Battle of Mogadishu, the French and Belgians had announced that their 2,050 soldiers would be leaving by December 1993. The Swedish hospital contingent would depart with them. In and of itself, this was not necessarily a major problem. The Belgians and French occupied Baidoa and Kismayo, a huge swath of territory, but replacing them was Brigadier M. P. Bhagat's newly arrived 66th Mountain Brigade from the Indian Army. With four infantry battalions, one of them mechanized, plus helicopters, artillery, and a squadron of T-72 main battle tanks, Bhagat's brigade was the most capable and powerful contingent in UNOSOM.[72] Bir shifted forces around to balance new arrivals with imminent departures. The Indian brigade headquartered itself and one of the infantry battalions in Baidoa, taking over from the French on 13 November.[73] Another battalion was split between Waajid and Oddur. A third, with the armored squadron, went to Kismayo to relieve the Belgians. To compensate for the departure of the American QRF, the fourth battalion relieved the Moroccans in Baledogle, who in turn relieved the Pakistani battalion in Merka, which joined the rest of the Pakistani brigade in managing Mogadishu. By December 1993, Bhagat's brigade was spread over 173,000 square kilometers of southern Somalia, or 70 percent of UNOSOM's area of responsibility; this territory encompassed five of the nine former UNITAF HRSs and one-third of Somalia's population. It was quite a dispersal, but the interior was peaceful. As Indian units assumed control of villages and towns, they were greeted with well-intentioned shouts of "Mohammed Gandhi."[74]

The biggest withdrawal by far was that of the United States. JTF Somalia had 17,700 personnel, but there were also 2,800 US troops serving in UNOSOM's Logistics Support Command. All Americans were scheduled to leave by 31 March 1994. Clinton sent a personal message to the heads of state of all NATO members, Security Council members, and troop contributors "to ask that you assist us in providing additional forces to augment the capabilities of the United Nations force in Somalia."[75] He argued, rather disingenuously, that if the UN was not supported in Somalia, instability would spread. He justified America's withdrawal to other world leaders by highlighting his administration's new focus on the Bosnian War. It would be hard to commit US forces to stop violence in the Balkans while still being involved in Somalia. Clinton was simultaneously asking the international community to help the United States leave Somalia and to ensure that UNOSOM did not fail.

In New York, Kofi Annan worked to find more troops. At a meeting of representatives from troop-contributing countries on 26 October, Annan justified the campaign against Aidid by arguing the necessity of maintaining security in Mogadishu. He acknowledged to all present, though, that the 383 dead and wounded peacekeepers were not "sustainable or acceptable."[76] Italian Ambassador Paolo Fulci dismissed rumors of Italy's departure from Somalia. In a barely veiled critique of Clinton's knee-jerk withdrawal announcement, Fulci said that any such departure would be in full consultation with the UN. A handwritten note on his speech elaborated, "in other words, [there] will be no unilateral moves on our side."[77] The next day, in a marked contrast to Mubarak's comments to Boutros-Ghali, Egypt agreed to increase its commitment, honoring its promise to send a three-battalion brigade by the end of November. Pakistan pledged to send two more battalions, and Nepal, a new member of UNOSOM, agreed to send another.[78]

Excluding JTF Somalia, the initial losses for UNOSOM amounted to a modest five thousand troops, who were replaced by the five thousand–strong Indian brigade, with Egypt, Pakistan, and Nepal committing an additional four thousand personnel. UNOSOM was still sizable and capable. With the American withdrawal, though, UNOSOM would lose almost all air support and air transport capabilities, as well as the most advanced military logistics system in the world, which was vital to supply the disparate contingents dispersed across southern Somalia. These were major problems. Annan and his military adviser Maurice Baril searched for countries to replace these key capabilities. Fifteen nations were approached to contribute helicopters, and forty-two governments were contacted about providing logistics units. None agreed.[79]

UNOSOM had substantial contingents, but political considerations heavily influenced where and how they could be employed. On 7 October, in the immediate aftermath of the Battle of Mogadishu, Bir ordered the Zimbabwean contingent from Beledweyne to Mogadishu to "concentrate forces in the city." The Zimbabwean government countermanded Bir's order. When Baril conveyed this to Bir, his response was, the "order stands."[80] Ultimately, Annan bypassed Bir and told Howe that the Zimbabwean government refused to allow its troops to be deployed "anywhere near Mogadishu." The inference was that if Bir insisted, Zimbabwe might withdraw too.[81]

The most significant example of political priorities trumping operational capabilities involved the German contingent. The deployment of seventeen hundred German troops had been politically polarizing and even caused a brief constitutional crisis. Nevertheless, Defense Minister Volker Ruehe argued that it boosted the image of the *Bundeswehr* and reinforced Germany's commitment to the international community. There was one key caveat: German troops were not to be used by UN-OSOM for combat operations. The German contingent was a logistics task force stationed in Beledweyne by the Ethiopian border, far from the turbulent streets of Mogadishu. UNOSOM's operational plan was to eventually expand northward to cover the rest of Somalia. As such, the Germans were stationed at Beledweyne to logistically support this expansion once the Indian brigade arrived. The historic nature of the deployment attracted more than four hundred journalists and dozens of politicians to Beledweyne.[82] However, the Indian brigade did not arrive until November 1993. With no UNOSOM expansion and no brigade to support, the Germans remained stuck in Beledweyne for months. By October 1993, Annan wrote to Howe and informed him that the "near inactivity of the contingent has become a major political issue."[83]

For Howe and Bir, the issue was far from political. The Summer War made expansion impossible, and the strict conditions set down by the German government left few options for using them elsewhere. The German government's risk-averse nature caused an embarrassing episode when its contingent began to run out of fuel. The Germans were offered fuel, but they would have to pick it up from nearby Gialalassi. But because Gialalassi had not officially been declared secure, the German government would not allow its troops to go and collect the fuel. In New York, Baril told Howe to simply declare Gialalassi secure to "avoid having to deal with this problem on a daily basis."[84] Howe did so, and the German troops were resupplied, but only after the German ambassador to the UN was formally notified of the status change in writing.[85]

After the Battle of Mogadishu, the prospect of UNOSOM expanding north arose again, but the Indian brigade was now replacing the Belgians and the French. Hoping to ease political tensions, Annan suggested using the Italian brigade for the expansion instead, supported by the Germans at Beledweyne.[86] For Bir, this was not feasible, as the future shape of UNOSOM was unclear. To appease German political sensitivities, Bir ordered the Italians to move a battalion to Beledweyne to "provide a unit for the Germans to support."[87] This movement resulted in the Germans downsizing their contingent, as it was supporting only one battalion instead of a brigade-sized expansion. Again, dispelling the narrative of an exodus caused by the Battle of Mogadishu, the German government quickly pointed out that its reduction in forces "should in no way be perceived as a withdrawal of the German contingent."[88]

The Germans had the potential to solve one major problem. With the Americans leaving, Bir suggested that the Germans move to Baledogle and become UNOSOM's vital logistics nexus, collecting supplies from Mogadishu and distributing them in the interior. Bir asked Baril to broach this idea with the German government, promising that all routes in the city would be secured beforehand. The Germans refused. They stayed in Beledweyne, supporting an Italian battalion sent there specifically to be supported. Then, on 21 January 1994, German sentries shot and killed a Somali who had broken into a fuel dump. The opposition in the German government seized on the incident and demanded that the *Bundeswehr* be withdrawn. Caving under the pressure, the Germans informed Boutros-Ghali that their contingent would be leaving by March.[89] Germany had agreed to stay in Somalia after the Americans left. It was not 3 October that persuaded them to leave but the politically charged incident involving the first fatality caused by German troops since 1945.

The consequence of losing both US and German logistics was another wave of departures, also unrelated to the Battle of Mogadishu, by smaller contingents unable to support themselves logistically. In January 1994 Turkey, Norway, Saudi Arabia, the United Arab Emirates, Greece, and Tunisia all announced their withdrawal.[90] The biggest blow came when, despite Fulci's statements in October, Italy announced that its 2,576-strong brigade was leaving. Defense Minister Fabio Fabbri told journalists that the diplomatic progress had "not proven sufficient."[91] UNOSOM was losing another 6,206 troops. In nearly all cases, the withdrawal deadline was the same as that of the United States: March 1994.

As New Year's Day came and went, Boutros-Ghali celebrated the hundreds of thousands of Somali lives saved by UNITAF and UNOSOM. However, with departures exceeding new arrivals, he reiterated that the mission was still the full implementation of the Addis Ababa Agreement. But, he noted, "there are unmistakable signs of fatigue among the international community as it continues to be called upon" to assist Somalia.[92] Worse still, the UN secretary-general suggested that with several nations leaving Somalia, it was doubtful the mission could be achieved. Both the UN and United States had canvassed countries for more troops, to no avail. It was clear who was in and who was out. Reminding them of the three options he had proposed in November, he invited members of the Security Council to formally decide on the future of UNOSOM. Throughout January, Annan, Boutros-Ghali, and Baril gauged the attitudes of various member states toward Somalia in informal and formal discussions. After taking stock, Annan informed Howe that most nations were in favor of Boutros-Ghali's second option, a traditional peacekeeping force of sixteen thousand. The robust peace enforcement of 1993, Annan told him, had "been tried and found wanting."[93]

The Summer War had unsettled troop-contributing countries, but so had the nature of the mission. Representatives had complained to Annan that during the fighting there was little consultation between the Security Council and troop contributors in terms of how their forces were being used. Thus, most nations preferred a return to traditional peacekeeping with a reduced force. The Malaysians, Zimbabweans, and Nigerians remained committed, telling Annan that the UN "must not fail in Somalia." Other nations agreed to stay but voiced concerns that "the withdrawal of some countries was not encouraging."[94]

With the pulse of the member states taken, the Security Council crystallized the future course of UNOSOM with Resolution 897 in February 1994. Pursuit of the three-part goal enshrined in Resolution 865 would continue, and overall success was defined as "the installation of a democratically elected government" by March 1995.[95] Military tasks were limited to protecting ports and airports and safeguarding UN personnel and facilities. However, UNOSOM's mandate did not revert to traditional peacekeeping—it remained Chapter VII peace enforcement. Force could still be used to achieve the mission, although there was little political will to do so. But in a compromise, considering the degradation of military capabilities, the Security Council set the force level at twenty-two thousand instead of the sixteen thousand originally suggested. Resolution 897 set a high bar for UNOSOM in Somalia, especially as it came on the eve of the Western withdrawal.

The Western Withdrawal

On 7 February 1994, just days after Resolution 897 was passed, Montgomery formally resigned as UNOSOM's deputy force commander and assumed command of JTF Somalia, finally unifying all American forces under one commander.[96] On stepping down, he was quoted as saying, "It's time to get out . . . at some point in time you've got to stand up and take responsibility, and Somalis will not take responsibility."[97] This was a pointedly unfair judgment, considering that the vast majority of Somalis had never fought UNOSOM. One week later, as Turkey was leaving, Bir stepped down as force commander.[98] Montgomery then began the process of transferring responsibility for Mogadishu to the Pakistani brigade from UNOSOM and its new commander, Brigadier Saulat Abbas. Operation Quickdraw, the American departure from Somalia, had begun.

After completing readiness exercises, the Malaysian mechanized infantry battalion assumed the role of UNOSOM's QRF, taking over from the Americans. On 8 February US Army personnel held a "retreat" ceremony in the embassy compound. The next day, Victory Base was gifted to Abbas's Pakistanis. As JTF Somalia units were relieved by UNOSOM, they assembled at the port and the airport. On 4 March the 24th MEU, one of two MEUs loitering off the coast, came ashore in a repetition of the arrival of UNITAF's vanguard in December 1992, securing New Port and the airport to allow Montgomery's assembled units to begin loading their vehicles, equipment, and personnel on ships. The hive of activity increased as the Americans were joined by the Germans, Italians, Saudis, and other contingents that were also leaving. The Greeks donated their entire field hospital to the Waajid district council when they left.[99] With few exceptions, the countries leaving were NATO members. In an official memorandum on the future of UNOSOM, Ali Mahdi's Group of 12 claimed the withdrawal was "nothing but a selective pullout of all UN Euro-American troops, leaving behind Third World UN contingents with no proper logistical support and sufficient military back up . . . this amounts to a prelude of [an] ultimate abandonment of Somalia."[100]

To cover the American withdrawal, and ostensibly to ensure that UNOSOM had some defensive capabilities, the US government leased more than one hundred Vietnam War–era tanks and APCs to the Pakistani brigade, along with eight aging Cobra attack helicopters that had only basic armaments and were unable to fly at night.[101] Ironically, given his appeals for strong reinforcements six months previously, Montgomery argued this was enough for UNOSOM to "adequately take care of themselves."[102] Taking a very different view, Pakistan's foreign minister, Sardar Assef Ahmed Ali, bitterly complained that the Cobras were barely airworthy, capable of only forty-five minutes of flight at a time. Speaking to the media, he lambasted their quality, asking, "Are Pakistani lives worth less than those that come from the West?" Ali went on to claim that the Western withdrawal smacked of racism, saying, "It is beginning to look like Europeans for Bosnia, and Africans and Asians for Somalia. . . . Life in America is very good. Nobody in America wants to die for anybody else's causes." In a tone-deaf response, General John Shalikashvili, Powell's successor as chairman of the Joint Chiefs, told reporters "I leave here with a very good conscience . . . with a guarded optimism about what lies ahead . . . for the Somalis, well, we can't guarantee their safety for the rest of their lives."[103]

The West *was* abandoning Somalia, and the smaller contingents that could not support themselves logistically were going too. Of UNITAF's thirty-nine thousand coalition troops that arrived in December 1992, more than 75 percent had been Western military forces, with a minority of African and Middle Eastern partners. After the withdrawals between December 1993 and March 1994, the makeup of UNOSOM radically changed. Of the nineteen thousand troops remaining, barely four hundred were Western or European. There was a logistics platoon from New Zealand and a movement control unit from Australia, along with the only two remaining European contingents—an Irish transport company and a Romanian field hospital. Most of UNOSOM now came from Asia. Bhagat's Indian brigade and Abbas's Pakistani brigade, along with the Bangladeshis, Nepalese, and Malaysians, accounted for twelve thousand of those staying behind.

Even UNOSOM's leadership changed. Replacing Bir and Montgomery were Malaysian Lieutenant General Aboo Samah Bin Aboo Bakar as force commander and Zimbabwean Major General Michael Nyambuya as his deputy. On 8 March Howe stepped down. Kouyate was elevated to acting special representative of the secretary-general in his stead. At force headquarters, where Americans and Europeans had once led and dominated the personnel, intelligence, operations, and logistics cells, staff appointments were carefully balanced between erstwhile enemies Pakistan and India. UNOSOM's operations and communications staffs were led by Indian officers, both with Pakistani deputies. A Pakistani ran the logistics staff, and Pakistani officers dominated the personnel office under a Zimbabwean. A Malaysian ran planning with an Egyptian deputy, while intelligence was led by an Italian commander and a New Zealand deputy.[104]

By mid-March, most Americans were gone. There had been sporadic acts of violence. Marines at the K-4 Circle were fired on and killed four Somalis in response. But the last American casualties resulted not from enemy fire but from an accident. An AC-130 gunship crashed in Kenya, leaving seven dead crew members, six wounded, and one missing.[105] On 25 March the 24th MEU, having covered Montgomery's withdrawal, now did the same, conducting an amphibious retreat from Green Beach, where Newbold's 15th MEU had arrived fourteen months previously. Journalists were eager for a sound bite from the last American to leave. On Green Beach they found marine Lieutenant David Wolcott as he was boarding the last amphibious assault vehicle. Wolcott told the journalists, "We accomplished our mission: the safe withdrawal of our troops. I suggest you get out of here while you can."[106]

The period between the Battle of Mogadishu and the Western withdrawal saw the most progress toward implementing the Addis Ababa Agreement, coinciding with the highest number of international military personnel in Somalia. With the SNA weakened from the war, the presence of nearly fifty thousand troops forced Aidid and the SNA into inaction. However, with the Western withdrawal, UNOSOM lost the power to maintain that momentum, as well as the ability to influence the course of political reconciliation. It was not the Battle of Mogadishu that undermined the UN mission; it was the West's abandonment after so much progress had been made. As UNOSOM continued without the West, there was still hope, though, that a new Somalia could emerge.

11 | Left to Wither on the Vine
The End of UNOSOM in Somalia

Dear Brother Ali . . . as we said ourselves, we knew that the foreigners could not bring a solution to Somali problems and will eventually depart.
—Mohamed Farah Aidid, SNA chairman[1]

The international community offered a helping hand and, in the face of often violent opposition, firmly held that hand open for over two years, ready and willing to help. . . . UNOSOM has done its part.
—Madeleine Albright, US ambassador to the UN[2]

Somalia has been brought back from the precipice. It has been given another chance. The future is in their hands, but we cannot force them to grasp it.
—Colin Keating, New Zealand ambassador to the UN[3]

By March 1994, most Western nations had left Somalia. And this is the point at which many works on the intervention end their analysis. However, a much-diminished UNOSOM remained for an additional year, striving to fulfill the Addis Ababa Agreement, before it too finally withdrew in March 1995, its mission a failure. The suggestion that this failure was caused by political stalemate during the latter half of 1994 due to the clash of intractable personalities is an oversimplification.

Resolution 897 determined that UNOSOM would leave in 1995 after the successful "installation of a democratically elected government."[4] And there are three key reasons why this goal was unachievable. First, with the Western withdrawal, UNOSOM was limited militarily. But even so, under Resolution 897, UNOSOM's military mission was protecting ports, airports, lines of communication, and UN personnel and facilities. As such, there was no political will to use force to achieve the mandate. Second, the UN was experiencing a crippling financial crisis, an underappreciated situation that undermined not only its operations but also nations' willingness to continue in Somalia.

Finally, the evidence suggests that Aidid had developed a complex plan for 1994, once it became clear the UN was no longer willing to use force to achieve its mission. Aidid had secretly toured regional neighbors in 1993, seeking endorsement as Somalia's next president.[5] Beginning in early March 1994, just as the Western withdrawal commenced, Aidid launched a dual strategy of limited military actions and careful political maneuvers to position himself as the strongest candidate for the leadership of post-UNOSOM Somalia. UNOSOM had the force but not the will to stop Aidid's ascendance, and it disintegrated due to a crippling lack of finances and disillusionment with a seemingly unachievable mission. Withdrawal thus became the only viable option.

To understand UNOSOM's demise, it is vital to understand the SNA's political and military situation at the beginning of 1994. The SNA did not represent all of Somalia; it was a coalition of only four of the fifteen factions. Compared to the SNA, Ali Mahdi's Group of 12 was much stronger militarily and represented a much bigger constituency. Thus, through maneuvers both political and military, Aidid aimed to strengthen the SNA's position before any new government was finalized. His strategy was rooted in the recognition that UNOSOM was leaving, that there would be a power vacuum, and that the SNA was not yet ideally placed to fill it.

At first, Aidid shunned political initiatives that would marginalize the SNA. Then, recognizing that stalemate weakened his support within the SNA, he promised to participate in the formation of a new government, only to stall. Ongoing regional peace conferences needed to conclude, he said, before the negotiation of any new government. Through these peace conferences, the SNA bolstered its alliance and removed potential adversaries. Militarily, the biggest point of contention affecting the future stability of Somalia was which subclan would dominate the Hawiye—Ali Mahdi's Abgal or Aidid's Habr-Gidr. The Hawiye clan had other subclans as well, such as the Hawadle, which was neutral, and the Murusade, which was hostile to the SNA for encroaching on its territory in Mogadishu. Consequently, Aidid and the SNA launched limited attacks on the other Hawiye subclans—Ali Mahdi's Abgal, because he was Aidid's chief rival for leadership of the future government, and the Hawadle and Murusade, to bring them into the fold or remove them as potential Ali Mahdi supporters.

The UN's failure in Somalia was rooted less in Aidid's ambitions to lead and more in UNOSOM's unwillingness to stop him. He carefully exploited this to his own ends and avoided engaging UNOSOM unless victory was assured or it gave him leverage.

The Nairobi Declaration of March 1994

In the wake of the Battle of Mogadishu, emergency talks were held in Addis Ababa in December 1993 between the SNA and the Group of 12, chaired by Kouyate, who at that point was still UNOSOM's deputy special representative. In a controversial move seen as an American endorsement of Aidid's political standing, Oakley offered him the use of a State Department aircraft to fly to Addis Ababa. Oakley defended this offer by noting that one can only make peace with one's enemies.[6] In Addis Ababa, the two sides refused to meet face-to-face and remained polarized on divisive issues. The Group of 12 wanted UNOSOM to take a leading role in the political reconciliation process; the SNA wanted UNOSOM gone. Ali Mahdi's coalition supported district and regional councils and the goal of implementing the Addis Ababa Agreement; Aidid wanted both the councils and the agreement revised.[7] It was a stalemate.

Part of the reason Aidid resisted the councils was that the SNA had little influence on them. By January 1994, nine of the fifteen factions had submitted their chosen candidates for the Transitional National Council (TNC) to UNOSOM. Somalia was marching inexorably toward implementing the Addis Ababa Agreement and creating a government in which the SNA was a minority. However, it was in Addis Ababa that Aidid's political ascendancy began. During the talks, Ethiopian President Meles Zenawi took a pronounced pro-Aidid stance. Although this alienated Ali Mahdi personally, Kouyate reported that some members of his coalition were considering breaking ranks in favor of the SNA.[8] Arguably, with Aidid endorsed by Zenawi and UNOSOM's departure date set, some of Ali Mahdi's erstwhile allies were evaluating which way the wind was blowing for a post-UN Somalia.

While sitting at a coffee shop in Nairobi in January 1994, Babiker Khalifa, UNOSOM's political liaison officer, was surprised to be approached by Osman Atto and Omar Salad, two senior SNA officials who had recently been released after being captured by Task Force Ranger. Salad was one of the targets on 3 October 1993. In the spur-of-the-moment conversation that ensued, Atto told Khalifa that there was division within the SNA; the hard-liners wanted UNOSOM to leave, but a sizable cohort believed that, after the Summer War, which Atto claimed cost fifteen thousand lives, enough was enough. It was time to cooperate with the UN.[9] The UN mission still appealed to most Somalis, especially outside of Mogadishu, and to SNA moderates in the capital.

In early March Egyptian President Hosni Mubarak, acting as chair of the Organisation for African Unity, invited the Group of 1 2 and the SNA to Cairo to break the deadlock. Once again, Aidid's paranoia surrounding Egypt's past support of Barre's regime surfaced. The SNA rejected Mubarak's invitation due to "problems with the Egyptian leadership," which it did not want involved in Somali affairs.[10] The Group of 1 2 sent a delegation that proposed forming an interim Transitional National Salvation Council, a much smaller version of the more representative TNC. That proposal was doomed from the start. Composed of seventeen members—the chairpersons of all fifteen factions plus the SNM in Somaliland and Ali Mahdi—the Salvation Council totally excluded representatives from the wider population and the various intellectual and women's advocacy groups. But the key flaw was that the council's chair would be elected from among the seventeen members.[11] With Ali Mahdi's Group of 1 2 dominating, there was no chance that Aidid and the three factions making up the SNA would be anything other than isolated.

The Salvation Council proposal went nowhere, but its rejection by the SNA was a visible snub of peaceful reconciliation. Kouyate emphasized to Aidid that if UNOSOM left Somalia, the relief organizations would soon follow, meaning that the eleven thousand Somalis employed by the UN in Mogadishu would lose their jobs.[12] This left Aidid with a complex choice: he could continue his obstructionist behavior and risk alienating SNA moderates and eroding his authority, or he could participate in reconciliation. Faced with internal dissent and the perception that he was the chief obstacle to progress, Aidid chose cooperation—or at least the appearance of it.

One week after the Cairo conference, Kouyate arranged for Aidid and Ali Mahdi to meet in Nairobi from 15 to 23 March 1994. The result was the Nairobi Declaration, signed just two days before the Western withdrawal from Somalia was complete. Faction leaders from the Group of 1 2 and the SNA gave Aidid and Ali Mahdi "power of attorney" to sign on their behalf.[13] As a statement of intent, all factions recommitted themselves to a cease-fire, the preservation of democratic principles, voluntary disarmament, and creation of the last remaining district and regional councils. In a sense, it was simply a renewal of the Addis Ababa Agreement. But far more significant was the commitment to a conference on 15 May 1994, hereafter referred to as the May Conference, to elect a president, vice president, and prime minister and then form a National Legislative Assembly, skipping the formation of the long-awaited TNC altogether.[14]

The Nairobi Declaration was the most compelling sign that Somalia was back on track to achieve political reconciliation, the cornerstone of UNOSOM's mission. But Aidid could afford to be conciliatory, as the March withdrawals of Western forces meant the degradation of UN military capabilities. If the United States and others had decided to stay, Aidid and the SNA may have been coerced to deliver on these promises. But once those forces left, Aidid repeatedly postponed the May Conference.

Publicly, his excuse for postponement was that ongoing regional peace conferences in Somalia should be finalized before the May Conference formed a government. No national government could be created while regional conflict was ongoing. The logic was sound, and even Ali Mahdi agreed with it. Negotiations were taking place at two principal conferences, both relating to Kismayo. Despite the regional stability achieved by the Jubbaland conference in August 1993, talks had reconvened when fighting broke out again between Aidid's ally Omar Jess and Hersi Morgan in February 1994. Even though the Hawiye population in Kismayo was negligible, Osman Atto, Aidid's right-hand man, was the chief negotiator for the SNA. It was Atto who signed a new cease-fire agreement, the Lower Jubba Agreement, with Morgan in June 1994, which promised power sharing among the nineteen clans and subclans in Kismayo.

The SNA then sponsored the Absaame conference, resulting in an agreement in July that reunited both wings of the SPM—Jess's SPM-Ogadeni and Morgan's SPM-Harti—which had been fighting over Kismayo for years.[15] Building on the Lower Jubba Agreement, the Absaame conference transformed a cease-fire into Morgan's permanent loss of SPM-Harti militia. By July, the May Conference had still not happened, but Aidid's political strategy had yielded success. Both the Lower Jubba Agreement and the Absaame conference improved the SNA's military position by ending a prolonged conflict on the SNA's southern flank and reducing a long-standing rival's ability to fight in the future. And by the end of July, Aidid and the SNA had enjoyed military successes as well.

The Western withdrawal reduced UNOSOM's strength by a third, leaving severe shortfalls in critical areas such as air support and logistics. In early April 1994, however, UNOSOM was still formidable.

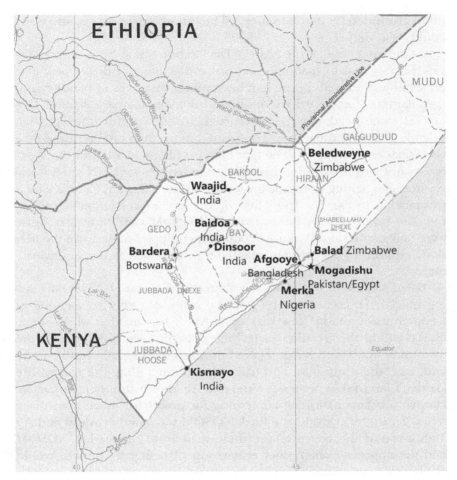

UNOSOM Garrisons, June 1994

General Aboo Bakar, UNOSOM's new force commander, reported to Maurice Baril in New York that his force mustered twenty-four well-armed battalions with more than 320 APCs. Abbas's Pakistani brigade included a tank regiment of forty American-built Patton tanks in Mogadishu, while Bhagat's Indian brigade had fourteen Soviet-built T-72s in Kismayo. Airpower was lacking though. The Indians and Pakistanis had a combined fleet of thirty-eight helicopters, but only the eight aging Cobras leased from America were armed, and half of them were often grounded for maintenance.[16] The rest were transports, and none could fly at night.

At the same time, if the Nairobi Declaration was to be believed, UNOSOM only had to maintain security and stability until the new government was formed. There had been minor instances of banditry and complaints of lax security that allowed Somalis to roam around UNOSOM force headquarters unescorted. In one month, the Egyptian brigade guarding the airport confiscated more than one hundred fake visitor passes from locals. The first high-profile incident after the Western withdrawal occurred in Kismayo when bandits took UN relief workers hostage. Setting domestic grievances aside, Pakistani Cobras joined troop-laden Indian transport helicopters in a successful air assault to free the hostages.[17] In Bakar's view, UNOSOM's military capabilities were "substantial and they are adequately equipped to perform the mission required by the present mandate, in the current threat environment."[18]

Bakar's cautious optimism was shared by Kouyate, UNOSOM's acting special representative and political head. Attending a meeting of troop contributors in New York on 8 April, he said that while Somalia was still at the "conflict stage," the cease-fire was holding, and the upcoming May Conference seemed promising. The main problem, he said, was "the acquisition and use of power, including the role of the Hawiye Clan in that process." Aidid and Ali Mahdi and their respective Hawiye subclans had been competing for power for more than three years. Thus, the critical issue for UNOSOM was whether Aidid and Ali Mahdi stayed the course. Nevertheless, Kouyate revealed, UNOSOM had developed an emergency evacuation plan that he hoped "would not become necessary."[19]

Kouyate faced tough questions from the representatives of the troop contributors: Realistically, what were the chances of Aidid and Ali Mahdi working together? Why could this progress not have been made sooner? Kouyate replied that the two rivals had been fighting for three years: "two different personalities pitted against each other in combat . . . this fact has not changed fundamentally." But, he continued, "both men were now tired of war. Each wanted peace, but simultaneously wished to be President of Somalia." Their struggle on the battlefield, Kouyate explained, had ended; they would now focus on politics.[20] Encouragingly, Ali Mahdi had informed Kouyate just two days previously that thirteen of Mogadishu's fourteen districts were willing to voluntarily hand their weapons over to UNOSOM.[21] As to why progress could not have been made sooner, the simple answer was the Summer War. This prompted some desultory remarks about the UN Commission of Inquiry report, which had been finalized in February and detailed the highly flawed basis for that conflict but was still being kept confidential.[22] Even so, Bakar and Kouyate were right to feel confident. All UNOSOM had to do was to maintain stability in a benign environment until the goals of the Nairobi Declaration were met. This confidence was shattered when Aidid and the SNA commenced their military campaign.

The SNA Military Campaign

On 5 March 1994, just prior to the Western withdrawal, heavy concentrations of SNA militia mobilized near Merka, held by the Group of 12.[23] They stayed until the West's withdrawal was complete. On 10 April the SNA took the port town in fighting that resulted in heavy casualties for both sides. This meant the SNA had secured the main road linking Kismayo and Mogadishu, but even more important, Merka became a gateway to receive arms shipments over the following months.[24] In another indication of Aidid's awareness of the SNA's relative weaknesses, when the Group of 12 gathered forces to retake Merka, he launched another attack elsewhere to keep Ali Mahdi off balance.[25] He chose the Medina District of Mogadishu, right beside the airport and the embassy and university compounds.

The Medina District exemplified the complexities of political reconciliation in Somalia and the lack of support for Aidid and the SNA. The population of Medina was Hawiye, predominantly the Abgal subclan, of which Ali Mahdi was a member, and the Hawadle subclan, which was broadly neutral in the contest between the Abgal and Aidid's Habr-Gidr. The Hawadle had negotiated the handover of Mogadishu airport to Imtiaz Shaheen and UNOSOM back in 1992, to Aidid's outrage. Medina had never been under SNA sway; it had its own militia, its own local governance, and even an Islamic-based justice system, and it had taken no part in the Summer War. On 18 April SNA militia clashed with the other Hawiye subclans in Medina. For a week, there was heavy and inconclusive fighting in the neighborhoods right beside the airport and UNOSOM force headquarters.[26]

Any UN optimism about succeeding in Somalia evaporated. The UN-

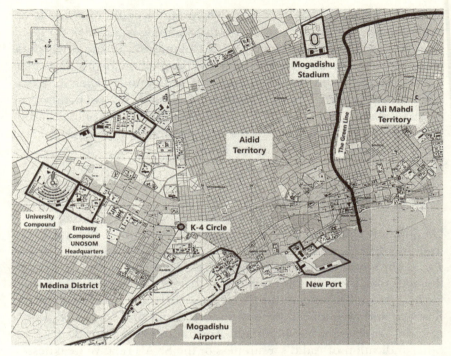

The Medina District of Mogadishu

OSOM intelligence summary at the end of April 1994 told the tale. Of UNOSOM's six operational sectors, two, Mogadishu and Kismayo, were designated "Amber—Unstable," with "Amber" indicating that "violence could occur." Merka, firmly in SNA hands, was "Amber—Stable," with "Stable" indicating a low-level police presence and local governance. The other three, Baidoa, Balad, and Afgooye, were "Green," meaning no violence was expected. But none of the six sectors was designated "Secure."[27] The fighting in April between the SNA and the Group of 12 provided another reason to delay the May Conference to establish a Somali government. Ali Mahdi refused to participate until the SNA withdrew from Merka.[28] The SNA held firm.

An intelligence report from the Irish contingent noted that technicals were becoming more common on the streets of Mogadishu, passing through UNOSOM checkpoints unchallenged. Rumors circulated that UNOSOM would confiscate heavy weapons, but the intelligence report observed, "Whether the will is there to introduce and enforce these changes remains to be seen. If these changes come about, it could mean a restart of serious anti-UNOSOM hostilities, at least in the Mogadishu area."[29] Even though Resolution 897 gave UNOSOM enforcement authority, there was no political will to forcibly disarm the factions nor much enthusiasm among the military contingents to do so.

The first phase of Aidid's military campaign was a success. Merka had been captured, and UNOSOM had not reacted. But there were unintended consequences of his political maneuvering. In June a sequence of events took place that ensured Medina became a war zone for months, with fighting spreading to other parts of Mogadishu as well. First, the Medina militia captured four SNA members who had fired on a UNOSOM convoy; they were sentenced to death, increasing tensions between Medina and the SNA. Then dissent emerged from within the SNA itself. The Ayr subclan of Aidid's Habr-Gidr, which made up a sizable portion of the SNA militia, revolted against Aidid's leadership. Protesting his recent endorsement of the Lower Jubba Agreement with Hersi Morgan, the Ayr denounced any peace with remnants of the former Barre regime. The Ayr declared that the Hawiye subclans should unite against Aidid. On 24 June, within a day of this call to arms, there was an assassination attempt as Aidid traveled from Merka to Mogadishu. Two of his bodyguards were killed, and Aidid claimed the Group of 12 was responsible. Medina descended into widespread fighting between the SNA and the other Hawiye subclans in an open revolt against Aidid's leadership.[30] It was, as one report described, the "most intense fighting in Mogadishu since 1992."[31]

Mogadishu was once again a city at war. UNOSOM units were put on full alert, and UN agencies ceased operations as the violence spread. The city's water system had to be shut down, and a dozen peacekeepers were wounded by stray gunfire. Convoys were ambushed, including the one escorting the new UN special representative, Ghanian Ambassador Victor James Gbeho, who was touring Somalia before taking over from Kouyate at the end of July. Gbeho's vehicle was caught in the cross fire while returning to the capital from Kismayo on 1 July. In another incident, local Somalis working for UNOSOM were abducted from a convoy and one of them was executed, prompting UN civilian staff to say that they had lost faith in the military's ability to protect them.[32] Another ambush saw two Malaysian peacekeepers killed and four more wounded, while the head of UNOSOM intelligence, Colonel Fulvio Vizzalini, was briefly taken prisoner and robbed of all his valuables.[33]

The fighting in Medina continued well into July, but it did not go Aidid's way. On 3 July Hisham Omayad, Kouyate's deputy, asked Ali Mahdi to declare a cease-fire. He agreed but demanded that Aidid and the SNA withdraw from Medina before the fighting spread to the rest of the city. Ali Mahdi also complained that instead of taking a leadership role in facilitating peace, UNOSOM was no longer peacekeeping or peacemaking but "peace-waiting."[34] He was not wrong. Omayad "politely declined" an offer to tour the positions of Ali Mahdi's militias, which, according to the Group of 12's leader, were poised to destroy the SNA. Later that day, more than eighty technicals carrying hundreds of militiamen left Medina along 21 October Road, heading toward SNA strongholds.[35] Aidid was retreating.

Given his now tenuous military position, Aidid took to the airwaves on 7 July. He advocated peace and cooperation, for "there can be no development where there is no peace and security." Warning his listeners that "repeated attempts by foreigners to disrupt the peace and reconciliation process . . . have not yet ceased," Aidid asked the international community to support the principle of self-determination and allow "Somalis alone to decide the future of their country." He signed off with the SNA motto of "Peace, Justice, Unity, and Development."[36] Whether due to his setbacks in Mogadishu or to drum up popular support for the SNA, Aidid's broadcasts took a pronounced anti-UNOSOM tone as July progressed. On 12 July, the anniversary of the Abdi house attack, he told listeners, "This day and 1993 are important to us because it is when US/UNOSOM targeted politicians, elders, youths, and women . . . they intended a collective massacre of an unarmed people that could not defend themselves."[37] A week later, he sought to "expose and declare the foreign interference" in the fighting in Mogadishu, baselessly claiming that the Egyptians and Pakistanis had provided the Abgal, Hawadle, and Murusade with weapons and logistics support.[38] Kouyate and Bakar denied all these accusations. It was really all UNOSOM could do.

UNOSOM's Inability to Respond

The security situation in Mogadishu rapidly worsened between April and July, despite the presence of half of UNOSOM's military contingents. Resolution 897 prevented UNOSOM from using force for anything other than defending the ports and airport and protecting UN personnel and installations, none of which had been attacked. There was no political will for a return to the violence of the previous year. But even if that will had existed, the forces did not. Kouyate had cabled Kofi Annan in April, the day before the fighting erupted in Medina, expressing concern that coalition forces were being reduced when the intervention was at its most crucial stage. It was vital that no more countries withdraw from Somalia, and Kouyate and Bakar implored Annan to stave off any further departures. Bakar had only eighteen thousand troops. And, given the growing international fatigue toward the mission in Somalia and the UN's preoccupation with the outbreak of the Rwandan Genocide that month, Boutros-Ghali was unsure how long even that number could be maintained.[39]

With the renewed fighting between the SNA and the Group of 12, Bakar's confidence that UNOSOM had the forces necessary to achieve the mission disappeared. The threat environment had fundamentally changed. Worse still, UNOSOM was heavily reliant on Brown & Root, a civilian logistics company, to keep the various contingents supplied, and Bakar worried that it might evacuate if the violence increased. With the bulk of UNOSOM garrisoning cities and towns across southern Somalia or escorting relief convoys, Bakar had no additional forces to contain the fighting, let alone deal with a renewed civil war. He soberly warned Kouyate that UNOSOM was now "stretched very thinly," and the "ability to achieve the mandated tasks has become limited." Worse still, just to carry out existing operations, Bakar needed the force increased to twenty-two thousand.[40] By July, Bakar conceded that it was becoming "increasingly difficult to maintain the required range and number of escorts for humanitarian relief and logistical convoys."[41] At best, UNOSOM could only secure the ports and airports in Somalia, with limited patrolling of key routes and areas.

The UNOSOM of mid-1994 barely resembled the force of 1993, and in no way did it have the capabilities of UNITAF. When the Nigerian government tried to send APCs to reinforce its contingent, the consequences of the Western withdrawal became glaringly obvious. Nigeria had no aircraft capable of moving armored vehicles and neither did UNOSOM, and UN headquarters' attempts to contract private aircraft proved a nightmare.[42] The result was scathing criticism from the Nigerian defense adviser in New York. Colonel M. B. Marwa wrote to Annan that Nigeria was very concerned about how its troops in Somalia would be resupplied after the "withdrawal en masse of the West." The UN's inability to arrange air transportation, Marwa wrote, "has confirmed our worst fears," as "no one is sure when the plane will be available." He warned that the situation could result in Nigeria pulling out of Somalia and that it was rethinking its participation with the UN mission in Rwanda, writing, "one failure is bad enough, who needs his forces stranded in two places?"[43] The APCs arrived, but only after a glacial contracting process that clearly demonstrated UNOSOM's inability to react quickly to events on the ground.

In New York, Boutros-Ghali still championed the potential for success because most Somalis and the Group of 12 still supported UNOSOM's mission. Somalia was not regressing; only Mogadishu was. UNOSOM was at "a defining moment in its complex and stormy history," Boutros-Ghali argued to the Security Council in May.[44] The Nairobi Declaration had created hope, but the SNA was fighting for a better negotiating position at a future conference that no longer had a set date. The Security Council was considering whether to renew UNOSOM's mandate, but Boutros-Ghali remained steadfast. Leaving would let the country slide back into civil war. To the Security Council he wrote, "The Somali people deserve a last chance." The mandate was extended until the end of September 1994, pending further review.[45]

Boutros-Ghali's appeal to continue in Somalia and the Security Council's extension of UNOSOM's mandate were not based on blind idealism. It was true that, despite the fifteen factions' commitment to voluntary disarmament, the complete opposite was happening as many factions rearmed in the uncertain environment. But regardless of SNA retrenchment in Mogadishu, real progress was being made elsewhere in building a new police force, creating a new judiciary, and establishing local governance. By July 1994, eight thousand police were serving across southern Somalia, trained by a fifty-strong UN Civilian Police Task Force from nine countries. Teams from the US Department of Justice's International Criminal Investigative Training Assistance Program had refurbished police academies in Baidoa and Mogadishu. UNOSOM' Police Division was still working toward the goal, set out in the judicial reconstruction plan, of having ten thousand police by the end of 1994. In July, this seemed attainable. In addition, a two thousand–strong rapid-deployment paramilitary police force, the *Darawishta*, was being trained.[46]

Progress was not limited to law enforcement. Fifty-four courthouses had been repaired and were operating in twenty-eight districts. Another

fifty-four were planned. UNOSOM's Justice Division identified and enlisted 146 judges for the new courts, and it worked with district councils
to refurbish and staff fourteen prisons. Critically, by July, only seven of
the sixty-six districts outside Mogadishu lacked a district council. Politically, the Lower Jubba Agreement and Absaame conference had ended
the fighting in Kismayo, and Ali Mahdi repeatedly wrote to Kouyate to
reiterate the Group of 12's readiness to attend the May Conference,
whenever it was scheduled. Progress had slowed, but it was still being
made. Boutros-Ghali hinted at who was to blame when he noted that
"*certain* Somali leaders are still not prepared to subordinate their personal ambitions for power to the cause of peace and stability in Somalia."[47] By July, there were still indicators that a government could be
formed, but there was enough skepticism for Boutros-Ghali to ask Kouyate and his replacement, Gbeho, to prepare an in-depth assessment of
whether political reconciliation could realistically be achieved.[48] Just a
week later, Aidid demonstrated how weak UNOSOM really was.

The Seizure of Beledweyne

The intra-Hawiye fighting in Medina had forced the SNA to retreat in
Mogadishu, but Aidid made up for it in Beledweyne. Deep in the interior, close to the Ethiopian border, Beledweyne was historically divided
between the Hawadle and the Habr-Gidr. Aidid had been born there in
1934. Ali Mahdi had recently traveled to the region to meet with Hawadle leaders, possibly to form an alliance against the SNA. On 24 July
Aidid responded as the SNA launched a series of successful attacks on
the Hawadle militia in Beledweyne. Under UNITAF, Beledweyne had
been home to nearly one thousand Canadians, who were replaced by an
even larger contingent of Germans under UNOSOM. But by July 1994,
Beledweyne was the UN's smallest and most isolated outpost, manned
by a single company of 142 Zimbabwean light infantrymen. The Zimbabweans were split between the UN compound in the town and their
base at the nearby airfield. On 26 July, having cleared the town of Hawadle, SNA militia approached the UN compound and demanded that
all property and vehicles be handed over. The Zimbabwean commander
refused. The compound was then surrounded by hundreds of SNA militiamen who proceeded to loot the buildings and vehicles.[49]

Overwhelmingly outnumbered, the Zimbabweans withdrew to their base at the airfield and joined the rest of their contingent there. The SNA arrived soon after and surrounded the Zimbabwean camp, which was also sheltering more than five hundred locals fleeing the SNA advance. A tense standoff ensued. The local SNA commander came forward and apologized to the Zimbabwean commander for looting UN property. He executed four of the perpetrators to demonstrate his sincerity. The Zimbabweans were then told they could not withdraw without SNA permission, and only after all weapons, vehicles, and equipment had been surrendered. This was an impossible position. The nearest UNOSOM garrison was three hundred kilometers away in Balad. In Mogadishu, Bakar and his staff developed a plan to send aircraft to evacuate the Zimbabweans, but the SNA blocked the runway, and UNOSOM could not launch a sufficiently large air assault to mount a rescue. On 30 July hundreds of SNA militia stormed the camp and disarmed the Zimbabweans at gunpoint, killing one soldier who resisted. The SNA now had 141 UNOSOM peacekeepers as hostages.[50]

The Beledweyne seizure was the first test of UNOSOM's new—and final—special representative, Ghanian Ambassador Victor James Gbeho. Gbeho had not officially taken over from Kouyate and was having lunch with Ali Mahdi in Mogadishu when the SNA swept into Beledweyne. The day before the Zimbabweans were taken hostage, Gbeho had been in Nairobi so that Kouyate could formally introduce him to the leaders of the Group of 12. Gbeho was blunt, asking the assembled leaders why they were paralyzing the reconciliation process. He warned that the international community was tired of Somalia and that UNOSOM resources were dwindling. The Group of 12 needed to stop "seeing UNOSOM as a government" and start taking responsibility for rebuilding Somalia. The Group of 12 pledged its full support to Gbeho and urged him to be more evenhanded than Kouyate, whose personal relationship with Aidid had been a source of suspicion, even though there is no evidence it was inappropriate. Gbeho was told that "only one man remained the problem of Somalia."[51] The Zimbabweans were captured the next day, and in this context, Gbeho had his first interaction with Aidid.

Meeting with Gbeho, Aidid displayed none of his usual antagonistic bluster. He did not deflect or debate the SNA's responsibility. Instead, he claimed he was "embarrassed" by what had happened and promised Gbeho he would investigate.[52] The next day, 31 July, Colonel S. B. Moyo, the senior Zimbabwean officer in Somalia, boarded a plane in Mogadishu bound for Beledweyne. He was accompanied by a platoon of his countrymen and fifteen senior SNA officials provided by Aidid to negotiate the release of the captured peacekeepers. They were freed, but without their weapons, equipment, or any UN property. On 1 August Moyo and his Zimbabweans flew back to Mogadishu. UNOSOM had officially abandoned Beledweyne.[53]

While the behind-the-scenes machinations cannot be definitively known, the capture of the Zimbabweans was arguably part of Aidid's strategy. A fait accompli against UNOSOM's smallest garrison was a low-risk gamble that would allow Aidid to save face and leverage his way back into a solid negotiating position by facilitating the captives' release. That the SNA made no demands to ransom the Zimbabweans suggests that another motive was in play. It was a major military victory for the SNA, but not just against the Hawadle. UNOSOM had been unable to prevent the seizure or to free the Zimbabweans. It was clear to all that UNOSOM either would not or could not fight. Even those who did not support Aidid realized that he and the SNA were controlling military and political events in Somalia. Ali Mahdi's supporters believed that the lack of Zimbabwean resistance meant that UNOSOM had deliberately ceded Beledweyne to the SNA. General Bakar was informed that in Ali Mahdi's portion of Mogadishu, "the general feeling is that UNOSOM wants to impose Aideed on the rest of Somalia and then leave."[54] An intelligence report from the Irish contingent noted that the seizure "emphasizes the increasingly blatant aggression towards UNOSOM, especially by S.N.A. This reflects a growing confidence . . . that Aideed can form the next government."[55] Beledweyne was a major propaganda coup in terms of identifying who might win a leadership contest in post-UNOSOM Somalia. Aidid's gamble worked. He had fought the Hawadle and won, challenged UNOSOM and got away with it, and stoked anti-UN sentiment among his rival's supporters.

For reasons that remain unclear, Boutros-Ghali's August report to the Security Council did not mention the seizure of Beledweyne at all. Instead, he focused on Gbeho's realistic appraisal of the potential for political reconciliation. This assessment emphasized the progress achieved outside Mogadishu, such as the regional peace conferences and the establishment of police, judiciary, and local governance. "The Somali people in general are tired of war and anarchy," Gbeho wrote, but "conflicts within the dominant Hawiye clan constitute the major obstacle to national reconciliation and that no meaningful progress can be made in the political process without first finding a solution to the conflict in Mogadishu."⁵⁶ To test Gbeho's assessment, Babiker Khalifa, UNOSOM's political liaison officer in Nairobi, met with senior officials from all the factions to gauge their willingness to form a government. General Aden Abdullahi Nur, leader of the SPM, told Khalifa that the faction leaders, including himself, should be tried as "criminals" for destroying their own country. Others argued that, with the Addis Ababa Agreement and the Nairobi Declaration, UNOSOM was focusing too much on political factions rather than clans, which were the foundation of Somali society. For many, Ali Mahdi and Aidid's rivalry was not political per se; it was a clan issue first and foremost.⁵⁷

Using Khalifa's litmus test of the faction leaders, Gbeho argued that national reconciliation was still a possibility, but UNOSOM needed to focus on clan and community leaders in collaboration with faction leaders, not the factions alone. He thus committed UNOSOM to reconciling the hostilities within the Hawiye clan and finally settle the intraclan animosities, end the fighting, and pave the way to national reconciliation. Gbeho proposed a Hawiye reconciliation conference as a vehicle for peace. Ali Mahdi had proposed a similar initiative on the same day the SNA attacked the Hawadle in Beledweyne.⁵⁸ Flush from the propaganda victory over UNOSOM and the actual victory over the Hawadle, Aidid agreed, but the reconciliation conference never happened. Bilateral meetings between subclans were held first, in yet another attempt to delay the May Conference on government formation until the SNA was in a position of maximum influence. In August, and supported by UNOSOM, Ali Mahdi's Abgal and Aidid's Habr-Gidr agreed to withdraw their respective militias from contested areas of the city to end the fighting. Meetings between the Habr-Gidr and the Murusade and Hawadle in Medina were also successful in reducing tensions. There was a pan-Hawiye cease-fire in the capital, but just like the May Conference, the Hawiye reconciliation conference kept getting postponed.⁵⁹

Boutros-Ghali's August report proposed two actions that ended up encouraging Aidid's delaying tactics and ceding more territory to the SNA. To convince Aidid and Ali Mahdi to reconcile, Boutros-Ghali tried to increase the pressure on them. He announced that UNOSOM would reduce its forces to fifteen thousand troops by the end of October. He then drew a line in the sand. If there was no progress on the May Conference or Hawiye reconciliation by the end of September, the Security Council would have to decide how long peacekeepers should remain to protect humanitarian efforts in the absence of political progress.[60] Those in New York saw this as a way to spur the factions into finally making headway. But on the ground, it backfired.

Liquidity Problems

Boutros-Ghali was not blinded by idealism; nor was he naïve. There had been genuine progress in Somalia, and the UN secretary-general was providing every opportunity to ensure that a sustainable government would emerge. The reduction of UNOSOM forces and the September deadline were driven by practical issues within the UN. In Boutros-Ghali's words, "many troop contributing countries, have conveyed to me . . . they are not prepared to continue indefinitely" in Somalia.[61] This international fatigue manifested in a financial crisis. The UN was running out of money. Peacekeeping operations were entirely dependent on member states' financial contributions. In the post–Cold War world, the size and scale of these operations had risen drastically, increasing costs exponentially. By November 1993, UNOSOM was $140 million in the red.[62] By January 1994, of the estimated $413 million needed to finance UNOSOM until the end of March, only one-quarter had been paid by the member states.[63]

The Tunisians exemplified how this financial crisis bled over into operations. They withdrew from Somalia because they were logistically dependent on the US military. The Tunisian government had been willing to increase its UNOSOM contingent and become self-sustaining, but it pointed out that the UN still owed it for a previous deployment in Cambodia. Unless payment was guaranteed, the Tunisians could not afford to continue in Somalia. At the time, an official in the Department of Peacekeeping Operations told Howe that the Tunisians were a "reflection of a much broader problem, namely, the financial situation of the organization (or should I say 'crisis')."[64]

By July 1994, UNOSOM was $500 million in debt. An Irish government memorandum identified the biggest debtors as Russia, Britain, France, Italy, and the United States; the US alone owed the UN $1.4 billion.[65] Like the Tunisians, the Irish suggested that if the crisis continued, it would jeopardize future participation of the Irish Defence Forces in UN missions. On 6 July Joseph Connor, the undersecretary-general for administration and management, told the UN General Assembly that all peacekeeping operations, including UNOSOM, were in a financially "precarious position."[66] Work on rebuilding Mogadishu's water system had stopped because funds ran out. So UNOSOM began supplying jerry cans of undrinkable desalinated water to peacekeepers instead of bottled water, citing "economic reasons."[67] This earned a strongly worded letter to General Bakar from Commandant D. J. Conway, commander of the Irish contingent, who said that waiting until after the Americans and other Western nations had withdrawn before supplying undrinkable water to a primarily Asian and African force smacked of racism.[68] But the crisis deepened. By November 1994, a paltry request for $7,200 to transport Somali delegates to a conference was refused due to "budgetary constraints."[69]

It really was a race against time for Aidid and Ali Mahdi to make progress before member states' patience—and UNOSOM's money—ran out. And from New York, Boutros-Ghali's line in the sand seemed a good way to cajole the factions into cooperating. What they failed to see was that, for Aidid, delaying progress until patience ran out was precisely his goal. Furthermore, the reduction to fifteen thousand peacekeepers meant that UNOSOM had to abandon certain sectors. To swiftly decrease troop numbers, the smaller contingents were leaving Somalia: Botswana, Ireland, Romania, Nepal, Nigeria, and a battalion of Pakistanis. Bakar could now garrison only Mogadishu, Baidoa, and Kismayo, reducing UNOSOM's territory by half. This caused a concurrent reduction in relief activities, as agencies were unwilling to work without UN protection.[70]

UNOSOM Shrinks, Aidid Rises

UNOSOM's territorial contraction destabilized the areas that had shown the most promise as the SNA, militias from other factions, and bandits rushed to fill the void. It was a free-for-all. Just five days after Boutros-Ghali announced his line in the sand, an Irish logistics convoy with Indian escorts was attacked near Baledogle. The unidentified force (suspected to be the SNA) used a quad-barreled antiaircraft cannon that tore the vehicles apart. Seven Indians were killed and nine were wounded. On 9 September there was an attempt to repeat the Beledweyne seizure as the Zimbabweans prepared to redeploy from Balad to Mogadishu. More than one hundred local militia with technicals attacked the UN compound, but this time the Zimbabweans fought back, killing four and capturing thirty-nine. Their reputation vindicated, the Zimbabweans departed Balad the next day with all their equipment, leaving nothing for the looters who swarmed the bare camp buildings. The same thing happened when the Indians left Oddur, the Botswanans left Bardera, and the Nigerians left Merka. Local militia and bandits immediately descended to claim anything of value.[71]

UNOSOM's contraction was heavily criticized. In a September press conference, SNF chairman General Omar Haji, speaking on behalf of the Group of 12, called on the international community "not to turn the historic rescue operation 'Restore Hope' into operation 'Destroy Hope.'" Calling Aidid "a killer and a looter," Haji rounded on UN officials for fixating on Mogadishu and the Aidid–Ali Mahdi rivalry when "the people in other regions are ready for peace and reconciliation." Haji's comments were dismissed by UNOSOM officials as an "organized show . . . to find a scapegoat for [the SNF's] failure to reconcile their differences with the SNA."[72] His criticisms were well founded, though. UNOSOM had given too much credence to a leader and a faction that represented a bare minority of Somalis. At the same time, Haji ignored that Aidid and the SNA had the power to undermine any peace that was not to their liking and to shape initiatives they favored—as demonstrated by the efficacy of Aidid's dual strategy throughout 1994 and UNOSOM's inability to hold him to account.

By mid-October, UNOSOM, which had once occupied fifty villages, towns, and cities and patrolled countless more, was concentrated in just four locations: Mogadishu, Afgooye, Baidoa, and Kismayo. Everywhere else, banditry returned and factional competition increased. Boutros-Ghali's hope for a new government gave way to fears that UNOSOM's mission would end in dismal failure. He wrote to the Security Council and warned of the possibility that, "following the withdrawal of UNOSOM, Somalia will plunge again into anarchy and chaos. A viable and acceptable peace," he conceded, "can only come from the Somalis themselves. [We] cannot impose peace."[73] Meanwhile, Kofi Annan traveled to Mogadishu to personally meet with Aidid in September, hoping to finally schedule the May Conference and the Hawiye reconciliation conference. Aidid enthusiastically assured him that both would be convened in October. Aidid was only partially truthful, because what resulted was not what Annan or anyone else had been hoping for.[74]

In October 1994, on the anniversary of the Battle of Mogadishu, Ai-

did delivered an impassioned speech commemorating the "victory day
. . . which marked the end of the war by the coalition of foreign troops
on the Somali people . . . under the auspices, the name and flag of the
United Nations to bring Somalia under a new form of colonialism."[75]
Aidid then made his move to become the gatekeeper of the nation's future. He declared that the Hawiye reconciliation conference was no longer necessary, and on 14 October he announced that he was unilaterally
convening the May Conference on the twenty-seventh of the month.
The SNA widely distributed a memorandum to that effect, signed by
eleven factions in addition to Aidid's.[76] The results of his dual strategy
were being unveiled.

The timing was highly significant. UNOSOM analysts had argued
that Aidid's political maneuvers and military campaign suggested the
SNA was trying to split the Group of 12 into pro-Aidid and pro-Mahdi
factions.[77] This would alter the political balance that, up to that point,
had favored the Group of 12. The SNA had previously comprised only
USC-Aidid, Jess's wing of the SPM, the SDM, and the SSNM. However,
by October, this balance had fundamentally shifted, and the context
is critical to understanding why. UNOSOM was in decline, with an
advertised departure date and no willingness to use military force to
achieve national reconciliation. All Gbeho and Annan could do was repeatedly ask Ali Mahdi and Aidid to make progress—the UN had no
leverage. The SNA had shown itself capable of exerting major influence
on regional and national political initiatives and had demonstrated its
military ability by taking Merka and Beledweyne. Whatever the post-
UNOSOM Somalia looked like, it was clear that Aidid and the SNA were
a force to be reckoned with, even if that future meant renewed civil war.
For that reason, by October, seven factions within the Group of 12 had
indeed split into pro-Aidid and pro-Mahdi factions. Moreover, in the
self-declared independent region of Somaliland, the SNM and other
northern factions had decided that secession was no longer desirable.
They voiced their willingness to join the May Conference to propose a
federal system of government for Somalia.[78] The SNM and all but one of
the northern factions threw their weight behind Aidid. Hence, when Aidid announced his unilateral conference, he had the support of eleven
factions, not just the original four that made up the SNA.

Politically and militarily, Aidid had redressed the imbalance to near
parity. And by unilaterally announcing that he would take the lead in
government formation, he was winning the propaganda contest. Aidid's

14 October memorandum benevolently asked Ali Mahdi and the remaining factions that were still opposed to the SNA to join the conference. To add legitimacy, Aidid even requested that Gbeho, on behalf of UNOSOM, issue the invitations to all the relevant faction leaders.[79] In the week that followed, the political landscape was thrown into chaos. The pro-Mahdi wings of the seven divided factions lambasted the pro-Aidid wings for claiming to represent them. Three factions that had been part of the Group of 12 issued press releases stating that it was "illegal for Ali Mahdi to claim that he is the spokesman of our movements without our consent."[80] With his coalition now thoroughly divided, Ali Mahdi consolidated the fragments that remained loyal to him into a new Somali Salvation Alliance under his chairmanship. Gbeho, for his part, appealed to Aidid not to go ahead with the conference and refused to issue invitations to splinter groups that did not, in the UN's view, represent the recognized factions that had signed the Addis Ababa Agreement.[81] Aidid was resolute—his conference would proceed.

The Security Council Visits Mogadishu

It was into this political chaos that a delegation from the UN Security Council arrived in Mogadishu. The suggestion of a council visit had arisen months before, when Ali Mahdi wrote to Boutros-Ghali on the eve of the SNA offensive in Beledweyne and stated it was "high time" the council "take stock of the present situation."[82] But the real momentum came days after Aidid's 14 October memorandum, when the chair of the UN's Arab Group of Member States, Tunisian Ambassador Slaheddine Abdellah, specifically asked the Security Council to go to Somalia. Invoking the highly provocative example of the Rwandan Genocide only months before, Abdellah worried that UNOSOM might suddenly be withdrawn, increasing the chances of renewed civil war.[83] With Abdellah's plea, and given the political chaos in Mogadishu, the president of the Security Council, British Ambassador David Hannay, announced that seven council members would go to Somalia. The future of UN involvement awaited the delegation's return with a direct measure of the situation.[84]

They landed in Mogadishu on 26 October, led by Ambassador Colin Keating of New Zealand. Keating was joined by Ambassadors Wang Xuexian of China, Herve Ladsous of France, Isaac Ayewah of Nigeria,

Kamran Niaz of Pakistan, Yuriy Fedotov of Russia, and Karl Inderfurth of the United States.[85] Only hours before their arrival, Gbeho had convinced a reluctant Aidid to postpone his conference, due to start the next day, until 1 November. The Security Council delegation first met with Gbeho, who warned that Aidid's conference had the real potential to cause a new civil war. Then the ambassadors met with Ali Mahdi.

The two-hour meeting was acrimonious to say the least. Keating delivered a prepared statement to the leader of the Somali Salvation Alliance and the self-proclaimed chairmen of the pro-Mahdi wings of eleven factions.[86] Somalia was at a "crossroads," Keating said, and the UN was about to make decisions that would "profoundly" affect the future of UNOSOM. He emphasized that all the leaders must recognize that "what will now happen to their country will rest squarely on their shoulders."[87] Conveying profound disappointment over the lack of progress, Keating said that UNOSOM's continued deployment could not be justified beyond March 1995. If Somalis wanted assistance with political efforts, the UN would oblige, but the inclusive conference promised by the Nairobi Declaration must be delivered. The UN, he said, was not abandoning Somalia, but UNOSOM was leaving.

Keating's speech was measured and direct and delivered plainly. Ali Mahdi's long-winded response was at first amicable, thanking Keating for the "historic humanitarian intervention and peace mission to rescue our people and assist Somalia to stand again on its feet." Somalia still needed the UN to rebuild and, Ali Mahdi pointed out, there had never been conflict between UNOSOM and the majority of factions that he represented. He pleaded with the delegation not to "abandon Somalia only because of the obstructive policies of one of the faction leaders."[88] He then descended into a litany of criticisms against the UN for assuming that Aidid and the SNA were central to any political solution, for legitimizing Aidid over and above his station, and for ignoring the popular support behind the Group of 12. Ali Mahdi blamed Aidid's rise and the current predicament on the Security Council. UNOSOM, he charged, had abdicated its role of mediator and become Aidid's facilitator when it failed to challenge his postponement of the May Conference. Even when the SNA seized the Zimbabwean contingent in Beledweyne, the UN responded with meaningless condemnations, he said. The Somali Salvation Alliance was willing to attend any conference under UN supervision, but, Ali Mahdi concluded, the Security Council needed to make UNOSOM honor UN resolutions and act as a genuine mediator.

The delegation retired for the night in preparation for an audience with Aidid the next day. Whereas Ali Mahdi had bloviated, blustered, and blamed, Aidid was magnanimity personified; flanked by the leaders of the pro-SNA wings of twelve factions, he was charming and charismatic.[89] Keating delivered the same prepared statement, with an added hint, aimed at Aidid's unilateral conference, that any government not based on broad representation would lack legitimacy and international recognition. Before delivering his own remarks to the delegation, Aidid responded directly to Keating's speech. Promising not to interfere with UNOSOM's withdrawal, he said he would do whatever he could to be inclusive. Aidid was more than happy to include Ali Mahdi and his factions in the plans for government formation. His rival was even free to compete for a role in said government. In an obvious exaggeration, he assured Keating that the assembled leaders in the room represented 95 percent of the population but, in an unassailable counter, said he could not be expected to secure 100 percent support, as no government in the world—not even the Western democracies—could meet that standard.

Aidid then delivered his statement, which had been signed by all the leaders present. Compared to Ali Mahdi's, it was much shorter and softer in tone. There were no criticisms of UNOSOM whatsoever. He opened, ironically, by welcoming the delegation at a time when "the myth that Somalis were hopelessly divided into two opposing camps has been proven wrong." He thanked the UN for all it had done and for the "sustained pressure of the international community to prod us towards making peace instead of war."[90] He then justified the legitimacy of his upcoming conference. In his view, it conformed point by point to the Nairobi Declaration and had attracted more than one thousand delegates from thirteen of the factions that had signed the Addis Ababa Agreement, in addition to intellectuals, legal experts, and women's advocacy groups. All that remained, he said, as if to suggest that the roles of peace enabler and obfuscator had always been thus, was Ali Mahdi and his holdouts.

Summing up the visit, Keating wrote, "Everything that the mission saw left its members with a profound sense of unease and a fear that, whether or not UNOSOM leaves, political reconciliation or the emergence of a government that enjoys widespread acceptance is far from certain. The risk of a return to civil war is real."[91] Nevertheless, he concluded that leaving by March 1995 was the right decision. Neither Ali Mahdi nor Aidid had asked UNOSOM to stay. Before flying back to New

York on 27 October, the delegation met with the last key stakeholders in the intervention: representatives from the humanitarian relief organizations. They did not ask the Security Council to reconsider leaving either. They merely voiced concern about the security environment after UNOSOM left and expressed their commitment to continuing their operations.[92]

The United States held the presidency of the Security Council that month, so the 4 November meeting to authorize UNOSOM's final withdrawal was convened by Madeleine Albright. Gone was the optimism and idealism of twenty months ago when the same council members, Albright included, had lauded Resolution 814's mandate for UNOSOM to rebuild Somalia from the ground up. Instead, the rhetoric was self-congratulatory. Keating offered consolation, thanking Boutros-Ghali and Gbeho for their noble efforts. "Nothing like the Unified Task Force and UNOSOM had ever been tried before," he said, and "mistakes along the way were inevitable. Somalia has been brought back from the precipice. It has been given another chance. The future is in their hands, but we cannot force them to grasp it." On behalf of Britain, Hannay echoed Keating: "It was of course an ambitious mission to begin with. . . . We made a start . . . which helped to give a measure of stability and security to the Somali people that they had not experienced for years."[93]

That the UN bore some blame for its failure was not discussed. The opposite happened. The responsibility was pushed broadly onto the Somalis themselves. Ambassador Al-Khussaiby of Oman said the withdrawal "reflects . . . the failure of the Somali people to benefit from the efforts of the international community." Both Ambassador Gambari of Nigeria and Ambassador Merimee of France specifically stated that the UN had not failed in Somalia. Every council member attempted to improve on the preceding speakers' claims that no one in the room was responsible for what had happened. Even Albright, speaking last as council president, joined in. "The hundreds of thousands of Somali survivors," she said, "will be a living monument to the fallen United Nations peacekeepers in the years ahead . . . the international community offered a helping hand and, in the face of often violent opposition, firmly held that hand open for over two years, ready and willing to help. . . . UNOSOM has done its part." That the violent opposition in 1993 resulted from a disastrous course charted by the American leadership in UNOSOM and supported by the Clinton administration was not considered. Instead, the members unanimously passed Resolution 954, ordering UNOSOM's withdrawal by March 1995. If Aidid and Ali Mahdi wanted assistance in achieving political reconciliation before then, UNOSOM would oblige, but its sole remaining mission was now the safe departure of all UN forces from Somalia.[94]

Aidid ultimately went ahead with his conference on 1 November, promising a government within forty-five days. Gbeho did not attend; nor did he issue invitations to any delegates. Because Ali Mahdi's factions chose not to participate, Gbeho reasoned, the conference was not inclusive, and UNOSOM could not support it. This earned him condemnation from the SNA, which called him hypocritical for criticizing its "lack of determination to push the peace process forward," only to boycott a conference among the majority of factions for its lack of inclusivity.[95] Ali Mahdi wrote to Aidid, hoping to sway him. He pointed out that the UN was leaving because of the constant political fragmentation and that if Aidid pressed ahead with his conference, the resulting civil war would be his responsibility. Ali Mahdi called on Aidid "to rediscover [his] nationalism. Then we can go beyond attachment to personal interest and assist the Somali people whom we lead."[96]

Aidid's response was flowery, and it could afford to be. "Dear Brother Ali . . . as we said ourselves, we knew that the foreigners could not bring a solution to Somali problems and will eventually depart. I have always respected your role as leader . . . it is no secret that it is too difficult for me . . . to establish a government . . . without you and your supporters."[97] Most factions, Aidid said, had accepted his invitation to join the conference, and he asked Ali Mahdi to follow suit. Ali Mahdi could have agreed, but instead the Somali Salvation Alliance announced that it would convene its own conference. And so it was that two separate conferences to form two separate governments in Mogadishu began in November. All attempts to reconcile the two—by Gbeho, by Abdullahi Yusuf of the SSDF, and even by Hersi Morgan, the "Butcher of Hargeisa"—had failed.[98]

It was an intractable stalemate. Ali Mahdi was both too weak and, like his rival, too stubborn. Perceiving himself to be the best candidate to lead Somalia in the post-UN vacuum, Aidid pressed on. With supportive factions and wings of factions on his side, he had the political and military power to do so and no real opponents to stop him. An internal UNOSOM memorandum reported an alleged meeting between the SNA and officials from the US embassy in Mogadishu suggesting that if a government was formed quickly, American recognition might be forthcoming. The memorandum concluded that this endorsement convinced Aidid that the Security Council was not as unified as it wanted the world to believe, boosting his determination to go ahead with his conference.[99] If the reports were true, it was not just Aidid and the SNA who believed he was the best choice to lead the country. By the time UNOSOM left in March 1995, the two conferences were still ongoing. Regardless of Aidid's promise of a government in forty-five days, the stalemate persisted.

Operation United Shield

The UN decision to leave Somalia came in November 1994, but planning for it had started a year before. The two UNOSOM force commanders—Cevik Bir and his successor Aboo Bakar—oversaw different iterations of how to get out of Somalia if the escalating violence necessitated the evacuation of all UN civilian staff, relief organizations, and the various embassies in Mogadishu. UNOSOM would fall back to both Mogadishu and Kismayo; the latter would be evacuated first, before the final departure from the capital. Where the plans differed was that Bir's January 1994 plan, before the Western withdrawal, envisaged the United States providing strategic military airlift and sealift for the exodus. In contrast, Bakar's April 1994 plan, after the Western withdrawal, relied on civilian aircraft and shipping or, if necessary, moving UNOSOM overland into Kenya. Bakar estimated that with open airports and seaports, UNOSOM could evacuate with all its equipment in seventy-five days, using 59 cargo ships and 168 wide-bodied passenger aircraft.[100] The eventual pullout was a hybrid of the two plans. The seizure of Beledweyne and the attempted seizure of Balad highlighted the danger UNOSOM might face while leaving, along with the vulnerability of civilian airliners and ships in the case of violence. As such, in August 1994 Boutros-Ghali started to approach nations with naval and air capabilities and asked them to assist in the evacuation whenever it happened.[101] Given the UN's financial crisis, Annan worked behind the scenes, asking various nations to help on a "pro-bono" basis.[102]

Brigadier General Anthony Zinni had arrived in Somalia as UNITAF's director of operations in December 1992. He left in May 1993 when UNOSOM took over but returned to Mogadishu in October with Robert Oakley to personally negotiate with Aidid following the Battle of Mogadishu. When he left for a second time, Zinni returned to the

Marine Corps Combat Development Command in Quantico as deputy commanding general. On the day he was officially promoted to major general, expecting to take command of the 1st Marine Division, the commandant of the Marine Corps, General Carl E. Mundy, informed Zinni with a curt "don't let it go to your head" that he was being promoted to lieutenant general and would command I Marine Expeditionary Force (I MEF) instead. This was the same post Robert Johnston had held two years earlier, leading the same force that made up the core of UNITAF.[103]

Although the Battle of Mogadishu soured the American public and policymakers on Somalia, many within the Clinton administration felt an obligation to ensure the safe departure of UNOSOM. After all, as Anthony Lake reminded Clinton in a memo, many nations whose contingents remained in Somalia had joined the mission or stayed the course at the urging of the United States. "They are quick to remind us," Lake said, "that US persuaded many of them to go to Somalia. If abandoned in a pinch, allies are unlikely to forgive us. The implications . . . could be grave."[104] A debt was owed, and as such, General John Shalikashvili, chairman of the Joint Chiefs of Staff, told Zinni in August 1994 that I MEF would lead Operation United Shield, pulling UNOSOM out of Somalia.[105]

Zinni wasted no time. The months between August 1994 and March 1995 were spent meticulously planning every aspect of United Shield, the largest amphibious retreat under hostile conditions since the Korean War. In the interim, when Keating's delegation to Somalia made it clear that UNOSOM was leaving, Bakar went to work immediately, not waiting for Resolution 954 to pass a week later. The bulk of Bhagat's Indian brigade was headquartered in Baidoa, with some units also garrisoning Kismayo. The Pakistani and Egyptian brigades, along with the Bangladeshis, Zimbabweans, and Malaysians, held Mogadishu. The Bangladeshis also held Afgooye, just outside Mogadishu, and controlled access to the roads to Kismayo and Baidoa. Bakar's task was to move all UNOSOM forces to Mogadishu and Kismayo and then reduce troop levels to the absolute minimum before Zinni arrived with I MEF to cover the final departure.

Starting on 26 October, Bhagat's Indian brigade decamped from Baidoa for Mogadishu. They handed over all remaining humanitarian supplies and whatever equipment that could not be moved to the Baidoa district council. By 30 November, the last Indian units had left what was once termed the epicenter of the "Triangle of Death." Thanks to UNITAF and UNOSOM, Baidoa had been transformed into a thriving city and was well on its way to recovery. On 6 December the Indian Navy arrived off Kismayo to evacuate its garrison by sea to Mogadishu. The Kismayo district council ensured the evacuation's peaceful completion on 11 December. It was not peaceful everywhere, though. The Bangladeshis in Afgooye were surrounded by a militia force in a repeat of Beledweyne. A Bangladeshi and Pakistani armored relief force sortied from Mogadishu and, with the aging Cobras overhead, broke the encirclement after heavy fighting. Afgooye was evacuated with three UN casualties.[106]

By 11 December, Mogadishu was the sole remaining UNOSOM enclave, and no movement was allowed outside the city into the interior. Bakar and Gbeho then turned to the task of reducing troop strength to the bare minimum. The Indian brigade, having loaded its equipment onto naval vessels, flew out of Mogadishu between 10 and 23 December, reducing UNOSOM by a third. As 1995 dawned, UNOSOM dwindled even further. The Malaysians and Zimbabweans left in the first week of January, and the staff at force headquarters was reduced by half when it relocated to the airport on 15 January. By the start of February, there were only 7,956 troops left in Somalia from three countries—Pakistan, Egypt, and Bangladesh. The US embassy compound, Mogadishu University, and Hunter, Sword, and Victory Bases had all been abandoned, as had all the checkpoints and strongpoints in the city. The last UN fatality was a Pakistani soldier killed by a reversing vehicle during the move to the new security perimeters established around the airport and New Port.[107]

As UNOSOM's footprint in Mogadishu shrank, violence and banditry increased. Abgal and Murusade militia clashed around the K-4 Circle. Looters swarmed into former UN facilities, including the residential compound for civilian staff, a luxury complex complete with swimming pool and leisure facilities that had cost $100 million to build. Gunfire once again lit up the streets, technicals drove with impunity in sight of the airport perimeter, and stray rounds wounded peacekeepers. In several instances, locals who were losing their jobs due to the evacuation barricaded UN offices and demanded payment of their wages, in some cases resorting to violence. By mid-February, Gbeho had no choice but to inform all remaining relief workers that the UN could no longer guarantee their safety, and he recommended they evacuate to Nairobi by

14 February.[108] Behind the security perimeter, more and more troops flew out of Mogadishu. By 20 February, 1,750 Pakistanis and the entire Egyptian contingent were gone. Fewer than five thousand peacekeepers remained when, on 22 February, a fleet of twenty-three warships appeared on the horizon. Zinni and Combined Task Force United Shield had arrived.

When Boutros-Ghali asked for assistance in UNOSOM's withdrawal and the Clinton administration offered to take the lead, several other nations volunteered to join Operation United Shield. Vessels from six nations formed the impressive fleet that arrived off Mogadishu. The nine ships from the US Navy included Amphibious Group Three, carrying Zinni's landing force; the 13th MEU from I MEF; and reinforcements from III MEF in Okinawa. The Italian Navy sent the aircraft carrier *Giuseppe Garibaldi*, along with a frigate, two amphibious assault ships, and a marine battalion for the landing force. They were joined by destroyers, frigates, and support ships from France, Pakistan, Malaysia, and Britain.[109]

Given the American public's outrage over the Battle of Mogadishu, one of Zinni's key concerns was to avoid friendly casualties. As the fleet steamed toward Somalia, reporters on board were fascinated as they watched marines on the flight deck of Zinni's command ship, USS *Belleau Wood*, training with nonlethal munitions designed to counter women and children being used as human shields and to prevent protests from turning deadly. Marines practiced with rubber bullets, pepper spray, beanbag rounds, and a "sticky foam gun" for gluing unruly opponents to the ground. Emblematic of Americans' exhaustion with Somalia, one marine colonel sardonically joked, "If we just fired beans instead of bean bags, we could call it a feeding program."[110]

The tactical situation in late February 1995 was almost identical to that when Newbold's marines landed in December 1992. UNOSOM was surrounded at the airport and preparing to link up with a marine amphibious landing. But this time, the marines were not the vanguard of thirty-nine thousand troops; they were there to safeguard the way out. The last flights out of Mogadishu would reduce UNOSOM to just enough troops to hold the perimeter. Then Zinni's marines, Italian and American, would land on Green Beach—just as Newbold's had years before—to set up a defensive perimeter on the sand berms just south of the airport that also included New Port. It would be akin to a giant collapsing bag. UN troops at New Port would board contracted shipping under marine protection, while those at the airport moved to Green Beach before heading to New Port to depart. Once all UN forces had left, Zinni's landing force would evacuate amphibiously from Green Beach.

With Zinni's fleet offshore, another twenty-five hundred Pakistanis and the remaining force headquarters staff flew out of Mogadishu. All that was left of UNOSOM was a rear guard of twenty-five hundred. During the cruise to Somalia, Kofi Annan had flown out to *Belleau Wood* to visit Zinni. For the withdrawal to work, all forces in Mogadishu needed to be unified under one command. Given the anti-UN sentiment in the wake of the Battle of Mogadishu, there was no question of Zinni and his marines being under UN command. Annan explained that in the final stages, Bakar would relinquish command of UNOSOM to Zinni, the first time UN forces were under non-UN command since Douglas MacArthur in the Korean War. As a symbolic gesture, Annan presented Zinni with a blue UN beret.[111] On 27 February Zinni came ashore to attend the transfer-of-command ceremony with Bakar, taking charge of the UNOSOM rear guard of Pakistani and Bangladeshi troops. With that, Bakar and Gbeho, UNOSOM's last force commander and special representative, boarded the last flight out of Mogadishu.[112] The stage was now set for the final departure.

To ensure that Operation United Shield ran as smoothly as possible, Zinni called a meeting at the airport for all the faction leaders and militia commanders in Mogadishu. The scene was surreal as they gathered on a rise within the comparative oasis of the airport perimeter; there was a clear view of both the fleet offshore and the surrounding city and the sound of frequent gunfire. Zinni made it clear to the leaders that UNOSOM was leaving; his troops were not looking for a fight, but any hostility would earn a decisive response. Promises not to interfere were proffered. One leader was brought to tears, telling Zinni, "Look at this [referencing the unstable city] look at how many years we tried, from when you first came, and it didn't work out . . . it was our hope that we would have a Somalia that would work."[113]

Zinni then went to meet with Aidid one last time. He would have preferred to go alone but was accompanied by Vice Admiral John Scott Redd and Ambassador Daniel H. Simpson, Gosende's successor as US special envoy to Somalia. Zinni had hoped to calmly deliver the same message given to the other leaders, but Simpson took an aggressive stance with the famously temperamental SNA leader. The meeting ended abruptly before tensions escalated to outbursts. As Zinni walked to his vehicle, Aidid pulled him back and said, "Don't worry about me, none of my people will interfere."[114] However, he warned Zinni, there were non-SNA militias near the airport and Green Beach that "will give you trouble."[115]

On the night and early morning of 27–28 February, the 13th MEU and the Italian San Marcos battalion landed on Green Beach and established a strong defensive beachhead that included New Port. The Bangladeshi battalion holding the port was relieved by Zinni's marines and departed at 08:30 that morning aboard civilian cargo ships contracted by the UN. All that remained now were the four understrength battalions of Abbas's Pakistani brigade. The Pakistanis had been the first peacekeepers to arrive in 1992 and suffered the highest casualties of any UNOSOM contingent, with nearly forty dead and a hundred wounded. They would now be the last to leave.[116] Their withdrawal to Green Beach was the most dangerous aspect of United Shield, as Zinni's marines would be unable to differentiate friend from foe if any hostile group attacked the Pakistanis as they retreated. To minimize the risk, Abbas moved in the early-morning darkness of 1 March. Over the course of three hours, columns of Pakistani APCs, M60 tanks, and other vehicles moved inside Zinni's perimeter on the beach, finishing ten minutes before the sun rose.[117]

From his position on the beach, Zinni watched as the local populace awoke to the sudden realization that the airport was unoccupied. "The looters came in hot and heavy, and also the militias," he remembered. Firefights broke out between militia and looters and between the militias themselves in a contest to dominate the real estate and capture anything UNOSOM had left behind. Within the beachhead Abbas's brigade moved to New Port to board more UN-contracted cargo ships. But then there was a delay. As it was coming into the dock, the MV *Vergina* struck the pier. The captain was found to be drunk. Worse still, there was no food or water on board for the Pakistanis. Precious time was lost as US Navy personnel surveyed the ship's hull and transferred supplies from Zinni's fleet. All the while, fighting around the airport escalated. Some bandits fired on the marines, provoking an overwhelming response. It was not until the next evening, 2 March, that the *Vergina* and the Pakistanis departed. Now just the 13th MEU and the San Marcos battalion were left in Somalia.[118]

At 17:00 the landing force withdrew to Green Beach. The Italians evacuated first. Zinni's marines waited for the cover of darkness. But as the sun set over Mogadishu, Aidid's warning came true. Rogue militia attacked in waves, shattering the darkness with the staccato of automatic rifle fire and the streaks of RPGs. Each wave was beaten back by the marines, Cobra attack helicopters, and AC-130 gunships loitering in the skies above. During a lull between attacks, Zinni and his two remaining marine companies made their escape, piling into their amphibious assault vehicles (AAVs), which then trundled en masse into the surf and headed for the *Belleau Wood*. The marine line had been engaged nearly thirty times during Operation United Shield, with not a single friendly casualty. Zinni boarded the last AAV on Green Beach, leaving at 00:59 on 3 March 1995.[119]

Soon after entering the Indian Ocean, in a grim metaphor for the intervention, Zinni's AAV started to belch smoke and take on water. The engine had died. Another AAV arrived to tow it, but it too broke down. Both AAVs were helplessly drifting back toward Green Beach, now lit up by the headlights of roving technicals and overrun by militia. Luckily, a landing craft dispatched by Zinni's deputy arrived to rescue the marines and tow the two stricken AAVs.

On 20 October 1944 one of the most iconic propaganda images of the Second World War captured US Army General Douglas MacArthur wading ashore in Leyte Gulf. Having fled the Philippines in 1942, MacArthur famously announced, "I have returned," signifying a key watershed in the campaign for victory in the Pacific. Half a century later, Zinni's landing craft was the last to enter the long well deck of the massive *Belleau Wood*, where it suddenly stopped halfway and lowered its ramp into waist-deep water. Confused, Zinni asked the chief of the boat why he was stopping short. "Sir," the chief replied, "I want you to go in there like MacArthur."[120]

UNOSOM had come to Somalia on 10 July 1992 as Imtiaz Shaheen's military observers arrived to monitor the cease-fire in Mogadishu. Now, 966 days later, the aft ramp on the *Belleau Wood* was raised, and the fleet left Somalia behind. During that time, UNITAF, UNOSOM II, and US forces suffered 649 casualties, including 169 dead. For the Somalis, civilian and militia casualties are impossible to calculate but were probably in the thousands. Having played a critical role in UNITAF, negotiating in the aftermath of the Battle of Mogadishu, and successfully completing the final evacuation of UNOSOM, Zinni jumped down and walked the final steps through the waist-deep water while dozens of journalists in the gantry above looked on. Unlike MacArthur's victorious return to the Philippines, though, Zinni's final steps signaled the end of the most ambitious experiment in nation building in history up to that point. And while getting out of Somalia was seen as a victory for the United States and the world, the reality was that the mission had ended in tragic failure.

Epilogue
Dancing on the Corpse of a Helicopter

When the definitive history of peacekeeping is written, [one] of the most important dates in that chronicle will be . . . October 3, 1993.
—Dennis C. Jett[1]

Our goals were well intentioned; we were very idealistic. The days of the UN had arrived; multilateralism was in, and the world was going to be saved.
—Ambassador Robert B. Oakley,
US presidential envoy to Somalia[2]

As Zinni's fleet disappeared over the horizon, Gbeho and his personal staff, all that remained of UNOSOM, waited in an office in Nairobi for a phone call from Mogadishu that never came. Neither Ali Mahdi nor Aidid would meet with any UN envoys. Finally, when maintaining a full-time special representative became too expensive for the UN, Gbeho and his staff flew home on 19 April 1995.[3] Not many noticed as the last vestiges of UNOSOM disappeared. Somalia had ceased making headlines in a world now beset by UN debacles in Bosnia and the tragedy and horror of the Rwandan Genocide. The world would soon be shocked again by the massacre at Srebrenica.

As the world moved on, Aidid's rise continued. On 15 June 1995, during his ongoing conference, delegates from fifteen factions (or pro-Aidid wings of them) elected him president of the Republic of Somalia, with five vice presidents each representing one of the five major clans. Aidid's presidency did not bring stability to Somalia. That September, the SNA seized control of Baidoa, prompting the emergence of a Rahanweyn-based insurgency against him. His rivalry with Ali Mahdi continued in Mogadishu, and Osman Atto, his chief lieutenant, rebelled. In the end, unlike in Tom Clancy's novel, it was not CIA operatives that got him. On 25 July 1996 Aidid was hit by a stray round purportedly fired by one of Atto's men. He died on 1 August.[4] Emblematic of the importance of clan politics in Somalia, Habr-Gidr elders offered the presidency to Aidid's son Hussein Mohamed Farrah. Thirty-four-year-old Farrah was a US citizen and had served both as a US marine with UNITAF and in the SNA campaign around Baidoa.[5] It was hoped that his dual citizenship would heal some of the wounds between America and Somalia. As president, he sent a letter to Zinni, who by 1997 had become commanding general at CENTCOM: "I want you to know," Farrah wrote, "that I am still continuing our work that we started here together all these years ago."[6] Farrah's presidency was unrecognized by many, least of all Ali Mahdi, who still clung to his title of interim president, and Farrah resigned after just one year in office. Ali Mahdi eventually renounced his own claim to the presidency in 2000. Outliving his rival by almost a quarter of a century, he contracted COVID-19 and died in Nairobi on 10 March 2021.

Tragically, the civil war that started in 1988 never ended. Weak governments rose and fell as the country was rocked by clan competition. After 2001, Somalia became just another theater in the Global War on Terror as a series of weak governments fought against Islamic extremists. Consequently, there have been nine Battles of Mogadishu over the past thirty years, each one numbered to differentiate them from the first on 3 October 1993. In 2007 the African Union sent twenty thousand troops into Somalia to support the fledgling Transitional Federal Government in its fight against Islamic insurgents. Eighteen years later, they are still there, having suffered well over a thousand fatalities in the struggle to stabilize the country.

The Specter of Somalia

In the aftermath of Somalia, most countries strived to ensure something similar could never happen again. Before the Summer War, the Clinton administration had been drafting Presidential Decision Direction 25. Reflecting the early 1993 optimism about multilateralism in the post–Cold War world, it was supposed to set out the US military's enthusiastic participation in UN peacekeeping operations going forward. However, after the Battle of Mogadishu, it was revised and became an exhaustive list of conditions to be met before American troops would serve with the UN. There were two nonnegotiable criteria: the operation had to be under American command, and the mission had to relate to vital US interests.[7] With such impossible constraints, UNOSOM was the first and last UN mission in which American troops served in large numbers.

For the United States, Somalia created an acutely risk-averse paranoia about sending troops overseas, and it lasted for the rest of the
1990s. It became politically indefensible for Americans to die abroad
where no vital interests were at stake. What was missed, though—forgotten even—was that UN success in Somalia would ease the post–Cold
War burden on the United States, which was itself a vital interest. Nevertheless, when the 10th Mountain Division deployed to Haiti in 1994,
soldiers hunkered down in protected complexes, interacting little with
the local populace. In Bosnia and Kosovo, American soldiers were committed only after peace negotiations had ended the fighting on the
ground. Then they were ridiculed by fellow NATO and coalition personnel and called "ninja turtles" because they wore body armor everywhere,
even on their own bases.[8] But the most egregious consequence of this
aversion to casualties was the deliberate decision not to act in Rwanda.
When the genocide began in April 1994, Canadian Lieutenant General Romeo Dallaire's small UN force tried to save as many as it could.
Dallaire begged for reinforcements, but several representatives on the
Security Council blocked this request, chief among them the United
States. America had proactively intervened in Somalia to avoid having
to extricate UNOSOM if the operation foundered, but there was no
willingness to do the same in Rwanda. As Clinton's Secretary of Defense
William J. Perry recalled, Somalia "foreclosed" acting in Rwanda. "Congress would have exploded," he remembered, "had anybody proposed
it to them, they would have been summarily dismissed as smoking dope
or something. . . . The specter of Somalia was very powerful."[9]

This specter haunted the UN as much as it did the United States. On
25 January 1995, just weeks before Operation United Shield, Boutros-
Ghali amended his landmark policy set out in *An Agenda for Peace.*
Peacekeeping had become more complex and more expensive, but the
biggest problem for the future of UN operations, he wrote in the revised
version, was the somber reality that the UN cannot impose itself on nations that do not want help: "Legally and politically [states'] request for,
or at least acquiescence in, United Nations action is a sine qua non."[10]
Consent, the onetime watchword of UN peacekeeping that had been
discarded due to the unprecedented crisis in Somalia, was now firmly
back as a principle of future operations.[11] In addition, in the short term,
the failure in Somalia convinced many countries to withhold enforcement powers from the UN mission in Bosnia. This meant, as Thijs Zaalberg wrote, that "UN peacekeepers who . . . came under fire from, or

were taken hostage by, Serb forces . . . were expected to turn the other cheek for fear" of crossing the so-called Mogadishu Line.[12] This fear persisted until the atrocities at Srebrenica could no longer be ignored.

In many ways, Boutros-Ghali himself became the final casualty of the UN experiment in Somalia. In keeping with tradition, he ran for a second term as secretary-general in 1996, only to be thwarted by Madeleine Albright and the Clinton administration. Albright made a weak claim that Boutros-Ghali's personality was the reason UN-US relations had soured and that Congress would not pay its substantial UN arrears if he continued as secretary-general.[13] Left unsaid was that he had been damaged by the failure in Somalia and the frustrations in Bosnia. He was now a political liability for a Clinton administration, which was hoping for a second term in the White House.[14] After Boutros-Ghali initially bowed out of the race, the African nations in the UN demanded that he run for a second term, as he was the first secretary-general from the African continent. In solidarity, other potential African candidates refused to put themselves forward, prompting Albright to candidly announce to the Security Council that the United States "would like to see an African Secretary-General who wants to reform the United Nations and lead it into the 21st century . . . if there are no names presented, at some stage the vacuum will be filled by non-African candidates. That's not a threat. It's just a statement of fact." After agreeing at first to contest his election, fourteen of the fifteen members of the Security Council voted for Boutros-Ghali; Albright then vetoed him at the behest of the Clinton administration. Despite outrage within the UN and public accusations of "diplomatic 'mugging,'" the United States held the Security Council hostage until Boutros-Ghali accepted the inevitable and bowed out in favor of another African candidate, Kofi Annan.

In many countries, the memory of Somalia remains irreversibly colored by scandal, pain, outrage, and shame. For some, the legacy of the intervention was the accusation of postcolonial racism. Italian Generals Bruno Loi and Carmine Fiore resigned in 1997 after photos emerged of Italian paratroopers raping Somali women. Belgian soldiers were tried when images showed them urinating on a dead Somali and holding a boy over an open fire to deter him from thievery. In Canada, the brutal killing of Shidane Arone resulted in a political scandal that saw the entire Canadian Airborne Regiment disbanded in disgrace.[15] In the United States, Somalia became synonymous with images of the mutilated bodies of American soldiers being dragged through the streets of Mogadishu and of "grinning Somalis dancing on the corpse of a helicopter."[16] The indelible marks left on the American psyche engendered lasting and thoroughly undeserved bitterness toward the UN and altered the perception of the mission in Somalia from a manhunt against a recalcitrant rogue to a futile attempt to help a seemingly ungrateful people too stubborn and backward to recognize the opportunity the world was trying to give them.

What Went Wrong in Somalia?

There is an oft-cited Somali proverb: "Me and my nation against the world. Me and my clan against my nation. Me and my family against the clan. Me and my brother against the family. Me against my brother."[17] It inspired the title of the official history published by the US Army's Combat Studies Institute, *"My Clan against the World": US and Coalition Forces in Somalia*, and was directly quoted in the US Forces Somalia after-action report to explain what went wrong.[18] Although the proverb describes the hierarchy of Somali society, it has been used instead to portray Somalis as habitually uniting against foreign interlopers: the harder the outside world tried to help, the more the Somali clans resisted. But this is wrong. The whole country did not unite against the intervention. Far from it. Most Somalis supported UNITAF and UNOSOM throughout their time in Somalia, and only an absolute minority took up arms against the intervention.

Nor, as Jane Boulden argued, was failure attributable to the everchanging mandates.[19] UNOSOM II's goals were just as clear as UNITAF's, though wholly more ambitious in scope. The UN mandate changed only twice over the course of two years: in June 1993 to hunt down Aidid, and then in November to call off the manhunt. It remained a Chapter VII peace enforcement mission for the duration of the intervention. Although some contingents were reluctant to enforce these mandates, they were not confused about the mission. Was a lack of consent the problem? No. Unlike traditional UN consent-based peacekeeping missions, both UNITAF and UNOSOM II were peace enforcement operations that did not require consent. Despite the lack of consent, there was no real resistance to UNITAF's presence. And UNOSOM *did* have the consent of the faction leaders, including Aidid, who entrusted the UN with implementing the Addis Ababa Agreement. As for suggestions that the disparity between UNITAF and UNOSOM II encouraged Aidid to attack, this book has demonstrated there is little evidence to support this argument.

This brings us to Michael Rose, the commander of UN forces in Bosnia, and his widely cited argument of "crossing the Mogadishu Line"—the conceptual Rubicon between peacekeeping and warfighting where UN impartiality is irrevocably lost. Although Rose sanctified the concept of impartiality, his views on the use of force in UN operations are littered with irreconcilable contradictions. He lauded a "major battle" between UN forces under his command and the Serbs because it showed "the UN was prepared to use extreme levels of force . . . within the constraints of peacekeeping." Rose then observed that it "is impossible to draw a clear line between the permissible use of force in a peacekeeping mission and an act of war." Nevertheless, he drew one anyway before sharing his belief that "peacekeepers will not be able to afford to be pacifists in the hostile situations they are likely to face."[20]

Many who cite Rose's "Mogadishu Line" ignore the context in which he coined the phrase. In Bosnia, Rose was confronted by a large and well-equipped conventional Serb military. Crossing this Mogadishu Line would have been fatal for Rose; the UN would have been soundly defeated if outright hostilities with the Serbs had broken out. The Mogadishu Line thus became a conceptual vehicle for Rose to manage the complexities of his own frustrating mission. And a potent way to counter those encouraging him to take more decisive action against the Serbs was to critique UNOSOM's actions in Somalia. In stark contrast to Bosnia, UNOSOM faced an insurgency by a much smaller irregular force. Despite the Summer War, UNOSOM retained its impartial status among most of the population and most of the factions. It did not simply become another party in the civil war. Howe ensured that the other factions did not take advantage of the hostilities, warning them not to attack Aidid while he was down. We know that UNOSOM's impartiality endured because after the Battle of Mogadishu, the UN mission continued to progress and still enjoyed broad support in Somalia.

In a chart of his own making, Rose described that crossing the Mogadishu Line in any UN mission meant the end of any ongoing peace process and the widening of conflict, such that aid to the population ceases and the safety of the UN force is at risk.[21] The peace process did not end in Somalia during the Summer War, nor did UN aid to the population cease. Critically, at no point was the safety of UNOSOM itself at risk. In

Bosnia, all these conditions would have been met if Rose had opted to use force against the Serbs, but in Somalia, the Mogadishu Line was not crossed at all.

The desire to identify a conceptual reason for the failure of the UN venture in Somalia is understandable. Concepts can be altered, refined, and perfected. But it is too often forgotten that at the ground level, the day-to-day execution of such concepts comes down to individual decision makers. Somalia was an unprecedented effort with no institutional memory to provide guidance for success. Instead, UNITAF and UNOSOM learned as they went. Boutros-Ghali was right: mistakes were going to be made. Some of those mistakes were honest, based on the best of intentions. Others were ill informed and damaging. And ultimately, what went wrong was all too human. In Somalia, both the Bush and Clinton administrations pushed to demonstrate the emergence of a newly invigorated and robust post–Cold War UN—a UN that could step up, step in, and shoulder some of the burdens previously carried by the United States. American and UN credibility was on the line in the Horn of Africa. Colin Powell cautioned against making UNOSOM an "American show" but warned, do not let it fail.[22] It became an American show nonetheless, and not letting it fail became a zero-sum game. Despite the UN's stated purpose to assist the Somalis, every step of reconstruction was meticulously controlled when Howe and Glaspie decided to prioritize national interests and policies over the UN mission by excluding Aidid, a recognized and influential political leader. Aidid had supported UNITAF's arrival, was pivotal in formalizing the Addis Ababa Agreement, and tried to work with a UNOSOM whose flawed policy, poor leadership, and lack of foresight made it completely unwilling to compromise. Contrary to Rose's views, Somalia was not an example of why the UN should not take action; it was a warning against making impulsive decisions in a complex environment without a strategy.

The intervention was working until American decision makers, fully aware of the political tensions they stoked in pursuit of an irrational policy, decided to target Radio Mogadishu under the guise of an inspection, seemingly without any appreciation of how it could all go horribly wrong. This transformed a precedent-setting UN operation into a war in the pursuit of that most nebulous of currencies: credibility. The demonization of the faction leaders meant that the international community could not be seen as bending to intimidation by, or considering a negotiated peace with, a bloodthirsty "warlord." Escalation thus became the only credible option. War was forced on Aidid because the precedent-setting win in Somalia had to be achieved, no matter the cost; the Abdi house strike clearly demonstrated that resolve. And when that resolve waned after four months of bloody stalemate, Hoar authorized Task Force Ranger's raid on 3 October 1993 knowing full well that the US policy toward Aidid had changed to negotiation and the war was over. Personalities mattered far more in Mogadishu than any concept or doctrine, and the easy solution, from a Western perspective, was to blame a recalcitrant, power-hungry African warlord and a seemingly ungrateful people from a far-away place. The far more uncomfortable truth is that American decision makers, charged with achieving success so that the UN could establish its credibility on the world stage, put that goal ahead of achieving its mission. The decisions they made were not just poor; they were terrible. The tragedy of Somalia is not that it all went wrong but that it was all so blatantly avoidable.

Could UNOSOM have succeeded if not for the abysmal decisions made in May, June, and October 1993? It is hard to say. Success was certainly made impossible. Astonishingly, despite the Summer War, the intervention recovered temporarily after the Battle of Mogadishu. And that is where the true impact of those decisions was felt. When UNOSOM limped forward despite the financial crisis, the political will to continue would have made all the difference. But the Summer War had burned up all the patience, tolerance, resources, and optimism the international community was willing to devote to Somalia. Aidid recognized that Somalia would soon have to fend for itself, so he maneuvered to fill the impending vacuum. We do not have to like Aidid, but we do have to understand him. Once it was clear in 1994 that UNOSOM would not or could not use force to achieve the mission or curtail Aidid's rise, many factions threw their weight behind the SNA to survive in post-UNOSOM Somalia. Survival is not a uniquely Somali trait.

Why Somalia Mattered

Despite the tragic failure, Somalia stands today not only as an ambitious experiment in nation building but also as a trailblazing attempt by the UN to change the conceptions of peacekeeping, peace enforcement, and multilateralism in action. Hundreds of thousands of lives were undoubtedly saved by UNITAF's and UNOSOM's efforts to end the civil war and the famine. Somalia *mattered.* So too did the experiences of the many militaries deployed there, though many, including the United States and UN, chose to repress that experience rather than learn from it. Somalia was not one of the many case studies of past counterinsurgencies included in the 282-page US Army manual *FM 3–24: Counterinsurgency*, published in 2006; nor did it appear in the 2014 or 2021 versions. Yet in 1993 the US military was fighting an insurgency in Mogadishu during a nation-building mission. There were lessons to be learned from Somalia, as just ten years later, American troops were dealing with insurgencies in simultaneous nation-building operations in Iraq and Afghanistan. Unlike those populations, many Somalis in the 1990s at least remembered living under a democracy, corrupt as it was.

Somalia demonstrated the inherent complexity of nation building, even with the support of the populace. It showed that nations can only be built or rebuilt around *existing* centers of power that are valued first and foremost by the population, not defined solely by the intervener. Somalis crafted the Addis Ababa Agreement, but then UNOSOM dictated what that agreement meant in practice. Even more so, nation building in the aftermath of a civil war requires an acknowledgment, however uncomfortable, that no groups or leaders emerge with clean hands. In Somalia, labeling the faction leaders "warlords" only galvanized public and political opinion against the same individuals who were chosen to represent their various clans and subclans and who were needed by the UN for political reconciliation.

Somalia exemplified the difficulties of inserting an occupation force into a society divided by clan and historic rivalries. Any patchwork map of ethnicities in Afghanistan would look just as jumbled as any clan map of Somalia. There were no quick and easy solutions when any clan or faction was alienated from the reconstruction process. Emotive opinions on Aidid aside, he played the chief role in defeating the Barre regime, and he had support among the population and the SNA. It took the four-month Summer War to learn there could be no political solution in Somalia that excluded Aidid and his clan. What was true for Somalia was true for Iraq. But in the effort to avoid a repeat of Somalia, that lesson was ignored. It was three years into the Iraq War before US forces started enlisting Sunni militias to be part of the solution rather than fighting them as part of the problem. The epiphany that the Sunnis had to be included in the new Iraq came just as soldiers started to receive copies of a new manual on counterinsurgency. Though replete with lessons from

Vietnam, Malaya, and even 1840s Ireland, it included no insights whatsoever into what had gone wrong in Somalia, America's most recent brush with insurgency. Perhaps the epiphany could have come sooner.

The venture into Somalia marked the end of an era. The Cold War was over, and the Gulf War had suggested that quality could beat quantity, that military power based not on size but on advanced technology could overcome any potential adversary. Somalia dashed this optimism, showing that the civil wars and uncertainty of the post–Cold War world were not as susceptible to military power as Saddam's Iraq. It was in Somalia that many countries cut their teeth on the controversial concepts and buzzwords that would define the next three decades of conflict: nation building and counterinsurgency. In that world, success yields returns slowly, but mistakes can be instantly fatal and unrecoverable. The enemy is not so easily identified, and the conditions for victory are not measured on a map or a calendar. Looking back on the 1990s, Somalia thus stands today not only as an ambitious experiment in nation building that stumbled into an insurgency, but also as a herald of the shape of things to come.

Appendix A
Major Somali Clans and Subclans and Their Political Factions

Darood Clan

- Marehan—Somali National Front (SNF)
- Majerteen—Somali Salvation Democratic Front (SSDF)
- Dolbohante—United Somali Party (USP)
- Ogadeni—Somali Patriotic Movement (SPM-Ogadeni)
- Harti—Somali Patriotic Movement (SPM-Harti)
- Warsangeli—United Somali Party (USP)
- Lil Kassir—Somali National Democratic Union (SNDU)

Hawiye Clan

- Abgal—United Somali Congress–Rome (USC–Ali Mahdi)
- Habr-Gidr—United Somali Congress–Ethiopia (USC–Aidid)
- Hawadle—Variously aligned with both USC wings
- Murusade—Pro-USC–Ali Mahdi

Dir Clan

- Ise—United Somali Front (USF)
- Gadabursi—Somali Democratic Association (SDA)
- Bimal—Southern Somali National Movement (SSNM)

Issaq Clan

- Somali National Movement (SNM)

Rahanweyn Clan

- Somali Democratic Movement (SDM)

Appendix B
Coalition Forces Deployment List

Following is a list of coalition units deployed to Somalia during the several phases of the intervention. Certain countries referred to their deployments by unique operational names; these are indicated where relevant.

Operation Eastern Exit: US Noncombatant Evacuation Operation of Mogadishu, January 1991

Amphibious Squadron Six
    USS *Guam* (LPH-9), Iwo Jima–class Amphibious Assault Ship
    USS *Trenton* (LPD-14), Austin-class Amphibious Transport Dock
Marine Air Ground Task Force from 4th Marine Expeditionary Brigade
    1st Battalion/2nd Marine Regiment
        Headquarters and Headquarters Company and C Company
    Marine Medium Helicopter Squadron (HMM-263)
    Marine Medium Helicopter Squadron (HMM-365)
    Marine Wing Support Squadron (MWSS-274)
    Detachment, Marine Light Attack Helicopter Squadron (HMLA-269)
    Detachment, Marine Heavy Helicopter Squadron (HMH-461)
    Detachment, Brigade Service Support Group 4

Operation Provide Relief: US and Coalition Relief Airlift into Somalia, August–December 1992

Canada (Operation Relief)
    429 Transport Squadron, Royal Canadian Air Force (RCAF)
        September–October 1992
    453 Transport Squadron, RCAF October–December 1992

Germany
   Luftwaffe detachment of three C-160 Transall transport aircraft
United Kingdom
   Royal Air Force detachment of two C-130 Hercules transport
      aircraft
United States
   2nd Airlift Squadron/23rd Wing, US Air Force (USAF)
   62nd Airlift Squadron/314th Airlift Wing, USAF
   2nd Battalion/5th Special Forces Group, US Army (Airborne QRF)
      Detachments from A and C Companies

United Nations Operations in Somalia (UNOSOM): Chapter VI Peacekeeping and Cease-fire Observer Mission, April 1992–May 1993

Military Cease-fire Observers
   Fifty observers from Austria, Bangladesh, Czechoslovakia, Egypt,
      Fiji, Finland, Indonesia, Jordan, Morocco, Pakistan, and
      Zimbabwe
UN Security Force
   7th Battalion/Frontier Force Regiment (Pakistan)
   Movement Control Platoon, Royal Australian Air Force (Operation
      Iguana)

Unified Task Force (UNITAF): US-Led Multinational Military Intervention in Somalia, 7 December 1992–4 May 1993

United States (Operation Restore Hope)
Headquarters, I Marine Expeditionary Force/UNITAF Headquarters
   US Army Forces Somalia (ARFOR) Occupied HRS Kismayo, HRS
      Baledogle, and HRS Merka
         10th Mountain Division—"Task Force Mountain"
            Division/ARFOR Headquarters and Headquarters Company
            41st Engineer Battalion
            33rd Finance Support Unit
            10th Personnel Services Company
            No. 1 Platoon, 10th Military Police Company

60th Military Police Detachment (CID)
280th Military Police Detachment (CID)
129th Postal Company
711th Postal Company
28th Public Affairs Team
10th Field Artillery Target Acquisition Detachment
Detachment, B Company, 110th Military Intelligence
    Battalion

2nd "Commando" Brigade/10th Mountain Division
    Brigade Headquarters and Headquarters Company
    2nd Battalion/87th Infantry Regiment
    3rd Battalion/14th Infantry Regiment (TF Kismayo)
    A and E Companies, 1st Battalion/87th Infantry Regiment
    A Company, 41st Engineer Battalion (TF Kismayo)
    B Company, 41st Engineer Battalion
    Detachments of A and B Batteries, 3rd Battalion/62nd Air
        Defense Artillery Regiment
    Civil Affairs Detachments, C Company, 96th Civil Affairs
        Battalion
    27th Public Affairs Team
    No. 2 Platoon, 10th Military Police Company (TF Kismayo)
    No. 3 Platoon, 10th Military Police Company
    Detachment, B Company, 110th Military Intelligence
        Battalion

10th "Falcon" Aviation Brigade/10th Mountain Division
    Brigade Headquarters and Headquarters Company
    3rd Squadron/17th Cavalry Regiment
    Task Force 5-158 (From 12th Aviation Brigade, V Corps, US
        Army Europe)
        Headquarters and Headquarters Company
        B Company, 3rd Battalion/25th Aviation Regiment
        C Company, 7th Battalion/158th Aviation Regiment
        A Company, 2nd Battalion/227th Aviation Regiment
        D Company, 502nd Aviation Battalion
        E Intermediate Maintenance Company, 25th Aviation
            Regiment
        I Intermediate Maintenance Company, 7th
            Battalion/159th Aviation Regiment

10th Mountain Divisional Artillery
  Headquarters and Headquarters Battery (TF Kismayo)
  Fire Support Element, 2nd Battalion/7th Field Artillery
    Regiment (TF Kismayo)
10th Mountain Division Support Command
  Headquarters and Headquarters Company
  210th Forward Support Battalion
  710th Main Support Battalion
  59th Chemical Company
  200th Supply Detachment
Signals Task Force
  10th Signal Battalion
  C Company, 327th Signal Battalion (TF Kismayo)
  209th Signal Company, 40th Signal Battalion
  Headquarters Company and 516th Signal Company, 86th
    Signal Battalion
  Platoon, B Company, 63rd Signal Battalion
  Platoon, B Company, 67th Signal Battalion
  Detachment, 50th Signal Battalion
  Detachment, 82nd Signal Battalion
36th Engineer Group
  Headquarters and Headquarters Company
  43rd Engineering Battalion (Combat Heavy)
  63rd Engineering Company (Combat Support Equipment)
  642nd Engineering Company (Combat Support Equipment)
  74th Engineer Detachment (Diving)
  95th Engineer Detachment (Firefighting)
  520th Engineer Detachment (Firefighting)
  597th Engineer Detachment (Firefighting)
4th Psychological Operations Group
  Detachment, 8th Psychological Operations Battalion
  Detachment, 9th Psychological Operations Battalion (TF
    Kismayo)
*US Marine Corps Forces Somalia (MARFOR) Occupied HRS Mogadishu,
HRS Baidoa, and HRS Bardera*
  1st Marine Division
    Division/MARFOR Headquarters Battalion
    Headquarters and Headquarters Company, 7th Marine
      Regiment

1st Battalion/7th Marine Regiment (C Company with TF Mogadishu)

3rd Battalion/9th Marine Regiment (K Company with TF Mogadishu)

3rd Battalion/11th Marine Regiment (TF Mogadishu) Headquarters and Headquarters Battery and I Battery

3rd Light Armored Infantry Battalion (TF Mogadishu)

3rd Amphibious Assault Battalion (TF Mogadishu)

Reconnaissance Company, 5th Marine Regiment (TF Mogadishu)

1st Combat Engineer Battalion

Military Police Company, 1st Marine Division (TF Mogadishu)

C Company, 1st Tank Battalion

Civil Affairs Detachments, C Company, 96th Civil Affairs Battalion, US Army

3rd Marine Aircraft Wing
   Marine Aircraft Group 16
      Headquarters and Headquarters Company
      Marine Light Attack Helicopter Squadron (HMLA-369)
      Marine Heavy Helicopter Squadron (HMH-363)
      Marine Aerial Transport Refueler Squadron (VMGR-352)
      Detachment, Marine Heavy Helicopter Squadron (HMH-466)
      Marine Wing Support Squadron (MWSS-372)
   Marine Air Control Group 38
      Marine Air Traffic Control Squadron (MACS-38)
      3rd Low Altitude Air Defense Battalion

1st Surveillance, Reconnaissance, and Intelligence Group
   9th Communications Battalion
   1st Radio Battalion
   1st Air Naval Gunfire Liaison Company
   National Intelligence Support Team

1st Force Service Support Group
   Headquarters and Service Battalion
   7th Engineer Support Battalion
   7th Motor Transport Battalion
   1st Landing Support Battalion
   1st Supply Battalion

1st Maintenance Battalion
1st Medical Battalion
1st Dental Battalion
30th Naval Construction Regiment
    Headquarters and Headquarters Company
    Naval Mobile Construction Battalion 1 (Horizontal Construction)
    Naval Mobile Construction Battalion 40 (Vertical Construction)

US Army Joint Task Force Support Command (JTFSC)
13th Corps Support Command (JTFSC Headquarters)
    Headquarters and Headquarters Company
    49th Transportation Movement Control Center
    4th Support Center Material Management
    Detachment, 54th Quartermaster Company (Graves Registration)
    546th Personnel Services Company
    720th Military Police Battalion
        Headquarters and Headquarters Detachment
        511th Military Police Company
        571st Military Police Company (TF Mogadishu)
        978th Military Police Company
        984th Military Police Company (TF Kismayo)
    Air Traffic Control Detachment, B Company, 1st Battalion/58th Aviation Regiment
    542nd EOD Control Team
62nd Medical Group
    Headquarters and Headquarters Company
    86th Evacuation Hospital
    159th Medical Company (Air Ambulance)
    423rd Medical Company (Clearing) (one platoon with TF Kismayo)
    514th Medical Company (Ambulance)
    61st Medical Detachment (Preventive Medicine) (TF Kismayo)
    73rd Medical Detachment (Veterinary)
    224th Medical Detachment (Preventive Medicine)
    227th Medical Detachment (Epidemiology)
    229th Medical Detachment (Air Ambulance) (TF Kismayo)

248th Medical Detachment (Veterinary)
257th Medical Detachment (Dental)
485th Medical Detachment (Preventive Medicine
　　Entomology)
528th Medical Detachment (Combat Stress Team)
555th Medical Detachment (Surgical)
Detachment, 32nd Medical Logistics Battalion
Detachment, 513th Military Intelligence Brigade
593rd Area Support Group
　Headquarters and Headquarters Company
　240th Terminal Operations Battalion
　　Headquarters and Headquarters Detachment
　　110th Quartermaster Company
　　267th Terminal Operations Company
　　360th Transportation Company
　　418th Transportation Company
　　364th Supply Company
　　22nd Quartermaster Laboratory
　　26th Quartermaster Detachment (ROWPU Barge Team)
　　30th Quartermaster Detachment (ROWPU Barge Team)
　　82nd Quartermaster Detachment (Water Purification
　　　Team)
　548th Combat Support Battalion
　　Headquarters and Headquarters Detachment
　　57th Transportation Company
　　62nd Supply Company
　　157th Field Service Company
　　226th Supply Company
　　602nd Maintenance Company
　　13th Ordnance Detachment (EOD)
　　608th Ammunition Management Platoon
7th Transportation Group
　Headquarters and Headquarters Company
　6th Transportation Battalion
　　Headquarters and Headquarters Detachment
　　24th Transportation Company
　　100th Transportation Company
　　870th Cargo Transfer Company
　　22nd Transportation Detachment

406th Transportation Detachment
24th Terminal Service Battalion
    Headquarters and Headquarters Detachment
    119th Terminal Service Company
    710th Transportation Company (TF Kismayo)
    169th Transportation Detachment
    491st Transportation Detachment

US Air Forces Somalia
22nd Air Refueling Wing
    6th Air Refueling Squadron
    9th Air Refueling Squadron
60th Airlift Wing
    22nd Airlift Squadron
    75th Airlift Squadron
351st Air Refueling Squadron/100th Air Refueling Wing
437th Airlift Wing
    14th Airlift Squadron
    17th Airlift Squadron
    20th Airlift Squadron
    76th Airlift Squadron
Wing Operations Center/463rd Airlift Wing
314th Air Refueling Squadron/940th Air Refueling Wing, USAFR
52nd Combat Communications Squadron/5th Combat Communications Group
823rd Civil Engineering Squadron (REDHORSE)
317th Airlift Control Squadron
701st Air Mobility Support Squadron
362nd Airlift Support Group (Cargo Handling)

US Army Special Operations Forces Somalia
5th Special Forces Group
    C Company, 2nd Battalion (TF Kismayo), *First Rotation*
    B Company, 1st Battalion, *Second Rotation*
3rd Special Forces Group
    Detachment, A Company, 3rd Battalion
10th Special Forces Group
    Detachments from 2nd and 3rd Battalions

US Naval Forces Somalia
Ranger Carrier Group—covered initial UNITAF deployment

USS *Ranger* (CV-61), Forrestal-class Aircraft Carrier
  Carrier Air Wing Two
    Fighter Squadron (VF-1)
    Fighter Squadron (VF-2)
    Attack Squadron (VA-145)
    Attack Squadron (VA-155)
    Air Anti-Submarine Squadron (VS-38)
    Tactical Electronic Warfare Squadron (VAQ-131)
    Helicopter Anti-Submarine Squadron (HS-14)
    Carrier Airborne Early Warning Squadron (VAW-116)
    Detachment 2, Helicopter Anti-Submarine Squadron
      Light (HSL-47)
    Detachment 10, Helicopter Combat Support
      Squadron (HC-11)
USS *Valley Forge* (CG-50), Ticonderoga-class Guided Missile
  Cruiser
USS *Kinkaid* (DD-965), Spruance-class Destroyer
USS *Wabash* (AOR-5), Wichita-class Oiler
Naval Beach Group One
  Assault Craft Unit One
  Beachmaster Unit One
  Amphibious Construction Battalion One
  Cargo Handling Group One
Military Sealift Command
  Maritime Prepositioning Ships
    MV *1st Lt Alex Bonneyman* (T-AK-3003), Corporal Louis J.
      Hauge Jr.–class Cargo Ship
    MV *1st Lt Jack Lummus* (T-AK-3011), 2nd Lt. John P.
      Bobo–class Cargo Ship
    MV *American Cormorant* (T-AK-2062)
    MV *PFC James Anderson Jr* (T-AK-3002), Hauge Jr.–class
    MV *Private Franklin J Phillips* (T-AK 3004), Hauge Jr.–class
    MV *Sheldmond*
    MV *Strong Virginian* (T-AKR-9205)
    SS *American Osprey* (T-AOT-5076)
    SS *Green Harbor* (T-AK-2064), Type C9–class Cargo Ship
    SS *Green Valley* (T-AK-2049)
  Fast Sea Lift Ships
    SS *Algol* (T-AKR-287), Algol-class Vehicle Cargo Ship

SS *Altair* (T-AKR-291), Algol-class
SS *Bellatrix* (T-AKR-288), Algol-class
SS *Capella* (T-AKR-293), Algol-class
SS *Denebola* (T-AKR-289), Algol-class
SS *Pollux* (T-AKR-290), Algol-class
SS *Gopher State* (T-ACS-4), Gopher State–class Crane Ship
SS *American Eagle* (T-AK-2044), Vehicle Cargo Ship

UNITAF Coalition Forces

Australia (Operation Solace) Occupied HRS Baidoa
    1st Battalion/Royal Australian Regiment
    B Squadron, 3/4th Cavalry Regiment
    107 Field Battery, 4th Field Artillery Regiment
    17 Field Troop, 18 Combat Engineer Squadron, 3rd Combat
        Engineering Regiment
    Detachment, 103rd Signals Squadron, 3rd Combat Signal
        Regiment
    1st Battalion Logistics Support Group
    HMAS *Canberra* (FFG-02), Adelaide-class Guided Missile
        Frigate
    HMAS *Jervis Bay* (GT-203), Roll-On/Roll-Off Vehicle Ferry
    HMAS *Tobruk* (L-50), Round Table–class Landing Ship
        Heavy
Belgium (Operation Equator Kiss) Occupied HRS Kismayo
    1st Parachute Battalion
    3rd Airborne Reconnaissance Squadron
    Zinnia (A961), Logistics Supply Ship
Botswana
    330th Light Infantry Company (TF Mogadishu)
    Mechanized Platoon and Mortar Platoon, 77th Mechanized
        Battalion (TF Mogadishu)
Canada (Operation Deliverance) Occupied HRS Beledweyne
    Canadian Airborne Regiment
        Headquarters and Headquarters Commando
        Commando, Royal 22nd Regiment
        Commando, Princess Patricia's Canadian Light Infantry
        Commando, Royal Canadian Regiment
        Service Commando
        A Squadron, Royal Canadian Dragoons Regiment
        23rd Field Squadron, 2nd Combat Engineer Regiment

Detachment, 1st Canadian Division Headquarters Signals
Regiment

93rd Rotary Wing Aviation Flight, 427 Tactical
Helicopter Squadron

HMCS *Preserver* (AOR-510), Protecteur-class
Replenishment Ship (TF Kismayo)

423 Helicopter Anti-Submarine Squadron

Egypt

245th Mechanized Infantry Battalion (TF Mogadishu)

France (Operation Oryx) Occupied HRS Oddur

Headquarters, 9th Marine Infantry Division

13th Foreign Legion Demi-Brigade

3rd Engineer Company, 6th Foreign Legion Engineer
Regiment

3rd Company Amphibious Company, 2nd Foreign
Legion Parachute Regiment

Special Operations Company

5th Combined Arms Overseas Regiment

1st Infantry Company

4th Armored Squadron

3rd Marine Infantry Regiment

3rd and 4th Infantry Companies

Detachment, 5th Combat Helicopter Regiment

Detachment, Logistics Support Battalion

Georges Leygues (D640), F70 Anti-Submarine Frigate

Dupleix (D641), F70 Anti-Submarine Frigate

La Grandiere (L9034), Champlain-class Landing Ship

Foudre (L9011), Foudre-class Landing Platform Dock

Var (A608), Durance-class Replenishment Oiler

Greece (served with the French in HRS Oddur)

Field Hospital

India

INS *Kuthar* (P46), Kukri-class Corvette

INS *Sukanya* (P50), Sukanya-class Patrol Ship

INS *Cheetah* (L18), Tank Landing Ship

INS *Deepak* (A50), Fleet Tanker

Italy (Operation Ibis) Occupied HRS Gialalassi

Parachute Brigade Folgore

Brigade Headquarters

183rd Parachute Regiment Nembo
186th Parachute Regiment Folgore
187th Parachute Regiment Folgore
9th Parachute Assault Battalion Col Moschin
1st Carabinieri Parachute Battalion Tuscania
185th Parachute Artillery Regiment Folgore
Paratroopers Logistics Battalion Folgore
Paratroopers Engineer Company Folgore
Company, 32nd Tank Regiment
Centauro Field Hospital
San Marco Marine Infantry Battalion
Antares Composite Helicopter Regiment/46th Aviation
    Brigade
24th Naval Group
    Vittorio Veneto (C550), Helicopter Cruiser
    Grecale (F571), Maestrale-class Frigate
    San Giorgio (L9892), San Giorgio–class Landing Ship
    Vesuvio (A5329), Stromboli-class Oiler
Kuwait
    Composite Motorized Company (TF Mogadishu)
Morocco, Occupied HRS Baledogle
    3rd Motorized Infantry Regiment
New Zealand
    Detachment, 42 Squadron, Royal New Zealand Air Force
Nigeria
    245 Reconnaissance Battalion (TF Mogadishu)
Pakistan
    6th Independent Infantry Brigade
        1st Battalion/Sind Regiment
        6th Battalion/Punjab Regiment
        7th Battalion/Frontier Force Regiment
        10th Battalion/Baloch Regiment
Saudi Arabia
    5th Airborne Battalion, Royal Saudi Land Forces (TF
        Mogadishu)
Sweden
    1st Field Hospital (Served with JTFSC)
Tunisia
    Light Infantry Battalion (served with JTFSC)

Turkey
>8th Mechanized Infantry Battalion (TF Mogadishu)
>TCG *Fatih* (F242), Yavuz-class Frigate
>TCG *Ertugrul* (L402), Tank Landing Ship
>TCG *Derya* (A576), Supply Ship

United Arab Emirates
>750th Mechanized Infantry Battalion (TF Mogadishu)

Zimbabwe
>S Company, 42nd Infantry Battalion (TF Mogadishu)

United Nations Operations in Somalia (UNOSOM) II: Chapter VII Peace Enforcement Mission, May 1993–March 1995

UNOSOM II Force Headquarters
>Headquarters staff from Australia, Bangladesh, Belgium, Botswana, Canada, Egypt, France, Germany, Ireland, Italy, South Korea, Malaysia, Morocco, Nepal, New Zealand, Nigeria, Pakistan, Saudi Arabia, Tunisia, Turkey, UAE, United States, and Zimbabwe
>Force Headquarters Company (Norway)
>Force Headquarters Security Company (Turkey)
>Movement Control Platoon (Australia)
>Military Police Platoon (Bangladesh)
>Military Police Platoon (India)
>Military Police Platoon (Italy)
>Military Police Platoon (Morocco)
>Military Police Platoon (Nigeria)
>Military Police Platoon (Pakistan)
>Logistics Platoon (New Zealand)
>Logistics Platoon (Zimbabwe)
>Air Traffic Control Detachment (Australia)

United Nations Logistics Support Command (UNLSC)
First Rotation, April–August 1993
>43rd Corps Support Group (United States)
>>Headquarters and Headquarters Company (UNLSC Headquarters)
>>33rd Finance Support Unit
>>280th Military Police Detachment

711th Postal Company
546th Personnel Services Company
260th Corps Support Battalion
    53rd Quartermaster Company
    10th Transportation Company
    Detachment, 493rd Supply and Service Company
    Detachment, 54th Quartermaster Company (Graves
        Registration)
    541st Transportation Company
    23rd Quartermaster Detachment
24th Terminal Service Battalion Task Force
    870th Cargo Transfer Company
    155th Transportation Company
68th Corps Support Battalion
    Detachment, 493rd Supply and Service Company
    183rd Maintenance Company
    12th Transportation Company
    155th Transportation Company
    358th Transport Detachment
    24th Quartermaster Detachment
    60th EOD Detachment
    63rd Ordnance Company
    295th Quartermaster Company
    568th Engineer Company (Combat Support Equipment)
Signals Task Force, 11th Signal Brigade
42nd Medical Task Force
    42nd Field Hospital
    Company, 261st Area Support Medical Battalion
    45th Medical Company (Air Ambulance)
    105th Medical Detachment (Sanitation)
    248th Medical Detachment (Veterinary)
    528th Medical Detachment (Combat Stress Control)
    Detachment, 147th Medical Logistics Battalion
Second Rotation, August 1993–January 1994
507th Corps Support Group (United States)
    Headquarters and Headquarters Company (UNLSC
        Headquarters)
    561st Corps Support Battalion
    Headquarters and Headquarters Company

        40th Transportation Company
        102nd Quartermaster Company
        362nd Engineer Company (Combat Support Equipment)
        594th Transportation Company
        196th Quartermaster Detachment (Water Purification)
        Detachment, 79th Quartermaster Company (Graves
           Registration)
    13th Corps Support Battalion
        Headquarters Detachment
        27th Quartermaster Company
        508th Ordnance Company (Ammunition Supply)
        533rd Transportation Company
        598th Maintenance Company
        57th EOD Detachment
        Detachment, 406th Quartermaster Company
    24th Terminal Service Battalion Task Force
        67th Terminal Services Transportation Company
        551st Cargo Transfer Company
    Signals Task Force, 11th Signal Brigade
46th Medical Task Force
    46th Combat Support Hospital
    Company, 261st Area Support Medical Battalion
    82nd Medical Company (Air Ambulance)
    47th Medical Company (Forward Support)
    926th Medical Detachment (Preventive Medicine)
    248th Medical Detachment (Veterinary)
    528th Medical Detachment (Combat Stress Control)
    Detachment, 32nd Medical Logistics Battalion
Logistics Task Force (Germany)
    Headquarters Company
    Two Airborne Infantry Companies
    Transport Company
    Supply and Service Company
    Field Engineer Company
    Field Hospital
    Signals Company
    Military Police Company
No. 1 Transport Company (Ireland), *First Rotation*
Engineer Battalion (South Korea)

Field Hospital (Romania)
Field Hospital (Sweden)
UNOSOM II National Force Contingents
Bangladesh
    5th Battalion/East Bengal Regiment, *First Rotation*
    9th Battalion/East Bengal Regiment, *Second Rotation*
Belgium
    Brigade Headquarters
    1st Parachute Battalion, *First Rotation*, carried over from
        UNITAF
    3rd Parachute Battalion, *Second Rotation*
Botswana
    330th Light Infantry Company, carried over from UNITAF
Egypt
    245th Mechanized Infantry Battalion, carried over from
        UNITAF
    Infantry Brigade of three battalions from 1994 to 1995
France
    Headquarters, 9th Marine Infantry Division
        13th Foreign Legion Demi-Brigade
            3rd Engineer Company, 6th Foreign Legion Engineer
                Regiment
            3rd Company Amphibious Company, 2nd Foreign Legion
                Parachute Regiment
        Special Operations Company
        Detachment, 5th Combat Helicopter Regiment
        Detachment, Logistics Support Battalion
Greece
    Field Hospital (attached to the French and then Indian
        brigade)
India
    66th Mountain Brigade/20th Mountain Division
        Brigade Headquarters
        1st Battalion/Bihar Regiment
        2nd Battalion/Jammu and Kashmir Light Infantry Regiment
        3rd Battalion/Mechanized Infantry Regiment
        5th Battalion/Mahar Regiment
        1st Armored Squadron, 7th Cavalry Regiment
        8722nd Light Battery, The Regiment of Artillery

176th Field Engineers Company
66th Brigade Group Signal Company
5055th Army Service Corps Company
55th Infantry Brigade Group Ordnance Company
203rd Field Workshop, Electrical and Mechanical Engineers
320th Field Ambulance, Army Medical Corps
No. 6 Reconnaissance and Air Observation Flight, Army Aviation
Air Force Missile Detachment
Detachment, 111th Helicopter Unit, Indian Air Force
INS *Ganga* (F22), Godavari-class Guided Missile Frigate
INS *Godavari* (F20), Godavari-class Guided Missile Frigate
INS *Shakti* (A57), Deepak-class Fleet Tanker
Ireland
No. 2 Transport Company, *Second Rotation*
Italy
Parachute Brigade Folgore, *First Rotation*, carried over from UNITAF
Brigade Headquarters
183rd Parachute Regiment Nembo
186th Parachute Regiment Folgore
187th Parachute Regiment Folgore
9th Parachute Assault Battalion Col Moschin
1st Carabinieri Parachute Battalion Tuscania
185th Parachute Artillery Regiment Folgore
Logistics Battalion Folgore
Paratroopers Engineer Company Folgore
Company, 32nd Tank Regiment
Centauro Field Hospital
Antares Composite Helicopter Regiment/46th Aviation Brigade
Mechanized Brigade Legnano, *Second Rotation*
Brigade Headquarters
2nd Bersaglieri Regiment
3rd Bersaglieri Regiment
28th Bersaglieri Battalion Oslavia
Infantry Company, 1st Regiment Granatieri di Sartegna
Infantry Company, 2nd Regiment Granatieri di Sartegna
Armored Squadron, 5th Cavalry Regiment Lancieri di Novara

Armored Squadron, 19th Cavalry Regiment Cavalleggeri
Guide
Logistics Battalion Legnano
Engineer Company Legnano
Centauro Field Hospital
Antares Composite Helicopter Regiment/46th Aviation Brigade
Kuwait
Infantry Company
Malaysia
19th Battalion/Royal Malay Regiment (Mechanized)
Morocco
3rd Motorized Infantry Regiment, carried over from UNITAF
Nepal
Infantry Battalion
Nigeria
245 Reconnaissance Battalion, carried over from UNITAF
Unidentified Reconnaissance Battalion, *Second Rotation*
243 Reconnaissance Battalion, *Third Rotation*
Pakistan
6th Independent Infantry Brigade, *First Rotation,* carried over
from UNITAF
1st Battalion/Sind Regiment
6th Battalion/Punjab Regiment
7th Battalion/Frontier Force Regiment
10th Battalion/Baloch Regiment
59th Field Engineers Company
637th Supply and Transport Company
135th Infantry Workshop Company
41st Military Police Company
122nd Field Ambulance
115th Ordnance Company
6th Independent Infantry Brigade, *Second Rotation*
4th Battalion/Sind Regiment
4th Battalion/Punjab Regiment
5th Battalion/Frontier Force Regiment
8th Battalion/Frontier Force Regiment
15th Battalion/Frontier Force Regiment
19th Battalion/The Lancer's Regiment
3rd Combat Aviation Squadron

Saudi Arabia
    Infantry Battalion
Tunisia
    Infantry Company
United Arab Emirates
    Infantry Battalion (Reduced to a company in January 1994)
Zimbabwe
    Light Infantry Battalion

Operation Continue Hope: US Quick Reaction Force for UNOSOM II, May 1993–January 1994

First Rotation, April–August 1993
    1st "Warrior" Brigade/10th Mountain Division
        Brigade Headquarters and Headquarters Company
        1st Battalion/22nd Infantry Regiment
        Task Force "Safari"
            Headquarters and Headquarters Company, 3rd
                Battalion/25th Aviation Regiment
            C Company, 2nd Battalion/25th Aviation Regiment
            C Company, 5th Battalion/101st Aviation Regiment
            K Aviation Intermediate Maintenance Company, 7th
                Battalion/159th Aviation Regiment
            Air Traffic Control Detachment, B Company, 1st
                Battalion/158th Aviation Regiment
            10th Forward Support Battalion
            Platoon, 300th Military Police Company
            No. 2 Platoon, C Company, 41st Engineer Battalion
            Detachment, B Company/110th Military Intelligence
                Battalion
            B Company, 1st Battalion/5th Special Forces Group
Second Rotation, August 1993–January 1994
    10th "Falcon" Aviation Brigade/10th Mountain Division
        Brigade Headquarters and Headquarters Company
        2nd Battalion/14th Infantry Regiment
        Platoon, C Company, 1st Battalion/87th Infantry Regiment
        Task Force "Raven"

Headquarters and Headquarters Company, 2nd
Battalion/25th Aviation Regiment
A and B Companies, 2nd Battalion/25th Aviation Regiment
Team Courage, 9th Battalion/101st Aviation Regiment
Platoon, D Intermediate Maintenance Company, 25th
Aviation Regiment
H Intermediate Maintenance Company, 159th Aviation
Regiment
Air Traffic Control Detachment, B Company, 1st
Battalion/158th Aviation Regiment
46th Forward Support Battalion
977th Military Police Company
No. 1 Platoon, C Company, 41st Engineer Battalion
Detachment, 201st Military Intelligence Battalion
C Company, 3rd Battalion/5th Special Forces Group

Operation Gothic Serpent: US Special Operations Deployment, August–October 1993

Task Force "Ranger"
US Joint Special Operations Command Headquarters Element
B Company, 3rd Battalion/75th Ranger Regiment
C Squadron, 1st Special Forces Operational Detachment Delta
D Company, 1st Battalion/160th Special Operations Aviation
Regiment
Detachment, 24th Special Tactics Squadron, USAF
Detachment, SEAL Team Six, US Navy

Joint Task Force Somalia: US Reinforcement Deployment to Somalia, October 1993–March 1994

Army Forces
Joint Task Force Somalia Headquarters
10th "Falcon" Aviation Brigade/10th Mountain Division
Brigade Headquarters and Headquarters Company
Task Force "Rogue"
B and C Companies, 1st Battalion/64th Armor Regiment

A and D Companies, 3rd Battalion/15th Infantry Regiment

C Battery, 1st Battalion/41st Field Artillery

C Company, 3rd Engineer Battalion

Platoon, B Company, 24th Signal Battalion

Platoon, 24th Military Police Company

Detachment, 224th Forward Support Battalion

Task Force "Raven"

Headquarters and Headquarters Company, 2nd
Battalion/25th Aviation Regiment

A and B Companies, 2nd Battalion/25th Aviation Regiment

Team Courage, 9th Battalion/101st Aviation Regiment

Platoon, D Intermediate Maintenance Company, 25th
Aviation Regiment

H Intermediate Maintenance Company, 159th Aviation
Regiment

Air Traffic Control Detachment, B Company, 1st
Battalion/158th Aviation Regiment

Task Force 4-4 (replaced Task Force Raven January 1994)

Headquarters and Headquarters Company, 4th
Battalion/4th Aviation Regiment

C and D Troops, 1st Squadron/10th Cavalry Regiment

B Company, 9th Battalion/101st Aviation Regiment

F Intermediate Maintenance Company, 4th Aviation Regiment

Air Traffic Control Detachment, B Company, 1st
Battalion/158th Aviation Regiment

Task Force 2-14

A, B, and C Companies, 2nd Battalion/14th Infantry
Regiment

C Company, 3rd Battalion/15th Infantry Regiment

Platoon, C Company, 1st Battalion/87th Infantry Regiment

No. 1 Platoon, C Company, 41st Engineer Battalion

Task Force 2-22 (replaced Task Force 2-14 January 1994)

B and C Companies, 2nd Battalion/22nd Infantry Regiment

B Company, 1st Battalion/87th Infantry Regiment

A Company, 41st Engineer Battalion

No. 1 Platoon, 10th Military Police Company

46th Forward Support Battalion

43rd Engineer Battalion (Combat Heavy)

C Company, 3rd Battalion/5th Special Forces Group

Naval Forces

    Abraham Lincoln Carrier Group—covered JTF Somalia deployment, October 1993

        USS *Abraham Lincoln* (CVN-72), Nimitz-class Aircraft Carrier

            Carrier Air Wing Eleven

                Fighter Squadron (VF-213)

                Strike Fighter Squadron (VFA-22)

                Strike Fighter Squadron (VFA-94)

                Marine Fighter Attack Squadron (VMFA-314)

                Attack Squadron (VA-95)

                Air Anti-Submarine Squadron (VS-29)

                Tactical Electronic Warfare Squadron (VAQ-135)

                Helicopter Anti-Submarine Squadron (HS-6)

                Carrier Airborne Early Warning Squadron (VAW-117)

        USS *Fox* (CG-33), Belknap-class Guided Missile Cruiser

        USS *Princeton* (CG-59), Ticonderoga-class Guided Missile Cruiser

        USS *Ingraham* (FFG-61), Perry-class Guided Missile Frigate

        USS *Pasadena* (SSN-752), Los Angeles–class Attack Submarine

        USS *Willamette* (AO-180), Cimarron-class Oiler

        USS *Mount Hood* (AE-29), Kilauea-class Ammunition Ship

        USS *White Plains* (AFS-4), Mars-class Combat Stores Ship

    America Carrier Group—relieved *Lincoln* Carrier Group in late October 1993

        USS *America* (CV-66), Kitty Hawk–class Aircraft Carrier

            Carrier Air Wing One

                Fighter Squadron (VF-102)

                Strike Fighter Squadron (VFA-82)

                Strike Fighter Squadron (VFA-86)

                Attack Squadron (VA-85)

                Air Anti-Submarine Squadron (VS-32)

                Tactical Electronic Warfare Squadron (VAQ-137)

                Helicopter Anti-Submarine Squadron (HS-11)

                Carrier Airborne Early Warning Squadron (VAW-123)

                Detachment 3, Fleet Logistics Support Squadron (VRC-40)

                Detachment A, Marine Medium Helicopter Squadron (HMM-162)

        USS *Simpson* (FFG-56), Perry-class Guided Missile Frigate

Marine Forces Somalia
  New Orleans Amphibious Ready Group (embarking 13th MEU) —
      covered JTF Somalia deployment, October 1993
      USS *New Orleans* (LPH-11), Iwo Jima–class Amphibious Assault
          Ship
      USS *Denver* (LPD-9), Austin-class Amphibious Transport Dock
      USS *Comstock* (LSD-45), Whidbey Island–class Dock Landing
          Ship
      USS *Cayuga* (LST-1186), Newport-class Tank Landing Ship
  13th Marine Expeditionary Unit on board *New Orleans* ARG
          Headquarters, 13th MEU
          Battalion Landing Team, 1st Battalion/9th Marine Regiment
          Marine Medium Helicopter Squadron (HMM-268)
          13th MEU Service Support Group
  Guadalcanal Amphibious Ready Group (embarking 22nd MEU) —
      covered JTF Somalia deployment, October–November 1993
      USS *Guadalcanal* (LPH-7), Iwo Jima–class Amphibious Assault
          Ship
      USS *Shreveport* (LPD-12), Austin-class Amphibious Transport
          Dock
      USS *Ashland* (LSD-48), Whidbey Island–class Dock Landing
          Ship
  22nd Marine Expeditionary Unit on board *Guadalcanal* ARG
      Headquarters, 22nd MEU
      Battalion Landing Team, 1st Battalion/8th Marine Regiment
      Marine Medium Helicopter Squadron (HMM 162)
      22nd MEU Service Support Group

**Operation United Shield: US-Led Multinational Withdrawal of
UNOSOM II from Somalia, February–March 1995**

United States
  Essex Amphibious Ready Group (embarking 13th MEU)
      USS *Essex* (LHD-2), Wasp-class Landing Helicopter Dock
      USS *Belleau Wood* (LHA-3), Tarawa-class Amphibious Assault
          Ship
      USS *Fort Fisher* (LSD-40), Anchorage-class Dock Landing Ship
      USS *Ogden* (LPD-5), Austin-class Amphibious Transport Dock

13th Marine Expeditionary Unit on board *Essex* ARG
    Headquarters, 13th MEU
    Battalion Landing Team, 3rd Battalion/1st Marine Regiment
    Marine Medium Helicopter Squadron (HMM-161)
    13th MEU Service Support Group
    USS *Lake Erie* (CG-70), Ticonderoga-class Guided Missile Cruiser
    USNS *Walter S Diehl* (T-AO-193), Henry J. Kaiser–class Oiler
    USNS *John Ericsson* (T-AO-194), Henry J. Kaiser–class Oiler
    USNS *Kiska* (T-AE-35), Kilauea-class Ammunition Ship
    USNS *Spica* (T-AFS-9), Sirius-class Combat Stores Ship
    16th Special Operations Squadron, USAF
France
    Commandant Bory (F726), Commandant Riviere–class Frigate
    D'Estienne d'Orves (F781), D'Estienne d'Orves–class Corvette
    Champlain (L9030), Champlain-class Landing Ship
Italy
    Giuseppe Garibaldi (551), Aircraft Carrier
    Libeccio (F572), Maestrale-class Frigate
    San Marco (L9893), San Giorgio–class Landing Ship
    San Giorgio (L9892), San Giorgio–class Landing Ship
    Stromboli (A5327), Stromboli-class Oiler
    San Marco Marine Infantry Battalion
Malaysia
    KD *Sri Indera Sakti* (1503), Sri Indera Sakti–class Support Ship
    KD *Mahawangsa* (1504), Sri Indera Sakti–class Support Ship
Pakistan
    PNS *Tughril* (D167), Gearing-class Destroyer
    PNS *Shamsheer*, Leander-class Frigate
    PNS *Nasr* (A47), Type 905 Oiler
United Kingdom
    HMS *Exeter* (D89), Type 42 Destroyer
UN Contracted Ships
    MV *Vergina*

Other US Units Associated with the Intervention

Initial lodgment of UNOSOM's Security Force, September 1992:
    Tarawa Amphibious Ready Group (embarking 11th MEU)

USS *Tarawa* (LHA-1), Tarawa-class Amphibious Assault Ship
USS *Fort Fisher* (LSD-40), Anchorage-class Dock Landing Ship
USS *Ogden* (LPD-5), Austin-class Amphibious Transport Dock
USS *Schenectady* (LST-1185), Newport-class Tank Landing Ship
11th Marine Expeditionary Unit on board *Tarawa* ARG
  Headquarters, 11th MEU
  Battalion Landing Team, 1st Battalion/4th Marine Regiment
  Marine Medium Helicopter Squadron (HMM-161)
  11th MEU Service Support Group
Initial lodgment of UNITAF, December 1992:
  Tripoli Amphibious Ready Group (embarking 15th MEU)
    USS *Tripoli* (LPH-10), Iwo Jima–class Amphibious Assault Ship
    USS *Juneau* (LPD-10), Austin-class Amphibious Transport Dock
    USS *Rushmore* (LSD-47), Whidbey Island–class Landing Ship
    USS *Niagara Falls* (AFS-3), Mars-class Supply Ship
  15th Marine Expeditionary Unit on board *Tripoli* ARG
    Headquarters, 15th MEU
    Battalion Landing Team, 2nd Battalion/9th Marine Regiment
    Marine Medium Helicopter Squadron (HMM-164)
    Battery D, 2nd Battalion/12th Marine Regiment
    C Company, 1st Reconnaissance Battalion
    15th MEU Service Support Group
Covering UNITAF's withdrawal, May 1993:
  Wasp Amphibious Ready Group (embarking 24th MEU)
    USS *Wasp* (LHD-1), Wasp-class Amphibious Assault Ship
    USS *Nashville* (LPD-13), Austin-class Amphibious Transport Dock
    USS *El Paso* (LKA-117), Charleston-class Cargo Ship
    USS *Barnstable County* (LST-1197), Newport-class Tank Landing Ship
  24th Marine Expeditionary Unit on board *Wasp* ARG
    Headquarters, 24th MEU
    Battalion Landing Team, 1st Battalion/2nd Marine Regiment
    Marine Medium Helicopter Squadron (HMM-263)
    24th MEU Service Support Group
  Kitty Hawk Carrier Group
    USS *Kitty Hawk* (CV-63), Kitty Hawk–class Aircraft Carrier
      Carrier Air Wing Fifteen
        Fighter Squadron (VF-111)

Fighter Squadron (VF-51)
Fighter/Attack Squadron (VFA-27)
Fighter/Attack Squadron (VFA-97)
Attack Squadron (VA-52)
Air Anti-Submarine Squadron (VS-37)
Tactical Electronic Warfare Squadron (VAQ-134)
Helicopter Anti-Submarine Squadron (HS-4)
Carrier Airborne Early Warning Squadron (VAW-114)
USS *Leahy* (CG-16), Leahy-class Cruiser
USS *Worden* (CG-18), Leahy-class Cruiser
USS *Horne* (CG-30), Belknap-class Cruiser
USS *William H Standley* (CG-32), Belknap-class Cruiser
USS *Cowpens* (CG-63), Ticonderoga-class Guided Missile
Cruiser
USS *Jarrett* (FFG-33), Oliver Hazard Perry–class Guided
Missile Frigate
USS *Reid* (FFG-30), Perry-class Guided Missile Frigate
USS *Rodney M Davis* (FFG-60), Perry-class Guided Missile
Frigate
USS *Samuel B Roberts* (FFG-58), Perry-class Guided Missile
Frigate
USS *Sacramento* (AOE-1), Sacramento-class Combat Support
Ship
Covering the US withdrawal from Somalia, March 1994:
Inchon Amphibious Ready Group (embarking 24th MEU), relieved
13th MEU in February 1994
USS *Inchon* (LPH-12), Iwo Jima–class Amphibious Assault Ship
USS *Trenton* (LPD-14), Austin-class Amphibious Transport Dock
USS *Portland* (LSD-37), Anchorage-class Dock Landing Ship
USS *Spartanburg County* (LST-1192), Newport-class Tank
Landing Ship
24th Marine Expeditionary Unit on board *Inchon* ARG
Headquarters, 24th MEU
Battalion Landing Team, 3rd Battalion/6th Marine Regiment
Marine Medium Helicopter Squadron (HMM-266)
24th MEU Service Support Group
Peleliu Amphibious Ready Group (embarking 11th MEU)
USS *Peleliu* (LHA-5), Tarawa-class Amphibious Assault Ship
USS *Duluth* (LPD-6), Austin-class Amphibious Transport Dock

USS *Anchorage* (LSD-36), Anchorage-class Dock Landing Ship
USS *Frederick* (LST-1184), Newport-class Tank Landing Ship
11th Marine Expeditionary Unit on board *Peleliu* ARG
Headquarters, 11th MEU
Battalion Landing Team, 2nd Battalion/5th Marine Regiment
Marine Medium Helicopter Squadron (HMM-263)
11th MEU Service Support Group

Notes

Introduction

1. Tom Clancy, *Debt of Honor* (New York: Berkeley Books, 1995), 20–27.
2. Gerald B. Helman and Steven R. Ratner, "Saving Failed States," *Foreign Policy* 89, 3 (1992): 3–20.
3. John R. Bolton, "Wrong Turn in Somalia," *Foreign Affairs* 73, 1 (February 1994): 66.
4. Mark Bowden, *Black Hawk Down: A Story of Modern War*, 1st ed. (New York: Grove Press, 1999); 2nd ed. (New York: Grove Press, 2010).
5. *Delta Force: Black Hawk Down* (NovaLogic, 2003).
6. See Karin Von Hippel, *Democracy by Force: US Military Intervention in the Post–Cold War World* (New York: Cambridge University Press, 2000); Taylor B. Seybolt, *Humanitarian Military Intervention: The Conditions for Success or Failure* (New York: Oxford University Press, 2007); Lise Morjé Howard, *UN Peacekeeping in Civil Wars* (New York: Cambridge University Press, 2008); Thomas R. Mockaitis, *Peace Operations and Intrastate Conflict: The Sword or the Olive Branch?* (Westport, CT: Praeger, 1999). For similar policy-oriented analyses, see Jane Boulden, *Peace Enforcement: The United Nations Experience in Congo, Somalia, and Bosnia* (Westport, CT: Praeger, 2001); Robert M. Cassidy, *Peacekeeping in the Abyss: British and American Peacekeeping Doctrine and Practice after the Cold War* (Westport, CT: Praeger, 2004); Thijs W. Brocades-Zaalberg, *Soldiers and Civil Power: Supporting or Substituting Civil Authorities in Modern Peace Operations* (Amsterdam: Amsterdam University Press, 2006); David A. Lake, *The Statebuilder's Dilemma: On the Limits of Foreign Intervention* (Ithaca, NY: Cornell University Press, 2016); Norrie MacQueen, *Humanitarian Intervention and the United Nations* (Edinburgh: Edinburgh University Press, 2011); Susan L. Woodward, *The Ideology of Failed States: Why Intervention Fails* (New York: Cambridge University Press, 2017).
7. Boulden, *Peace Enforcement*, 74. This suggestion was also made by Von Hippel, *Democracy by Force*, 78–83; Frederick H. Fleitz, *Peacekeeping Fiascoes of the 1990s: Causes, Solutions, and U.S. Interests* (Westport, CT: Praeger, 2002), 133; Trevor Findlay, *The Use of Force in UN Peace Operations* (New York: Oxford University Press, 2002), 204–206.
8. Michael Wesley, *Casualties of the New World Order: The Causes of Failure of UN Missions to Civil Wars* (Boulder, CO: St. Martin's, 1997), 73. See also How-

ard, *UN Peacekeeping in Civil Wars*, 21; Fleitz, *Peacekeeping Fiascoes*, 130; Seybolt, *Humanitarian Military Intervention*, 57.

9. Cassidy, *Peacekeeping in the Abyss*, 168.

10. See Fleitz, *Peacekeeping Fiascoes*, 131; Cassidy, *Peacekeeping in the Abyss*, 166; Mockaitis, *Peace Operations*, 61; Ray Murphy, *UN Peacekeeping in Lebanon, Somalia, and Kosovo* (Cambridge: Cambridge University Press, 2007), 186; Brocades-Zaalberg, *Soldiers and Civil Power*, 242; Daniel P. Bolger, *Savage Peace: Americans at War in the 1990's* (Novato, CA: Presidio Press, 1995), 299; Peter Huchthausen, *America's Splendid Little Wars: A Short History of U.S. Military Engagements, 1975–2000* (New York: Viking, 2003), 175; Findlay, *Use of Force*, 187; Seybolt, *Humanitarian Military Intervention*, 57.

11. Mockaitis, *Peace Operations*, 59.

12. Michael Rose, *Fighting for Peace: Bosnia 1994* (London: Harvill Press, 1998), 126.

13. See Howard, *UN Peacekeeping in Civil Wars*, 28; Boulden, *Peace Enforcement*, 75; Cassidy, *Peacekeeping in the Abyss*, 168; Mockaitis, *Peace Operations*, 64; Von Hippel, *Democracy by Force*, 73; Findlay, *Use of Force*, 166, 204–206; MacQueen, *Humanitarian Intervention*, 218–219; Lake, *Statebuilder's Dilemma*, 169–170.

14. U.N. SCOR, 49th sess., 3447th mtg., U.N. Doc. S/PV.3447 (4 November 1994), 7, https://undocs.org/en/S/PV.3447.

1. The Collapse of Somalia: The Long Dark Road through Anarchy to Intervention

1. Mohamed Sahnoun, *Somalia: The Missed Opportunities* (Washington, DC: United States Institute for Peace Press, 1994), 9.

2. General Anthony C. Zinni, USMC (retired), interview by the author, 20 December 2019.

3. Mohammed Farah Aidid, "Democracy in Somalia: Its Roots and Its Future Scenario," in *Preferred Future Development in Somalia*, ed. Mohammed Farah Aidid and Satya Pal Ruhela (New Delhi: Vikas, 1993), 24–25.

4. John Drysdale, *Whatever Happened to Somalia?* 2nd ed. (London: Haan, 2001), 16, 21–23.

5. Gerald B. Helman and Steven R. Ratner, "Saving Failed States," *Foreign Policy* 89, 3 (1992): 3–20.

6. The works on Somalia that use the term "warlord" are too numerous to list here, but the most recent example is Stephen Biddle, *Nonstate Warfare: The Military Methods of Guerillas, Warlords, and Militias* (Princeton, NJ: Princeton University Press, 2021), 182–223.

7. For scholarship focusing on Somalia in the colonial period, the short-lived republic, and the Barre regime, see Catherine Besteman, *Unraveling Somalia: Race, Class, and the Legacy of Slavery* (Philadelphia: University of Pennsylvania

Press, 1999); Lee V. Cassanelli, "Explaining the Somali Crisis," in *The Struggle for Land in Southern Somalia: The War behind the War*, ed. Catherine Besteman and Lee V. Cassanelli (London: Haan, 1996), 13–26; John Drysdale, "Reflections 1943–1963," in *Milk and Peace, Drought and War: Somali Culture, Society and Politics*, ed. Markus Hoehne and Virginia Luling (London: Hurst, 2010), 19–33; Gerard Prunier, "Benign Neglect versus *La Grande Somalia*: The Colonial Legacy and the Post-Colonial State," in Hoehne and Luling, *Milk and Peace*, 35–49; Mohamed Haji Ingiriis, *The Suicidal State in Somalia: The Rise and Fall of the Siad Barre Regime, 1969–1991* (Lanham, MD: University Press of America, 2016); Ioan M. Lewis, *Blood and Bone: The Call of Kinship in Somali Society* (Trenton, NJ: Red Sea Press, 1994).

8. Cassanelli, "Explaining the Somali Crisis," 14.

9. Ingiriis, *Suicidal State*, 35.

10. Walter S. Clarke, *Background Information for Operation Restore Hope* (Carlisle, PA: Strategic Studies Institute, US Army War College, 1992), 6.

11. Terrence Lyons and Ahmed I. Samatar, *Somalia: State Collapse, Multilateral Intervention, and Strategies for Political Reconstruction* (Washington, DC: Brookings Institution, 1995), 9–11.

12. Clarke, *Background Information*, 3.

13. Helen Chapin Metz, *Somalia: A Country Study* (Washington, DC: Federal Research Division, Library of Congress, 1993), 11–12.

14. Lyons and Samatar, *Somalia: State Collapse*, 11; Piero Ignazi, Giampiero Giacomello, and Fabrizio Coticchia, *Italian Military Operations Abroad: Just Don't Call It War* (New York: Palgrave Macmillan, 2012), 98; Brian R. Sullivan, Institute for National Security Studies report on Somalia, sent to General Gordon R. Sullivan by Lieutenant General Paul G. Cerjan, 22 December 1992, folder 2, box 117, Gordon R. Sullivan Papers, US Army Heritage and Education Center, Carlisle, PA; Ingiriis, *Suicidal State*, 38.

15. Metz, *Somalia*, 13.

16. Ignazi, Giacomello, and Coticchia, *Italian Military Operations*, 98; Metz, *Somalia*, 14.

17. Metz, *Somalia*, 14–19; Drysdale, "Reflections 1943–1963," 26.

18. Metz, *Somalia*, 19–22; Sullivan, Institute for National Security Studies report.

19. Lyons and Samatar, *Somalia: State Collapse*, 13; Metz, *Somalia*, 27, 35.

20. Prunier, "Benign Neglect," 36–43.

21. John L. Hirsch and Robert B. Oakley, *Somalia and Operation Restore Hope: Reflections on Peacemaking and Peacekeeping* (Washington, DC: Institute of Peace Press, 1995), 4–5. Oakley was US ambassador to Somalia from 1982 to 1984 and US presidential envoy and political head of the US-led Unified Task Force in Somalia in December 1992. Hirsch served as Oakley's deputy. Ingiriis, *Suicidal State*, 39–45.

22. Ingiriis makes a compelling case that Barre was linked to the assassination plot and the planning of the coup. See Ingiriis, *Suicidal State*, 45–55.

23. Metz, *Somalia*, 30–36.

24. Lewis, *Blood and Bone*, 150–152.

25. Brian Crozier, *The Soviet Presence in Somalia* (London: Centre for Security and Conflict Studies, 1975), 8–9; Metz, *Somalia*, 37, 49; Lyons and Samatar, *Somalia: State Collapse*, 14–18; Ingiriis, *Suicidal State*, 73–75.

26. Lewis, *Blood and Bone*, 166–167, 171–172; Catherine Besteman, "Representing Violence and 'Othering' Somalia," *Cultural Anthropology* 11, 1 (February 1996): 125; Ingiriis, *Suicidal State*, 73–75.

27. Ingiriis, *Suicidal State*, 77.

28. Metz, *Somalia*, 37; Crozier, *Soviet Presence*, 5–6; Ingiriis, *Suicidal State*, 96–98.

29. Ingiriis, *Suicidal State*, 109–113.

30. Metz, *Somalia*, 49; Crozier, *Soviet Presence*, 8–9.

31. Clarke, *Background Information*, 4; Ingiriis, *Suicidal State*, 144.

32. Herman J. Cohen, *Intervening in Africa: Superpower Peacemaking in a Troubled Continent* (New York: St. Martin's Press, 2000), 197–200. Cohen was US undersecretary of state for African affairs from 1989 to 1993. Drysdale, *Whatever Happened*, 134–136; Ingiriis, *Suicidal State*, 146.

33. Lidwien Kapteijns, *Clan Cleansing in Somalia: The Ruinous Legacy of 1991* (Philadelphia: University of Pennsylvania Press, 2013), 90; Ingiriis, *Suicidal State*, 158–163.

34. Human Rights Watch, *Somalia: A Government at War with Its Own People; Testimonies about the Killings and the Conflict in the North* (New York: Human Rights Watch, 1990), 29–31; Lyons and Samatar, *Somalia: State Collapse*, 18; Drysdale, *Whatever Happened*, 138; Hirsch and Oakley, *Somalia and Operation Restore Hope*, 9; Michael Maren, *The Road to Hell: The Ravaging Effects of Foreign Aid and International Charity* (New York: Free Press, 1997), 99.

35. Hirsch and Oakley, *Somalia and Operation Restore Hope*, 9; Cohen, *Intervening in Africa*, 197–200; Lyons and Samatar, *Somalia: State Collapse*, 16–17.

36. Hirsch and Oakley, *Somalia and Operation Restore Hope*, 9; Cohen, *Intervening in Africa*, 197–200; Eugene G. Piasecki, "If You Liked Beirut, You'll Love Mogadishu: An Introduction to ARSOF in Somalia," *Veritas* 3, 2 (2007): 5.

37. Human Rights Watch, *Somalia: Government at War*, 30; Ingiriis, *Suicidal State*, 194.

38. Hirsch and Oakley, *Somalia and Operation Restore Hope*, 12; Lyons and Samatar, *Somalia: State Collapse*, 18; Drysdale, *Whatever Happened*, 134–136; Human Rights Watch, *Somalia: Government at War*, 30–31; Clarke, *Background Information*, 14; Lewis, *Blood and Bone*, 179.

39. Metz, *Somalia*, 47.

40. Kapteijns, *Clan Cleansing*, 82–83; Mohamed Haji Mukhtar and Margaret Castagno, *Historical Dictionary of Somalia* (Oxford: Scarecrow Press, 2003), 181.

41. Maren, *Road to Hell*, 95–99, 106; Lyons and Samatar, *Somalia: State Collapse*, 18.

42. Mohammed Farah Aidid, "Foreign Aid for the Somali Nation's Development: A Challenge to Our Integrity and Future," in Aidid and Ruhela, *Preferred Future Development in Somalia*, 243–244.

43. Aidid, 246–247.

44. Metz, *Somalia*, 49; Lewis, *Blood and Bone*, 214; Ingiriis, *Suicidal State*, 192–193.

45. References to Morgan's letter can be found in Human Rights Watch, *Somalia: Government at War*, 44–45, 124.

46. Human Rights Watch, 99–104; James Reinl, "Investigating Genocide in Somaliland," *Al Jazeera*, 6 February 2014.

47. Cohen, *Intervening in Africa*, 200–201; Human Rights Watch, *Somalia: Government at War*, 128.

48. Lyons and Samatar, *Somalia: State Collapse*, 18; Sahnoun, *Somalia: Missed Opportunities*, 7; Human Rights Watch, *Somalia: Government at War*, 196; Kapteijns, *Clan Cleansing*, 90–91; Lewis, *Blood and Bone*, 226.

49. Human Rights Watch, *Somalia: Government at War*, 142.

50. Sahnoun, *Somalia: Missed Opportunities*, 6; Drysdale, *Whatever Happened*, 138; Glenn M. Harned, *Stability Operations in Somalia, 1992–1993: A Case Study* (Carlisle, PA: Peacekeeping and Stability Operations Institute, 2016), 127; Human Rights Watch, *Somalia: Government at War*, 140.

51. Cohen, *Intervening in Africa*, 202; Sahnoun, *Somalia: Missed Opportunities*, 7; Maren, *Road to Hell*, 178–184.

52. Lyons and Samatar, *Somalia: State Collapse*, 18–19; Drysdale, *Whatever Happened*, 15–18; Ingiriis, *Suicidal State*, 211–213; Mohamed Haji Ingiriis, "From Grievance to Greed in Somalia," *Cahiers d'Études Africaines* 59, 3 (2019): 789–790; Lewis, *Blood and Bone*, 211–213.

53. Ingiriis, *Suicidal State*, 69.

54. United Nations, *The Blue Helmets: A Review of United Nations Peace-keeping*, 3rd ed. (New York: UN Department of Public Information, 1996), 287; Zinni interview. Zinni served as the Unified Task Force's director of operations, cultivating personal relationships with key Somali participants, including Aidid. Ignazi, Giacomello, and Coticchia, *Italian Military Operations*, 98; Drysdale, *Whatever Happened*, 21–24; Mukhtar and Castagno, *Historical Dictionary*, 179; Clarke, *Background Information*, 30; British Foreign and Commonwealth Office, Research and Analysis Department Note on Somali Clans and Their Political Role, April 1992, 10, S-1830-0011-06, AG-050, United Nations Archives, New York; Ingiriis, "From Grievance to Greed," 791.

55. The SNA included Aidid's wing of the USC, SPM-Ogadeni, the SDM, and the SSNM.

56. Sahnoun, *Somalia: Missed Opportunities*, 7–8; Drysdale, *Whatever Happened*, 21–23; Ingiriis, *Suicidal State*, 210.

57. Ingiriis, *Suicidal State*, 215.

58. Drysdale, *Whatever Happened*, 21–23; Mukhtar and Castagno, *Historical Dictionary*, 74.

59. Walter Clarke, "Failed Visions and Uncertain Mandates in Somalia," in *Learning from Somalia: The Lessons of Armed Humanitarian Intervention*, ed. Walter Clarke and Jeffrey Herbst (Boulder, CO: Westview Press, 1997), 5; Drysdale, *Whatever Happened*, ix–xi, 16–26.

60. Drysdale, *Whatever Happened*, 16–26.

61. S. L. Arnold, "Somalia: An Operation Other Than War," *Military Review* 73, 12 (December 1993): 27.

62. James K. Bishop, "Escape from Mogadishu," *Foreign Service Journal* 6 (March 1991): 27.

63. Gary J. Ohls, *Somalia . . . From the Sea* (Newport, RI: Naval War College Press, 2009), 27–33.

64. Bishop, "Escape from Mogadishu," 27–31; Ohls, *Somalia . . . From the Sea*, 27–38; Ignazi, Giacomello, and Coticchia, *Italian Military Operations*, 99.

65. Drysdale, *Whatever Happened*, 27; Ingiriis, *Suicidal State*, 224–226.

66. Ignazi, Giacomello, and Coticchia, *Italian Military Operations*, 98; Ingiriis, *Suicidal State*, 245–248.

67. John Drysdale, "Foreign Military Intervention in Somalia: The Root Cause of the Shift from UN Peacekeeping to Peacemaking and Its Consequences," in Clarke and Herbst, *Learning from Somalia*, 124; Hirsch and Oakley, *Somalia and Operation Restore Hope*, 12; Drysdale, *Whatever Happened*, 28–31, 43–44.

68. British Foreign and Commonwealth Office, Note on Somali Clans, 3–11.

69. Ingiriis, *Suicidal State*, 231.

70. Cassanelli, "Explaining the Somali Crisis," 19–21.

71. I. M. Lewis, "Doing Violence to Ethnography: A Response to Catherine Besteman's 'Representing Violence and "Othering" Somalia,'" *Cultural Anthropology* 13, 1 (February 1998): 102.

72. Besteman, "Representing Violence," 124.

73. Kaptiejns, *Clan Cleansing*, 226–229.

74. Ingiriis, *Suicidal State*, 233.

75. Ingiriis, 241.

76. Lewis, *Blood and Bone*, 227–228.

77. Ingiriis, *Suicidal State*, 252.

78. Africa Watch Women's Rights Project, *Seeking Refuge, Finding Terror: The Widespread Rape of Somali Women Refugees in North Eastern Kenya* (New York: Human Rights Watch, 1993), 11–19; Steven Hansch, Scott Lillibridge, Grace

Egeland, Charles Teller, and Michael Toole, *Lives Lost, Lives Saved: Excess Mortality and the Impact of Health Interventions in the Somalia Emergency* (Washington, DC: Center for Policy Analysis and Research on Refugee Issues, 1994), 10–11; Drysdale, "Foreign Military Intervention," 124; Hirsch and Oakley, *Somalia and Operation Restore Hope*, 12.

79. Smith Hempstone, *Rogue Ambassador: An African Memoir* (Sewanee, TN: University of the South Press, 1997), 207.

80. Hempstone, 204.

81. Cohen, *Intervening in Africa*, 206–207; Andrew S. Natsios, "Humanitarian Relief Intervention in Somalia: The Economics of Chaos," in Clarke and Herbst, *Learning from Somalia*, 80–81.

82. Drysdale, "Foreign Military Intervention," 124; Hirsch and Oakley, *Somalia and Operation Restore Hope*, 12; Hansch et al., *Lives Lost, Lives Saved*, 12–13.

83. United Nations, *The United Nations and the Situation in Somalia* (New York: UN Department of Public Information, 1994), 1; Hansch et al., *Lives Lost, Lives Saved*, 10–13.

84. Hansch et al., *Lives Lost, Lives Saved*, 24.

85. Drysdale, *Whatever Happened*, 28–31.

86. Sahnoun, *Somalia: Missed Opportunities*, 9.

87. Drysdale, *Whatever Happened*, 140–141.

88. Drysdale, 30–32.

89. Ken Menkhaus, "International Peacebuilding and the Dynamics of Local and National Reconciliation in Somalia," in Clarke and Herbst, *Learning from Somalia*, 47; Clarke, *Background Information*, 32–34; Drysdale, *Whatever Happened*, 32; Drysdale, "Foreign Military Intervention," 119; Lewis, *Blood and Bone*, 227.

90. Drysdale, "Foreign Military Intervention," 119; Ingiriis, *Suicidal State*, 253–254.

91. Clarke, *Background Information*, 32–34.

92. Sahnoun, *Somalia: Missed Opportunities*, 10–11.

93. Drysdale, *Whatever Happened*, ix–xiv.

94. Aidid, "Democracy in Somalia," 16, 20.

95. Letter from Javier Perez de Cuellar, UN Secretary-General, to the UN Security Council, 27 December 1991, in United Nations, *The United Nations and Somalia, 1992–1996* (New York: UN Department of Public Information, 1996), 113; United Nations Security Council, letter dated 20 January 1992 from the Chargé d'Affaires of the Permanent Mission of Somalia to the United Nations addressed to the President of the Security Council, S/23445 (20 January 1992), undocs.org/en/S/23445.

2. A Tale of Two Bureaucracies: The United Nations and United States Decide to Intervene in Somalia

1. United Nations, Security Council, Letter from the Secretary-General Addressed to the President of the Security Council, S/24868 (30 November 1992), 2–3, available from undocs.org/en/S/24868; hereafter, S/24868.

2. John Luke Hills, memorandum on congressional review on the situation in Somalia, 16 September 1992, S-1086-0101-09, AG-028, United Nations Archives, New York (UNA).

3. Javier Perez de Cuellar, UN Secretary-General, Letter to the UN Security Council, 27 December 1991, in United Nations, *The United Nations and Somalia, 1992–1996* (New York: UN Department of Public Information, 1996), 113.

4. Peter Hansen, Report of the Technical Mission to Somalia, 4–17 August 1992, S-1086-0100-01, AG-028, UNA.

5. Walter Clarke, "Failed Visions and Uncertain Mandates in Somalia," in *Learning from Somalia: The Lessons of Armed Humanitarian Intervention*, ed. Walter Clarke and Jeffrey Herbst (Boulder, CO: Westview Press, 1997), 5; United Nations, Security Council, *The Situation in Somalia: Report of the Secretary General*, S/23693 (11 March 1992), 17, available from undocs.org/en/S/23693; hereafter, S/23693.

6. United Nations, Security Council, Letter dated 20 January 1992 from the Chargé d'Affaires of the Permanent Mission of Somalia to the United Nations Addressed to the President of the Security Council, S/23445 (20 January 1992), available from undocs.org/en/S/23445; letter from Perez de Cuellar to UN Security Council, 27 December 1991.

7. Herman J. Cohen, *Intervening in Africa: Superpower Peacemaking in a Troubled Continent* (New York: St. Martin's Press, 2000), 206.

8. Paul Lewis, "How U.N. Nominee Won: 4 Switched," *New York Times*, 23 November 1991.

9. Marc Grossman, memorandum for Anthony Lake, 22 February 1993, National Security Council and NSC Records Management System, "Declassified Documents Concerning U.N. Secretary General Boutros Boutros-Ghali and Somalia," Clinton Digital Library, accessed 3 January 2024, https://clinton.presidentiallibraries.us/items/show/101838.

10. Marrack Goulding, *Peacemonger* (London: John Murray, 2002), 276.

11. Jonathan Stevenson, "Hope Restored in Somalia?" *Foreign Policy* 91 (Summer 1993): 144.

12. S/23693, 5–10, 22; U.N. SCOR, 47th sess., 3039th mtg, U.N. Doc. S/PV.3039 (23 January 1992), available from undocs.org/en/S/PV/3039; United Nations, Security Council Resolution 733, S/RES/733 (23 January 1992), available from https://digitallibrary.un.org/record/135713?ln=en.

13. United Nations, Security Council Resolution 746, S/RES/746 (17 March 1992), available from https://digitallibrary.un.org/record/139714?ln=en.

14. United Nations, Security Council, *The Situation in Somalia: Report of the Secretary General*, S/23829 (21 April 1992), 6–7, available from undocs.org/en/S/23829; hereafter, S/23829.

15. S/23829, 9–10.

16. United Nations, Security Council Resolution 751, S/RES/751 (24 April 1992), available from https://digitallibrary.un.org/record/141599?ln=en; Boutros Boutros-Ghali, *Unvanquished: A US-UN Saga* (New York: Random House, 1999), 54.

17. United Nations, Security Council, Letter from the Secretary-General Addressed to the President of the Security Council, S/24179 (25 June 1992), available from undocs.org/en/S/24179; United Nations, Security Council, Letter from the Secretary-General Addressed to the President of the Security Council, S/24180 (29 June 1992), available from undocs.org/en/S/24180.

18. United Nations, *United Nations and Somalia, 1992–1996*, 18–20.

19. Mohamed Sahnoun, handwritten fax to Boutros Boutros-Ghali, 5 May 1992, S-1000-0024-02, AG-024, UNA.

20. Mohamed Sahnoun, *Somalia: The Missed Opportunities* (Washington, DC: United States Institute for Peace Press, 1994), 16; Boutros-Ghali, *Unvanquished*, 54.

21. S/23829, 21–22.

22. S/23693, 3, 9–10; Boutros-Ghali, *Unvanquished*, 54.

23. John Drysdale to Hassan Conteh, 22 December 1992, S-1000-0028-02, AG-024, UNA.

24. John Drysdale, "Foreign Military Intervention in Somalia: The Root Cause of the Shift from UN Peacekeeping to Peacemaking and Its Consequences," in Clarke and Herbst, *Learning from Somalia*, 120.

25. Sahnoun, *Somalia: Missed Opportunities*, 39; Drysdale, "Foreign Military Intervention," 122–124.

26. Sahnoun, *Somalia: Missed Opportunities*, 18–19; Allen G. Sens, *Somalia and the Changing Nature of Peacekeeping: The Implications for Canada; a Study Prepared for the Commission of Inquiry into the Deployment of Canadian Forces to Somalia* (Ottawa: Ministry of Public Works and Government Services, 1997), 73.

27. Sahnoun, *Somalia: Missed Opportunities*, 20.

28. Mort Rosenblum, "Somalia Slips Back into the Stone Age," Associated Press, 30 August 1992, folder INFO-041, box 12, Somalia Crisis Collection, US Army Heritage and Education Center, Carlisle, PA (SCC/USAHEC).

29. Greg Myre, "In Somalia's War, the Surreal Mixes with the Tragic," Associated Press, 13 September 1992, folder INFO-041, box 12, SCC/USAHEC.

30. S/23693, 14; Sahnoun, *Somalia: Missed Opportunities*, 17–18; letter from

Boutros Boutros-Ghali, UN Secretary-General, to the President of the Security Council, 5 June 1992, in United Nations, *United Nations and Somalia, 1992–1996,* 168.

31. S/23829, 16, 19.

32. S/23829, 8.

33. S/23829, 8.

34. This is a perception articulated by Sahnoun, *Somalia: Missed Opportunities,* 39; John L. Hirsch and Robert B. Oakley, *Somalia and Operation Restore Hope: Reflections on Peacemaking and Peacekeeping* (Washington, DC: Institute of Peace Press, 1995), 26; and Drysdale, "Foreign Military Intervention," 124. Sahnoun laments the months between the authorization for the UN security force and its deployment, which is echoed by Hirsch and Oakley and by Drysdale. Sahnoun should have been intimately acquainted with such matters, but he often heard about UN developments only after the fact, and he was rarely party to consultations or Security Council deliberations in New York, which may account for this misunderstanding. The current US Army history of the intervention also inaccurately presents the security force as being created by Resolution 751. See Robert F. Baumann, Lawrence A. Yates, and Versalle F. Washington, *"My Clan against the World": US and Coalition Forces in Somalia 1992–1994* (Fort Leavenworth, KS: Combat Studies Institute Press, 2004), 18.

35. Security Council Resolution 751.

36. Cohen, *Intervening in Africa,* 206–207; Andrew S. Natsios, "Humanitarian Relief Intervention in Somalia: The Economics of Chaos," in Clarke and Herbst, *Learning from Somalia,* 81.

37. "Why Not Save Somalis," *New York Times,* 29 April 1992; "Somalia, Too, Needs Help," *Washington Post,* 13 May 1992.

38. Nancy Kassebaum and Paul Simon, "Save Somalia from Itself," *New York Times,* 2 January 1992.

39. Jane Perlez, "Deaths in Somalia Outpace Delivery of Food," *New York Times,* 19 July 1992.

40. United Nations, Security Council, *Report of the Secretary-General on the Situation in Somalia,* S/24343 (22 July 1992), 11–12, available from undocs.org/en/S/24343; hereafter, S/24343.

41. United Nations, Security Council Resolution 767, S/RES/767 (24 July 1992), available from https://digitallibrary.un.org/record/146263?ln=en.

42. Smith Hempstone, "Dispatch from a Place Near Hell," *Washington Post,* 23 August 1992.

43. Smith Hempstone, *Rogue Ambassador: An African Memoir* (Sewanee, TN: University of the South Press, 1997), 229.

44. Walter Poole, *The Effort to Save Somalia, August 1992–March 1994* (Washington, DC: Joint History Office, Office of the Chairman of the Joint Chiefs of Staff, 2005), 7.

45. Cohen, *Intervening in Africa*, 209.

46. Statement by Governor Clinton on the crisis in Somalia, 28 August 1992, Office of the Press Secretary and Dee Dee Myers, "Somalia [2]," Clinton Digital Library, accessed 3 January 2024, https://clinton.presidentiallibraries.us/items/show/100064.

47. Cohen, *Intervening in Africa*, 207-209; Natsios, "Humanitarian Relief Intervention," 82; "Why Not Save Somalis"; *Humanitarian Aid in Somalia, September 1990-May 1993* (Washington, DC: Center for Policy Analysis and Research on Refugee Issues, 1994), 16-18, folder 801/4H, box 77, Frederick C. Cuny Collection, Cushing Library, Texas A&M University (hereafter, Cuny Collection); Don Oberdorfer, "The Path to Intervention," *Washington Post*, 6 December 1992; US Army War College, *Campaign Analysis Course Case Study: Somalia* (Carlisle, PA: US Army War College, Department of Military Strategy, Planning, and Operations, 2005), 10.

48. Cuny famously disappeared in Chechnya in 1995 amidst global speculation that he was an American intelligence agent who ran afoul of either the Chechens or the Russians in an area that supposedly housed an underground nuclear weapons storage site. Scott Anderson, *The Man Who Tried to Save the World: The Dangerous Life and Mysterious Disappearance of Fred Cuny* (New York: Doubleday, 1999), 20-27.

49. US Army War College, *Campaign Analysis*, 11-13; Colin Powell, *My American Journey* (New York: Ballantine Books, 1996), 565.

50. Oberdorfer, "Path to Intervention."

51. US Army War College, *Campaign Analysis*, 15; *Humanitarian Aid in Somalia*, 15; Said S. Samatar, "How to Save Somalia," *Washington Post*, 1 December 1992; Gary J. Ohls, *Somalia . . . From the Sea* (Newport, RI: Naval War College Press, 2009), 47; Hirsch and Oakley, *Somalia and Operation Restore Hope*, 24-25.

52. Natsios, "Humanitarian Relief Intervention," 84; Hempstone, *Rogue Ambassador*, 218-223; Joseph P. Hoar, "A CINC's Perspective," *Joint Forces Quarterly* 1, 2 (Autumn 1993): 57.

53. World Food Program, *The Problems with the UN Airlift into Somalia as Seen from Mogadishu*, n.d., folder 602, box 65, Cuny Collection; Hoar, "CINC's Perspective," 57; Ohls, *Somalia . . . From the Sea*, 58; Joseph D. Celeski, "A History of SF Operations in Somalia: 1992-1995," *Special Warfare* 15, 2 (June 2002): 17; J. P. Jensen, "Airlift Control Element (ALCE) I," in *In the Line of Duty: Canadian Joint Forces Somalia, 1992-1993* (St. Catherine's, ON: Vanwell, 2001), 36-37.

54. World Food Program, *Problems with the UN Airlift.*

55. Ohls, *Somalia . . . From the Sea*, 58; Joint Task Force Somalia, J-3 Operations Situation Report, 21 April 1993, folder 35, box 1, Operation Restore Hope Collection (ORHC), COLL/3708, Archives Branch, Marine Corps History Division, Quantico, VA (MCHD).

56. Natsios, "Humanitarian Relief Intervention," 84.

57. *Humanitarian Aid in Somalia,* 24.

58. Philip Johnston, *Somalia Diary* (Atlanta: Longstreet Press, 1994), 16–17, 62.

59. Mort Rosenblum, "Lawlessness, Gunplay Thrive in Once-Pretty Somalian City," Associated Press, 2 September 1992, folder INFO-041, box 12, SCC/USAHEC. The "technicals" Rosenblum mentions were specific to the Somali intervention. The factions found it cost-effective to mount heavy weapons—machine guns, recoilless rifles, or salvaged aerial weaponry—on pickup trucks or any vehicle with a cargo bed. Somalis themselves never referred to these ersatz fighting vehicles as technicals. The term originated with UN and relief agencies that frequently hired Somalis equipped with technicals as security. They categorized paying for this security as "technical assistance." Thus, "technical" entered the lexicon of the international actors and media working in Somalia.

60. "2 UN Observers Shot as Somalis Loot Supplies," *International Herald Tribune,* 29 August 1992; United Nations, Security Council, *The Situation in Somalia: Report of the Secretary General,* S/24480 (24 August 1992), 5, available from undocs.org/en/S/24480; hereafter, S/24480.

61. S/24480, 5; "Statement by Press Secretary Fitzwater on the Military Airlift for Humanitarian Aid to Somalia," White House, 13 August 1992, available from https://www.presidency.ucsb.edu/documents/statement-press-secretary-fitzwater-the-military-airlift-for-humanitarian-aid-somalia.

62. Mohamed Sahnoun, Fax to Boutros Boutros-Ghali, 5 May 1992, S-1000-0024-02, AG-024, UNA.

63. Sahnoun, Report on the Meetings with the USC Delegation, 5 May 1992, S-1830-0011-07, AG-050, UNA; Sahnoun, Report of the Meeting with General Aidid, 9 May 1992, S-1830-0011-07, AG-050, UNA.

64. Sahnoun, *Somalia: Missed Opportunities,* 26–27; Boutros-Ghali to President of the Security Council, 5 June 1992, 168, 25–27.

65. S/24480; United Nations, Security Council, *The Situation in Somalia: Report of the Secretary General, Addendum,* S/24480/Add.1 (28 August 1992), available from undocs.org/en/S/24480/Add.1.

66. United Nations, Security Council, Letter from the Secretary-General Addressed to the President of the Security Council, S/24451 (14 August 1992), available from undocs.org/en/S/24451; United Nations, Security Council Resolution 775, S/RES/775 (28 August 1992), available from https://digitallibrary.un.org/record/149086?ln=en.

67. Hirsch and Oakley, *Somalia and Operation Restore Hope,* 26–27; Sahnoun, *Somalia: Missed Opportunities,* 39.

68. Drysdale to Hassan Conteh, 22 December 1992; John Drysdale, *Whatever Happened to Somalia?* 2nd ed. (London: Haan, 2001), 65; "2 UN Observers Shot."

69. Colonel Michael W. Hagee, USMC, commander 11th MEU, interview

by Captain D. A. Dawson, 6 January 1994, 2–3, RHIT-C-367, Somalia Oral History Interview Collection, US Army Center of Military History, Washington, DC; Ohls, *Somalia . . . From the Sea*, 64.

70. John Connor, "Intervention and Domestic Politics," in *Australian Peacekeeping: Sixty Years in the Field*, ed. David Horner, Peter Londey, and Jean Bou (Melbourne: Cambridge University Press, 2009), 73–74.

71. Tughral Yamin, *UN Peacekeeping Operations in Somalia: The Pakistani Perspective* (Karachi: Paramount Books, 2019), 75.

72. Brigadier Imtiaz Shaheen, Fax to Marrack Goulding, 9 November 1992, S-1829-0016-01, AG-050, UNA.

73. Bob Breen, *A Little Bit of Hope: Australian Force Somalia* (St. Leonard's, NSW: Allen & Unwin, 1998), 2–3, 15–16. Breen deployed to Somalia as the command historian for the Australian contingent of UNITAF.

74. Mohamed Farah Aidid, Letter to Ismat Kittani, 30 November 1992, S-1000-0024-02, AG-024, UNA; Johnston, *Somalia Diary*, 47.

75. Memorandum on the threat to the UN Pakistani Battalion in Mogadishu, 18 November 1992, National Security Council Meeting Files, NSC/DC 395, Bush Presidential Records, George Bush Presidential Library (GBPL).

76. Breen, *Little Bit of Hope*, 15–16.

77. Edith M. Lederer, "Food Isn't Going Far in Somalia," Associated Press, 25 October 1992, folder INFO-041, box 12, SCC/USAHEC.

78. "The 100-Day Action Programme for Accelerated Humanitarian Assistance for Somalia," 6 October 1992, in United Nations, *United Nations and Somalia, 1992–1996*, 194–196. The Geneva conference raised $67.3 million in donations for the program.

79. Johnston, *Somalia Diary*, 30–31; United Nations, *United Nations and Somalia, 1992–1996*, 23.

80. George H. W. Bush, Letter to Mohamed Sahnoun, 21 September 1992, S1086-0101-09, AG-028, UNA.

81. Hirsch and Oakley, *Somalia and Operation Restore Hope*, 30.

82. Drysdale to Hassan Conteh, 22 December 1992.

83. Sahnoun, *Somalia: Missed Opportunities*, 41; Goulding, *Peacemonger*, 277.

84. Trevor Rowe, "Somali-Relief Official Said to Quit after Criticism by Boutros-Ghali," *Washington Post*, 27 October 1992; Sahnoun, *Somalia: Missed Opportunities*, 41; Boutros-Ghali, *Unvanquished*, 57; Drysdale, *Whatever Happened*, 66.

85. President of the Security Council, statement on persons hampering the deployment of UNOSOM, 16 October 1992, in United Nations, *United Nations and Somalia, 1992–1996*, 196.

86. United Nations, *United Nations and Somalia, 1992–1996*, 27–28; Drysdale to Hassan Conteh, 22 December 1992; United Nations, Security Council, Letter from the Secretary-General Addressed to the President of the Security Council,

S/24859 (27 November 1992), available from undocs.org/en/S/24859, 2–3; hereafter, S/24859.

87. S/24859, 1; Boutros-Ghali, *Unvanquished*, 57; Drysdale, *Whatever Happened*, 79, 81–82; Drysdale to Hassan Conteh, 22 December 1992.

88. Drysdale, *Whatever Happened*, 77; Boutros-Ghali, *Unvanquished*, 57; Johnston, *Somalia Diary*, 47; S/24859, 2–3.

89. S/24859, 2–3; Johnston, *Somalia Diary*, 63–64; Drysdale, *Whatever Happened*, 77–78.

90. S/24859, 3–4.

91. D. J. Hurley, "Operation Solace," *Australian Defence Force Journal* 104, 1 (February 1994): 32. Lieutenant Colonel Hurley commanded the 1st Battalion/Royal Australian Regiment in Somalia with the UNITAF coalition.

92. S/24859, 5.

93. United Nations, Security Council Resolution 82, S/1501 (25 June 1950), available from https://digitallibrary.un.org/record/112025?ln=en; United Nations, Security Council Resolution 502, S/RES/502 (3 April 1982), available from https://digitallibrary.un.org/record/34455?ln=en; United Nations, Security Council Resolution 678, S/RES/678 (29 November 1990), available from https://digitallibrary.un.org/record/102245?ln=en.

94. United Nations, General Assembly/Security Council, *An Agenda for Peace*, A/47/277-S/24111 (17 June 1992), available from undocs.org/en/A/47/277-S/24111; hereafter, *Agenda for Peace*.

95. *Agenda for Peace*, 1.

96. *Agenda for Peace*, 5; emphasis added. Though formalized in *An Agenda for Peace*, challenging the notion of absolute sovereignty was a long-held view within the UN dating back to the 1950s. See Margot Tudor, *Blue Helmet Bureaucrats: United Nations Peacekeeping and the Reinvention of Colonialism, 1945–1971* (Cambridge: Cambridge University Press, 2023); Brian Drohan, "Retaining Flexibility: Dag Hammarskjöld, the 1958 Summary Study, and the History of UN Peacekeeping," *Global Governance: A Review of Multilateralism and International Organizations* 29, 2 (2023): 119–135.

97. *Agenda for Peace*, 12–13.

98. S/24868, 2–3.

99. S/24868, 4–6; memorandum on the threat to the UN Pakistani Battalion in Mogadishu, GBPL.

100. S/24868, 3.

101. S/24868, 5.

102. Oberdorfer, "Path to Intervention"; Ohls, *Somalia . . . From the Sea*, 66.

103. Ambassador Smith Hempstone, State Department Cable Reference 385838 to Under Secretary of State Frank Wisner, 1 December 1992, folder 1, box 3, ORHC, MCHD.

104. Leslie H. Gelb, "U.S. Forces Should Go to Somalia," *International Her-*

ald Tribune, 20 November 1992; Anderson, *Man Who Tried to Save the World*, 120–127.

105. Frederick C. Cuny, Intertect, Operational Concept Plan 2: Military Intervention in Somalia, 21 November 1992, folder 37, box 5, Cuny Collection.

106. Cuny, Operational Concept Plan 2.

107. State Department discussion paper for the Deputies Committee, "The Need for Action in Somalia," November 1992, National Security Council Meeting Files, NSC/DC 395, GBPL; US Army War College, *Campaign Analysis*, 15.

108. Director of Central Intelligence, "National Intelligence Council Memorandum: Can United Nations Forces Successfully Carry out Their Mission in Somalia?" 10 November 1992, National Security Council Meeting Files, NSC/DC 395, Bush Presidential Records, GBPL; State Department discussion paper, "Need for Action in Somalia."

109. Deputies Committee of the National Security Council, memorandum on the next steps in Somalia, 23 November 1992, National Security Council Meeting Files, NSC/DC 396, Bush Presidential Records, GBPL; Director of Central Intelligence, "Can United Nations Forces Successfully Carry out Their Mission in Somalia?"; memorandum from John Ordway to Jonathan Howe on discussion points for the 20 November 1992 Deputies Committee meeting on Somalia, 19 November 1992, National Security Council Meeting Files, NSC/DC 395, Bush Presidential Records, GBPL; State Department discussion paper, "Need for Action in Somalia"; US Army War College, *Campaign Analysis*, 15.

110. State Department discussion paper, "Need for Action in Somalia"; Cohen, *Intervening in Africa*, 210–211. Wisner had a strong relationship with Boutros-Ghali from his tenure as US ambassador to Egypt.

111. Memorandum from Ordway to Howe.

112. State Department discussion paper, "Need for Action in Somalia."

113. Powell, *My American Journey*, 564.

114. Stefano Recchia, "Pragmatism over Principle: US Intervention and Burden Shifting in Somalia, 1992–1993," *Journal of Strategic Studies* 43, 3 (2018): 342, 355, citing personal interviews with Powell.

115. Deputies Committee, memorandum on next steps in Somalia.

116. Recchia, "Pragmatism over Principle," 349–352; Cohen, *Intervening in Africa*, 212; US Army War College, *Campaign Analysis*, 16–17.

117. Recchia, "Pragmatism over Principle," 353, citing personal interviews with Powell; Brent Scowcroft interview, 10–11 August 2000, 98, George H. W. Bush Presidential History Project, Miller Center, University of Virginia; Boutros-Ghali, *Unvanquished*, 58–59; Powell, *My American Journey*, 565.

118. Clarke, "Failed Visions," 9.

119. U.N. SCOR, 47th sess., 3145th mtg., U.N. Doc. S/PV.3145 (3 December 1992), 7, 19, available from undocs.org/en/S/PV/3145; hereafter, S/PV/3145.

120. United Nations, Security Council Resolution 794, S/RES/794 (3 December 1992), available from https://digitallibrary.un.org/record/154648?ln=en.

121. S/PV/3145, 36–37.

122. Robert G. Patman, *Strategic Shortfall: The Somali Syndrome and the March to 9/11* (Denver: Praeger, 2010), 38. This altruism argument was also made by Thomas H. Henriksen in *America's Wars: Interventions, Regime Change, and Insurgencies after the Cold War* (Cambridge: Cambridge University Press, 2022), 59.

123. See, for example, Lise Morjé Howard, *UN Peacekeeping in Civil Wars* (New York: Cambridge University Press, 2008), 25; Dennis C. Jett, *Why Peacekeeping Fails* (New York: Palgrave, 2001), 30.

124. Matthew A. Baum, "How Public Opinion Constrains the Use of Force: The Case of Operation Restore Hope," *Presidential Studies Quarterly* 34, 2 (June 2004): 204–205.

125. Jon Western and Robert Patman both advanced this Somalia versus Bosnia argument but provided little evidence that it existed. See Jon Western, "Sources of Humanitarian Intervention: Beliefs, Information, and Advocacy in the U.S. Decisions on Somalia and Bosnia," *International Security* 26, 4 (2002): 112–142; Patman, *Strategic Shortfall*, 39.

126. US Army War College, *Campaign Analysis*, 16.

127. Recchia, "Pragmatism over Principle," 356, citing personal interviews with Powell.

128. "Bush Sends Force to Somalia, with Clinton's Support for Mercy Mission," *International Herald Tribune*, 5–6 December 1992.

129. George H. W. Bush, address on Somalia, 4 December 1992, transcript from the Miller Center at the University of Virginia, available from https://millercenter.org/the-presidency/presidential-speeches/december-4-1992-address-somalia.

3. Deploying to the Moon: The Formation and Arrival of the Unified Task Force

1. Joseph P. Hoar, "A CINC's Perspective," *Joint Forces Quarterly* 1, 2 (Autumn 1993): 60.

2. Tom Clancy, Tony Zinni, and Tony Koltz, *Battle Ready* (New York: Berkley Books, 2004), 255.

3. Major General Steven L. Arnold, USA, Commanding General, 10th Mountain Division and Army Forces Somalia, interview by Major Robert K. Wright and Captain Drew R. Meyerowich, 26 February 1993, 13, RHIT-JHT-048, Somalia Oral History Interview Collection, US Army Center of Military History, Washington, DC (SOHIC/USACMH); hereafter, Arnold interview.

4. Daniel P. Bolger, *Savage Peace: Americans at War in the 1990's* (Novato, CA: Presidio Press, 1995), 291.

5. Lieutenant Colonel Heumphreus, 10th Division Support Command, Joint Uniform Lessons Learned System (JULLS) Long Report 11527-80658, 15 January 1993, folder ARFR-005, box 9, Somalia Crisis Collection, US Army Heritage and Education Center, Carlisle, PA (SCC/USAHEC).

6. Major General Charles E. Wilhelm, Commanding General MARFOR Somalia, interview by Lieutenant Colonel Charles H. Curitan and Captain D. A. Dawson, 11 March 1993, 18, transcript in folder 6, box 6, Operation Restore Hope Collection (ORHC), COLL/3708, Archives Branch, Marine Corps History Division, Quantico, VA (MCHD); hereafter, Wilhelm interview.

7. S. L. Arnold, "Somalia: An Operation Other Than War," *Military Review* 73, 12 (December 1993): 29.

8. General Anthony C. Zinni, USMC (retired), interview by the author, 7 February 2020.

9. Colonel James Brian Egan, UNITAF J-3, interview by Lieutenant Colonel Charles Keritan and Major Robert K. Wright, 11 March 1993, 2, transcript in folder 8, box 4, ORHC, MCHD (hereafter, Egan interview); Hoar, "CINC's Perspective," 56; Colonel E. R. Bedard, Commanding Officer RCT-7, interview by Lieutenant Colonel Charles Keritan and Captain D. A. Dawson, 12 March 1993, 2, transcript in folder 4, box 4, ORHC, MCHD; hereafter, Bedard interview.

10. Marine Forces Somalia/I Marine Expeditionary Force, Command Chronology, 7 December 1992–28 February 1993, section 2.3, folder 16, box 2, ORHC, MCHD (hereafter, MARFOR Command Chronology); Lieutenant General Robert B. Johnston, Commanding General UNITAF, interview by Lieutenant Colonel Charles H. Cureton and Major Robert K. Wright, 16 March 1993, 61, RHIT-JHT-085, SOHIC/USACMH; hereafter, Johnston interview.

11. General Anthony C. Zinni, USMC (retired), interview by the author, 20 December 2019; Johnston interview, 30.

12. Office of the White House Press Secretary, press release on the nomination of Robert B. Oakley as US Ambassador to Pakistan, 18 August 1988, folder 29, box 4, Robert B. Oakley Collection, Coll 437, Northwest Louisiana Archives, Noel Memorial Library, Louisiana State University, Shreveport; Robert B. Oakley, interview by Charles Stuart Kennedy and Thomas Stern, 7 July 1992, 155, Association for Diplomatic Studies and Training Foreign Affairs Oral History Project, transcript available at https://www.loc.gov/item/mfdipbib000876/.

13. Boutros Boutros-Ghali, *Unvanquished: A US-UN Saga* (New York: Random House, 1999), 105.

14. Boutros Boutros-Ghali, UN Secretary-General, Letter to President George H. W. Bush, 8 December 1992, in United Nations, *The United Nations and Somalia, 1992–1996* (New York: UN Department of Public Information, 1996), 216–217.

15. US Army War College, *Campaign Analysis Course Case Study: Somalia* (Car-

lisle, PA: US Army War College, Department of Military Strategy, Planning, and Operations, 2005), 22–24.

16. Brian R. Sullivan, Institute for National Security Studies Report on Somalia, sent to General Gordon R. Sullivan by Lieutenant General Paul G. Cerjan, 22 December 1992, folder 2, box 117, Gordon R. Sullivan Papers (GRSP), USAHEC; hereafter, Sullivan report.

17. US Army War College, *Campaign Analysis*, 24.

18. Zinni interview, 20 December 2019.

19. F. M. Lorenz, "Law and Anarchy in Somalia," *Parameters* 23, 4 (Winter 1993–94): 28.

20. Hoar, "CINC's Perspective," 58.

21. Zinni interview, 20 December 2019.

22. Hoar, "CINC's Perspective," 58 (emphasis added); US Army War College, *Campaign Analysis*, 24.

23. Robert F. Baumann, Lawrence A. Yates, and Versalle F. Washington, *"My Clan against the World": US and Coalition Forces in Somalia 1992–1994* (Fort Leavenworth, KS: Combat Studies Institute Press, 2004), 26.

24. MARFOR Command Chronology, section 2.20.

25. Johnston interview, 58–59.

26. Zinni interview, 20 December 2019.

27. Arnold, "Somalia: Operation Other Than War," 28–29.

28. 10th Mountain Division, Report on Deployment Issues from Restore Hope, n.d., 2, folder INFO-002, box 10, SCC/USAHEC.

29. Kevin M. Kennedy, "The Relationship between the Military and the Humanitarian Organizations in Operation Restore Hope," in *Learning from Somalia: The Lessons of Armed Humanitarian Intervention*, ed. Walter Clarke and Jeffrey Herbst (Boulder, CO: Westview Press, 1997), 100.

30. Frederick C. Cuny, Intertect, Operational Concept Plan 2: Military Intervention in Somalia, 21 November 1992, folder 37, box 5, Frederick C. Cuny Collection, Cushing Library, Texas A&M University.

31. MARFOR Command Chronology, section 2.3; Egan interview, 25–28.

32. Lieutenant Colonel Meyer, JULLS Long Report 11442-06430, 15 January 1993, folder OBS-006, box 2, SCC/USAHEC; Arnold interview, 14.

33. John L. Hirsch and Robert B. Oakley, *Somalia and Operation Restore Hope: Reflections on Peacemaking and Peacekeeping* (Washington, DC: Institute of Peace Press, 1995), 65.

34. Combined Arms Assessment Team Somalia, Operation Restore Hope Lessons Learned draft, n.d., 11, folder AAR-004, box 1, SCC/USAHEC.

35. MARFOR Command Chronology, section 2.3.

36. Baumann, Yates, and Washington, *"My Clan,"* 29–30.

37. Headquarters, Military Sealift Command, Operation Restore Hope Historical Chronology, 30 November–18 December 1992, folder 1, box 1, Joint

History Team Somalia Collection (JHT), USACMH; Third Army/USARCENT Somalia Relief Chronology Briefing, 10 February 1993, folder BRF-012, box 6, SCC/USAHEC.

38. Press briefing on Operation Restore Hope by US Secretary of Defense Richard B. Cheney and Chairman of the Joint Chiefs of Staff General Colin Powell, 4 December 1992, folder 2, box 1, Operation Restore Hope Press Releases Collection, USACMH.

39. Hoar, "CINC's Perspective," 60; Operation Restore Hope, Roster of Personnel, circa 2007, OCLC 68859171, USAHEC; Joint Task Force Support Command Mission Briefing, 21 January 1993, folder BRF-009, box 6, SCC/USAHEC; Joint Task Force Somalia, Somalia Force List, 4 January 1993, folder 36, box 1, ORHC, MCHD.

40. Clancy, Zinni, and Koltz, *Battle Ready,* 254–255.

41. Hoar, "CINC's Perspective," 62; Waldo D. Freeman, Robert B. Lambert, and Jason D. Mims, "Operation Restore Hope: A US CENTCOM Perspective," *Military Review* 73, 9 (September 1993): 69.

42. Allen G. Sens, *Somalia and the Changing Nature of Peacekeeping: The Implications for Canada; a Study Prepared for the Commission of Inquiry into the Deployment of Canadian Forces to Somalia* (Ottawa: Ministry of Public Works and Government Services, 1997), 103–105; Colonel Richard T. Strickland, "Crisis to Catalyst: The Strategic Effects of the Somalia Affair on the Canadian Armed Forces" (master's thesis, School of Advanced Military Studies, US Army Command and General Staff College, 2017), 8, https://cgsc.contentdm.oclc.org/digital/collection/p4013coll3/id/3665/rec/1.

43. John Connor, "Intervention and Domestic Politics," in *Australian Peacekeeping: Sixty Years in the Field,* ed. David Horner, Peter Londey, and Jean Bou (Melbourne: Cambridge University Press, 2009), 75; Bob Breen, *A Little Bit of Hope: Australian Force Somalia* (St. Leonard's, NSW: Allen & Unwin, 1998), 21–29.

44. Statement by the Prime Minister, the Honorable P. J. Keating, on the commitment of Australian forces to Somalia, 15 December 1992, folder 2, box 117, GRSP, USAHEC.

45. Letter from Lieutenant General John C. Grey to General Gordon R. Sullivan, 15 December 1992, folder 2, box 117, GRSP, USAHEC.

46. Alan Riding, "Somalia Stirs French Opposition," *International Herald Tribune,* 10 December 1992.

47. Egan interview, 30; MARFOR Command Chronology, section 2.3; Piero Ignazi, Giampiero Giacomello, and Fabrizio Coticchia, *Italian Military Operations Abroad: Just Don't Call It War* (New York: Palgrave Macmillan, 2012), 96–102; Colonel Wallace S. Grayson, UNITAF Deputy J-3, interview by Lieutenant Colonel Charles Keritan and Major Robert K. Wright, 13 March 1993, 26, transcript in folder 10, box 4, ORHC, MCHD; hereafter, Grayson interview.

48. Grayson interview, 26; United Nations, Security Council, Letter dated 19 February 1993 from Ambassador Mohammad Abulhasan, Permanent Representative of Kuwait Addressed to the President of the Security Council, S/25312 (19 February 1993), available from undocs.org/en/S/25312; Joint Task Force Somalia, Somalia Force List, 4 January 1993.

49. Satish Nambiar, *For the Honour of India: A History of Indian Peacekeeping* (New Delhi: Centre for Armed Forces Historical Research, United Service Institution of India, 2009), 262; Joint Task Force Somalia, Somalia Force List, 4 January 1993.

50. Andrew Hill, "Western Planes Swoop over Mogadishu," Reuters, 7 December 1992, box 104, Cuny Collection.

51. Captain John Peterson, Commander PHIBRON 3, interview by Dr. John Partin, 18 June 1993, 5-6, transcript in folder 16, box 5, ORHC, MCHD; hereafter, Peterson interview.

52. Peterson interview, 12-14.

53. MARFOR Command Chronology, section 2.3.

54. Hirsch and Oakley, *Somalia and Operation Restore Hope*, 54.

55. Jonathan Clayton, "Somali Warlord Pledges No Resistance to U.N. Force," Reuters, 8 December 1992, box 104, Cuny Collection; Hirsch and Oakley, *Somalia and Operation Restore Hope*, 46, 54.

56. General Gordon R. Sullivan, memorandum to commanding officers, 4 December 1992, box 117, GRSP, USAHEC.

57. Hirsch and Oakley, *Somalia and Operation Restore Hope*, 54.

58. Colonel R. B. McKittrick, I MEF G-3, memorandum on statistical data for Operation Restore Hope, 29 July 1993, folder 5, box 1, James B. Egan Papers, COLL/5672, MCHD.

59. Peterson interview, 12-14.

60. Donatella Lorch, "Lights, Camera and . . . Land 'Em," *International Herald Tribune*, 10 December 1992.

61. Lorch.

62. Captain John Peterson, USN, quoted in Gary J. Ohls, *Somalia . . . From the Sea* (Newport, RI: Naval War College Press, 2009), 87.

63. Alan Riding, "Somalia Stirs French Opposition," *International Herald Tribune*, 10 December 1992.

64. Colonel Gregory Newbold, Commanding Officer 15th MEU, interview by Captain D. A. Dawson, 13 January 1993, 15-17, transcript in folder 13, box 5, ORHC, MCHD; hereafter, Newbold interview.

65. Philip Johnston, *Somalia Diary* (Atlanta: Longstreet Press, 1994), 74.

66. Newbold interview, 15-17.

67. McKittrick, memorandum on statistical data for Operation Restore Hope; Ohls, *Somalia . . . From the Sea*, 100; Hirsch and Oakley, *Somalia and Operation Restore Hope*, 59.

68. Clancy, Zinni, and Koltz, *Battle Ready*, 245.

69. Ismat Kittani, Cable to Marrack Goulding, 11 December 1992, S-1000-0024-02, AG-024, United Nations Archives, New York.

70. Hirsch and Oakley, *Somalia and Operation Restore Hope*, 55–57.

71. Hirsch and Oakley, 55–57; General Anthony C. Zinni, USMC (retired), interview by the author, 1 May 2020; UNITAF J-3 Command Operations Center Log, 17 December 1992, folder 7, box 4, JHT, USACMH.

72. Baumann, Yates, and Washington, *"My Clan,"* 48.

73. UNITAF J-3 Command Operations Center Log, 11 December 1992; Freeman, Lambert, and Mims, "Operation Restore Hope," 64.

74. Baumann, Yates, and Washington, *"My Clan,"* 43.

75. Martin Stanton, *Somalia on Five Dollars a Day: A Soldier's Story* (Novato, CA: Presidio, 2001), 81.

76. MARFOR Command Chronology, section 2.3; UNITAF J-3 Command Operations Center Log, 13 December 1992; Newbold interview, 19–22.

77. MARFOR Command Chronology, section 2.4.

78. Newbold interview, 19–22; MARFOR Command Chronology, section 2.3, 24–25.

79. Tony Zinni and Tony Koltz, *The Battle for Peace: A Frontline Vision of America's Power and Purpose* (New York: Palgrave Macmillan, 2006), 101.

80. Zinni and Koltz, 105.

81. Corporal Brian M. Keltner, "Somalia: A Portrait," unpublished personal diary, n.d., folder 104, box 1A22, Personal Papers Collection (PPC), MCHD.

82. Benjamin C. McGraw, daily diary of Operation Restore Hope, entries for 18 and 22 December 1992, folder 5B15, PPC, MCHD; emphasis added.

83. Egan interview, 30–31.

84. Newbold interview, 19–22.

85. Grayson interview, 17.

86. MARFOR Command Chronology, section 2.3; Egan interview, 23.

87. Johnston interview, 16.

88. Major R. Boatman, Combined Arms Assessment Team, script for deployment operations video—Somalia, n.d., folder AAR-004, box 1, SCC/USA-HEC.

89. Martin N. Stanton, "Operational Considerations for Sub-Saharan Africa," *Infantry* 86, 5 (October 1996): 29.

90. Waldo D. Freeman, "Operation Restore Hope: A Logistical Challenge," *Field Artillery* (June 1993): 6.

91. Colonel Ray Cole, MARFOR G-3, interview by Captain D. A. Dawson, 23 January 1993, 21, transcript in folder 1, box 4, ORHC, MCHD; hereafter, Cole interview.

92. Egan interview, 30–31.

93. Hoar, "CINC's Perspective," 60; emphasis added.

94. Boatman, script for deployment operations video; Peterson interview, 19–20.

95. Restore Hope Lessons Learned draft, 35, 43; Major Boatman, JULLS Long Report 11937-95994, 19 January 1993, folder OBS-006, box 2, SCC/USAHEC.

96. Heumphreus, JULLS Long Report 11527-80658.

97. Restore Hope Lessons Learned draft, 43.

98. Boatman, script for deployment operations video.

99. Jean Bou, Bob Breen, David Horner, Garth Pratten, and Miesje De Vogel, *The Official History of Australian Peacekeeping, Humanitarian and Post–Cold War Operations*, vol. 4, *The Limits of Peacekeeping, Australian Missions in Africa and the Americas, 1992–2005* (Port Melbourne: Cambridge University Press, 2019), 171.

100. Message 3651632 from 463rd TALCE to Air Mobility Element Somalia, n.d., folder 10, box 1, JHT, USACMH; Master Sergeant G. R. Mays, MCLLS Long Report 23043-17868, 29 January 1993, folder 17, box 2, ORHC, MCHD; Colonel Walter S. Evans, UNITAF Director of Mobility Forces, memorandum on operations at Mogadishu airport, 31 December 1992, folder 10, box 1, JHT, USACMH.

101. Colonel William T. Johnson, MWSS 372, interview by Captain D. A. Dawson, 1 February 1993, 14, 18, transcript in folder 5, box 5, ORHC, MCHD (hereafter, Johnson interview); Wilhelm interview, 11; Colonel John J. Holly, MARFOR G-3, interview by Captain D. A. Dawson, 29 January and 21 February 1993, 34–35, transcript in folder 2, box 4, ORHC, MCHD; hereafter, Holly interview.

102. Major McWethy, ARFOR G3, JULLS Long Report 02553-20561, 21 January 1993, folder ARFR-018, box 9, SCC/USAHEC.

103. Katherine A. W. McGrady, *The Joint Task Force in Operation Restore Hope* (Alexandria, VA: Center for Naval Analyses, 1994), 33.

104. Hirsch and Oakley, *Somalia and Operation Restore Hope*, 59; US Air Force Somalia, Mogadishu Airport Total Operations Count, 3 February 1993, folder 1, box 2, JHT, USACMH.

105. Restore Hope Lessons Learned draft, 12–13.

106. Task Force Mountain briefing slides, 2 March 1993, box 121, GRSP, USAHEC; Arnold interview, 7.

107. Restore Hope Lessons Learned draft, 62–64; Holly interview, 34–35; Lieutenant Colonel Power, JULLS Long Report 11519-27835, 10 January 1993, folder OBS-006, box 2, SCC/USAHEC.

108. Johnson interview, 11–12.

109. Major Clark, Army Medical Department, Center, and School, JULLS Long Report 11914-10882, 19 January 1993, folder OBS-020, box 4, SCC/USAHEC.

110. Restore Hope Lessons Learned draft, 66–68; Lieutenant Colonel Wegmann, JULLS Long Report 12548-43071, 25 January 1993, folder OBS-019, box 4, SCC/USAHEC; Lieutenant Colonel Kapinos, JULLS Long Report 03016-98334, 15 January 1993, folder ARFR-008, box 9, SCC/USAHEC.

111. Restore Hope Lessons Learned draft, 15–16; Boatman, script for deployment operations video; Headquarters, Military Sealift Command, Operation Restore Hope Historical Chronology; McGrady, *Joint Task Force*, 39.

112. Holly interview, 12–13; McGrady, *Joint Task Force*, 43.

113. Boatman, JULLS Long Report 11937-95994.

114. Briefing on MARFOR to Joint Task Force Support Command Transition, n.d., folder BRF-006, box 6, SCC/USAHEC; Major Walter J. Leitmeyer, USMC, interview by Major Robert K. Wright and Captain D. A. Dawson, 13 February 1993, 7, transcript in folder 8, box 5, ORHC/MCHD; hereafter, Leitmeyer interview.

115. Major Boatman, CALL, JULLS Long Report 11606-89748, 16 January 1993, folder OBS-006, box 2, SCC/USAHEC; Lieutenant Colonel Power, CALL, JULLS Long Report 12423-17355, 10 January 1993, folder OBS-006, box 2, SCC/USAHEC.

116. Holly interview, 36–37.

117. Major Stahl, JULLS Long Report 10117-10742, 14 January 1993, folder ARFR-003, box 9, SCC/USAHEC; McGrady, *Joint Task Force*, 54; Lieutenant Colonel Dressel, JULLS Long Report 30135-67597, 27 February 1993, folder ARFR-028, box 9, SCC/USAHEC; Restore Hope Lessons Learned draft, 62.

118. Third Army/USARCENT Somalia Relief Chronology Briefing; Major Stahl, JULLS Long Report 10712-67477, 22 March 1993, folder ARFR-002, box 9, SCC/USAHEC; Stanton, *Somalia on Five Dollars*, 73.

119. Colonel James S. Gavitt, memorandum to the Chief of Staff, 10th Mountain Division, 8 December 1992, folder 8, box 3, Kevin M. Born Papers (KBP), USAHEC.

120. S. L. Arnold and David T. Stahl, "A Power Projection Army in Operations Other Than War," *Parameters* 23, 4 (Winter 1993–94): 12; Stanton, *Somalia on Five Dollars*, 73; Arnold interview, 7; McGrady, *Joint Task Force*, 34–37.

121. Holly interview, 27.

122. ARFOR G3, JULLS Long Report 12161-25098, 21 January 1993, folder ARFR-019, box 9, SCC/USAHEC.

123. Restore Hope Lessons Learned draft, 12–16; McGrady, *Joint Task Force*, 34–37.

124. Boatman, JULLS Long Report 11937-95994; 1st Forward Service Support Group, draft report on lessons learned during Operation Restore Hope, "Runway Expansion and Repair," n.d., folder 8, box 3, ORHC, MCHD; Lieutenant Colonel Gary L. Holmquist, Commanding Officer 1st Combat Engineer

Battalion, interview by Captain D. A. Dawson, 30 January 1993, 4–5, transcript in folder 12, box 4, ORHC, MCHD; Lieutenant Hall, 36th Engineer Group, JULLS Long Report 21274-60007, 16 January 1993, folder ARFR-012, box 9, SCC/USAHEC; Captain Blackman, JULLS Long Report 03002-29418, 15 January 1993, folder ARFR-007, box 9, SCC/USAHEC.

125. Leonard J. Sly, "62nd Medical Group's Deployment to Somalia" (personal experience monograph, US Army War College, 1995), 3–10, 21–33, 40–51, OCLC 49945811, US Army War College Student Papers Collection, USAHEC.

126. McGrady, *Joint Task Force*, 37.

127. Keltner, "Somalia: A Portrait."

128. Lieutenant Colonel Daniel Spurlock, Commanding Officer HMH 363, interview by Captain D. A. Dawson, 1 February 1993, 10, transcript in folder 3, box 5, ORHC, MCHD.

129. Zinni interview, 1 May 2020.

130. Leitmeyer interview, 9–10; Marine Forces Somalia/I Marine Expeditionary Force, Command Chronology, 1 March–30 April 1993, section 1.5, supplied to the author by Archives Branch, MCHD.

131. Coalition Forces Support and Coordination Team, n.d., folder DRPT-020, box 7, SCC/USAHEC.

132. Leitmeyer interview, 5–6.

133. Zinni interview, 1 May 2020.

134. Fax from Robert B. Johnston to Gordon Rudd, 24 May 2002, Gordon Rudd Papers, supplied to the author; Cole interview, 12.

135. Leitmeyer interview, 26.

136. Major Patrick, JULLS Long Report 12055-81418, 20 January 1993, folder ARFR-014, box 9, SCC/USAHEC.

137. Leitmeyer interview, 9–10, 25–33.

138. ARFOR Executive Summary, Operation Restore Hope, Integration of Coalition Forces, 1 March 1993, folder DRPT-028, box 7, SCC/USAHEC.

139. UNITAF J-3 Command Operations Center Log, 20 December 1992; 10th Mountain Division Artillery, Report on Combined Task Force Kismayo, n.d., folder AAR-005, box 1, SCC/USAHEC; MARFOR Command Chronology, section 2.4.

140. MARFOR Command Chronology, section 2.5.

141. Bedard interview, 13–20, 27.

142. MARFOR Command Chronology, section 2.5; Johnston interview, 16.

143. Sens, *Somalia and the Changing Nature of Peacekeeping*, 106; account of Chief Warrant Officer Bud Jardine, Regimental Sergeant Major, Canadian Airborne Battle Group, in Ron Pupetz, *In the Line of Duty: Canadian Joint Forces Somalia, 1992–1993* (St. Catherine's, ON: Vanwell, 2001), 212; Arnold, "Somalia: Operation Other Than War," 32.

144. Stanton, *Somalia on Five Dollars*, 100-103.

145. McGrady, *Joint Task Force*, 24.

146. ARFOR Significant Acts Chronology, 23 December 1992-7 June 1993, folder 4, box 3, KBP, USAHEC; Breen, *Little Bit of Hope*, 43, 64, 72-74.

147. Report on Humanitarian Relief Sector Populations, 9 January 1993, folder 23, box 2, ORHC, MCHD.

148. UNITAF J-3 Command Operations Center Log, 31 December 1992 entry.

149. UNITAF J-3 Command Operations Center Log, 2 January 1992 entry; Clancy, Zinni, and Koltz, *Battle Ready*, 268.

4. Pacification, Presence, and Overwhelming Force: Securing Somalia

1. Colonel Jack W. Klimp, Commander, Task Force Mogadishu, interview by Captain D. A. Dawson, 11 and 25 January 1993, 47, transcript in folder 7, box 5, Operation Restore Hope Collection (ORHC), COLL/3708, Archives Branch, Marine Corps History Division, Quantico, VA (MCHD); hereafter, Klimp interview.

2. Robert B. Oakley quoted in George J. Church and Ann Blackman, "Mission Half Accomplished," *Time*, May 17, 1993.

3. Klimp interview, 1.

4. Keith B. Richburg, *Out of Africa: A Black Man Confronts Africa* (San Diego, CA: Harcourt Brace, 1998), 73.

5. Marine Forces Somalia/I Marine Expeditionary Force, Command Chronology, 7 December 1992-28 February 1993, section 2.6. folder 16, box 2, ORHC, MCHD; hereafter, MARFOR Command Chronology.

6. Major General Charles E. Wilhelm, Commanding General MARFOR Somalia, interview by Lieutenant Colonel Charles H. Curitan and Captain D. A. Dawson, 11 March 1993, 30-32, transcript in folder 6, box 6, ORHC, MCHD; hereafter, Wilhelm interview.

7. Colonel Jeffrey E. Schefferman, MARFOR G-2, interview by Captain D. A. Dawson, 21 January 1993, 8, transcript in folder 18, box 5, ORHC, MCHD.

8. MARFOR Command Chronology, section 2.6; Robert F. Baumann, Lawrence A. Yates, and Versalle F. Washington, *"My Clan against the World": US and Coalition Forces in Somalia 1992-1994* (Fort Leavenworth, KS: Combat Studies Institute Press, 2004), 67.

9. MARFOR Command Chronology, section 2.6.

10. Klimp interview, 1.

11. Commander MARFOR Somalia, Fragmentary Order 15 to Operation Order 2-92 (Operation Restore Hope), 8 January 1993, folder 2, box 1, ORHC, MCHD; emphasis added.

12. Task Force Mogadishu also included C Company, 1st Battalion/7th Marines, and Reconnaissance Company, 5th Marines. Colonel Jack W. Klimp, Task Force Mogadishu Command Chronology, 21 December 1992–22 January 1993, 3 February 1993, 1–2, folder 1, box 1, ORHC, MCHD (hereafter, TF Mogadishu Command Chronology); Task Force Mogadishu, S1 Overview Summary, n.d., folder 18, box 1, ORHC, MCHD; Captain M. O. Hewett, Task Force Mogadishu, S4 Overview Summary, 25 January 1993, folder 18, box 1, ORHC, MCHD.

13. TF Mogadishu Command Chronology, section 2.2.

14. Hewett, S4 Overview Summary; TF Mogadishu Command Chronology, section 2.4.

15. Colonel J. W. Klimp, memorandum on Task Force Mogadishu after-action report, 31 January 1993, 3, folder 32, box 1, ORHC, MCHD; Major General Charles Wilhelm, Operational Situation Report, 14 January 1993, folder 6, box 1, ORHC, MCHD.

16. Task Force Mogadishu, Commanders Patrol Guidance, 14 January 1993, folder 27, box 1, ORHC, MCHD; Captain Robert S. Abbott, 3rd Light Armored Infantry, interview by Captain D. A. Dawson, 17 September 1993, 65, transcript in folder 3, box 4, ORHC, MCHD; hereafter, Abbott interview.

17. Major MacIntyre, 3rd Amphibious Assault Battalion, Unit Operations Overview, 21 January 1993, folder 22, box 1, ORHC, MCHD; Klimp, memorandum on Task Force Mogadishu after-action report, 8.

18. Wilhelm interview, 34; Captain Greg Saroka, Task Force Mogadishu S2 Overview Summary, 24 January 1993, folder 18, box 1, ORHC, MCHD.

19. Mr. L. Aldrich, JULLS Long Report 33338-67600, 3 March 1993, folder OBS-015, box 4, Somalia Crisis Collection (SCC), US Army Heritage and Education Center, Carlisle, PA (USAHEC); Chief Warrant Officer 3 G. Leopold, JULLS Long Report 33337-42900, 3 March 1993, folder OBS-015, box 4, SCC/USAHEC.

20. General Anthony C. Zinni, USMC (retired), interview by the author, 7 February 2020.

21. Lieutenant Colonel Edward J. Lesnowicz, interview by Major Robert K. Wright and Captain D. A. Dawson, 13 February 1993, 54, transcript in folder 15, box 5, ORHC, MCHD (hereafter, Lesnowicz interview); Commander MARFOR Somalia, Fragmentary Order 11 to Operation Order 2-92 (Operation Restore Hope), 5 January 1993, folder 2, box 1, ORHC, MCHD.

22. Lesnowicz interview, 20, 40–41; Task Force Mogadishu, handwritten situation report, 9 January 1993, folder 7, box 1, ORHC, MCHD; 3rd Light Armored Infantry Battalion, Daily Sitrep to TF Mogadishu, 14 January 1993, folder 7, box 1, ORHC, MCHD; Lieutenant Colonel Tarik Salem Malik, 6th Battalion, Punjab Regiment, Pakistani Army, interview by Captain David Dawson and Major Robert Wright, 13 March 1993, 13, JHT-RHIT-088, Somalia Oral

History Interview Collection, US Army Center of Military History (SOHIC/US-ACMH); Lieutenant Colonel Samir Heikal and Major Khalid, Egyptian Army, interview by Captain David Dawson and Major Robert Wright, 23 February 1993, 5–7, JHT-RHIT-042, SOHIC/USACMH; Lieutenant Colonel Olagunsoye Oyinlola, 245 Reconnaissance Battalion, Nigerian Army, interview by Captain David Dawson and Major Robert Wright, 4 March 1993, 2, 7, JHT-RHIT-056, SOHIC/USACMH.

23. 3rd Battalion, 11th Marine Regiment, Fragmentary Order 7-93, 11 January 1993, folder 4, box 1, ORHC, MCHD; 3rd Battalion, 11th Marine Regiment, Fragmentary Order 5-93, 9 January 1993, folder 4, box 1, ORHC, MCHD.

24. Task Force Mogadishu, Analysis of Possible Reasons for Attacks upon U.S. Marines Operating in Mogadishu, 14 January 1993, folder 30, box 1, ORHC, MCHD; Abbott interview, 56–58; Lieutenant Colonel Michael W. Sullivan, 3rd Amphibious Assault Battalion, interview by Captain D. A. Dawson, 17 February 1993, 5–6, transcript in folder 2, box 6, ORHC, MCHD (hereafter, Sullivan interview); Task Force Mogadishu, Chronological Listing of Action, January 1993, folder 19, box 1, ORHC, MCHD.

25. Tom Clancy, Tony Zinni, and Tony Koltz, *Battle Ready* (New York: Berkley Books, 2004), 257.

26. TF Mogadishu Command Chronology, sections 2.5, 3.8; Staff Sergeant R. T. Boretti, handwritten report on the 12 January 1993 engagement in Mogadishu in which PFC Arroyo was killed, folder 3, box 1, ORHC, MCHD; Reconnaissance Company, 5th Marine Regiment, Summary of Events, January 1993, 21 January 1993, folder 23, box 1, ORHC, MCHD.

27. Leonard J. Sly, "62nd Medical Group's Deployment to Somalia" (personal experience monograph, US Army War College, 1995), 121, OCLC 49945811, US Army War College Student Papers Collection, USAHEC; MARFOR Command Chronology, section 2.13.

28. Sly, "62nd Medical Group's Deployment," 102, 111.

29. MARFOR Command Chronology, section 2.13.

30. 3rd Battalion, 11th Marine Regiment, handwritten situation report, 14 January 1993, folder 7, box 1, ORHC, MCHD; Lesnowicz interview, 66.

31. Lesnowicz interview, 19–20.

32. Colonel Fred Peck, press briefing, 22 February 1993, folder 14, box 3, Joint History Team Somalia Collection (JHT), USACMH.

33. Colonel Fred Peck, press briefing, 10 February 1993, folder 14, box 3, JHT, USACMH.

34. Major Ken Roberts, press briefing, 16 February 1993, folder 14, box 3, JHT, USACMH; emphasis added.

35. Richburg, *Out of Africa*, 70–71.

36. Major F. D. Houston, Memorandum for the Record: Minutes of Local Elders Meeting, 12 January 1993, folder 9, box 1, ORHC, MCHD.

37. Captain B. T. Wright, Memorandum for the Record: Minutes of Local Elders Meeting, 14 January 1993, folder 9, box 1, ORHC, MCHD.

38. Task Force Mogadishu, Situation Report, 6 January 1993, folder 3, box 1, ORHC, MCHD.

39. Task Force Mogadishu, Situation Report, 16 January 1993, folder 3, box 1, ORHC, MCHD; 3rd Light Armored Infantry Battalion, Daily Sitrep to TF Mogadishu, 17 January 1993, folder 7, box 1, ORHC, MCHD; Task Force Mogadishu, handwritten situation report, 9 and 11 January 1993, folder 7, box 1, ORHC, MCHD; Benjamin C. McGraw, Daily Diary of Operation Restore Hope, 15 December 1992, folder 5B15, Personal Papers Collection (PPC), MCHD; Martin Stanton, *Somalia on Five Dollars a Day: A Soldier's Story* (Novato, CA: Presidio, 2001), 138, 148. Stanton served as the operations officer for the US Army's 2nd Battalion, 87th Infantry Regiment, in HRS Merka.

40. Bob Breen, *A Little Bit of Hope: Australian Force Somalia* (St. Leonard's, NSW: Allen & Unwin, 1998), 150; UNITAF J-3 Command Operations Center Log, 15 December 1992, folder 7, box 4, JHT, USACMH.

41. G. Peterson, "Human Intelligence and Somalia—A Cost Effective Winner for a Small Army," *Australian Defence Force Journal* 104, 1 (1994): 38; John L. Hirsch and Robert B. Oakley, *Somalia and Operation Restore Hope: Reflections on Peacemaking and Peacekeeping* (Washington, DC: Institute of Peace Press, 1995), 50; Staff Sergeant Cindy Killion, press release, "Bero Method," 21 January 1993, folder 10, box 3, Kevin M. Born Papers (KBP), USAHEC.

42. Major Walter J. Leitmeyer, interview by Major Robert K. Wright and Captain D. A. Dawson, 13 February 1993, 13, transcript in folder 8, box 5, ORHC, MCHD.

43. UNITAF, Psychological Operations Media Assessment, n.d., folder 9, box 2, JHT, USACMH.

44. UNITAF, Psychological Operations Concept Briefing, 9 January 1993, folder 4, box 2, JHT, USACMH; Hirsch and Oakley, *Somalia and Operation Restore Hope*, 62.

45. UNITAF, Psychological Operations Media Assessment.

46. UNITAF, *Rajo* articles, January 1993, folder 4, box 2, JHT, USACMH; David Evans, "Calvin and Hobbes, Somali Style," *Chicago Tribune*, 29 December 1992.

47. Colonel William T. Johnson, interview by Captain D. A. Dawson, 1 February 1993, 25, transcript in folder 5, box 5, ORHC, MCHD.

48. Sly, "62nd Medical Group's Deployment," 134.

49. Staff Sergeant Cindy Killion, press release, untitled, n.d. folder 10, box 3, KBP, USAHEC.

50. Laura L. Miller and Charles Moskos, "Humanitarians or Warriors? Race, Gender, and Combat Status in Operation Restore Hope," *Armed Forces & Society* 21, 4 (Summer 1995): 615–637.

51. Susan Ferriss, "Marines Apprehensive About Expedition to Somalia," *San Francisco Examiner*, 7 December 1992.

52. Gary Lee, "For Some GI's, a Personal Mission," *International Herald Tribune*, 10 December 1992.

53. Barton Gellman, "Military's Relief Role Questioned," *Washington Post*, 8 December 1992.

54. Corporal Brian M. Keltner, "Somalia: A Portrait," unpublished personal diary, n.d., 11, folder 104, box 1A22, PPC, MCHD.

55. Lieutenant Andrew R. Milburn, memorandum to the commanding office of Weapons Company, Battalion Landing Team 2/9, on lessons learned in Operation Restore Hope, 11 January 1993, folder 5B15, PPC, MCHD.

56. MARFOR Command Chronology, section 2.10.

57. Sly, "62nd Medical Group's Deployment," 114.

58. F. M. Lorenz, "Law and Anarchy in Somalia," *Parameters* 23, 4 (Winter 1993–94): 33; UNITAF J-3 Operations, Spot Report 77, 4 February 1993, folder 14, box 3, JHT, USACMH. Lorenz was the staff judge advocate in UNITAF headquarters.

59. Baumann, Yates, and Washington, *"My Clan,"* 68.

60. Task Force Mogadishu, handwritten situation report, 9 January 1993.

61. Stanton, *Somalia on Five Dollars*, 147.

62. Breen, *Little Bit of Hope*, 107.

63. Lorenz, "Law and Anarchy," 33; UNITAF J-3 Operations, Spot Report 77, 4 February 1993; Clancy, Zinni, and Koltz, *Battle Ready*, 266.

64. Baumann, Yates, and Washington, *"My Clan,"* 69.

65. Sly, "62nd Medical Group's Deployment," 82.

66. Clancy, Zinni, and Koltz, *Battle Ready*, 266–267.

67. Abbott interview, 21.

68. Operation Restore Hope Operational Chronology, folder 4, box 159, Warfighting Development Integration Division Collection, MCHD.

69. Letter from Colonel J. S. Labbe, Commander, Canadian Forces Somalia, to UNITAF Headquarters, 23 April 1993, folder 2, box 1, James B. Egan Papers (JEP), COLL/5672, MCHD.

70. *Dishonored Legacy: The Lessons of the Somalia Affair; Report of the Commission of Inquiry into the Deployment of Canadian Forces to Somalia*, vol.1 (Ottawa: Commission of Inquiry into the Deployment of Canadian Forces to Somalia, 1997), 183–185, 194–197.

71. "2 Italian Generals Resign over Somali Scandal," *Tampa Bay Times*, 15 June 1997.

72. Raf Casert, "In Italy, Belgium, and Canada, Somalia Peacekeeping Scandals Growing," Reuters, 23 June 1997.

73. MARFOR Command Chronology, section 2.10.

74. Headquarters, 2nd Brigade, 10th Mountain Division, draft Lessons

Learned Report, 16 January 1993, folder DRPT-003, box 7, SCC/USAHEC; Lieutenant Colonel Paul D. Eaton, Incident Report of Investigation, n.d., folder DRPT-003, box 7, SCC/USAHEC.

75. TF Mogadishu Command Chronology, sections 2.5–2.6.

76. Dr. Robert D. Campbell, Matrix Corporation, Preliminary Report: Analysis of the Marine Pacification System, 19 April 1968, 5, folder 1, box 170, Studies and Reports Collection (S&R), COLL/3746, MCHD.

77. Bruce C. Allnutt, *Constabulary Capabilities of the United States Marine Corps: The Counterinsurgency Mission*, vol. 1, *The CAP Experience in Vietnam*, report by Human Sciences Research, December 1969, iii, folder 6, box 171, S&R, MCHD.

78. Allnutt, 8, 20.

79. Allnutt, 45–46.

80. Joseph C. Story and Herbert H. Vreeland III, *Implementation of the Marine Combined Action Concept in Future Contingencies*, report by Human Sciences Research, November 1971, 84–87, 153, folder 8, box 173, S&R, MCHD.

81. TF Mogadishu Command Chronology, section 3.8.

82. TF Mogadishu Command Chronology, section 2.6; MARFOR Command Chronology, section 2.11.

83. Abbott interview, 68, 99.

84. Abbott interview, 80–81.

85. Abbott interview, 85–87.

86. Lesnowicz interview, 62.

87. Lesnowicz interview, 58–60.

88. MARFOR Command Chronology, section 2.11

89. Klimp interview, 47.

90. Hirsch and Oakley, *Somalia and Operation Restore Hope*, 81.

91. Task Force Mogadishu, handwritten situation report, 22 January 1993, folder 3, box 1, ORHC, MCHD.

92. Commander MARFOR Somalia, Fragmentary Order 14 to Operation Order 2-92 (Operation Restore Hope), 5 January 1993, folder 2, box 1, ORHC, MCHD; Wilhelm interview, 28; TF Mogadishu Command Chronology, section 2.7; Piero Ignazi, Giampiero Giacomello, and Fabrizio Coticchia, *Italian Military Operations Abroad: Just Don't Call It War* (New York: Palgrave Macmillan, 2012), 103.

93. Hirsch and Oakley, *Somalia and Operation Restore Hope*, 71.

94. Martin R. Rupiya, "The Bakara Market Arms Clearance Operation of 1993: The Zimbabwe National Army in Somalia," *International Peacekeeping* 4, 1 (1997): 116–120.

95. Breen, *Little Bit of Hope*, 68, 72–74, 164–165; Sullivan interview, 7–8.

96. Lieutenant Colonel Jean Vautrey, French Army, interview by Captain David Dawson and Major Robert Wright, 6 March 1993, 36, JHT-RHIT-069, SOHIC/USACMH.

97. Ron Pupetz, *In the Line of Duty: Canadian Joint Forces Somalia, 1992–1993* (St. Catherine's, ON: Vanwell, 2001), 16–18.

98. Paolo Tripodi, *The Colonial Legacy in Somalia* (London: Macmillan, 1999), 144; Dennis P. Mroczkowski, *Restoring Hope: In Somalia with the Unified Task Force, 1992–1993* (Washington, DC: History Division, US Marine Corps, 2005), 87.

99. Staff Sergeant Cindy Killion, press release, "Living in Jilib," 24 January 1993, folder 10, box 3, KBP, USAHEC.

100. 10th Mountain Division Artillery, Report on Combined Task Force Kismayo, n.d., folder AAR-005, box 1, SCC/USAHEC; hereafter, TF Kismayo AAR.

101. TF Kismayo AAR; Brigadier General Lawson Magruder, interview by Major Robert K. Wright, Major Robert L. Furu, and Captain Drew Meyerowich, 17 February 1993, 7–8, RHIT-JHT-014, SOHIC/USACMH; hereafter, Magruder interview.

102. ARFOR Significant Acts Chronology, 23 December 1992–7 June 1993, folder 4, box 3, KBP, USAHEC; Staff Sergeant Cindy Killion, press release, "3–14 Moves to Jilib," 21 January 1993, folder 10, box 3, KBP, USAHEC.

103. Staff Sergeant Cindy Killion, press release, "Labadad Holds the Answer," 19 February 1993, folder 10, box 3, KBP, USAHEC; Staff Sergeant Cindy Killion, press release, "Jamaame Method," 4 February 1993, folder 10, box 3, KBP, USAHEC; Staff Sergeant Cindy Killion, press release, "Jilib Food Drop," 21 January 1993, folder 10, box 3, KBP, USAHEC; Staff Sergeant Cindy Killion, press release, "TF Durham Fixes Somali Roads," 6 February 1993, folder 10, box 3, KBP, USAHEC; Mr. Lowrey, JULLS Long Report 12620-15979, 26 January 1993, folder OBS-022, box 4, SCC/USAHEC; Headquarters, 10th Mountain Division, *US Army Forces Somalia: 10th Mountain Division (LI) After Action Report Summary* (Fort Drum, NY: Headquarters, 10th Mountain Division, 1993), 24.

104. Lawson W. Magruder, *A Soldier's Journey Living His Why* (Coppell, TX: independently published, 2020), 203.

105. Undersecretary-General Kofi Annan, Daily Report to the Secretary-General on Somalia, 11 December 1992, S-1834-0021-07, AG-050, United Nations Archives, New York (UNA).

106. Magruder, *Soldier's Journey*, 206–207; Hirsch and Oakley, *Somalia and Operation Restore Hope*, 76–77.

107. Magruder, *Soldier's Journey*, 206–207; TF Kismayo AAR.

108. Magruder, *Soldier's Journey*, 209; Chronology of Events in Kismayo, 19 January–21 February 1993, folder 4, box 3, KBP, USAHEC.

109. 10th Mountain Division, Operation Restore Hope Log of Events as of 12 April 1993, folder 4, box 3, KBP, USAHEC; Chronology of Events in Kismayo; Staff Sergeant Cindy Killion and Private Bernadette Paris, press release, "Aviators Recount Morgan Engagement," 28 January 1993, folder 10, box 3, KBP, USAHEC; Magruder interview, 27–32.

110. Chronology of Events in Kismayo; Lieutenant Colonel Bob Thompson, Spot Report, 5 February 1993, folder DRPT-025, box 7, SCC/USAHEC.

111. Chronology of Events in Kismayo; TF Kismayo AAR; 10th Mountain Division, Operation Restore Hope Log of Events.

112. Thompson, Spot Report, 5 February 1993.

113. Commander, Joint Special Operations Forces Somalia, Situation Reports to UNITAF J-2, 21 and 22 February 1993, folder 4, box 4, JHT, USACMH.

114. Commander, Joint Special Operations Forces Somalia, Situation Report to UNITAF J-2, 22 February 1993.

115. Colonel Mark R. Hamilton, interview by Commander Roger T. Zeimet, 28 February 1993, 6–11, RHIT-JHT-051, SOHIC/USACMH.

116. Chronology of Events in Kismayo.

117. CIA memorandum on the February 1993 SPM-Jess Executive Committee meeting, 22 February 1993, folder 4, box 4, JHT, USACMH.

118. Chronology of Events in Kismayo.

119. Task Force Kismayo, Tactical Operations Center Log, 22 February 1993, folder 6, box 2, JHT, USAMCH.

120. TF Kismayo AAR; Colonel Fred Peck, press briefing, 24 February 1993, folder 14, box 3, JHT, USACMH.

121. Peck press briefing, 24 February 1993.

122. Magruder, *Soldier's Journey*, 212–215; Captain Bob Stone, press release on curfew in Kismayo, 22 February 1993, folder 6, box 2, JHT, USACMH.

123. Stanton, *Somalia on Five Dollars*, 231; TF Kismayo AAR.

124. 10th Mountain Division, Operation Restore Hope Log of Events.

125. Commander, Joint Special Operations Forces Somalia, Situation Report to UNITAF J-2, 22 February 1993; Staff Sergeant Cindy Killion, press release, "TF Kismayo Redeployment Delayed," 23 February 1993, folder 10, box 3, KBP, USAHEC; Stanton, *Somalia on Five Dollars*, 222.

126. Letter from Lieutenant General Robert Johnston and Ambassador Robert Oakley to General Hersi Morgan, 23 February 1993, folder 6, box 2, JHT, USACMH.

127. Lieutenant General Robert B. Johnston, Commanding General UNITAF, interview by Lieutenant Colonel Charles H. Cureton and Major Robert K. Wright, 16 March 1993, 13, RHIT-JHT-085, SOHIC/USACMH.

128. Staff Sergeant Cindy Killion, press release, "Psyops Informs Kismayo Residents," 26 February 1993, folder 10, box 3, KBP, USAHEC; TF Kismayo AAR.

129. Message from Major General S. L. Arnold to General Gordon R. Sullivan, 4 March 1993, box 121, Gordon R. Sullivan Papers (GRSP), USAHEC.

130. Captain Bob Stone, press release, "Morgan Agrees," 24 February 1993, folder 10, box 3, KBP, USAHEC.

131. Letter from "Morgan Elders" to Major General Steven Arnold, 24 February 1992, folder 6, box 2, JHT, USACMH.

132. 10th Mountain Division, Operation Restore Hope Log of Events.

133. Arnold to Sullivan, 4 March 1993; Magruder, *Soldier's Journey*, 212–215.

134. Colonel Hussein Siad Farah, chair SNA Cease-fire Observing Committee, Letter to Ambassador Robert Oakley, 28 February 1993, S-1000-0028-02, AG-024, UNA.

135. Hussein Siad Farah to Oakley, 28 February 1993; John Drysdale, *Whatever Happened to Somalia?* 2nd ed. (London: Haan, 2001), 111–113; Rear Admiral Skip Bowman, Spot Report on Kismayo Infiltration, n.d., box 119, GRSP, USAHEC; Hirsch and Oakley, *Somalia and Operation Restore Hope*, 76–77.

136. Translation of leaflet handed out in Mogadishu, 23 February 1993, folder 6, box 2, JHT, USACMH.

137. Diana Jean Schemo, "Rioting by Warlord's Supporters Creates Havoc in Somali Capital," *New York Times*, 25 February 1993.

138. Office of the Commandant of the Marine Corps, Public Affairs Manager, News Summary 09-93, 26 February 1993, folder 14, box 3, JHT, USACMH.

139. MARFOR Command Chronology, section 2.15.

140. Office of the Commandant of the Marine Corps, News Summary 09-93.

141. Zinni interview, 7 February 2020.

142. MARFOR Command Chronology, section 2.16; Bowman, Spot Report on Kismayo Infiltration; Office of the Commandant of the Marine Corps, News Summary 09-93; Colonel E. R. Bedard, RCT-7, interview by Lieutenant Colonel Charles Keritan and Captain D. A. Dawson, 12 March 1993, 56, transcript in folder 4, box 4, ORHC, MCHD; Hirsch and Oakley, *Somalia and Operation Restore Hope*, 78–79.

143. Hirsch and Oakley, *Somalia and Operation Restore Hope*, 78–79; Baumann, Yates, and Washington, *"My Clan,"* 82–83; Diana Jean Schemo, "Somali Warlord's Supporters on Rampage for Second Day," *New York Times*, 26 February 1993.

144. Drysdale, *Whatever Happened*, 113–114.

145. MARFOR Command Chronology, section 2.16.

146. Colonel Wallace S. Grayson, interview by Lieutenant Colonel Charles Keritan and Major Robert K. Wright, 13 March 1993, 20, transcript in folder 10, box 4, ORHC, MCHD.

147. Colonel Michael W. Hagee, 11th MEU, interview by Captain D. A. Dawson, 6 January 1994, 34, RHIT-C-367, SOHIC/USAMCH.

148. Task Force Mogadishu, Analysis of Possible Reasons for Attacks upon US Marines Operating in Mogadishu, 14 January 1993, folder 30, box 1, ORHC, MCHD.

149. Briefing delivered to Lieutenant General Cevik Bir on the status of

each HRS in advance of UN handover, 23 February 1993, folder 2, box 3, JHT, USACMH.

150. Wilhelm interview, 42.

151. Colonel James Brian Egan, UNITAF J-3, interview by Lieutenant Colonel Charles Keritan and Major Robert K. Wright, 11 March 1993, 34–38, transcript in folder 8, box 4, ORHC, MCHD.

152. Colonel R. B. McKittrick, memorandum on statistical data for Operation Restore Hope, 29 July 1993, folder 5, box 1, JEP, MCHD.

153. UNITAF Summary of Casualties Resulting in Death, n.d., folder 9, box 2, JEP, MCHD.

5. Jump-Starting a Nation: UNITAF and Embryonic Nation Building

1. Martin Stanton, *Somalia on Five Dollars a Day: A Soldier's Story* (Novato, CA: Presidio, 2001), 156.

2. Statement by Lieutenant General Martin Brandtner, Hearings on Operation Restore Hope and Military Operations in Somalia before the Committee on Armed Services, United States Senate, 102nd Cong., 9 December 1992, 25.

3. Lieutenant Colonel Michael W. Sullivan, 3rd Amphibious Assault Battalion, interview by Captain D. A. Dawson, 17 February 1993, 50, transcript in folder 2, box 6, Operation Restore Hope Collection (ORHC), COLL/3708, Archives Branch, Marine Corps History Division, Quantico, VA (MCHD); hereafter, Sullivan interview.

4. Jim Hoagland, "Prepared for Non-Combat," *Washington Post*, 15 April 1993.

5. Tony Zinni and Tony Koltz, *Before the First Shot Is Fired: How America Can Win or Lose off the Battlefield* (New York: Palgrave Macmillan, 2014), 38.

6. General Anthony C. Zinni, USMC (retired), interview by the author, 20 December 2019.

7. John L. Hirsch and Robert B. Oakley, *Somalia and Operation Restore Hope: Reflections on Peacemaking and Peacekeeping* (Washington, DC: Institute of Peace Press, 1995), 50, 83.

8. D. J. Hurley, "Operation Solace," *Australian Defence Force Journal* 104, 1 (February 1994): 31.

9. George H. W. Bush, address on Somalia, 4 December 1992, transcript from the Miller Center at the University of Virginia, available from https://millercenter.org/the-presidency/presidential-speeches/december-4-1992-address-somalia.

10. Brigadier General Anthony C. Zinni, interview by Lieutenant Colonel Charles H. Cureton and Major Robert K. Wright, 11 March 1993, 18, RHIT-

JHT-081, Somalia Oral History Interview Collection, US Army Center of Military History, Washington, DC (SOHIC/USACMH).

11. Zinni and Koltz, *Before the First Shot*, 212.

12. Hirsch and Oakley, *Somalia and Operation Restore Hope*, 50-58.

13. Colonel Wallace S. Grayson, interview by Lieutenant Colonel Charles Keritan and Major Robert K. Wright, 13 March 1993, 12-13, transcript in folder 10, box 4, ORHC, MCHD; hereafter, Grayson interview.

14. Hirsch and Oakley, *Somalia and Operation Restore Hope*, 59.

15. Minutes from an intelligence community debrief by Ambassador Robert B. Oakley, 29 December 1992, folder 34, box 5, Robert B. Oakley Collection, COLL/437, Northwest Louisiana Archives, Noel Memorial Library, Louisiana State University, Shreveport; hereafter, Oakley Collection.

16. Bob Breen, *A Little Bit of Hope: Australian Force Somalia* (St. Leonard's, NSW: Allen & Unwin, 1998), 208; Stanton, *Somalia on Five Dollars*, 126; account of Chief Warrant Officer Bud Jardine, Canadian Airborne Battlegroup, in Ron Pupetz, *In the Line of Duty: Canadian Joint Forces Somalia, 1992-1993* (St. Catherine's, ON: Vanwell, 2001), 212; Michael J. Kelly, *Peace Operations: Tackling the Military, Legal and Policy Challenges* (Canberra: Australian Government Publishing Service, 1997), 8.5-8.6; Hirsch and Oakley, *Somalia and Operation Restore Hope*, 71.

17. Special State Department briefing on Somalia by Ambassador Robert B. Oakley, 5 January 1993, folder 34, box 5, Oakley Collection.

18. S. L. Arnold, "Somalia: An Operation Other Than War," *Military Review* 73, 12 (December 1993): 33; 10th Mountain Division, Operation Restore Hope Log of Events as of 12 April 1993, folder 4, box 3, Kevin M. Born Papers (KBP), US Army Heritage and Education Center, Carlisle, PA (USAHEC); Dennis P. Mroczkowski, *Restoring Hope: In Somalia with the Unified Task Force, 1992-1993* (Washington, DC: History Division, US Marine Corps, 2005), 84-87; Colonel Serge Labbe, Canadian Forces Somalia, addressing the UNITAF press briefing, 19 February 1993, folder 14, box 3, Joint History Team Somalia Collection (JHT), USACMH; Jardine account in Pupetz, *In the Line of Duty*, 212; Breen, *Little Bit of Hope*, 137-139; Marine Forces Somalia/I Marine Expeditionary Force, Command Chronology, 7 December 1992-28 February 1993, section 2.24-2.25, folder 16, box 2, ORHC, MCHD (hereafter, MARFOR Command Chronology); Gerard Prunier, "The Experience of European Armies in Operation Restore Hope," in *Learning from Somalia: The Lessons of Armed Humanitarian Intervention*, ed. Walter Clarke and Jeffrey Herbst (Boulder, CO: Westview Press, 1997), 139-141.

19. 10th Mountain Division, Restore Hope Log of Events.

20. Stanton, *Somalia on Five Dollars*, 126.

21. Jardine account in Pupetz, *In the Line of Duty*, 212.

22. Lieutenant General Robert B. Johnston, interview by Lieutenant Colo-

nel Charles H. Cureton and Major Robert K. Wright, 16 March 1993, 10, RHIT-JHT-085, SOHIC/USACMH; hereafter, Johnston interview.

23. Jonathan T. Dworken, *Military Relations with Humanitarian Relief Organizations: Observations from Restore Hope* (Alexandria, VA: Center for Naval Analyses, 1993), 14. Dworken worked for the Center for Naval Analyses, assisting I MEF in Mogadishu.

24. Dworken, 17–19; Hirsch and Oakley, *Somalia and Operation Restore Hope*, 67; Philip Johnston, *Somalia Diary* (Atlanta: Longstreet Press, 1994), 76; Kevin M. Kennedy, "The Relationship between the Military and the Humanitarian Organizations in Operation Restore Hope," in Clarke and Herbst, *Learning from Somalia*, 101–104.

25. Dworken, *Military Relations*, 21; Breen, *Little Bit of Hope*, 197, 203; Kelly, *Peace Operations*, 8.8–8.13; Pupetz, *In the Line of Duty*, 60–61; Combined Arms Assessment Team Somalia, Operation Restore Hope Lessons Learned draft, n.d., 73, folder AAR-004, box 1, Somalia Crisis Collection (SCC), USAHEC.

26. Major Martin Stanton, After Action Report: Wanlaweyne Incident 30 December 1992, 2 January 1993, folder 4, box 3, KBP, USAHEC.

27. Stanton, *Somalia on Five Dollars*, 115.

28. Breen, *Little Bit of Hope*, 70, 104.

29. Dworken, *Military Relations*, 24–25; Kennedy, "Relationship between the Military and Humanitarian Organizations," 110.

30. Statement by Lieutenant General Martin Brandtner, Joint Chiefs of Staff briefing on current military operations in Somalia, Iraq, and Yugoslavia, 103rd Cong., 29 January 1993, 29.

31. Lieutenant Colonel Moase, JULLS Long Report 12457-88301, 24 January 1993, folder ARFR-017, box 9, SCC/USAHEC; Major Knox, JULLS Long Report 10684-73278, 7 January 1993, folder ARFR-022, box 9, SCC/USAHEC; Kennedy, "Relationship between the Military and Humanitarian Organizations," 101.

32. Breen, *Little Bit of Hope*, 190.

33. MARFOR Command Chronology, section 2.29.

34. Stanton, *Somalia on Five Dollars*, 126–127; Breen, *Little Bit of Hope*, 77, 194–195; Colonel Gregory Newbold, interview by Captain D. A. Dawson, 13 January 1993, 27–28, transcript in folder 13, box 5, ORHC, MCHD.

35. Dworken, *Military Relations*, 38.

36. Dworken, 39.

37. Kennedy, "Relationship between the Military and Humanitarian Organizations," 109.

38. Martin R. Ganzglass, "The Restoration of the Somali Justice System," in Clarke and Herbst, *Learning from Somalia*, 21; General Anthony C. Zinni, USMC (retired), interview by the author, 7 February 2020; Hirsch and Oakley, *Somalia and Operation Restore Hope*, 89–92.

39. Robert B. Oakley, "The Urban Area during Support Missions Case Study: Mogadishu, the Strategic Level," in *Capital Preservation: Preparing for Urban Operations in the Twenty-First Century*, ed. Russell W. Glenn (Santa Monica, CA: RAND Corporation, 2001), 332.

40. Johnston interview, 35; Lynn Thomas and Steve Spataro, "Peacekeeping and Policing in Somalia," in *Policing the New World Disorder: Peace Operations and Public Security*, ed. Robert B. Oakley, Michael J. Dziedzic, and Eliot M. Goldberg (Washington, DC: National Defense University Press, 1998), 188–192; Hirsch and Oakley, *Somalia and Operation Restore Hope*, 89–92; Johnston, *Somalia Diary*, 98–100.

41. The Police Committee consisted of the following members: Brigadier General Ahmed Jama, former SNPF commandant; Brigadier General Ahmed Jilao, the last governor of Mogadishu under the Barre regime and a senior career officer in Barre's National Security Service; Brigadier General Ali Mohamed Elmi, former head of the SNPF Criminal Investigations Division; Brigadier General Elmi Sahal, former SNPF communications and transport chief; Colonel Oman Omar, SNPF Criminal Investigations Division; Colonel Abrahim Shekh, National Army engineer trained in the Soviet Union; Colonel Mohamed Mohamud, former National Army officer trained at the US Army Armor School; Colonel Kholuf Addawe, SNPF lawyer; Colonel Abdullahi Gafo, SNPF; and Colonel Mohamed Abls, National Army. CIA Report on Biographic Information on Members of the Mogadishu Security Committee, 17 February 1993, folder 8, box 2, JHT, USACMH.

42. Lieutenant Colonel Stephen M. Spataro, memorandum to UNITAF J-3 on Auxiliary Security Force, 27 January 1993, folder 8, box 2, JHT, USACMH.

43. Thomas and Spataro, "Peacekeeping and Policing," 190.

44. Spataro, memorandum on Auxiliary Security Force, 27 January 1993.

45. Spataro, memorandum on Auxiliary Security Force; Colonel Fred Peck, press briefing, 10 February 1993, folder 14, box 3, JHT, USACMH; Lieutenant Colonel Stephen M. Spataro, memorandum to UNITAF J-3 on Auxiliary Security Force, 13 February 1993, folder 8, box 2, JHT, USACMH; Zinni interview, 7 February 2020; Ganzglass, "Restoration of Somali Justice," 24; Lieutenant Colonel J. D. Theeuwen, interview by Captain D. A. Dawson, 28 February 1993, 2, transcript in folder 5, box 6, ORHC, MCHD; hereafter, Theeuwen interview.

46. Thomas and Spataro, "Peacekeeping and Policing," 195–196.

47. Theeuwen interview, 12.

48. Johnston, *Somalia Diary*, 98–100.

49. Spataro, memorandum on Auxiliary Security Force, 13 February 1993; Lieutenant Colonel Stephen M. Spataro, memorandum to Lieutenant General Robert Johnston on Auxiliary Security Force weapons policy, 14 February 1993, folder 8, box 2, JHT, USACMH.

50. Spataro, memorandum on Auxiliary Security Force, 27 January 1993.

51. Handwritten minutes of the General Security Committee meeting, 14 January 1993, folder 8, box 2, JHT, USACMH.

52. The participating humanitarian relief organizations were CARE, World Concern, Irish Concern, Swedish Church Relief, International Development and Relief Board, ACCORD, Comitatio Internationale per lo Suivppo Die Populi, Manzumat Al Dawa Al Islamia, Islamic African Relief Agency, Adventist Relief and Development Agency, and GOAL. Memorandum on Mass Distribution Site Program, 21 April 1993, folder 37, box 1, ORHC, MCHD.

53. Theeuwen interview, 4; Johnston, *Somalia Diary*, 98–102; Ganzglass, "Restoration of Somali Justice," 25.

54. Letter from Colonel Gregory S. Newbold to Brigadier General E. H. Simmons, Director of Marine Corps History & Museums, 26 June 1995, folder 2, box 18, Field Historians Collection, COLL./4300, Archives Branch, MCHD.

55. Kelly, *Peace Operations*, 8.20; Lieutenant Colonel Stephen M. Spataro, memorandum to UNITAF J-3 on Auxiliary Security Force in Baidoa, 13 February 1993, folder 8, box 2, JHT, USACMH; Hirsch and Oakley, *Somalia and Operation Restore Hope*, 50.

56. Brigadier General Lawson Magruder, interview by Major Robert K. Wright, Major Robert L. Furu, and Captain Drew Meyerowich, 17 February 1993, 17–18, RHIT-JHT-014, SOHIC/USACMH.

57. Lieutenant Colonel Stephen M. Spataro, memorandum to UNITAF J-3 on Auxiliary Security Force in Oddur, 13 February 1993, folder 8, box 2, JHT, USACMH; Lieutenant Colonel Stephen M. Spataro, memorandum to UNITAF J-3 on Auxiliary Security Force in Gialalassi, 16 February 1993, folder 8, box 2, JHT, USACMH; Pupetz, *In the Line of Duty*, 62; account of Colonel J. S. Labbe in Pupetz, 267; Sullivan interview, 14, 47–48.

58. Oakley, "Urban Area," 336.

59. Spataro, memorandum on Auxiliary Security Force, 13 February 1993.

60. Ganzglass, "Restoration of Somali Justice," 26–27; Lieutenant Colonel Stephen M. Spataro, memorandum to UNITAF J-3 on Auxiliary Security Forces in UNITAF AOR, 15 February 1993, folder 8, box 2, JHT, USACMH; Kelly, *Peace Operations*, 8.13.

61. The ASF was established in Mogadishu, Bardera, Baidoa, Beledweyne, Matabaan, Gialalassi, Giola, Balcad, Bullo Barde, Oddur, Wajeed, Teeglo, Afgooye, Wanlaweyne, Merka, and Kismayo. Thomas and Spataro, "Peacekeeping and Policing," 194; Tom Clancy, Tony Zinni, and Tony Koltz, *Battle Ready* (New York: Berkley Books, 2004), 263.

62. Kelly, *Peace Operations*, 7.27–7.31, 8.5–8.6; Lieutenant General Robert Johnston, memorandum to potential users of Somali airspace, n.d., folder 7, box 3, JHT, USACMH; F. M. Lorenz, "Law and Anarchy in Somalia," *Parameters* 23, 4 (Winter 1993–94): 28–29; Kelly, *Peace Operations*, 7.27.

63. Kelly, *Peace Operations*, 7.32.

64. Commander, Joint Task Force Somalia, "Commander's Policy Guidance, Civilian Detainees, Vehicle Accidents, Medical Care, and Reporting Requirements," 24 December 1992, quoted in Kelly, *Peace Operations*, 7.33.

65. Colonel E. R. Bedard, interview by Lieutenant Colonel Charles Keritan and Captain D. A. Dawson, 12 March 1993, 42, transcript in folder 4, box 4, ORHC, MCHD; hereafter, Bedard interview.

66. Lieutenant Colonel Edward J. Lesnowicz, interview by Major Robert K. Wright and Captain D. A. Dawson, 13 February 1993, 50-51, transcript in folder 15, box 5, ORHC, MCHD; hereafter, Lesnowicz interview.

67. Kelly, *Peace Operations*, 7.39; Breen, *Little Bit of Hope*, 47, 100-101.

68. Lieutenant General Johnston, memorandum to all subordinate Unified Task Force commanders, "Detainee Policy," 9 February 1993, quoted in Kelly, *Peace Operations*, 7.33; Spataro, memorandum on Auxiliary Security Force, 27 January 1993.

69. Lieutenant Colonel Dubia, JULLS Long Report 10639-80895, 6 January 1993, folder OBS-016, box 4, SCC/USAHEC; Thomas and Spataro, "Peacekeeping and Policing," 190; Kelly, *Peace Operations*, 7.34-7.35.

70. Spataro, memorandum on Auxiliary Security Force in Baidoa, 13 February 1993; Kelly, *Peace Operations*, 7.37.

71. Kelly, *Peace Operations*, 8.15-8.21.

72. Kelly, 8.22-24, 8.32; Zinni interview, 7 February 2020.

73. Labbe account in Pupetz, *In the Line of Duty*, 267.

74. Labbe, UNITAF press briefing, 19 February 1993; Pupetz, *In the Line of Duty*, 62, 233.

75. Paolo Tripodi, *The Colonial Legacy in Somalia* (London: Macmillan, 1999), 144-146; Colonel Major Omar Ess Akalli, Royal Moroccan Army, interview by Major Robert Rue, 22 February 1993, 11-12, JHT-RHIT-033, SOHIC/USACMH.

76. MARFOR Command Chronology, section 2.33.

77. Lieutenant General Robert Johnston, memorandum on medical support to civilians, 19 December 1992, folder DRPT-035, box 11, SCC/USAHEC; M. L. Cowan, memorandum on regulating patients to medical treatment facilities, 6 January 1993, folder DRPT-035, box 11, SCC/USAHEC.

78. Lois M. Davis, Susan D. Hosek, Michael G. Tate, Mark Perry, Gerard Hepler, and Paul S. Steinberg, *Army Medical Support for Peace Operations and Humanitarian Assistance* (Santa Monica, CA: RAND Corporation, 1996), 57-58.

79. UNITAF J-3 Command Operations Center Log, 2 January 1992, folder 7, box 4, JHT, USACMH; Leonard J. Sly, "62nd Medical Group's Deployment to Somalia" (personal experience monograph, US Army War College, 1995), 142, OCLC 49945811, US Army War College Student Papers Collection, USAHEC.

80. Lesnowicz interview, 58-60.

81. Lesnowicz interview, 58-60.

82. United States Forces Somalia, *After Action Report and Historical Overview* (Washington, DC: US Army Center of Military History, 2003), 102.

83. Lorenz, "Law and Anarchy," 31; transcript of Joseph P. Hoar, interview with the Columbia Center for Oral History, 13 March 2013, 119, https://www.ccohr.incite.columbia.edu/joseph-p-hoar.

84. Press briefing on Operation Restore Hope by US Secretary of Defense Richard B. Cheney and Chairman of the Joint Chiefs of Staff General Colin Powell, 4 December 1992, folder 2, box 1, Operation Restore Hope Press Releases Collection (PRC), USACMH.

85. Office of the Assistant Secretary of Defense for Public Affairs, press briefing by General Joseph P. Hoar, 18 December 1992, folder 1, box 1, PRC, USACMH.

86. Special State Department briefing on Somalia by Ambassador Robert B. Oakley, 5 January 1993.

87. Boutros Boutros-Ghali, Letter to President George H. W. Bush, 8 December 1992, in United Nations, *The United Nations and Somalia, 1992–1996* (New York: UN Department of Public Information, 1996), 216–217.

88. Boutros Boutros-Ghali, *Unvanquished: A US-UN Saga* (New York: Random House, 1999), 60.

89. MARFOR Intelligence Cell, memorandum on authorized weapons storage sites, 7 January 1993, folder 4, box 1, ORHC, MCHD; Stanton, *Somalia on Five Dollars*, 140–141; Breen, *Little Bit of Hope*, 81; Labbe, UNITAF press briefing, 19 February 1993; CIA memorandum on the Italian Intelligence and Military Security Service Situation Report on Somalia, 20 February 1993, folder 4, box 4, JHT, USACMH.

90. Stanton, *Somalia on Five Dollars*, 140–141; Jardine account in Pupetz, *In the Line of Duty*, 212; Arnold, "Somalia: Operation Other Than War," 31; Lorenz, "Law and Anarchy," 31.

91. Captain Robert S. Abbott, interview by Captain D. A. Dawson, 17 September 1993, 38–40, transcript in folder 3, box 4, ORHC, MCHD; hereafter, Abbott interview.

92. Sullivan interview, 2–4; Katherine A. W. McGrady, *The Joint Task Force in Operation Restore Hope* (Alexandria, VA: Center for Naval Analyses, 1994), 88.

93. MARFOR Command Chronology, section 2.9.

94. Captain Michael F. Belcher, Lieutenant John A. Van Messel, and Gunnery Sergeant David C. Phillips, interview by Captain D. A. Dawson, 10 January 1993, 9–14, transcript in folder 5, box 4, ORHC, MCHD; Colonel Jack W. Klimp, Task Force Mogadishu Command Chronology, 21 December 1992–22 January 1993, section 2.4, folder 1, box 1, ORHC, MCHD; Task Force Mogadishu, Situation Report, 8 January 1993, folder 3, box 1, ORHC, MCHD.

95. Task Force Mogadishu, Situation Report, 8 January 1993.

96. Staff Judge Advocate, Commander's Policy Guidance #3: Weapons Confiscation and Disposition, 8 January 1993, folder 4, box 1, ORHC, MCHD.

97. 3rd Battalion, 11th Marine Regiment, Fragmentary Order 9-93, 16 January 1993, folder 4, box 1, ORHC, MCHD.

98. Task Force Mogadishu, Situation Reports, 10–20 January 1993, folder 3, box 1, ORHC, MCHD; 3rd Light Armored Infantry Battalion, Daily Sitrep to TF Mogadishu, 13 January 1993, folder 7, box 1, ORHC, MCHD.

99. Task Force Mogadishu, Operation Order "Bakara," 9 January 1993, folder 26, box 1, ORHC, MCHD.

100. Grayson interview, 3.

101. Task Force Mogadishu, Situation Report, 12 January 1993, folder 3, box 1, ORHC, MCHD; ARFOR Significant Acts Chronology, 23 December 1992–7 June 1993, folder 4, box 3, KBP, USAHEC.

102. Sullivan interview, 5–6.

103. UNITAF J-3 Command Operations Center Log, 11 January 1992, folder 7, box 4, JHT, USACMH.

104. Stanton, *Somalia on Five Dollars*, 172–181; Abbott interview, 43, 48.

105. Lieutenant Colonel Walsh, 3rd Battalion/9th Marines, interview by Captain D. A. Dawson, 21 January 1993, 14, transcript in folder 4, box 6, ORHC, MCHD.

106. ARFOR Significant Acts Chronology; UNITAF J-3 Command Operations Center Log, 16 January 1992, folder 7, box 4, JHT, USACMH; Breen, *Little Bit of Hope*, 81, 156–168; Mroczkowski, *Restoring Hope*, 84–85; Tripodi, *Colonial Legacy*, 144.

107. Colonel Fred Peck, press briefing, 24 February 1993, folder 14, box 3, JHT, USACMH.

108. Lieutenant Colonel Gary L. Holmquist, 1st First Combat Engineer Battalion, interview by Captain D. A. Dawson, 30 January 1993, 7, transcript in folder 12, box 4, ORHC, MCHD; Mr. Lowrey, JULLS Long Report 1159-54030, 17 January 1993, folder OBS-022, box 4, SCC/USAHEC; Breen, *Little Bit of Hope*, 173.

109. Staff Sergeant Cindy Killion, press release, "Psyops Informs Kismayo Residents," 26 February 1993, folder 10, box 3, KBP, USAHEC; Staff Sergeant Cindy Killion, press release, "Kismayo Weapons Sweep," 1 March 1993, folder 10, box 3, KBP, USAHEC; Staff Sergeant Cindy Killion, press release, "360th Hauls Weapons," 3 March 1993, folder 10, box 3, KBP, USAHEC.

110. Colonel James Brian Egan, UNITAF J-3, interview by Lieutenant Colonel Charles Keritan and Major Robert K. Wright, 11 March 1993, 14, transcript in folder 8, box 4, ORHC, MCHD; hereafter, Egan interview.

111. Memorandum on revising UNITAF weapons policies, 28 February 1993, folder 5, box 2, James B. Egan Papers (JEP), COLL/5672, MCHD.

112. UNITAF J-3 Command Operations Center Log, 2 and 15 January 1992,

folder 7, box 4, JHT, USACMH; memorandum on revising UNITAF weapons policies, 28 February 1993; Dworken, *Military Relations*, 29–31.

113. Lieutenant Colonel Veach, JULLS Long Report 12242-02959, 22 January 1993, folder OBS-025, box 4, SCC/USAHEC.

114. Kennedy, "Relationship between the Military and Humanitarian Organizations," 112.

115. Kennedy, 117.

116. Bedard interview, 18–20.

117. Kennedy, "Relationship between the Military and Humanitarian Organizations," 112, 114; memorandum on revising UNITAF weapons policies, 28 February 1993.

118. Headquarters, 10th Mountain Division, *US Army Forces Somalia: 10th Mountain Division (LI) After Action Report Summary* (Fort Drum, NY: Headquarters, 10th Mountain Division, 1993), 49.

119. Briefing slides included in Colonel R. B. McKittrick, I MEF G-3, memorandum on statistical data for Operation Restore Hope, 29 July 1993, folder 5, box 1, JEP, MCHD.

120. Lieutenant Colonel Meyer, JULLS Long Report 11324-60546, 13 January 1993, folder OBS-006, box 2, SCC, USAHEC.

121. Bedard interview, 48–49.

122. Egan interview, 22.

123. Grayson interview, 1–2, 5.

124. Hurley, "Operation Solace," 30.

125. Stanton, *Somalia on Five Dollars*, 156.

126. Hirsch and Oakley, *Somalia and Operation Restore Hope*, xvii; United States Institute of Peace, *Special Report on Somalia, December 8th, 1992* (Washington, DC: United States Institute of Peace, 1992), 2–4, folder 801/4H, box 77, Frederick C. Cuny Collection, Cushing Library, Texas A&M University, College Station.

127. Minutes from an intelligence community debrief by Ambassador Robert B. Oakley, 29 December 1992, Oakley Collection.

128. Memorandum for the record on discussions with Ambassador Robert Oakley, 16 March 1993, "FOIA 2012-0659-F—Peacekeeping Operations in Somalia," National Archives Digital Catalog, https://catalog.archives.gov/id/312197677.

129. Tom Cohen, "U.S. 'Plucking the Bird' of Violence to Reduce Warlord's Power," Associated Press, 19 February 1993.

130. Zinni interview, 20 December 2019.

6. The Reluctant Crusader: UNOSOM II Takes over in Somalia

1. Letter from General Gordon R. Sullivan to General Colin Powell, 5 January 1993, box 118, Gordon R. Sullivan Papers (GRSP), US Army Heritage and Education Center, Carlisle, PA (USAHEC).

2. United Nations, *The United Nations and Somalia, 1992–1996* (New York: UN Department of Public Information, 1996), 44.

3. Lieutenant General Robert Johnston, Commander's Assessment of Operation Restore Hope, January 1993, folder 1, box 3, Joint History Team Somalia Collection (JHT), US Army Center of Military History, Washington, DC (USACMH).

4. William J. Clinton, remarks on Operation Restore Hope, 5 May 1993, transcript from the Miller Center at the University of Virginia, available from https://millercenter.org/the-presidency/presidential-speeches/may-5-1993 -remarks-operation-restore-hope.

5. Colin Powell, *My American Journey* (New York: Ballantine Books, 1996), 586.

6. United Nations, Security Council, Letter dated 19 January 1993 from Ambassador Edward Perkins, Permanent Representative of the United States of America, Addressed to the President of the Security Council, S/25126 (19 January 1992), available from undocs.org/en/S/25126; United Nations, Security Council Resolution 794, S/RES/794 (3 December 1992), available from https://digitallibrary.un.org/record/154648?ln=en.

7. Jonathan T. Dworken, *Operation Restore Hope: Preparing and Planning the Transition to UN Operations* (Alexandria, VA: Center for Naval Analyses, 1994), 17–18.

8. Security Assessments—HRS Baidoa, HRS Bardera, HRS Belet Uen, HRS Oddur, 13 January 1993, folder 5, box 2, JHT, USACMH.

9. Security Assessments—HRS Kismayo and HRS Mogadishu, 13 January 1993, folder 5, box 2, JHT, USACMH.

10. Lieutenant General Robert Johnston, Commander's Assessment of Operation Restore Hope, 28 January 1993, "FOIA 2012-0659-F—Peacekeeping Operations in Somalia," National Archives Digital Catalog, https://catalog.ar chives.gov/id/312197575.

11. "Humanitarian Aid in Somalia, September 1990–May 1993," draft discussion paper (Washington, DC: Center for Policy Analysis and Research on Refugee Issues, 1994), 44, folder 801/4H, box 77, Frederick C. Cuny Collection, Cushing Library, Texas A&M University, College Station.

12. United Nations, Security Council, Letter from the Secretary-General Addressed to the President of the Security Council, S/24868 (30 November 1992), 5, available from undocs.org/en/S/24868.

13. Walter Poole, *The Effort to Save Somalia, August 1992–March 1994* (Wash-

ington, DC: Joint History Office, Office of the Chairman of the Joint Chiefs of Staff, 2005), 29; United Nations, Security Council, The Situation in Somalia: Report of the Secretary General, S/24992 (19 December 1992), 11–12, available from undocs.org/en/S/24992; hereafter, S/24992.

14. S/24992, 8.

15. John L. Hirsch and Robert B. Oakley, *Somalia and Operation Restore Hope: Reflections on Peacemaking and Peacekeeping* (Washington, DC: Institute of Peace Press, 1995), 65.

16. United Nations, Security Council, The Situation in Somalia: Report of the Secretary General, S/25168 (26 January 1993), 3–5, available from undocs. org/en/S/25168; hereafter, S/25168.

17. UNITAF J-3 Command Operations Center Log, 3 January 1992, folder 7, box 4, JHT, USACMH.

18. Jean Bou, Bob Breen, David Horner, Garth Pratten, and Miesje De Vogel, *The Official History of Australian Peacekeeping, Humanitarian and Post–Cold War Operations*, vol. 4, *The Limits of Peacekeeping: Australian Missions in Africa and the Americas, 1992–2005* (Port Melbourne: Cambridge University Press, 2019), 147.

19. Secretary of State to USLO Mogadishu, State Department Cable 013493, Somalia Contributors Group Briefing, 16 January 1993, folder DRPT-027, box 7, Somalia Crisis Collection (SCC), USAHEC.

20. "1993-02-05, Minutes of the Principals Committee Meeting on Bosnia, February 5, 1993," Clinton Digital Library, https://clinton.presidentiallibraries.us/items/show/12307.

21. Madeleine Albright, *Madam Secretary* (New York: Miramax Books, 2003), 142.

22. Colonel James Brian Egan, UNITAF J-3, interview by Lieutenant Colonel Charles Keritan and Major Robert K. Wright, 11 March 1993, 5, transcript in folder 8, box 4, Operation Restore Hope Collection (ORHC), Archives Branch, Marine Corps History Division, Quantico, VA (MCHD) (hereafter, Egan interview); Marine Forces Somalia/I Marine Expeditionary Force, Command Chronology, 7 December 1992–28 February 1993, section 2.7, Archives Branch, MCHD (hereafter, MARFOR Command Chronology); Bob Breen, *A Little Bit of Hope: Australian Force Somalia* (St. Leonard's, NSW: Allen & Unwin, 1998), 64.

23. Katherine A. W. McGrady, *The Joint Task Force in Operation Restore Hope* (Alexandria, VA: Center for Naval Analyses, 1994), 22–24.

24. Colonel Fred Peck, press briefing, 19 February 1993, folder 14, box 3, JHT, USACMH; Combined Arms Assessment Team Somalia, Operation Restore Hope Lessons Learned draft, n.d., 96, folder AAR-004, box 1, SCC/USAHEC; Lieutenant General Robert B. Johnston, interview by Lieutenant Colonel Charles H. Cureton and Major Robert K. Wright, 16 March 1993, 45–46,

RHIT-JHT-085, Somalia Oral History Interview Collection, USACMH; hereafter, Johnston interview.

25. United Nations, Security Council, Letter dated 10 February 1993 from Secretary General Boutros-Boutros Ghali to the President of the Security Council, S/25295 (10 February 1993), available from undocs.org/en/S/25295; United Nations, Security Council, Letter dated 16 February 1993 from President of the Security Council Ahmed Snoussi to Secretary General Boutros-Boutros Ghali, S/25296 (16 February 1993), available from undocs.org/en/S/25296.

26. United States Central Command History Office, "USCENTCOM in Somalia: Operations Provide Relief and Restore Hope," November 1994, 34–35, folder 33, box 2, ORHC, MCHD.

27. Memorandum from Wisner to Aspin quoted in Poole, *Effort to Save Somalia*, 34.

28. Memorandum of conversation, meeting with Secretary General Boutros Boutros-Ghali of the United Nations, 26 February 1993, National Security Council and NSC Records Management System, "Declassified Documents Concerning U.N. Secretary General Boutros Boutros-Ghali and Somalia," Clinton Digital Library, https://clinton.presidentiallibraries.us/items/show/101838.

29. William H. Itoh, memorandum for Marc Grossman, "Additional Somalia Points for Meeting with Boutros-Ghali," 30 January 1993 (emphasis in original), National Security Council and NSC Records Management System, "Declassified Documents Concerning U.N. Secretary General Boutros Boutros-Ghali and Somalia," Clinton Digital Library, https://clinton.presidentiallibraries.us/items/show/101838.

30. Joseph P. Hoar, transcript of interview with the Columbia Center for Oral History, 13 March 2013, 120–121, https://www.ccohr.incite.columbia.edu/joseph-p-hoar; hereafter, Hoar interview.

31. US Army Military History Institute, "An Oral History of General Gordon R. Sullivan," ed. Colonel John R. Dabrowski, 2009, 295, OCLC 299160035, USAHEC; Robert F. Baumann, Lawrence A. Yates, and Versalle F. Washington, *"My Clan against the World": US and Coalition Forces in Somalia 1992–1994* (Fort Leavenworth, KS: Combat Studies Institute Press, 2004), 103, referencing Baumann's interviews with Montgomery.

32. Briefing delivered to Lieutenant General Cevik Bir on the status of each HRS in advance of UN handover, 23 February 1993, folder 2, box 3, JHT, US-ACMH.

33. F. M. Lorenz, "Law and Anarchy in Somalia," *Parameters* 23, 4 (Winter 1993–94): 37; Baumann, Yates, and Washington, *"My Clan,"* 103, referencing Baumann's interviews with Montgomery.

34. United Nations, Security Council, *The Situation in Somalia: Report of the Secretary General*, S/25354 (3 March 1993), 19, 21, available from undocs.org/en/S/25354; hereafter, S/25354.

35. S/25354, 22.

36. S/25354, 13.

37. S/24992, 5; S/25168, 2–3. The fourteen factions invited were USC-Aidid, USC-Mahdi, Somali Africans Muke Organization (SAMO), SDA, SDM, SNF, SNM, SPM-Harti, SPM-Ogadeni, Somali National Democratic Union (SNDU), SSDF, SSNM, USF, and United Somali Party (USP).

38. Hirsch and Oakley, *Somalia and Operation Restore Hope*, 95.

39. S/25168.

40. General Agreement of 8 January 1993, included in annex II of S/25168.

41. Agreement on Implementing the Ceasefire and on Modalities of Disarmament, 8 January 1993, included in annex III of S/25168.

42. S/25168, 2.

43. John Drysdale, *Whatever Happened to Somalia?* 2nd ed. (London: Haan, 2001), 125–127.

44. Drysdale, 115–120.

45. Addis Ababa Agreement, 27 March 1993, S-1000-0004-04, AG-024, United Nations Archives, New York (UNA).

46. Lansana Kouyate, Report on Addis II, 9 April 1993, S-1000-0004-04, AG-024, UNA.

47. Addis Ababa Agreement. The signatories were the Somali Africans Muke Organization (SAMO), SDA, SDM, SDM-SNA, Somali National Democratic Union (SNDU), SNF, Somali National Union (SNU), SPM, SPM-SNA, SSDF, SSNM, USC-SNA, USC, USF, and United Somali Party (USP).

48. Addis Ababa Agreement.

49. Addis Ababa Agreement.

50. Operation Restore Hope Operational Chronology, S/26317, 4, folder 4, box 159, Warfighting Development Integration Division Collection, MCHD.

51. Hirsch and Oakley, *Somalia and Operation Restore Hope*, 97.

52. S/25354, 4.

53. Lansana Kouyate, memorandum on Addis II to Jonathan Howe, 1 April 1993, S-1000-0004-04, AG-024, UNA; Kouyate, Report on Addis II, 9 April 1993; letter from Boutros Boutros-Ghali to President Meles Zenawi, 29 March 1993, in United Nations, *United Nations and Somalia, 1992–1996*, 267; Hirsch and Oakley, *Somalia and Operation Restore Hope*, 98–99; John Drysdale, "Foreign Military Intervention in Somalia: The Root Cause of the Shift from UN Peacekeeping to Peacemaking and Its Consequences," in *Learning from Somalia: The Lessons of Armed Humanitarian Intervention*, ed. Walter Clarke and Jeffrey Herbst (Boulder, CO: Westview Press, 1997), 131.

54. Leonard Kapungu, Addis Ababa Agreement analysis, 30 March 1993, S-1000-0004-04, AG-024, UNA.

55. Kouyate, memorandum on Addis II to Howe, 1 April 1993.

56. State Department discussion paper for the Deputies Committee, "The

Need for Action in Somalia," November 1992, National Security Council Meeting Files, NSC/DC 395, Bush Presidential Records, George Bush Presidential Library.

57. Sullivan to Powell, 5 January 1993; emphasis added.

58. Anthony Lake interview, 21 May 2002, 73, William J. Clinton Presidential History Project, Miller Center, University of Virginia; hereafter, Lake interview.

59. Statement by Ambassador David Shinn, Hearings on Current Military Operations in Somalia before the Committee on Armed Services, United States Senate, 103rd Cong., 25 March 1993, 8.

60. Clinton, remarks on Operation Restore Hope, 5 May 1993.

61. General Anthony C. Zinni, USMC (retired), interview by the author, 30 July 2020.

62. Drysdale, *Whatever Happened*, 6–7.

63. Keith B. Richburg, "U.S. Envoy in Somalia Viewed as Linchpin of Reconciliation," *Washington Post*, 2 February 1993.

64. Marc Grossman, memorandum for Anthony Lake, 22 February 1993, National Security Council and NSC Records Management System, "Declassified Documents Concerning U.N. Secretary General Boutros Boutros-Ghali and Somalia," Clinton Digital Library, https://clinton.presidentiallibraries.us/items/show/101838.

65. Richard A. Clarke, memorandum to Peter Tarnoff and Walt Slocombe, 25 March 1993, "FOIA 2012-0659-F—Peacekeeping Operations in Somalia," National Archives Digital Catalog, https://catalog.archives.gov/id/312197891; United Nations, *The United Nations and the Situation in Somalia* (New York: UN Department of Public Information, 1994), 9; Drysdale, *Whatever Happened*, 6–7; Boutros Boutros-Ghali, *Unvanquished: A US-UN Saga* (New York: Random House, 1999), 92.

66. Lake interview, 74.

67. Keith B. Richburg, "Somalia's Scapegoat," *Washington Post*, 18 October 1993.

68. Boutros-Ghali, *Unvanquished*, 92.

69. Scott Peterson, *Me against My Brother: At War in Somalia, Sudan, and Rwanda* (New York: Routledge, 2001), 75.

70. Itoh, memorandum for Grossman, 30 January 1993.

71. Interviews with Lieutenant General Barry McCaffrey and Major General Waldo Freeman quoted in Poole, *Effort to Save Somalia*, 38.

72. Transcript of "Ambush in Mogadishu, Interview with Admiral Jonathan Howe," *Frontline*, PBS, September 1998, https://www.pbs.org/wgbh/pages/frontline/shows/ambush/interviews/howe.html; hereafter, Howe interview.

73. "Terms of Reference for US Forces Somalia, United Nations Operation in Somalia Force Command," 29 April 1993, in Leslie L. Ratliff, "Joint Task

Force Somalia: A Case Study" (personal experience monograph, US Naval War College, 1995), https://apps.dtic.mil/sti/citations/ADA283478.

74. Transcript of "Ambush in Mogadishu, Interview with General Thomas Montgomery," *Frontline*, PBS, September 1998, https://www.pbs.org/wgbh/pages/frontline/shows/ambush/interviews/montgomery.html.

75. Itoh, memorandum for Grossman, 30 January 1993.

76. UNOSOM Force Headquarters Nominal Roll, 31 October 1993, S-1000-0022-01, AG-024, UNA.

77. Itoh, memorandum for Grossman, 30 January 1993.

78. Hoar interview, 121; Albright, *Madam Secretary*, 142.

79. United Nations, Security Council, Letter dated 2 April 1993 from Secretary General Boutros-Boutros Ghali to the President of the Security Council, S/25532 (1 April 1993), available from undocs.org/en/S/25532.

80. Bou et al., *Official History of Australian Peacekeeping*, 4:148–151; Michael J. Kelly, *Peace Operations: Tackling the Military, Legal and Policy Challenges* (Canberra: Australian Government Publishing Service, 1997), 8.7; Elisabeth Lindenmayer, fax to Jonathan Howe, 25 May 1993, S-1000-0020-03, AG-024, UNA.

81. Ambassador M. H. Ansari, Permanent Representative of India to the UN, Letter to Boutros Boutros-Ghali, 18 May 1993, S-1000-0020-03, AG-024, UNA; United Nations, Security Council, Further Report of the Secretary-General Submitted in Pursuance of Paragraph 18 of Resolution 814 (17 August 1993), 3, available from undocs.org/en/S/26317.

82. Lieutenant-General Richard Chilcoat, memorandum to General Gordon R. Sullivan, 8 May 1993, folder 1, box 123, GRSP, USAHEC.

83. Kerry Longhurst, *Germany and the Use of Force* (Manchester, UK: Manchester University Press, 2004), 57–58, 61–64; Anja Dalgaard-Nielsen, *Germany, Pacifism and Peace Enforcement* (Manchester, UK: Manchester University Press, 2006), 61–62.

84. Longhurst, *Germany and the Use of Force*, 57–58, 61–64; Dalgaard-Nielsen, *Germany, Pacifism and Peace Enforcement*, 61–62.

85. S/25354, 15–18.

86. Johnston interview, 45–46.

87. S/25354, 17–19; Lynn Thomas and Steve Spataro, "Peacekeeping and Policing in Somalia," in *Policing the New World Disorder: Peace Operations and Public Security*, ed. Robert B. Oakley, Michael J. Dziedzic, and Eliot M. Goldberg (Washington, DC: National Defense University Press, 1998), 199; Colonel James B. Egan, memorandum on the UNITAF-UNOSOM II transition, 3 March 1993, folder 5, box 1, James B. Egan Papers (JEP), MCHD.

88. Walter Clarke, "Failed Visions and Uncertain Mandates in Somalia," in Clarke and Herbst, *Learning from Somalia*, 9.

89. U.N. SCOR, 48th sess., 3188th mtg., U.N. Doc. S/PV.3188 (26 March 1993), 26, available from undocs.org/en/S/PV/3188; hereafter, S/PV.3188.

a (New York: Random House, 1999), 94; Robert F. Baumann, Lawrence A. ?s, and Versalle F. Washington, *"My Clan against the World": US and Coalition ?es in Somalia 1992-1994* (Fort Leavenworth, KS: Combat Studies Institute ss, 2004), 108; Ed Wheeler and Craig Roberts, *Doorway to Hell: Disaster in ?alia* (London: Frontline Books, 2012), 91; Leigh Neville, *Day of the Rangers: ? Battle of Mogadishu 25 Years On* (New York: Osprey, 2018), 26; Daniel P. ?ger, *Savage Peace: Americans at War in the 1990's* (Novato, CA: Presidio Press, ?5), 300; Peter Huchthausen, *America's Splendid Little Wars: A Short History U.S. Military Engagements, 1975-2000* (New York: Viking, 2003), 175; David Lake, *The Statebuilder's Dilemma: On the Limits of Foreign Intervention* (Ithaca, ?: Cornell University Press, 2016), 168; Trevor Findlay, *The Use of Force in ? Peace Operations* (New York: Oxford University Press, 2002), 193; Taylor B. ?ybolt, *Humanitarian Military Intervention: The Conditions for Success and Failure* ?ew York: Oxford University Press, 2007), 58; Thomas H. Henriksen, *America's ?ars: Interventions, Regime Change, and Insurgencies after the Cold War* (Cambridge: ?ambridge University Press, 2022), 60.

7. Walter Poole, *The Effort to Save Somalia: August 1992–March 1994* (Washington, DC: Joint History Office, Office of the Chairman of the Joint Chiefs of Staff, 2005), 41.

8. United States Forces Somalia, *After Action Report and Historical Overview* (Washington, DC: US Army Center of Military History, 2003), 9; hereafter, USFORSOM AAR.

9. John L. Hirsch and Robert B. Oakley, *Somalia and Operation Restore Hope: Reflections on Peacemaking and Peacekeeping* (Washington, DC: Institute of Peace Press, 1995), 116-117.

10. United Nations, Security Council, *Report Pursuant to Paragraph 5 of Security Council Resolution 837 (1993) on the Investigation into the 5 June 1993 Attack on United Nations Forces in Somalia Conducted on Behalf of the Secretary-General,* S/26351 (24 August 1993), 7, available from undocs.org/en/S/26351; hereafter, Farer Report.

11. Poole, *Effort to Save Somalia*, 41; Baumann, Yates, and Washington, *"My Clan,"* 107; transcript of "Ambush in Mogadishu, Interview with Ambassador Robert Oakley," *Frontline*, PBS, September 1998, https://www.pbs.org/wgbh/pages/frontline/shows/ambush/interviews/oakley.html; hereafter, Oakley interview.

12. Neville, *Day of the Rangers*, 24.

13. Mark Bowden, *Black Hawk Down: A Story of Modern War*, 2nd ed. (New York: Grove Press, 2010), 92-93.

14. Joseph P. Hoar, interview with the Columbia Center for Oral History, 13 March 2013, 123, https://www.ccohr.incite.columbia.edu/joseph-p-hoar.

15. Oakley interview.

16. Baumann, Yates, and Washington, *"My Clan,"* 107-108.

17. Agreements reached between the political leaders at the consultations held in Addis Ababa, 30 March 1993, S-1000-0004-04, AG-024, UNA.

18. Under Secretary General for Political Affairs James Jonah, Cable to Jonathan Howe, 22 April 1993, S-1000-0004-04, AG-024, UNA.

19. Lieutenant General Cevik Bir, Letters to Ahmed Omar Jess and Siad Hersi Morgan, 4 May 1993, S-1000-0004-04, AG-024, UNA; Ahmed Omar Jess, Letters to Lieutenant General Cevik Bir, 6 and 8 May 1993, S-1000-0028-03, AG-024, UNA; Lieutenant General Cevik Bir, Letter to Ahmed Omar to Jess, 7 May 1993, S-1000-0028-03, AG-024, UNA.

20. Walid Musa, minutes of meeting with Mohamed Farah Aidid, 8 May 1993, S-1000-0028-03, AG-024, UNA.

21. USFORSOM AAR, 84; Headquarters, 1st Brigade, 10th Mountain Division, *Task Force Mountain Warrior After Action Report Operation Restore Hope/Continue Hope Somalia 10 April–7 August 1993* (Fort Drum, NY: Headquarters, 10th Mountain Division, 1993), 4 (hereafter, TF Mountain AAR); United Nations, Security Council, *Further Report of the Secretary-General Submitted in Pursuance of Paragraph 18 of Resolution 814 (1993)*, S/26317 (17 August 1993), 4–5, available from undocs.org/en/S/26317 (hereafter, S/26317); Commission of Inquiry Report, 18.

22. Major John R. Evans, "Task Force 1–22 Infantry from Homestead to Port-au-Prince" (master's thesis, US Army Command and General Staff College, 2000), 35–36, https://apps.dtic.mil/sti/citations/ADA384044; TF Mountain AAR, 4.

23. Walid Musa, note to the file, 4 April 93, S-1000-0020-03, AG-024, UNA.

24. Lansana Kouyate, Letter to Mohamed Farah Aidid, 8 May 1993, S-1000-0003-04, AG-024, UNA.

25. John Drysdale, *Whatever Happened to Somalia?* 2nd ed. (London: Haan, 2001), 168–172; Ken Menkhaus, "International Peacebuilding and the Dynamics of Local and National Reconciliation in Somalia," in *Learning from Somalia: The Lessons of Armed Humanitarian Intervention*, ed. Walter Clarke and Jeffrey Herbst (Boulder, CO: Westview Press, 1997), 52.

26. Mohamed Farah Aidid, Letter to Jonathan Howe, 10 May 1993, S-1000-0028-03, AG-024, UNA.

27. Glaspie is mentioned only in Tughral Yamin, *UN Peacekeeping Operations in Somalia: The Pakistani Perspective* (Karachi: Paramount Books, 2019), 93; Brian Cloughley, *A History of the Pakistan Army: Wars and Insurrections*, 4th ed. (Karachi: Oxford University Press, 2014), 521; Stanley Meisler, *United Nations: A History*, 2nd ed. (New York: Grove Press, 2011), 304; Drysdale, *Whatever Happened*, 8–9; Scott Peterson, *Me against My Brother: At War in Somalia, Sudan, and Rwanda* (New York: Routledge, 2001), 72, 160.

28. Rupert Cornwell, "How the Heroine of 1985 Took the Rap for Gulf War," *Independent*, 13 March 1995.

29. Paul Houston, "April in Mogadishu," *Los Angeles Times*, 28 June 1993.

30. Cornwell, "How the Heroine of 1985."

31. John Drysdale, memorandum on meeting with Yusuf Omar Al-Azahari, SSDF, 7 June 1993, S-1000-0028-03, AG-024, UNA.

32. Drysdale, *Whatever Happened*, 168–172.

33. S/26317, 11.

34. United Nations, Security Council Resolution 814, S/RES/814 (26 March 1993), available from https://digitallibrary.un.org/record/164678?ln=en.

35. Commission of Inquiry Report, 14–15.

36. USFORSOM AAR, 84–85.

37. Menkhaus, "International Peacebuilding," 52; Commission of Inquiry Report, 18–20.

38. Lieutenant Colonel Thomas J. Daze, US Army (retired), interview by the author, 10 May 2024; hereafter, Daze interview.

39. USFORSOM AAR, 84–85; Drysdale, *Whatever Happened*, 168–172.

40. Daze interview.

41. "Walter," memorandum to Jonathan Howe on UNOSOM II political strategy, 16 May 1993, S-1000-0028-03, AG-024, UNA.

42. Commission of Inquiry Report, 18–20.

43. Drysdale, *Whatever Happened*, 168–172.

44. Meisler, *United Nations*, 304.

45. Halim, minutes of meeting with Awale, 2 June 1993.

46. Halim, minutes of meeting with Awale.

47. Drysdale, *Whatever Happened*, 177; United Nations, Security Council, *Report of the Security Council Mission to Somalia on 26 and 27 October 1994*, S/1994/1245 (3 November 1994), Annex VII, available from undocs.org/en/S/1994/1245; Ahmed Abdullahi Yusuf and Mohamed Farah Aidid, Letter to Jonathan Howe, 3 June 1993, S-1000-0028-03, AG-024, UNA.

48. Commission of Inquiry Report, 20–21.

49. USFORSOM AAR, 39, 84–85.

50. Drysdale, *Whatever Happened*, 174–175.

51. Commission of Inquiry Report, 20–21.

52. Michael Maren, *The Road to Hell: The Ravaging Effects of Foreign Aid and International Charity* (New York: Free Press, 1997), 226.

53. Drysdale, *Whatever Happened*, 174–175.

54. Naulu Mataitini, meeting with Abdi Osman Farah, 12 May 1993, S-1000-0028-03, AG-024, UNA.

55. Commission of Inquiry Report, 20–21; Center for Army Lessons Learned, *U.S. Army Operations in Support of UNOSOM II*, October 1994, final draft, F-3, folder 5, box 2, Operation Restore Hope Press Releases Collection, US Army Center of Military History, Washington, DC.

56. Lieutenant General Cevik Bir, daily situation reports to Jonathan Howe,

13-18 May 1993, S-1000-0020-03, AG-024, UNA; Lieutenant General Cevik Bir, Fax to Major General Maurice Baril, 14 May 1993, S-1000-0020-03, AG-024, UNA; Jonathan Howe, Fax to Kofi Annan, 29 May 1993, S-1000-0021-01, AG-024, UNA.

57. United Nations Operations in Somalia (UNOSOM) II, Summary of Significant Events, 5, AWM260 3/6-AWM2019.8.1256, Somalia (UNOSOM/UNITAF) Collection, Australian War Memorial Digital Archives, https://www.awm.gov.au/collection/C2688006; hereafter, UNOSOM AAR.

58. USFORSOM AAR, 86.

59. Commission of Inquiry Report, 20-21, 71.

60. USFORSOM AAR, 87; Daze interview.

61. Commission of Inquiry Report, 22-23.

62. Drysdale, *Whatever Happened*, 180-181.

63. Commission of Inquiry Report, 20-21.

64. Jean Bou, Bob Breen, David Horner, Garth Pratten, and Miesje De Vogel, *The Official History of Australian Peacekeeping, Humanitarian and Post-Cold War Operations*, vol. 4, *The Limits of Peacekeeping: Australian Missions in Africa and the Americas, 1992-2005* (Port Melbourne: Cambridge University Press, 2019), 158.

65. Commission of Inquiry Report, 22-23; Drysdale, *Whatever Happened*, 180-181.

66. Curiously, in the section on 5 June 1993, not a single official is named. Key individuals are referred to only by their job titles. USFORSOM AAR, 85-90; Commission of Inquiry Report, 23; Yamin, *UN Peacekeeping Operations*, 94-96.

67. Center for Army Lessons Learned, *U.S. Army Operations in Support of UNOSOM II*, F-3-F-6; Yamin, *UN Peacekeeping Operations*, 96.

68. Bou et al., *Official History of Australian Peacekeeping*, 4:158-160.

69. United Nations, Security Council, *The Situation in Somalia: Report of the Secretary General*, S/26022 (1 July 1993), 3, available from undocs.org/en/S/26022; hereafter, S/26022.

70. Commission of Inquiry Report, 24-25; Yamin, *UN Peacekeeping Operations*, 94-96, based on interviews and 7th Frontier Force's war diary.

71. Bou et al., *Official History of Australian Peacekeeping*, 4:158-160; transcript of "Ambush in Mogadishu, Interview with General Thomas Montgomery," *Frontline*, PBS, September 1998, https://www.pbs.org/wgbh/pages/frontline/shows/ambush/interviews/montgomery.html.

72. Howe interview.

73. Bou et al., *Official History of Australian Peacekeeping*, 4:158-160.

74. Yamin, *UN Peacekeeping Operations*, 97.

75. Commission of Inquiry Report, 24-25.

76. Evans, "Task Force 1-22," 37-38; TF Mountain AAR, 4-6.

77. Commission of Inquiry Report, 24-25.

78. S/26022, 4–5; Sly, "UN Raises the Ante."

79. Howe interview.

80. Mohamed Farah Aidid, Letter to Jonathan Howe, 7 June 1993, S-1000-0028-03, AG-024, UNA.

81. Jonathan Howe, draft code cable to Kofi Annan, 5 June 1993, S-1000-0028-03, AG-024, UNA.

82. Jonathan Howe, final code cable to Kofi Annan, 5 June 1993, S-1000-0028-03, AG-024, UNA; emphasis added.

83. Drysdale, *Whatever Happened*, 185.

84. Farer Report, 7.

85. Farer Report, 7.

86. Farer Report, 6.

87. Central Intelligence Agency, intelligence memorandum, "Somalia: Dealing with Aideed," 12 July 1993, National Security Council and Records Management Office, "Declassified Documents Concerning Somalia," Clinton Digital Library, https://clinton.presidentiallibraries.us/items/show/49436.

88. Maren, *Road to Hell*, 226.

89. Transcript of "Ambush in Mogadishu, Interview with General Anthony Zinni," *Frontline*, PBS, September 1998, https://www.pbs.org/wgbh/pages/frontline/shows/ambush/interviews/zinni.html.

90. General Anthony C. Zinni, USMC (retired), interview by the author, 30 July 2020.

91. Stanley Meisler, "Peacekeeping: A Red-Faced United Nations Keeps Lid on Somalia Report," *Los Angeles Times*, 21 May 1994; Commission of Inquiry Report, 7–8.

92. Commission of Inquiry Report, 35, 36–41.

93. Commission of Inquiry Report, Annex 1, 50–55.

94. Commission of Inquiry Report, 36, 41.

95. Meisler, "Peacekeeping: Red-Faced United Nations."

96. Commission of Inquiry Report, 25.

97. UNOSOM AAR, 9.

98. Drysdale, *Whatever Happened*, 183.

99. United Nations, Security Council, Letter Dated 5 June 1993 from the Permanent Representative of Pakistan to the United Nations Addressed to the President of the Security Council, S/25888 (6 June 1993), available from un-docs.org/en/S/25888.

100. Permanent Mission of Pakistan to the United Nations, draft resolution for consideration by the UN Security Council, 5 June 1993, S-1000-0028-03, AG-024, UNA.

101. Poole, *Effort to Save Somalia*, 42.

102. U.N. SCOR, 48th sess., 3229th mtg., U.N. Doc. S/PV.3188 (6 June 1993), available from undocs.org/en/S/PV/3229.

103. U.N. Doc. S/PV.3188.

104. Albright, *Madam Secretary*, 143.

105. United Nations, Security Council Resolution 837, S/RES/837 (6 June 1993), available from https://digitallibrary.un.org/record/166972?ln=en.

106. Leonard Kapungu, note to General Godfrey on meeting with Mr. Awale, 8 June 1993, S-1000-0028-03, AG-024, UNA.

8. The Fatal Attraction of Mogadishu: The Summer War, June–October 1993

1. Theodore C. Sorensen and Christopher B. Jochnik, "Aidid's Arrest Is Crucial to UN Principle," *Los Angeles Times*, 20 July 1993.

2. Kofi Annan, interview with Lucia Annunziata, 16 July 1993, S-1000-0020-04, AG-024, United Nations Archives, New York (UNA).

3. Charles Krauthammer, "The Immaculate Intervention," *Time*, 26 July 1993.

4. Major F. Pascal, Intelligence Summary on Islam and Fundamentalism in Somalia, 30 December 1993, S-1000-0010-05, AG-024, UNA.

5. Sorensen and Jochnik, "Aidid's Arrest Is Crucial."

6. Donatella Lorch, "U.N. Moves Troops to Somali City and Vows Punishment for Attack," *New York Times*, 8 June 1993; United Nations, Security Council, *The Situation in Somalia: Report of the Secretary General*, S/26022 (1 July 1993), 5, available from undocs.org/en/S/26022 (hereafter, S/26022); United Nations Operations in Somalia (UNOSOM) II, Summary of Significant Events, 9, AWM260 3/6–AWM2019.8.1256, Somalia (UNOSOM/UNITAF) Collection, Australian War Memorial Digital Archives, https://www.awm.gov.au/collection/C2688006; hereafter, UNOSOM AAR.

7. Headquarters, 1st Brigade, 10th Mountain Division, *Task Force Mountain Warrior After Action Report Operation Restore Hope/Continue Hope Somalia 10 April–7 August 1993* (Fort Drum, NY: Headquarters, 10th Mountain Division, 1993), 4–6; hereafter, TF Mountain AAR.

8. See Trevor Findlay, *The Use of Force in UN Peace Operations* (New York: Oxford University Press, 2002), 195. For Glaspie's role in this meeting, Findlay cites J. Chopra, A. Eknes, and T. Nordbo, "Fighting for Hope in Somalia," *Peacekeeping and Multinational Operations* 6 (1995): 44.

9. State Department, outgoing telegram to US Mission to the UN, 10 June 1993, "FOIA 2012-0659-F—Peacekeeping Operations in Somalia," National Archives Digital Catalog, https://catalog.archives.gov/id/312197677.

10. Walter Poole, *The Effort to Save Somalia, August 1992–March 1994* (Washington, DC: Joint History Office, Office of the Chairman of the Joint Chiefs of Staff, 2005), 43.

11. S/26022, 5.

12. United States Forces Somalia, *After Action Report and Historical Overview* (Washington, DC: US Army Center of Military History, 2003), 92–93 (hereafter, USFORSOM AAR); United Nations, Security Council Resolution 837, S/RES/837 (6 June 1993), available from https://digitallibrary.un.org/record/166972?ln=en.

13. Babefemi Badejo, note to General Godfrey on meeting with leaders from G-11, 8 June 1993, S-1000-0028-03, AG-024, UNA.

14. S/26022, 5–6; Major John R. Evans, "Task Force 1-22 Infantry from Homestead to Port-au-Prince" (master's thesis, US Army Command and General Staff College, 2000), 39–40, https://apps.dtic.mil/sti/citations/ADA384044; TF Mountain AAR, 6; United Nations, Security Council, *Report of the Commission of Inquiry Pursuant to Security Council Resolution 885 (1993) to Investigate Armed Attacks on UNOSOM II Personnel which Led to Casualties among Them*, S/1994/653 (24 February 1994), 72, available from https://digitallibrary.un.org/record/189847?ln=en (hereafter, Commission of Inquiry Report); UNOSOM AAR, 10–11.

15. Jonathan T. Howe, Statement to the People of Somalia, 12 June 1993, "FOIA 2012-0659-F—Peacekeeping Operations in Somalia," National Archives Digital Catalog, https://catalog.archives.gov/id/312197587.

16. Press talking points, 14 June 1993, "FOIA 2012-0659-F—Peacekeeping Operations in Somalia," National Archives Digital Catalog, https://catalog.archives.gov/id/312197677.

17. S/26022, 6; John Drysdale, *Whatever Happened to Somalia?* 2nd ed. (London: Haan, 2001), 198; Commission of Inquiry Report, 29; Keith B. Richburg, "U.N. Unit Kills 14 Somali Civilians," *Washington Post*, 14 June 1993.

18. S/26022, 7.

19. USFORSOM AAR, 94–95; Tughral Yamin, *UN Peacekeeping Operations in Somalia: The Pakistani Perspective* (Karachi: Paramount Books, 2019), 103; Poole, *Effort to Save Somalia*, 44; TF Mountain AAR, 7–8.

20. USFORSOM AAR, 94–95.

21. Commission of Inquiry Report, 74–75, Annex 4, 60–61; USFORSOM AAR, 94–95; UNOSOM AAR, 11; Keith B. Richburg, "In War on Aidid, UN Battled Itself," *Washington Post*, 6 December 1993; S/26022, 7.

22. Statement by Jonathan Howe, special representative of the secretary-general, 17 June 1993, S-1000-0028-03, AG-024, UNA.

23. Transcript of "Ambush in Mogadishu, Interview with Admiral Jonathan Howe," *Frontline*, PBS, September 1998, https://www.pbs.org/wgbh/pages/frontline/shows/ambush/interviews/howe.html (hereafter, Howe interview); Jean Bou, Bob Breen, David Horner, Garth Pratten, and Miesje De Vogel, *The Official History of Australian Peacekeeping, Humanitarian and Post–Cold War Operations*, vol. 4, *The Limits of Peacekeeping: Australian Missions in Africa and the Americas, 1992–2005* (Port Melbourne: Cambridge University Press,

2019), 161; Keith B. Richburg, "Somalia's Scapegoat," *Washington Post*, 18 October 1993.

24. Boutros Boutros-Ghali, Letter to Presidents Hassan Gouled Aptidon, Issaias Affwerki, Daniel Toroitich arap Moi, and Meles Zenawi, 22 June 1993, in United Nations, *The United Nations and Somalia, 1992–1996* (New York: UN Department of Public Information, 1996), 270–271.

25. Commission of Inquiry Report, 74–75.

26. Bou et al., *Official History of Australian Peacekeeping*, 4:161.

27. Jennifer Parmelee, "Waltzing with Warlords," *Washington Post*, 20 June 1993.

28. Somalia After Action Review Briefing for US Secretary of Defense, 16 June 1994, Gordon Rudd Papers, supplied to the author; USFORSOM AAR, 28–29, 96.

29. Fabbio Fabbri, Italian Minister of Defense, Letter to Kofi Annan, 13 May 1993, S-1834-0026-02, AG-050, UNA; Ambassador F. Paulo Fulci, Letter to Annan, 7 June 1993, S-1834-0026-02, AG-050, UNA; Unidentified Author, "Tension Rises between Italian and U.S. Peacekeepers," Reuters, 23 June 1993, S-1834-0026-02, AG-050, UNA; Kofi Annan, Letter to Fulci, 30 June 1993, S-1834-0026-02, AG-050, UNA; Fulci, Letter to Annan, 5 July 1993, S-1834-0026-02, AG-050, UNA; S. Igbal Riza, note to the Secretary-General, 11 August 1993, S-1834-0026-02, AG-050, UNA; Beniamino Andreatta, Letter to Boutros-Ghali, 3 July 1993, S-1834-0026-02, AG-050, UNA.

30. For such allegations, see Captain Lee A. Rysewyk, "The Battle of the Black Sea," Infantry Officers' Advanced Course 2-94, May 1994, 3, Personal Experience Monographs Collection, Donovan Research Library, Maneuver Center of Excellence, Fort Benning, GA (hereafter, PEMC); Boutros Boutros-Ghali, *Unvanquished: A US-UN Saga* (New York: Random House, 1999), 97; Bou et al., *Official History of Australian Peacekeeping*, 4:162; Ken Menkhaus, "International Peacebuilding and the Dynamics of Local and National Reconciliation in Somalia," in *Learning from Somalia: The Lessons of Armed Humanitarian Intervention*, ed. Walter Clarke and Jeffrey Herbst (Boulder, CO: Westview Press, 1997), 52.

31. UNOSOM AAR, 14; Commission of Inquiry Report, 77; Vincenzo Nigro, "The Battle for Checkpoint Pasta," *La Republicca*, 5 July 2013; TF Mountain AAR, 9.

32. USFORSOM AAR, 96.

33. Piero Ignazi, Giampiero Giacomello, and Fabrizio Coticchia, *Italian Military Operations Abroad: Just Don't Call It War* (New York: Palgrave Macmillan, 2012), 104; Commission of Inquiry Report, 29; Lieutenant Colonel Thomas J. Daze, US Army (retired), interview by the author, 10 May 2024; hereafter, Daze interview. Daze was Bir's military assistant.

34. Commission of Inquiry Report, 29.

35. Annan interview.

36. Letter from Fabio Fabbri to Les Aspin, 22 July 1993, "FOIA 2012-0659-F—Peacekeeping Operations in Somalia," National Archives Digital Catalog, https://catalog.archives.gov/id/312197675.

37. United Nations, Security Council, *Further Report of the Secretary-General Submitted in Pursuance of Paragraph 18 of Resolution 814 (1993)*, S/26317 (17 August 1993), 19, available from undocs.org/en/S/26317; hereafter, S/26317.

38. Paolo Fulci, Letter to Boutros-Ghali, 12 August 1993, S-1834-0026-02, AG-050, UNA; Richard Bernstein, "Italian General Who Refused Order in Somalia Is Removed," *New York Times*, 14 July 1993; Alan Cowell, "Italy, in U.N. Rift, Threatens Recall of Somalia Troops," *New York Times*, 16 July 1993.

39. Poole, *Effort to Save Somalia*, 82, fn. 6, based on interviews with Montgomery.

40. Rick Atkinson, "U.S. to Leave Somalia with Its Guard Up," *Washington Post*, 8 December 1993; Somalia After Action Briefing for Secretary of Defense, 16 June 1994; USFORSOM AAR, 28–29.

41. UNOSOM AAR, 15–20.

42. Commission of Inquiry Report, 29–30, Annex 4, 60–63.

43. William Perry interview, 21 February 2006, 16, William J. Clinton Presidential History Project, Miller Center, University of Virginia.

44. Howe interview.

45. Howe interview.

46. Keith B. Richburg, "U.N. Helicopter Assault in Somalia Targeted Aidid's Top Commanders," *Washington Post*, 16 July 1993; Richburg, "In War on Aidid."

47. Transcript of "Ambush in Mogadishu, Interview with General Thomas Montgomery," *Frontline*, PBS, September 1998, https://www.pbs.org/wgbh/pages/frontline/shows/ambush/interviews/montgomery.html; hereafter, Montgomery interview.

48. Commission of Inquiry Report, 79; Drysdale *Whatever Happened*, xiii, 199–204.

49. Evans, "Task Force 1–22," 45; UNOSOM AAR, 16; TF Mountain AAR, 9–10.

50. UNOSOM II press release, 19 July 1993, S-1000-0028-04, AG-024, UNA.

51. Extracts from Report on Aidid Propaganda and Misinformation, 23 July 1993, S-1000-0028-04, AG-024, UNA.

52. Richburg, "U.N. Helicopter Assault in Somalia."

53. The four were Dan Eldon, Hos Maina, and Anthony Macharia from Reuters and Hansi Krause from Associated Press.

54. African Rights, *Somalia: Human Rights Abuses by the United Nations Forces* (London: African Rights, 1993), 6.

55. Drysdale, *Whatever Happened*, xiii.

56. Howe interview.

57. USFORSOM AAR, 96.

58. Paul Holmes, "Italy Calls for Suspension of Combat in Somalia," Reuters, 12 July 1993, S-1834-0026-02, AG-050, UNA.

59. Cowell, "Italy, in U.N. Rift."

60. Natalia Megas, "Did the U.S. Cover up a Civilian Massacre before Black Hawk Down?" *Daily Beast*, 5 January 2019; Keith B. Richburg, "U.N. Report Criticizes Military Tactics of Somalia Peacekeepers," *Washington Post*, 5 August 1993.

61. UNOSOM II Justice Division memorandum to Howe on legal and human rights aspects of UNOSOM military operations, 13 July 1993, S-1000-0029-01, AG-024, UNA.

62. Richburg, "In War on Aidid"; Richburg, "U.N. Report Criticizes Military Tactics"; James Jonah, Fax to Jonathan Howe, 5 August 1993, S-1000-0029-01, AG-024, UNA.

63. USFORSOM AAR, 41, 132.

64. Richburg, "In War on Aidid."

65. S/26317, 4; Commission of Inquiry Report, Annex 4, 60–66; UNOSOM AAR, 15; United Nations Peacekeeping Operations Fatalities in 1993, 6 January 1994, S-1000-0022-02, AG-024, UNA; Mike Horan, *Eyes over Mogadishu* (Bloomington, IN: Xlibris, 2003), 60–61; Michael Whetstone, *Madness in Mogadishu: Commanding the 10th Mountain Division's Quick Reaction Company during Black Hawk Down* (Mechanicsburg, PA: Stackpole Books, 2015), 34.

66. Daze interview.

67. TF Mountain AAR, 10; Headquarters, 2nd Battalion (Attack), 25th Aviation Regiment, *Task Force Raven After Action Report Operation Continue Hope Somalia 27 August 1993–9 January 1994* (Fort Drum, NY: Headquarters, 10th Mountain Division, 1993), Appendixes 2, 5 (hereafter, TF Raven AAR); Horan, *Eyes over Mogadishu*, 62; Whetstone, *Madness in Mogadishu*, 79.

68. Captain Jeffrey Riedel, US Army (retired), and Chief Warrant Officer Benjamin Johnson, US Army (retired), interview by the author, 11 August 2020 (hereafter, Riedel and Johnson interview); Horan, *Eyes over Mogadishu*, 71; Whetstone, *Madness in Mogadishu*, 73; USFORSOM AAR, 99–100; UNOSOM AAR, 20; Lawrence E. Casper, *Falcon Brigade: Combat and Command in Somalia and Haiti* (Boulder, CO: Lynne Rienner, 2001), 113.

69. S/26317, 5; UNOSOM AAR, 19–20; Commission of Inquiry Report, 79–81, Annex 4, 62–63; Whetstone, *Madness in Mogadishu*, 47.

70. Central Intelligence Agency, intelligence memorandum, "Somalia: Dealing with Aideed," 12 July 1993, National Security Council and Records Management Office, "Declassified Documents Concerning Somalia," Clinton Digital Library, https://clinton.presidentiallibraries.us/items/show/49436.

71. Madeleine K. Albright, "Yes, There Is a Reason to Be in Somalia," *New York Times*, 10 August 1993.

72. Bou et al., *Official History of Australian Peacekeeping*, 4:164; Montgomery interview.

73. Evans, "Task Force 1–22," 44–45.

74. TF Raven AAR, 3.19.

75. Montgomery interview.

76. Poole, *Effort to Save Somalia,* 45–46.

77. Poole, 45–46.

78. Daze interview.

79. Rick Atkinson, "The Raid That Went Wrong," *Washington Post,* 30 January 1994; Poole, *Effort to Save Somalia,* 47–49; Colin Powell, *My American Journey* (New York: Ballantine Books, 1996), 584; US Department of State, Briefing on the Situation in Somalia, 10 August 1993, National Security Council, Office of Press and Communications, and Philip "PJ" Crowley, "Somalia [3]," Clinton Digital Library, https://clinton.presidentiallibraries.us/items/show/48605.

80. Bill Clinton, *My Life* (New York: Alfred A. Knopf, 2004), 550; Lynne Duke, "President Promises 'Appropriate' Response," *Washington Post,* 9 August 1993.

81. Task Force Ranger comprised C Squadron, 1st Special Forces Operational Detachment—Delta; B Company/3rd Ranger Battalion; D Company, 1st Battalion/160th Special Operations Aviation Regiment; and a detachment from SEAL Team Six and US Air Force Special Tactics. Statement by Major General William Garrison, in *Hearings on U.S. Military Operations in Somalia before the Committee on Armed Services, United States Senate,* 103rd Cong., 12 May 1994, 39; Atkinson, "Raid That Went Wrong"; Captain Larry D. Perino, "The Battle of the Black Sea," 9, PEMC.

82. Captain Thomas DiTomasso, "The Battle of the Black Sea, Bravo Company, 3rd Ranger Battalion, 75th Ranger Regiment, 3–4 October 1993," Infantry Officers' Advanced Course 4-94, May 1994, 2, PEMC.

83. Mark Bowden, *Killing Pablo: The Hunt for the World's Greatest Outlaw* (New York: Grove Press, 2001), 195–197, 288.

84. William G. Boykin, *Never Surrender* (New York: Faith Words, 2008), 252; Atkinson, "Raid That Went Wrong"; Rysewyk, "Battle of the Black Sea," 5; Howard E. Wasdin and Stephen Templin, *SEAL Team Six: Memoirs of an Elite Navy SEAL Sniper* (New York: St. Martin's Press, 2011), 179.

85. Atkinson, "Raid That Went Wrong"; USFORSOM AAR, 137–138.

86. Boykin, *Never Surrender,* 258.

87. Perino, "Battle of the Black Sea," 4–5.

88. Report of Larry De Boice, faxed to Howe by Luiz Maria-Gomez, 30 August 1993, S-1000-0021-02, AG-024, UNA.

89. United States Information Agency, Foreign Media Reaction Digest, 8 September 1993, "FOIA 2012-0659-F—Peacekeeping Operations in Somalia," National Archives Digital Catalog, https://catalog.archives.gov/id/312197927.

90. Atkinson, "Raid That Went Wrong"; USFORSOM AAR, 137–138.

91. Horan, *Eyes over Mogadishu,* 32; Casper, *Falcon Brigade,* 135–136; Wasdin and Templin, *SEAL Team Six,* 194–196; Atkinson, "Raid That Went Wrong."

92. Wasdin and Templin, *SEAL Team Six*, 206.

93. Jonathan Howe, Fax to UN Department of Peacekeeping Operations, 7 January 1994, S-1000-0022-02, AG-024, UNA.

94. Wasdin and Templin, *SEAL Team Six*, 217.

95. Atkinson, "Raid That Went Wrong."

96. USFORSOM AAR, 137–138.

97. USFORSOM AAR, 137–138.

98. Yamin, *UN Peacekeeping Operations*, 125; UNOSOM AAR, 26; Wasdin and Templin, *SEAL Team Six*, 215.

99. Major General Maurice Baril, Fax to Jonathan Howe, 19 August 1993, S-1000-0021-02, AG-024, UNA.

100. Lieutenant General Cevik Bir, Fax to Jonathan Howe on UNOSOM II force requirements, 6 August 1993, S-1000-0021-02, AG-024, UNA.

101. Somalia After Action Briefing for Secretary of Defense, 16 June 1994; Major General Maurice Baril, Fax to Jonathan Howe, 26 July 1993, S-1000-0020-04, AG-024, UNA; Major General Norman E. Williams, UN Logistics Support Command, interview by Major Michael W. Byrne, 9 February 1994, 15, RHIT-C-362, Somalia Oral History Interview Collection, US Army Center of Military History, Washington DC (USACMH) (hereafter, Williams interview); Ambassador T. P. Sreenivasan, Pakistani Permanent Mission to the UN, Letter to Kofi Annan, 28 September 1993, S-1000-0021-03, AG-024, UNA.

102. Major General Maurice Baril, Fax to Jonathan Howe on force build up, 19 August 1993, S-1000-0021-02, AG-024, UNA; Bir to Howe, Fax on UNOSOM II Force Requirements, 6 August 1993.

103. Lieutenant General Cevik Bir, Fax to Major General Maurice Baril on Pakistani offer to UNOSOM II, 20 September 1993, S-1000-0021-03, AG-024, UNA; Major General Maurice Baril, Fax to Jonathan Howe, 24 September 1993, S-1000-0021-03, AG-024, UNA.

104. Bir to Howe, Fax on UNOSOM II Force Requirements, 6 August 1993; fax from Bir to Baril, 20 September 1993; fax from Baril to Howe, 24 September 1993.

105. Lieutenant General Cevik Bir, Memorandum to Jonathan Howe on force plans and requirements, 13 September 1993, S-1000-0021-03, AG-024, UNA.

106. Lieutenant General Cevik Bir, Fax to Major General Maurice Baril on Indian brigade, 30 September 1993, S-1000-0021-03, AG-024, UNA.

107. United Nations, Security Council, *Further Report of the Secretary-General Submitted in Pursuance of Paragraph 19 of Resolution 814 (1993) and Paragraph A5 of Resolution 865 (1993)*, S/26738 (12 November 1993), 17, available from undocs.org/en/S/26738 (hereafter, S/26738); USFORSOM AAR, 103–104; Commission of Inquiry Report, 82.

108. The commission found no evidence of any Italian involvement in the 5 September firefight. Commission of Inquiry Report, 31.

109. Yamin, *UN Peacekeeping Operations*, 127.

110. First Lieutenant Kennard M. Murphy, "Multinational Combined Arms Breaching (MOUT) in Somalia," unpublished personal experience monograph, Infantry Officers' Advanced Course 4-94, 20 May 1994, 10–11, PEMC.

111. Commission of Inquiry Report, 86.

112. TF Raven AAR, Appendix 2.

113. Murphy, "Multinational Combined Arms Breaching," 14–17; S/26738; UNOSOM AAR, 24; TF Raven AAR, Appendix 2.

114. Casper, *Falcon Brigade*, 120.

115. TF Mountain AAR, 10; Whetstone, *Madness in Mogadishu*, 51.

116. Whetstone, *Madness in Mogadishu*, 39, 43.

117. Whetstone, 52–59.

118. Captain Dennis C. Williams, Summary of 13 September 1993 Engagement in Mogadishu, Somalia, n.d., folder 1, box 2, Contingency Operations Collection: Operation Restore Hope (ORH), USACMH; Whetstone, *Madness in Mogadishu*, 83–90.

119. TF Raven AAR, Appendix 2.

120. Horan, *Eyes over Mogadishu*, 59.

121. UNOSOM AAR, 24–25; TF Raven AAR, Appendix 2; Williams, Summary of 13 September 1993 Engagement.

122. TF Raven AAR, Appendix 4.

123. Colonel Lawrence E. Casper, Valorous Unit Award Recommendation for 2nd Battalion (Attack)/25th Aviation Regiment to Major General Thomas Montgomery, deputy commander United Nations Operation in Somalia (UNOSOM), 4 December 1993, folder 3, box 4, Kevin M. Born Papers, US Army Heritage and Education Center, Carlisle, PA (USAHEC).

124. Atkinson, "U.S. to Leave Somalia."

125. General Anthony Zinni, USMC (retired), interview by the author, 30 July 2020. For more on the tired tactics argument, see Jonathan Carroll, "Courage under Fire: Reevaluating Black Hawk Down and the Battle of Mogadishu," *War in History* 29, 3 (2022): 704–726.

126. Williams interview, 41; TF Raven AAR, 2–3.

127. Horan, *Eyes over Mogadishu*, 40.

128. Whetstone, *Madness in Mogadishu*, 33.

129. Statement by Garrison, 38; Atkinson, "Raid That Went Wrong."

130. Carroll, "Courage under Fire," 713.

131. UNOSOM AAR, 21–22.

132. Commission of Inquiry Report, Annex 4, 62–63; Riedel and Johnson interview.

133. TF Raven AAR, 3.16.

134. TF Mountain AAR, Tab G.

135. Perino, "Battle of the Black Sea," 4–5.

136. Riedel and Johnson interview. Shrader was awarded the Distinguished Flying Cross for landing his stricken aircraft and the Silver Star for carrying his wounded copilot to safety while under fire. Letter from Colonel Randall F. Cochran to the Honorable Edward Whitfield, Representative to the First District, State of Kentucky, 20 May 1999, supplied to the author.

137. Captain Michael L. Whetstone, sworn statement on the 25 September 1993 engagement in Mogadishu, Somalia, 25 September 1993, folder 1, box 2, ORH, USACMH.

138. Summary of 25 September 1993 engagement in Mogadishu, Somalia, n.d., folder 1, box 2, ORH, USACMH; UNOSOM AAR, 26; TF Raven AAR, Appendix 2.

139. Summary of 25 September 1993 engagement in Mogadishu.

140. Captain Tim McDavitt, UNOSOM II press briefing, 25 September 1993, folder 2, box 128, Gordon R. Sullivan Papers, USAHEC.

141. Carroll, "Courage under Fire," 718.

142. Ray D. Leoni, *Black Hawk: The Story of a World Class Helicopter* (Reston, VA: American Institute of Aeronautics & Astronautics, 2007), 10, 103–114.

143. Femi Badejo, deputy SRSG's meeting with the Political Division, 16 July 1993, S-1000-0028-04, AG-024, UNA.

144. Anthony Lake, Letter to Jimmy Carter, 1 September 1993, "FOIA 2012-0659-F—Peacekeeping Operations in Somalia," National Archives Digital Catalog, https://catalog.archives.gov/id/312197581.

145. Handwritten remarks by Richard A. Clarke on news article describing Aidid's plan to mediate through Jimmy Carter, 22 August 1993, "FOIA 2012-0659-F—Peacekeeping Operations in Somalia," National Archives Digital Catalog, https://catalog.archives.gov/id/312197581.

146. Boutros Boutros-Ghali, "Don't Make the UN's Hard Job Harder," *New York Times*, 20 August 1993.

147. Keith B. Richburg, "U.N. Rejected Somali Overture," *Washington Post*, 17 October 1993.

148. Barton Gellman, "The Words behind a Deadly Decision," *Washington Post*, 31 October 1993; Poole, *Effort to Save Somalia*, 50.

149. Keith B. Richburg, "US Somalia Envoy Urged Policy Shift before 18 GIs Died," *Washington Post*, 11 November 1993.

150. Gellman, "Words behind a Deadly Decision."

151. Richburg, "US Somalia Envoy Urged Policy Shift."

152. Poole, *Effort to Save Somalia*, 50–53.

153. Samuel P. Huntington, "New Contingencies, Old Roles," *Joint Forces Quarterly* 1, 2 (Autumn 1993): 42.

154. Tom Farer, "From Warlord to Peacelord? Like It or Not, the West Needs to Enlist Aideed, or Face Disaster," *Washington Post*, 12 September 1993.

155. Poole, *Effort to Save Somalia*, 52–53; Boutros-Ghali, *Unvanquished*, 99–101.

156. Boutros Boutros-Ghali, Letter to Warren Christopher, 25 September 1993, "FOIA 2012-0659-F—Peacekeeping Operations in Somalia," National Archives Digital Catalog, https://catalog.archives.gov/id/312197671.

157. Poole, *Effort to Save Somalia*, 52–56.

158. William J. Clinton, "Remarks to the 48th Session of the United Nations General Assembly in New York City," 27 September 1993 (emphasis added), American Presidency Project, https://www.presidency.ucsb.edu/node/217952.

159. Elaine Sciolino, "Pentagon Changes Its Somalia Goals as Effort Falters," *New York Times*, 28 September 1993.

160. Montgomery interview.

161. USFORSOM AAR, 35.

162. Statement by Major General Thomas Montgomery, in *Hearings on U.S. Military Operations in Somalia before the Committee on Armed Services, United States Senate*, 103rd Cong., 12 May 1994, 48–51; Montgomery interview; Gellman, "Words behind a Deadly Decision."

163. *Hearings on Current Military Operations before the Committee on Armed Services, United States Senate*, 103rd Cong., 7 October 1993, 101–102.

164. *Hearings on Current Military Operations*, 13 October 1993, 145.

165. Gellman, "Words behind a Deadly Decision."

166. USFORSOM AAR, 35; Poole, *Effort to Save Somalia*, 56.

167. USFORSOM AAR, 42–43; Poole, *Effort to Save Somalia*, 55–57; United States Senate, *Review of the Circumstances Surrounding the Ranger Raid on October 3–4, 1993 in Mogadishu, Somalia* (Washington, DC: Senate Armed Services Committee, 1995), 45–46.

9. The Battle of Mogadishu

1. Sean J. Darragh, memorandum to Jeremy D. Rosner on conversation with General Garrison, 7 October 1993, "FOIA 2012-0659-F—Peacekeeping Operations in Somalia," National Archives Digital Catalog, https://catalog.archives.gov/id/312197727.

2. Rick Atkinson, "U.S. to Leave Somalia with Its Guard Up," *Washington Post*, 8 December 1993.

3. Keith B. Richburg, "Somali's Cease-Fire Takes Hold," *Washington Post*, 11 October 1993.

4. Headquarters, 2nd Battalion (Attack), 25th Aviation Regiment, *Task Force*

Raven After Action Report Operation Continue Hope Somalia 27 August 1993–9 January 1994 (Fort Drum, NY: Headquarters, 10th Mountain Division, 1993), Appendix 2 (hereafter, TF Raven AAR); Captain Jeffrey Riedel, US Army (retired), and Chief Warrant Officer Benjamin Johnson, US Army (retired), interview by the author, 11 August 2020; Colonel Randall F. Cochran, US Army (retired), interview by the author, 15 June 2020.

5. Jonathan Carroll, "Courage under Fire: Reevaluating Black Hawk Down and the Battle of Mogadishu," *War in History* 29, 3 (2022): 704–726.

6. William G. Boykin, *Never Surrender* (New York: Faith Words, 2008), 260–262.

7. Statement by Major General William Garrison, in *Hearings on U.S. Military Operations in Somalia before the Committee on Armed Services, United States Senate,* 103rd Cong., 12 May 1994, 7–9.

8. Captain Kurt J. Smith, "Task Force Ranger in Somalia, 1st Special Forces Operational Detachment—Delta, 3–4 October 1993," Personal Experience Monographs Collection, Donovan Research Library, Maneuver Center of Excellence, Fort Benning, GA; hereafter, PEMC.

9. Rick Atkinson, "The Raid That Went Wrong," *Washington Post,* 30 January 1994.

10. Captain James O. Lechner, "A Monograph of Combat Operations in Mogadishu, Somalia, Conducted by Task Force Ranger," Advanced Course 4-94, 19 September 1994, 16, PEMC; Captain Lee A. Rysewyk, "The Battle of the Black Sea," Infantry Officers' Advanced Course 2-94, May 1994, 9–13, PEMC; Garrison statement, 7–9; Captain Larry D. Perino, "The Battle of the Black Sea," 7, PEMC.

11. Atkinson, "Raid That Went Wrong."

12. Michael J. Durant and Steven Hartov, *The Night Stalkers* (New York: G. P. Putnam's Sons, 2006), 224.

13. Durant and Hartov, 226.

14. Rysewyk, "Battle of the Black Sea," 9–13; Garrison statement, 7–9.

15. Atkinson, "Raid That Went Wrong"; Rysewyk, "Battle of the Black Sea," 9–13; Perino, "Battle of the Black Sea," 7.

16. Atkinson, "Raid That Went Wrong"; Rick Atkinson, "Night of a Thousand Casualties," *Washington Post,* 31 January 1994.

17. Rysewyk, "Battle of the Black Sea," 9–13; Garrison statement, 2–9.

18. Rysewyk, "Battle of the Black Sea," 9–13; Garrison statement, 2–7.

19. First Lieutenant Chris Hornbarger, "TF Raven's Role on 3 October," in TF Raven AAR, 4.

20. Atkinson, "Raid That Went Wrong"; Atkinson, "Night of a Thousand Casualties"; Rysewyk, "Battle of the Black Sea," 9–13; TF Raven Tactical Operations Cell Log 3–4 October, in TF Raven AAR; Major Michael D. Ellerbe, Summary of 3–4 October 1993 Engagement in Mogadishu, Somalia, n.d., folder 1,

box 2, Contingency Operations Collection: Operation Restore Hope (ORH), US Army Center of Military History, Washington, DC (USACMH); Falcon Brigade Quick Reaction Force Summary of Combat Operation on 3 October 1993, in TF Raven AAR, 2.

21. United Nations, Security Council, *Report of the Commission of Inquiry Pursuant to Security Council Resolution 885 (1993) to Investigate Armed Attacks on UNOSOM II Personnel which Led to Casualties among Them*, S/1994/653 (24 February 1994), 87–89, available from https://digitallibrary.un.org/record/189847?ln=en (hereafter, Commission of Inquiry Report); Falcon Brigade Quick Reaction Force Summary, 2.

22. Falcon Brigade Quick Reaction Force Summary, 3; Tughral Yamin, *UN Peacekeeping Operations in Somalia: The Pakistani Perspective* (Karachi: Paramount Books, 2019), 138.

23. Hornbarger, "TF Raven's Role," 7; Captain Dennis C. Williams, 2nd Battalion/14th Infantry Regiment, Tactical Operations Cell Watch Officer Log, 4 October 1993, folder 1, box 2, ORH, USACMH; TF Raven Tactical Operations Cell Log 3–4 October; TF Raven AAR, Appendix 2; Ellerbe, Summary of 3–4 October 1993 Engagement.

24. Durant and Hartov, *Night Stalkers*, 231.

25. Hornbarger, "TF Raven's Role," 13.

26. Hornbarger, 14; TF Raven Tactical Operations Cell Log 3–4 October; Ellerbe, Summary of 3–4 October 1993 Engagement; Commission of Inquiry Report, 89.

27. Williams, Tactical Operations Cell Watch Officer Log, 4 October 1993; TF Raven Tactical Operations Cell Log 3–4 October; Hornbarger, "TF Raven's Role," 7; Ellerbe, Summary of 3–4 October 1993 Engagement.

28. Williams, Tactical Operations Cell Watch Officer Log, 4 October 1993; TF Raven Tactical Operations Cell Log 3–4 October; Hornbarger, "TF Raven's Role," 7; Ellerbe, Summary of 3–4 October 1993 Engagement.

29. Williams, Tactical Operations Cell Watch Officer Log, 4 October 1993; TF Raven Tactical Operations Cell Log 3–4 October; Hornbarger, "TF Raven's Role," 7, 22; Ellerbe, Summary of 3–4 October 1993 Engagement; Commission of Inquiry Report, 32–33.

30. Carroll, "Courage under Fire," 722–725.

31. United Nations, Security Council, Letter Dated 4 October 1993 from the Chargé d'Affaires A.I. of the Permanent Mission of Somalia to the United Nations Addressed to the President of the Security Council, S/26530 (4 October 1993), available from undocs.org/en/S/26530.

32. Perino, "Battle of the Black Sea," 1.

33. Michael Whetstone, *Madness in Mogadishu: Commanding the 10th Mountain Division's Quick Reaction Company during Black Hawk Down* (Mechanicsburg, PA: Stackpole Books, 2015), 196.

34. Message from General C. E. Mundy to General Gordon R. Sullivan, 29 October 1993, box 129, Gordon R. Sullivan Papers, US Army Heritage and Education Center, Carlisle, PA.

35. United States Forces Somalia, *After Action Report and Historical Overview* (Washington, DC: US Army Center of Military History, 2003), 111.

36. Matt Eversmann, "Operation Gothic Serpent," in *The Battle of Mogadishu: Firsthand Accounts from the Men of Task Force Ranger*, ed. Matt Eversmann and Dan Schilling (New York: Ballantine Books, 2004), 35.

37. Major General Norman E. Williams, UN Logistics Support Command, interview by Major Michael W. Byrne, 9 February 1994, 44, RHIT-C-362, Somalia Oral History Interview Collection, USACMH.

38. Robert F. Baumann, Lawrence A. Yates, and Versalle F. Washington, *"My Clan against the World": US and Coalition Forces in Somalia 1992–1994* (Fort Leavenworth, KS: Combat Studies Institute Press, 2004), 165.

39. Bill Clinton, *My Life* (New York: Alfred A. Knopf, 2004), 551.

40. William J. Clinton, Remarks on Operation Restore Hope, 5 May 1993, transcript from the Miller Center at the University of Virginia, available from https://millercenter.org/the-presidency/presidential-speeches/may-5-1993-remarks-operation-restore-hope.

41. CNN televised news broadcast, 4 October 1993.

42. ABC televised news broadcast, 4 October 1993.

43. *Hearings on Current Military Operations before the Committee on Armed Services, United States Senate*, 103rd Cong., 4 October 1993, 58.

44. *Time*, 18 October 1993, front cover.

45. George J. Church, "Somalia: Anatomy of a Disaster," *Time*, 18 October 1993.

46. Letter from House Republicans to President Bill Clinton, 6 October 1993, "FOIA 2012-0659-F—Peacekeeping Operations in Somalia," National Archives Digital Catalog, https://catalog.archives.gov/id/312197995.

47. Statement by Senator Strom Thurmond, in *Hearings on Current Military Operations*, 4 October 1993.

48. *Hearings on Current Military Operations*, 56–59.

49. Statement by Senator Robert Smith, in *Hearings on Current Military Operations*, 4 October 1993, 57.

50. Statement by Lieutenant General John Sheehan, in *Hearings on Current Military Operations*, 7 October 1993, 94.

51. Statement by Major General Thomas Montgomery, in *Hearings on Current Military Operations*, 7 October 1993, 99–100.

52. Sheehan statement, 78–80.

53. Baumann, Yates, and Washington, *"My Clan,"* 166, based on the authors' interview with Montgomery.

54. Montgomery statement, 99–100.

55. *Hearings on Current Military Operations,* 7 October 1993, 101–102.

56. *Hearings on Current Military Operations,* 13 October 1993, 145.

57. Statement by Major General Thomas Montgomery, in *Hearings on U.S. Military Operations in Somalia,* 12 May 1994, 12.

58. Garrison statement, 35.

59. Garrison statement, 7.

60. United States Senate, *Review of the Circumstances Surrounding the Ranger Raid on October 3–4, 1993 in Mogadishu, Somalia* (Washington, DC: Senate Armed Services Committee, 1995), 5, 9; hereafter, *Review of Circumstances.*

61. *Review of Circumstances,* 5.

62. *Review of Circumstances,* 25–27.

63. *Review of Circumstances,* 44.

64. White House Press Secretary, remarks by the president before departing the White House for New Jersey, 8 October 1993, National Security Council, Office of Press and Communications, and Philip "PJ" Crowley, "Department of Defense [2]," Clinton Digital Library, https://clinton.presidentiallibraries.us/items/show/48487.

65. Bill Clinton, handwritten note to Anthony Lake, 12 November 1993, "FOIA 2012-0659-F—Peacekeeping Operations in Somalia," National Archives Digital Catalog, https://catalog.archives.gov/id/312197551.

66. Keith D. Hahn, notes from June 12 meeting with Joyce/Smith/Pilla family, 18 May 1994, "FOIA 2006-1021-F—Peacekeeping Operations in Somalia," Clinton Digital Library, https://clinton.presidentiallibraries.us/items/show/14594.

67. Elizabeth Drew, *On the Edge: The Clinton Presidency* (New York: Simon & Schuster, 1994), 316–317.

68. Memorandum of telephone conversation between Bill Clinton and Tony Blair, 10 April 1999, National Security Council and Records Management Office, "Declassified Documents Concerning Tony Blair," Clinton Digital Library, https://clinton.presidentiallibraries.us/items/show/48779.

69. Clinton, *My Life,* 552.

70. Nancy Soderberg, memorandum to Anthony Lake on crisis management, 19 October 1993, "FOIA 2012-0659-F—Peacekeeping Operations in Somalia," National Archives Digital Catalog, https://catalog.archives.gov/id/312197829.

71. Thomas W. Lippmann and Barton Gellman, "Distracted Clinton Administration Missed Signs of 'Peacemaking' Gone Sour," *Washington Post,* 10 October 1993.

72. R. Jeffrey Smith and Ann Devroy, "Somalia Inattention Led to US Deaths," *Washington Post,* 17 October 1993.

73. Church, "Somalia: Anatomy of a Disaster."

74. White House Office of the Press Secretary, press conference by Presi-

dent Bill Clinton, 14 October 1993, "FOIA 2012-0659-F—Peacekeeping Operations in Somalia," National Archives Digital Catalog, https://catalog.archives.gov/id/312197633.

75. Clinton, *My Life*, 551.

76. Letter reproduced in Mark Bowden, *Black Hawk Down: A Story of Modern War*, 2nd ed. (New York: Grove Press, 2010), 337–338.

77. White House Office of the Press Secretary, press briefing by Secretary of Defense Les Aspin, 7 October 1993, "FOIA 2012-0659-F—Peacekeeping Operations in Somalia," National Archives Digital Catalog, https://catalog.archives.gov/id/312197633.

78. R. James Woolsey interview, 13 January 2010, 51–53, William J. Clinton Presidential History Project, Miller Center, University of Virginia.

79. Josh King, memorandum to Roy Neel, 5 October 1993, "FOIA 2012-0659-F—Peacekeeping Operations in Somalia," National Archives Digital Catalog, https://catalog.archives.gov/id/312197825.

80. Rod von Lipsey, memorandum to Mack McLarty, 16 October 1993, "FOIA 2012-0659-F—Peacekeeping Operations in Somalia," National Archives Digital Catalog, https://catalog.archives.gov/id/312197547.

81. Commission of Inquiry Report; United Nations Operations in Somalia (UNOSOM) II, Summary of Significant Events, 29, AWM260 3/6–AWM2019.8.1256, Somalia (UNOSOM/UNITAF) Collection, Australian War Memorial Digital Archives, https://www.awm.gov.au/collection/C2688006.

82. Church, "Somalia: Anatomy of a Disaster."

83. William J. Clinton, address on Somalia, 7 October 1993, transcript from the Miller Center at the University of Virginia, available from https://millercenter.org/the-presidency/presidential-speeches/october-7-1993-address-somalia.

84. Whetstone, *Madness in Mogadishu*, 196.

85. Commission of Inquiry Report, 32–33.

10. Caught in a Dangerous Interlude: Charting the Course for UNOSOM amidst the Settling Dust

1. Lieutenant General Cevik Bir, code cable to Jonathan Howe on end states, 16 November 1993, S-1000-0022-01, AG-024, United Nations Archives, New York (UNA).

2. Boutros Boutros-Ghali, *Unvanquished: A US-UN Saga* (New York: Random House, 1999), 119–120.

3. Mark Fineman, "Aging U.S. Coptors Sent to Somalia, Pakistan Charges," *Los Angeles Times*, 14 March 1994.

4. Major F. Pascal, Intelligence Summary on Islam and Fundamentalism in Somalia, 30 December 1993, S-1000-0010-05, AG-024, UNA.

5. Martin R. Ganzglass, "The Restoration of the Somali Justice System," in *Learning from Somalia: The Lessons of Armed Humanitarian Intervention*, ed. Walter Clarke and Jeffrey Herbst (Boulder, CO: Westview Press, 1997), 31.

6. Marc Grossman, memorandum to William H. Itoh, Executive Secretary, National Security Council, 26 July 1993, "FOIA 2012-0659-F—Peacekeeping Operations in Somalia," National Archives Digital Catalog, https://catalog.archives.gov/id/312197675.

7. United Nations, Security Council, *Annex I to Further Report of the Secretary-General Submitted in Pursuance of Paragraph 18 of Resolution 814 (1993)*, S/26317 (17 August 1993), 25-28, available from undocs.org/en/S/26317 (hereafter, S/26317); Ganzglass, "Restoration of Somali Justice System," 29-30; Michael J. Kelly, *Peace Operations: Tackling the Military, Legal and Policy Challenges* (Canberra: Australian Government Publishing Service, 1997), 8.33-8.35.

8. Kelly, *Peace Operations*, 9.5.

9. Ganzglass, "Restoration of Somali Justice System," 29-31.

10. S/26317, 10.

11. S/26317, 10-11; Ken Menkhaus, "International Peacebuilding and the Dynamics of Local and National Reconciliation in Somalia," in Clarke and Herbst, *Learning from Somalia*, 50-52.

12. Angelina Eichhorst, Letter to Omar Halim, 14 July 1993, S-1000-0028-04, AG-024, UNA.

13. Babefemi Badejo, note to General Godfrey on meeting with leaders from G-11, 8 June 1993, S-1000-0028-03, AG-024, UNA.

14. Note to the file, 20 July 1993, S-1000-0028-03, AG-024, UNA.

15. Eichhorst to Halim, 14 July 1993.

16. United Nations, Geospatial Information Section, *UNOSOM II Deployment as of September 1993*, E416/10/1993 (September 1993), available from https://digitallibrary.un.org/record/175490?ln=en.

17. United Nations Operations in Somalia (UNOSOM) II, Summary of Significant Events, 2-3, 13-15, AWM260 3/6-AWM2019.8.1256, Somalia (UNOSOM/UNITAF) Collection, Australian War Memorial Digital Archives, https://www.awm.gov.au/collection/C2688006; hereafter, UNOSOM AAR.

18. Brigadier General Maurice Quadri, Commander French Forces Somalia, Letter to Bir, 9 August 93, S-1000-0021-02, AG-024, UNA.

19. UNOSOM AAR, 17-23.

20. United Nations, *The United Nations and Somalia, 1992-1996* (New York: UN Department of Public Information, 1996), 55.

21. United States Forces Somalia, *After Action Report and Historical Overview* (Washington, DC: US Army Center of Military History, 2003), 100-101; hereafter, USFORSOM AAR.

22. United Nations, *United Nations and Somalia*, 55-58.

23. Kelly, *Peace Operations*, 9.7.

24. S/26317, 6, 22-23.

25. United Nations, Security Council Resolution 865, S/RES/865 (22 September 1993), available from https://digitallibrary.un.org/record/173064?ln=en.

26. Carl F. Ernst, "The Urban Area during Support Missions Case Study: Mogadishu, the Operational Level," in *Capital Preservation: Preparing for Urban Operations in the Twenty-First Century*, ed. Russell W. Glenn (Santa Monica, CA: RAND Corporation, 2001), 376; Joint Task Force Somalia: After Action Report, 14 October 1993 to 31 March 1994, 1-2, 8-9, Personal Papers of Professor Gordon W. Rudd, School of Advanced Warfighting, Marine Corps University, Quantico, supplied to the author (hereafter, JTF Somalia AAR); Gary J. Ohls, *Somalia . . . From the Sea* (Newport, RI: Naval War College Press, 2009), 161-162.

27. Transcript of "Ambush in Mogadishu, Interview with Admiral Jonathan Howe," *Frontline*, PBS, September 1998, https://www.pbs.org/wgbh/pages/frontline/shows/ambush/interviews/howe.html.

28. United Nations, Security Council, *Further Report of the Secretary-General Submitted in Pursuance of Paragraph 19 of Resolution 814 (1993) and Paragraph A5 of Resolution 865 (1993)*, S/26738 (12 November 1993), 11, available from undocs.org/en/S/26738; hereafter, S/26738.

29. JTF Somalia AAR, 8-9; Ernst, "Urban Area during Support Missions," 360.

30. JTF Somalia AAR, 4.

31. A. J. Plunkett and William H. McMichael, "Fort Monroe General Told to Lead Troops in Somalia," *Daily Press*, 14 October 1993; Walter Poole, *The Effort to Save Somalia, August 1992–March 1994* (Washington, DC: Joint History Office, Office of the Chairman of the Joint Chiefs of Staff, 2005), 86 (Poole's interview with Montgomery); JTF Somalia AAR, 10.

32. Lawrence E. Casper, *Falcon Brigade: Combat and Command in Somalia and Haiti* (Boulder, CO: Lynne Rienner, 2001), 102; Ohls, *Somalia . . . From the Sea*, 161-162.

33. General Anthony C. Zinni, USMC (retired), interview by the author, 30 July 2020; transcript of "Ambush in Mogadishu, Interview with Ambassador Robert Oakley," *Frontline*, PBS, September 1998, https://www.pbs.org/wgbh/pages/frontline/shows/ambush/interviews/oakley.html; hereafter, Oakley interview.

34. Zinni interview, 30 July 2020.

35. Zinni interview.

36. Zinni interview.

37. S/26738, 18.

38. Zinni interview, 30 July 2020; Oakley interview.

39. Zinni interview, 30 July 2020.

40. Zinni interview; Oakley interview.

41. This argument has entered both the public and the academic domain.

Yet while researching the Somali intervention, I saw no documents mentioning al-Qaeda. For example, see James Gordon Meek, "Black Hawk Down Anniversary: Al Qaeda's Hidden Hand," https://abcnews.go.com/Blotter/black-hawk-anniversary-al-qaedas-hidden-hand/story?id=20462820; Robert G. Patman, "The Roots of Strategic Failure: The Somalia Syndrome and Al Qaeda's Path to 9/11," *International Politics* 52, 1 (2015): 89–109; Daniel P. Bolger, *Why We Lost: A General's Inside Account of the Iraq and Afghanistan Wars* (New York: Houghton, Mifflin, Harcourt, 2014), 16.

42. Scott Peterson, *Me against My Brother: At War in Somalia, Sudan, and Rwanda* (New York: Routledge, 2001), 151.

43. Babiker Khalifa, memorandum to Victor James Gbeho, 23 November 1994, S-1000-0003-05, AG-024, UNA.

44. Zinni interview, 30 July 2020.

45. Jonathan Howe, Letter to Beniamino Andreatta, 30 September 1993, S-1834-0026-02, AG-050, UNA.

46. Keith B. Richburg, "Somali Faction Frees U.S. Pilot," *Washington Post*, 15 October 1993.

47. White House Office of the Press Secretary, press conference by President Bill Clinton, 14 October 1993, "FOIA 2012-0659-F—Peacekeeping Operations in Somalia," National Archives Digital Catalog, https://catalog.archives.gov/id/312197633.

48. David Gergen, memorandum to Anthony Lake on General Aideed, 19 October 1993, "FOIA 2012-0659-F—Peacekeeping Operations in Somalia," National Archives Digital Catalog, https://catalog.archives.gov/id/312197547.

49. United Nations, Security Council Resolution 885, S/RES/885 (16 November 1993), available from https://digitallibrary.un.org/record/242009?ln=en.

50. Boutros-Ghali, *Unvanquished*, 119–120.

51. S/26738, 3, 7, 21, 23.

52. S/26738, 24.

53. United Nations, Security Council Resolution 886, S/RES/886 (18 November 1993), available from https://digitallibrary.un.org/record/177296?ln=en.

54. Bir, code cable to Howe, 16 November 1993.

55. United Nations, Security Council, *Further Report of the Secretary-General Submitted in Pursuance of Paragraph 4 of Resolution 886 (1993)*, S/1994/12 (6 January 1994), 5–6, available from undocs.org/en/S/1994/12; hereafter, S/1994/12.

56. Runo Bergstrom, fax status report of District and Regional Council, 21 March 1994, S-1000-0007-02, AG-024, UNA.

57. Casper, *Falcon Brigade*, 117.

58. Ernst, "Urban Area during Support Missions," 361.

59. Robert F. Baumann, Lawrence A. Yates, and Versalle F. Washington, *"My Clan against the World": US and Coalition Forces in Somalia 1992–1994* (Fort

Leavenworth, KS: Combat Studies Institute Press, 2004), 184; Casper, *Falcon Brigade*, 117.

60. JTF Somalia AAR, 4–5, 20, 44; Ernst, "Urban Area during Support Missions," 367–371; Casper, *Falcon Brigade*, 102.

61. JTF Somalia AAR, 24: Joe Frescura, "Mechanized Platoon and Company Operations in Somalia: October 1993 to March 1994," 4, unpublished personal experience monograph, Infantry Officers' Advanced Course 2-96, 5 June 1996, Personal Experience Monographs Collection, Donovan Research Library, Maneuver Center of Excellence, Fort Benning, GA.

62. JTF Somalia AAR, 11.

63. Ernst as quoted in Baumann, Yates, and Washington, *"My Clan,"*186.

64. JTF Somalia AAR, 14.

65. JTF Somalia AAR, 12–15; Ernst, "Urban Area during Support Missions," 384–385.

66. Casper, *Falcon Brigade*, 117; JTF Somalia AAR, 16–17; Baumann, Yates, and Washington, *"My Clan,"*190–191; Poole, *Effort to Save Somalia*, 63–64; Lieutenant Colonel Thomas J. Daze, US Army (retired), interview by the author, 10 May 2024; hereafter, Daze interview.

67. Daze interview.

68. Rick Atkinson, "Some Heavy Symbolism in Somalia," *Washington Post*, 22 November 1993.

69. S/26738, 11.

70. Boutros-Ghali, *Unvanquished*, 111.

71. USFORSOM AAR, 44.

72. Satish Nambiar, *For the Honour of India: A History of Indian Peacekeeping* (New Delhi: Centre for Armed Forces Historical Research, United Service Institution of India, 2009), 263.

73. UNOSOM AAR, 31.

74. S/26738; Nambiar, *For the Honour*, 262–269.

75. Message by William J. Clinton, 18 October 1993, S-1000-0021-04, AG-024, UNA.

76. Statement by Kofi Annan, Undersecretary-General for Peacekeeping Operations, to UNOSOM Troop Contributors Meeting, 26 October 1993, S-1000-0021-04, AG-024, UNA.

77. Statement of Ambassador Fulci to UNOSOM Troop Contributors Meeting, 26 October 1993, S-1000-0021-04, AG-024, UNA.

78. Major General Maurice Baril, Fax to Jonathan Howe on Egyptian deployment, 27 October 1993, S-1000-0021-04, AG-024, UNA; S/26738.

79. Briefing on logistics issues related to U.S. withdrawal, n.d., S-1000-0022-02, AG-024, UNA; Major General Maurice Baril, Fax to Lieutenant General Aboo Bakar, 11 April 1994, S-1000-0023-01, AG-024, UNA; S/1994/12, 11.

80. Lieutenant General Cevik Bir, Fax to Major General Maurice Baril, 7 October 1993, S-1000-0021-04, AG-024, UNA.

81. Kofi Annan, code cable to Jonathan Howe, 13 October 1993, S-1000-0021-04, AG-024, UNA.

82. Anja Dalgaard-Nielsen, *Germany, Pacifism and Peace Enforcement* (Manchester, UK: Manchester University Press, 2006), 105, 122; Rick Atkinson, "Somalia Mission Fuels German Debate," *Washington Post*, 25 February 1994.

83. Kofi Annan, code cable to Jonathan Howe, 29 October 1993, S-1000-0021-04, AG-024, UNA.

84. Major General Maurice Baril, Fax to Jonathan Howe on German contingent, 8 October 1993, S-1000-0021-04, AG-024, UNA.

85. S. Iqbal Riza, Letter to Ambassador Detlev Graf Zu Rantzau, 13 October 1993, S-1000-0021-04, AG-024, UNA.

86. Annan, code cable to Howe, 29 October 1993.

87. Lieutenant General Cevik Bir, Fax to Major General Maurice Baril on German issue, 28 October 1993, S-1000-0021-04, AG-024, UNA.

88. Major General Maurice Baril, Fax to Jonathan Howe, 19 November 1993, S-1000-0022-01, AG-024, UNA.

89. Fax from Bir to Baril, 28 October 1993; Lieutenant General Cevik Bir, Letter to Major General Maurice Baril, 6 November 1993, S-1000-0022-01, AG-024, UNA; S/1994/12, 11; Atkinson, "Somalia Mission Fuels German Debate."

90. Elisabeth Lindenmayer, Fax to Jonathan Howe, 7 January 1994, S-1000-0022-02, AG-024, UNA.

91. Daniela Salvati, Letter to Juan Carlos Brandt, 20 December 1993, S1834-0026-02, AG-050, UNA.

92. S/1994/12, 12.

93. Kofi Annan, code cable to Jonathan Howe, 19 January 1994, S-1000-0022-02, AG-024, UNA.

94. Kingsley Moghalu, meeting notes from UNOSOM troop contributing countries meeting, 20 January 1994, S-1000-0022-02, AG-024, UNA.

95. United Nations, Security Council Resolution 897, S/RES/897 (4 February 1994), available from https://digitallibrary.un.org/record/180890?ln=en.

96. JTF Somalia AAR, 10.

97. Poole, *Effort to Save Somalia*, 66.

98. S/1994/12.

99. JTF Somalia AAR, 18–19; Falcon Brigade, Somalia update, January 1994, folder 6, box 3, Kevin M. Born Papers, US Army Heritage and Education Center, Carlisle, PA; UNOSOM AAR, 39; Lansana Kouyate, Letter to Major Botonakis, Hellenic Contingent, 5 March 1994, S-1000-0022-03, AG-024, UNA.

100. Somali Salvation Alliance (G12), Review of the United Nations Role in

Somalia: Comment and Suggestions, 3 January 1994, S-1000-0001-01, AG-024, UNA.

101. Kofi Annan, Fax to Lieutenant General Aboo Bakar, 7 April 1994, S-1000-0023-01, AG-024, UNA; Tughral Yamin, *UN Peacekeeping Operations in Somalia: The Pakistani Perspective* (Karachi: Paramount Books, 2019), 155.

102. Rick Atkinson, "U.N. Force in Somalia Changes Guard," *Washington Post*, 20 March 1994.

103. Fineman, "Aging U.S. Coptors Sent to Somalia."

104. United Nations, Security Council, Letter Dated 6 January 1994 from the Secretary-General Addressed to the President of the Security Council, S/1994/21 (11 January 1994), 1, available from undocs.org/en/S/1994/21; UNOSOM AAR, 34; UNOSOM Force Headquarters Nominal Roll, 15 April 1993, S-1000-0022-04, AG-024, UNA; United Nations, Security Council, *Further Report of the Secretary-General on the United Nations Operation in Somalia Submitted in Pursuance of Paragraph 14 of Resolution 897 (1994)*, S/1994/614 (24 May 1994), 1, undocs.org/en/S/1994/614.

105. Falcon Brigade, Somalia update, January 1994.

106. Michael Maren, *The Road to Hell: The Ravaging Effects of Foreign Aid and International Charity* (New York: Free Press, 1997), 235–236.

11. Left to Wither on the Vine: The End of UNOSOM in Somalia

1. Mohamed Farah Aidid, Letter to Ali Mahdi Mohamed, 11 November 1994, S-1000-0003-05, AG-024, United Nations Archives, New York (UNA).

2. U.N. SCOR, 49th sess., 3447th mtg., U.N. Doc. S/PV.3447 (4 November 1994), 15, available from https://undocs.org/en/S/PV.3447; hereafter, S/PV.3447.

3. S/PV.3447, 7.

4. United Nations, Security Council Resolution 897, S/RES/897 (4 February 1994), available from https://digitallibrary.un.org/record/180890?ln=en.

5. UNOSOM Information and Operations Center, Assessment of USC/SNA "One," 30 November 1994, S-1000-0003-05, AG-024, UNA.

6. John L. Hirsch and Robert B. Oakley, *Somalia and Operation Restore Hope: Reflections on Peacemaking and Peacekeeping* (Washington, DC: Institute of Peace Press, 1995), 140.

7. Lansana Kouyate, Situation Report to Jonathan Howe, 11 December 1993, S-1000-0004-04, AG-024, UNA.

8. United Nations, Security Council, *Further Report of the Secretary-General Submitted in Pursuance of Paragraph 4 of Resolution 886 (1993)*, S/1994/12 (6 January 1994), 5, available from undocs.org/en/S/1994/12 (hereafter, S/1994/12); Lansana Kouyate, Situation Report to Jonathan Howe, 6 December 1993.

S-1000-0004-04, AG-024, UNA; Ken Menkhaus, "International Peacebuilding and the Dynamics of Local and National Reconciliation in Somalia," in *Learning from Somalia: The Lessons of Armed Humanitarian Intervention*, ed. Walter Clarke and Jeffrey Herbst (Boulder, CO: Westview Press, 1997), 47.

9. Babiker Khalifa, telefax transmission to Leonard Kapungu, 31 January 1994, S-1000-0003-04, AG-024, UNA.

10. Babiker Khalifa, telefax transmission to Ambassador Ataul Karim, 26 February 1994, S-1000-0001-01, AG-024, UNA.

11. Results of the Consultations amongst the Somali G12 Political Organizations, Cairo, March 1994, 1–7, S-1000-0001-01, AG-024, UNA.

12. United Nations, Security Council, *Further Report of the Secretary-General on the United Nations Operation in Somalia Submitted in Pursuance of Paragraph 14 of Resolution 897 (1994)*, S/1994/614 (24 May 1994), 1, available from undocs. org/en/S/1994/614 (hereafter, S/1994/614); Menkhaus, "International Peacebuilding," 53.

13. Group of 12, Delegation of Authority, 23 March 1994, S-1000-0001-01, AG-024, UNA; memorandums on power of attorney written by Mahamed Nur Alio, Chairman of the SDM, and Abdulaziz Yusuf, Chairman of the SSNM, 24 March 1994, S-1000-0003-04, AG-024, UNA.

14. Declaration by the Leaders of the Somali Political Organizations, Nairobi, 24 March 1994, S-1000-0001-01, AG-024, UNA; S/1994/614; Ken Menkhaus, "Getting out vs. Getting Through: U.S. and U.N. Policies in Somalia," *Middle East Policy* 3, 1 (March 1994): 160.

15. United Nations, Security Council, *Further Report of the Secretary-General on the United Nations Operation in Somalia Submitted in Pursuance of Paragraph 2 of Resolution 923 (1994)*, S/1994/839 (18 July 1994), 7, available from undocs .org/en/S/1994/839 (hereafter, S/1994/839); Menkhaus, "International Peacebuilding," 52.

16. Major General Michael Nyambuya, Situation Report 493, 23–24 August 1994, S-1000-0024-03, AG-024, UNA; Major General Michael Nyambuya, Situation Report 488, 18–19 August 1994, S-1000-0024-03, AG-024, UNA; Major General Michael Nyambuya, Situation Report 487, 17–18 August 1994, S-1000-0024-03, AG-024, UNA.

17. Sue Bicknell, memo on Gate 1A control arrangements to Camp Commandant, 16 April 1994, S-1000-0023-01, AG-024, UNA; Colonel Aly Helmy Soliman, Egyptian Brigade, Security Statistics, July 1994, S-1000-0024-01, AG-024, UNA; Tughral Yamin, *UN Peacekeeping Operations in Somalia: The Pakistani Perspective* (Karachi: Paramount Books, 2019), 160.

18. Lieutenant General Aboo Bakar, Weekly Report to Major General Maurice Baril, 7 April 1994, S-1000-0023-01, AG-024, UNA.

19. Minutes of meeting of UNOSOM Troop Contributing Countries, 8 April 1994, S-1000-0030-02, AG-024, UNA.

20. Minutes of meeting of UNOSOM Troop Contributing Countries, 8 April 1994.

21. Ataul Karim, note to Lansana Kouyate, 6 April 94, S-1000-0001-01, AG-024, UNA.

22. Minutes of meeting of UNOSOM Troop Contributing Countries, 8 April 1994.

23. United Nations Operations in Somalia (UNOSOM) II, Summary of Significant Events, 37, AWM260 3/6–AWM2019.8.1256, Somalia (UNOSOM/UNITAF) Collection, Australian War Memorial Digital Archives, https://www.awm.gov.au/collection/C2688006; hereafter, UNOSOM AAR.

24. Commandant D. J. Conway, Officer Commanding No. 2 Transport Company, G2 Monthly Report, June 1994, ACS-145/06, Irish Defence Forces Military Archives, Cathal Brugha Barracks, Dublin (IDFMA).

25. UNOSOM AAR, 37, 40; Huntley G. Anderson, memorandum to Lansana Kouyate, 26 April 1994, S-1000-0001-01, AG-024, UNA.

26. Anderson memorandum to Kouyate, 26 April 1994; S/1994/614; UNOSOM AAR, 40, 43.

27. UNOSOM Security Assessments, 25 April 1994, S-1000-0022-04, AG-024, UNA.

28. UNOSOM AAR, 40.

29. Commandant D. J. Conway, Officer Commanding No. 2 Transport Company, G2 Monthly Report, May 1994, ACS-145/06, IDFMA.

30. Decree issued by the officers and leaders of Habr Gedir, 24 June 1994, S-1000-0003-04, AG-024, UNA; UNOSOM Policy and Planning Group, The Medina Conflict, 26 June 1994, S-1000-0003-04, AG-024, UNA; UNOSOM Information and Operations Center, Assessment of USC/SNA "One," 30 November 1994.

31. Conway, G2 Monthly Report, June 1994.

32. William Clive, memorandum to Bjornsson, 15 July 1994, S-1000-0024-01, AG-024, UNA.

33. S/1994/839, 6; United Nations, *The United Nations and Somalia, 1992–1996* (New York: UN Department of Public Information, 1996), 68–69; UNOSOM AAR, 45–46; Lieutenant General Aboo Bakar, Fax to Kofi Annan, 18 July 1994, S-1000-0024-01, AG-024, UNA; Lieutenant General Aboo Bakar, Fax to Kofi Annan, 20 July 1994, S-1000-0024-01, AG-024, UNA.

34. Hisham Omayad, code cable to Kofi Annan, 3 July 1994, S-1000-0001-01, AG-024, UNA.

35. Lieutenant General Aboo Bakar, Weekly Situation Report, 27 June–3 July 1994, S-1000-0035-03, AG-024, UNA.

36. Somali National Alliance, radio address by Mohamed Farah Aidid, 7 July 1994, S-1000-0003-05, AG-024, UNA.

37. Mohamed Farah Aidid, speech delivered on 12 July 1994, S-1000-0003-04, AG-024, UNA.

38. Mohamed Farah Aidid, Letter to Lansana Kouyate, 21 July 1994, S-1000-0003-04, AG-024, UNA.

39. Lansana Kouyate, code cable to Kofi Annan, 20 April 1994, S-1000-0023-01, AG-024, UNA; Lieutenant General Aboo Bakar, memorandum to Lansana Kouyate on UNOSOM II force structure, April 1994, S-1000-0023-01, AG-024, UNA.

40. UNOSOM Force Headquarters Daily Strength Return, 30 April 1994, S-1000-0022-04, AG-024, UNA; Bakar, memorandum to Kouyate, April 1994.

41. S/1994/839, 8.

42. Douglas Manson, Fax to D. Beissel, 5 May 1994, S-1000-0023-02, AG-024, UNA.

43. Colonel M. B. Marwa, Nigerian Ministry of Defence, message to DPKO, May 1994, S-1000-0023-02, AG-024, UNA.

44. S/1994/614, 16-17.

45. United Nations, Security Council Resolution 923, S/RES/923 (31 May 1994), available from https://digitallibrary.un.org/record/188055?ln=en.

46. S/1994/614, 7-11; S/1994/839, 10-12; Martin R. Ganzglass, "The Restoration of the Somali Justice System," in Clarke and Herbst, *Learning from Somalia,* 33-34.

47. S/1994/839, 14; emphasis added.

48. S/1994/839, 14; Ganzglass, "Restoration of Somali Justice," 33-34; Ali Mahdi Mohamed, Letters to Lansana Kouyate, 12 and 19 May 1994, S-1000-0001-01, AG-024, UNA.

49. UNOSOM Policy and Planning Group, Medina Conflict, 26 June 1994; Lieutenant General Aboo Bakar, Weekly Situation Report, 25-31 July 1994, S-1000-0035-03, AG-024, UNA; UNOSOM AAR, 47-48; Lieutenant General Aboo Bakar, Special Situation Report No. 16, 1 August 1994, S-1000-0024-02, AG-024, UNA.

50. Lieutenant General Aboo Bakar, Weekly Situation Report, 25-31 July 1994, S-1000-0035-03, AG-024, UNA; UNOSOM AAR, 47-48; Bakar, Special Situation Report No. 16, 1 August 1994.

51. Record of meeting with G-12 leaders in Nairobi, 29 July 1994, S-1000-0001-01, AG-024, UNA.

52. Note to the file, SRSG's meeting with General Aidid, 1 August 1994, S-1000-0003-05, AG-024, UNA.

53. UNOSOM AAR, 49.

54. Hassan Conteh, Zone Director North Mogadishu, memo to Lieutenant General Aboo Bakar, 8 August 1994, S-1000-0024-02, AG-024, UNA.

55. G2 Monthly Report, No. 2 Transport Company, 1 July–17 August 1994, ACS-145/06, IDFMA.

56. Office of the SRSG, Assessment of the Prospects for National Reconciliation, 1994, S-1000-0007-04, AG-024, UNA.

57. Babiker Khalifa, Fax to Ambassador Ataul Karim, 26 July 1994, S-1000-0030-04, AG-024, UNA.

58. Ali Mahdi Mohamed, Letter to Boutros Boutros-Ghali, 24 July 1994, S-1000-0001-01, AG-024, UNA.

59. United Nations, Security Council, *Report of the Secretary-General to the Security Council on Somalia,* S/1994/977 (17 August 1994), 2–4, available from undocs.org/en/S/1994/977; hereafter, S/1994/977.

60. S/1994/977, 6.

61. S/1994/977, 6.

62. United Nations, Security Council, *Further Report of the Secretary-General Submitted in Pursuance of Paragraph 19 of Resolution 814 (1993) and Paragraph A5 of Resolution 865 (1993),* S/26738 (12 November 1993), 24, available from undocs.org/en/S/26738.

63. S/1994/12, 14.

64. Elisabeth Lindenmayer, Fax to Jonathan Howe, 7 January 1994, S-1000-0022-02, AG-024, UNA.

65. Anthony Lake, memorandum to Clinton, 19–24 September 1994, National Security Council, Speechwriting Office, and Robert Boorstin, "Declassified Documents Concerning Robert Boorstin, NSC Speechwriter," Clinton Digital Library, https://clinton.presidentiallibraries.us/items/show/36629.

66. Memorandum for the Government, Approval to Withdraw Defense Forces Personnel from UNOSOM II in Somalia, 11 July 1994, DOPS-TEMP-4526, IDFMA.

67. Commandant D. J. Conway, Officer Commanding No. 2 Transport Company, G4 Monthly Report, March 1994, ACS-145/06, IDFMA.

68. Commandant D. J. Conway, Officer Commanding No. 2 Transport Company, Letter to Lieutenant General Aboo Bakar, 6 April 1994, ACS-145/06, IDFMA.

69. Abdul Rahman Turay, telefax transmission to Igor Khvorostiany, 3 November 1994, S-1000-0003-05, AG-024, UNA.

70. United Nations, Security Council, *Report by the Secretary-General Concerning the Situation in Somalia,* S/1994/1068 (17 September 1994), 5, available from undocs.org/en/S/1994/1068; hereafter, S/1994/1068.

71. Victor James Gbeho, Weekly Situation Report, 22–28 August 1994, S-1000-0035-03, AG-024, UNA; Memorandum on the SNA response to the 22 August attacks, 9 September 1994, S-1000-0003-05, AG-024, UNA; Lieutenant General Aboo Bakar, Weekly Situation Report, 5–11 September 1994, S-1000-0035-03, AG-024, UNA; Victor James Gbeho, Weekly Situation

Report, 10–16 October 1994, S-1000-0035-03, AG-024, UNA; UNOSOM AAR, 50–52.

72. Babiker Khalifa, telefax transmission to Ambassador Ataul Karim, 6 September 1994, S-1000-0001-01, AG-024, UNA.

73. United Nations, Security Council, *Report by the Secretary-General Concerning the Situation in Somalia,* S/1994/1166 (14 October 1994), 7, available from undocs.org/en/S/1994/1166; hereafter, S/1994/1166.

74. S/1994/1166, 3.

75. Somali National Alliance, An Address to the Nation to Mark the First Anniversary of the Great Victory Day, 3 October 1994, S-1000-0003-05, AG-024, UNA.

76. United Nations, Security Council, *Report of the Security Council Mission to Somalia on 26 and 27 October 1994,* S/1994/1245 (3 November 1994), 2, available from undocs.org/en/S/1994/1245; hereafter, S/1994/1245.

77. Office of the DSRSG, summary of biweekly activities, 2–14 August 1994, S-1000-0035-03, AG-024, UNA.

78. S/1994/1068, 3.

79. United Nations, Security Council, *Report of the Secretary-General on the Situation on Somalia Submitted in Pursuance of Paragraph 13 of Resolution 954 (1994),* S/1995/231 (28 March 1995), 2, available from undocs.org/en/S/1995/231; hereafter, S/1995/231.

80. Press statement by SAMO, SSNM, and SNU, 19 October 1994, S-1000-0003-05, AG-024, UNA.

81. S/1995/231, 2.

82. Ali Mahdi Mohamed, Letter to Boutros Boutros-Ghali, 24 July 1994, S-1000-0001-01, AG-024, UNA.

83. United Nations, Security Council, Letter Dated 18 October 1994 from the Permanent Representative of Tunisia to the United Nations Addressed to the President of the Security Council, S/1994/1204 (22 October 1994), available from undocs.org/en/S/1994/1204.

84. United Nations, Security Council, note by the president of the Security Council, S/1994/1194 (21 October 1994), available from undocs.org/en/S/1994/1194 (hereafter, S/1994/1194); United Nations, Security Council Resolution 946, S/RES/946 (30 September 1994), available from https://digitallibrary.un.org/record/161993?ln=en; United Nations, Security Council Resolution 953, S/RES/953 (31 October 1994), available from https://digitallibrary.un.org/record/163379?ln=en.

85. S/1994/1194.

86. In addition to Ali Mahdi, also present were the chairmen of the SSDF, SPM, SDM, SAMO, SNU, USP, and SSV; vice-chairmen of the SNF, SSNM, and SDA; and, notably, Abdinasir Ahmed Adan Serjito, who had reportedly replaced Aidid as chairman of USC-SNA.

87. S/1994/1245, Annex II.

88. S/1994/1245, Annex V.

89. In addition to Aidid as chairman of the USC-SNA, also present were the chairmen of the SSDF, SPM-SNA, SDM-SNA, SSNM-SNA, SAMO, USF, USP, USC, SNDU, SNU, and SDA and the vice-chairman of the SNM. S/1994/1245, Annex VI.

90. S/1994/1245, Annex VII.

91. S/1994/1245, 9.

92. S/1994/1245, 8.

93. S/PV.3447, 7, 14.

94. S/PV.3447, 7, 18, 19.

95. Press statement by the official spokesmen of the National Reconciliation Conference in Mogadishu, 4 November 1994, S-1000-0003-05, AG-024, UNA; S/1995/231; Babiker Khalifa, telefax transmission to Victor James Gbeho, 3 November 1994, S-1000-0003-05, AG-024, UNA.

96. Ali Mahdi Mohamed, Letter to General Mohamed Farah Aidid, 4 November 1994, S-1000-0003-05, AG-024, UNA.

97. Mohamed Farah Aidid, Letter to Ali Mahdi Mohamed, 11 November 1994, S-1000-0003-05, AG-024, UNA.

98. S/1995/231, 3; Babiker Khalifa, memorandum to Victor James Gbeho, 23 November 1994, S-1000-0003-05, AG-024, UNA.

99. Internal memorandum from Marian Dinu, Political Affairs Officer, to Salimatu Kahn, Deputy Director, UNOSOM Political Affairs, 31 October 1994, S-1000-0003-05, AG-024, UNA.

100. Lieutenant General Cevik Bir, memorandum to Jonathan Howe on Force Command Planning for UNOSOM Withdrawal, 17 January 1994, S-1000-0022-02, AG-024, UNA; UNOSOM II Withdrawal Plan, 10 April 1994, S-1000-0023-01, AG-024, UNA.

101. S/1994/1166, 5.

102. Kofi Annan, note to the Secretary-General on withdrawal of UNOSOM II, 20 October 1994, S-1831-0011-12, AG-050, UNA.

103. General Anthony C. Zinni, USMC (retired), interview by the author, 30 October 2020; Gary J. Ohls, *Somalia . . . From the Sea* (Newport, RI: Naval War College Press, 2009), 177-178.

104. Lake, memo to Clinton, 19-24 September 1994.

105. Zinni interview, 30 October 2020; Major Gregory F. Kliene, "Operation United Shield: A Case Study" (master's thesis, US Marine Corps Command and Staff College, 1999), 15.

106. Lieutenant General Aboo Bakar, Weekly Situation Report, 5-11 December 1994, S-1000-0035-03, AG-024, UNA; Satish Nambiar, *For the Honour of India: A History of Indian Peacekeeping* (New Delhi: Centre for Armed Forces Historical Research, United Service Institution of India, 2009), 274-275.

107. Nambiar, *For the Honour*, 274; Victor James Gbeho, Weekly Situation Reports, 2 January–5 February 1995, S-1000-0035-03, AG-024, UNA; S/1995/231.

108. Victor James Gbeho, Weekly Situation Reports, 9 January–19 February 1995, S-1000-0035-03, AG-024, UNA; Rick Atkinson, "Marines Close Curtain on U.N. in Somalia," *Washington Post*, 3 March 1995; S/1995/231, 14.

109. Zinni interview, 30 October 2020; Ohls, *Somalia . . . From the Sea*, 183–192; S/1994/1166; Kliene, "Operation United Shield," 11–15.

110. Rick Atkinson, "Lean, Not-So-Mean Marines Set for Somalia," *Washington Post*, 25 February 1995; Zinni interview, 30 October 2020.

111. Zinni interview, 30 October 2020.

112. S/1995/231, 14.

113. Zinni interview, 30 October 2020.

114. Zinni interview.

115. Ohls, *Somalia . . . From the Sea*, 193.

116. UNOSOM Force Headquarters, Fax to DPKO Situation Room, 12 January 1994, S-1000-0022-02, AG-024, UNA.

117. Kliene, "Operation United Shield," 36–39; Zinni interview, 30 October 2020; Ohls, *Somalia . . . From the Sea*, 184–189.

118. Kliene, "Operation United Shield," 36–39; Zinni interview, 30 October 2020; Ohls, *Somalia . . . From the Sea*, 184–189.

119. Kliene, "Operation United Shield," 36–39; Zinni interview, 30 October 2020; Ohls, *Somalia . . . From the Sea*, 184–189.

120. Zinni interview, 30 October 2020; Ohls, *Somalia . . . From the Sea*, 189.

Epilogue: Dancing on the Corpse of a Helicopter

1. Dennis C. Jett, *Why Peacekeeping Fails* (New York: Palgrave, 2001), 3.

2. Robert B. Oakley, interview by Charles Stuart Kennedy and Thomas Stern, 7 July 1992, 162, Association for Diplomatic Studies and Training Foreign Affairs Oral History Project, https://www.loc.gov/item/mfdipbib000876/.

3. Steinar Bjornsson, telefax to Hocine Medili, 19 April 1995, S-1831-0011-12, AG-050, United Nations Archives, New York; United Nations, Security Council, *Report of the Secretary-General on the Situation on Somalia Submitted in Pursuance of Paragraph 13 of Resolution 954 (1994)*, S/1995/231 (28 March 1995), 16–17, available from undocs.org/en/S/1995/231.

4. Mohamed Haji Mukhtar, *Historical Dictionary of Somalia* (Lanham, MD: Scarecrow Press, 2003), xliii–xliv; Haroun M. Hassan, "Somali Faction Leader Gen. Aidid Is Dead, Radio Says," Associated Press, 2 August 1996.

5. James C. McKinley Jr., "How a U.S. Marine Became Leader of Somalia," *New York Times*, 12 August 1996; Blake Stilwell, "This U.S. Marine Went

to Somalia and Became a Warlord," We Are the Mighty, 17 July 2020, https://www.wearethemighty.com/mighty-trending/us-marine-went-somalia-became-warlord/.

6. General Anthony C. Zinni, USMC (retired), interview by the author, 30 October 2020.

7. National Security Council and National Security Council Records Management Office, "PDD-25—U.S. Policy on Reforming Multilateral Peace Operations, 5/3/1994," Clinton Digital Library, https://clinton.presidentiallibraries.us/items/show/12749.

8. David Fitzgerald, *Learning to Forget: US Army Counterinsurgency Doctrine and Practice from Vietnam to Iraq* (Stanford, CA: Stanford University Press, 2013), 104–105.

9. William Perry interview, 21 February 2006, 18–19, William J. Clinton Presidential History Project, Miller Center, University of Virginia.

10. United Nations, Security Council, *Supplement to An Agenda for Peace: Position Paper of the Secretary-General on the Occasion of the Fiftieth Anniversary of the United Nations*, S/1995/1 (25 January 1995), 8, available from undocs.org/en/S/1995/1.

11. United Nations, Security Council, *Supplement to An Agenda for Peace*, 9.

12. Thijs W. Brocades-Zaalberg, *Soldiers and Civil Power: Supporting or Substituting Civil Authorities in Modern Peace Operations* (Amsterdam: Amsterdam University Press, 2006), 243.

13. Madeleine Albright, *Madam Secretary* (New York: Miramax Books, 2003), 207–216.

14. Barbara Crossette, "U.N. Leader Halts Bid for New Term but Does Not Quit," *New York Times*, 5 December 1996.

15. "2 Italian Generals Resign over Somali Scandal," *Tampa Bay Times*, 15 June 1997; Raf Casert, "In Italy, Belgium, and Canada, Somalia Peacekeeping Scandals Growing," Reuters, 23 June 1997.

16. Lance Morrow, "The Trouble with Good Intentions: In Feeding Somalia and Backing Yeltson, America Discovers the Limits of Idealism," *Time*, 18 October 1993.

17. United States Forces Somalia, *After Action Report and Historical Overview* (Washington, DC: US Army Center of Military History, 2003), 55.

18. Robert F. Baumann, Lawrence A. Yates, and Versalle F. Washington, *"My Clan against the World": US and Coalition Forces in Somalia 1992–1994* (Fort Leavenworth, KS: Combat Studies Institute Press, 2004).

19. Jane Boulden, *Peace Enforcement: The United Nations Experience in Congo, Somalia, and Bosnia* (Westport, CT: Praeger, 2001).

20. Michael Rose, *Fighting for Peace: Bosnia 1994* (London: Harvill Press, 1998), 126–127, 241.

21. Rose, 242.

22. Walter Poole, *The Effort to Save Somalia, August 1992–March 1994* (Washington, DC: Joint History Office, Office of the Chairman of the Joint Chiefs of Staff, 2005), 42.

Bibliography

Africa Watch Women's Rights Project. *Seeking Refuge, Finding Terror: The Wide-spread Rape of Somali Women Refugees in North Eastern Kenya.* New York: Human Rights Watch, 1993.

Aidid, Mohammed Farah. "Democracy in Somalia: Its Roots and Its Future Scenario." In *Preferred Future Development in Somalia,* edited by Mohammed Farah Aidid and Satya Pal Ruhela, 12-25. New Delhi: Vikas, 1993.

———. "Foreign Aid for the Somali Nation's Development: A Challenge to Our Integrity and Future." In *Preferred Future Development in Somalia,* edited by Mohammed Farah Aidid and Satya Pal Ruhela, 243-255. New Delhi: Vikas, 1993.

———. "Opening a New Chapter in the Lives of the Somali Nomads and Minorities." In *Preferred Future Development in Somalia,* edited by Mohammed Farah Aidid and Satya Pal Ruhela, 53-84. New Delhi: Vikas, 1993.

———. "The Virgin Land of Somalia: Prospects of Indo-Somali Technological Cooperation." In *Preferred Future Development in Somalia,* edited by Mohammed Farah Aidid and Satya Pal Ruhela, 217-242. New Delhi: Vikas, 1993.

Albright, Madeleine. *Madam Secretary.* New York: Miramax Books, 2003.

Allard, C. Kenneth. "Lessons Unlearned: Somalia and Joint Doctrine." *Joint Forces Quarterly* 3, 3 (Autumn 1995): 105-109.

Allard, Kenneth. *Somalia Operations: Lessons Learned.* Washington, DC: National Defense University Press, 1995.

Anderson, Scott, *The Man Who Tried to Save the World: The Dangerous Life and Mysterious Disappearance of Fred Cuny.* New York: Doubleday, 1999.

Arnold, S. L. "Somalia: An Operation Other Than War." *Military Review* 73, 12 (December 1993): 26-35.

Arnold, S. L., and David T. Stahl. "A Power Projection Army in Operations Other Than War." *Parameters* 23, 4 (Winter 1993-94): 4-26.

Bacevich, Andrew J. *America's War for the Greater Middle East: A Military History.* New York: Random House, 2016.

Baum, Matthew A. "How Public Opinion Constrains the Use of Force: The Case of Operation Restore Hope." *Presidential Studies Quarterly* 34, 2 (June 2004): 187-226.

Baumann, Robert F., Lawrence A. Yates, and Versalle F. Washington. *"My Clan against the World": US and Coalition Forces in Somalia 1992-1994.* Fort Leavenworth, KS: Combat Studies Institute Press, 2004.

Belemy, Alex J., and Paul D. Williams. *Understanding Peacekeeping*. Cambridge: Polity Press, 2016.

Belman, John. "What Was Left Behind." In *The Battle of Mogadishu: Firsthand Accounts from the Men of Task Force Ranger*, edited by Matt Eversmann and Dan Schilling, 107–126. New York: Ballantine Books, 2004.

Bercuson, David. *Significant Incident: Canada's Army, the Airborne, and the Murder in Somalia*. Toronto: McClelland & Stewart, 1996.

Besteman, Catherine. "Primordialist Blinders: A Reply to I. M. Lewis." *Cultural Anthropology* 13, 1 (February 1998): 109–120.

———. "Representing Violence and 'Othering' Somalia." *Cultural Anthropology* 11, 1 (February 1996): 120–133.

———. *Unraveling Somalia: Race, Class, and the Legacy of Slavery*. Philadelphia: University of Pennsylvania Press, 1999.

Biddle, Stephen. *Nonstate Warfare: The Military Methods of Guerillas, Warlords, and Militias*. Princeton, NJ: Princeton University Press, 2021.

Bishop, James K. "Escape from Mogadishu." *Foreign Service Journal* 6 (March 1991): 26–31.

Blaxland, John C. "Strategic Cousins: Canada, Australia and Their Use of Expeditionary Forces from the Boer War to the War on Terror." Doctoral diss., Royal Military College of Canada, 2003.

Bolger, Daniel P. *Savage Peace: Americans at War in the 1990's*. Novato, CA: Presidio Press, 1995.

Bolton, John R. "Wrong Turn in Somalia." *Foreign Affairs* 73, 1 (February 1994): 56–66.

Borner, Karl-Heinz. "The Future of German Operations outside NATO." *Parameters* 26, 1 (Spring 1996): 66–72.

Bou, Jean, Bob Breen, David Horner, Garth Pratten, and Miesje De Vogel. *The Official History of Australian Peacekeeping, Humanitarian and Post–Cold War Operations*. Vol. 4, *The Limits of Peacekeeping: Australian Missions in Africa and the Americas, 1992–2005*. Port Melbourne: Cambridge University Press, 2019.

Boulden, Jane. *Peace Enforcement: The United Nations Experience in Congo, Somalia, and Bosnia*. Westport, CT: Praeger, 2001.

Boutros-Ghali, Boutros. *Unvanquished: A US-UN Saga*. New York: Random House, 1999.

Bowden, Mark. *Black Hawk Down: A Story of Modern War*. 2nd ed. New York: Grove Press, 2010.

———. *Killing Pablo: The Hunt for the World's Greatest Outlaw*. New York: Grove Press, 2001.

Boykin, William G. *Never Surrender*. New York: Faith Words, 2008.

Breen, Bob. *A Little Bit of Hope: Australian Force Somalia*. St. Leonard's, NSW: Allen & Unwin, 1998.

Brocades-Zaalberg, Thijs W. *Soldiers and Civil Power: Supporting or Substituting*

Civil Authorities in Modern Peace Operations. Amsterdam: Amsterdam University Press, 2006.

Carroll, Jonathan. "Courage under Fire: Re-evaluating Black Hawk Down and the Battle of Mogadishu." *War in History* 29, 3 (2022): 704-726.

Cash, Raleigh. "Sua Sponte: Of Their Own Accord." In *The Battle of Mogadishu: Firsthand Accounts from the Men of Task Force Ranger,* edited by Matt Eversmann and Dan Schilling, 37-60. New York: Ballantine Books, 2004.

Casper, Lawrence E. *Falcon Brigade: Combat and Command in Somalia and Haiti.* Boulder, CO: Lynne Rienner, 2001.

Cassanelli, Lee. "Explaining the Somali Crisis." In *The Struggle for Land in Southern Somalia: The War behind the War,* edited by Catherine Besteman and Lee V. Cassanelli, 13-26. London: Haan, 1996.

Cassidy, Robert M. *Peacekeeping in the Abyss: British and American Peacekeeping Doctrine and Practice after the Cold War.* Westport, CT: Praeger, 2004.

Celeski, Joseph D. "A History of SF Operations in Somalia: 1992-1995." *Special Warfare* 15, 2 (June 2002): 16-27.

Clancy, Tom. *Debt of Honor.* New York: Berkeley Books, 1995.

Clancy, Tom, Tony Zinni, and Tony Koltz. *Battle Ready.* New York: Berkley Books, 2004.

Clarke, Walter. "Failed Visions and Uncertain Mandates in Somalia." In *Learning from Somalia: The Lessons of Armed Humanitarian Intervention,* edited by Walter Clarke and Jeffrey Herbst, 3-19. Boulder, CO: Westview Press, 1997.

Clarke, Walter, and Jeffrey Herbst. "Somalia and the Future of Humanitarian Intervention." In *Learning from Somalia: The Lessons of Armed Humanitarian Intervention,* edited by Walter Clarke and Jeffrey Herbst, 239-254. Boulder, CO: Westview Press, 1997.

Clarke, Walter S. *Background Information for Operation Restore Hope.* Carlisle, PA: Strategic Studies Institute, US Army War College, 1992.

Clinton, Bill. *My Life.* New York: Alfred A. Knopf, 2004.

Cloughley, Brian. *A History of the Pakistan Army: Wars and Insurrections.* 4th ed. Karachi: Oxford University Press, 2014.

Cohen, Herman J. *Intervening in Africa: Superpower Peacemaking in a Troubled Continent.* New York: St. Martin's Press, 2000.

Connor, John. "Intervention and Domestic Politics." In *Australian Peacekeeping: Sixty Years in the Field,* edited by David Horner, Peter Londey, and Jean Bou, 60-83. Melbourne: Cambridge University Press, 2009.

Criggler, Frank T. "The Peace-Enforcement Dilemma." *Joint Forces Quarterly* 1, 2 (Autumn 1993): 64-70.

Crozier, Brian. *The Soviet Presence in Somalia.* London: Centre for Security and Conflict Studies, 1975.

Dalgaard-Nielsen, Anja. *Germany, Pacifism and Peace Enforcement.* Manchester, UK: Manchester University Press, 2006.

Dallaire, Romeo. *Shake Hands with the Devil: The Failure of Humanity in Rwanda.* New York: Carroll & Graf, 2003.

David, William C. "Preparing a Battalion for Combat: Combat Leadership Lessons Learned." *Infantry* 85, 6 (December 1995): 32–35.

———. "Preparing a Battalion for Combat: Maneuver Live-Fire Training." *Infantry* 85, 5 (October 1995): 23–27.

———. "Preparing a Battalion for Combat: Marksmanship." *Infantry* 85, 4 (August 1995): 27–30.

———. "Preparing a Battalion for Combat: Physical Fitness and Mental Toughness." *Infantry* 85, 3 (June 1995): 25–30.

Davis, Lois M., Susan D. Hosek, Michael G. Tate, Mark Perry, Gerard Hepler, and Paul S. Steinberg. *Army Medical Support for Peace Operations and Humanitarian Assistance* (Santa Monica, CA: RAND Corporation, 1996).

Dawson, Grant. *Here Is Hell: Canada's Engagement in Somalia.* Vancouver, BC: University of British Columbia Press, 2007.

DeLong, Kent, and Steven Tuckey. *Mogadishu! Heroism and Tragedy.* Westport, CT: Praeger, 1994.

Diehl, Paul F. "With the Best of Intentions: Lessons from UNOSOM I and II." *Studies in Conflict and Terrorism* 19 (1996): 153–177.

Dobbins, James, Seth G. Jones, Keith Crane, Andrew Rathmell, Brett Steele, and Richard Teltschik. *The UN's Role in Nation-Building: From the Congo to Iraq.* Santa Monica, CA: RAND Corporation, 2004.

Dobbins, James, John G. McGinn, Keith Crane, Seth G. Jones, Rollie Lal, Andrew Rathmell, Rachel Swanger, and Anga Timilsina. *America's Role in Nation-Building: From Germany to Iraq.* Santa Monica, CA: RAND Corporation, 2003.

Dobbins, James, Michele A. Poole, Austin Long, and Benjamin Runkle. *After the War: Nation-Building from FDR to George W. Bush.* Santa Monica, CA: RAND Corporation, 2008.

Drew, Elizabeth. *On the Edge: The Clinton Presidency.* New York: Simon & Schuster, 1994.

Drohan, Brian. "Retaining Flexibility: Dag Hammarskjöld, the 1958 Summary Study, and the History of UN Peacekeeping." *Global Governance: A Review of Multilateralism and International Organizations* 29, 2 (2023): 119–135.

Drysdale, John. "Foreign Military Intervention in Somalia: The Root Cause of the Shift from UN Peacekeeping to Peacemaking and Its Consequences." In *Learning from Somalia: The Lessons of Armed Humanitarian Intervention*, edited by Walter Clarke and Jeffrey Herbst, 118–134. Boulder, CO: Westview Press, 1997.

———. "Reflections 1943–1963." In *Milk and Peace, Drought and War: Somali Culture, Society and Politics*, edited by Markus Hoehne and Virginia Luling, 19–33. London: Hurst, 2010.

———. *Whatever Happened to Somalia?* 2nd ed. London: Haan, 2001.

Durant, Michael J., and Steven Hartov. *In the Company of Heroes.* New York: G. P. Putnam's Sons, 2003.

———. *The Night Stalkers.* New York: G. P. Putnam's Sons, 2006.

Dworken, Jonathan T. *Military Relations with Humanitarian Relief Organizations: Observations from Restore Hope.* Alexandria, VA: Center for Naval Analyses, 1993.

———. *Operation Restore Hope: Preparing and Planning the Transition to UN Operations.* Alexandria, VA: Center for Naval Analyses, 1994.

Ernst, Carl F. "The Urban Area during Support Missions Case Study: Mogadishu, the Operational Level." In *Capital Preservation: Preparing for Urban Operations in the Twenty-First Century,* edited by Russell W. Glenn, 355–412. Santa Monica, CA: RAND Corporation, 2001.

Eversmann, Matt. "Operation Gothic Serpent." In *The Battle of Mogadishu: Firsthand Accounts from the Men of Task Force Ranger,* edited by Matt Eversmann and Dan Schilling, 3–36. New York: Ballantine Books, 2004.

Ferry, Charles P. "Mogadishu, October 1993: A Company XO's Notes on Lessons Learned." *Infantry* 84, 6 (December 1994): 31–38.

———. "Mogadishu, October 1993: Personal Account of a Rifle Company XO." *Infantry* 84, 5 (October 1994): 23–31.

Findlay, Trevor. *The Use of Force in UN Peace Operations.* New York: Oxford University Press, 2002.

Finnemore, Martha. *The Purpose of Intervention: Changing Beliefs about the Use of Force.* Ithaca, NY: Cornell University Press, 2003.

Fitzgerald, David. *Learning to Forget: US Army Counterinsurgency Doctrine and Practice from Vietnam to Iraq.* Stanford, CA: Stanford University Press, 2013.

Fleitz, Frederick H. *Peacekeeping Fiascoes of the 1990s: Causes, Solutions, and U.S. Interests.* Westport, CT: Praeger, 2002.

Freeman, Waldo D. "Operation Restore Hope: A Logistical Challenge." *Field Artillery* (June 1993): 5–8.

Freeman, Waldo D., Robert B. Lambert, and Jason D. Mims. "Operation Restore Hope: A US CENTCOM Perspective." *Military Review* 73, 9 (September 1993): 61–72.

Ganzglass, Martin R. "The Restoration of the Somali Justice System." In *Learning from Somalia: The Lessons of Armed Humanitarian Intervention,* edited by Walter Clarke and Jeffrey Herbst, 20–41. Boulder, CO: Westview Press, 1997.

George, John M. "The Politics of Peace: The Challenge of Civil-Military Cooperation in Somalia." *Policy and Management Review* 2, 2 (2002): 1–34.

Goulding, Marrack. *Peacemonger.* London: John Murray, 2002.

Granatstein, J. L. *Canada's Army: Waging War and Keeping Peace.* Toronto: University of Toronto Press, 2002.

Hackworth, David H. *Hazardous Duty.* New York: William Morrow, 1996.

Halberstam, David. *War in a Time of Peace: Bush, Clinton, and the Generals.* New York: Scribner, 2001.

Hansch, Steven, Scott Lillibridge, Grace Egeland, Charles Teller, and Michael Toole. *Lives Lost, Lives Saved: Excess Mortality and the Impact of Health Interventions in the Somalia Emergency.* Washington, DC: Center for Policy Analysis and Research on Refugee Issues, 1994.

Hardy, Mat. "UN-Consistent: A Comparison of Australia's Military Interventions in Somalia and Rwanda." *Small Wars & Insurgencies* 18, 3 (2007): 467–491.

Harned, Glenn M. *Stability Operations in Somalia, 1992–1993: A Case Study.* Carlisle, PA: Peacekeeping and Stability Operations Institute, 2016.

Head, William, P. *Night Hunters: The AC130s and Their Role in US Airpower.* College Station: Texas A&M University Press, 2014.

Helman, Gerald B., and Steven R. Ratner. "Saving Failed States." *Foreign Policy* 89, 3 (1992): 3–20.

Hempstone, Smith. *Rogue Ambassador: An African Memoir.* Sewanee, TN: University of the South Press, 1997.

Henriksen, Thomas H. *America's Wars: Interventions, Regime Change, and Insurgencies after the Cold War.* Cambridge: Cambridge University Press, 2022.

Hirsch, John L., and Robert B. Oakley. *Somalia and Operation Restore Hope: Reflections on Peacemaking and Peacekeeping.* Washington, DC: Institute of Peace Press, 1995.

Hoar, Joseph P. "A CINC's Perspective." *Joint Forces Quarterly* 1, 2 (Autumn 1993): 56–63.

Holbrooke, Richard. *To End a War.* New York: Random House, 1998.

Hollis, Mark A. B. "Platoon under Fire: Mogadishu, October 1993." *Infantry* 88, 1 (April 1998): 27–34.

Horan, Mike. *Eyes over Mogadishu.* Bloomington, IN: Xlibris, 2003.

Horner, David, and John Connor. *The Official History of Australian Peacekeeping, Humanitarian and Post–Cold War Operations.* Vol. 3, *The Good International Citizen: Australian Peacekeeping in Asia, Africa and Europe, 1991–1993.* Port Melbourne, VIC: Cambridge University Press, 2014.

Howard, Lise Morjé. *UN Peacekeeping in Civil Wars.* New York: Cambridge University Press, 2008.

Howe, Jonathan T. "Relations between the United States and United Nations in Dealing with Somalia." In *Learning from Somalia: The Lessons of Armed Humanitarian Intervention,* edited by Walter Clarke and Jeffrey Herbst, 173–190. Boulder, CO: Westview Press, 1997.

Huchthausen, Peter. *America's Splendid Little Wars: A Short History of U.S. Military Engagements, 1975–2000.* New York: Viking, 2003.

Human Rights Watch. *Somalia: A Government at War with Its Own People; Testimonies about the Killings and the Conflict in the North.* New York: Human Rights Watch, 1990.

Huntington, Samuel P. "New Contingencies, Old Roles." *Joint Forces Quarterly* 1, 2 (Autumn 1993): 38–43.

Hurley, D. J. "Operation Solace." *Australian Defence Force Journal* 104, 1 (February 1994): 29–33.

Ignazi, Piero, Giampiero Giacomello, and Fabrizio Coticchia. *Italian Military Operations Abroad: Just Don't Call It War*. New York: Palgrave Macmillan, 2012.

Ingiriis, Mohamed Haji. "From Grievance to Greed in Somalia." *Cahiers d'Études Africaines* 59, 3 (2019): 783–814.

———. *The Suicidal State in Somalia: The Rise and Fall of the Siad Barre Regime, 1969–1991*. Lanham, MD: University Press of America, 2016.

Jett, Dennis C. *Why Peacekeeping Fails*. New York: Palgrave, 2001.

Johnston, Harry, and Ted Dagne. "Congress and the Somalia Crisis." In *Learning from Somalia: The Lessons of Armed Humanitarian Intervention*, edited by Walter Clarke and Jeffrey Herbst, 191–206. Boulder, CO: Westview Press, 1997.

Johnston, Philip. *Somalia Diary*. Atlanta: Longstreet Press, 1994.

Kaempf, Sebastian. "US Warfare in Somalia and the Trade-off between Casualty-Aversion and Civilian Protection." *Small Wars & Insurgencies* 23, 3 (2012): 388–413.

Kalyvas, Stathis N. *The Logic of Violence in Civil War*. New York: Cambridge University Press, 2006.

Kapteijns, Lidwien. *Clan Cleansing in Somalia: The Ruinous Legacy of 1991*. Philadelphia: University of Pennsylvania Press, 2013.

———. "Test-firing the 'New World Order' in Somalia: The US/UN Military Humanitarian Intervention of 1992–1995." *Journal of Genocide Research* 15, 4 (2013): 421–442.

Kassing, David. *Transporting the Army for Operation Restore Hope*. Santa Monica, CA: RAND Corporation, 1994.

Kelly, Michael J. *Peace Operations: Tackling the Military, Legal and Policy Challenges*. Canberra: Australian Government Publishing Service, 1997.

Kendrick, William A. "Peacekeeping Operation in Somalia." *Infantry* 85, 3 (June 1995): 31–35.

Kennedy, Kevin M. "The Relationship between the Military and the Humanitarian Organizations in Operation Restore Hope." In *Learning from Somalia: The Lessons of Armed Humanitarian Intervention*, edited by Walter Clarke and Jeffrey Herbst, 99–117. Boulder, CO: Westview Press, 1997.

Kirkpatrick, Charles E. *"Ruck It Up!" The Post–Cold War Transformation of V Corps, 1990–2001*. Washington, DC: Department of the Army, 2006.

Klarevas, Louis J. "American Public Opinion on Peace Operations: The Cases of Somalia, Rwanda, and Haiti." Doctoral diss., American University, 1999.

Kurth, Mike. "Through My Eyes." In *The Battle of Mogadishu: Firsthand Accounts from the Men of Task Force Ranger,* edited by Matt Eversmann and Dan Schilling, 61–106. New York: Ballantine Books, 2004.

Lake, David A. *The Statebuilder's Dilemma: On the Limits of Foreign Intervention.* Ithaca, NY: Cornell University Press, 2016.

Lennox, William J., and Charles B. Allen. "The 24th Div Arty in Somalia." *Field Artillery* (August 1994): 14–17.

Lewis, Ioan M. *Blood and Bone: The Call of Kinship in Somali Society.* Trenton, NJ: Red Sea Press, 1994.

———. "Doing Violence to Ethnography: A Response to Catherine Besteman's 'Representing Violence and "Othering" Somalia.'" *Cultural Anthropology* 13, 1 (February 1998): 100–108.

Longhurst, Kerry. *Germany and the Use of Force.* Manchester, UK: Manchester University Press, 2004.

Lorenz, F. M. "Confronting Thievery in Somalia." *Military Review* 74, 8 (August 1994): 46–55.

———. "Law and Anarchy in Somalia." *Parameters* 23, 4 (Winter 1993–94): 27–41.

Loring, Denise L. "Support in Somalia." *Ordnance* 9, 3 (August 1993): 21–23.

Lyons, Terrence, and Ahmed I. Samatar. *Somalia: State Collapse, Multilateral Intervention, and Strategies for Political Reconstruction.* Washington, DC: Brookings Institution, 1995.

MacKinnon, Michael G. *The Evolution of US Peacekeeping Policy under Clinton: A Fairweather Friend?* Portland, OR: Frank Cass, 2000.

MacQueen, Norrie. *Humanitarian Intervention and the United Nations.* Edinburgh: Edinburgh University Press, 2011.

———. *United Nations Peacekeeping in Africa since 1960.* London: Pearson Education, 2002.

Magruder, Lawson W. *A Soldier's Journey Living His Why.* Coppell, TX: independently published, 2020.

Maren, Michael. *The Road to Hell: The Ravaging Effects of Foreign Aid and International Charity.* New York: Free Press, 1997.

Marra, Michael A., and William G. Pierce. "Somalia 20 Years Later—Lessons Learned, Re-learned and Forgotten." *Small Wars Journal* (2013). https://smallwarsjournal.com/jrnl/art/somalia-20-years-later-%E2%80%93-lessons-learned-re-learned-and-forgotten.

McGowan, Patrick D. "Operations in Somalia: Changing the Light Infantry Training Focus." *Infantry* 83, 6 (December 1993): 23–25.

McGrady, Katherine A. W. *The Joint Task Force in Operation Restore Hope.* Alexandria, VA: Center for Naval Analyses, 1994.

Meisler, Stanley. *United Nations: A History.* 2nd ed. New York: Grove Press, 2011.

Menkhaus, Ken. "Getting out vs. Getting Through: U.S. and U.N. Policies in Somalia." *Middle East Policy* 3, 1 (March 1994): 146–162.

———. "International Peacebuilding and the Dynamics of Local and National Reconciliation in Somalia." In *Learning from Somalia: The Lessons of Armed Humanitarian Intervention*, edited by Walter Clarke and Jeffrey Herbst, 42–66. Boulder, CO: Westview Press, 1997.

Metz, Helen Chapin. *Somalia: A Country Study*. Washington, DC: Federal Research Division, Library of Congress, 1993.

Miller, Laura L., and Charles Moskos. "Humanitarians or Warriors? Race, Gender, and Combat Status in Operation Restore Hope." *Armed Forces & Society* 21, 4 (Summer 1995): 615–637.

Mockaitis, Thomas R. *Peace Operations and Intrastate Conflict: The Sword or the Olive Branch?* Westport, CT: Praeger, 1999.

Mroczkowski, Dennis P. *Restoring Hope: In Somalia with the Unified Task Force, 1992–1993*. Washington, DC: History Division, US Marine Corps, 2005.

Mukhtar, Mohamed Haji, and Margaret Castagno. *Historical Dictionary of Somalia*. Lanham, MD: Scarecrow Press, 2003.

Murphy, Ray. *UN Peacekeeping in Lebanon, Somalia, and Kosovo*. Cambridge: Cambridge University Press, 2007.

Nambiar, Satish. *For the Honour of India: A History of Indian Peacekeeping*. New Delhi: Centre for Armed Forces Historical Research, United Service Institution of India, 2009.

Natsios, Andrew S. "Humanitarian Relief Intervention in Somalia: The Economics of Chaos." In *Learning from Somalia: The Lessons of Armed Humanitarian Intervention*, edited by Walter Clarke and Jeffrey Herbst, 77–98. Boulder, CO: Westview Press, 1997.

Neville, Leigh. *Day of the Rangers: The Battle of Mogadishu 25 Years On*. New York: Osprey, 2018.

Oakley, David P. *Subordinating Intelligence: The DOD/CIA Post–Cold War Relationship*. Lexington: University Press of Kentucky, 2019.

Oakley, Robert B. "An Envoy's Perspective." *Joint Forces Quarterly* 1, 2 (Autumn 1993): 44–55.

———. "The Urban Area during Support Missions Case Study: Mogadishu, the Strategic Level." In *Capital Preservation: Preparing for Urban Operations in the Twenty-First Century*, edited by Russell W. Glenn, 309–354. Santa Monica, CA: RAND Corporation, 2001.

Ohls, Gary J. *Somalia . . . From the Sea*. Newport, RI: Naval War College Press, 2009.

Oloya, Opiyo. *Black Hawks Rising: The Story of AMISOM's Successful War against Somali Insurgents, 2007–2014*. Solihull, UK: Helion, 2016.

Palazzo, Albert. *The Australian Army: A History of Its Organisation, 1901–2001*. Melbourne: Oxford University Press, 2001.

Patman, Robert G. "Disarming Somalia: The Contrasting Fortunes of United States and Australian Peacekeepers during United Nations Intervention, 1992–1993." *African Affairs* 96 (1997): 509–533.

————. *Strategic Shortfall: The Somali Syndrome and the March to 9/11*. Denver: Praeger, 2010.

Peterson, G. "Human Intelligence and Somalia—A Cost Effective Winner for a Small Army." *Australian Defence Force Journal* 104, 1 (February 1994): 35–37.

————. "Psyops and Somalia—Spreading the Good News." *Australian Defence Force Journal* 104, 1 (February 1994): 38–40.

Peterson, Scott. *Me against My Brother: At War in Somalia, Sudan, and Rwanda*. New York: Routledge, 2001.

Piasecki, Eugene G. "If You Liked Beirut, You'll Love Mogadishu: An Introduction to ARSOF in Somalia." *Veritas* 3, 2 (2007): 1–11.

Poole, Walter S. *The Effort to Save Somalia: August 1992–March 1994*. Washington, DC: Joint History Office, Office of the Chairman of the Joint Chiefs of Staff, 2005.

Powell, Colin. *My American Journey*. New York: Ballantine Books, 1996.

Powell, Colin L. "U.S. Forces: Challenges Ahead." *Foreign Affairs* 71, 5 (Winter 1992–93): 32–45.

Proctor, Pat. "Lessons Unlearned: Army Transformation and Low-Intensity Conflict." *Parameters* 47, 4 (Winter 2017–18): 33–45.

Prunier, Gerard. "Benign Neglect versus *La Grande Somalia*: The Colonial Legacy and the Post-Colonial State." In *Milk and Peace, Drought and War: Somali Culture, Society and Politics*, edited by Markus Hoehne and Virginia Luling, 35–49. London: Hurst, 2010.

————. "The Experience of European Armies in Operation Restore Hope." In *Learning from Somalia: The Lessons of Armed Humanitarian Intervention*, edited by Walter Clarke and Jeffrey Herbst, 135–147. Boulder, CO: Westview Press, 1997.

Pupetz, Ron. *In the Line of Duty: Canadian Joint Forces Somalia, 1992–1993*. St. Catherine's, ON: Vanwell, 2001.

Recchia, Stefano. "Pragmatism over Principle: US Intervention and Burden Shifting in Somalia, 1992–1993." *Journal of Strategic Studies* 43, 3 (2018): 341–365.

Richburg, Keith B. *Out of Africa: A Black Man Confronts Africa*. San Diego, CA: Harcourt Brace, 1998.

Rose, Michael. *Fighting for Peace: Bosnia 1994*. London: Harvill Press, 1998.

Rupiya, Martin R. "The Bakara Market Arms Clearance Operation of 1993: The Zimbabwe National Army in Somalia." *International Peacekeeping* 4, 1 (1997): 115–121.

Rutherford, Kenneth R. *Humanitarianism under Fire: The US and UN Intervention in Somalia*. Sterling, VA: Kumarian Press, 2008.

Sahnoun, Mohamed. *Somalia: The Missed Opportunities*. Washington, DC: United States Institute for Peace Press, 1994.

Schilling, Dan. "On Friendship and Firefights." In *The Battle of Mogadishu: First-

hand Accounts from the Men of Task Force Ranger, edited by Matt Eversmann and Dan Schilling, 157–208. New York: Ballantine Books, 2004.

Sens, Allen G. *Somalia and the Changing Nature of Peacekeeping: The Implications for Canada; a Study Prepared for the Commission of Inquiry into the Deployment of Canadian Forces to Somalia.* Ottawa: Ministry of Public Works and Government Services, 1997.

Seybolt, Taylor B. *Humanitarian Military Intervention: The Conditions for Success and Failure.* New York: Oxford University Press, 2007.

Stanton, Martin. *Somalia on Five Dollars a Day: A Soldier's Story.* Novato, CA: Presidio, 2001.

Stanton, Martin N. "Letter from Somalia: An S-3's Observations." *Infantry* 85, 1 (February 1995): 13–14.

———. "Operational Considerations for Sub-Saharan Africa." *Infantry* 86, 5 (October 1996): 28–36.

———. "Riot Control in the 1990s." *Infantry* 86, 1 (February 1996): 22–29.

Stevenson, Jonathan. "Hope Restored in Somalia?" *Foreign Policy* 91 (Summer 1993): 138–154.

———. *Losing Mogadishu: Testing U.S. Policy in Somalia.* Annapolis, MD: Naval Institute Press, 1995.

Stewart, Richard D., *The United States Army in Somalia, 1992–1994.* Washington, DC: US Army Center for Military History, 2003.

Strickland, Richard T. "Crisis to Catalyst: The Strategic Effects of the Somalia Affair on the Canadian Armed Forces." Master's thesis, School of Advanced Military Studies, US Army Command and General Staff College, 2017.

Thakur, Ramesh. "From Peacekeeping to Peace Enforcement: The UN Operation in Somalia." *Journal of Modern African Studies* 32, 3 (September 1994): 387–410.

———. *The United Nations, Peace and Security: From Collective Security to the Responsibility to Protect.* 2nd ed. New York: Cambridge University Press, 2017.

Thomas, Lynn, and Steve Spataro. "Peacekeeping and Policing in Somalia." In *Policing the New World Disorder: Peace Operations and Public Security*, edited by Robert B. Oakley, Michael J. Dziedzic, and Eliot M. Goldberg, 175–214. Washington, DC: National Defense University Press, 1998.

Tripodi, Paolo, *The Colonial Legacy in Somalia.* London: Macmillan, 1999.

Tudor, Margot. *Blue Helmet Bureaucrats: United Nations Peacekeeping and the Reinvention of Colonialism, 1945–1971.* Cambridge: Cambridge University Press, 2023.

United Nations. *The Blue Helmets: A Review of United Nations Peace-keeping.* 3rd ed. New York: UN Department of Public Information, 1996.

———. *The United Nations and the Situation in Somalia.* New York: UN Department of Public Information, 1994.

———. *The United Nations and Somalia, 1992–1996.* New York: UN Department of Public Information, 1996.

US Army War College. *Campaign Analysis Course Case Study: Somalia.* Carlisle, PA: US Army War College, Department of Military Strategy, Planning, and Operations, 2005.

Von Hippel, Karin. *Democracy by Force: US Military Intervention in the Post–Cold War World.* New York: Cambridge University Press, 2000.

Wasdin, Howard E., and Stephen Templin. *SEAL Team Six: Memoirs of an Elite Navy SEAL Sniper.* New York: St. Martin's Press, 2011.

Wesley, Michael. *Casualties of the New World Order: The Causes of Failure of UN Missions to Civil Wars.* Boulder, CO: St. Martin's, 1997.

Western, Jon. *Selling Intervention and War: The Presidency, the Media, and the American Public.* Baltimore: Johns Hopkins University Press, 2005.

———. "Sources of Humanitarian Intervention: Beliefs, Information, and Advocacy in the U.S. Decisions on Somalia and Bosnia." *International Security* 26, 4 (2002): 112–142.

Western, Jon, and Joshua S. Goldstein. "Humanitarian Intervention Comes of Age." *Foreign Affairs* 90, 6 (2011): 48–59.

Wheeler, Ed, and Craig Roberts. *Doorway to Hell: Disaster in Somalia.* London: Frontline Books, 2012.

Whetstone, Michael. *Madness in Mogadishu: Commanding the 10th Mountain Division's Quick Reaction Company during Black Hawk Down.* Mechanicsburg, PA: Stackpole Books, 2015.

Wilkinson, Tim. "Be Careful What You Wish For." In *The Battle of Mogadishu: Firsthand Accounts from the Men of Task Force Ranger,* edited by Matt Eversmann and Dan Schilling, 127–156. New York: Ballantine Books, 2004.

Williams, Paul D. *Fighting for Peace in Somalia.* New York: Oxford University Press, 2018.

Winslow, Donna. "Rites of Passage and Group Bonding in the Canadian Airborne." *Armed Forces & Society* 25, 3 (Spring 1999): 429–457.

Woods, James L. "U.S. Government Decisionmaking Processes during Humanitarian Operations in Somalia." In *Learning from Somalia: The Lessons of Armed Humanitarian Intervention,* edited by Walter Clarke and Jeffrey Herbst, 151–172. Boulder, CO: Westview Press, 1997.

Woodward, Susan L. *The Ideology of Failed States: Why Intervention Fails.* New York: Cambridge University Press, 2017.

Yamin, Tughral. *UN Peacekeeping Operations in Somalia: The Pakistani Perspective.* Karachi: Paramount Books, 2019.

Zinni, Tony, and Tony Koltz. *The Battle for Peace: A Frontline Vision of America's Power and Purpose.* New York: Palgrave Macmillan, 2006.

———. *Before the First Shot is Fired: How America Can Win or Lose off the Battlefield.* New York: Palgrave Macmillan, 2014.

Zockler, Markus. "Germany in Collective Security Systems—Anything Goes." *European Journal of International Law* 6, 2 (1995): 274–286.

Index

128; relationship with UNITAF, 108, 126–128, 141, 270; Somali guards hired by, 51, 142, 146–147; views on disarmament, 65–66

reverse osmosis water purification unit (ROWPU), 84–85

Richburg, Keith, 96, 101, 177, 222, 261

Riedel, Jeffrey, 237, 246–247

Romania, 180, 290, 310

Rose, Michael, 4, 5, 7, 331–332. *See also* Mogadishu Line

ROWPU. *See* reverse osmosis water purification unit

Ruehe, Volker, 286

Ryan, Jack (fictional character), 1

Rwandan Genocide, 3, 303, 313, 326

Sahnoun, Mohamed, 9, 39, 41, 48–52

SAMO. *See* Somali African Muki Organisation

Saudi Arabia, 72, 96, 99, 287

Schwarzkopf, H. Norman, 21, 64, 81

scientific socialism (ideology), 14–15

Scowcroft, Brent, 123, 167

SDA. *See* Somali Democratic Association

SDM. *See* Somali Democratic Movement

2nd Battalion/14th Infantry Regiment (US Army), 225, 233, 251–255, 272

2nd Battalion/87th Infantry Regiment (US Army), 77, 93

Senate Armed Services Committee, 176, 238, 243, 257, 260–261

seven-point agreement, 76–77, 143–144, 172

7th Frontier Force Battalion (Pakistan), 36, 42, 48–50, 52–53, 55, 75, 198–202

7th Transportation Group (US Army), Shaheen, Imtiaz, 39–41, 48–55, 76–77, 170

Shalikashvili, John, 265, 290, 319

Sheehan, John J., 257–259

Shermarke, Abdirashid Ali, 14

Shinn, David, 176, 226

Shrader, Dale, 237–238

Shughart, Randall, 250–253

Simpson, Daniel H., 322

6th Battalion/Punjab Regiment (Pakistan), 199

62nd Medical Group (US Army), 70, 89, 100

66th Mountain Brigade (India), 284. *See also* India

Social Democratic Party (SPD) (Germany), 181

Somalia: colonization of, 10–12; Global War on Terror and, 327; independence, 12; popularity of print media and radio, 103; public attitudes towards United Nations, 12; relations with Soviet Union, 13–16, 19; religious tensions with UNITAF, 102; UN interests in, 13, 55, 333; US interests in, 12, 17, 19–21, 37, 55, 60, 176

Somali African Muki Organisation (SAMO), 410n37, 410n47, 445n86, 446n89

Somali Civil War, 19–21, 24, 26–30, 32–35

Somali Democratic Association (SDA), 27, 410n37, 410n47, 445n86, 446n89

Somali Democratic Movement (SDM), 125, 179, 312, 326

Somali Democratic Republic, 14–21

Somaliland, 18, 21, 31–32, 68, 181, 279, 295, 312

Somali National Alliance (SNA): Addis Ababa Agreement and, 172–173; al-Qaeda and, 275–276; anti-aircraft capabilities, 276; attacks on UNOSOM, 220, 224–225; authorized weapons storage sites of, 187–188, 197–200; Battle of Checkpoint Pasta and, 217; Battle of Mogadishu and, 211, 247–256; bounties on American soldiers, 224; capture of Merka, 299; ceasefire negotiation attempts, 238–241, 243; division within, 295, 301; 8 August 1993 bombing and, 224; 5 June 1993 attacks and, 186–187, 201–205; 5 September 1993 attacks and, 231; formation and composition, 23, 312; estimates of capabilities, 55,